ROUTLEDGE HANDBOOK OF DEMOCRACY AND SECURITY

This handbook explores how democracies around the world seek to balance democratic values with the requirement to protect their citizens from the threat of politically motivated violence.

Over the past few decades, the majority of the world's democracies have had to confront serious security threats, and in many instances these challenges have not come from rival states but from violent groups. This volume offers readers an overview of how some democracies have responded to such threats. It examines the extent to which authorities have felt compelled to modify laws to evade what would ordinarily be regarded as protected rights, such as personal privacy, freedom of movement and freedom of speech. Grounded in historical analysis, each of the sections addresses past and emerging security threats; legal and legislative responses to them; successful and unsuccessful efforts to reconcile democracy and security; and a range of theoretical questions. The case studies provided vary in terms of the durability of their democratic systems, level of economic development and the severity of the threats with which they have been confronted.

The volume is divided into three thematic parts:

- Strong democracies: United States, Great Britain, France, Germany, Italy, Spain, Australia, New Zealand and Israel
- Challenged democracies: India, South Africa, Brazil, Argentina and Romania
- Fragile democracies: the Philippines and Nigeria.

This book will be of much interest to students of democracy, security studies, political philosophy, Asian politics, Middle Eastern politics, African politics, West European politics and IR in general.

Leonard Weinberg is Emeritus Foundation Professor of Political Science at the University of Nevada, Reno, USA.

Elizabeth Francis is an Associate Professor of English and Judicial Studies at the University of Nevada, Reno, USA.

Eliot Assoudeh is Adjunct Professor of Political Science at the University of Nevada, Reno, USA.

ROUTLEDGE HANDBOOK OF DEMOCRACY AND SECURITY

Edited by Leonard Weinberg, Elizabeth Francis and Eliot Assoudeh

Routledge
Taylor & Francis Group
LONDON AND NEW YORK

First published 2021
by Routledge
2 Park Square, Milton Park, Abingdon, Oxon OX14 4RN

and by Routledge
52 Vanderbilt Avenue, New York, NY 10017

Routledge is an imprint of the Taylor & Francis Group, an informa business

British Library Cataloguing in Publication Data
A catalogue record for this book is available from the British Library

Library of Congress Cataloging-in-Publication Data
A catalog record has been requested for this book

ISBN: 978-1-138-79998-1 (hbk)
ISBN: 978-1-315-75572-4 (ebk)

Typeset in Bembo
by Taylor & Francis Books

CONTENTS

ILLUSTRATIONS

Figures

Tables

CONTRIBUTORS

Rogelio Alonso is Professor of Political Science, King Juan Carlos University, Madrid, Spain

Eliot Assoudeh is Adjunct Professor of Political Science, the University of Nevada, Reno, US

Rouben Azizian is Director of the Centre for Defence and Security Studies, Massey University, Manawata, New Zealand

Thomas C. Bruneau is Distinguished Professor Emeritus of the Department of National Security Affairs, the Naval Postgraduate School, Monterey, California, US

Raphael Cohen-Almagor is Professor and Chair of Political Science, and Director of the Middle East Study Group, the University of Hull, UK

Elizabeth A. Francis is Associate Professor English and Judicial Studies, the University of Nevada, Reno, US

Lawrence Friedman is Professor of Law, the New England School of Law, Boston, Massachusetts, US

Jeffrey A. Griffin is a Lecturer in Political Science, the University of Nevada, Reno, US

Amos N. Guiora is Professor of Law, the J.J. Quinney College of Law at the University of Utah, US

Christopher Harmon, formerly Professor at the Marine Corps University, US, is now in government service

Terry Johanson is a Lecturer at the Centre for Defence and Security Studies, Massey University, Manawata, New Zealand

Juliette Legendre is a Research Associate at the Center on Budget and Policy Priorities, Washington, DC, US

Florina Cristiana Matei is a Lecturer in the Department of National Security Affairs, the Naval Postgraduate School, Monterey, California, US

Ajay K. Mehra is Professor of Political Science, the University of Delhi, India

Robert L. Ostergard, Jr. is Professor of Political Science, the University of Nevada, Reno, US

Vittorio Emanuele Parsi is Professor of Political Science and Director of International Relations at the Catholic University of the Sacred Heart, Milan, Italy

David Pion-Berlin is Professor of Political Science, the University of California, Riverside, US

Steffen Schneider is a member of the Department of Political Science, Universität Bremen, Germany

Sudha Setty is Dean of the School of Law, Western New England University, Springfield, MA, US

Robin Simcox is Margaret Thatcher Fellow at the Heritage Foundation Center for Freedom, London, UK

Ari Tobi-Aiyemo is a retired Magistrate Judge, Lagos, Nigeria, called to the Nigerian bar as solicitor and advocate of the Supreme Court of Nigeria in 2002

Leonard B. Weinberg is Foundation Professor of Political Science Emeritus, the University of Nevada, Reno, US

Antonio Zotti is a Lecturer in European Institutions, the Catholic University of the Sacred Heart, Milan, Italy.

DEMOCRACY, SECURITY AND THE RULE OF LAW

An introduction

Leonard Weinberg, Elizabeth Francis and Eliot Assoudeh

We come to this project at a time when democracy is experiencing a recession on a worldwide basis. Not all that long ago, at the end of the Cold War, it appeared to many as though the democratic prospect could not be brighter. In 1989–1990 the countries of Eastern Europe, formerly part of the now defunct Soviet Union, underwent transitions to democratic rule after experiencing the largely peaceful (Romania was an exception) replacement of one-party dictatorships by promising, newly installed democracies.

The ex-Yugoslavia was another story. In that Balkan republic the end of communism led to the end of the country itself. During the period 1990–1992 Yugoslavia broke apart, fragmenting into various ethnic mini-states: Serbia, Croatia, Slovenia, Montenegro, Macedonia, Bosnia–Herzegovina, and later Kosovo. Exceptionally brutal civil wars broke out in the course of Yugoslavia's disintegration. Despite episodes of mass murder, mass rape and other genocidal incidents, the newly independent mini-states evolved into ethnically based democracies.

Democracy returned, by and large, to Latin America. After undergoing bouts of military dictatorship or bureaucratic authoritarianism during the 1970s, Argentina, Brazil, Peru, Chile, Uruguay, Colombia, Venezuela and the rest of the continent restored democratic rule. The situation in Central America was far more problematic.

In South and East Asia, India sustained its democracy despite violent Hindu vs. Muslim clashes, a severe wave of terrorism launched by Sikh separatists in the Punjab and a continuing struggle with Pakistan over Jammu-Kashmir. In East Asia, South Korea, Taiwan, Indonesia and Malaysia evolved democratic institutions – typically following from or accompanying dramatic economic growth. In the Philippines democracy was restored when the Marcos dictatorship toppled under pressure from largely peaceful protests, with some assistance from the United States.

Sub-Saharan Africa offered one major success story. In 1994, under the leadership of Nelson Mandela, South Africa abandoned its system of Apartheid to become a multi-racial democracy ('the rainbow nation'). Change was achieved with a minimum of violence. In East Africa, Kenya – along with Ghana, Nigeria and certain other West African states – also achieved democratic rule despite inter-tribal and inter-religious conflicts.

The Middle East was an exception. After a period of military rule, Turkish democracy was restored when the country's military returned to its barracks. Lebanon's civil war ended in

1989–1990 and a semblance of democratic rule returned, albeit structured along sectarian lines. Israel's continued occupation of the West Bank and Gaza marred its democratic credentials, but no serious effort to replace the Jewish state's democratic institutions occurred. Elsewhere in the region there were democratic stirrings, but little was achieved by way of replacing existing authoritarian systems – either secular (Syria) or religious (Iran).

These developments led various observers to conclude that the democratic wave was irreversible. History had finally rendered its judgement in favor of democracy, a conclusion based on more than vapors floating in the *zeitgeist.*

Observers martialed evidence to support this claim.[1] Wealth, they asserted, was a crucial component in the trend towards democracy. Poor countries typically were unable to develop or sustain democratic rule. Situations in which the many were poor and an elite possessed most of the country's wealth created a dynamic under which the poor would be driven to revolt, assuming there were leaders prepared to steer them in that direction. The wealthy, on the other hand, would become fearful of just such a prospect and enlist the help of the military and para-military forces to prevent such an outcome.

During the 1990s it appeared as if the world in general was becoming wealthier. Increasing per capita income brought with it an expanding middle class, a growing segment of the population both literate and politically attentive. Analysts suggested the middle class would become invested in the rule of law and political freedoms: the wealthier national populations became, the greater the pressures towards democracy.

The political scientist Ron Inglehart borrowed from Abraham Maslow's well-known 'hierarchy of human needs' to forecast the impact of growing prosperity on the things people valued.[2] The more successfully basic human needs for food, clothing and shelter were met, the more people were likely to commit themselves to such 'higher values' as social and political involvement in public life. Material considerations would count for less as 'post-materialist' values emerged and gained in significance. The democratic cause would concurrently gain in strength.

Religious considerations also played a role. Religious values tend towards the absolute and the uncompromising, at least as far as the Abrahamic ones are concerned. Confucian values seem less likely to ignite the same degree of passion but nonetheless stress the need for order and hierarchy, so that ideas about political equality appear alien to its proponents. Students of political development reasoned that as countries became more secular the chances for popular acceptance of the give-and-take of democratic politics would improve. Such reasoning was challenged when the 1979 Iranian revolution that toppled the monarchy and brought the Ayatollah Khomeini and his followers to power offered a warning that a decline in the role of uncompromising religion in politics was hardly inevitable.

We should not forget the impact of urban growth. Thomas Jefferson, arguing with Alexander Hamilton, claimed that the survival of democratic governance was largely contingent on yeomen, independent farmers whose values and interests were not only congruent with, but essential to, rule by and for the citizens of a democracy. Large landowners, plantation owners – in today's language agribusiness – do not provide the social basis for democratic governance. If we regard Jefferson's claims from a comparative perspective, we see that they have rarely proven to be true. In the developing world of the twentieth century, landless peasants repeatedly supported anti-democratic revolutions that produced authoritarian regimes (e.g. China and Vietnam). Instead of, and despite Marx's predictions to the contrary, farmers and peasants provided the social basis for most twentieth-century revolutionary upheavals. The fact that urbanization occurred throughout much of the world over the past century became a cause for democratic optimism. The literature suggests that rapid urbanization creates populations vulnerable to recruitment by anti-democratic movements. But once urban populations stabilize, sympathy for democratic values increases and becomes a basis for commitment to democracy.

Finally, two obvious alternatives to liberal democracy – fascism and communism – both failed dramatically, the first mid twentieth century, the second during the late twentieth century. Their failure seemed to suggest there were virtually no options to democratic rule.

What could go wrong?

Before attempting to answer this question, we should pause and take a closer look at democracy's components. Political scientists from Robert Dahl to Yascha Mounk have observed that liberal democracy consists of two elements. The first element includes the rule of law and the protection of civil liberties (such as rights to freedom of expression and thought, among them the right to contest peacefully the policies of those in power). The second element of liberal democracy is the right of mass participation in political life: the right of all adults (citizens at least) to vote in free and open elections. The very idea of 'citizenship' suggests that political passivity and indifference to public affairs are incompatible with liberal democratic rule.[3]

These two elements of democracy may not be compatible with one another. A long list of writers, including James Madison and John Stuart Mill, recognized that popular involvement in political life carries with it the risk that the 'masses,' or popular majorities in the population, may not or will not abide by the self-restraining rules of constitutional democracy. Unless a majority of the population develops and adheres to a set of often informal norms of conduct involving (among other things) mutual trust and respect, democratic rule will be put in jeopardy whenever a country is confronted by a crisis, internally or externally generated.

Wealth and its distribution are also at issue. As Aristotle and another long list of analysts have written, vast differences in the distribution of wealth within a society are incompatible with the development and persistence of democratic rule. It is hardly true in every case, but a large middle class is the *sine qua non* of democratic stability.

A partial answer to the 'what could go wrong' question is the appearance of what Fareed Zakaria and others have labelled 'illiberal democracy'.[4] Illiberal democracy represents a continuation of mass involvement in politics, but shorn of its liberal component. Symptoms of 'illiberal' or authoritarian democracy reflect the outlook of a country's rulers: (1) Do rulers reject or display weak commitment to the democratic rules of the game? (2) Do they deny the legitimacy of political opponents? (3) Do they tolerate or encourage violence? (4) Are they ready to curtail the civil liberties of their opponents?[5]

A number of democracies have gone down this path in recent years. Thanks to their manipulative and demagogic skills the leaders of Venezuela, Ecuador, Hungary, Poland, Romania, Turkey, the Philippines and several of the other new or newly restored democracies have become the victims of illiberal democratic rule. The growing power of right-wing populist parties in the long-standing democracies, including France, Germany, Austria and Italy, represents cause for concern. The willingness of the American President Donald Trump and his followers to attack the free press, the country's own Justice Department and the independent judiciary are clearly worrisome.

Observers have come forward with a variety of answers to explain the bad news. Here are the most salient.

In many of the industrialized democracies, economic growth has slowed and the income gap between rich and poor has widened, reaching a point where working-class folk and a wealthy elite – made up of the enterprising, the well-born, the well-educated and the well-connected – now live almost completely separate lives. Prosperous elites have been increasingly able to pass their advantages along to their offspring and their offspring's offspring. Even in such places as the United States rates of upward social mobility have slowed to a crawl. Furthermore, in the newly formed democracies of the Balkans and other parts of Eastern Europe, a widespread sentiment initially prevailed, claiming that the advent of democracy would yield enormous economic benefits. When benefits failed to materialize, at least not at the pace widely expected, disenchantment followed. Democracy had not paid off. A certain nostalgia for the old communist system or for some form of strong-man authoritarian rule developed.

Equally important, fear of mass immigration spread on both sides of the old 'iron curtain'. Because of lagging economic development and explosions of civil strife in North Africa, the Middle East and parts of Sub-Saharan Africa (the Sahel especially), the prosperous democracies of Europe became the destination for millions of émigrés fleeing their countries of origin. This vast surge of new immigrants produced a serious political backlash. Voters in France, Germany and the other Western democracies turned to support right-wing populist parties whose leaders amplified popular fears by articulating a heightened and renewed commitment to nationalism. Keeping foreigners out became an important element in Brexit, Britain's decision to withdraw from the European Union. In the United States, hostility toward new 'undocumented' immigrants from Central America and Mexico contributed to the 'Make America Great Again' presidential campaign of Donald Trump in 2016.

We turn now to the functioning of democracy itself. As Francis Fukuyama and others note, many of the long-standing democracies have suffered serious political decay. Their democratic institutions no longer seem to work – at least not very well. Italy comes to mind. Corruption and institutional paralysis became so rampant in the second decade of the twenty-first century that large numbers of voters turned to the Five Star Movement, a party created by a professional comedian to express popular contempt for the country's party political establishment. In the Philippines during 2016 presidential voters turned to Roderigo Duterte, out of frustration with his predecessor's inability to deal effectively with widespread epidemics of drug use and violent crime. Turkey, under the domination of President Erdoğan, came close to losing its democratic credentials altogether following a failed coup attempt by the country's military. In the United States, many voters turned to Donald Trump because of his promise to 'drain the swamp', to reduce the influence of Washington lobbyists and influence peddlers whose impact on Congress and various federal agencies had warped the policy-making process from Trump's point of view.

We should also mention an important democratization experience that failed: the Arab Spring. Beginning in Tunisia in 2011, many of the countries of the Middle East and North Africa experienced popular uprisings. In Egypt crowds gathered in Tahir Square to demand the resignation of President Mubarak and an end to one-party rule. Popular protests broke out in Algeria, Yemen, Syria and Bahrain. The results of these episodes were disheartening. Protests led to widespread turmoil and chaos, especially bloody civil wars and the re-imposition of strong-man rule. Only Tunisia has been able to retain its liberal democratic institutions.

Certainly, part of the reason for the Arab Spring's failure had to do with Islamism or Salafism. Literal-minded followers of the Prophet Mohammad fashioned a doctrine maintaining that liberal democracy was a heresy because it advocated rule by the people and secular law as against the Koran and Sharia law. To the extent that this doctrine achieved widespread support in the Arab world, efforts to establish and maintain liberal democracy became exceedingly difficult.

We come now to the matter of terrorism. In the Western world at least, modern terrorist violence appeared during the late 1960s. It represented a convergence of three elements. First among them was the failure of the student protest movements of the late 1960s to bring an end to the Vietnam War, and the inability of young protesters to create what they conceived to be more equal and just societies. Such failures produced frustration and disillusion. For many protestors, the works of Mao and Lenin had offered direction; the Viet Cong and Che Guevara, a highly romanticized revolutionary in Cuba, provided inspiration. As the massive protests waned, small groups of diehard revolutionaries turned towards violence. In Italy, Germany (or what was then West Germany), France and the United States such groups waged 'urban guerrilla' warfare against 'establishment' targets. Typically, this meant bombings, kidnappings and assassinations of the wealthy and powerful carried out by such groups as the Red Brigades, the Red Army Faction and the Weather Underground. In South America – Argentina, Brazil, Colombia and Uruguay – young revolutionaries created small bands, e.g. the Tupamaros, which used terrorist means to end what they viewed as the continued exploitation of the continent's poor.

Second, nationalist-based causes produced terror and violence. In Northern Ireland, the Basque Country of Spain and even to some extent the Netherlands (over the status of the ex-Dutch colony of South Molucca/Maluku) violence erupted. The Irish Republican Army (IRA) and Basque Homeland and Liberty (ETA) employed terrorist tactics in an effort to detach their regions from British and Spanish control – to achieve national independence in the case of ETA and to achieve a united Ireland in the case of the IRA. Violence enacted by ETA and the IRA deliberately threatened the security of civilian targets.

Third is the Palestinian problem. Following the defeat of Arab armies in the June 1967 Arab–Israeli war, Palestinian groups emerged under the general umbrella of the Palestinian Liberation Organization (PLO). Their cause was the destruction of Israel and its replacement by a democratic secular state, so their 1968 program said. Some of the groups – notably the Popular Front for the Liberation of Palestine (PFLP) and later the late Abu Nidal organization – carried out attacks in Western Europe and the Middle East, including and especially the skyjacking of commercial airliners. Violence at the 1972 Munich Olympic Games focused the world's attention on Palestinian issues. Using the label 'Black September', Palestinian gunmen took members of the Israeli Olympic team hostage. This event captured a worldwide television audience, and culminated in the deaths of the athletes Black September had seized.

In Western Europe and North America, the terrorist wave provoked a substantial reaction. Multiple countries passed new legislation to weaken civil liberty protections and to relax habeas corpus rules and various policies governing the right of privacy, e.g. search and seizure. New counter-terrorism agencies were created. The UN and other international organizations took up the issue. The result was a long list of international and regional agreements concerning air piracy, attacks on 'internationally protected' persons and related matters.

In the Latin American democracies, severe measures were undertaken. 'States of emergency' were declared in Argentina, Uruguay and Brazil. The military took control of the countries, and liberal democratic practices were suspended. Measures suspending civil liberty guarantees seemed to enjoy popular support, at least for a while.

When the Cold War ended, terrorism appeared to be on a downward trajectory, but subsequent events promoted a resurgence of the violence. The US decision to liberate

Kuwait from Iraqi occupation in 1990–1991 involved the stationing of American forces in Saudi Arabia, a decision which infuriated a wealthy young Saudi, Osama bin Laden (and others), and caused them to form al Qaeda, an organization committed to the expulsion of the United States and other Western powers from the House of Islam.

To achieve that goal, al Qaeda launched a series of spectacular terrorist attacks against the American presence, notably the bombing of US embassies in Kenya and Tanzania (1997) and the attack on the USS *Cole* at anchor in the port of Aden (2000).

Far and away the most spectacular terrorist acts initiated by al Qaeda were the September 11, 2001 attacks on the World Trade Center in New York and the Pentagon in Washington, attacks which killed some 3000 people. The effect of these disasters was enormous. A new unit of the US federal government was established, the Department of Homeland Security (really a consolidation of already existing agencies). Congress quickly enacted the Patriot Act to make it easier for federal law enforcement agencies to investigate suspected terrorist operations. The Bush administration committed itself to waging a global war on terrorism, during which virtually anything went, including a successful effort to expel al Qaeda from its protected space in Afghanistan.

The September 11 attacks should not be viewed in isolation. In the years immediately following 2001, Osama bin Laden's followers carried out major multi-casualty bombings in Bali, Madrid, Morocco and London, attacks that left hundreds dead. Most democracies followed the American lead in enacting more stringent anti-terrorism legislation and by developing better coordination of their mutual struggle to weaken al Qaeda. International organizations, e.g. Interpol and Europol, engaged in the effort and coordinated their activities.

Al Qaeda was not the only Salafist/jihad organization to wage a terrorist campaign against Western democracies and against both Shia- and Sunni-led governments (whose leaders al Qaeda militants regarded as heretical). A power vacuum occurred in the aftermath of the Anglo-American invasion of Iraq in 2003 and the resulting defeat of Saddam Hussein's regime. Sunni and Shia conflicted. A Sunni-based terrorist group appeared, al Qaeda in Mesopotamia, which carried out particularly bloody attacks on Shiite holy sites as well as upon symbols of the American presence.

Al Qaeda in Mesopotamia morphed into the Islamic State (ISIS) after the outbreak of the Syrian civil war in 2011–2012. In the midst of the fighting ISIS appeared, representing an amalgam of Iraqi and Syrian jihadists. Neither the government in Baghdad nor the government in Damascus was able to control areas of either country where ISIS had encysted itself. ISIS's leader proclaimed a new caliphate and its forces took control of territory overlapping Syria and Iraq. ISIS became an inspiration for young jihadists throughout the Western world and the Middle East, jihadists who enacted their commitment by joining forces in the Middle East or by emulation from abroad.

Though ISIS jihadists were ultimately expelled from the lands they had conquered (2015–2016), ISIS was hardly a spent force. Often inspired by its extensive online presence on the Web, young jihadists carried out numerous terrorist attacks on civilian targets in Western Europe (e.g. in France and Germany) and North America, all of which challenged the legitimacy of democratic process and rule. The most dramatic and lethal of these attacks were carried out in France and Belgium, targeting Parisian concert goers, Bastille Day celebrants and the wickedly satirical *Charlie Hebdo* magazine's editors, killed for their profanation of the Prophet's teachings.

The Islamic State's use of the Internet and the World Wide Web calls attention to another threat to liberal democratic values. From approximately the mid-1990s forward advances in computer technology have created a situation in which cyberspace has become a venue for serious political conflict. The extensive use of the Internet for malicious purposes has taken a variety of different forms. ISIS and other Islamist groups have used it to spread propaganda on behalf of their political doctrines. This use has not been confined to the dissemination of jihadist ideas. In Europe and North America, groups and individuals on the far right have created websites, e.g. Stormfront, to promote ultra-nationalist, white racist and anti-Semitic ideas. In addition, sophisticated extremist websites recruit new militants and prepare them to carry out violent attacks on selected targets. Further, radical groups use cyberspace to create ersatz communities. Individuals who may feel isolated are able to feel part of a community of the like-minded, and encouraged to act as a result.

Most ominous is the emergence of cyber warfare between and among nations. Insofar as liberal democracy is concerned, cyber war, usually waged via Facebook, Google and Twitter, becomes a modality hostile countries use to undermine the conduct of free and open elections, e.g. the Russian Federation's efforts to undermine the 2016 American and 2017 French presidential elections. If democratic institutions require freedom and openness, the prospect of cyber warfare goes to their heart.

Threats to security

Based on what we have observed above we can cluster current major threats to the security of liberal democracies under the following broad headings.

First is the tendency for citizens of the democracies to support restrictions on the exercise of liberty when they perceive an immediate threat to their health, safety or well-being. At present, fear of outsiders, newcomers and their offspring, fear of ethnic minorities has created a favorable environment for right-wing populism. Exponents of right-wing populism in Europe and North America stoke fears that a country's traditional culture is being threatened and denigrated. For those who follow the headlines it will hardly come as a surprise that many of the liberal democracies have become corrupted by groups seeking to achieve public benefits by paying public officials, in cash or in kind, to receive those benefits. Such manifestations of 'political decay' serve to reduce the public's commitment to affected democratic institutions.

Second, matters involving counter-insurgency and counter-terrorism.[6] In some democracies – India, Colombia and the Philippines for example – democratic governments face armed insurgencies by groups whose goal is to topple the freely elected government by force. Elsewhere, democracies face the threat of terrorism – home-grown, launched from abroad or arising from some combination of both.[7]

Third, when confronted by such challenges, decision-makers in the democracies often enact laws and issue special regulations to eliminate perceived threats. In the course of taking such steps, they have at times seriously compromised individual liberties. In the American struggle against al Qaeda, for instance, the CIA and the US armed forces were willing to use targeted killings, via Predator drones and Hellfire missiles, against American citizens belonging to jihadist organizations – without offering the accused trials or other due process protections. Also, during the war on terrorism the US established special prisons, so-called 'black-sites', where 'enemy combatants' were subject to 'enhanced interrogation' – i.e. torture, in violation of the laws of war. The more severe the threat, the more willing democratic policy-makers are to waive accepted rules. In some cases in the not too distant past citizens of the more fragile democracies have supported seizures of power by the military or placed their faith in a 'strong man' to purge a nation of corrupt or inept politicians.

Cyber warfare has clearly become a significant threat to the conduct of political life in the advanced democracies.[8] Adversaries of the democracies who use the Internet to manipulate and control the political views of computer users threaten the integrity of elections, alter democratic process and threaten democracy itself. The United States would be 'Exhibit A' in this regard.

Chapters in this volume

Democracies are hardly alike. They vary in terms of strength (their ability to apply and enforce law) and durability (how long they last.) Some are interrupted by military interventions, then resume. Some are resilient; others falter as they confront critical challenges of the types described above, challenges of either foreign or domestic origin. Of particular interest to us is the frequency and severity of democracies' resort to extra-legal or extra-judicial means to achieve security. Equally interesting is the balance democracies establish between security and the rule of law (rule of law conceived from both legislative and judicial perspectives).

Based on these standards we have divided the countries included in our analysis into three categories: strong democracies, challenged democracies and fragile democracies. Strong democracies include the United States, Great Britain, France, Germany, Italy, Spain, Australia, New Zealand and, at least arguably, Israel. These democracies are far from perfect, to put it mildly. Certainly, America's performance under the Trump administration has demonstrated certain glaring weaknesses with respect to democracy. Nevertheless democratic institutions in this group of nations have shown a repeated ability to withstand challenges and threats from within and from abroad.

By contrast, Argentina, India, South Africa, Brazil and Romania face serious challenges to the stability of the democratic order. With the exception of South Africa and Romania, challenged democracies have either been displaced by the military in the not too distant past or may be vulnerable to coups in the event they suffer serious economic downturns. Brazil is currently led by President Bolsonaro, a former army officer, who has expressed contempt for Brazil's democratic norms. India has been able to sustain democratic rule since its national independence in 1947. Nevertheless we regard India as challenged because its democratic institutions have had to control serious armed opposition from both its Sikh minority in the Punjab and a sustained violent separatist movement in Jammu-Kashmir. From time to time India also has experienced serious waves of violence inflicted upon the country's large Muslim minority by radical elements within the Hindu population. South African and Romanian democracies have been marred by widespread corruption; corruption alienates many voters from the prevailing order.

We consider democracy in the Philippines and Nigeria to be fragile. In the former case President Duterte (in the second half of his six-year term) openly advocates violation of the rule of law by endorsing the extra-judicial killing of suspected drug dealers and other alleged wrong-doers. Manila is also confronted by at least two armed insurgencies that have plagued the country for many years. The first, a Maoist insurgency pursued by the New Peoples' Army, has declined recently. The second, launched by Muslim separatists on Mindanao and other southern islands, has waxed and waned. Abu Sayyaf, a jihadist group, continues to kidnap and kill local opponents and foreign tourists.

Nigeria has oscillated between democracy and military dictatorship since it achieved independence from British rule in 1960. Not only has its democracy experienced massive waves of corruption based on its vast oil resources, but Nigeria's democracy still struggles to overcome profound tribal and religious cleavages that result in widespread violence throughout the country. Boko Haram, a violent jihadist movement, continues to threaten populations in the Muslim northeast region of the country. Given our concern about the means democracies employ to achieve security, we should note that the Nigerian military has carried out indiscriminate killings of villagers alleged to have ties to Boko Haram.

Our distinguished group of contributors tackles the problems posed by security threats to democratic governance by placing them in historical and/or legal context. Whether the writers are political scientists or scholars schooled in the law, they all seek to understand current threats by placing them against the background of earlier experiences. In general, the countries we label 'strong' have had to confront threats posed by terrorist activity, either home-grown or international. The more 'challenged' or 'fragile' democracies have had to respond to threats posed by internal wars, as in the cases of India, Nigeria and the Philippines – wars which oftentimes include insurgents who receive support from outside forces (e.g. Pakistan in the case of India). The volume is selective rather than comprehensive; contributors write from a variety of theoretical perspectives and employ a range of analytic methods. It is time to let them speak for themselves.

Notes

1 See especially, Francis Fukuyama, The End of History and the Last Man (New York: Free Press, 1992).

2 Ronald Inglehart, Modernization and Postmodernization (Princeton NJ: Princeton University Press, 1997).

3 Fareed Zakaria, *The Future of Freedom: Illiberal Democracy at Home and Abroad* (New York: Norton, 2003).

4 Fareed Zakaria, *The Post American World* (New York: Norton, 2008).

5 Steven Levitsky and Daniel Ziblatt, *How Democracies Die* (New York: Crown, 2018) pp. 23–24.

6 See Antonia Chayes, *Borderless Wars* (New York: Cambridge University Press, 2015) pp. 5–14.

7 See for example, Leonard Weinberg (Ed.), *Democratic Responses to Terrorism* (New York: Routledge, 2008).

8 Richard Clarke and Robert Knake, *Cyber War* (New York: HarperCollins, 2010).

PART I

Strong democracies: United States, Great Britain, France, Germany, Italy, Spain, Australia and New Zealand, Israel

1

DEMOCRACY AND SECURITY IN THE UNITED STATES

Leonard Weinberg and Elizabeth Francis

This chapter confronts what is usually depicted as a classic dilemma of democratic rule. If democratic rule is threatened, whether by an internal or an external challenge, how best can a democracy defeat the threat without jeopardizing the very core principles on which the democracy is based? If 'the rules of the game' are to be suspended, for how long and to what degree of severity must this 'state of exception' persist? Who decides? How 'exceptional' does a threat have to be?[1]

Consider another problem: it is always possible that those holding power in a democracy will manufacture a threat or exaggerate that threat in order to enhance the government's own power. The events of 9/11 and subsequent terrorist attacks on Americans, both at home and abroad, have excited an intense, sometimes hysterical, debate about how the country should respond to such events. Central to the debate has been the matter of balance. How many rights of individual citizens should be compromised in order to enhance the security of other citizens or the community in general?[2] Those engaging in the debate often suggest a 'delicate balance' is to be struck between security and liberty. In effect, a commitment to heightened security leads inevitably to less liberty (see the congressional debates over the passage of the 2001 Patriot Act). How much liberty must be sacrificed to achieve more security? Should a balance be struck based on 'bad tendency' or 'gravity of the danger' doctrines, or some other legal formulation? Does it make a difference if the threat to the country is internal, external or a combination of both? Does a long-standing democracy really have to compromise its own principles in order to deal with small bands of terrorists whose chances of gaining terrestrial power are infinitesimal, except in their own minds?

Recently these questions have entangled themselves with vast changes wrought by the computer revolution and the advent of the new social media. The ability of government agencies, the National Security Agency (NSA) in the United States especially, to achieve surveillance (at least apparently) over virtually all individuals within the country has drawn widespread attention. So has the capacity of terrorist-minded groups to evade detection through encryption and related means. Often the mouse has been able to evade the cat.

In our view, debates over the 'delicate balance' presumption often present us with a false dichotomy. More often than not, recent terrorist events involve efforts by a democratic government to react quickly and publicly to citizen pressure by apprehending or killing members, authentic or aspirational, of al Qaeda (AQ) or the Islamic State (ISIS). Aspirational groups typically consist of no more than a handful of individuals acting on behalf of some wider religious or political cause. In an increasing number of instances 'lone wolves', radicalized via social media, commit the terrorist act, lone wolves whose attachment to the larger group is largely imaginary.

Terrorist episodes normally do not pit the government or law enforcement agencies against the People, where significant segments of the population support the killers. Instead the situation usually involves demands on the part of popular majorities for the government to act rapidly and effectively to eliminate a terrorist threat. If the affected government is perceived as not responding rapidly and effectively enough to terrorist attacks, popular opposition mounts and opposition parties are likely gain votes at the next elections. Certainly in the American context no national administration (e.g. Clinton, Bush, Obama, Trump) wishes to be perceived as weak or insufficiently vigorous in its pursuit of a 'killer elite' out to harm the public. This seems to be particularly true when clandestine bands of terrorists or 'lone wolves' are viewed as foreign, or inspired by foreign organizations.

The current situation (circa 2020) in the United States is not unprecedented. So far as attempts to counter terrorism are concerned, the 'modern' struggle dates to the Nixon administration (1969–1974). Readers may recall the Vietnam War era. During the late 1960s and early 1970s the United States faced a series of terrorist threats. Domestically the Vietnam War caused the formation of a widespread 'peace movement'. The war, in other words, led to a cycle of mass protests aimed initially at persuading the powers that be to withdraw American forces from Southeast Asia on pain of massive disruptions to public life.

As American involvement in the war wound down in the early 1970s, so did the mass anti-war protests, particularly following the killings of students at Kent State University by Ohio National Guardsmen (1970). In place of mass protests, new 'revolutionary' groups appeared, the most conspicuous of which were the Weathermen, the Black Liberation Army and the Symbionese Liberation Army. Rather than pursue peace, these groups sought to ignite a violent revolution, no matter how far-fetched their aim. Small bands carried out a series of terrorist attacks on various publicity-winning targets – including newspaper heiress Patty Hearst, who was kidnapped, and Marcus Foster, the first African-American superintendent of the Oakland CA school system, who was murdered. The randomized murder of police officers also caught the public's attention.

During this period terrorism was hardly confined to the home front. Following the June 1967 Arab–Israeli war, Palestinian groups (especially the Popular Front for the Liberation of Palestine, PFLP), acting under the umbrella of the Palestinian Liberation Organization (PLO), launched a terrorist campaign against Israeli targets in Europe. Most spectacular among them was the 1972 Black September attack on Israeli athletes at the Munich Olympic Games. The PLO's operations quickly spread to the Jewish State's perceived friends and allies. Consequently, PLO groups began to target Americans and their diplomatic installations and commercial aircraft in Europe and elsewhere.

The Nixon administration reacted to such threats (including the murder of a US diplomat during a 1973 reception at the Saudi Embassy in Khartoum by a PLO group) by issuing executive orders, encouraging Congress to pass legislation and encouraging international cooperation (e.g. the International Conventions on Airline Skyjacking), initiatives all designed to stop terrorist attacks foreign and domestic.[3]

After this initial outburst of terrorist activity in the early 1970s, American security services, armed forces and law enforcement agencies have sought to eliminate a succession of terrorist threats. Terrorist groups have come and gone (especially at the end of the Cold War), but threats have persisted. If anything, the level of threat to America and American interests by the Islamic State and its jihadist cohorts during the second decade of the 21st century has been as substantial as it was during the earlier revival of terrorism in the 1970s.

Earlier 20th-century security threats

Over the course of the 20th century the United States faced a number of threats to its security by enemies foreign and domestic, real and imaginary. That history is worth examining in detail. To undertake the analysis we should begin by defining the nature of the specific security threat with which the United States was confronted and ask ourselves whether the response was proportionate to the threat.

First, we should consider whether the threat posed to the US was primarily foreign, domestic or a combination of both. It appears that reaching a plausible conclusion about this distinction is much more difficult than it might seem initially. Take the case of the Korean War (1950–1954). In June 1950 the Truman administration deployed American forces to South Korea in order to prevent the communist North from overrunning the government in Seoul and seizing control of the whole peninsula. The deployment was sanctioned by the UN Security Council. At first glance the Korean 'police action' appears to have been a case where the threat to American security was exclusively foreign. Kim Il Sung, the North Korean ruler, had few admirers or followers in the United States ready to sabotage or undermine the war effort. Nor did the North Korean dictator possess the military means to strike at the United States. Nevertheless, the Korean fighting did have serious domestic ramifications involving mass fear of communism as manifested by the Soviet Union, the People's Republic of China and agents or alleged agents of those countries operating in the United States. Such fears led to various anti-communist investigations conducted by members of congressional and state legislative committees committed to eliminating 'subversive activities'. During the Korean War era even private organizations and popular journalists (e.g. Red Channels, the *New York Journal American* and the American Legion) committed themselves to rooting out the Red threat to American society.

Neither the Korean War nor more generally the conflict between the US and the USSR and its allies involved terrorist operations of the sort with which we are familiar today. Of course the threat to American national security posed by the Soviet bloc countries was far more serious than that offered by ISIS and al Qaeda in recent years. The latter's terrorist acts have been and are profoundly disturbing to American and other Western publics; but they are hardly existential challenges, and do not involve the potential destruction of the countries involved.

Second, as suggested above, beyond the distinction between foreign and domestic events we need to evaluate the severity and extent to which terrorism was involved. For example, World War II drew millions of Americans into the fighting in both the European and Asian theatres of operations but involved virtually no terrorism on the North American mainland, even though the fighting appeared at one point to represent a serious threat to the country.

The consequences of World War I were not the same. World War I ended with an Armistice agreement in November 1918. The United States emerged relatively unscathed by the fighting. In Europe, on the other hand, WWI left millions dead, destroying a whole generation of young men. The German, Austro-Hungarian, Ottoman and Russian Empires came to an end as a result of the fighting. Perhaps of greatest consequence was the 1917 Russian Revolution, which resulted in the victory of the Bolsheviks under V.I. Lenin.

The Red Revolution led to the formation of revolutionary communist parties throughout the industrialized world, including the United States, and the Third

Communist International. Communists, revolutionary socialists and revolutionary anarchists launched violent uprisings in Hungary, Italy, Germany (e.g. Bavaria, Berlin) and elsewhere. All were ultimately repressed, and most revolutionary leaders lost their lives in the process.

As elsewhere in the industrialized world, many of America's leaders worried about the threat of Red Revolution within the United States (the postwar atmosphere is captured in John Dos Passos' 1932 novel, *1919*). During World War I Congress passed the Espionage Act, which criminalized speech that appeared to undermine the war effort. Those who spoke out against US involvement faced prosecution. The socialist leader Eugene Debs was imprisoned. His conviction was subsequently upheld by the Supreme Court.

In the aftermath of the war substantial economic and social dislocation occurred. Unemployment became widespread, and many ex-soldiers had great difficulty finding jobs and adjusting to private life.

> There were deep divisions within the population. The growth of industry had produced vast wealth, but it was unevenly distributed, and the great mansions that graced Fifth Avenue were shadowed by slum districts where tuberculosis, alcoholism, and industrial accidents exacted a heavy toll.[4]

Against this background, the country experienced the 'Red Scare' of 1919–1920. The view became widespread that revolutionaries, like their European counterparts, intended to overthrow the capitalist system and replace it with something approximating the new Soviet Union or, for the anarchists, no state at all. Sufficient violence occurred to raise popular suspicions that such plans were not sheer fantasy.

Among the most visible of the anarchist groups was the Industrial Workers of the World (IWW), or 'Wobblies', whose leadership had opposed American entry into WWI and who also favored direct action ('Propaganda by Deed') to bring about the revolution they believed they could ignite. Using the Espionage Act, the Justice Department prosecuted the Wobblies' leaders for their public advocacy of revolution. Violence followed: bombs were detonated by anarchists at a number of places around the country, including the offices of the *Los Angeles Times* and the *Wall Street Journal*, and spectacularly in front of the home of A. Mitchell Palmer, the US Attorney General. 'Foreigners' or recent immigrants were blamed for causing most of the revolutionary agitation. These events led Palmer's Justice Department to undertake the deportation of hundreds of immigrants suspected of sympathy with or active support for the revolutionary cause. The inspirational anarchist figure Emma Goldman was among those deported. In most cases, deportees were not afforded judicial hearings before being expelled from the country. One estimate put around 10,000 as the number of people expelled in this way.

The Depression era of the 1930s was another occasion on which the threat to civil liberty was tested. In terms of foreign developments, this was a period during which the Soviet Union fell under the complete control of Joseph Stalin. Using his role of party secretary Stalin launched a series of brutal purges involving, at first, many of the party's old Bolshevik leadership (Trotsky, Kamenev, Bukharin, Radek, Zinoviev). After torture by the secret police, these figures were subjected to 'purge trials' and then executed. By the late 1930s the purges had spread to wide swaths of the Soviet population.

Despite or perhaps because of the havoc created by this 'great terror', Stalin expressed the concept 'socialism in one country'. Given the USSR's encirclement by hostile capitalist powers, the country needed to consolidate its control over its own territory and build up its military-industrial capacity. The goal of world-wide revolution as advocated by Trotsky and his followers would have to be put aside for a more propitious occasion.

Despite its self-restricted approach to revolution the Stalinist regime hardly withdrew from the international arena. The Moscow-dominated Comintern or Third International (1919–1943) was an organization of communist parties whose objective was to defend and protect the Soviet Union from all threats posed by the encircling capitalist powers. This meant, so far as the United States in the 1930s was concerned, the formation of an extensive spy network inside the US government. It also meant the development of an American Communist Party as an above-ground operation that sought votes for its candidates for public office. In addition, the party was extremely active in the labor movement, where its cadres became influential in the newly formed Congress of Industrial Organizations (CIO).

We should not forget that the Depression also prompted the formation of a variety of radical right movements throughout the country. Some of these were home-grown copies of European fascist groups. Among the most visible were the Defenders of the Christian Faith, led by Gerald Winrod, 'the Jayhawk Nazi'; William Dudley Pelley's Silver Shirts; Huey 'the Kingfish' Long's Share Our Wealth Movement; and Father Charles Coughlin's Social Justice and Christian Front organizations.[5]

With the exception of Huey Long's Share Our Wealth movement, the other formations were led by individuals who expressed admiration for Hitler and Mussolini and their dynamic fascist regimes. With the exception of Share our Wealth, these figures were all intensely anti-Semitic, holding Jews responsible for the spread of communism both in Europe and North America in their alleged quest for world domination.

Admiration for fascism is one thing, but direct emulation is something else. Following the Nazis' rise to power in Germany at the end of January 1933, recent emigrants from the Hitler state formed the German American Bund.[6] The Bund's fuehrer for most of this prewar period was Fritz Kuhn, a recently naturalized American citizen. The New York-centered Bund performed a number of functions, the most important of which was campaigning to keep the US out of European conflicts – often citing George Washington ('no foreign entanglements') in support of its position.

The emergence of both far-right movements during the Depression and the penetration of communists into American life caught the attention of US congressional leaders. Accordingly, in 1934 a temporary House Committee on Un-American Activities (HUAC) was formed under the leadership of Representatives John McCormack and Martin Dickstein. Dickstein, a Jew from New York, was the prime mover. To many observers it was not completely clear what 'un-American activities' meant. Despite the elusive character of the term, the committee called witnesses and took testimony over the next several years. Also, during the mid-1930s the Federal Bureau of Investigation (FBI) became interested in the Bund and home-grown fascist groups.

In the late 1930s the committee was changed into a permanent House committee and switched political focus. Under the new leadership of Martin Dies, a conservative Texan, the HUAC became especially interested in the Communist Party and its links to the Soviet Union. The Smith Act (1940) was the result of these inquiries. The Smith Act, along with earlier legislation requiring foreign agents to register with the authorities (1938), was intended to criminalize public speech and expression that advocated the violent overthrow of the American government.

After American entry into World War II at the end of December 1941, the Justice Department dissolved the German American Bund. Fritz Kuhn, its leader, fled into exile in Mexico. The Justice Department also undertook to prosecute a long list of pro-fascist figures

(*McWilliams vs. US* 1944), some of whom are mentioned above. The pro-fascists were accused of sedition and brought to trial in 1944. But Justice Department lawyers evidently bungled the prosecution and the charges were dismissed.

We should also point out that, following the Japanese attack at Pearl Harbor in December 1941, hatred and fear of people of Japanese ancestry living on the West Coast became widespread. Were these people possibly 'Fifth Columnists' preparing to aid an invasion of the US by Japanese forces? The result of such fears was an executive order signed by President Roosevelt permitting the American military to round up all Japanese Americans living on the West Coast and transport them to 'relocation' centers built in isolated areas of the inter-mountain West. The constitutionality of this policy was later upheld by the Supreme Court in *Hirabayashi vs. US* (1943) and *Korematsu vs. US* (1944), but overturned decades later under the Carter and Reagan administrations.

During World War II the US and Britain committed themselves to building an atomic bomb. Major work on this vast project centered on Los Alamos, an isolated area in the New Mexico desert not far from Santa Fe. It was not long before leaders in the Kremlin discovered what their wartime allies were up to. This knowledge led the Soviets to successfully plant a network of spies in Los Alamos and related facilities. The major figures were Klaus Fuchs and Theodore Hall, both important atomic physicists; of much less significance were Julius Rosenberg and his wife Ethel. Ethel's brother, David Greenglass, an army machinist, also played a role.

World War II ended at the beginning of September 1945 (VJ Day), when the Japanese surrendered unconditionally to the Allies. The war produced two clear-cut victors: the United States and the Soviet Union. At this point these 'superpowers' remained allies. But within a brief period they became geopolitical adversaries in what became a four-decade long 'Cold War'.

At least four major events appear to have ignited this new conflict. In 1948 the Russians blocked Anglo-American land access to Berlin, resulting in the Berlin Blockade. The Western allies reacted by staging an around-the-clock airlift to keep the three Western sectors of the city supplied with food and fuel. Then in 1949 the USSR was able to develop and test a nuclear weapon of its own, only a few years after the American deployment. Third, also in 1949, Chinese communists under Mao defeated the American-supported nationalists, ushering in a Chinese People's Republic.

The Truman administration reacted to these evident Soviet successes by orchestrating the North Atlantic Treaty Organization (NATO), sending American troops to Korea to prevent a communist victory (see above), and providing economic assistance (the Marshall Plan) to various countries threatened by domestic communist parties and labor unions (e.g. Italy).

Within the US reaction took the form of a second Red Scare. The perception became widespread that the US was threatened by a massive communist conspiracy whose goal was the transformation of the country into a People's Republic governed by a dictatorship of the proletariat. For many inside and outside of American political life such negative developments came as a shock.[7] In turn, shock led to widespread suspicion that communist agents operating within the United States had acted as 'subversives', stealing secrets and in general seeking to undermine American democracy.

Acting under the Smith Act and later the Internal Security Act (1950), plus a number of executive orders, the Justice Department tried and convicted a dozen leaders of the Communist Party USA. In the middle of the Korean War federal officials arrested Julius and Ethel Rosenberg and accused them of supplying atomic secrets to the USSR. David Greenglass, Ethel Rosenberg's brother, was also accused. After a lengthy trial and appeal process, the

Rosenbergs were convicted and later executed in 1953. Greenglass furnished evidence for the prosecution and was given a lengthy prison sentence. The top-level Soviet spies at Los Alamos were not prosecuted and emerged virtually unscathed. Klaus Fuchs fled to communist East Germany and Theodore Hall spent the rest of his career working in England at Cambridge.

The US Congress played a substantial role in pursuing communist subversion. HUAC drew widespread attention by holding hearings about communist penetration of the film industry. Some screen writers, 'the Hollywood Ten', were prosecuted for contempt because of their unwillingness to testify. HUAC members also pursued the case of Alger Hiss. Based on the testimony of two ex-communists, Whittaker Chambers and Elizabeth Bentley, Hiss, a long time State Department official, was accused of passing secrets to the Soviets. Under oath Hiss denied the allegation. HUAC investigators (including then Congressman Richard Nixon) discovered Hiss had lied. Hiss was later convicted of perjury and sent to federal prison.

During 1950 and over the next several years, the foremost investigator of communists in government was Senator Joseph McCarthy of Wisconsin. In his role as Chair of a Senate subcommittee McCarthy and his staff launched one investigation after another focused on communists in the State Department, the US armed forces and other government agencies. Virtually all federal employees whose backgrounds McCarthy and his free-wheeling staff found questionable were open to investigation. McCarthy's reign as a Red baiter lasted until 1955 when the US Senate voted to censure him for his often reckless charges. (During one speech McCarthy accused General George Marshall, one of the principal architects of American victory in World War II, of being 'a disgrace to his uniform'.)

The censure of McCarthy was not the end of what came to be known as 'McCarthyism'. State legislators in California, Indiana, New York, Texas and other states pursued their own hunts for subversive elements at the state and local level. School teachers and college professors were frequent targets. And the major device used in these inquiries was the loyalty oath. In many states public employees were required to sign an oath stipulating that they were not, nor had they ever been, a member of the Communist Party; nor, in many instances, had they belonged to any group on the US Attorney General's list of 'subversive' organizations. This requirement was ultimately broadened to all those seeking licenses to practice the trades and professions. For example, if someone wanted a license to become a barber or beautician in Texas, that person was required to sign an oath denying proscribed memberships. In Indiana professional boxers and wrestlers were required to disavow Communist Party membership before they were permitted to enter the ring.

Eventually cooler heads prevailed. The federal courts, especially the Supreme Court under Chief Justice Earl Warren, found most of the federal and state legislation and other government actions described above to be unconstitutional because they violated the First, Fourth and Fifth Amendments to the Constitution.

The courts also played a decisive role in the next major crises facing the country: the civil rights movement and anti-Vietnam protests. Surprisingly, neither movement managed to unleash the waves of political paranoia linked to and characteristic of the earlier Red Scares.[8] It was not for lack of trying.

In the case of movements during the 1960s to achieve racial integration of America's public institutions on the basis of non-violent public protests, several institutions and political constituencies tried to revive the Red baiting of earlier decades. Certain politicians from the Southern states claimed that white organizers from the North were really communists out to undermine the region's way of life. Long-serving FBI director J. Edgar Hoover believed that

Dr. Martin Luther King Jr. and his immediate followers were subversives, despite their professions of non-violent civil disobedience. As a consequence the FBI monitored the private lives of King and his aides.

By the mid-1960s the civil rights movement was challenged, some would say superseded, by the Black Power movement, which elicited authentically radical opposition groups, perhaps most notably the Ku Klux Klan and other white racial supremacist organizations. The result of the struggle over racial equality was serious inter-racial conflict that took a variety of forms.

Beginning in the fall of 1965 in the Watts section of East Los Angeles the form that achieved the most attention was the urban riot. After Watts, African-American neighborhoods in Newark, Detroit, Chicago, Milwaukee and other major cities went up in flames. Thousands of protestors burned and looted in response to triggering events. The April 1968 assassination of Martin Luther King produced the most widespread rioting.

Despite the intensity and widespread distribution of the riots and other manifestations of race conflict during the 1960s there was little to report by way of 'political paranoia'. Unlike circumstances during the two Red Scares, the civil rights movement was rarely perceived as a communist or foreign effort to undermine the American system – with the notable exception of certain political figures in the South. Many Southern political figures maintained that Northerners, both black and white, who came south to help register newly enfranchised African-Americans (Freedom Summer 1963), were communists in reality, there to do the bidding of the Kremlin.

About the same might be said about the almost decade-long protests (1966–1973) against America's military involvement in the Vietnam War. The US military effort to prevent South Vietnam from falling to the Vietcong and communist North Vietnam failed. This failure was helped, at least to a certain extent, by the massive agitation and protest against the war in the US. Students for a Democratic Society (SDS) and a host of other groups staged sit-ins, rallies and marches in an effort to force American withdrawal from Southeast Asia.

The struggle over Vietnam occurred at a time when China and the Soviet Union were embroiled in a dispute over the inevitability of anti-capitalist revolutions, and in an era when East and West were armed with nuclear weapons. One effect of the Sino-Soviet struggle was the appearance of Maoist or pro-Chinese communist parties all over the non-communist world, including the United States. The Maoist Progressive Labor Party played an active role in the anti-Vietnam mass protests in the US.[9] None of its activities were particularly clandestine. Nor were the activities of groups that waved North Vietnamese flags and chanted pro-Vietcong slogans ('Ho, Ho Chi Minh the Vietcong is going to win') at rallies in front of the Pentagon, or at the Republican and Democratic national conventions in 1968.

In contrast to the two Red Scare episodes following the world wars, Vietnam War-era protesters made little attempt to hide their political sympathies. In fact, they gloried in their links to radical movements on a world-wide basis. In an era of American–Soviet détente, many youthful protesters regarded the USSR and the communist parties aligned with it as bureaucratic, stodgy and out of touch.[10] New revolutionary parties, well to the left of pro-Soviet ones, sprang up in Western Europe and Latin America.

Security agencies in the US did not let Vietnam-era protests go unnoticed. Both the FBI and the Central Intelligence Agency (CIA) engaged in surveillance of the anti-war movement. They also conspired to plant agents inside the more radical and violence-prone of the groups. On occasion CIA and FBI agents acted as *agents provocateurs*, encouraging militants to carry out acts likely to get all concerned arrested.

The US Senate reacted to disclosures about such FBI and CIA operations by appointing a special committee, chaired by Idaho Senator Frank Church, to investigate abuses of the First and Fourth Amendments, to consider congressional oversight and to define somewhat stricter limitations on what these agencies could and could not do, stressing that the CIA could not engage in secret operations within the United States. The Freedom of Information Act (1966) permitted private citizens (journalists especially) to obtain access to many previously secret government documents.[11]

Responses to terrorism

This brings us to the problem of terrorism. During the mid-1960s and thereafter terrorist activity, both domestic and international, became a serious concern for American authorities. So far as the United States is concerned, the diversion of American-based commercial airliners (skyjacking) to Cuba became a common phenomenon. From the mid-1960s onward, individuals with political axes to grind seized control of airliners bound for Miami or New Orleans and demanded they be flown to Havana. At that time the US and the Castroite regime did not have diplomatic relations. Cuban authorities felt under no obligation to extradite the skyjackers to the US for prosecution, although the other passengers were permitted to return to the US.[12]

There were few disincentives for would-be skyjackers. Copy-cat behavior or behavior contagion followed as individuals with various agendas or psychological problems headed for Havana. American and Cuban authorities eventually concluded that this wave of skyjackings was intolerable. Accordingly, the governments entered into a bilateral agreement to extradite or prosecute skyjackers and return both the affected planes and passengers to the US.

The seizure and diversion of airliners had become a world-wide problem by the late 1960s and early 1970s. There were also cases in which a handful of terrorists threw bombs at or shot up the gate areas of airports in attempts to kill as many passengers as possible, a strategy that did not require seizing control of a plane mid-flight. Another practice that became common during the 1970s involved planting bombs in the stowed luggage of airline passengers, bombs that detonated mid-flight. A number of Israel-bound airliners were destroyed in this way.

Initial reactions to such criminal enterprises were the Montreal and Tokyo international conventions on air piracy. The US played a leading role in their approval. Signatory states to the conventions were under obligation to extradite or prosecute the skyjackers they apprehended. And states that refused to comply with this rule (e.g. Libya, South Yemen) were subject to boycott by, *inter alia*, the International Airline Pilots Association.

Overall, initial responses among the Western democracies to the onset of what Walter Laqueur labeled 'the age of terrorism' were to treat terrorist acts more or less as prosecutable crimes, rather than acts of war requiring military or paramilitary reaction. After all, kidnapping individuals and holding them for ransom were crimes no matter what the kidnapper's motivation – political or otherwise.

We should also consider the phenomenon of the 'poisoned pawn'. In the early 1970s governments that arrested and then prosecuted individuals suspected of committing crimes in the name of a political cause faced problems not normally associated with common crimes. First, the person arrested and charged with a crime (in Northern Ireland for example) might claim to be a 'political prisoner' and therefore not bound by the rules governing normal criminal prosecutions. Second, if the state went ahead and convicted the terrorist and put him/her in prison, other members of the terrorist group might stage another kidnapping or skyjacking and attempt to use hostages thus acquired to blackmail the government into releasing fellow members on threat of executing the newly kidnapped.

As terrorism became a significant problem during the Nixon administration, American policy became one of no blackmail and no concessions to terrorism. In cases involving the kidnapping of prominent individuals or the sequestration of numbers of airline passengers, a succession of American presidents refused to deal with their terrorist captors. The logic of this position was that negotiations and concessions to one group of terrorists offered incentives to other terrorist groups to do likewise.

Terrorist activity within the US and against Americans traveling abroad continued to increase during the 1970s and 1980s. Domestically, a number of far left groups, such as the Symbionese Liberation Army and Weather Underground, sought to ignite a revolution in hopes of toppling the capitalist system. Black and Puerto Rican nationalist groups also carried out terrorist attacks on behalf of their secessionist demands.

Those on the left had no monopoly on the use of terrorism. Racist and radical right-wing groups surfaced or resurfaced during these decades as well.[13] Groups such as the Aryan Nations, Ku Klux Klan, White Aryan Resistance and Posse Comitatus defined the US as under the control of Zionist Occupation Government (ZOG) or a similar malevolent cabal. They claimed that ZOG and its surrogates used racial minorities (so-called 'mud' people) to displace white Aryans from their rightful place as North America's natural rulers. To restore the natural order of things it was necessary to ignite a Racial Holy War (RAHOWA).

One of the federal government's responses to this radicalization at the fringes of American political life was COINTELPRO, a plan developed by the Justice Department and the FBI led by J. Edgar Hoover. COINTELPRO involved the recruitment or assignment of agents to penetrate extremist groups, both left and right, in order to keep the government informed about the groups' plans. Bribery, an often overlooked tool, proved successful on occasion.

During the 1970s and 1980s Americans living or traveling abroad became targets of terrorist attacks. At first these operations were staged by ideologically driven revolutionary groups that perpetrated crimes such as the kidnapping of US General James Dozier in Italy and the murder of Dan Mitrione, a US police trainer, in Uruguay. Such attacks subsided as left-wing revolutionary ideologies lost their appeal.

This was not true, however, with attacks emanating from the Middle East and responding to the Palestinian issue. A variety of groups committed to 'armed struggle' against Israel; some outside the Palestinian Liberation Organization umbrella regarded Americans and American entities in Europe and elsewhere as appropriate targets because of US support for Israel. Thus identified, American embassies and diplomatic personnel became legitimate and worthwhile targets.

As these attacks mounted, American officials gradually reached the conclusion that the policy of treating terrorist attacks as simple law enforcement problems should give way to a more militarized outlook. The CIA and 'special forces' elements of the US military became involved.

Following the 1982 invasion of Lebanon by Israeli forces, the PLO groups headquartered in Beirut, or at least their leaders, were compelled to move their headquarters to Tunis. At that time Yasser Arafat and other PLO leaders reached the conclusion that they ought to seek dialogue with the US, especially since the US had brokered a peace agreement between Egypt and Israel. For many on the Palestinian side, it looked as if continued terrorism was a blind alley.

The consequence of this reasoning was the Camp David Accords of 1994. It appeared as if the violence between Israel and Palestine might have passed. But this was not to be. New forces entered the picture, presenting themselves as grounded in religious inspiration. In Lebanon a Shiite organization, Hezbollah (Party of God), entered the fray. This 'Party of God' not only attacked Israeli and Sunni Lebanese targets but staged terrorist attacks on American targets as well. Americans and American institutions, the US Embassy in Beirut, the Marine Corps barracks at the Beirut Airport and employees of the American University in Beirut were all targeted by Hezbollah, which was also responsible for introducing the tactic of suicide bombing into the repertoire of terrorist organizations.

Despite rhetoric about being tough and uncompromising towards terrorism, the Reagan administration withdrew US forces from Lebanon and entered into secret negotiations with the Iranian theocracy. American negotiators recognized that Hezbollah would follow Tehran's lead. In exchange for military equipment and hard currency, Iran's clerical leadership agreed to have Hezbollah release American hostages it had kidnapped from the streets of Beirut.

This blood money was then used in Central America to support the pro-American Contras in Nicaragua (1986–1987) in their armed conflict with the pro-communist Sandinistas. The transfer of funds was in clear violation of the law which prohibited American aid to the right-wing Contras because of their frequent violations of human rights. The episode became known as the 'Iran-Contra Scandal' and led to several criminal prosecutions, including those of Admiral John Poindexter and Michael Ledeen, National Security Council staff members.

Islamic terrorism – really Salafist/jihadi terrorism – became a significant problem in the following years subsequent to the American-led military campaign to expel Iraqi forces from Kuwait in 1991. Osama bin Laden, a wealthy Saudi businessman and veteran of the anti-Soviet fighting in Afghanistan, was deeply offended by Riyadh's decision to invite American forces to enter the Kingdom and protect it against further Iraqi aggression. From bin Laden's perspective this decision to allow the American military (including women) to enter 'the land of the two holy sites' was profoundly anti-Islamic.

The result was the formation of al Qaeda, an organization aimed at expelling the Americans along with other 'Crusaders and Jews' from the House of God (*Dar al Islam*), and also aimed at toppling the corrupt Arab regimes the US supported. The US, 'the far enemy', became bin Laden's principal target. Blood-curdling threats were often followed by terrorist operations.

Before 9/11 al Qaeda's major operations included attacks on American forces in Mogadishu (1993), the bombing of the New York World Trade Center (1993), the bombing of US embassies in Nairobi and Dar es Salaam (1998) and the attack on the American warship US *Cole* in Aden harbor (2000). How did the US react to these attacks?

Based on recommendations made by presidential commissions appointed by presidents Bush and Clinton, the executive proposed new congressional action. The result was the omnibus 1996 Antiterrorism Act. The Act made it a crime for citizens and noncitizens alike to provide any material support to the lawful political or humanitarian activities of any foreign group designated by the Secretary of State as 'terrorist'. Thus, the Act reintroduced to federal law the principle of 'guilt by association.' Three consequences resulted from the Secretary of State's decision to designate a foreign entity as a terrorist organization:

> (1) it is a crime for anybody to contribute money or other material support or resources to a designated group … (2) all members of the group are barred from entering the United States, and are deportable if they were members prior to entry … (3) banks must freeze the funds of any designated group.[14]

The Act gave the Attorney General and the Justice Department wide latitude in defining and applying the term 'terrorist group'. Once designated as 'terrorist' a group became exposed to the sanctions listed above. These sanctions had a limited effect. Some Americans and permanent residents were prosecuted for attempting to raise money for Middle Eastern terrorist groups, Hamas in particular. But designated groups had other sources of funding from Iran and wealthy contributors from Saudi Arabia and the Persian Gulf Sheikdoms.

The CIA and other American security agencies succeeded in achieving enhanced cooperation among the Western democracies in response to terrorism. Officials on both sides of the Atlantic met frequently to discuss common problems in combating the threat. They also cooperated with some of the least savory Middle Eastern autocracies (e.g. Mubarak's Egypt), regimes that employed torture against suspects on a routine basis. These measures failed to stop terrorist operations.

Al Qaeda in particular evolved into a global network of groups operating from Algeria in West Africa to Indonesia and the Philippines in the East. By the late 1990s Osama bin Laden and his followers had been able to establish training camps in Taliban-controlled Afghanistan. Suicide bombing became the preferred method of attack against the network's numerous enemies. And, despite all the attention AQ enjoyed and the variety of counter-terrorism measures the US and its allies developed to deal with terrorism, no tactic, by itself or in combination, managed to forestall the 9/11 spectacular.

Responses to 9/11

'9/11' is, of course, shorthand for the worst single act of terrorism in American history. Under bin Laden's overall control, skyjackers destroyed the twin World Trade Center Towers in New York, along with part of the Pentagon. The attacks were carried out by 19 individuals, most of Saudi background, who had managed to enter the United States by using normal visa provisions. After entry they evaded close scrutiny by the FBI, some even receiving flight training along the way. On September 11, 2001 these jihadi seized control of four commercial airliners and proceeded to crash them into their targets (a fourth plane, United 93, crashed into a rural area in Pennsylvania). Close to 3000 people died.[15]

Reactions were quick in coming. At the international level, leaders of NATO invoked its Treaty provisions on mutual defense and offered to come to the aid of the United States. The United Nations Security Council quickly passed resolution #1368 condemning the attacks specifically and terrorism in general (without yet agreeing on a definition of the term 'terrorism'). All UN member states were encouraged to take steps to crack down on terrorist operations within their borders. The Bush administration demanded that the Taliban 'government' in Kabul give up bin Laden and his associates so they could be prosecuted for their crimes. The Taliban refused. What then followed was an American-aided attack on the Taliban by its opponent – the Northern Alliance. By the end of November 2001 this Alliance had driven the Taliban from power and forced bin Laden and some hundreds of his followers into Pakistan, its northern tribal areas especially.

The American response to 9/11 represented the most substantial government reorganization since the end of World War II. The response was both organizational and legislative.[16] Disentangling organizational from legislative responses is not all that easy since the former largely depends on the latter. Nonetheless it is helpful to attempt the distinction. The most substantial administrative changes involved the formation of a new cabinet-level Department of Homeland Security. This new department represented a merger of over 20 existing entities, among them the Secret Service, Coast Guard, Citizenship and Naturalization,

Science and Technology, Infrastructure Protection, Emergency Preparedness and Border Security. The FBI and CIA retained their independent status, although a Director of National Intelligence was appointed to channel FBI and CIA reports directly to the president.

One of the problems identified by the National Commission was a failure of coordination. The FBI, CIA, NSA and other agencies had failed to share important information about the 9/11 skyjackers, information they possessed prior to the attacks. To overcome this problem President Bush created the National Counter-Terrorism Center (NCTC), whose purpose was to encourage the sharing of terrorism-related information among the still autonomous intelligence bodies.

The major piece of legislation growing out of 9/11 was the Patriot (or PATRIOT) Act. With a few exceptions the Act simply modified and updated laws already in force at the time of 9/11. The document is 352 pages in length, so it is no mean feat for interested parties to make their way through it. The most important provisions appear to be the following. The FBI is able to secretly gain access to the personal information of American citizens and residents alike without having to demonstrate that those individuals have any involvement in terrorism or espionage. Banks, libraries and other third parties may be issued administrative subpoenas to induce their compliance. A second highly controversial provision amends the Foreign Intelligence Surveillance Act (1978). The Patriot Act permits intelligence agencies to bypass the normal judicial warrant requirement and requires, instead, that they obtain permission from a special secret court, Foreign Intelligence Surveillance Court (FISA Court), for electronic surveillance or physical search of a suspect's premises. The Patriot Act contains a 'sunset provision', meaning that Congress must re-authorize its provisions every three years. To date Congress has eliminated some of its more draconian provisions but has sustained the legislation in general.

We should also consider the even more contentious issue of 'enemy combatants'. In the months following 9/11, the Bush administration issued a military order permitting US forces to detain terrorist 'non-citizens' if there was reason to believe the individual in question is 'a member of al Qaeda, is involved in international terrorism, or has knowingly harbored such members or terrorists'.[17] Such 'enemy combatants' were detained at a military prison at Guantanamo Bay, Cuba, and subject to prosecution by military tribunals rather than the civilian court system. Congress resisted President Obama's efforts to change the system, close the Guantanamo Bay facility and house its inmates in prisons within the US, which would have made them subject to US constitutional protections (e.g. habeas corpus).

Observations and conclusions

Since the end of World War I in 1918 the United States has been confronted by several challenges and crises. They have varied in their severity, their perceived origins and their ability to incite panic and suspicion. It seems relatively clear that cases where foreign threats have been seen as having domestic collaborators have been most damaging to individual rights and protections afforded by the US Constitution, the First, Fourth and Fifth Amendments in particular.

The Red Scares following both World Wars were inflamed by the fact that foreign revolutionaries came to be understood as having domestic supporters, 'Reds' or Bolsheviks who were conspiring to weaken the US or even turn the country over to some alien power. These vastly exaggerated fears evoked what the late historian Richard Hofstadter described as 'the paranoid style in American politics'.[18] According to this view, a powerful conspiracy can be detected that intends to turn the country over to foreign elements.

The country's recent confrontation with Islamic terrorist groups and so-called 'lone wolves' understandably enough captures these fears, but with a major difference. Certainly one thing the US has not been confronting is an existential threat posed by a nuclear-armed superpower whose leaders threaten to bury the country, and plausibly enough have had the means to do so. Instead, the US has confronted al Qaeda and Islamic State (IS), terrorist networks whose jihadi have sought to carry out suicide attacks on American targets and make use of secret agents active within the US. These actors have also sought to induce intense fear via social media (e.g. displaying beheadings). The threat itself may have been somewhat exaggerated, but the disruptions and fears associated with this 'age of terrorism' appear real enough, relatively speaking.

While the terrorist threat to US security posed by jihadist groups appears to be subsiding, another challenge is emerging. Recently the FBI warned of the danger posed by conspiracy theories that appear on social media and produce domestic terrorism.[19] The United States is of course no stranger to conspiratorial interpretations of political developments (see above). They have been the stock-in-trade of far-right groups for many years. But the circulation of these typically far-fetched views has been vastly accelerated thanks to the Internet, impacting potential 'lone-wolf' actors and extreme right groups throughout the country. The fears such theories arouse may be and have been translated into action. In October 2018, a Pittsburgh man, believing that a Jewish organization was leading a caravan of Central Americans towards the US southern border as part of a conspiracy to destroy the white race, walked into the Tree of Life Synagogue and killed 11 worshippers. During the presidential contest of 2016, a right-wing website reported that Hillary Clinton, the Democratic Party's presidential nominee, was part of a group engaged in the kidnapping and sale of white children. The basement of a Washington DC pizzeria was the alleged headquarters of the operation. Intending to rescue white children, a man walked into the restaurant and began shooting at diners. Such violence seems likely to recur, as recent shootings in Ohio and El Paso demonstrate.

We cannot end this account without mentioning two emerging security threats to American democracy. First, as reported by the country's security agencies, the Russian government made a massive effort to intervene in the 2016 presidential election campaign on behalf of the winner, Donald Trump. The principal vehicles for this intervention were the new social media. Using a variety of subterfuges, Russian intelligence organizations were able to use Internet-linked platforms to send distorted messages of one type or another to influence citizens' voting decisions. As of this writing, various efforts, both public and private, are underway to thwart such efforts to subvert the electoral process during the 2020 election cycle. Second, as of this writing, the United States and the world face the existential health security threat posed by pandemic. We have yet to see its effects on rule of law, democratic governance and security issues in their multiple dimensions.

Notes

1 For an extended discussion see David Cole and James Dempsey, *Terrorism and the Constitution* (New York: New Press, 2006) pp. 1–21.

2 See the work of John Stuart Mill, *Considerations on Representative Government* (London: Electric Books, 2001).

3 See for example, Neil Livingstone and Terrell Arnold (eds.), *Fighting Back: Winning the War against Terrorism* (Lexington, MA: Lexington Books, 1986) pp. 50–83.

4 Christopher Finan, *From the Palmer Raids to the Patriot Act* (Boston: Beacon Press, 2007) p. 7.

5 See for example, Seymour Lipset and Earl Raab, *The Politics of Unreason* (New York: Harper & Row, 1970) pp. 150–208.
6 Arnie Bernstein, *Swastika Nation* (New York: St. Martin's Press, 2013).
7 See David Caute, *The Great Fear: The Anti-Communist Purge under Truman and Eisenhower* (New York: Simon and Schuster, 1978).
8 Caute, *The Great Fear.*
9 Robert Jackson Alexander, *Maoism in the Developed World* (Westport, CT: Greenwood Press, 2001).
10 The Soviet–American détente began in 1971 and took 'Decisive Form' with the visit of President Nixon to Moscow in May 1972. Nixon met with Secretary Brezhnev. The détente ended with the Soviet invasion of Afghanistan in 1980.
11 The Church Select Committee's first report was issued in April 1976, and was entitled 'Intelligence Activities and the Rights of Americans'. See also Loch Johnson, *A Season of Inquiry* (Chicago: Dorsey Press, 1988).
12 Walter Laqueur, *Terrorism* (Boston: Little, Brown, 1977).
13 See for example, George Michael, *Confronting Right-Wing Extremism and Terrorism in the USA* (New York: Routledge, 2003) pp. 93–128.
14 Cole and Dempsey, *Terrorism and the Constitution*, pp. 137–238.
15 For a thorough account of the events see, *The 9/11 Commission Report: Final Report of the National Commission on Terrorist attacks upon the United States* (New York: Norton, 2004) pp. 145–173.
16 For a summary see Donald Kettl, *System under Stress: Homeland Security and American Politics*, 2nd edn (Washington DC: CQ Press, 2007) p. 54.
17 William Banks, "The United States Responses to 9/11" in Victor Ramraj, Michael Hor and Kent Roach (eds.), *Global Anti-Terrorism Law and Policy* (New York: Cambridge University Press, 2005) p. 495.
18 Richard Hofstadter, *The Paranoid Style in American Politics* (New York: Knopf, 1966).
19 Jeff Murdock, "FBI says QAnon Conspiracy Theories Pose a Domestic Terrorism Threat", *Washington Post* (August 1, 2019).

Further reading

Bernstein, Arnie, *Swastika Nation* (New York: St. Martin's Press, 2013)

Caute, David, *The Great Fear: The Anti-Communist Purge under Truman and Eisenhower*(New York: Simon & Schuster, 1978)

Cole, David and James Dempsey, *Terrorism and the Constitution* (New York: New Press, 2006)

Finan, Christopher, *From the Palmer Raids to the Patriot Act* (Boston, MA: Beacon Press, 2007)

Hofstadter, Richard, *The Paranoid Style in American Politics* (New York: Knopf, 1966)

Kettl, Donald, *System under Stress: Homeland Security and American Politics*, 2nd edn (Washington DC: CQ Press, 2007)

Laqueur, Walter, *Terrorism* (Boston, MA: Little, Brown, 1977)

Lipset, Seymour and Earl Raab, *The Politics of Unreason* (New York: Harper & Row, 1970)

Livingstone, Neil and Terrell Arnold (eds), *Fighting Back: Winning the War against Terrorism* (Lexington, MA: Lexington Books, 1986)

Michael, George, *Confronting Right-Wing Extremism and Terrorism in the USA* (New York: Routledge, 2003)

Ramaj, Victor, Michael Hor and Kent Roach (eds), *Global Anti-Terrorism Law and Policy* (New York: Cambridge University Press, 2005)

2

SURVEILLANCE AND THE INVERSION OF DEMOCRATIC TRANSPARENCY

Sudha Setty[1]

Introduction

The traditional structure of a democracy includes the people who have the right to live largely private lives, and a government that has few secrets because it is empowered by the people to act in their name and its workings are transparent to the government's constituents. Yet national security-related surveillance and the secrecy with which it is conducted invert the democratic structure of transparency in ways that corrode the polity and its underlying assumptions.

In the United States, post-9/11, fear of terrorism has influenced not only substantive laws and policies but also the manner in which they are constructed. The results are evident in the laws governing mass data collection and retention programs—such as those made public by former National Security Agency (NSA) contractor Edward Snowden from 2013 onward. Vaguely worded laws have become enabling and justifying mechanisms for intrusive data collection programs that are largely kept secret from the public. The unwillingness or political inability of the Obama administration and Congress to consider curtailing these controversial and arguably unconstitutional surveillance programs until a high-profile leak occurred suggested that asserting significant democratic control over such programs, once implemented, was unlikely. Simultaneously, the unwillingness of the judiciary to allow for litigation on secret surveillance programs until the Snowden leak occurred suggested the lack of a judicial avenue toward transparency as well. This dynamic has become more pronounced under the Trump administration: secrecy claimed over various government programs has increased, and the ability to marshal any meaningful accountability over those programs has diminished significantly.

Absent a multifaceted response in which transparency of the law is considered a priority by Congress, the judiciary and the public, it seems unlikely that the United States will be able to address the issue of democratic transparency effectively from a structural standpoint.

This chapter addresses the issue of secret surveillance as an inversion of democracy. First, it considers recent debate over secret surveillance programs and discusses the role that leaked information has played in giving the public greater understanding of what kinds of surveillance programs exist. Second, it considers the sometimes vague and opaque legal authorities that have been relied upon in the post-September 11 context to justify surveillance. Third, it argues that national security surveillance, when justified in secret and without adequate accountability measures in place, undermines the transparency norms that a liberal democracy demands.

2.1 The current debate on secret surveillance

The terrorist attacks of September 11, 2001 led to a significant increase in U.S. domestic and foreign surveillance efforts, partly as a response to the perception that intelligence agencies failed to gather intelligence that could have prevented the attacks.[2] There was significant disagreement within the U.S. government and intelligence community as to whether the failure was due primarily to existing legal constraints,[3] or to an inability to analyze the available intelligence accurately and thoroughly.[4] The 9/11 Commission[5] agreed with the latter view, concluding that whatever pre-9/11 failures the intelligence community suffered, they were not attributable to a lack of legal authority to collect data and to conduct surveillance.[6] Nonetheless, political and public pressure to prevent another large-scale terrorist attack on U.S. soil led to the loosening of legal and policy constraints on intelligence gathering, despite an understanding of the potential adverse effects of such loosening on civil liberties and constitutional rights.

As part of this shift, broad programs were implemented without significant understanding by the public and, at times, by members of Congress, as to their scope and details. As discussed below, the secret collection and storage of domestic telephony and internet metadata[7] and the collection and content searches of substantial amounts of foreign telephone and internet communications was arguably statutorily authorized,[8] giving the intelligence community a much larger "haystack" of information within which to investigate possible emerging and ongoing terrorist threats.[9] For many years, critics of these expanded statutory authorities were unable to secure significant and lasting victories in curtailing surveillance powers, either through judicial action[10] or legislative initiative. One of the key reasons behind this inability to challenge surveillance effectively was the secret nature of the programs: without public knowledge of the extent to which surveillance existed, Congress was unable or unwilling to act, and plaintiffs looking to challenge domestic surveillance in court were almost uniformly found to lack standing to bring their claims.

The public debate shifted in June 2013, when then-NSA contractor Edward Snowden began revealing classified documents as to the scope of NSA surveillance on foreign and U.S. persons, with the stated purpose of prompting public scrutiny and debate over the programs. Snowden revealed, among other things,[11] that the NSA was engaged in the practice of collecting and retaining the metadata of all U.S. telephone customers for five years, and had been running searches through that metadata when there was a "reasonable, articulable suspicion" that a particular telephone number was associated with potential terrorist activity (the "NSA Metadata Program").[12] One of Snowden's stated intents in revealing the details of this program—its secret operations, broad scope, lack of particularized suspicion, and lengthy duration of data retention—was to allow "the public to be able to have a say in how they are governed."[13] In other words, Snowden sought, at least in part, to restore democratic transparency with regard to a program that was largely unknown and unknowable to the public prior to his disclosures.

If increasing democratic discourse and discussion of potential accountability was one of Snowden's objectives, then this was achieved to some extent by public demands for better oversight of the NSA.[14] The Obama administration initiated various review mechanisms;[15]

Congress discussed and debated its oversight role;[16] and former judges on the Foreign Intelligence Surveillance Court (FISC), tasked with determining whether government requests for surveillance authority should be authorized, weighed in on matters of secrecy and government accountability.[17]

2.2 National security's domestic surveillance authorities

The legal architecture constructed to support arguments as to the domestic authorization of the NSA Metadata Program was extensive.[18] A significant number of laws—such as the 2001 Authorization for the Use of Military Force,[19] provisions of the USA PATRIOT Act ("Patriot Act"),[20] the Protect America Act and the FISA Amendments Act of 2008[21]—were enacted by Congress and interpreted by the NSA as providing ample statutory authority for the capture and storage of data.[22] Compounding these statutory authorities, the executive branch likely sought its own non-public legal guidance in the form of secret legal opinions from the Office of Legal Counsel[23] and other Department of Justice memoranda defending the legality and efficacy of the surveillance program.[24]

After the Snowden disclosures began, public pressure mounted for the Obama administration and Congress to take action to better protect individual privacy rights from government overreaching. This led to the passage of the USA FREEDOM Act in mid-2015 that curtailed the scope of metadata collection starting in December 2015.[25] When the USA FREEDOM Act came into effect, it mandated that intelligence agencies such as the NSA stop gathering and storing metadata for their own use without further judicial oversight. Instead, when an intelligence agency needs to gather metadata on an individual or group, it must seek it from the telecommunications companies that store such data, and only after obtaining an individualized warrant from the FISC to do so.[26] The USA FREEDOM Act also encourages the publication of FISC opinions under some circumstances,[27] and gives FISC judges the opportunity to appoint amici curiae to argue against the government's request for surveillance authorities,[28] thereby offering, in some circumstances, an adversarial process before that court. As discussed below, the Snowden disclosures also encouraged administrative measures, such as the staffing and funding of a Privacy and Civil Liberties Oversight Board, to give advice on whether certain surveillance activities impermissibly infringed on the privacy rights of both U.S. citizens and non-citizens.

Courts also took on a more active role with regard to providing meaningful oversight after June 2013. Prior to the start of the Snowden disclosures, the surveillance and data collection that are part of the NSA Metadata Program were upheld by two forms of relatively weak judicial review. Ordinary federal courts largely refused to hear the merits of cases challenging government surveillance, instead finding that plaintiffs were unable to satisfy the standing requirement,[29] or dismissed suits at the pleadings stage due to invocations of the state secrets privilege by the government.[30] The FISC had operated largely in secret and without an adversarial process to contest the government's arguments. When the U.S. government first sought and received FISC approval for the NSA Metadata Program in 2006, the NSA argued that U.S. national security interests demanded non-public access to vast swaths of data, since one of the "greatest challenges" faced by the government was the identification of potential threats from al Qaeda,[31] and that individualized data collection would be insufficient to counter the potential terrorist threat.[32] The government further argued[33] that it would be insufficient to allow telecommunications companies to hold the metadata and have the government make individualized metadata requests, since the possibility of the companies not saving the data for a sufficiently long period of time might jeopardize intelligence-gathering efforts.[34] The government's justification for the vast, non-public collection of data it was seeking was simple and powerful: "the government's interest is the most compelling imaginable: the defense of the Nation in wartime from attacks that may take thousands of lives."[35] This argument was convincing to the FISC. Not only did it approve the NSA Metadata program, but it overwhelmingly acquiesced to government requests for surveillance authorities over the years.[36]

After the Snowden disclosures began in June 2013, however, the government's justification for the NSA Metadata Program shifted away from identifying al Qaeda as a near-existential threat to simply stating that bulk metadata collection was still a necessary part of the U.S. counterterrorism strategy.[37] Cases litigated after June 2013, but prior to the USA FREEDOM Act taking effect, suggest that the judicial deference offered to the government in many previous counterterrorism cases softened in some jurisdictions in favor of a somewhat more rights-protective stance, particularly in light of public attention and critique of the NSA Metadata Program, as well as a reinvigorated judicial embrace of the privacy protections embodied in the Fourth Amendment.[38] One federal circuit court continued the deferential posture of dismissing suits seeking to challenge the government's collection of their metadata at an early stage,[39] and the FISC validated its own previous authorization of bulk metadata collection.[40] Yet, for other courts, the issue of the secret surveillance authorities was anathema[41] to the idea of democracy and, therefore, could not be legal. One court rejected the Obama administration's contention that the NSA Metadata Program must be legal because it was being run under the auspices of Section 215 of the USA PATRIOT Act, stating simply that "Congress cannot reasonably be said to have ratified a program of which many members of Congress—and all members of the public—were not aware."[42]

The Supreme Court, although not weighing in on the NSA Metadata Program per se, has made clear in the years since the passage of the USA FREEDOM Act that it, too, is wary of government surveillance conducted in secrecy and without appropriate accountability mechanisms in place. Perhaps the most prominent recent example of this dynamic is the 2018 case of *Carpenter v. United States*, [43] which held that historical cell tower data that could pinpoint the location of individuals carrying cell phones cannot be accessed by law enforcement without a judicial warrant, and that the appropriate standard for getting a warrant is a showing of probable cause. Although U.S. courts have been largely deferential to law enforcement and intelligence agency claims that any limitation on their ability to collect data might lead to another large-scale terrorist attack, the *Carpenter* court resisted, acknowledging the need for limits as to what the government can surveil, as well as for accountability.

2.3 Broad, secret surveillance inverts democratic transparency

The post-9/11 government use of extremely intrusive surveillance technology, along with the secrecy of these programs from the public, resulted in an inversion of the transparency on which democracy ordinarily relies.[44] The deployment of powerful and intrusive surveillance technology essentially renders citizens of liberal democratic nations, who are normally afforded the right to privacy, transparent to the government. The scope of government surveillance and the legal basis on which that surveillance has been justified has been opaque to the public absent the benefit of leaked information. These two forces combine to create a Panopticon-like surveillance regime in which the government has the ability to watch and collect vast amounts of data on the population secretly. Since the populace is unable to ascertain the parameters of when the surveillance might occur, they must operate under the belief that all of their telephonic and internet activity may be examined by the government at any time.[45]

Particularly since the early years of the Cold War, the public, Congress, and the judiciary have ceded large swaths of security-related decision-making authority to the executive branch,[46] often allowing security-related decisions to be made in secret, without the traditional transparency on which democracy relies.[47] Despite this shift in policy-making authority, security policies that have led to broad, secret surveillance and data collection have been historically viewed by politicians and judges as antithetical to the democratic foundation of the United States. Several important examples stem from the contentious discussions around secret surveillance and democratic transparency in the 1970s. When the Supreme Court decided to uphold a warrant requirement for domestic surveillance in the 1972 *Keith* case, the tenor and language of the opinion focused on the need to uphold the privacy rights of Americans as a bulwark of a democratic society: "Nor must the fear of unauthorized official eavesdropping deter vigorous citizen dissent and discussion of government action in private conversation. For private dissent, no less than open public disclosure is essential to our free society."[48]

In 1976, the Church Committee's investigations into the National Security Agency and its domestic intelligence-gathering operations yielded the conclusion that:

> Americans have rightfully been concerned since before World War II about the dangers of hostile foreign agents likely to commit acts of espionage. Similarly, the violent acts of political terrorists can seriously endanger the rights of Americans. Carefully focused intelligence investigations can help prevent such acts.
>
> But too often intelligence has lost this focus and domestic intelligence activities have invaded individual privacy and violated the rights of lawful assembly and political expression. Unless new and tighter controls are established by legislation, domestic intelligence activities threaten to undermine our democratic society and fundamentally alter its nature.[49]

Further, when Congress debated the enactment of the Foreign Intelligence Surveillance Act of 1978, a significant amount of legislative discourse focused on the extent to which warrantless surveillance might undermine democratic values.[50] The concern centered on the corrosion of democracy that occurs when the scope of the government's actions and legal authority ceases to be transparent to the public, thereby unmooring the government's actions from any form of democratic accountability. The extent to which Congress could function as a democratically elected source of constraint on the intelligence community was stifled by the structure of FISA, which vested sole control in the Foreign Intelligence Surveillance Court, with its closed hearings and secret body of law.[51]

In the post-9/11 era, the same kind of deliberation and debate should have occurred; but a combination of factors—including genuine concerns for national security, broad claims of executive authority, an overly deferential judiciary, and political fear of seeming to be "soft on terror" during an election cycle—stifled essential debate on questions of secret law and the undermining of the rule of law. Instead, the enormous technological capabilities available to the government, the murky statutory authority on which surveillance programs are predicated, the secrecy of the intelligence community, and the lack of access to FISA decisions rendered the Panopticon complete.

In this context, democratic control mechanisms ordinarily available are not effective in restoring transparency over the surveillance apparatus. First, the public is not given enough information to create informed opinion as to the types of surveillance policies adopted and utilized by the government. Therefore the public cannot be realistically expected to serve as a source of democratic accountability. Instead the public relies on leaks such as those regarding the Terrorist Surveillance Program in 2005[52] and the disclosures by Edward Snowden in 2013 and onward[53] for specific information about the broad surveillance measures being taken unannounced in the name of national security. These leaks engaged the public in debate, and have led to some reforms that limited surveillance and data collection authority. Still it is notable that such reforms under the George W. Bush and Obama administrations stemmed from the executive branch first,[54] with Congress following and curbing programs to parameters with which each administration felt comfortable.[55] Even then, it was clear that ad hoc leaking of classified information was not an adequate substitute for a structural means by which democratic accountability can exist.[56] Given the Obama administration's crackdown on leaking and the treatment of whistleblowers as criminals,[57] as well as heightened security measures in the wake of leaking, reliance on leaking as a means of achieving democratic discourse, and as a meaningful check on government actions, proved to be misplaced. Under the Trump administration, adherence to democratic norms and values has been largely abandoned,[58] leaks continue to be prosecuted aggressively,[59] and secrecy over national security matters has grown significantly.[60] Reliance on the administration to maintain transparency would be misplaced, and reliance on leaks does not serve as a substitute for genuine accountability.

Ideally, Congress could serve as another possible means of exercising oversight and democratic control. Relying on Congress is an appealing option to prevent disclosure of sensitive material or to discipline unwarranted surveillance in an effort to prevent disclosure of sensitive or classified national security information. But Congress has been hamstrung by its inability and unwillingness to make informed decisions with regard to surveillance programs. First, absent high-profile leaks, Congress itself has not been particularly well-informed by more than one administration with regard to the parameters of surveillance programs: limitations on briefings to certain congressional committees, misleading responses to congressional oversight hearings, and the inability of members of Congress to consult with staff on certain programs create an information deficit that hampers effective oversight.[61]

Second, even when information is made available, most members of Congress do not avail themselves of opportunities to improve their understanding of surveillance programs utilized by the intelligence community.[62] Third, and relatedly, it may be politically expedient for Congress to exercise willful blindness when it comes to the more controversial aspects of surveillance programs; if those programs become public later and are met with anger or discontent, as with the case of the NSA Metadata Program, members of Congress can use plausible deniability as political cover and lay blame on the administration and the intelligence community.[63] This arguably explains some of the congressional furor over the NSA Metadata Program, and part of the righteous impetus behind the USA FREEDOM Act. Fourth, under certain circumstances Congress can later assert itself in a limited fashion as a rights-protective body. As with the USA FREEDOM Act, this may be based largely on information provided through the administration and through leaking, and/or with the approval of the administration.

As an alternative to reliance on somewhat unreliable democratic controls, two non-democratic mechanisms exist as potential means of restoring a semblance of democratic transparency: the judiciary and independent oversight mechanisms operating within an administration. As discussed above, ordinary federal courts and the FISC have been largely reluctant to engage with matters administrations deem to involve national security secrets.

Relying solely on administrations to self-police seems to have been ineffective in curtailing numerous practices that undermine the rule of law, including the development of secret law and policy governing national security and related matters. By contrast, the Privacy and Civil Liberties Oversight Board (PCLOB), born out of a 9/11 Commission recommendation, is one potential avenue for accountability over some national security matters.

The PCLOB's mission is to assess aspects of the government's national security programs for efficacy and for potentially unnecessary incursions into civil liberties. The PCLOB has some independence from the executive branch.[64] Initially, its promise to curb potential abuses seemed significant. With regard to the NSA Metadata Program, the PCLOB issued a highly critical report in January 2014 that added pressure on the Obama administration to curtail this program, and encouraged congressional debate on what eventually passed as the USA FREEDOM Act.[65] Prospectively, it seemed possible that an intelligence agency would consult the PCLOB if the agency itself considered an issue it faced to be new or novel (the NSA Metadata Program was labeled novel prior to its inception).[66] In such cases, decision makers within an agency generally ask whether the contemplated program is useful or necessary, technologically feasible, and legal, and only implement a program if all three questions are answered affirmatively. If a contemplated program is considered new or novel by an intelligence agency, a best-case scenario for maintaining government accountability would involve consultation with the PCLOB at some stage of the process. This nonpartisan external input may improve self-policing within the intelligence community, help intelligence agencies avoid implementing controversial programs, or, even if such programs are implemented, set better parameters for new programs.[67] Because the PCLOB issues public reports, this non-democratic institution offers the possibility of restoring some level of transparency to inform the public about the types of surveillance programs the government operates.

Still, the Board's potential influence in protecting civil liberties is based on soft power. Its resources are limited by its position as an advisory body: it cannot mandate any changes. The ability to have a high level of access to information surrounding counterterrorism surveillance programs and to recommend changes in such programs is important and should be lauded. But reliance on the PCLOB's non-binding advice to the intelligence community to fully resolve the accountability and transparency gap with regard to these programs would be a mistake. The PCLOB's soft power is further limited when the Board is insufficiently resourced to do its work. The PCLOB was fully staffed in 2013, after the Snowden disclosures were made, at which point it began to investigate and produce significant reports. In 2017 PCLOB staff shrank from its full complement of five board members to one. Only in 2019, after several years of dormancy, was the PCLOB again fully staffed and thus able to set an agenda for new investigations and oversight efforts.[68]

Conclusion

The idea that secret law is anathema to a liberal democracy is well-established in the United States. Yet transparency with regard to national security surveillance programs has been and will continue to be a challenge. Particularly at times of heightened stress over national security, as in the wake of a large-scale terrorist attack, the political and public imperative shifts to further empowering the surveillance apparatus without transparency requirements and other safeguards against potential abuse that would be considered more carefully when governments are not on an emergency or war footing. Like other nations, the United States has depended on leaking as a form of unauthorized transparency to engage the public in debate over improved accountability measures. However, unlike other countries that struggle with similar issues in terms of counterterrorism powers and the need for democratic transparency, the absence of supranational or effective international controls upon the United States puts it in a more precarious situation in that it has an even greater dependence on leaking to force a measure of transparency. Under these circumstances it becomes all the more necessary for each branch of the U.S. government to engage more fully and proactively in matters of national security surveillance in an effort to provide accountability and transparency that would otherwise be lacking but for the leak of government information. The unwillingness and inability thus far of Congress and the judiciary to do so represent a systemic failure to safeguard the democratic value of transparency. Passage of the USA FREEDOM Act, the restaffing of the PCLOB in 2019, and recent jurisprudence that indicates an interest in curbing government surveillance authorities suggest the possibility of a future that values transparency more fully. The efficacy and durability of those developments are yet to be seen.

Notes

1 Some elements of this chapter are drawn from a previous work: Sudha Setty, *Surveillance, Secrecy, and the Search for Meaningful Accountability*, 51 STAN. J. INT'L L. 69 (2015) © Sudha Setty 2015. I deeply appreciate the comments and suggestions offered on this project by participants at workshops at the University of Connecticut School of Law and the University of South Carolina School of Law, both held in March 2015. I am grateful to Matthew H. Charity, Richard S. Kay, Mark Weston Janis, Molly Land, Peter L. Lindseth, the late Robert Prasch, Wadie E. Said and Falguni A. Sheth for thoughtful comments and insights. Finally, I thank Ryan O'Hara and Joseph Greenhalgh for fine research assistance.

2 *See Final Report of the National Commission on Terrorist Attacks Upon the United States* 339–60 (2004) [hereinafter *9/11 Commission Report*], www.9-11commission.gov (discussing the inability of U.S. intelligence agencies to synthesize relevant data prior to the September 11 attacks).

3 *See* Testimony of Attorney General John Ashcroft Before the National Commission on Terrorist Attacks Upon the United States 2 (Apr. 13, 2004), http://govinfo.library.unt.edu/911/hearings/hearing10/ashcroft_statement.pdf (noting that "[t]he single greatest structural cause for September 11 was the wall that segregated criminal investigators and intelligence agents. Government erected this wall Government buttressed this wall. And before September 11, government was blinded by this wall").

4 *See* Testimony of Professor Stephen J. Schulhofer Before the National Commission on Terrorist Attacks Upon the United States 1 (Dec. 8, 2003), http://govinfo.library.unt.edu/911/hearings/hearing6/witness_schulhofer.htm (noting that intelligence "capabilities are largely determined by non-legal constraints—technical, budgetary and human resources, the training and priorities of our officers and the organization and cultures of the relevant agencies—all areas where our deficits have been, and continue to be, enormous").

5 The National Commission on Terrorist Attacks Upon the United States is also known as the "9/11 Commission."

6 *See 9/11 Commission Report, supra* note 2, at 339–60.

7 The telephony metadata authorized for collection is defined as: "includ[ing] comprehensive communications routing information, including but not limited to session identifying information (e.g., originating and terminating telephone number, International Mobile Subscriber Identity (IMSI) number, International Mobile station [*sic*] Equipment Identity (IMEI) number, etc.), trunk identifier, telephone calling card numbers, and time and duration of call. Telephony metadata does not include the substantive content of any communication … or the name, address, or financial information of a subscriber or customer." *See In re Application of the Federal Bureau of Investigation for an Order Requiring the Production of Tangible Things From* [Redacted], 3 n.1 (FISA Ct. 2013), www.dni.gov/files/documents/PrimaryOrder_Collection_215.pdf.

8 *See* Uniting and Strengthening America by Providing Appropriate Tools Required to Intercept and Obstruct Terrorism Act of 2001, Pub. L. No. 107–56, § 215, 115 Stat. 287 [hereinafter PATRIOT Act] (arguably authorizing the collection and storage of bulk metadata); *id.* at § 702 (authorizing the

targeted collection of data, including content, from overseas targets). When various provisions of the Patriot Act were up for renewal in 2010, debates on the utility, invasiveness, and potential abuse of the surveillance provisions ended in congressional reauthorization of the Act without alternation. *See* David Kravets, *Lawmakers Punt Patriot Act to Obama*, WIRED (Feb. 26, 2010), www.wired.com/2010/02/lawmakers-renew-patriot-act/.

9 *See* Gil Press, *The Effectiveness of Small vs. Big Data Is Where the NSA Debate Should Start*, FORBES, (June 12, 2013), www.forbes.com/sites/gilpress/2013/06/12/the-effectiveness-of-small-vs-big-data-is-where-the-nsa-debate-should-start/ (discussing need to understand whether a larger or smaller "haystack" of data better enables intelligence-gathering and analysis efforts).

10 *E.g.*, Clapper v. Amnesty Int'l, No. 11–1025 (U.S. Feb 26, 2013) (holding that plaintiffs alleging unconstitutional and illegal surveillance lacked standing to bring their complaint because they had no publicly available proof of their surveillance). Cases that challenge these surveillance programs on constitutional and statutory grounds are still being litigated.

11 Of course, the U.S. intelligence community has engaged in numerous programs involving warrantless surveillance, and this chapter only addresses the bulk metadata collection that was arguably authorized under Section 215 of the Patriot Act. Other warrantless surveillance—of non-U.S. persons or on non-U.S. territory—falls under the auspices of other authorities, such as Executive Order 12333 or Section 702 of the Foreign Intelligence Surveillance Act. Those surveillance and data collection efforts are beyond the scope of this chapter. Nonetheless, the structural accountability questions raised with regard to the NSA Metadata Program can be extrapolated to consider other domestic surveillance questions because of analogous legal and political frameworks.

12 *See* Glenn Greenwald, *NSA Collecting Phone Records of Millions of Verizon Customers Daily*, GUARDIAN (June 6, 2013), www.theguardian.com/world/2013/jun/06/nsa-phone-records-verizon-court-order.

13 Bridie Jabour, *Edward Snowden Declares "Mission Accomplished" in Moscow Interview*, GUARDIAN (Dec. 24, 2013), www.theguardian.com/world/2013/dec/24/edward-snowden-i-already-won.

14 *See* James Ball & Spencer Ackerman, *NSA Loophole Allows Warrantless Search for U.S. Citizens' Emails and Phone Calls*, GUARDIAN (Aug. 9, 2013), www.theguardian.com/world/2013/aug/09/nsa-loophole-warrantless-searches-email-calls; Michael Birnbaum & Ellen Nakashima, *German Leader Calls Obama About Alleged Cellphone Tapping*, WASH. POST (Oct. 23, 2013), www.washingtonpost.com/world/german-leader-calls-obama-about-alleged-cellphone-tapping/2013/10/23/2edb4aa2-3c10-11e3-b0e7-716179a2c2c7_story.html; James Risen & Laura Poitras, *N.S.A. Gathers Data on Social Connections of U.S. Citizens*, N.Y. TIMES (Sept. 28, 2013), www.nytimes.com/2013/09/29/us/nsa-examines-social-networks-of-us-citizens.html?pagewanted=all.

15 *E.g.*, PRIVACY & CIVIL LIBERTIES OVERSIGHT BD., REPORT ON THE TELEPHONE RECORDS PROGRAM CONDUCTED UNDER SECTION 215 OF THE USA PATRIOT ACT AND ON THE OPERATIONS OF THE FOREIGN INTELLIGENCE SURVEILLANCE COURT 10–11 (2014), www.pclob.gov/Library/215-Report_on_the_Telephone_Records_Program-2.pdf; PRESIDENT'S REVIEW GRP. ON INTELLIGENCE & COMMUNICATIONS, LIBERTY AND SECURITY IN A CHANGING WORLD 17–21 (2013), www.whitehouse.gov/sites/default/files/docs/2013-12-12_rg_final_report.pdf.

16 *See* Senator Ron Wyden & Senator Mark Udall, *Wyden, Udall Statement on Reports of Compliance Violations Made Under NSA Collection Programs*, RON WYDEN SENATOR FOR OREGON (Aug. 16, 2013), www.wyden.senate.gov/news/press-releases/wyden-udall-statement-on-reports-of-compliance-violations-made-under-nsa-collection-programs (noting that the disclosures of thousands of violations by the NSA are "just the tip of a larger iceberg" and that they are prohibited from discussing the further problematic aspects of the NSA surveillance program by Senate rules).

17 E.g., *See* Carol Leonnig, *Court: Ability to Police U.S. Spying Program Limited*, WASH. POST (Aug. 15, 2013), www.washingtonpost.com/politics/court-ability-to-police-us-spying-program-limited/2013/08/15/4a8c8c44-05cd-11e3-a07f-49ddc7417125_story.html (quoting Judge Reggie Walton as lamenting that "[t]he FISC is forced to rely upon the accuracy of the information that is provided to the Court … . The FISC does not have the capacity to investigate issues of noncompliance"). Judge James Carr, *A Better Secret Court*, N.Y. TIMES (July 22, 2013), www.nytimes.com/2013/07/23/opinion/a-better-secret-court.html.

18 There are ongoing questions as to whether the practice of mass data collection, storage and mining by governments violates international legal standards, such as those articulated in the International Convention on Civil and Political Rights. *See, e.g.*, U.N. Secretary-General, *Promotion and Protection of Human Rights and Fundamental Freedoms While Countering Terrorism*, U.N. Doc. A/69/397 (Sept. 23, 2014). The question of the NSA's international law compliance is beyond the scope of this project.

19 *See* Authorization for the Use of Military Force (AUMF), Pub. L. No. 107–40, 115 Stat. 224 (2001).

20 *See* Patriot Act, Pub. L. No. 107–56, § 218, 115 Stat. 287 (amending the Foreign Intelligence Surveillance Act of 1978 such that electronic surveillance and physical searches need only be justified in "significant" part by the goal of obtaining foreign intelligence); *id.* at §§ 215, 702.

21 *See* Protect America Act of 2007, Pub. L. No. 110–55, 121 Stat. 552 (amending Foreign Intelligence Surveillance Act of 1978 (FISA)); Foreign Intelligence Surveillance Act of 1978 Amendments Act of 2008, Pub. L. No. 110–261, 122 Stat. 2436 (2008). *See generally* AUMF; Patriot Act § 215.

22 *See* Letter from Ronald Weich to the Honorable Dianne Feinstein and the Honorable Saxby Chambliss (Feb. 2, 2011), www.dni.gov/files/documents/2011_CoverLetters_Report_Collection.pdf (discussing the legislative basis for the NSA bulk metadata collection program).

23 *See* Michael J. Glennon, *National Security and Double Government*, 5 HARV. NAT'L SECURITY J. 1, 78 (2014) (describing the existence and possible content of such an Office of Legal Counsel memorandum).

24 *See* Weich, *supra* note 22 (including Justice Department analysis of the legislative authority supporting the NSA's bulk metadata collection program).

25 Uniting and Strengthening America by Fulfilling Rights and Ending Eavesdropping, Dragnet-Collection and Online Monitoring Act ("USA FREEDOM Act") of 2015, Pub. L. No. 114–23, § 501.

26 USA FREEDOM Act of 2015, Pub. L. No. 114–23, § 501.

27 USA FREEDOM Act of 2015, Pub. L. No. 114–23, § 402.

28 USA FREEDOM Act of 2015, Pub. L. No. 114–23, § 401.

29 *See* Clapper v. Amnesty Int'l, No. 11–1025 (U.S. Feb 26, 2013).

30 *See* Al-Haramain Islamic Found. v. Obama, 705 F.3d 845 (9th Cir. 2012).

31 Memorandum of Law in Support of Application for Certain Tangible Things for Investigations to Protect Against Int'l Terrorism, *In re* [REDACTED] (hereinafter "NSA Memo") (FISA Ct. May 23, 2006) (No. 06–05), at 1.

32 *Id.* at 1–2.

33 Some arguments for the NSA Metadata Program that were heard by the FISC in 2006 have yet to be disclosed. *See id.* at 10–11 (a heavily redacted portion of the NSA Memo).

34 *Id.* at 9–10.

35 *Id.* at 3.

36 For example, in 2012 the FISC authorized every one of the 1,788 government requests to conduct electronic surveillance that it was asked to rule on. *See* Letter from Peter J. Kadzik, Principal Deputy Assistant Attorney General, to Senator Harry S. Reid (Apr. 30, 2013), http://fas.org/irp/agency/doj/fisa/2012rept.pdf.

37 ADMINISTRATION WHITE PAPER: BULK COLLECTION OF TELEPHONY METADATA UNDER SECTION 215 OF THE USA PATRIOT ACT (Aug. 9, 2013).

38 *See, e.g., Klayman v. Obama*, Civ. No. 13–851 (D.D.C. Nov. 9, 2015) (holding that the NSA Metadata Program violates the Fourth Amendment); *see also* Riley v. California, 134 S.Ct. 2473, 2429 (2014) (holding that a warrantless search of an arrested individual's cell phone contents violated the Fourth Amendment).

39 *Obama v. Klayman*, No. 14–5004 (D.C. Cir. Aug. 28, 2015; consolidated with Nos. 14–5005, -5016, -5017) (allowing metadata collection to continue for a limited time).

40 *In re* Application of the FBI for an Order Requiring the Production of Tangible Things, Nos. BR 15–75, Misc. 15–01 (FISA Ct. June 29, 2015) (same).

41 *ACLU v. Clapper*, 785 F.3d 787, 792 (2d Cir. 2015) (holding that the NSA Metadata Program was not statutorily authorized); *Klayman v. Obama*, F. Supp. 2d 1 (D.D.C. 2013) (finding that the Section 215 metadata collection program was illegal).

42 *ACLU v. Clapper*, 785 F.3d at 819.

43 138 S.Ct.2206 (2018). See also *United States v. Jones*, 565 U.S.400 (2012) (holding that long-term GPS tracking required a warrant).

44 Although this chapter focuses on the NSA Metadata Program, the inversion of democratic transparency exists with regard to other federal surveillance programs, as well as the surveillance efforts of state and local police departments that now have access to powerful surveillance technology because of federal government largess. *See* Matt Richtel, *A Police Gadget Tracks Phones? Shhh! It's Secret*, N.Y. TIMES (March 16, 2015), http://nyti.ms/18Qewm5 (noting that local police departments have been purchasing powerful surveillance technology using Homeland Security grants, and that purchase of the technology was predicated on municipalities agreeing not to demand access to detailed information about the technology and signing broad non-disclosure agreements).

45 The Panopticon—a plan for a prison proposed by utilitarian philosopher Jeremy Bentham in the late 18th century, in which prisoners could not be aware of when they were being watched by guards and, therefore, would always feel pressured to act as though their captors were watching them—was invoked by 20th-century philosopher Michel Foucault as an example of the way in which governments seek to categorize and control their subjects. *See* Michel Foucault, DISCIPLINE AND PUNISH: THE BIRTH OF THE PRISON 135–48 (Vintage Books 1995).

46 *See* Aziz Rana, *Who Decides on Security?* 44 CONN. L. REV. 1419 (2012). Rana argues that this post-World War II posture marked a significant change from the democratic grounding of security-related decisions in the early Republic and 19th century. *Id.* at 1442–43.

47 *See* Sudha Setty, *The Rise of National Security Secrets*, 44 CONN. L. REV. 1565, 1567–68 (2012) (noting the contemporary discomfort in some quarters at the shift toward secrecy and, therefore, away from democratic control).

48 United States v. United States District Court, 407 U.S. 297, 314 (1972).

49 United States Senate, Final Report of the Select Committee to Study Governmental Operations with Respect to Intelligence Activities, Intelligence Activities and the Rights of Americans, Book II, at 1 (April 24, 1976).

50 *See* Jeffrey S. Brand, *Eavesdropping on Our Founding Fathers: How a Return to the Republic's Core Democratic Values Can Help Us Resolve the Surveillance Crisis*, 6 Harv. Nat'l Security J. 1, 22–26 (2015).

51 *Id.* at 46–47.

52 *See* James Risen and Eric Lichtblau, *Bush Lets U.S. Spy on Callers Without Courts*, N.Y. TIMES (Dec. 16, 2005), www.nytimes.com/2005/12/16/politics/16program.html?_r=0 (disclosing the existence of the Bush Administration's warrantless Terrorist Surveillance Program).

53 *See* Glenn Greenwald, *NSA Collecting Phone Records of Millions of Verizon Customers Daily*, GUARDIAN (June 6, 2013), www.theguardian.com/world/2013/jun/06/nsa-phone-records-verizon-court-order.

54 In February 2015, the Director of National Intelligence announced new limits to the scope of Section 215 surveillance and intelligence-gathering that largely reflected the type of limitations suggested by President Obama in 2014. *See* ODNI General Counsel Robert Litt's As Prepared Remarks on Signals Intelligence Reform at the Brookings Institute, Feb. 4, 2015, http://icontherecord.tumblr.com/post/110632851413/odni-general-counsel-robert-litts-as-prepared.

55 USA FREEDOM Act of 2015, Pub. L. No. 114–23, § 501.

56 *Cf.* Rahul Sagar, SECRETS AND LEAKS: THE DILEMMA OF STATE SECRECY (Princeton Univ. Press 2013) (arguing that the status quo of incomplete oversight coupled with sporadic leaks is the best realistic option for national security accountability); David Pozen, *The Leaky Leviathan: Why the Government Condemns and Condones Unlawful Disclosures of Information*, 127 HARV. L. REV. 512 (2013) (describing ways in which leaks are an integral and adaptive mechanism of information disclosure for the US federal government).

57 *See* Sue Halpern, *Partial Disclosure*, NEW YORK REVIEW OF BOOKS (July 10, 2014), www.nybooks.com/articles/archives/2014/jul/10/glenn-greenwald-partial-disclosure/. Halpern offers some detail on how NSA whistleblowers from several years prior to Snowden's disclosures did not have their concerns taken seriously but were subjected to FBI interrogation, searches of their homes, and/or threats of prosecution. As such, Halpern argues, Snowden acted as he did after being "[s]tymied by an unresponsive bureaucracy, seeing the fate of earlier NSA whistleblowers, and finding no adequate provisions within the system to challenge the legality of government activity if that activity was considered by the government to touch on national security."

58 See Dawn Johnsen, *Toward Restoring Rule-of-Law Norms*, 97 TEX. L. REV. 1205 (2019).

59 See James Risen, *The Leaks That Trump's Justice Department Prosecutes Are Mostly About Trump, His Cronies, and Russia*, theintercept.com (Feb. 27, 2019), https://theintercept.com/2019/02/17/trump-russia-leaks-mueller-investigation/.

60 E.g. Kate Oh, *Trump's Year of Secrecy*, justsecurity.org (Dec.12, 2017), www.justsecurity.org/48932/trumps-year-secrecy/.

61 *See* Weich, *supra* note 22, at 25.

62 This information was gleaned from interviews with current and former officials within the NSA; notes on file with the author.

63 *See* Rana, *supra* note 46, at 1422 (arguing that Congress tends to cede decision-making power back to the executive branch on national security matters, giving the administration little oversight but providing a "constitutional imprimatur" to security programs).

64 *See* Garrett Hatch, Cong. Research Serv., RL34385, Privacy and Civil Liberties Oversight Board: New Independent Agency Status (2012) (describing the establishment of the PCLOB).
65 privacy & civil liberties oversight bd., report on the telephone records program conducted under section 215 of the usa patriot act and on the operations of the foreign intelligence surveillance court 10–11 (2014), www.pclob.gov/Library/215-Report_on_the_Telephone_Records_Program-2.pdf.
66 Sudha Setty, national security secrecy: comparative effects on democracy and the rule of law 31 (Cambridge Univ. Press 2017).
67 In some national security contexts, it has been clear that government officials would refuse to engage in potentially illegal behavior without the "golden shield" of protection against civil and criminal liability. *See* Glennon, *supra* note 23, at 78 (President Bush's decisions with regard to initiating and suspending metadata collection were dependent on Office of Legal Counsel guidance at the time).
68 Privacy and Civil Liberties Oversight Board, *Active Oversight Projects and Other Engagements* (July, 2019), www.pclob.gov/library/Agency%20July%202019.pdf.

3

NATIONAL SECURITY AND PRIVACY IN THE UNITED STATES THROUGH A LITIGATION LENS

Lawrence Friedman

In the constitutional democracy that is the United States, the people are expected to hold their representatives in the legislative and executive branches accountable through the electoral process. The ability of the people to perform this checking function is in turn premised upon the existence of certain conditions: access to the information necessary to make judgments about what their government is doing in their name; and a private space in which to digest the information available to them, and to plan how, or whether, to act on that information. When one or both of these conditions is not satisfied, any power the people possess to enforce some kind of accountability will be diminished.

Litigation about national security and privacy issues can tell us a great deal about the extent to which these conditions are satisfied—that is, about the extent to which Americans have access to information about particular governmental policies and programs, and the extent to which they enjoy protection from governmental intrusion into their deliberations. Over the past several decades, two distinct litigation arcs have become apparent: the federal government's ability to keep information related to national security policies from the public is growing; at the same time, the compass of individual privacy as against government intrusion is shrinking. In those cases where security and privacy interests intersect, the government typically prevails—both when it asserts an interest in keeping information in its possession from disclosure and when it asserts that individuals have no reasonable expectation of privacy with respect to the information they possess. The trajectory of judicial decision-making in the last half-century, in other words, has led to more privacy for the government, and less for the citizenry.

In the first two sections of this chapter, I review both litigation arcs, beginning with the government's efforts to keep close what it regards as national security secrets, then moving on to the issue of individual privacy.[1] In the final section, I discuss the potential consequences of these developments, as well as the ability of the judiciary to ensure that conditions necessary for constitutional democracy are not irretrievably diminished.

I

National security is among the most important concerns of any citizenry. While in the United States the details of security efforts might be beyond the scope of most citizens' experience or understanding, still citizens must be prepared to evaluate the overall thrust of such efforts. In this policy realm, as in all others, citizens remain the ultimate check on the federal government—in particular on the executive branch, which inevitably directs national security and foreign affairs policy efforts.[2] To voice their approval or disapproval, moreover, they need to know *something* about the substance of the nation's security policies. But how much do the people need to know in order to restrain executive policy and power? Information must flow for the ordinary processes of democracy to function—for the people to act effectively to check the excesses of their leaders; but where national security is concerned, there lies the danger that the indiscriminate release of information will serve only to "imperil the environment of physical security which a functioning democracy requires."[3]

The history of litigation touching on issues of national security reveals an executive that prefers to shield from public disclosure information about particular programs. The ability of the government to keep such information private today corresponds to the reach of the state secrets doctrine, first addressed by the U.S. Supreme Court in a Cold War-era case called *United States v. Reynolds.* [4] *Reynolds* arose from the October 1948 crash of a B-29 aircraft in which six crew members and three civilian observers lost their lives. The plaintiffs—widows of three of the deceased—sued the Air Force for wrongful death. When they sought production of the official accident investigation report, as well as statements by the surviving crew members that had been taken in connection with the investigation, the Air Force objected, arguing that, because the crew had been engaged in a highly secret mission, the requested material could not be furnished "without seriously hampering national security."[5]

The Supreme Court agreed that the state secrets doctrine immunizes certain materials relevant to national security from disclosure in litigation. Under the doctrine, the government enjoys a privilege to withhold information when a court is satisfied "from the implications of [a] question, in the setting in which it was asked, that a responsive answer to the question or an explanation of why it could not be answered might be dangerous because injurious disclosure could result."[6] Once the government has invoked the privilege, there need be no automatic disclosure of information; and, indeed, there may be cases in which the government's demand for secrecy cannot be overcome by "even the most compelling necessity."[7] As to the government's claim in *Reynolds*, the Court accepted that there existed a reasonable danger the accident investigation report at issue would contain references to secret electronic equipment—the primary concern of the mission.

To be sure, *Reynolds* was not the first time the Court addressed the issue of state secrets.[8] *Totten v. United States,* [9] an 1875 case, involved a claim by the estate of a Union spy against the government for payment for services rendered. There, the Court concluded that the mere revelation of such an arrangement could compromise or embarrass the government, undermining its ability to perform important national security functions. The *Totten* Court went so far as to suggest that, in particular cases, public policy may forbid any suit in which a trial "would inevitably lead to the disclosure of matters which the law itself regards as confidential."[10] *Totten* remains good law today. In the 2005 case *Tenet v. Doe*, the Court concluded that—as in *Totten*—public policy forbids former spies from suing the United States for failing to provide them with "the assistance it had promised in return for their espionage services"[11] because the suit concerned information that, were it disclosed, would compromise national security operations. And in the 2011 case *General Dynamics Corp. v. United States*, the

Court similarly concluded that, under *Totten*, both parties to a suit by the government against one of its defense contractors effectively "assumed the risk that state secrets would prevent the adjudication of [their contract] claims."[12]

Reynolds arguably announced a more limited rule than the one embraced by the *Totten* Court—a rule to govern only the potential disclosure of state secrets through litigation requests and the admission of evidence into court.[13] But the courts have applied *Reynolds* in numerous cases to much the same effect.[14] Consider, for example, *Zuckerbraun v. General Dynamics Corp.* [15] With Iran and Iraq at war, the United States maintained a naval presence in the Persian Gulf to protect shipping. An Iraqi fighter jet struck the U.S.S. *Stark* with two missiles, and thirty-seven crewmen died, including Earl Patton Ryals. The administrator of Ryals' estate brought a wrongful death action against General Dynamics, asserting it had negligently designed, manufactured, and tested the *Stark*'s weapons systems.

The government intervened, arguing that the state secrets doctrine protected information pertaining to the details and specifications of particular weapons and procedures, the disclosure of which would cause "grave damage" to U.S. security interests by enabling potential enemies to exploit weaknesses in those weapons systems and to develop appropriate countermeasures.[16] The Court of Appeals for the Second Circuit affirmed dismissal of the case, emphasizing that the courts must accord the "utmost deference" to the executive's determination of the impact of disclosure on military or diplomatic security.[17] Echoing *Reynolds*, the Court stated that "[e]ven the most compelling necessity [could] not overcome the claim of privilege if the court [wa]s ultimately satisfied that military secrets [were] at stake."[18] Indeed, the Court acknowledged that, in cases like *Zuckerbraun*, dismissal was appropriate because the factual questions at issue—regarding the design, performance, and tactics associated with particular weapons systems—could not be resolved without access to classified information. In other words, the Court deemed the very subject matter of the action to be a state secret, leaving the plaintiff no available evidence with which to establish a prima facie case.

Zuckerbraun was no anomaly. Following September 11, the assertion of the state secrets privilege by the government, as well as defense contractors and related private parties, became virtually automatic—even when much of the information sought was already publicly available. In *Al-Haramain Islamic Foundation, Inc. v. Bush,* [19] for instance, a non-profit foundation filed suit against the government following a December 2006 radio address in which President George W. Bush responded to a the *New York Times* article revealing the existence of a hitherto unknown domestic electronic surveillance program. The President acknowledged he had authorized "the interception of international communications of people with known links to al Qaeda and related terrorist organizations" after the September 11 attacks.[20] The Attorney General later clarified that the government only intercepted communications in which "one party to the communication is outside the United States and the government has a reasonable basis to believe that at least one party to communication is affiliated with, or working in support of, al Qaeda."[21]

The plaintiff alleged, among other things, that in March and April 2004 the National Security Agency (NSA) orchestrated the electronic surveillance of conversations between its director and its attorneys without first obtaining a court order or following the procedures set out in the Foreign Intelligence Surveillance Act (FISA)—the statute enacted by Congress to govern the acquisition of foreign intelligence. In addition, it alleged that, in May 2004, the NSA provided logs of these communications to the Office of Foreign Assets Control, which identified Al-Haramain as a "specially designated global terrorist," due to its allegedly having provided support to al Qaeda.[22] The government sought dismissal of the suit, arguing the very subject matter of the case was a state secret.

The district court characterized the outright dismissal of a suit based upon the state secrets doctrine as a "drastic" or "draconian" remedy,[23] noting that, "whenever possible, sensitive information must be disentangled from non-sensitive information to allow for the release of the latter."[24] Nonetheless, the Court acknowledged the inherent limitations of this approach, comparing contemporary electronic intelligence-gathering to the compilation of a "mosaic" which would allow "seemingly innocuous information" to be analyzed and compiled to reveal a fuller picture.[25] Ultimately, the Court concluded that disclosure of the information contained in one specific document presented no reasonable public danger, but that disclosure of information indicating whether the government had subjected the plaintiff to other surveillance efforts potentially could harm national security.

The executive also successfully invoked the state secrets doctrine in cases challenging the United States' extraordinary rendition program—the program pursuant to which foreign nationals suspected of involvement in terrorism were transferred by U.S. intelligence agencies to countries where local rules would provide greater flexibility with respect to detention and interrogation. In *El-Masri v. United States*, [26] the plaintiff, a German citizen of Lebanese descent, claimed that in December 2003 Macedonian officials handed him to the Central Intelligence Agency (CIA), who then detained him at a facility near Kabul, Afghanistan, until May 2004, when he was transported to Albania and released in a remote area. Albanian officials picked him up and took him to an airport, from which he returned to Germany. El-Masri alleged that, while detained, he was tortured and subjected to inhumane treatment.

When the government sought dismissal on the ground that the state secrets doctrine precluded litigation of El-Masri's complaint, El-Masri responded that information about U.S. rendition operations—including his own—had been discussed publicly. The district court nonetheless dismissed. On appeal, the Court of Appeals for the Fourth Circuit affirmed, following *Reynolds* and concluding that the privilege required dismissal because the plaintiff's claims and the government's defenses could not be adequately litigated absent the disclosure of information that remained, by government designation, a state secret.

Courts have not been unaware of the consequences of the government's invocation of the state secrets privilege. The Court of Appeals for the Ninth Circuit in *Mohamed v. Jeppesen Dataplan, Inc.* [27] recognized the tension between the government's perceived need to shroud many details of its counterterrorism efforts and "fundamental principles of our liberty, including justice, transparency, accountability, and national security."[28] The plaintiffs in that case alleged the defendant, a U.S. corporation and subsidiary of the Boeing Company, supplied flight planning and logistical support services to the aircraft and crew responsible for transporting each of them to the various detention locations. The government intervened, maintaining that further litigation would undermine national security interests, notwithstanding that much of the evidence needed to try the case was—as in El Masri's case—publicly available.

The Ninth Circuit ultimately focused on questions of whether and to what extent the matters requested should be regarded as state secrets, and, if they were, whether the suit could be litigated absent that evidence. After reviewing the government's public and classified declarations, the Court concluded at least some of the matters at issue qualified as state secrets—but of course it could not explain which matters were privileged, "lest [it] jeopardize the secrets [it was] bound to protect."[29] *Reynolds*, the Court concluded, required dismissal because there was "no feasible way to litigate Jeppesen's alleged liability without creating an unjustifiable risk of divulging state secrets."[30] In other words, Jeppesen's alleged role and attendant liability could not be isolated from the protected information; and, the Court reasoned, any plausible effort by Jeppesen to defend against the plaintiff's allegations would create an unjustifiable risk of divulging state secrets.

The Supreme Court in *Reynolds* suggested governmental assertions of the state secrets doctrine should be considered carefully: courts, Chief Justice Vinson stated, should not relinquish control of the information at issue "to the caprice of executive officers."[31] Yet, as the cases discussed here (and there are many others) illustrate, the courts essentially have permitted the government to wield the privilege as a blunt instrument, especially in the years following September 11 and even in light of public revelations of the policies—such as extraordinary rendition—that the government pursued during that time. Indeed, Laura Donohue has concluded that, "from January 2001 to January 2009, the privilege played a significant role in the executive branch's national security litigation strategy."[32] Her research shows, moreover, that the reach of the privilege in actuality extends well beyond the reported cases in which the government has invoked it. Today, she notes, corporations engaged in matters related to national security will, in commercial disputes, assert "state secrets as an affirmative defense," thus giving themselves "a significant tactical advantage by raising its specter"[33]—and, at the same time, enhancing the privacy the government enjoys with respect to the national security policies and programs in which those entities are involved.

II

While the executive's arguments for governmental privacy vis-à-vis the state secrets doctrine have been well-received by the courts over the last half-century, the same cannot be said for the privacy claims of individuals. This notwithstanding the textual anchor such claims arguably enjoy: the Fourth Amendment specifically provides for a right "of the people to be secure in their persons, houses, papers, and effects, against unreasonable searches and seizures." Like the First Amendment's protection of free speech, the Fourth Amendment's privacy protection serves a distinctly political function: it creates a space in which citizens may deliberate about their government—its leaders and their policies and programs—without fear of surveillance by the government's agents.[34] It creates a space, in other words, where citizens are free to think critical or even dissident thoughts, and to preserve those thoughts in their "papers" and "effects," which today might include their laptops, personal digital assistants, and cellular telephones.

The space protected by the Fourth Amendment is defined by a person's "reasonable expectation of privacy." The formulation comes from *Katz v. United States.* [35] There, a criminal defendant challenged the introduction into evidence of telephone conversations in which he had engaged and which government agents had intercepted. The court held that the Fourth Amendment "protects people, not places," and what a person "seeks to preserve as private, even in an area accessible to the public, may be constitutionally protected."[36] Katz, though visible when making calls from a telephone booth, could "rely upon the protection of the Fourth Amendment," for "[o]ne who occupies [the booth,] shuts the door behind him, and pays the toll that permits him to place a call is surely entitled to assume that the words he utters into the mouthpiece will not be broadcast to the world."[37] In his concurring opinion, Justice John Marshall Harlan articulated the test for which *Katz* has come to be known: a person has a protectable privacy interest when she has "exhibited an actual (subjective) expectation of privacy and, second, … the expectation [is] one that society is prepared to recognize as 'reasonable.'"[38] Under this test, the telephone booth qualified as "a temporarily private place whose momentary occupants' expectations of freedom from intrusion" were reasonable.[39]

When, under *Katz*, there exists a reasonable expectation of privacy, the Fourth Amendment's specific protections come into play. Before invading an individual's privacy, agents of the government must demonstrate to a neutral and detached magistrate that they have some level of suspicion that evidence of criminal activity will be found in the particular place to be searched. This requirement permits the judiciary to serve as a check on the executive, and secures for citizens a measure of the privacy the Fourth Amendment was designed to protect.

One problem with this framework is that courts have tended to apply the same rules to all searches, regardless of the importance of the privacy interests at stake relative to the Fourth Amendment's political function.[40] It follows that judicial applications of the Fourth Amendment which diminish the compass of individual privacy in one context—say, surveillance of individuals suspected, because of their known associates and actions, of dealing drugs—also diminish it in others—say, surveillance of individuals suspected, because of their known associates and actions, of materially supporting terrorism. This is not to say that terrorism poses less of a danger to the public than drug-dealing—far from it. But we should acknowledge that any judicial ruling that makes it easier for the government to intercept communications which reflect our private conversations and thoughts is likely to diminish the space within which citizens may innocently deliberate and communicate about national policies and programs.

Consider, in this regard, *In re Directives*, [41] a case concerning a directive issued under the Protect America Act of 2007 (PAA). PAA required communications service providers to assist the government in acquiring foreign intelligence about individuals—including United States persons—reasonably believed to be located outside the United States. The Foreign Intelligence Surveillance Court (FISC) rejected an unnamed service provider's constitutional challenge to the law and the provider appealed to the Foreign Intelligence Surveillance Court of Review, arguing that the Fourth Amendment requires the government to obtain a warrant before acquiring its customers' communications and, alternatively, that the surveillance requested was unreasonable.

The provider argued, first, that the requested surveillance violated the Fourth Amendment because there was no foreign intelligence exception to the warrant clause. The Court of Review did not disagree, but noted that the Supreme Court "has recognized a comparable exception, outside the foreign intelligence context, in so-called 'special needs' cases."[42] Under that exception, the warrant requirement does not apply "when the purpose behind the governmental action [goes] beyond routine law enforcement and insisting upon a warrant would materially interfere with the accomplishment of that purpose."[43] Foreign intelligence surveillance, the Court concluded, presents just such a special need. The court here elided the distinctions between situations in which the Supreme Court had found special needs and those implicated by foreign intelligence surveillance, even though the latter are different not just in degree but in kind. Approved special needs regimes have addressed situations in which the government is interested in, and generally seeks to obtain, one species of personal information—whether, for example, an individual has been drinking alcohol, or using drugs. Foreign intelligence surveillance, on the other hand, by design may uncover numerous bits of personal information entirely unrelated to an individual's alleged involvement in questionable activities—bits that, collectively, can paint a surprisingly rich picture of the target's life in all its facets.[44]

Again, this is not to say that national security—in particular counterterrorism efforts—does not represent (as the Court of Review put it) a governmental interest "of the highest order of magnitude."[45] But it is not clear why that reality in itself should serve to justify a search regime that would allow the government to obtain *all* of an individual's personal communications based upon mere suspicion (as dictated by the PPA itself) that the individual was linked to a foreign power. Arguably, the threat of foreign terrorism does not represent a special need divorced from the ordinary aims of law enforcement—terrorism is, in a real sense, criminal conduct.

Another problem to consider is that the protections provided by the Fourth Amendment are relevant only when, under *Katz*, an individual has a reasonable expectation of privacy. Within little more than a decade after the *Katz* decision, the limits of Harlan's test became apparent. In a 1979 case, *Smith v. Maryland*, [46] the defendant sought to suppress evidence derived from the use of a pen register to record the numbers dialed from his telephone because the police had failed to obtain a warrant prior to the device's installation. On appeal, the Supreme Court affirmed the defendant's conviction, concluding that an individual maintains no "actual expectation of privacy in the numbers [he or she] dial[s]."[47] Telephone users, the Court observed, know they must convey numbers to a telephone company for calls to be completed, and that the companies can make records of the numbers dialed. Given that individuals have no reasonable expectation of privacy in information they voluntarily convey to third parties, the Court concluded they assume the risk that the telephone company may convey the numbers dialed to the government. Thus *Smith* announced what has come to be known as "the third-party doctrine"—the rule that individuals have no reasonable expectation of privacy in information voluntarily transmitted to others.

Smith discarded the normative understanding of privacy embraced in *Katz*—the understanding that some information is private, even when it may be seen or overheard—and traded it for a descriptive understanding of privacy premised upon the idea that, whenever an individual shares information, she loses any claim she might have that that information be considered private going forward. On this understanding, and given the way in which twenty-first century individuals rely upon third parties to facilitate information-sharing relationships, the third-party doctrine threatens to make irrelevant in many instances the very protection the framers intended the Fourth Amendment to afford us.[48] This is because the third-party doctrine creates a zone in which government need not secure prior judicial approval to search, because individuals have no reasonable expectation of privacy. And that zone is expanding in the United States, for the third-party doctrine eliminates any expectation of privacy except when individuals disclose information either out of ignorance or compulsion. As Judge Alex Kozinski and Eric Nguyen put it,

> If speaking to friends, putting money in a bank account and making telephone calls routed through a phone company waive the privacy of information so disclosed, then very little indeed can remain private in a world that is becoming more electronically interconnected.[49]

Not long after Kozinski and Nguyen made this pronouncement in 2011–2012, the U.S. District Court for the Southern District of New York addressed the constitutionality of governmental efforts to obtain foreign intelligence related to potential terrorist threats through a program designed to collect domestic telephone metadata in bulk—the digital equivalent of the telephone numbers captured by a pen register device. The Court in *American Civil Liberties Union v. Clapper* recognized that, "[i]f plumbed," the metadata could "reveal a rich profile of every individual as well as a comprehensive record of people's associations with one another."[50] Nonetheless, the Court concluded that individuals voluntarily convey this information to communications services providers, and even the "[t]he collection of breathtaking amounts of information unprotected by the Fourth Amendment does not transform that sweep into a Fourth Amendment search."[51] Earlier in 2013, the FISC had similarly reasoned that, "where one individual does not have a Fourth Amendment interest, grouping together a large number of similarly-situated individuals cannot result in a Fourth Amendment interest springing into existence *ex nihilo*."[52]

The logic of these cases may have been undermined by the Supreme Court's 2018 decision in *Carpenter v. United States.* [53] There, the Court determined that individuals maintain some reasonable expectation of privacy in cell site location data, though this information is available to a third party—the cell phone service provider. The Court reasoned that the quantity and quality of the information conveyed—from which a far clearer picture of an individual's days could be constructed than from the information acquired by a pen register device—and the fact that the information is transmitted by cell phones automatically, distinguish this sharing of information from *Smith*. But the Court notably confined its holding to cell site location data, and specifically noted that a warrant will be required only "in the rare case where the suspect has a legitimate privacy interest in records held by a third party."[54] Still, it is possible the Court's reasoning in *Carpenter* might at least slow courts that would otherwise blindly extend the *Smith* rationale to national security regimes that involve the acquisition of personal information through sweeping communications surveillance.

III

Whether the consequences of the litigation arcs involving the state secrets and third-party doctrines should be considered alarming is a separate question. It could be argued that greater privacy for the government and less for individuals represents a positive development for national security. The late William J. Stuntz, for example, in an essay published in 2006, viewed a fixation on privacy as one reason why government struggles to keep the citizenry safe: "We have too much privacy," he wrote, "and those who govern us have too little."[55] The protection of individual privacy, he argued, impedes efficient law enforcement—particularly with respect to counterterrorism efforts—while an emphasis on transparency prevents government from "act[ing] aggressively when action is needed."[56] These assertions are debatable. The administration of President George W. Bush carried out many of its counterterrorism programs in secret, to no discernible advantage. But when viewed through the lens of litigation implicating issues of privacy and security, it would be difficult to argue that Stuntz's prescription—more government secrecy and less individual privacy—hasn't been effectively realized.

To support reducing the levels of both government transparency and individual privacy requires a belief that government leaders—and particularly executive branch officials—will inevitably act honorably, in the best interests of the nation. The courts have long adhered to such a belief. In *In re Directives*, for instance, the Court of Review discounted the possibility that the PAA's foreign intelligence surveillance regime would "invite abuse," for the Court declined to assume, in the absence of evidence to the contrary, that the government would implement its surveillance program in bad faith.[57] It took comfort in the fact that "the government ha[d] instituted several layers of serviceable safeguards against unwarranted harms."[58]

Of course, a judicial assumption that the government will operate in good faith is really a necessary concomitant of the decision to rule in the government's favor in cases like *In re Directives*. The assumption would be unwarranted if there existed a real possibility that agents of the executive might act dishonorably. Such an assumption, moreover, finds no basis in the frameworks for law- and policy-making the Constitution establishes, which generally require that executive action be constitutionally susceptible, at some point in time, to an extra-departmental check. It is difficult to square an executive promise to self-police its power to search individuals with the Fourth Amendment's textual commitment to pre-search authorization by a neutral and detached magistrate—even when that authorization comes from a magistrate specially designated to review applications for warrants to pursue precisely this kind of surveillance, a role the FISC historically has filled.[59]

But we need not rely on formalist views of separation of powers to question a judicial assumption that the executive will in good faith assert the state secrets privilege or cabin its broad-based communications surveillance efforts. History has shown government officials do not always act in the citizenry's best interests in these and like matters. Famously, the government's invocation of the state secrets privilege in the *Reynolds* litigation served not to protect mission-critical state secrets but, rather, to hide the Air Force's own negligence.[60] And, to take a more recent example, the National Security Agency during the Bush administration exceeded a mandate to acquire only the telephone and e-mail metadata of non-U.S. persons, or of messages that could be linked to terrorism. In fact, the agency was also gathering, in secret, much more.[61] Such action at least suggests that the executive's internal safeguards and procedures with respect to foreign intelligence surveillance—like the measures the Court of Review approved in similar circumstances in *In re Directives* [62]—should not necessarily be considered adequate substitutes for the extra-departmental check that the Fourth Amendment contemplates will precede such efforts.

An assumption of good faith on the government's part should be understood as a form of judicial deference.[63] Such deference is pronounced in the state secrets cases, where courts have been particularly reluctant to question the government's claims. And we see it in the search and seizure cases concerning the vast surveillance apparatus created in the wake of September 11, cases where courts have tended to accept executive assertions regarding the need for the desired surveillance.

At bottom, it is not difficult to appreciate that very human insecurities may be at work. Where national security is concerned, the President and other executive branch officials tend to live moment to moment, respectful of the price they will pay should they neglect to address national security issues that pose potentially imminent threats to American lives.[64] Federal judges are not, merely by virtue of their institutional positions (protected by life-tenure and theoretically remote from the vicissitude of electoral politics), immune from such thinking. When the government's lawyers contend that a particular program—its details classified and confidential, its effect on privacy destructive—is necessary to avert the next disaster, in order to save lives, how should a court respond?

Justice Robert Jackson recognized that judges can fall prey in matters of national security to the self-serving claims of the executive. In *Korematsu v. United States*, he urged his colleagues to step outside the legal dilemma created by the government when it sought to confine American citizens without due process because they were of Japanese descent. The problem, he reasoned, is that, in cases involving allegations of military necessity, the "courts can never have any real alternative to accepting the mere declaration [by the government] that it was reasonably necessary."[65] Justice Jackson accordingly dissented from the holding that national security concerns justified restrictions on the liberty interests of Japanese Americans, arguing that the Court should not "distort the Constitution to approve all that the military may deem expedient"[66] by "enforc[ing] an order which violates constitutional limitations even if it is a reasonable exercise of military authority."[67]

Decisions like *Clapper* and *In re Directives* can be traced to *Korematsu*. There, the Court assumed it could objectively review the due process implications of national security policy determinations in the midst of crisis. But, as Justice Jackson warned, such review tends to be shallow, given the human reluctance to undermine any effort the executive claims is necessary to protect citizens from the harm posed by an external threat. Jackson urged his colleagues to stay the Court's hand in *Korematsu* because, in the end, he preferred they not "lead people to rely on th[e] Court for a review that seems … wholly delusive."[68] Consider, in this light, the *Clapper* court's statement that the government after September 11 "adapted to confront a new enemy" by launching a bulk telephony metadata collection program that "only works because it collects everything."[69] This assertion appeared in the decision's opening paragraphs, at a point where one might reasonably believe its truth had yet to be proved. The court's tone signals for the reader the essentially uncritical constitutional review of the bulk metadata collection program that will follow.

And yet: the U.S. Supreme Court, even after September 11, has in a few notable instances struck down the executive's national security policy determinations. Perhaps most famously in *Hamdi v. Rumsfeld*, Justice Sandra Day O'Connor, writing for the plurality, explained that the executive could not detain U.S. citizens suspected of being enemy combatants absent some process—and that the existence of "a state of war is not a blank check for the President when it comes to the rights of the Nation's citizens."[70] In that spirit, perhaps there are arguments to be made in litigating the reach of the state secrets and third-party doctrines to which courts will be amenable. Heidi Kitrosser has suggested that, notwithstanding *Reynolds*, "advocates have a strong doctrinal basis on which to urge courts, case-by-case, to review disputed evidence themselves, and to demand that the government defend its privilege claims with some precision."[71]

With respect to the third-party doctrine, advocates might point to *Klayman v. Obama*, decided two weeks before *Clapper*. There, the District Court for the District of Columbia concluded *Smith v. Maryland* didn't support the constitutionality of the government's bulk telephony metadata collection program, because "present-day circumstances" are "so thoroughly unlike those considered by the Supreme Court [in *Smith*]."[72] The court continued: "[N]ot only is the Government's ability to collect, store, and analyze phone data greater now than it was in 1979, but the nature and quantity of the information contained in people's telephony metadata is much greater as well."[73]

Importantly, the Court of Appeals for the Second Circuit overturned the lower court's decision in *Clapper*—but on statutory, not constitutional grounds.[74] The court held the program exceeded the scope of the surveillance program that Congress had authorized under Section 215 of the PATRIOT Act. The government had argued the statute allowed the collection of metadata that could be used for some purpose by the National Security Agency and at some unknown time in the future. The Court concluded Congress had not authorized the collection of metadata "concerning every telephone call made or received in the United States using the services of the recipient service provider … for an indefinite period extending into the future."[75]

Though the Court resolved the surveillance issue on statutory grounds, it noted that "whether Congress has considered and authorized a program such as this one is not irrelevant to its constitutionality."[76] The court went on to discuss the importance to any Fourth Amendment analysis of the extent to which Congress was involved in crafting a surveillance regime, given that body's capacity to appreciate both the "intricacies and competing concerns involved in protecting our national security," and the effect such a program could have on reasonable expectations of privacy.[77] These observations suggest that Congress may yet serve as a check on executive policymaking when the judiciary, for one reason or another, cannot. Congress, after all, may be in the best position to police the executive's national security efforts: it enjoys access to information that the President is constitutionally obligated to share;

and has the ability, through its investigatory powers, to appropriately monitor the operations that flow from the executive's policymaking choices.[78]

As the Second Circuit's decision demonstrates, moreover, the courts may be more likely to review critically the question of whether executive action comports with statutory, as opposed to constitutional authority, for the simple reason that the stakes are lower: Congress can always act afterward either to confirm or correct judicial understanding of the relevant grant of power. In this way, relationships between security and privacy, and between those matters and the larger issue of government accountability, may still be influenced by the courts through litigation—but indirectly, as refracted through the prism of statutory construction. And, with a little distance, judges might be more inclined to relax the reflexive deference they have shown the executive through decades of constitutional litigation over conflicts between national security and privacy.

★ ★ ★

William Stuntz had a point: it would be folly to argue that the government may never claim a state secret, that every bit of surveillance undermines reasonable expectations of privacy. Executive officials—and their legislative counterparts in Congress, for that matter—need some privacy within which to make difficult decisions regarding national security. As Alan Dershowitz has observed, "[n]o reasonable person can dispute the reality that there are 'necessary secrets,' like the names of spies, the movement of troops, the contents of codes and ciphers, the location of satellites and the nature of secret weapons."[79] It would not be unreasonable to conclude, though, that today the ability of the American people to hold their leaders appropriately accountable for national security decisions is diminished. To keep the government accountable, we must know something about what it is doing—at least enough to be able to participate in debates about whether we should approve of what it is doing. And we must feel secure in knowing that we can discuss what our government is doing without fear of surveillance. The litigation arcs discussed in this chapter suggest that judicial decision-making has contributed to the erosion of both these conditions.

Notes

1 These reviews are not intended to be, and within the confines of this chapter could not be, comprehensive.
2 *See, e.g.*, Zivotofsky v. Kerry, 135 S.Ct. 2076 (2015) (discussing exclusive executive power under the Constitution to recognize foreign nations).
3 United States v. Morrison, 844 F.2d 1057, 1082 (4th Cir. 1988) (Wilkinson, J., concurring).
4 345 U.S. 1 (1953).
5 *Id.* at 5.
6 *Id.* at 9 (quoting Hoffman v. United States, 341 U.S. 479, 486–87 (1951)).
7 *Id.*
8 *See* Laura K. Donohue, *The Shadow of State Secrets*, 159 U. PA. L. REV. 77, 83 (2010).
9 92 U.S. 105 (1875).
10 *Id.* at 107.
11 544 U.S. 1, 3 (2005).
12 131 S. Ct. 1900, 1909 (2011).
13 *See id.* at 1906 ("*Reynolds* was about the admission of evidence").
14 See HEIDI KITROSSER, RECLAIMING ACCOUNTABILITY: TRANSPARENCY, EXECUTIVE POWER, AND THE U.S. CONSTITUTION 122 (2015) (discussing modern cases in which "state secrets doctrine can prove supremacist in application").
15 935 F.2d 544 (2d Cir. 1991).

16 *Id.*
17 *Id.* at 548.
18 *Id.* at 547 (quoting United States v. Reynolds, 345 U.S. 1, 7–11 (1953)).
19 451 F.Supp. 2d 1215 (D. Or. 2006).
20 *Id.* at 1218.
21 *Id.*
22 *Id.*
23 *Id.* at 1220.
24 *Id.* at 1220 (quoting Ellsberg v. Mitchell, 709 F.2d 51, 57 (1983)).
25 *Id.* (quoting Halkin v. Helms, 598 F.2d 1, 8 (D.C. Cir. 1978)).
26 479 F.3d 296 (4th Cir. 2007).
27 614 F.3d 1070, 1073 (9th Cir. 2010).
28 *Id.* at 1073.
29 *Id.*
30 *Id.*
31 United States v. Reynolds, 345 U.S. 1, 10 (1953).
32 *See* Donohue, *supra* note 8 at 87.
33 *Id.* at 214.
34 *See* Thomas P. Crocker, *The Political Fourth Amendment*, 88 WASH. U. L. REV. 303, 311 (2010) (discussing role of Fourth Amendment in protecting political liberty).
35 389 U.S. 347 (1967).
36 *Id.* at 351.
37 *Id.* at 352.
38 *Id.* at 361 (Harlan, J., concurring).
39 *Id.*
40 *Cf.* William J. Stuntz, *O.J. Simpson, Bill Clinton, and the Transsubstantive Fourth Amendment*, 114 HARV. L. REV. 842, 843 (2001) (noting that "Fourth Amendment law mostly ignores substantive criminal law; distinctions among crimes are usually irrelevant when it comes to regulating criminal investigations").
41 *In re Directives*, 551 F.3d 1004, 1006 (FISC 2008).
42 *Id.* at 1010.
43 *Id.*
44 *See* ACLU v. Clapper, 785 F.3d 787 (2nd Cir. 2015) (observing that, "[t]he more metadata the government collects and analyzes … the greater the capacity for such metadata to reveal ever more private and previously unascertainable information about individuals").
45 *In re Directives*, 551 F.3d at 1016.
46 442 U.S. 735 (1979).
47 *Id.* at 742.
48 *See* Lawrence Friedman, Commonwealth v. Augustine *and the Future of the Third-Party Doctrine*, 41 N. E. JOURNAL ON CRIMINAL AND CIVIL CONFINEMENT 271, 283 (2015).
49 *See* Alex Kozinski & Eric S. Nguyen, *Has Technology Killed the Fourth Amendment?*, 2011–2012 CATO SUP. CT. REV. 15, 29; see also id. at 30 ("If the courts continue to apply [the third-party] rationale, then pretty much nothing will be private"), *see also* United States v. Jones, 132 S. Ct. 945, 957 (2012) (Sotomayor, J., concurring) (observing that the third-party doctrine "is ill suited to the digital age, in which people reveal a great deal of information about themselves to third parties in the course of carrying out mundane tasks").
50 American Civil Liberties Union v. Clapper, 959 F. Supp.2d 724, 730 (S.D.N.Y. 2013).
51 *Id.* at 752.
52 *In re FBI*, 2013 WL 5307991, *2 (FISC 2013).
53 138 S. Ct. 2206 (2018).
54 *Id.* at 2222.
55 William J. Stuntz, *Against privacy and transparency*, THE NEW REPUBLIC (April 17, 2006), www.newrepublic.com/article/against-privacy-and-transparency.
56 *Id.*
57 *In re Directives*, 551 F.3d 1004, 1014–1015 (FISC 2008).
58 *Id.* at 1016.
59 *See* Global Relief Foundation, Inc. v. O'Neil, 207 F. Supp. 779, 788–89 (N.D. Ill. 2002) (discussing role of FISC under FISA).

60 *See* Kitrosser, *supra* note 14, at 97.

61 *See* Charlie Savage, *Bush Made Retroactive N.S.A. "Fix" After Hospital Room Showdown*, N.Y. TIMES, Sept. 20, 2015, at A13.

62 *See In re Directives*, 551 F.3d at 1016 (finding "the risks of error and abuse … within acceptable limits and effective minimization procedures … in place").

63 On judicial deference to the executive in respect to national security decision-making, see DAVID RUDENSTINE, THE AGE OF DEFERENCE: THE SUPREME COURT, NATIONAL SECURITY AND THE CONSTITUTIONAL ORDER (Oxford University Press 2016).

64 *See, e.g.*, RON SUSKIND, THE ONE PERCENT DOCTRINE: DEEP INSIDE AMERICA'S PURSUIT OF ITS ENEMIES SINCE 9/11 (Simon & Schuster 2006), at 62 (discussing the doctrine reportedly articulated by Vice President Dick Cheney: "[e]ven if there's just a one percent chance of the unimaginable coming due, act as if it is a certainty").

65 32 U.S. 214, 245 (1944) (Jackson, J., dissenting).

66 *Id.* at 244.

67 *Id.* at 247.

68 *Id.* at 248.

69 ACLU v. Clapper, 959 F.Supp.2d 724, 729–30 (S.D.N.Y. 2013).

70 542 U.S. 507, 536 (2004).

71 Kitrosser, *supra* note 14, at 122–23.

72 957 F.Supp.2d 1, 31 (D.D.C. 2013).

73 *Id.* at 34. It is worth noting that this is the argument that the U.S. Supreme Court accepted in *Carpenter v. United States*, 585 U.S. __ (2017), in which it held that individuals maintain a reasonably expectation of privacy in cell site location data communicated to cell phone service providers.

74 *See* 785 F.3d 787 (2nd Cir. 2015).

75 *Id.* at 813.

76 *Id.* at 824.

77 *Id.* at 824–25.

78 *See* Lawrence Friedman and Victor Hansen, *Secrecy, Transparency, and National Security*, 38 WM. MITCHELL L. REV. 1610, 1626–28 (2012). And, as it happens, Congress has acted to check the executive; in 2015, for example, it replaced the PATRIOT Act with the USA Freedom Act, which curtailed the executive's authority to conduct sweeping surveillance of domestic telephone communications. *See* Jennifer Steinhauer and Jonathan Wiseman, *U.S. Surveillance in Place Since 9/11 Is Sharply Limited*, N.Y. TIMES, June 2, 2015, at A1.

79 Alan M. Dershowitz, *Who Needs to Know?*, N.Y. TIMES BOOK REV., May 28, 2010, www.nytimes/com/2010/05/30/books/review/Dershowitz-t.html.

4
DEMOCRACY AND SECURITY IN THE UK

Leonard Weinberg

By contrast to its counterparts on the European Continent, the United Kingdom (UK) has not experienced mass revolutionary or counter-revolutionary violence over the last century and a half. Unlike Germany after World War I or Russia in the middle of that conflict – or even Italy, France and Spain during the first decades of the 20th century – Britain has come off relatively unscathed. In fact, at one point in the 19th century Britain's courts adhered to the idea of a 'political exemption' in extradition cases. If a state sought the extradition of one of its nationals resident in the UK, accusing him/her of a crime he/she had allegedly committed in the home country, the British courts could and did refuse to grant the request based on the fact that the crime had been committed for a clearly political motive.

Consequently, by the last third of the 19th century Britain had become a refuge for a long list of political radicals. Karl Marx, working in the reading room of the British Museum, was not an isolated figure. London abounded with anarchists and Marxists of one type or another, all committed to the destruction of the capitalist system. Joseph Conrad's novel *The Secret Agent* (1907) depicts the unsuccessful attempt by anarchists to blow up the Royal Observatory at Greenwich (the source of Greenwich Mean Time) in 1886 as a way of making 'propaganda by deed' and shattering the complacency of the bourgeoisie.

Ireland

It was not the cause of social revolution that ignited a wave of violence in the UK during the 19th century. Instead, it was Irish nationalism: the desire on the part of many Irishmen to separate their homeland from Great Britain. The most spectacular act in this regard was the Phoenix Park murders of May 6, 1882. On that date members of the Irish national 'Invincibles' assassinated London's newly appointed Chief Secretary for Ireland along with his secretary while they were on a stroll through Dublin.[1]

The cause for which these British officials were killed was Irish home rule and, eventually, national independence from Britain. The movement to achieve such goals led to numbers of violent attacks on government targets both in Ireland and on the British mainland. In the years leading up to World War I Irish nationalists, under a variety of names, launched a series of bombings intended to make the denial of self-government too painful for His Majesty's

Government on a long-term basis. Other Irishmen, led by Charles Parnell, sought to pursue this objective through parliamentary politics.

By the time World War I began in 1914 the UK government of Prime Minister Herbert Henry Asquith was prepared to grant home rule to Ireland. This willingness set off a backlash. The cause of Irish independence emanated largely, though not exclusively, from the island's majority Catholic population. Its Protestant minority, concentrated in Northern Ireland, strenuously objected to home rule and prepared to use violence to resist the Asquith government's policy. Led by the Protestant lawyer Edward Carson, the Unionists prepared to establish their own provisional government and declare their independence from the rest of Ireland.

Before a full-scale sectarian conflict could erupt Britain entered WWI, and implementation of home rule was suspended for the duration of the fighting. Then, in 1916, the 'Easter Rising' took place. Supporters of the Irish Republican Brotherhood (IRB), attempting to take advantage of the UK's wartime preoccupations, seized control of Dublin's central post office and proclaimed Irish national independence. The government in London reacted to the Easter Rising by deploying the military and crushing the rebellion. Many of the rebels were executed by firing squad for their treason. The effect of these executions was to transform the IRB rebels into martyrs. The British were unnecessarily cruel in their repression, which included round-ups of suspects on an Ireland-wide basis. By the time WWI ended in 1918 the Irish population was prepared for what amounted to civil war.[2]

Over the following years (1918–1923) the nationalists waged an internal war in support of their demand for complete independence. Michael Collins, one of the nationalists' key figures, and his followers launched a terrorist campaign against off-duty British military officers and government officials. London reacted by sending the 'Black and Tans'. These former members of the British Army employed exceptionally brutal tactics in an effort to put down the rebellion.

When the UK government concluded repression was not likely to be successful in the long run, it entered into negotiations with the Irish nationalists. Led by Collins and Eamon de Valera, the nationalists agreed to a solution involving the establishment of an Irish Free State to be ruled from Dublin. The northern region of the island, or Ulster, with its large Protestant majority, would retain its union with the UK.

This outcome in effect produced a war within a war. The Irish Republican Army (IRA) took up arms to resist the compromise settlement (1924). During the course of the fighting between the new Dublin government and the IRA, Michael Collins, the settlement's chief negotiator, was assassinated. When the fighting subsided, an Irish government headed by de Valera governed the 'Free State' while Northern Ireland retained its status as a UK province, its own regional government located at Stormont outside Belfast.

During the 1930s the IRA and the political party Sinn Fein with which it had close ties engaged in a two-sided conflict. In the Free State de Valera's government sought to repress the IRA because of its propensity for violence and its refusal to accept the legitimacy of the two-state solution to the Irish conflict. Between 1936 and 1940 the IRA launched a cross-border bombing campaign in Ulster. In both Ulster and across the Irish Sea in English cities, IRA 'active service units' set off bombs directed at civilians.[3]

For the duration of World War II (1939–1945) the Irish problem remained unresolved, at least to the IRA's satisfaction. The British government used three parliamentary measures to quell the unrest: the Special Powers Act (1922), the Public Order Act (1936) and the earlier Defense of the Realm Act (1914) (which supplied the Home Office with sufficient authority under emergency circumstances to control disorder and detain its perpetrators).

Following WWII and up to the 1960s the division of Ireland was not a major concern in the public mind. The Protestant (Presbyterian)-dominated provincial government in Stormont saw to it that Ulster's Catholic minority became the target of a number of discriminatory measures – in public housing, employment and political life. Furthermore, the province's police force, the Royal Ulster Constabulary (RUC), was virtually monopolized by Protestant unionists. An auxiliary police force, the so-called 'B Specials', were regarded as militant unionists. Catholics were in effect 'second-class' citizens, a situation not completely unlike that of African-Americans in the American South. This similarity did not go unnoticed by young Irish Catholics who observed the American civil rights movement led by Dr. Martin Luther King Jr.

By the mid-1960s a Northern Irish civil rights movement (the Campaign for Social Justice) emerged, led by such youthful republican activists as Bernadette Devlin, Patricia McCluskey, and Paddy O'Hanlon. Rights activists were committed to the principles of non-violent protest and peaceful civil disobedience in their effort to end anti-Catholic discrimination. At campaign rallies protesters often sang 'We Shall Overcome'. By 1968 this civil rights movement began to assert itself by staging peaceful marches through Belfast, Londonderry and other Ulster communities. As they paraded through Protestant neighborhoods the civil rights protesters were often met with violent opposition by Protestant young people who did what they could to disrupt the marches.

On the other side of Ulster's sectarian divide, in 1971 an ardently anti-Catholic Protestant clergyman, the Reverend Dr. Ian Paisley, organized his own movement aimed at countering the civil rights protesters. Paisley was jailed briefly for organizing violent anti-Catholic protests.

We must also take into account the 'marching season'. Every summer members of the Orange Order, Protestant loyalists, staged marches through Belfast and Londonderry to commemorate the 1746 victory of Protestants (the House of Hanover) over Catholics (Stuarts) at the Battle of Culloden for control of the British monarchy. When the marchers passed through Catholic neighborhoods, they were often met by Catholic republicans who used violent means to stop this degradation ritual.

By the early 1970s the fighting between loyalists and republicans had become a fact of everyday life throughout Northern Ireland. The fighting became so acute that in 1973 London suspended the Northern Irish provincial legislature and imposed direct rule from Westminster. Concomitantly, Parliament enacted the Northern Ireland Emergency Provisions Act and then, the following year, the Prevention of Terrorism Act.[4]

These parliamentary measures, among other things, provided for internment without charge for a limited period of time. They also loosened the rules of admissible evidence at trial. The emergency legislation established 'Diplock' courts throughout Northern Ireland. Named after Lord Diplock, chair of a commission reporting to Parliament, such courts eliminated trial by jury, leaving matters of guilt or innocence to a trial judge. Trial judges could admit the hearsay testimony of so-called 'super-grasses'. Super-grasses were jailed former members of one of the loyalist or republican paramilitary groups; they testified (in anonymity) against their former associates in exchange for reduced sentences.

The situation on the ground in Northern Ireland became so acute that in 1971 London sent the British Army there in an effort to restore order. Initially, the goal was also to protect Northern Ireland's Catholic population against mounting violence by the Protestant loyalists. Soon though, the Army became embroiled in a long-term fight with the IRA.

In the midst of the Northern Irish conflict, the IRA split into the 'Provisionals' (PIRA) and the 'Officials'. It was the former, the 'Provos', who opted for armed struggle. The PIRA leadership defined the British military presence in neo-colonial terms as an army of occupation. PIRA's goal then became the expulsion of the British military from Ulster and the reunification of Ireland under the auspices of a socialist Dublin government to be led by Sinn Fein, the IRA's political wing.

What followed over the course of the subsequent 15 years was a three-cornered cycle of violence involving the British military, PIRA and the Protestant loyalists e.g. the Ulster Defence Association (UDA).[5] Not only did bombs go off in the town centers of Belfast, Londonderry, and smaller Ulster communities, but the military lost control and carried out indiscriminate attacks on Republican civilians – 'Bloody Sunday', January 30, 1972. The fighting spread to Britain itself. Most spectacularly, PIRA detonated bombs in pubs frequented by English servicemen, as in Birmingham in January 1974, where 11 off-duty soldiers were killed. In 1984 PIRA almost succeeded in assassinating Prime Minister Margaret Thatcher while she was attending the Conservative Party's annual conference in Brighton.

During the 1970s and '80s there were a number of attempts to end the violence by means of negotiation involving power-sharing arrangements.[6] Secret negotiations, held in London in 1974–75 between PIRA representatives and Britain's Secretary of State for Northern Ireland, William Whitelaw, resulted in an agreement according to which Ulster's Catholic population would share power in running the province, commensurate with that population's size.

Leaders of the loyalist cause, notably Ian Paisley, reacted to the agreement with bitter hostility. Loyalist groups in Ulster organized a workers' strike to protest the new distribution of power. Business activity slowed substantially. The negotiations broke down and fighting resumed at unprecedented levels. In this violent context, Margaret Thatcher's government launched another initiative to find a peaceful solution, a solution allowing for democratic governance and public security. The British Prime Minister and her Republic of Ireland counterpart, Taoiseach Garret FitzGerald, discussed possible alternatives to achieve a settlement. These talks occurred against the background of hunger-strikes staged by PIRA inmates in Northern Irish prisons. Imprisoned PIRA members sought to achieve the status of 'political prisoners' rather than conventional criminals. They were willing to fast until death rather than concede the point. Led by Bobby Sands, 11 PIRA members died in this manner (1981–1982).

As the situation in Ulster intensified new anti-terrorism legislation, really updates of older laws, was enacted by Parliament. These measures widened and deepened the government's authority to investigate and prosecute terrorist threats. They included the following capacities:

1 Power for the home secretary to proscribe terrorist organizations and the definition of various offenses connected with such organizations (e.g. membership).
2 The creation of specific offenses connected with terrorism, such as fund-raising or training in the use of firearms for a terrorist act.
3 Enhanced "police powers to prevent and investigate terrorist acts, such as powers of investigation, arrest, stop and search. And detention."[7]

If not carte blanche, these measures came pretty close to it. Still they did not bring an end to the killings. On the other hand, PIRA's objectives of ending British rule in Northern Ireland and merging the province with the Republic did not seem to make much headway either. PIRA was unable to capture and hold any territory despite the violence it perpetrated. In short, by the mid-1990s the conflict had reached a stalemate whose continuation hurt all sides.

Complex and prolonged steps finally led to the opening of serious peace negotiations including all parties to the conflict. Suffice it to say that by 1995 the British and Irish governments – along with representatives of PIRA (whose leaders, Gerry Adams and Martin McGuiness, had agreed to a permanent ceasefire), spokesmen for the loyalist cause, and Northern Ireland's republican and loyalist political parties – began serious talks to end the fighting. The talks also involved an international presence including American, Canadian and Norwegian representatives. Former US Senator George Mitchell chaired this international commission.

The discussions proceeded by fits and starts. Finally, in April 1998 the 'Good Friday' Agreement was reached and signed in Belfast. The Agreement proposed that Northern Ireland be ruled by a power-sharing assembly, and that all the principal political parties would be represented permanently in a coalition government. A human rights commission was established to investigate cases of religious discrimination. Northern Ireland retained its separate status, but a North–South Ministerial Council was established to promote cooperation between the legislatures in Dublin and Stormont.[8]

All citizens of both Northern Ireland and the Republic were given copies of the Agreement, which was then subject to a popular referendum. The Agreement was approved overwhelmingly by voters in the Republic (91 percent of the vote). The margin in Ulster was narrower, but still over 70 percent of the electorate endorsed the settlement. Nevertheless this was not the end of the conflict. There was still the matter of 'decommissioning'. The Agreement called for all paramilitary groups to give up their weapons. PIRA especially was reluctant to do so. An international commission was created to supervise the process. Eventually the PIRA leadership, notably Gerry Adams, was sufficiently mollified to permit the commission's supervision of PIRA's disarmament.

Islamic extremism

As the Northern Irish conflict was resolved, more or less, Britons became aware that they faced an even more serious problem. The problem arose from the intent of some Muslim extremists to wage a jihad or holy war within Britain and to use the country as a haven from which to launch terrorist attacks on targets abroad.

From the early 1960s on the UK had become the destination of hundreds of thousands of immigrants from Britain's former colonies. Initially most of these individuals came from the Caribbean or the 'new nations' of sub-Saharan Africa. Later new waves of immigrants and asylum-seekers arrived from South Asia and the Middle East. By the 1980s these largely Muslim new populations had created separate enclaves in Britain's major cities, London especially. And by the beginning of the 21st century the pace of immigration picked up so that more than 200,000 people were entering the country on a yearly basis.

In 2006 the columnist Melanie Phillips summarized the situation: "Britain now has a net inflow of approximately 220,000 immigrants per year – four times the rate between 1985 and 1995."[9] She went on to assert that the newcomers or new newcomers had established very distinct Muslim communities throughout the UK. And, while earlier generations of Muslim immigrants sought assimilation into British society, recent arrivals displayed little such inclination. Instead they maintained their separate identities as believers first and foremost. To exacerbate this problem the UK offered asylum to dozens of Islamist Salafist imams, often veterans of various Pakistani and Middle Eastern conflicts, who preached the virtues of holy war against America, Britain, the West in general and such 'near enemies' as the regimes in Egypt, Iraq and Libya.

Sermons on the necessity and requirements of jihad typically did not have a major impact on the older generations of immigrants. They did, however, affect newer generations, especially young Muslims born in Britain who lacked ties to countries of family origin as well to any sense of British national identity. These young Muslims became especially vulnerable to the appeals of the imams and to new extremist groups that sprang up in London, Birmingham, Liverpool and other large cities.

Ed Husain, a defector from this new world of alienated militancy, describes how he gradually distanced himself from his conservative parents. Via the East London mosque he attended he gradually became caught up in the world of Islamic radicalism. His young friends encouraged him to read the works of such Islamist preachers as Abul Ala Maududi and to join Hizb ut-Tahrir, a militant organization of 'Brothers' who sought converts to the cause of Salafism and the translation of talk into action.[10]

By the end of the 20th century al Qaeda itself began to put down roots in Britain. The Finsbury Park mosque in North London (e.g. Imam Abu Hamza) and the East London mosque became important recruitment centers for jihadi prepared to die for the cause of militant Islam. In addition to street-corner preaching and the dissemination of Salafist literature throughout London and beyond, militants began to teach the need for violence, the need to defend the *Umma* (Muslim community) against non-believers both in the UK and elsewhere. The Russian government's brutal treatment of Chechens, the US and British invasion of Iraq in 2003, and the situation of the Palestinians under Israeli rule became rallying points for Islamic militants and their challenges to democracy.

Not always but typically, al Qaeda operatives established networks of Mujahideen (holy warriors) organized into cells. The jihadi themselves came from radical Islamist movements. Ostensibly non-violent movements, such as al-Muhajiroun, also provided a milieu from which the violent jihadi were drawn. Many, though not all, recruits went on to receive training at centers in Pakistan, Afghanistan and Yemen.[11]

The depiction of Muslim suffering at the hands of infidels led to marches and other street protests in London and elsewhere in the country. It also led to serious acts of terrorism both at home and abroad. To quote the terrorism analyst Lorenzo Vidino: "The United States' closest ally in the war on terror, Great Britain, is known to take an extremely soft line toward the Islamic terrorists operating on its soil; indeed, on occasion its level of tolerance borders on masochism."[12]

Tolerance 'bordering on masochism' led to terrorist attacks carried out by British citizens traveling abroad. For example, in 2002 Omar Sheikh, a Briton of Pakistani descent, participated in the beheading of *Wall Street Journal* journalist Daniel Pearl. The following year two British militants flew to Tel Aviv, where one staged a suicide attack on a local bar, killing three Israelis. A few years later a Briton detonated himself while standing in a group of young people waiting to enter a Tel Aviv nightclub. Then there were the spectacular attempts to blow up commercial airliners in flight. Both the English convert to Islam, Richard Reid (the 'shoe bomber', 2002) and the Nigerian-born but British-educated Umar Farouk Abdulmutallab (the 'underwear bomber', 2012) were subdued before they could detonate their hidden explosives.

Thereafter the Islamic State (ISIS) enjoyed some success in recruiting young Muslim Britons to fly typically from London to Istanbul, and from there make their way to the Turkish border and cross into Syria to join the terrorist group. The most widely known of these terrorists is 'Jihadi John': Mohammed Emwazi, whose family was from Kuwait and who grew up in London as a first-generation Briton. In a now familiar narrative, he became radicalized as he grew older, and travelled to Syria where he became an English-speaking executioner for ISIS. Before beheading his hapless victims, Jihadi John delivered blood-curdling messages over ISIS television outlets until he was himself killed in 2015.[13]

In August 2006 the British authorities arrested some two dozen individuals who were preparing to skyjack, almost simultaneously, six airliners over the Atlantic and blow them up over major American and Canadian cities. If this scheme had succeeded the number of people killed likely would have surpassed the 9/11 death toll.

To date the most lethal attacks carried out by al Qaeda operatives active in the UK were the July 7, 2005 early morning bombings of three underground rail stations. A fourth bomber detonated himself on the upper deck of one of London's buses. These explosions killed 56 passengers and injured over 500.[14] They served as the British 9/11, challenging the security of the country from within its own borders. If nothing else the 7/7 attacks alerted the British public that Britain had a serious and deadly problem to confront. The head of Britain's domestic intelligence agency, MI5, estimated in 2005 that there were over 1000 al Qaeda militants living in the UK at various stages of preparation to strike at targets around the country. No more masochism.

The Blair government and its successors developed a four-fold policy after 2005 to combat terrorism: Prevent, Pursue, Protect, Prepare – collectively known as CONTEST (see Simcox, Chapter 5 this volume). As the *Economist* concisely expressed,

> Prevent is one of four strands of counter-terror efforts, alongside Pursue (to stop attacks), Protect (to reduce vulnerability), and Prepare (to minimize the impact of attacks). The latter includes Channel, a program in which those identified as being at risk of radicalization are offered a tailored package of education, counseling and support.[15]

Thousands of public-sector workers spent much of their work time seeking to implement the strategy. By 2016 hundreds of thousands had gone through training programs aimed at identifying potential terrorists.

Prior to the turn of the 21st century Britain's anti-terrorism legislation was temporary in nature and focused on Northern Ireland and its violent secessionist minority. Following the 9/11 attacks in the United States, the Blair government enacted the Anti-Terrorism Crime and Security Act. This legislation amended and strengthened a law passed some months earlier. It broadened the definition of 'terrorism' and strengthened the powers of government to pursue and prosecute its perpetrators and promoters.[16] Among other things the Act extended the jurisdiction of British law to include terrorist acts carried out abroad by British subjects, so that, for example, Britons of Pakistani background could be prosecuted in British courts for terrorist acts committed in Israel or Pakistan itself. Further, membership in an organization listed by the Home Office as 'terrorist' was criminalized. Part 4 of the law, titled "Immigration and Asylum", permitted the Home Secretary

> to issue certificates against non-British individuals living in the UK were he or she to believe that the person's presence in the United Kingdom is a risk to national security and suspect that the person is a terrorist. In turn, this measure allowed the government to hold these individuals indefinitely without charging, trying or deporting them.[17]

This provision in particular aroused the opposition of many of the country's civil libertarians, who identified it as police state practice and who later drew parallels between British detainees and 'enemy combatants' held at Guantanamo Bay in Cuba by the American authorities.

Britain's courts agreed with the civil libertarians and overturned provisions on internment without charge. In 2005 the omnibus counterterrorism law was then changed to include 'control orders'. Instead of internment without trial, the law now stipulated that, on the basis of the Home Secretary's decision, terrorism suspects could be subject to 'house arrest'; they were not permitted to leave their homes or workplaces without the authorities' consent. 'Control orders' also prompted opposition from civil liberties organizations and members of both chambers of Parliament – as embodied in its Human Rights Commission. Among other things, civil libertarians pointed out that this provision was clearly in conflict with the European Human Rights Convention, to which Britain was a party, and would be challenged successfully at the Council of Europe's Court of Human Rights. The result was a 'sunset' stipulation: control orders would have to be re-authorized by Parliament on an annual basis to remain in force.

Objections to control orders and their implications for British parliamentary democracy became louder over the years. Consequently, in 2011 Parliament replaced them with less draconian means of preventing individuals from planning and implementing terrorist actions.[18] Also, under the Prevent component of its counterterrorism policy, the government offered subsidies to private organizations that appeared to provide Muslim youth with alternatives to radical militancy.

The newer legislation made it easier to deport individuals the government regarded as a threat to the country's safety and well-being. Accordingly, a number of Muslim clerics were returned to their countries of origin or extradited to countries (e.g., the United States) to face prosecution for crimes they had allegedly committed against that country's citizens – either at home or abroad.

On the especially sensitive issue of advocacy, the Blair government at first proposed the public prosecution of individuals who were deemed to have 'glorified' the use of terrorism in public speeches – a sweeping restriction on free speech and a clear violation of European human rights law (and also for example an obvious violation of the US Constitution's First Amendment). Because of opposition in Parliament the legislation was softened to cover merely what amounted to the incitement of violence.[19] It did allow the detention of individuals suspected of terrorism-related activity for up to 28 days without charge.

As in the United States, the threat of terrorism caused a substantial strengthening of the UK's security and police organizations. The *Economist* noted that in 2012–2013, 95,921 public employees were trained in how to identify future(!) terrorists. In subsequent years the figure reached over 243,000.[20] And, as in the United States, the need to protect the United Kingdom against terrorist threats has led to a significant reorganization of British government.

Still, nothing the British have done has been as sweeping as the creation of the Department of Homeland Security in the United States post-9/11 – an amalgam of many separate agencies whose secretary enjoys cabinet-level status. Nor did 7/7 lead to the creation of a Director of National Intelligence whose role is to channel security information coming from multiple intelligence organizations in the United States – e.g. CIA, FBI, Defense Intelligence Agency (DIA), National Counterterrorism Center (NCTC) – to the President.

By the end of first decade of the 21st century, Britain's counterterrorism apparatus appeared as follows:

- Initially, the police counterterrorism function was the responsibility of the Metropolitan Police's Special Branch.
- During the 1970s the Home Office (the UK equivalent of European interior ministries) added an anti-terrorism branch.

- Following the 7/7 attacks Britain consolidated the two police organizations into one, the Counter Terrorism Command.
- The Blair government, as part of the Cabinet Office (the UK's equivalent of the Office of the President in the US), created a security and intelligence coordinator.[21]

In addition to these police-based organizations, Britain has maintained long-standing agencies whose purpose is to gather information about domestic and foreign threats the security service MI5 for the former; and the secret intelligence service MI6 for the latter. The functions of MI6 abroad bear resemblance to the American CIA. Its agents seek to alert the UK government to terrorists emanating from South Asia, the Middle East and North Africa.

It is certainly worth mentioning that London, the center of terrorist threats in the UK, is the most publicly monitored major city in the world. Since the era of the Troubles in Northern Ireland, CCTV cameras have been placed in virtually every public space in London. All of them are constantly monitored by the police. This form of public surveillance may (or may not) have a deterrent effect on would-be terrorists. But it certainly makes deterrence easier.

Concluding observations

British counterterrorism policy did not prevent some hundreds of alienated young Muslims in London and cities in the Midlands from traveling to Iraq and Somalia to join ISIS and the militant group al-Shabab and become jihadi. We cannot forget that the executioner of some half-dozen ISIS captives spoke to his audience with a London accent before beheading his hapless victims. On the other hand, we should also recall that in 2016 London elected its first Muslim mayor, Sadiq Khan, a man who preaches peace and tolerance. We should also not forget that Prevent has likely convinced a not inconsiderable number of the country's Muslims to reconsider their political and religious attitudes. Finally, if we were to compare Britain's counterterrorism record on the domestic front to France's, we would necessarily have to conclude that, for all its problems, the former has been more successful than the latter, even taking into consideration the magnitude of the threats.

Notes

1 Tim Pat Coogan, *The IRA* (New York: Palgrave, 2002) p. 15.
2 Tim Pat Coogan, *The Troubles* (London: Random House, 1996) pp. 22–24.
3 Coogan, *The IRA*, pp. 113–131.
4 Laura Donohue, "Anti-Terrorism Legislation: Civil Liberty and Judicial Alteration" in Leonard Weinberg (Ed.), *Democratic Responses to Terrorism* (New York and Abingdon: Routledge, 2008) pp. 101–147.
5 Adrian Guelke, "Loyalist and Republican Perceptions of the Northern Ireland Conflict" in Peter Merkl (Ed.), *Political Violence and Terror* (Berkeley: University of California Press, 1986) pp. 91–122.
6 Louise Richardson, "Britain and the IRA" in Robert Art and Louise Richardson (Eds.), *Democracy and Counterterrorism* (Washington DC: Institute of Peace Press, 2007) pp. 63–104.
7 Terence Taylor, "United Kingdom" in Yonah Alexander (Ed.) *Combating Terrorism: Strategies of Ten Countries* (Ann Arbor: University of Michigan Press, 2002) pp. 188–189.
8 Roger Mac Ginty and John Darby, *Guns and Government: The Management of the Northern Ireland Peace Process* (New York: Palgrave, 2002) pp. 41–54.
9 Melanie Phillips, *Londonistan* (New York: Encounter Books, 2006) p. 59.
10 Ed Husain, *The Islamist: Why I Became an Islamic Fundamentalist, What I Saw Inside, and Why I Left* (London: Penguin, 2007) pp. 28–29.

11 Peter Neumann and Ryan Evans, "Operation Crevice in London" in Bruce Hoffman and Fernando Reinares (Eds.), *The Evolution of the Global Terrorist Threat: From 9/11 to Osama bin Laden's Death* (New York: Columbia University Press, 2014) pp. 61–80.
12 Lorenzo Vidino, *Al Qaeda in Europe* (Amherst NY: Prometheus Press, 2006) pp. 114–115.
13 Robert Verkaik, *Jihadi John* (London: Oneworld, 2016) pp. 160–189.
14 Bruce Hoffman, "The July 7, 2005 London Bombings" in Hoffman and Reinares, pp. 192–223.
15 "Counter-Terrorism: Driving away the Shadows" *Economist* (August 20–26, 2016) p. 47.
16 Taylor, "United Kingdom", pp. 221–223.
17 Steve Hewitt, *The British War on Terror* (London: Continuum, 2008) p. 38.
18 David Anderson, *Control Orders in 2011* (London: The Stationery Office, 2012).
19 David Cole, "Human Rights and the Challenge of Terror" in Weinberg, pp. 157–170.
20 *Economist*, "Counter-Terrorism".
21 Hewitt, pp. 96–97.

Further reading

Alexander, Yonah (ed.), *Combating Terrorism: Strategies of Ten Countries* (Ann Arbor: University of Michigan Press, 2002)
Anderson, David, *Control Orders in 2011* (London: The Stationery Office, 2012)
Art, Robert and Louise Richardson (eds.), *Democracy and Counterterrorism* (Washington DC: Institute of Peace Press, 2007)
Coogan, Tim Pat, *The IRA* (New York: Palgrave, 2002)
Coogan, Tim Pat, *The Troubles* (London: Random House, 1996)
Hoffman, Bruce and Fernando Reinares (eds.), *The Evolution of the Global Terrorist Threat: from 9/11 to Osama bin Laden's Death* (New York: Columbia University Press, 2014)
Husain, Ed, *The Islamist: Why I Became an Islamic Fundamentalist, What I Saw Inside, and Why I Left* (London: Penguin, 2007)
Mac Ginty, Roger and John Darby, *Guns and Government: The Management of the Northern Ireland Peace Process* (New York: Palgrave, 2002)
Merkl, Peter (ed.), *Political Violence and Terror* (Berkeley: University of California Press, 1986)
Phillips, Melanie, *Londonistan* (New York: Encounter Books, 2006)
Weinberg, Leonard (ed.), *Democratic Responses to Terrorism* (New York and Abingdon: Routledge, 2008)

5

PREVENT

The United Kingdom responds to terrorism

Robin Simcox

The Prevent strategy attempts "to stop people becoming terrorists or supporting terrorism."[1] There is an obvious reason for its existence: the UK has been targeted repeatedly by Islamist terrorists. Prevent is the UK's effort to win hearts and minds in its battle against extremism.[2]

Attempting to stop radicalization and, subsequently, to reduce the threat posed by terrorism is a theoretically uncontroversial aim. But theory and practice are not the same. Prevent has been vilified. The Institute of Race Relations labelled the program "discriminatory and divisive."[3] The Waltham Forest Council of Mosques in London claimed that Prevent was being used to "denigrate the Muslim community," as noted by David Anderson QC, the independent reviewer of terrorism legislation.[4] Academic Aminul Hoque has stated that Prevent is so hated it has actually become "counter-productive."[5] Then head of the Federation of Student Islamic Societies, Ibrahim Ali, referred to Prevent as "racist" and "Islamophobic."[6] The Islamist advocacy group, CAGE, accused Prevent of "contribut[ing] to the radicalisation process rather than counter[ing] it."[7] University lecturer Fahid Qurashi even claimed that "Prevent gives people permission to hate Muslims."[8]

Prevent has served as a lightning rod for a debate that transcends any one policy or any one government strategy: debate about the extent to which non-violent extremism (sometimes known as 'soft Islamism') can be co-opted, or perhaps even promoted, in order to reduce the threat from violent extremists who share the ideology of jihadist groups such as al-Qaeda.

This chapter examines the genesis of Prevent and the reasons for its introduction; tracks shifts within the policy; assesses the validity of criticisms leveled at Prevent; and concludes by examining the prospects for Prevent's longevity. It contends that while few would argue Prevent has been an unqualified success, the strategy has had some utility. Furthermore, certain criticisms of the program have not been made in good faith, and scrapping the initiative completely is neither realistic nor desirable.

I

In order to place Prevent in context, it is important to inspect the threat level in the UK and the nature of the government's response to it at specific moments post-1999.

The primary terrorist threat facing the UK today still comes from the Islamic State of Iraq and al-Sham (ISIS), al-Qaeda and radicalized individuals inspired by these groups. The official threat level, as set by the government's Joint Terrorism Analysis Centre, is 'severe', meaning an attack is "highly likely."[9]

There is ample reason for this concern. On 7 July 2005, four suicide bombings took place on the London transport network, killing 52. The murder of Drummer Lee Rigby, a British solider, by two radicalized British Nigerians in London in May 2013 also demonstrated terrorists' willingness to carry out simpler attacks (on occasion using machetes).

Yet the scope of threat to the United Kingdom is of longer duration and greater intensity than these events suggest. Between 1999 and 2010, eight major terrorism plots in the UK either resulted in convictions or in successful attacks.[10] They included a major plot in summer 2006 that targeted multiple transatlantic aircraft with liquid bombs concealed in soft-drink containers. Certain disrupted plots did not lead to UK prosecutions, such as al-Qaeda's 'Easter bomb plot' of 2009 which targeted the city of Manchester and led to the deportation of Pakistanis who had infiltrated the UK (cell ringleader Abid Naseer was eventually convicted in the US for his role in the plot).

Attack planning has continued over the past decade, leading to convictions in British courts. A cell was arrested in the autumn of 2011 whose members received training from al-Qaeda in Pakistan and planned to carry out suicide attacks with bombs concealed in rucksacks. ISIS-inspired plotters, arrested in September 2014, aimed to commit a series of drive-by shootings against police officers, soldiers and civilians.

Furthermore, from the 1990s onward, Britain has seen thousands of its citizens and residents fight or train in Bosnia, Chechnya, Pakistan, Afghanistan, Iraq, Somalia and Yemen. Between 2010 and 2015, approximately 850 UK citizens travelled to fight in Syria. Notorious among them was Mohammed Emwazi, who beheaded several people, including numerous American and British citizens, on grisly ISIS propaganda videos before being killed in Raqqa by a US airstrike in November 2015.

The UK's response to these challenges has extended beyond counter-terrorism, intelligence gathering and certainly beyond Prevent, to include military and legislative initiatives, all of which have provoked varying degrees of controversy and dissent within the UK. Britain's response was partially military and international. In total, over 50,000 British troops were dispatched to the wars in Afghanistan and Iraq, beginning in 2001 and 2003 respectively. Airstrikes have taken place against ISIS positions in both Iraq (from 2014) and Syria (from 2015). To varying degrees, these conflicts have proved controversial domestically, and have had uncertain outcomes in terms of reducing the terrorist threat at home.

Britain's response has not focused solely on foreign terrorists. After all, according to a 2011 study, more than two-thirds (69 percent) of Islamism-related offences that took place between 1999 and 2010 were perpetrated by British citizens and were domestic in nature.[11] Counter-terrorism, intelligence gathering and legislative initiatives have been necessary, and undertaken to protect the country. Prevent became one of four strands that comprised the government's comprehensive counter-terrorism strategy, called CONTEST, intended to achieve this goal.

Devised at the beginning of 2003, before the 2005 London bombings, Prevent was "concerned with tackling the radicalisation of individuals, both in the UK and elsewhere, which sustains the international terrorist threat." Prevent would take three specific approaches believed to contribute to radicalization: "tackling disadvantage and supporting reform by addressing structural problems … such as inequalities and discrimination"; deterrence through "changing the environment in which the extremists and those radicalising others can operate"; and "engaging in the battle of ideas" in order to defeat terrorist ideology.[12] At its inception Prevent was barely fleshed out beyond these stated goals. Its immediate focus was on stopping pre-existing networks actively attempting to carry out attacks on British soil.[13]

Prevent's focus began to change in October 2006 with the launch of the Preventing Extremism Pathfinder Fund, later renamed the Preventing Violent Extremism (PVE) Pathfinder Fund. Pathfinder was the genesis of what would eventually become the prevailing Prevent strategy. According to CONTEST language from 2010, Prevent's aim was simple post-2006: "to stop people becoming terrorists or supporting terrorism and violent extremism."[14] Prevent was about aiming to dissuade those on the verge of pursuing a violent path from doing so (those in the 'pre-criminal space', in civil service speak).

Prevent envisaged the government, police and local Muslim communities working together closely to challenge those who supported violent Islamist extremism and its surrounding narratives.[15] This challenge would be implemented by a locally led, grassroots campaign which included engagement with faith groups, working with local communities in schools and mosques, and strengthening various community ties with the police.[16]

Responsibility for Prevent's implementation lay with the Department for Communities and Local Government (DCLG).[17] The DCLG's first Secretary of State, Ruth Kelly, laid out a vision of how funding would be distributed in October 2006. Kelly warned that Muslim groups who did not promote "non-negotiable" values such as freedom of speech would see money cut.[18] But the Assistant General Secretary of the Muslim Council of Britain (MCB) – the largest Muslim group in the UK, an umbrella organization of mosques, charities and schools that work extremely closely with the government – made clear Prevent would "lose credibility with the Muslim community" by pushing this line.[19] The MCB response to the government hinted that problems in Muslim communities went deeper than terrorism, and actually concerned a lack of connection to broader liberal values. The MCB thus identified problems that would only appear in sharper contrast in years thereafter.

In April 2007, the DCLG launched its *action plan* – 'Preventing Violent Extremism: Winning Hearts and Minds'.[20] The plan emphasized the important role local councils would play in the delivery of Prevent, as it was local communities who understood their areas best. This plan was sensible in theory but troubled in practice, a problem highlighted in March 2009 by the Policy Exchange think tank: "government is asking municipal worthies to take the lead role in making extremely sophisticated decisions about ideological questions relating to the struggle against radical Islamism."[21] Local authorities – flush with Prevent funding – had no framework for how to spend the money, or on which types of initiatives. Inevitably, incoherence resulted – with respect to the types of group being funded, the values they held and what metrics would constitute successful use of funding.

Indeed, such systemic problems had not been solved before the government published its first Prevent *strategy* – 'Preventing Violent Extremism: A Strategy for Delivery' – in May 2008 (accompanied by 'The Prevent Strategy: A Guide for Local Partners in England'). The 2008 Strategy laid out five specific aims:

- challenging the violent extremist ideology and supporting mainstream voices;
- disrupting those who promote violent extremism and supporting the institutions where they are active;
- supporting individuals who are being targeted and recruited to the cause of violent extremism;
- increasing the resilience of communities to violent extremism; and
- addressing the grievances that ideologues are exploiting.[22]

Embedded in this approach was the assumption that if a twisted interpretation of Islam led to terrorism, then the answer was to push the 'correct' version of Islam. The Strategy highlighted its ability to "recognize and support people and organisations who speak authoritatively about Islam." It claimed that, as "theology is being distorted to justify violent extremist rhetoric," "Government should reinforce faith understanding ... to expose the paucity of the extremist message."[23]

First, this strategy rested on several uncertain, unexamined and untested assumptions: that the extremists' reading of certain parts of theology was indeed distorted, as opposed to at least plausible; that those who did speak most authoritatively about Islam agreed with the government on this reading; and that more theology for British Muslims – as opposed to a focus on shared British values – was part of the solution, as opposed to part of the problem.

Second, actors the government enlisted to advance this strategy were themselves problematic. For example, the individual assigned to "improve the quality of information about Islam" in English universities was Dr Ataullah Siddiqui, then Director of the Markfield Institute of Higher Education (MIHE).[24] By relying on the MIHE, the UK government was outsourcing its Islamic education policy to the Islamist sphere of influence.

Organizational connections are key to understanding this point. The parent organization of the MIHE was the Islamic Foundation (with which MIHE shared the same site in Leicestershire). The Islamic Foundation was the main publisher of works by Maulana Abu al-A'la al-Mawdudi, a key Islamist theologian whose politicized version of Islam deeply influenced the organization. It was Mawdudi's contention that Islam was not just a religion, but a "revolutionary ideology which seeks to alter the social order of the entire world." Mawdudi founded the highly conservative but highly influential South Asian Islamist revivalist movement, Jamaat-i-Islami.

Jamaat-i-Islami's influence among the bodies that the UK government was seeking to work with to prevent violent extremism was significant. For example, the Islamic Foundation's chairman and founder, Khurshid Ahmad, was formerly President of Jamaat-i-Islami's Pakistan branch.[25] The Foundation's former deputy director, Chowdhury Mueen Uddin, also a member of Jamaat, was sentenced to death *in absentia* by a Bangladeshi court for committing war crimes in the 1971 war of independence.[26] Uddin denies all charges.

The UK government's alignment with Islamism in 2008–2009 was not an outlier, but a theme. For example, a series of Working Groups established after the 7 July 2005 attacks came to the conclusion that a national advisory board that could regulate mosques needed to be established.[27] In June 2006 this manifested itself in the creation of the Mosques and Imams National Advisory Board (MINAB). The Jamaat-tinged MCB and the Muslim Association of Britain (MAB) – described by former Prime Minister David Cameron as a "political front for the Muslim Brotherhood" (the transnational Sunni Islamist group founded in Egypt) – comprised two of the four stakeholders charged with running the program.[28]

Third, the funds government dedicated to Prevent were also spent haphazardly. A review of the PVE Pathfinder Fund for the years 2007/08 revealed that only minimal amounts of Prevent funding actually went to those at risk of radicalization.[29] Instead, government funding was disseminated to organizations that promoted varying shades of Islamism. Those organizations included the London Muslim Centre (LMC), which was housed inside the East London Mosque (ELM) in Whitechapel. Both the LMC and ELM regularly hosted clerics who called for the murder of apostates, homosexuals and adulterers; and clerics who supported convicted terrorists, terror suspects and proscribed terrorist groups.[30] Funding also found its way to Strategy to Reach, Empower, and Educate Teenagers (STREET), an avowedly Salafist group; and to the Cordoba Foundation, a group aligned with the Muslim

Brotherhood.[31] Another group backed was the Jamaat-i-Islami aligned Islamic Forum Europe, whose literature placed on record its support for changing the "very infrastructure of society, its institutions, its culture, its political order and its creed … from ignorance to Islam."[32]

Only part of this outcome could be attributed to local council naivete. A clearly thought out rationale stood behind the state's alignment with such groups. Robert Lambert, former head of the Metropolitan Police Special Branch's Muslim Contact Unit, was an influential voice at the time. He believed that "Islamists can be powerful allies in the fight against al-Qaida influence … they can be the levers that help get young people away from the most dangerous positions."[33]

Lambert put this view into practice at Finsbury Park Mosque in north London. Following the arrest of Abu Hamza al-Masri – the hook-handed cleric who used the mosque as a place to radicalize, recruit and dispatch operatives to foreign jihadist conflict zones and training camps – Lambert helped facilitate the mosque's takeover by MAB, a group closely aligned with the Muslim Brotherhood. MAB's senior figures included Azzam Tamimi. Tamimi had said in an interview with the BBC that he supported Hamas and was prepared to become a suicide bomber (he was also a lecturer at the MIHE).[34] Lambert theorized that Islamists such as MAB and Jamaat-i-Islami, and Salafists such as STREET, may not have subscribed to values of equality, liberty or tolerance; but their willingness to at least temporarily eschew violence meant they should be perceived as groups that would help defuse the threat of jihadism. They could act as a bulwark against, or safety valve for, disaffected young Muslims.

Fourth, there was widespread confusion about Prevent's actual purpose among those it targeted. An article in *The Guardian* of 16 October 2009 alleged that Prevent was "being used to gather intelligence about innocent people who are not suspected of involvement in terrorism."[35] In another article from the same issue, Ed Husain, then a member of the anti-extremist organization the Quilliam Foundation, did not correct this false statement, but rather added to the mini-firestorm it produced by saying Prevent was indeed doing this and "it is good and it is right" that it was.[36]

Such assertions muddied the water about what precisely Prevent had been set up to do. The need for intelligence gathering to prevent terrorism and further killing was largely uncontroversial. Yet that was a job for security/intelligence services MI5, MI6 and the Government Communications Headquarters (GCHQ). Prevent had no such agenda, yet it was described by Shami Chakrabarti, former director of the human rights group Liberty, as "the biggest domestic spying program targeting the thoughts and beliefs of the innocent in Britain in modern times."[37]

Chakrabarti and Husain were not the only leaders who failed to fully understand Prevent. And even when a Prevent initiative achieved success, the successful initiative was too often conflated with less successful non-Prevent initiatives. Take, for example, Operation Nicole, a Prevent initiative designed by the Association of Chief Police Officers (ACPO). Operation Nicole was directed at the UK's Muslim communities, and "designed to break down barriers between police and communities by promoting an understanding of how counter-terrorism operations work." It was intended to provide a "safe space for community members to discuss their concerns," part of a broader attempt to demonstrate that the UK was by no means at war with Islam.[38] Operation Nicole was deemed a rare success, contributing to an improvement in relations between the police and Muslim communities, and enhancing police awareness of the dynamics within those communities.[39]

Yet the progress the police made via Prevent, including Operation Nicole, was mitigated by other, less successful, non-Prevent efforts. In 2010, for example, it was discovered that CCTV cameras operating in heavily Muslim areas of Birmingham were partially funded by Home Office counter-terrorism money. The BBC called this "one of the biggest knocks to Prevent."[40] In reality, the cameras were funded by the government's Terrorism and Allied Matters fund, administered by ACPO.[41] There was no connection to Prevent whatsoever, yet the incident was still swept up in the general Prevent discourse.

II

By 2009 there was a sense that Prevent was not working as well as it should. A report published in September by the Tax Payers' Alliance (TPA) into how Prevent money was spent by local authorities concluded that there "has been insufficient monitoring of how Prevent money is spent, with the Government unsure of what groups Councils have disbursed money to."[42]

An inquiry was established by the DCLG to assess Prevent's effectiveness. The results were troubling. Even by that point – mirroring an argument that would become increasingly common – there was a "lack of trust of the programme amongst those delivering and receiving services."[43] The committee concluded that large amounts of money had "been wasted on unfocused or irrelevant projects."[44] Placing the DCLG at the forefront for both cohesion and counter-terrorism work was a mistake, as it threatened to undermine "positive cross-cultural work on cohesion and capacity building to combat exclusion and alienation in many communities." This meant that the DCLG was "[t]ainted by its negative association with a counter-terrorism agenda."[45]

These were reasonable conclusions. Yet the committee also seemed to be doubling down on government engagement with Islamists. The committee heard "widespread criticism of the Government's failure to engage with more 'radical' voices which do not promote violent extremism." The committee favoured a 'big tent' approach, arguing that "[n]o organisation – unless proscribed – should be excluded from debate and discussions."[46] Rather than spending too much time engaging with non-violent extremists, actually the government was not engaging with them enough.

This conclusion went to the heart of the debate within government. When it came to engagement with Muslim communities, some believed that the government should be willing to partner with any organization willing to reject terrorism in the UK, no matter how extreme its views on other positions (such as homosexuality or the existence of Israel). Others believed that this was setting the bar far too low and the government should only be partnering with organisations that adhered to basic British values of democracy, liberty and equality.

The dispute came to the forefront in February 2009, when Daud Abdullah, the Deputy Secretary General of the MCB, signed the 'Istanbul Statement'. This document supported Hamas, called for jihad against Israel and called for Muslims to attack foreign navies aiming to prevent weapons being smuggled into Gaza. Just a month before, British Prime Minister Gordon Brown had offered the Royal Navy's services to do precisely that. Abdullah was, therefore, essentially calling for attacks against British service personnel.[47]

In February 2009, the Secretary of State at the DCLG was Hazel Blears, who had succeeded Ruth Kelly in June 2007. Blears fell into the camp of taking a tougher line on 'soft' Islamists and non-violent extremists the government had hitherto worked so closely with. Blears asked the MCB to distance itself from Abdullah. When it refused, she severed all relations with the organization.[48]

Blears was forced to resign in June 2009 following the parliamentary expenses scandal. Her replacement, John Denham, very much adhered to the 'big tent' approach. He delivered a speech in December of that year in which he stressed that Prevent's sole concern was terrorism "against Britain or British people overseas." Furthermore, while it "unequivocally" said that terrorism in Britain was unacceptable, it only sought to "challenge" those who believed it was acceptable overseas.[49] By implication, Denham admitted that stopping attacks against Americans in Afghanistan, Jews in Israel or government forces in Somalia (for example) would not be prioritized by the DCLG.

In short, by late 2009 Prevent appeared increasingly incoherent and inconsistent. It was no surprise that the author and commentator Douglas Murray labelled the strategy "a textbook example of how to alienate absolutely everybody."[50]

III

The Labour government's loss of power in the May 2010 General Election to a Conservative/Liberal Democrat alliance provided an opportunity for a fresh look at the effectiveness of Prevent. A review was quickly established, and reported back in June 2011. The review labelled previous versions of Prevent as "flawed." What Prevent would now focus on was laid out as being to:

- respond to the ideological challenge of terrorism and the threat we face from those who promote it ...
- prevent people from being drawn into terrorism and ensure that they are given appropriate advice and support ...
- work with sectors and institutions where there are risks of radicalization.[51]

If the role of ideology had been underplayed previously, it was now central to Prevent. Previous incarnations of the program had failed to "confront the extremist ideology at the heart of the threat we face."[52] Non-violent extremism now needed to be tackled with the same ferocity as violent extremism – and for the same reasons – as there was "evidence to indicate that support for terrorism is associated with rejection of a cohesive, integrated, multi-faith society and of parliamentary democracy."[53]

The government explicitly ruled out working with or funding extremists and, helpfully, defined what it meant by extremism: "vocal or active opposition to fundamental British values, including democracy, the rule of law, individual liberty and mutual respect and tolerance of different faiths and beliefs." Included in this definition were "calls for the death of members of our armed forces, whether in this country or overseas" – a clear repudiation of the approach taken by Denham.[54]

The process for funding groups was also lambasted, as "funding sometimes even reached the very extremist organisations that *Prevent* should have been confronting." Some groups had received funding from the Home Office as "they were able to relate to and therefore work with" those at risk of being radicalized (a nod to the approach espoused by Lambert), with "insufficient attention" paid to whether they subscribed to the British values the Prevent review defined. The review vowed that no government funds would go to groups "that hold extremist views or support terrorist-related activity of any kind, in this country or overseas," another pushback against the 'big tent' approach.[55]

It was also discovered that there had been precious little oversight on how Prevent money was spent and little ability to measure whether expenditures had been effective: "the monitoring and evaluation of *Prevent* projects has not been robust enough to justify the sums of public money spent on them."[56] The review concluded it was "unlikely" in some cases that Prevent funding had actually had a "direct impact" on those most likely to be recruited to terrorist causes. Unsatisfactory metrics were in place in terms of measuring impact (which was, admittedly, difficult to measure): the number of participants at a workshop, for example, as opposed to whether the workshop had in fact shaped those participants' views.[57] The threat was made to cut government funding if Prevent could not prove value for money.

Other structural changes were made. Conflating integration and security policy was seen as a mistake. Successful integration – while recognized as vital to reducing the terrorist threat and improving social cohesion – was no longer in Prevent's domain.[58] Integration projects would be the domain solely of the DCLG, and Prevent would be run out of the Office for Security and Counter-terrorism (OSCT) within the Home Office, with the Home Secretary now the lead Minister.

This was a striking new approach. The fresh focus on ideology, in particular, was a sea change in government thinking. However, the shift was not welcomed by Islamist pressure groups such as CAGE. Believing that the new focus typified a "neo-Conservative world-view," CAGE described Prevent's focus on ideology as "fundamentally flawed" as terrorism was caused by "the political struggle of Muslims in response to unrepresentative regimes, often aided by Western policy and occupations."[59]

Criticism also appeared in academic and political circles. Rizwaan Sabir, a British academic, claimed that "[t]here is no empirical evidence to prove a correlation between ideology and violence. But that is what Prevent is based on – an unverifiable, flawed premise."[60] The criticisms did not dissipate with time. Recycling the Lambert approach, Dr Peter Neumann from the International Centre for the Study of Radicalisation (ICSR) argued in 2015 that those the government had assessed to be extremists were actually the ones "who are working hard in the communities to make sure violent extremism didn't happen."[61] Neumann was echoing the thoughts of Baroness Warsi, the Conservative peer who in January 2015 lambasted the government for its "dangerously narrow engagement," rejection of the MCB and unwillingness to attend events with "unsavoury" speakers.[62]

IV

Following the brutal response of the Bashar al-Assad regime to the 'Arab Spring' protests of 2011, hundreds of British citizens and residents left to fight jihad in Syria. Many joined ISIS. In response, the UK attempted to ramp up its counter-terrorism and counter-radicalisation efforts.

One part of this was the Counter-Terrorism and Security Bill, which became law in February 2015. Much of the domestic focus was placed on provisions surrounding intelligence and law enforcement agencies' access to communications data. However, it was also a vote of confidence in Prevent. Section 26 of the Counter-Terrorism and Security Act placed a statutory duty on frontline workers at local councils, schools, universities, prisons and hospitals to have "due regard to the need to prevent people from being drawn into terrorism."[63] Frontline staff would be trained in awareness of issues around radicalization and extremism, why vulnerable individuals could be drawn into terrorism, and what could be done to help prevent it.

While previous versions of Prevent preferred teachers (for example) to identify at-risk pupils, it was not their legal obligation to do so. In schools this led to significant numbers not engaging with the program as it was suspected of being "anti-Islamic."[64] Now, reporting became a legal requirement. Furthermore, the government encouraged teachers and other workers to pay heed to "not just violent extremism but also non-violent extremism, which can create an atmosphere conducive to terrorism and can popularise views which terrorists exploit." By placing an actual statutory duty on the need to be cognizant of even non-violent extremism, the Counter-Terrorism and Security Act was a decisive repudiation of the Denham/Warsi approach taken to Prevent.[65]

V

Another previously voluntary initiative within Prevent was now to become statutory as well: 'Channel,' commonly referred to as the government's 'de-radicalization' program. Government documentation describes Channel as "an early intervention multi-agency process designed to safeguard vulnerable people from being drawn into violent extremist or terrorist behaviour."[66] It aims to dissuade radicalized individuals – ideally with support from that individual's family – from pursuing a violent path. This can include those inspired by violent Islamism, which make up the majority of cases, as well as the far right.[67]

According to government guidelines, Channel "may focus on a person's vulnerabilities around health, education, employment or housing, as well as specialist mentoring or faith guidance and broader diversionary activities such as sport."[68] Given Channel's work with vulnerable individuals, prisons, schools, colleges and hospitals were all particularly impacted by the legislation.

First tested in 2007, Channel was formally rolled out across England and Wales in 2012. There were a total of 3,882 referrals in 2015.[69] Approximately 20 percent of referrals received what Security Minister John Hayes described as "specialist intervention support."[70]

The long-term success of Channel remains unclear. As with any such program, a 100 percent success rate is impossible. For example, one British teenager referred to Channel in November 2013 was arrested almost 18 months later for directing an ISIS-inspired plot in Australia; another was jailed for planning to behead a British soldier.[71]

The statutory duty to report and refer led to particularly vocal, sustained and organized criticism by one sector impacted by the Prevent duty: education. This was the case with both schools and universities.

When it came to schools, prominent examples highlighted the need for vigilance. In February 2015 three teenage schoolgirls from Bethnal Green, east London, ran away from home and joined up with ISIS in Syria.[72] Another four pupils at the school were placed on a government watchlist over concerns they would attempt to do the same.[73] Then, in January 2016, photographs emerged showing six- and eight-year-old children posing with a sword in front of the black flag of Islam associated with jihadist movements.[74] The photograph was taken by their father, Ibrahim Anderson, who was convicted in January 2016 for inviting support for ISIS.

In the context of such incidents, as David Anderson noted, "it would be perverse to deny that schools have a potentially useful safeguarding role."[75] Government guidance outlined how safeguarding against radicalization should be incorporated into the schools' broader duty to be aware of the need to protect children from sexual exploitation, gangs and drugs.[76] There was some support for the new approach, including from the General Secretary of the National Association of Head Teachers (NAHT). However, there was a fierce pushback from others as well. CAGE labelled the bill an attempt by the state to "tak[e] away our children."[77] The General Secretary of the National Union of Teachers (NUT), Christine Blower, warned of the government turning teachers "into spies."[78] In April 2015, delegates at the NUT conference stated they were being transformed into "frontline Stormtroopers."[79] A year later, the NUT voted for a motion calling for Prevent's disbandment.[80]

The reaction on university campuses was arguably even more vitriolic. The problem of radicalization on campus had long been a cause for concern. A minimum of 30 percent of those who committed Islamism-related offences had attended university or another higher education institute.[81] This number included presidents of university Islamic societies, such as the 'underwear bomber' Umar Farouk Abdulmutallab, who was trained by al-Qaeda in Yemen and tried to detonate a bomb on an aircraft heading to Detroit on 25 December 2009.[82] Furthermore, according to the government's Extremism Analysis Unit, in 2014 alone a minimum of 70 university events involved extremist speakers.[83]

Given earlier events there was also a need to provide guidance to university staff with respect to addressing signs of radicalization. For example, Mohammed Atif Siddique, who was convicted of terrorism offenses in September 2007, accessed websites related to Osama bin Laden and suicide bombings at the college he attended. This was witnessed by staff members; yet according to Lord Osborne, the judge in a British Appeals Court dealing with Siddique's case, they "were reluctant to do anything for fear of some accusation of racist conduct."[84] Similarly, according to the former Chief Constable of West Yorkshire Police, Sir Norman Bettison, despite Hasib Hussain's schoolbooks being "littered … with supportive comments about al-Qaeda," no action was taken.[85] Hussain was one of the four suicide bombers who attacked the London transport network on 7 July 2005. The legally required Prevent duty to report aimed to stop such situations from occurring again.

Yet campaigners on campuses lined up to denounce the initiative. Their criticisms took two specific forms: that it was part of a campaign to spy on Muslims; and that it was the first step by government to crush all dissent on campus. Critics on campus did not take Prevent's stated aims ("to stop people becoming terrorists or supporting terrorism") at their word. Instead, Malia Bouattia – then President of the National Union of Students (NUS) – alleged in January 2015 that "academics are being trained to spy on students."[86] The union of which she was an officer, the NUS Black Students' Campaign, came up with its very own *Preventing Prevent* handbook in order to actively block attempts to address the situation on campus.[87] In this handbook, a NUS International Students Officer claimed that the Prevent duty would lead to deportations of foreigners.[88]

Such evidence illustrates not only just how greatly misunderstood what Prevent actually does remains, but also how criticisms of Prevent remained consistent year after year. In early 2011, for example, CAGE stated that "pressure is being applied to Universities to spy on their Muslim students."[89] In the same year, according to Liberty, Prevent had "outsourced" intelligence work to "teachers and other frontline service providers in a way that necessarily conflicts with their primary professional obligations and responsibilities."[90] The talking points used to criticize Prevent transcended whatever actual government policy was in place at the time.

Yet it was on the policing of dissent that arguments became most hyperbolic. In April 2015, the NUS passed a motion which claimed that Prevent was part of a vast government conspiracy that involved "manipulating public perceptions and current global events to scale back civil liberties and freedoms as part of a political agenda."[91] An open letter signed by dozens of British academics stated that Prevent would "have a chilling effect on open debate, free speech and political dissent" and result in an "environment in which political change can no longer be discussed openly." It voiced its concern that "anti-austerity and environmental campaigners" would eventually be targeted by Prevent.[92] The Black Students' handbook argued that while Prevent may have "targeted mostly Muslims" so far, its true intent was "a wider attack by the government against dissent" and, unless Prevent was "dismantled," the government could "criminalize anyone who challenges their domestic or foreign policy line."[93]

These campaigns worked. The NUS passed a motion pledging to block Prevent funding going to the NUS; to not "engage" with Prevent; and to "encourage" unions to not only not comply with Prevent, but actually to draw up guidelines on best practice when it came to not doing so.[94] A report by Student Rights, a non-partisan organization dedicated to monitoring campus extremism, concluded that students had "attempted to deliberately evade scrutiny, or have actively worked to hinder Prevent delivery."[95] It is clear that the arguments made by those opposing Prevent were not done in good faith. The independent reviewer of terrorism legislation, David Anderson QC, who was no public cheerleader for Prevent, told a Home Affairs Select Committee that it was "quite possible that some of those attacking Prevent … are motivated by a wish not to promote harmony but to sow grievance and division."[96] The cumulative effect, however, was that implementing the Prevent duty became enormously challenging.

Conclusion

There is no sign that Prevent will be disbanded in the future. This is not necessarily a bad thing as there is much to commend in Prevent. Channel is an imperfect initiative, but one attempting to address a clear problem. Operation Nicole is a vital recognition of the need to improve relations between the police and Muslim communities. And Prevent's recent willingness to take on both violent and non-violent extremism is vital in undercutting the ideology that animates Islamist terrorism.

Yet a host of valid criticisms remain. Hundreds of millions of pounds have been spent; and, as multiple assessments have concluded, much of that money has been spent very badly. Islamists have been brought into the heart of the government, given patronage and funding. Their views have been given a veneer of legitimacy solely because they agreed to denounce terrorism within the UK.

There are also invalid criticisms, which mainly revolve around bogus accusations of spying and a state desire to crush dissent. Such falsehoods have been spread by a small but effective lobby devoted to misrepresenting and distorting Prevent's true intent. The government has proven itself impotent in debunking such myths.

Lying somewhere in the middle is the argument that, for several years now, Prevent has been interpreted as discriminatory by a seemingly significant section of the UK's Muslim communities. Those claiming to speak for all of Britain's diverse Muslim communities should be treated with skepticism, though the claim is possibly true. Yet it was also probably unavoidable; the government makes reference to the dangers of far-right terrorism, but Prevent *does* focus primarily on Muslims. Equally unavoidable is the fact that the vast majority of counter-terrorism work carried out by the police and security services relates to threats emanating from Muslim communities, and the threat of far-right terrorism pales in comparison. Clearly the Prevent strategy would never have existed were it not for the terrorist threat that has emerged from followers of Islam.

No government initiative will be regarded as universally fair, proportionate, respectful of privacy and non-discriminatory. There is no perfect response to the problem of radicalization. Furthermore, Prevent may have got wrong as much as it has got right. Yet the scale of radicalization taking place in the UK means that doing nothing is simply not an option. A more sober debate centered on what Prevent actually does, a debate which debunks myths and focuses on how the strategy's efficacy can be improved, can only benefit the UK.

Notes

1 HM Government, *Prevent Strategy* (London: The Stationery Office [TSO], 2011) [hereafter *Prevent Strategy*]. www.gov.uk/government/uploads/system/uploads/attachment_data/file/97976/prevent-strategy-review.pdf.

2 Islamism defined as a belief that law should be made by God rather than man; and that Islam is not only a religion but an all-encompassing socio-political system.

3 www.irr.org.uk/pdf2/spooked.pdf.

4 David Anderson, 'Supplementary Written Evidence,' http://data.parliament.uk/writtenevidence/committeeevidence.svc/evidencedocument/home-affairs-committee/countering-extremism/written/27920.pdf, p. 1.

5 Frank Gardner, 'Prevent Strategy: Is It Failing to Stop Radicalisation?' BBC, 6 March 2015. www.bbc.com/news/uk-31756755.

6 Rupert Sutton, *Preventing Prevent? Challenges to Counter-Radicalisation Policy on Campus* (London: Henry Jackson Society, 2015). http://henryjacksonsociety.org/wp-content/uploads/2015/10/Preventing-Prevent_webversion3.pdf.

7 *Prevent Written Evidence*. www.london.gov.uk/sites/default/files/preventing_extremism_in_london_evidence_pack.pdf.

8 Fahid Qurashi, 'Prevent Gives People Permission to Hate Muslims – It Has No Place in Schools,' *Guardian*, 4 April 2016. www.theguardian.com/commentisfree/2016/apr/04/prevent-hate-muslims-schools-terrorism-teachers-reject.

9 www.mi5.gov.uk/threat-levels.

10 Robin Simcox, Hannah Stuart, Houriya Ahmed and Douglas Murray, *Islamist Terrorism: The British Connections* (London: Henry Jackson Society and Centre for Social Cohesion, 2011). http://henryjacksonsociety.org/wp-content/uploads/2011/07/Islamist+Terrorism+2011+Preview-1.pdf.

11 Ibid.

12 HM Government, *Countering International Terrorism: The United Kingdom's Strategy* (London: TSO, 2006). www.gov.uk/government/uploads/system/uploads/attachment_data/file/272320/6888.pdf.

13 UK Parliament, *Preventing Violent Extremism: Communities and Local Government Committee*. www.publications.parliament.uk/pa/cm200910/cmselect/cmcomloc/65/6504.htm.

14 HM Government, *The United Kingdom's Strategy for Countering International Terrorism Annual Report* (London: TSO, 2010). www.gov.uk/government/uploads/system/uploads/attachment_data/file/228907/7833.pdf.

15 Ibid.

16 Department for Communities and Local Government, *Preventing Violent Extremism: Winning Hearts and Minds* (London: DCLC, 2007). https://webarchive.nationalarchives.gov.uk/20070506201536/http://www.communities.gov.uk/pub/401/PreventingviolentextremismWinningheartsandminds_id1509401.pdf.

17 HM Government, *Pursue Prevent Protect Prepare: The United Kingdom's Strategy for Countering International Terrorism*(London: TSO, 2009). www.gov.uk/government/uploads/system/uploads/attachment_data/file/228644/7547.pdf.

18 Toby Helm, 'Back British Values or Lose Grants, Kelly Tells Muslim Groups,' *Telegraph*, 12 October 2006. www.telegraph.co.uk/news/uknews/1531226/Back-British-values-or-lose-grants-Kelly-tells-Muslim-groups.html.

19 Ibid.

20 DCLC, *Preventing Violent Extremism*.

21 Shiraz Maher and Martyn Frampton, *Choosing Our Friends Wisely: Criteria for Engagement with Muslim Groups* (London: Policy Exchange, 2009). www.policyexchange.org.uk/images/publications/choosing%20our%20friends%20wisely%20-%20mar%2009.pdf.

22 HM Government, *The Prevent Strategy: A Guide for Local Partners in England*(London: HMG). http://webarchive.nationalarchives.gov.uk/20130401151715/http://www.education.gov.uk/publications/eOrderingDownload/Prevent_Strategy.pdf.

23 HMG, 'Preventing Violent Extremism: A Strategy for Delivery', 2008. https://webarchive.nationalarchives.gov.uk/20080612052800/http://www.dfes.gov.uk/publications/violentextremism/downloads/Preventing%20Violent%20Extremism%20A%20Strategy%20for%20Delivery%203%20June%202008.pdf, p. 4.

24 DCLC, *Preventing Violent Extremism*, p. 6.

25 Sean O'Neill, 'The Colleges with Links to Islamist Movements: Campuses Connected to al-Qaeda Have Concerned Charity Workers,' *Times*, 29 July 2004. www.thetimes.co.uk/tto/news/uk/article1927007.ece.

26 'British Muslim Leader Sentenced to Death for War Crimes,' Channel 4 News, 3 November 2013. www.channel4.com/news/chowdhury-mueen-uddin-war-crimes-london-muslim.

27 'Preventing Extremism Together' Working Groups, *Working Together to Prevent Extremism* (London: Home Office, 2005). http://webarchive.nationalarchives.gov.uk/20120919132719/http://www.communities.gov.uk/documents/communities/pdf/152164.pdf.

28 Dominic Casciani, 'Watchdog for UK Mosques Launches,' BBC, 27 June 2006. http://news.bbc.co.uk/2/hi/uk_news/5120338.stm.

29 Jamie Bartlett and Jonathan Birdwell, *From Suspects to Citizens: Preventing Violent Extremism in a Big Society* (London: Demos, 2010). www.demos.co.uk/files/From_Suspects_to_Citizens_-_web.pdf?1279732377.

30 See, for examples, the following on the Harry's Place blog: http://hurryupharry.org/2015/08/11/khalid-khan-and-the-east-london-mosque/; http://hurryupharry.org/2011/02/16/the-london-muslim-centre-opposes-homophobia/; http://hurryupharry.org/2013/11/04/ismail-menk-on-homosexuality-worse-than-animals/; http://hurryupharry.org/2013/02/25/khalid-al-fikri-and-the-east-london-mosque/; http://hurryupharry.org/2013/12/19/shakeel-begg-and-the-east-london-mosque/.

31 Maher and Frampton, *Choosing Our Friends Wisely*.

32 Lord Alex Carlile, *Report to the Home Secretary of Independent Oversight of Prevent Review and Strategy* (London: HM Government, 2011), p. 6. www.gov.uk/government/uploads/system/uploads/attachment_data/file/97977/lord-carlile-report.pdf.

33 Seumas Milne, 'We Need to Listen to the Man from Special Branch,' *Guardian*, 14 February 2008. www.theguardian.com/commentisfree/2008/feb/14/uksecurity.terrorism.

34 Daniel Pipes Middle East Forum, 2 November 2004. www.danielpipes.org/2813/interview-with-dr-azzam-al-tamimi-institute-of-islamic.

35 Vikram Dodd, 'Government Anti-Terrorism Strategy "Spies" on Innocent.' www.theguardian.com/uk/2009/oct/16/anti-terrorism-strategy-spies-innocents.

36 Vikram Dodd, 'Spying Morally Right, Says Thinktank.' www.theguardian.com/uk/2009/oct/16/spying-morally-right-says-thinktank.

37 Dodd, 'Anti-Terrorism Strategy "Spies" on Innocent.'

38 www.npcc.police.uk/documents/TAM/Op%20Nicole.pdf.

39 *Prevent Strategy*, p. 48.

40 Dominic Casciani, 'Analysis: The Prevent Strategy and Its Problems,' 26 August 2014. www.bbc.com/news/uk-28939555.

41 Paul Lewis, 'Surveillance Cameras in Birmingham Track Muslims' Every Move,' *Guardian*, 4 June 2010. www.theguardian.com/uk/2010/jun/04/surveillance-cameras-birmingham-muslims.

42 *Council Spending Uncovered II No.5: The Prevent Strategy* (London: TPA, 2009). https://d3n8a8pro7vhmx.cloudfront.net/taxpayersalliance/pages/5596/attachments/original/1438000210/Prevent.pdf?1438000210.

43 Communities and Local Government Committee (CLGC), *Preventing Violent Extremism* (London: TSO, 2010). www.publications.parliament.uk/pa/cm200910/cmselect/cmcomloc/65/65.pdf, p. 63.

44 Ibid, p. 61.

45 Ibid, p. 3.

46 Ibid, p. 39.

47 Jamie Doward, 'British Muslim Leader Urged to Quit over Gaza,' *Guardian*, 8 March 2009. www.theguardian.com/world/2009/mar/08/daud-abdullah-gaza-middle-east.

48 Paul Bignell, 'Government Shuns Muslim Council over Link with Hamas,' *Independent*, 22 March 2009. www.independent.co.uk/news/uk/politics/government-shuns-muslim-council-over-link-with-hamas-1651323.html.

49 John Denham, Secretary of State for Communities and Local Government, Speech at National Prevent Conference, 8 December 2009. http://webarchive.nationalarchives.gov.uk/+/http://www.communities.gov.uk/speeches/corporate/nationalpreventconf.

50 31 March 2010. www.telegraph.co.uk/news/uknews/terrorism-in-the-uk/7540456/The-Prevent-strategy-a-textbook-example-of-how-to-alienate-just-about-everybody.html.

51 *Prevent Strategy*, p. 1.

52 Ibid.

53 Ibid, p. 107.
54 Ibid.
55 Ibid, pp. 1, 34, 35.
56 Ibid, p. 1.
57 Ibid, p. 50.
58 *Prevent Strategy.*
59 www.cageuk.org/wp-content/uploads/A4_PREVENT_CAGE_REPORT_WEB.pdf, p. 6–7.
60 www.london.gov.uk/sites/default/files/preventing_extremism_in_london_evidence_pack.pdf.
61 Homa Khaleeli, '"You Worry They Could Take Your Kids": Is the Prevent Strategy Demonising Muslim Schoolchildren? *Guardian*, 23 September 2015. www.theguardian.com/uk-news/2015/sep/23/prevent-counter-terrorism-strategy-schools-demonising-muslim-children.
62 Sayeeda Warsi, 'Muslims Will Speak Up for British Values Only When They Know They Will Be Heard,' *Guardian*, 24 January 2015. www.theguardian.com/world/2015/jan/24/sayeeda-warsi-muslims-british-values.
63 Home Office, *Prevent Duty Toolkit for Local Authorities and Partner Agencies: Supplementary Information to the Prevent Duty Guidance for England and Wales* (London: Home Office, 2018). https://assets.publishing.service.gov.uk/government/uploads/system/uploads/attachment_data/file/736759/Prevent_Duty_Toolkit_for_Local_Authorities.pdf, p. 1.
64 Alan Travis, 'Schools' Counter Terrorism Project Reviewed,' *Guardian*, 18 February 2011. www.theguardian.com/politics/2011/feb/18/schools-counter-terrorism-project-review.
65 Sean Coughlan, 'Schools Face New Legal Duties to Tackle Extremism,' BBC, 30 June 2015. www.bbc.com/news/education-33328377.
66 'Guidance on Prevent and the Channel Programme.' http://preventforfeandtraining.org.uk/wp-content/uploads/2018/02/The-Prevent-Strategy-and-the-Channel-Programme-in-FE-Colleges.pdf.
67 BBC, 'Referrals over Radicalisation "Double in a Year",' 22 February 2016. www.bbc.com/news/uk-35633673.
68 'Guidance on Prevent and the Channel Programme.'
69 BBC, 'Referrals over Radicalisation.'
70 BBC, 'Deradicalisation Programme Referrals on Rise,' 8 October 2015. www.bbc.com/news/uk-34469331.
71 Tom Whitehead and Tomwhitehead, 'Channel Project under Fire after Conviction of Britain Youngest Terrorist,' *Telegraph*, 23 July 2015. www.telegraph.co.uk/news/uknews/terrorism-in-the-uk/11756822/Channel-Project-under-fire-after-conviction-of-Britain-youngest-terrorist.html.
72 Katrin Bennhold, 'Jihad and Girl Power: How ISIS Lured 3 London Girls,' *New York Times*, 17 August 2015. www.nytimes.com/2015/08/18/world/europe/jihad-and-girl-power-how-isis-lured-3-london-teenagers.html?_r=0.
73 Cahal Milmo, 'Missing Syria Schoolgirls: Four More Pupils at Bethnal Green Academy Being Monitored over Fears They Considered Joining Isis,' *Independent*, 6 March 2015. www.independent.co.uk/news/uk/home-news/missing-syria-schoolgirls-four-more-pupils-at-same-school-being-monitored-over-fears-they-considered-10091893.html.
74 Duncan Gardham and Omar Wahid, 'Age SIX and Groomed for Jihad in British Suburbia,' *MailOnline*, 23 January 2016. www.dailymail.co.uk/news/article-3413806/Age-SIX-groomed-jihad-British-suburbia-Shocking-image-UK-extremism-taken-little-boy-s-Muslim-convert-father.html.
75 Anderson, 'Supplementary Written Evidence,' p. 2.
76 Department for Education, 'The Prevent Duty: Departmental Advice for Schools and Childcare Providers,' June 2015. www.gov.uk/government/uploads/system/uploads/attachment_data/file/439598/prevent-duty-departmental-advice-v6.pdf.
77 www.cageuk.org/article/taking-away-our-children-counter-terrorism-and-security-bill-2014/.
78 Coughlan, 'Schools Face New Legal Duties.'
79 Khaleeli, 'You Worry They Could Take Your Kids.'
80 Richard Adams, 'Teachers Back Motion Calling for Prevent Strategy to Be Scrapped,' *Guardian*, 28 March 2016. www.theguardian.com/politics/2016/mar/28/teachers-nut-back-motion-calling-prevent-strategy-radicalisation-scrapped.
81 Simcox et al., *Islamist Terrorism*, p. xi.
82 Sutton, *Preventing Prevent?*

83 HM Government, 'PM's Extremism Taskforce: Tackling Extremism in Universities and Colleges Top of the Agenda.' Press release, 17 September 2015. www.gov.uk/government/news/pms-extremism-taskforce-tackling-extremism-in-universities-and-colleges-top-of-the-agenda.
84 Appeal Court, High Court of Justiciary, [2010] HCJAC 7, Appeal No. XC878/07. http://web.archive.org/web/20100716013623/http://www.scotcourts.gov.uk/opinions/2010HCJAC7.html.
85 CLGC, *Preventing Violent Extremism*, p. 17.
86 Sutton, *Preventing Prevent?*, p. 47.
87 NUS Black Students, *Preventing Prevent Handbook 2017*. Available to download at www.nusconnect.org.uk/articles/preventing-prevent-handbooks.
88 Ibid, p. 38.
89 www.cageuk.org/wp-content/uploads/CP_Good_Muslim_Bad_Muslim.pdf.
90 www.liberty-human-rights.org.uk/sites/default/files/response-to-home-office-consultation-on-prevent-january-2011.pdf.
91 Sutton, *Preventing Prevent?*, p. 48.
92 *Independent*, 10 July 2015. www.independent.co.uk/voices/letters/prevent-will-have-a-chilling-effect-on-open-debate-free-speech-and-political-dissent-10381491.html.
93 NUS Black Students, *Preventing Prevent Handbook*, p. 28.
94 Sutton, *Preventing Prevent?*
95 Ibid, p. 8.
96 Anderson, 'Supplementary Written Evidence,' p. 2.

6

IMMIGRATION AND EXTREMISM

Security challenges for France's Fifth Republic

Eliot Assoudeh and Juliette Legendre

Introduction

Crises – of the national and international types – have repeatedly tested democratic governance in France over the last century. Nazi Germany's invasion of France (1940), the Indochina War (1946–54) and the Algerian crisis (1958) not only threatened to undermine France's democracy but also led to the collapse of the Republic. All trials proved the resilient character of this nation, as each time a new and stronger Republic emerged. Out of each crisis arose a "heroic leader" (a phrase coined by political scientist Stanley Hoffmann), each with his peculiar statecraft.[1] Philippe Petain, Chief of Vichy France (1940–44), Pierre Mendes France, Prime Minister of France (1954–55), and Charles de Gaulle, founder of the Fifth Republic (1959–69) not only took revenge against the status quo, but also became agents of change. This chapter considers transitions between the Fourth and Fifth Republics, and the challenges the Fifth Republic currently faces, particularly security challenges arising from immigration and extremism.

Charles de Gaulle, a French military general and rightist statesman, played a key role in both interwar and post-WWII France. De Gaulle was the leader of Free France (1940–44), and head of the Provisional Government of the French Republic (1944–46). On October 4, 1958, he founded the Fifth Republic and was elected the 18th President of France, a position he held until his resignation in 1969. De Gaulle was the dominant figure of France during the Cold War era, and his memory continues to influence French politics.

One major area facing the post-WWII French government was the ideological question of the nature of state power. A provisional government under General de Gaulle was formed by the Resistance leadership following the Liberation of France in 1944. Inherently unstable, this makeshift government soon fractured over a spectrum of issues, from social inequalities to French colonial relationships, to political relations with the Soviet Union. De Gaulle advocated for a new, strong, decisive structure led by a single assembly and a powerful executive. The alternative would have been a moderated democratic republic, featuring greater accountability and power limits.[2]

The Fourth Republic, politically defined by instability, was characterized by central and centrist parties caught between extremes of anti-system parties. Italian political philosopher Giovanni Sartori described its fragmented politics as a "polarized pluralism". There is little doubt that the politics of the Fifth Republic later developed out of a recognized need for increased stability.[3] De Gaulle's personal ambitions increased rapidly, evolving from his original royalism to a broader romanticism grounded in his conception of "the Leader". A long article titled "On Prestige", written at the time, anticipated this evolution. The article concludes with the expectation that the excessive democracy of the Third Republic would likely trigger an opposite reaction, tending "toward equilibrium".[4]

De Gaulle's approach to both domestic and foreign politics was rooted in his wartime experience. He did not like to accept France's role as a subordinate partner in an international system. Given the events of the French defeat in 1940 by German forces – a catastrophe linked to a weak executive office – de Gaulle was certain of the need to allow a head of state to decisively seize power in major emergencies. Once de Gaulle returned to power in 1958, the project of drafting a new Constitution offered an opportunity to create this executive ability.

De Gaulle's approach to foreign policy was defined by a *politique de grandeur*: independent decision-making; insistence on strong international leadership; and a higher priority given to the nation-state than had been the case in the past.[5] Affirming domestic stability and national identity, de Gaulle's international revisionism and notions of grandeur became powerfully symbolic of his aspirations for unifying the French people around a common purpose – "the acceptability of the political system as a whole."[6]

That political system experienced significant challenges given France's status as a colonial power. As a colony of France, Algeria had confronted its own nationalist movements during colonial rule. Responding to poor educational opportunities, unemployment and malnutrition among Muslim populations in the 1930s, Algerian nationalist movements were not unified in their intent. Some sought greater assimilation, some greater independence. Algerian nationalists cooperated with de Gaulle during the Second World War. Only after celebrations of the Allied victory over Nazism concluded did conflicts between Algerian nationalists and the French state arise.[7]

For France's prominent philosophers, such as Albert Camus and Jean-Paul Sartre, "the Algerian revolution was also a French Revolution", reflecting inherent questions about citizenship, cultural identity and the nature of government.[8] Decolonization detached Algeria from the French national collective identity, and France was allowed to forget its shared past with Algeria and the implications of it. Thus emerged new definitions of French national identity in which race, ethnicity and religion were significant markers. Around 9 million Algerian-born French citizens had lost their citizenship by the end of 1963. De Gaulle himself spoke to the issue in 1959:

> It is very good that there are yellow Frenchmen, black Frenchmen, brown Frenchmen. They prove that France is open to all races and that she has a universal mission. But on condition that they remain a small minority. Otherwise, France would no longer be France. We are, after all, primarily a European people of the white race, Greek and Latin culture, and the Christian religion.[9]

Muslims (the majority) were assigned Algerian citizenship, while around 1 million "European" residents retained French citizenship. Policies that excluded Algeria and Algerians from both France's territory and identity allowed de Gaulle's government to drastically remodel the Fifth Republic.[10]

Since the 1970s another phenomenon has undermined liberal democratic values across Europe: populist radical right parties. Until recently, populist radical right parties, which are mainly single-issue parties, were marginalized as political groups. But socio-economic conditions, especially those resulting from European Union (EU) expansion and mass immigration, have provided populist radical right politicians a great opportunity to increase their popularity within European communities. Britain's Brexit departure from the European Union represents the most recent achievement of populist far-right parties in Europe. Marine Le Pen, head of the National Front in France, has likened Brexit to the falling of the Berlin Wall, a historic victory for freedom. European mainstream politicians such as Angela Merkel, the incumbent German Chancellor, François Hollande, a former President of France, and Herman Van Rompuy, the first president of the European Council, have delivered powerful warnings against populism and racism in European communities.

Over the past decade France, among Western European countries, has been particularly hard hit by Islamist assaults from both jihadists and radicalized citizens.[11] Perhaps ISIS networks in Europe have been particularly strong, or the French security forces (including the police) particularly weak; but, following William McCants and Christopher Meserole, we contend that French political culture should also be examined as a ground for such violence.[12]

On the one hand, France has an uncomfortable history of violence in the Middle East and North Africa; within the domestic Muslim community, discrimination, hostility and exclusion have fostered a tenuous peace, at best. On the other hand, as we discuss in this chapter, the "New Right", threatened by multiculturalism, has entered into a perceived culture war with its counterparts in mainstream politics. The New Right frames immigrants, especially Muslims, as a "moral panic", to use William Cohen's memorable term.[13] Often leading with anti-immigrant and anti-Muslim rhetoric, the French radical right movement seeks to influence the nation.[14]

According to Gilles Kepel, both the French Right and the French Left have empowered the rise of Muslim identity politics: the Right by tacitly accepting and thereby communicating the view that Muslims are unwelcome; the Left by oversimplifying French Muslim populations as victims, and failing to understand that identity politics would pose such an extreme threat to the French Republic.[15] What are the effects of identity politics on the rise of terrorism and extremism? Whether France's responses to these threats is democratic or not is the question we intend to answer, the story we propose to tell.

We turn back now to de Gaulle's accession to power in 1958.

May 1958: crisis and Article 16

On May 13, 1958 the French National Assembly approved the nomination of Pierre Pflimlin as Prime Minister. However, certain French generals, led by Jacques Massu in Algeria, who were concerned about any potential negotiation between Pflimlin and Algerian nationalists, not only did not recognize Pflimlin's cabinet but also planned a military coup. Protests incited a riot-fueled sacking of the Great Delegation, the highest organization of civil authority at the time. The "May Day" protest march began in honor of three French soldiers executed in Tunisia by National Liberation Front (FLN) troops. The executions had been carried out in retaliation for the French government's prior execution of seven suspected FLN activists. The outbreak of this uprising forced Pflimlin to resign on that same day. Shortly thereafter, Charles de Gaulle returned to France's political scene as the last Prime Minister of the Fourth Republic.

De Gaulle's personal credentials vouchsafed guarantees from Fourth Republic influencers upon the French Republic, respecting the arrangement and power structure provided by the Constitution.[16] De Gaulle's new constitutional government decisively consolidated leadership, and, due to the state of emergency precipitated by the Algeria crisis and military insubordination, gave de Gaulle near dictatorial power under Article 16, which defines the emergency powers of the President:

> Where the institutions of the Republic, the independence of the Nation, the integrity of its territory or the fulfilment of its international commitments are under serious and immediate threat, and where the proper functioning of the constitutional public authorities is interrupted, the President of the Republic shall take measures required by these circumstances, after formally consulting the Prime Minister, the Presidents of the Houses of Parliament and the Constitutional Council.[17]

One major reason why left-wing parties campaigned against the new Constitution during the referendum of 1958 was specifically because they feared that the power of Article 16 would be used against them. In fact, prior to President Hollande's declaration of a state of emergency due to terrorist attacks in Paris in 2015,[18] Article 16 had been actively used only twice: between 1961 and 1963 to stop an attempted coup; and in 1962 to intervene over French evacuees in the wake of Algerian independence. Article 16 was used sparingly, and never against the left; in fact, it was used in both instances on populations who would have been more likely to support de Gaulle.

Article 16 was subject to a number of checks and balances, designed by de Gaulle and Michel Jean-Pierre Debré – the first Prime Minister of the Fifth Republic – to increase the likelihood of approval for the 1958 Constitution. In order to initiate Article 16 provisions the President must first consult with the Prime Minister, the leaders of both chambers of Parliament and the Constitutional Council. The President is not required to act on the recommendations of these stakeholders, but they must be consulted; conceivably, if those consulted do not agree about a state of emergency, public opinion could be affected by an inappropriate use of Article 16.[19]

The efficacy and durability of Article 16 was tested in the early 1960s by dissident military officers and the formation of a short-lived dissident group of the French right-wing called the *Organisation armée secrete* (Secret Army Organization, or OAS).

On April 22, 1961, a group of French army officers carried out a coup in opposition to the independence of Algeria from France and seized power in Algeria. Responding in a public speech, de Gaulle acted on Article 16 and announced a state of national emergency, declaring that the coup compromised and challenged France's position in Africa, causing shame and humiliation for the nation. Citizen brigades formed in response to de Gaulle's speech, resisting the coup and supporting the president. Within a week the rebellion collapsed and certain coup members were arrested. But one officer, Raoul Salan, formed the OAS, whose motto was "Algeria is French and will remain so". Between April 1961 and April 1962 OAS activists conducted a series of violent acts that left more than 2000 casualties in both France and Algeria; and multiple times it plotted to assassinate de Gaulle. The OAS and other opponents of independence presented the case not as a matter of opposing freedom, but as a more effective decolonization process that would adopt Algerians into the rights and duties of French citizenship instead of expelling them.[20] The French government stood firm in opposing and ultimately destroying the OAS and executing some of its leaders.

May 1968: crisis and immigration

The events of May 1968 occurred at the peak of an immigration wave (1954–74), especially post Algeria's independence. More than 3 million immigrant workers, mainly from Southern Europe and North Africa, arrived in France. The crisis started as a student uprising on the Nanterre University campus during the Spring semester 1968, but soon turned into a widespread revolt against de Gaulle's authoritarian-style rule. The campus was close to one of the largest shanty towns in the suburbs of Paris, where immigrant workers lived in very poor economic conditions.

The French public was unaware for a long time of the lives of early immigrants in France; immigrants were quite isolated in the 1960s. As immigration and integration increased in political importance, such ignorance influenced the conversation.[21] In the midst of the crisis immigration became a politicized issue for the first time, interestingly in the minds of leftist intellectuals and activists. The primitively produced language and imagery of contemporary posters helped average citizens learn about and empathize with immigrants, and provided immigrants a sense of unity and empowerment to work together against oppression.[22] The 1968 rebellions represented and encouraged greater interest in strengthening smaller communities and social ties, where individuals could feel more tightly connected. Since then this focus on "subnational" identities has increased interest in, and tolerance of, the ideas behind a plural society.[23]

Post-de Gaulle immigration policies

The only European nation actively encouraging postwar permanent immigration as much as the United States was France. As in the US and Western Europe, immigration numbers fell in France in 1973, with the first oil shock. Since 1973, French immigration policy has been largely focused on controlling and discouraging permanent migration.[24] Let us consider French immigration policy post the crises of 1968.

Between 1971 and 1973 an advocacy movement for French immigration arose independently. Public awareness, triggered by several tragedies involving immigrants, led to mobilization influenced by major intellectual figures. Advocates for immigrant rights welcomed François Mitterrand's government, hoping that important reforms would be forthcoming. Initially, Mitterrand's immigration policies fell fairly closely in line with the demands of the left in 1968. Radical reform reversed some of the Giscard d'Estaing government's punitive policies; offered an amnesty accepted by more than 130,000 immigrants; eased naturalization and family meetings; made it impossible to deport foreigners born in France; and stopped requiring authorization from the Interior Minister for immigrants to form associations.[25]

The Mitterrand-led immigration policies reveal more complexity. While Mitterrand's restoration of a more classic French immigration policy leant on antiracist principles, overall immigration policy was given far less attention in relation to other governmental public policies, a circumstance that seems to have fostered a rise in racism.[26]

Hostility toward Islam and Islamic symbols, such as the construction of mosques, increased from 1979 onwards. While Islam had been fairly absent from public debate about immigration, it now took center stage, especially following a series of terrorist attacks aimed at Jewish targets. The politics of immigration in France began a new era of anti-immigration policies led by the Right, starting in the 1980s. In March of 1983 the Front National won its first local election, on the back of a conversation dominated by immigration concerns. Shiite Islamists became the new target of major suspicion, following the Iranian revolution of 1979.

This fact indicates a shift away from Cold War immigration concerns to those connected to conflict between Islam and the West. Prior to 1968, blame for strikes would have been attributed first to communism.[27]

The policies of Nicolas Sarkozy, himself another former French President, significantly impacted immigration and identity politics in the country. As an interior minister in Jacques Chirac's government, Sarkozy headed the newly established Ministry of Immigration, Integration, National Identity and Co-Development. His first new immigration control law (2003) increased restrictions on immigration control, yet still included provisions for existing immigrant integration. In fact, the former restriction was justified by the latter provision in that integration was to be facilitated to a greater degree by the restriction of new immigrants. Two objectives guided the legislation: the restriction of illegal immigration, under which the deportation goal was increased from 10,000 in 2002 to 25,000 in 2006; and a reduction in the number of refugee-status immigrants.

Whereas the 2003 legislation aimed to reduce illegal immigration, initiatives in 2005 were more concerned with France's economic, social and cultural capacity to receive and integrate immigrants. Speaking from the *Union pour un mouvement populaire* (Union for a Popular Movement, UMP) conference in 2005, Sarkozy specifically identified an objective to reverse the ratio of family immigrants to labor immigrants, a tougher position enabled by his 2004 election to the leadership of the UMP.

In 2006 emphasis was placed on selective immigration versus imposed immigration. France's economic requirements now levied a greater influence over immigration numbers. While previously the vast majority of French immigrants were family members and asylum seekers, the introduction of a new residence permit, called a "skills and talents" permit, for highly qualified workers increased the emphasis on labor and economic value-based immigration.[28]

Sarkozy was a proponent of constitutional reform that would formalize diversity as a value within the context of the Fifth Republic Constitution. He even established a commission to draft the change shortly after his election. The commission rejected the revision, anticipating that it could open the door to ethnically based policies of positive discrimination.[29]

In December 2009 Sarkozy initiated a debate over France's national identity. Indeed, initial polls revealed support for opening discussions about national identity. But poll numbers quickly reversed following media comments criticizing the debates and conservative town hall meetings for setting a tone of racism, xenophobia and suspicion of foreign influence. Some radical right politicians blamed Muslim immigrants as "unpatriotic" and for seeking a community to replace France's native population.[30]

As part of his national identity debate initiative, Sarkozy proposed banning the burqa and publicly recognizing France's Christian origins. The proposal to ban the burqa was presented by Sarkozy as a "law of liberation", not a ban, as it supported a French value (of women's freedom and dignity) that superseded the religious value it canceled. Sarkozy framed his proposal as a cultural value, not a religious freedom issue. Recognizing Christian origins openly, Sarkozy contended, would not preclude but rather support the power of the laity to protect free thinking and freedom of belief.[31]

Public attitudes towards immigration

A survey of attitudes towards immigration conducted by European Social Survey (ESS) in 2002 (wave 1) and 2014 (wave 7) in some European countries, including France, shows responses based on a Likert scale designed to measure qualifications for immigration

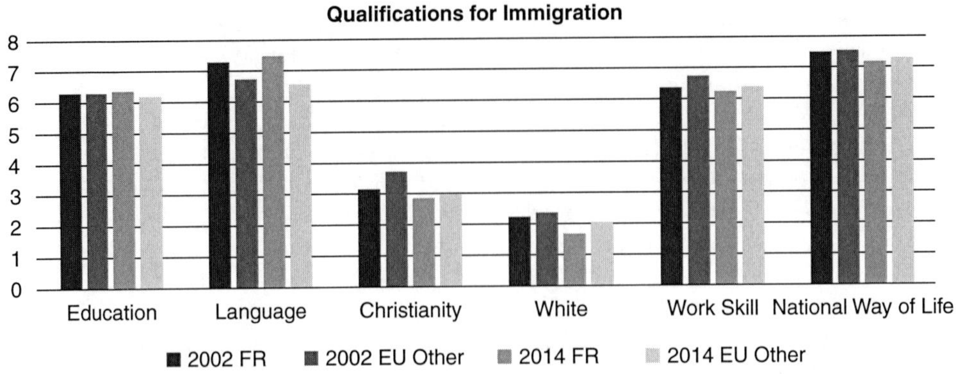

Figure 6.1 Public attitudes towards immigration
Source: European Social Survey (www.europeansocialsurvey.org)

(extremely unimportant to extremely important). Figure 6.1 reports the results for France and other European countries from a comparative perspective.

What these results suggest is that, on average, compared with other European populations, French citizens attach highest importance to immigrants' ability speak the country's official language. The next most important qualification for immigrants is a level of commitment to the French way of life. In addition, and consistent with attitudes in other European countries, the French public prefers educated immigrants with professional skills that meet a perceived national need of some kind. The survey also indicates that the French public, on average, does not believe that immigrants make France's crime problems worse or undermine dominant religious beliefs or practices. However, it does indicate a public feeling that immigrants might have some negative impact on French cultural life.

The presence of a large number of immigrants, particularly those of North African Arab origin, estimated to be as many as 3 million, has raised many questions about national identity. Some French citizens are resentful of or feel threatened by the influx of immigrants, who can compete with the established population for jobs, housing and social benefits. While in the past France has relied upon gradual assimilation to resolve immigration differences, recent immigrants seem so distinct in religion, race, social customs and heritage, and so great in number, that this process is now less efficient than it once might have been.[32]

While individual immigrants may be welcomed by many French citizens, immigrant families or communities may be less welcome as collectives. This inconsistency between individual and collective experience might suggest that matters of principle, such as welcoming new people, can be overridden, or at least influenced by, economic considerations such as job or benefit competition.[33] One study indicated that, while tolerance toward immigrants was increasing, ambivalence toward immigration as a political policy was simultaneously increasing as well. Respondents were positive about cultural enrichment, but identified concerns about the number of migrants allowed into the country.[34]

Far-right parties and immigration

The emergence of the National Front (FN) in 1972, under the leadership of Jean-Marie Le Pen, further divided the political right camp. The party became a beacon of hope for other European right-wing populist parties soon after its electoral victory in 1983. As a right-wing electoral party, the National Front has increasingly advocated against immigration, the

European Union and globalization.[35] Once a league made up of a small group of right-wing political activists, the National Front has consolidated its position over time to become the most influential populist radical right (PRR) party in France. Since its formation, the National Front has had an ambivalent relationship with the Fifth Republic.

In 1990 William Safran identified three distinct approaches to "national identity" among French political parties. Extreme-right movements, such as the National Front, react with a negative, defensive stance, prescribing a rigid approach to a kind of "membership" process. At the other end of the spectrum political opinion appears to be more optimistic, seeing the benefits of cultural pluralism, and often viewing strong French nationalism as the real problem. Moderate pluralists simply believe that it is plausible for a French national identity to co-exist with multiple subnational identities.[36]

In reaction to series of clashes between police forces and immigrants (mainly Arabs) in *banlieues*, the head of the National Front blamed the mainstream parties' immigration policies for "injustice, insecurity, corruption and decadence". Le Pen added that "the French want to be at home in France". Then President Mitterrand, while emphasizing the importance of the safety of suburbs, stated that "young immigrants should not be victims of permanent suspicion but should be respected and even loved".[37] In fact, it was Mitterrand, a socialist presidential candidate, who during his campaign in 1988 for the first time declared: "The sons and daughters of immigrants born in France are not immigrants; they are French. I will say it in a loud voice: 'They are at home!'"[38]. Mitterrand thus broadened the definition of "Frenchness" against Jean-Marie Le Pen's narrative.

According to Hannah Arendt, problems arise when promoters of an ideology are gaining influence and mobilizing people by strategically selecting scapegoats. The term "scapegoating" describes the process by which a hostility or grievance advanced by one group is turned into blame against another group, instead of addressing the real causes of the social problem. This strategy is often leveraged to promote an ideological or social goal since it draws scapegoaters together in unity against the scapegoated group. Whether the problem or grievance is real or imagined, or whether the accused party is truly innocent or guilty, the important characteristic of a scapegoated group is that the entire group is stereotyped into a single faceless enemy or blame-holder.[39] Immigrants – in particular those of Middle Eastern and African background – have been scapegoated in France by populist right-wing groups such as the National Front.

In post-9–11 rhetoric, "the face of evil" is commonly evoked in Islamophobic dialogue, especially dialogue surrounding international terrorism. The phrase also appears in local discussions of crime that specify the cultural or religious backgrounds of perpetrators. Identifying an act as "evil" oversimplifies the story, and even more so identifies perpetrators as the embodiment of evil. The function of identifying evil confirms a moral bias that needs to serve as collateral for good, often by designating whole communities, defined by religious or ethnic differences, as outsiders.[40]

Since the terrorist attacks on *Charlie Hebdo* in January 2015, the National Front has targeted the immigration issue even more sharply than it had earlier. To avoid racism charges, FN frames the issue on cultural and economic grounds. An analysis of the Twitter accounts for the National Front reveals a nativist ideology in the political agenda of the organization. FN believes that France's institutions should serve the French people first, and that one culture should prevail. In addition, FN blames immigrants for high unemployment rates and wage stagnation.

National Front monoculturalism has roots in the work of European far-right ideologues such as Renaud Camus and Alain de Benoist. Camus is a French writer known for his theory of the "great replacement"; Benoist stigmatizes Muslims as invaders and criminals. In 2014 Camus was condemned by Justice for inciting hate towards Muslims. Camus' definition of "Frenchness" is presented according to classical rationality, but engenders a historically uneasy perspective on colonialism, territorialism, cultural and religious differences. For Benoist, founder of the "New Right", immigration is actually a clearly negative process for all involved. From Benoist's standpoint, immigration turns immigrants into victims by an erasure of their cultural roots. Some unexpected paradoxes occur within Benoist's definition of "diversity". He both defends a Muslim immigrant's right to wear a head covering and opposes the policies by which she was able to emigrate.[41]

Marine Le Pen and Florian Philippot (Vice President of the National Front in charge of communication strategy) have proclaimed several times that "a multicultural society is a multi-conflictual society". The National Front blames immigrants for threatening the stability of French society in terms of security and culture. Its members focus even more extensively on immigration's impact on the economy.

National Front and its like-minded partners have constructed a culturally based "folk devil" out of Muslim immigrants and mapped that attribution to a sense of "collective insecurity". The result is "moral panic". Gilles Ivaldi conducted an empirical analysis of the National Front's political agenda between 1997 and 2012 which reveals that the share of economic recommendations has doubled during that period while cultural ones have decreased by almost half.[42] Similarly, Cécile Alduy and Stéphane Wahnich's lexical analysis of Marine Le Pen's speeches in comparison with her father's shows that 40 percent of her nominal expressions refer to economic issues, as opposed to 23 percent of her father's.[43]

Actual increasing polarization between population groups can make it difficult to balance real progress toward good democratic governance with diversely organized populations. The main beneficiaries of escalating intolerance and confrontational attitudes are populist and extremist leaders, who see the opportunity to polarize populations as a way to support political gains.[44]

Following the terrorist attacks in Paris and Brussels in 2015–2016, Gilles Kepel pointed to the "virtual and mental enclaves" that are increasingly splitting European and French societies, a situation characterized by both heightened marginalization and increasing rejection of common values – in a word, polarization. What makes Professor Kepel stand out among other scholars and intellectuals who support a theory of radicalism that is particularly Islamist in nature are the two main supports of his analysis: first, the increasing power of imported ideologies; and, second, the radicalization of suburban French Muslims.[45]

Immigration issues in France have garnered political attention for a longer time than in other European nations, aided by French electoral laws that reward a focus on immigration. While other European party systems encourage more complex policy coverage, France's electoral system has emphasized partisan issues.

A majority of French voters perceive the National Front as a political outsider, which makes cooperation across the rightist voting bloc a challenging task for elites. When the moderate Right join with the National Front in political contests, they have always risked losing centrist voters to the Left. The conflict and division between the three segments of the Right benefits the socialist camp the most.[46] By gaining centrist swing votes alienated from established parties – parties split by divisive issues – the National Front has raised immigration as a major topic of debate, and led the charge of contemporary racism in France. Moderate leaders have dealt with their loss of votes by mimicking the successful tactics of FN, including slurring and scapegoating immigrants. Politicians of almost every group affiliation have parroted the National Front's popular dogma that France must dramatically slow immigration.

Key differentiations among voters who sometimes swing to vote with the National Front are extremely high levels of concern with immigration and crime and low levels of concern with issues of disarmament and the environment.

Immigration and terrorism: a constructed nexus

Terrorism as an international crime was initiated in 1937 in the form of two draft conventions developed at the League of Nations. The first convention defined preventative and punitive measures for terrorism. Further, this convention proposed making acts of terror by assassination an international crime. Criminal responsibility for assassinations rested on the individual actors, who were prevented from gaining legal asylum in any state. The second draft convention established an international court for processing terrorism cases.[47]

An uptick in new terrorism legislation followed the events of 9/11, as many democracies expanded definitions of terrorism and extended the power of security organizations to investigate potential terrorist networks/organizations, and to apprehend individuals connected with them. The resulting increase in security measures has raised many questions about individual rights, freedom of speech and the freedom security authorities arrogate to themselves to use excessive force under the new laws.[48] Michael Ignatieff argues that a democratic war on terrorism should never supersede, in priority and authority, the individual, human right to dignity. For Ignatieff, nations who successfully balance democracy and authority pass the "dignity test".[49] Does France pass Ignatieff's dignity test?

Between 1970 and 2016, France experienced more than 2640 terror incidents (Figure 6.2). While a majority of these incidents were carried out by groups affiliated to Marxist, nationalist, far-right extremist (including neo-Nazi) and separatist groups (Figure 6.3), Islamist terrorism was present in France much earlier than in other European countries (ca. 1980). Islamist terrorist attacks are often tied to either France's colonial legacy or the country's foreign policy in the Middle East. Examples include the Iranian/Islamic Revolutionary Guard Corps (IRGC)-led assassination of Louis Delamare, the French Ambassador to Lebanon, in September of 1981 and the August 1982 attack on the Goldenberg restaurant in Paris' Jewish

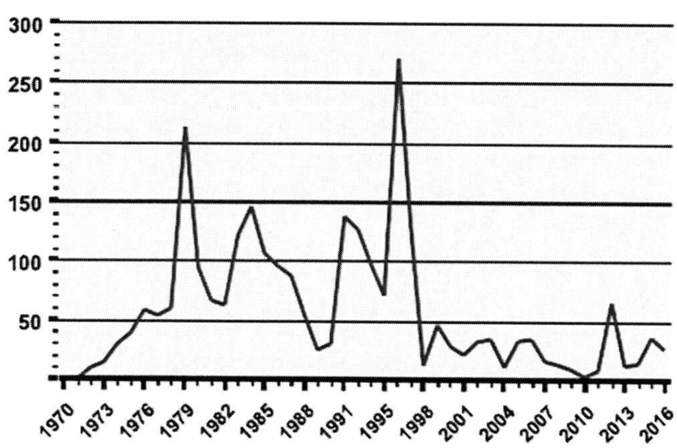

Figure 6.2 Number of terror incidents in France (1970–2016)

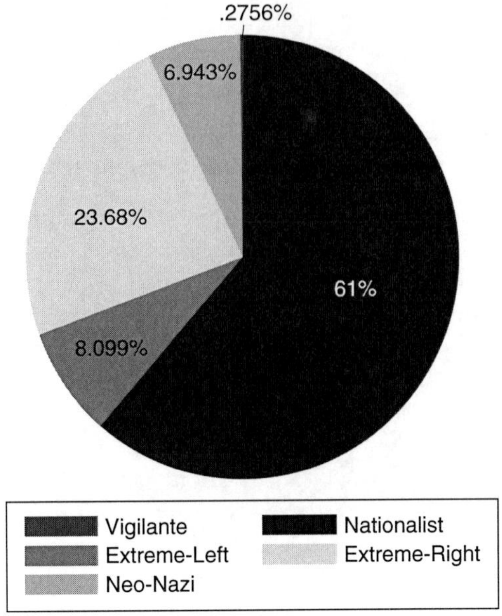

Figure 6.3 Number of domestic terror incidents in France (1973–2002)
Source: De la Calle, Luis and Ignacio Sánchez-Cuenca, "The Quantity and Quality of Terrorism: The Domestic Terrorism Victims (DTV) Dataset." *Journal of Peace Research* 48, no. 1 (2011): 49–58.
Note: Total of 151 incidents that left 215 casualties.

Quarter that left 6 dead and 22 injured.[50] The latter attack was led by Black June, a group affiliated to Abu Nidal's organization.

While France and other Western European nations experience similar threats, their responses to such threats are distinctly conditioned by cultural norms, guiding institutions and organizational processes. There are also distinct differences in these states' approaches to counterterrorist operations.[51] France has been targeted by terrorist attacks. Over time, French governments have reinforced the country's judicial and legislative systems to respond adequately and rapidly to terrorist incidents. Beginning in 1986, terrorist cases in France have been prosecuted by *examining magistrates* rather than ordinary civil courts.[52]

Legal responses to terrorism in France are quite consistent, empowered by this judicial system which includes a position that does not exist in the legal systems of countries such as Great Britain and the United States: a group of investigating magistrates who effectively coordinate the leadership of terrorism investigations, allowing for a much more coordinated effort between the judicial and executive branches. While the special legal category of investigating magistrate judges certainly expedites coordination of police and intelligence forces in France to direct legal action on Islamist terrorism cases, this integration also seems inconsistent with a democratic judicial system of checks and balances.[53]

Over the years, reforms have been conducted to give additional power to magistrates and police forces in order to facilitate their investigation and surveillance of terrorist suspects. The Penal Code has also been reformed to increase punishments for terrorist acts. Even more recently, laws have adapted to the development of new technologies and cyber-terrorism, allowing increased surveillance of data and communications systems. These measures aim to prevent terrorist attacks and limit radicalization of individual participants. In response to the

Paris terrorist attacks of November 2015, a 1955 law defining state of emergency requirements was re-enacted and reinforced.

In a press statement issued in July 2016 after the attacks in Nice, Vice President Manuel Valls and Interior Minister Bernard Cazeneuve reminded the population that the cabinet had done more to fight terrorism than any previous government. This "more" translates into increases in police personnel, budget, reforms of intelligence services, the creation of special units, new antiterrorism laws, and national prevention plans against radicalization.[54]

Former President François Hollande declared a state of emergency after the terrorist attacks in November 2015, which remained in place for several months. The Constitutional Law Act amended the Constitution in July of 2008. The committee at the time presented reflections and proposals on the amendment, which aimed to rebalance, and not eradicate, Article 16. The amendment establishes democratic control over the time period for which Article 16 can be applied, limiting the control of executive leadership. Now the Article may only be applied for thirty days, after which period the Constitutional Council, an assembly president or sixty deputies or senators must evaluate the conditions of application and provide public notice.[55] Modifications were made to the original text to respond to terrorism threats, e.g. the insertion of specific counterterrorism dispositions. The French government published a document on its website explaining what the current act allows.[56] The Interior Minister has the power to:

- Put under house arrest anyone whose activity is considered a threat to public order.
- Take all measures to shut down places that praise or encourage terrorist activities (including places of worship).
- Dissolve by decree in the Council of Ministers any associations or groups that participate in acts that endanger public order, or organizational activities that may facilitate or encourage these acts.

In all regions, the act enables prefects to:

- Restrict freedom of movement by creating special areas of protection and/or by prohibiting travel in some places (curfew).
- Prohibit travel in some part of national territory for anyone who might bring stress on public order.
- Requisition people or private means.
- Prohibit public meetings or temporarily shut down meeting places.
- Allow administrative searches in the presence of an officer of the judicial police. None of these searches can target places that operate with a parliamentary mandate or professional activities of lawyers, magistrates and journalists (can be done at any time, day or night).

This last point about administrative searches means, in other words, that police can carry out warrantless searches (without the approval of a judge).

This document does not give all the details regarding allowances of power in a state of emergency. After the Nice attacks in July 2016, the Assembly and the Senate voted to extend the state of emergency to six months, and new dispositions were added that extended police powers. One of them, detailed in Article 5 of the new version, allowed the police to seize data from computers and other electronic devices: "data stored in IT systems or equipment present in the premises can be copied or seized if [a] copy can't be processed or finished during the time of the search".[57] This measure had been found unconstitutional by the Constitutional Court in February 2015 but was, in fact, adopted in the new version.

In April 2016 Interior Minister Cazeneuve released a public statement on the results of the state of emergency:[58]

> In total, since the beginning of the state of emergency, 743 weapons had been neutralized, including 75 weapons of war. As of today, 592 administrative searches resulted in legal proceedings. As a result, 67 sentences were given out by the courts and 56 individuals have been taken into custody.

In another press statement released in July 2016, Cazeneuve, along with Manuel Valls, stated:

> Sixteen attempted terrorist attacks have been stopped on our territory since 2013. and 160 individuals linked to terrorist activities have been arrested since the beginning of the year in France thanks to the work of our security services. Since the restoration of border controls on November 13, 48 million individuals have been monitored/controlled … and 28,000 individuals were not allowed to enter the territory.

Numerous human rights non-governmental organizations (NGOs) and other civil society organizations (such as *La Quadrature du Net*) have been monitoring the state of emergency measures to denounce abusive situations. Violations of human rights by the authorities and a disproportionate tendency to target Muslims can be observed. In a report published in February 2016 Amnesty International stated that: "Some Muslims were targeted mainly on the basis of their religious practice, with no evidence pointing to their involvement in any criminal offence." This organization recommends that the French government "refrain from proposing to extend the current State of Emergency".[59]

The French National Consultative Commission on Human Rights (CNCDH) also published a report on the state of emergency measures. In the first section, the report lists issues associated with the administrative searches, such as: "failure to take into account the potential presence of minors or vulnerable persons in the premises being searched"; "the use of physical violence"; "psychological violence"; and issues about house-arrest measures that are "insufficiently individualized with respect to the situation of those under house-arrest" and "the impossibility of reconciling the obligation to attend a police station with working life has led to several dismissals".[60] Further, Amnesty International denounces the assigned residence order measures because of "the vague grounds on which [they] are usually adopted, the lack of transparency regarding the collection of information used to justify them, as well as their negative consequences to the human rights of those subjected to them".[61]

On October 30, 2017 Emmanuel Macron signed into law a new counterterrorism bill that replaced the state of emergency. For the political majority, this law put an end to the state of emergency and strengthened security measures without infringing civil liberties. However, for the opposition party, *La France Insoumise* (Unbowed or Untamed France), this law dangerously incorporated exceptional practices, which restrict several civil liberties, into ordinary law permanently.

Intelligence Act, May 2015

One especial concern of many in the EU, especially after documented revelations of surveillance by government services, is that the democratic balance of national security and individual liberty has been disrupted to the detriment of individual liberties.[62]

Even as legal powers, intelligence processing and more extensive security action have emerged in response to radical Islamist terrorism threats, perceived trends of increased authoritarian action are still governed, to some extent, by institutional and cultural norms. In the French case, it is institutional conventions and cultural norms that enable a severe response to terrorism.[63]

France was behind in terms of legislation over its surveillance system compared to other developed countries. In the context of terrorist threats, the government approved a new bill in July 2015 that extended the power of intelligence agencies to adapt to the era of new technologies. On its website, the government published a document that explains the main provisions of this Act (original emphases omitted).[64]

1 Limits to the analysis of online data monitoring

> The Act authorises the automatic analysis of connection data in the sole aim of detecting online patterns of behaviour typically displayed by terrorists. User anonymity will be preserved and message content will not be monitored. Only telephone conversations involving individuals designated by name will be intercepted, including those made using an "IMSI-catcher" device. Their number will remain limited, and the principle of prior individual consent will apply to the interception of international communications sent or received in France. Citizens believing themselves to be under illegal surveillance will be able to refer the matter to the Council of State, and a judge may not be prevented from discovering the purposes of surveillance on the grounds of national defense secrecy.

2 Limits to the monitoring of telecommunications

> Technical systems will be put in place in conjunction with telecommunications operators by a department reporting to the Prime Minister under the control of the National Commission for the Control of Intelligence Techniques (CNCTR – *Commission nationale de contrôle des techniques de renseignement*), an independent administrative authority which will be comprised of magistrates, parliamentarians and an engineer specialising in IT and digital technology. Except in rare emergency situations, it will always issue a prior opinion, and have oversight during and after implementation of the intelligence technology. It will also have the power to refer a matter to the Council of State.

3 Clarifying definition of terms

> [B]y identifying the purposes of surveillance measures, the Act specifies when they can and cannot be used. The monitoring of political parties, trade unions and peaceful protest movements is therefore clearly prohibited. France has set itself apart from its neighbours, who have adopted far broader conceptions. The bill is even more specific than the European Convention on Human Rights, which states that

> intrusion into privacy might be necessary "in the interests of national security, public safety or the economic well-being of the country, for the prevention of disorder or crime, for the protection of health or morals, or for the protection of the rights and freedoms of others". Given their missions and the secrecy that must surround some of their activity, certain professions will benefit from additional guarantees. These will include lawyers, journalists, magistrates and parliamentarians. The Commission's opinion will be compulsory and delivered by a full bench, and the confidentiality needed to work in these areas will be maintained. However, in order to prevent individuals using these professions to conceal their activities, no absolute ban on using intelligence techniques to investigate them can be imposed.

The Guardian reported that:

> The new law will allow authorities to spy on the digital and mobile phone communications of anyone linked to a "terrorist" inquiry without prior authorisation from a judge. It forces internet service providers and phone companies to give up data upon request. Intelligence services will have the right to place cameras and recording devices in private homes and install so-called "keylogger devices" that record every key stroke on a targeted computer in real time. The authorities will be able to keep recordings for a month and metadata for five years.[65]

The French government claims that its goal is to better target terrorist threats, but civil society is worried this bill allows generalized surveillance and reduces civil liberties.

In 2015 Amnesty International published an article in response to this new bill to object to the threats the bill poses to public liberties, including the following:[66]

- It allows the Prime Minister to authorize intrusive surveillance measures for broad and undefined goals such as "major foreign policy interests", protecting of France's "economic, industrial and scientific interests" and prevention of "collective violence" and "organized delinquency".
- For purposes of counterterrorism, the bill allows use of mass digital surveillance tools to capture mobile phone calls and black boxes maintained by internet service providers, thus permitting collection and analysis of the personal data of millions of internet users.
- Lack of independent oversight: instead of getting a judge's approval for such activity, the Prime Minister would only need to seek the views of a new body, the "National Committee of Intelligence Techniques Control", without any need to abide by those views.
- It will be very difficult, if not impossible, for people to find out whether they are being unlawfully spied on, or for whistle-blowers to expose abuse of surveillance powers.

Some say that the Intelligence Act of 2015 is France's Patriot Act. Like the American bill of 2001, it was approved in the wake of an attack (in particular the Islamist attacks on *Charlie Hebdo*). These types of bill are highly controversial because the tradeoff is significant: more security, but at the cost of loss of privacy and liberties for the population.

While many democracies remain preoccupied with individual liberties, in France there appears to be a clear consensus among influential actors that the security of the Republic is of first priority. Giving such a level of priority to security concerns creates the opportunity for French security forces to enact a much more authoritarian legal and operational response to threats than security forces in some other Western European governments, such as the UK.

Islamic terrorism is seen as a threat from both foreign and home-grown agents. France can point to a long history of targeting by foreign groups, from the Armed Islamic Group (GIA) to the Salafist Group for Preaching and Combat (GSPC) and Al-Qaeda. But French citizens who may have important foreign links are also identified as potential threats.

In order to reject society, according to Roy, groups of young men from poor urban communities have turned to Islamist extremism, refusing to defend and fight for the ideals of a society in which, as Roy says, "they have no place". Thus, France's real problem has not been with "the radicalization of Islam", but with "the Islamification of radicalism".[67] One of the most volatile population groups, as identified by Ismail Serageldin, director of Egypt's Bibliotheca Alexandrina, is also one of the most alienated and marginalized: young Muslims. The split between Muslim and non-Muslim worlds – together with the resulting flow of resentment and frustrations across generations – is especially strong among the young, who are more likely to feel marginalized, forgotten and resentful toward either culture, making them prime targets for extremist ideological indoctrination or recruitment.[68]

Kepel and Roy agree that "push factors" such as the lack of jobs and opportunities for children of immigrants, poor housing and underfunded educational systems do matter to the conversation. In order to limit the power of jihadist or extremist recruiters, Roy advocates that the French government allow greater bandwidth of expression to mainstream Islam.

This method was attempted in Britain following the London Transport bombings in 2005, allowing spokespeople opposed to jihadist violence a platform for reaching young Muslims. While an admirable attempt, the results were less than satisfactory, putting the British in the position of defining why some leaders were chosen and others were not.

Kepel favors assimilation over integration. The extreme emphasis on cultural assimilation in France is based on an ideology of unity around a national community, not on ethnic or racial exclusivity. From this perspective French values provide freedom from other value systems. Adopting an Anglo-Saxon model of multiculturalism would essentially mean a loss of identity for the French.

Conclusions

The official inception of the EU in 1991, accompanied by public demonstrations of solidarity and commitment to common values among diverse national cultures, embodied a belief held by European citizens of many nations – a belief in the transformational potential of democracy, human rights and the rule of law.

The fall of the Berlin Wall, while liberating many Europeans from the Soviet dictatorial system, ignited a series of conflicts and territorial disputes that not only challenged liberal European values, but also marked an identity crisis across the continent. Since 2010, as tensions in the Middle East increased and destabilization escalated, some young Europeans have identified with the cause and empathized with the sense of global complexity represented by conflicting cultures. As a result terrorism is not only an external force, but can also be sourced internally by dissenting groups or individuals who reject the values that united the EU.[69]

European opposition to immigration is not a factor of left or right political leanings, but rather an experiential reaction to the near-constant massive migration to Europe from the Middle East and Africa. Racism, nationalism and xenophobic tendencies can be found at every point across the political spectrum.[70]

To some large extent, democratic responses to threat are being decided by the battle of ideas, which engages advocates of civil liberties, the media, and legal and political elites to contend against government members who focus on expanding the authority of the state. Generating awareness of rights through public discussion is as much a pillar to hold up the standards of liberal democracy as it is an effective means of countering terrorist threats.[71]

Serageldin identifies not only a need for alliance between Western and Middle Eastern nations to confront threats, but also a need to change Western discourse around religion and culture. It is not military power, but cultural confrontation that will defeat terrorism.

Notes

1 Hoffmann, Stanley. "Heroic Leadership: The Case of Modern France". In Edinger, Lewis J., ed. *Political Leadership in Industrialized Societies: Studies in Comparative Analysis*. Wiley, 1967.

2 "From Fourth to Fifth Republic: France 1946–1969." https://eserve.org.uk/tmc/contem/fifth.htm.

3 Bell, David Scott. *Parties and Democracy in France: Parties under Presidentialism*. Dartmouth Publishing, 2000.

4 Mangan, Sherry. "Two Democracies in Crisis: France: Is de Gaulle Fascist?" *Commentary*, January 1, 1948. www.commentarymagazine.com/articles/two-democracies-in-crisis-france-is-de-gaulle-fascist/.

5 Gordon, Phillip H. *A Certain Idea of France: French Security Policy and Gaullist Legacy*. Princeton University Press, 1993.

6 Keeler, John T.S. "The Politics of Grandeur Ideological Aspects of de Gaulle's Foreign Policy. By Philip G. Cerny" *American Political Science Review* 75, no. 1 (1981): 263–264.

7 Bell, 2000.

8 Meany, Thomas. "The Colonist of Good Will: On Albert Camus." *The Nation*. August 27, 2013. www.thenation.com/article/colonist-good-will-albert-camus/.

9 Charles de Gaulle's letter to Alain Peyrefitte in 1959. Cited in Thomas Chatterton Williams. "The French Origins of 'You Will Not Replace Us': The European Thinkers behind the White-Nationalist Rallying Cry." *New Yorker*. December 4, 2017.

10 Shepard, Todd. *The Invention of Decolonization: The Algerian War and the Remaking of France*. Cornell University Press, 2008.

11 Malsin, Jared. "Why France Has Become the Number One Target for Terror." *Time*. http://time.com/4407810/nice-attack-france-target-jihadists-terrorism/.

12 McCants, William and Christopher Meserole. "The French Connection." *Foreign Affairs*. December 20, 2017. www.foreignaffairs.com/articles/2016-03-24/french-connection.

13 Cohen, Stanley. *Folk Devils and Moral Panics: The Creation of the Mods and Rockers*. Psychology Press, 2002.

14 Williams, 2017.

15 Klausen, Jytte. "Terror in the Terroir: The Roots of France's Jihadist Problem." *Foreign Affairs* 96 (2017): 166.

16 Shepard, 2008.

17 www.conseil-constitutionnel.fr/conseil-constitutionnel/english/constitution/constitution-of-4-october-1958.25742.html#TitleII.

18 Sharma, Swati. "'It Is Horror': French President Hollande's Remarks after Paris Attacks." *Washington Post*, November 13, 2015. www.washingtonpost.com/news/worldviews/wp/2015/11/13/it-is-horror-french-president-hollandes-remarks-after-paris-attacks/?utm_term=.c9b1efd0ea6d.

19 "State of Emergency in France: What is Article 16?" Center for European Politics. http://cep.rhul.ac.uk/cep-blog/2015/11/14/state-of-emergency-in-france-what-is-article-16.html.

20 Shepard, 2008.

21 Gordon, 1993.

22 McNamara, Sara. "Posters, Politics and Immigration during the May 1968 Protests in France." MA thesis, University of New Orleans, 2010. https://core.ac.uk/reader/216835040.

23 Safran, William. "The French and their National Identity: The Quest for an Elusive Substance?" *French Politics and Society* 8, no. 1 (1990): 56–67.

24 Guiraudon, Virginie. "Immigration Policy in France". Brookings Institution. July 1, 2001.

25 Gordon, 1993.

26 Weil, Patrick. "Immigration and the Rise of Racism in France: The Contradictions in Mitterrand's Policies." *French Politics and Society* 9, no. 3–4 (1991): 82–100.
27 Gordon, 1993.
28 Marthaler, Sally. "Nicolas Sarkozy and the Politics of French Immigration Policy." *Journal of European Public Policy* 15, no. 3 (2008): 382–397.
29 Taras, Raymond. *Xenophobia and Islamophobia in Europe*. Edinburgh University Press, 2012.
30 Crumley, Bruce. "Why France's National Identity Debate Backfired?" *Time*. February 12, 2010.
31 Taras, 2012.
32 Safran, 1990.
33 Safran, William. *The French Polity*. Routledge, 2015.
34 Taras, 2012.
35 Blee, Kathleen M. "Ethnographies of the Far Right." *Journal of Contemporary Ethnography* 36, no. 2 (2007): 119–128.
36 Safran, 1990.
37 Riding, Alan. "Immigrant Unrest Alarming French." *New York Times*. June 23, 1991.
38 Markham, James M. "Mitterrand Above the Campaign Trail". *New York Times*. April 12, 1988.
39 Berlet, Chip. "Christian Identity: The Apocalypse Style, Political Religion, Palingenesis and Neo-Fascism." *Totalitarian Movements and Political Religions* 5, no. 3 (2004): 469–506.
40 Noble, Greg. "Where's the Moral in Moral Panic? Islam, Evil and Moral Turbulence." In Morgan, George and Scott Poynting, eds. *Global Islamophobia: Muslims and Moral Panic in the West*. Ashgate, 2012.
41 Williams, 2017.
42 Ivaldi, Gilles. "Du néolibéralisme au social-populisme?" In Crépon, Sylvain, Alexandre Dézé, and Nonna Mayer, eds. *Les faux-semblants du Front national*, pp. 161–184. Presses de Sciences Po, 2015.
43 Alduy, Cécile, and Stéphane Wahnich. *Marine Le Pen prise aux mots. Décryptage du nouveau discours frontiste*. Seuil, 2015, p. 37.
44 Serageldin, Ismail. "Inaugural Debate on 'Countering Radicalization and Extremism'." Debates on Democratic Security (2015–2017). *Council of Europe*.
45 Kepel, Gilles. "'The Attacks in Paris and Brussels: Salafism and Jihadism in Europe'". Debates on Democratic Security (2015–2017). *Council of Europe*.
46 Veugelers, John W.P. "Right-Wing Extremism in Contemporary France: A 'Silent Counter-revolution'?" *Sociological Quarterly* 41, no. 1 (2000): 19–40.
47 Weinberg, Leonard. *Democracy and Terrorism: Friend or Foe?* Routledge, 2013.
48 Foley, Frank. *Countering Terrorism in Britain and France: Institutions, Norms and the Shadow of the Past*. Cambridge University Press, 2013; also, see Weinberg, 2013.
49 Ignatieff, Michael. *The Lesser Evil: Political Ethics in an Age of Terror*. Princeton University Press, 2013.
50 Kifner, John. "French Ambassador Is Slain in Beirut." *New York Times*, September 5, 1981. www.nytimes.com/1981/09/05/world/french-ambassador-is-slain-in-beirut.html.
51 For more information see Haubrich, Dirk. "September 11, Anti-Terror Laws and Civil Liberties: Britain, France and Germany Compared." *Government and Opposition* 38, no. 1 (2003): 3–28; Foley, 2013.
52 "Thirty Years of Anti Terrorism Legislations". www.vie-publique.fr/chronologie/chronos-thematiques/trente-ans-legislation-antiterroriste.html.
53 Foley, 2013.
54 "Joint Press Conference Manuel Valls and Bernard Cazeneuve." July 17, 2016. www.interieur.gouv.fr/Archives/Archives-des-dossiers/2016-Dossiers/La-lutte-contre-le-terrorisme/Communique-de-presse-commun-de-M.-Manuel-Valls-et-de-M.-Bernard-Cazeneuve.
55 "The Emergency Powers of the President." *vie-publique*, January 2, 2014. www.viepublique.fr/decouverteinstitutions/institutions/approfondissements/pouvoirsexceptionnelsdupresident.html.
56 www.gouvernement.fr/action/la-lutte-contre-le-terrorisme.
57 Law No. 55–385 of 3 April 1955 on the state of emergency. www.legifrance.gouv.fr/affichTexteArticle.do;jsessionid=072F36C018A2BDEDABE7BC259AA92F6B.tpdila10v_3?cidTexte=JORFTEXT000000695350&idArticle=LEGIARTI000032925311&dateTexte=20161105&categorieLien=id#LEGIARTI000032925311.
58 www.interieur.gouv.fr/Actualites/L-actu-du-Ministere/Prorogation-de-l-etat-d-urgence2.
59 Amnesty International (Feb. 2016). *Upturned Lives: The Disproportionate Impact of France's State of Emergency*. p. 7.

60 www.cncdh.fr/sites/default/files/english_avis_statement_of_opinion_on_the_state_of_emergency.pdf.
61 Amnesty International, 2016. p. 17.
62 Council of Europe Debates on Democratic Security (2015–2017). www.coe.int/en/web/policy-planning/democratic-security-debates.
63 Foley, 2013.
64 www.gouvernement.fr/en/parliament-adopts-the-intelligence-bill.
65 Crisafis, Angelique et al. "France Passes New Surveillance Law in Wake of Charlie Hebdo Attack." *Guardian*. May 5, 2015. www.theguardian.com/world/2015/may/05/france-passes-new-surveillance-law-in-wake-of-charlie-hebdo-attack.
66 www.amnesty.org/en/latest/news/2015/07/france-new-surveillance-law-a-major-blow-to-human-rights/.
67 Roy, Olivier. "Jihadism: A Generational and Nihilist Revolt." *Logos*, Spring (2020). http://logosjournal.com/2016/roy.
68 Serageldin, Ismail. "Inaugural Debate on 'Countering Radicalization and Extremism'." Debates on Democratic Security (2015–2017). *Council of Europe*. www.coe.int/en/web/policy-planning/-/inaugural-debate-on-countering-radicalisation-and-extremism-.
69 Council of Europe Debates on Democratic Security (2015–2017).
70 Williams, 2017.
71 Foley, 2013.

7

DEMOCRACY AND SECURITY IN GERMANY BEFORE AND AFTER REUNIFICATION

Steffen Schneider

Introduction

A recent history of the Federal Republic of Germany post-1949, entitled *Die Suche nach Sicherheit* (The Search for Security), suggests a close relationship between the development of (West) Germany's constitutional order, its foreign and domestic policy on the one hand, and various external and internal security challenges on the other.[1] The defeated, demoralized Germany of 1945 was, first of all, a security threat for its *neighbors* – several of which had been victims of German aggression not once, but twice in the first half of the 20th century – and for the occupation forces of the four Allied powers. The demilitarization and denazification efforts of the US, British and French military governments, but also their decision to support the re-establishment of a liberal democratic regime in the three Western zones of occupation, addressed these concerns. With the onset of the Cold War, a new security threat emerged, and the Federal Republic was quickly enlisted as a partner in the fight against Soviet totalitarianism and expansionism.

For the next four decades, the survival of the Federal Republic and its democratic political system *themselves* appeared to be premised on success in coping with this *external* security threat and related *internal* security challenge posed by anti-democratic forces from the left and right, forces which had already undermined and destroyed Germany's first democratic regime, the Weimar Republic. The public good of security is arguably a core (Hobbesian) state function and soon became – together with Germany's economic performance – an important (Weberian and Eastonian) output legitimation resource of Germany's second democratic regime. Yet the country has also undoubtedly experienced *tensions* between democratic values, legal principles and security policy objectives.[2]

This chapter first examines how security threats – and conflicts between "freedom" and security – were dealt with in the "old" Federal Republic up to the end of the Cold War and reunification in 1990.[3] It then probes the development of Germany's external and internal security challenges and policy in the post-reunification era.[4]

Democracy and security in the "old" Federal Republic of Germany (1949–1990)

When deliberations on a new democratic constitution for Germany began on 1 September 1948, the Soviets had already left the Allied Control Authority and initiated their blockade of Berlin. When the final text of the *Grundgesetz* (Basic Law, or GG) was adopted on 8 May 1949, exactly four years after the capitulation of Nazi Germany, the North Atlantic Treaty Organization (NATO) had just been founded. The birth of the Federal Republic made the separation of Germany into East and West fully apparent and consolidated it for the next four decades, despite the never relinquished (and ultimately achieved) objective of reuniting the country under conditions of *Frieden und Freiheit* (peace and security). Hence, the purview of the Basic Law remained limited to West Germany, its ten *Länder* (states) and (with restrictions) Berlin – de facto West Berlin. In line with the requirements of the Western powers, the Basic Law re-established the principles of rule of law (*Rechtsstaat*), liberal democracy and federalism.

Unlike the Weimar constitution, the text of the Basic Law begins with the notion of human dignity and the enumeration of basic – that is, human and civil – rights (in articles 1–19 GG). Amendments touching on the core principles and standards of basic rights protection, the rule of law and democracy – the *freiheitlich-demokratische Grundordnung* – are inadmissible (art. 20, 79 (3) GG). While the parliamentary arrangements and strong executive of the Federal Republic correspond to the Westminster model of democracy in the UK, its strong and constitutionally guaranteed federalism and bicameralism, as well as its highly influential Constitutional Court (*Bundesverfassungsgericht*), are closer to the US model of power-sharing, checks and balances, and judicial review. The *Länder* have their own democratic constitutions; participate in national legislation via the *Bundesrat* (Second Chamber of Parliament); and are, in the context of Germany's executive or intrastate type of federalism, largely responsible for the administration of federal law. With their own police forces and internal security agencies (*Verfassungsschutzämter*), the *Lander* are not least major players in the field of security policy. To make the Federal Republic "safe" for its European neighbors and democracy, and to prepare it for the external security challenges of the Cold War period, the Basic Law (art. 24) permits the transfer of authority to international organizations.

Finally, drawing lessons from the quasi-legal access of the Nazis to power, the Basic Law offers strong instruments against domestic enemies of its constitutional order. The provisions of *streitbare* or *wehrhafte Demokratie* (militant democracy) include the forfeiture of basic rights (art. 18 GG) and a right of resistance against attacks on the constitutional order (art. 20 (4)). They require the loyalty of public servants to the constitution (art. 33). Political organizations (art. 9 (2)) and parties (art. 21 (2)) with anti-constitutional objectives may be outlawed by the government or the Federal Constitutional Court, respectively. However, the original text of the Basic Law does not define or regulate a state of internal emergency. Any such emergency in the early years of the Federal Republic would presumably have triggered the intervention of the Allied High Commission based on its prerogatives under the 10 April, 1949 Occupation Statute. Due to these restrictions of West Germany's sovereignty, the Allied powers remained key players in its external and internal security policy.

Over the next four decades, the East–West conflict and West Germany's vulnerable location at the periphery of NATO – with the Iron Curtain running through the country itself – determined its external security context. National governments in the first twenty years of the Federal Republic were dominated by the newly established Christian Democratic Union (CDU) and its Bavarian sister party, the Christian Social Union (CSU). Against the backdrop of the Cold War, Chancellor Konrad Adenauer (1949–1963, followed by Ludwig Erhard) highly prioritized foreign and external security policy. Dealing with the consequences of the Nazi regime and the war – issues such as reparations, compensation for war victims and prisoners of war – required a minimum of exchange with the Soviet Union, and hence diplomatic relations were established in 1955; but otherwise a firm policy of integration into the West and its emerging, US-led security arrangements was pursued. The famous Stalin note on German unity in 1952, whose seriousness remains disputed, was thus ignored.

While the Federal Republic renounced ABC (atomic, biological, chemical) weapons in 1954 (confirmed in 1990), and thus remained fundamentally dependent on the military deterrence and troops provided by its NATO allies, two constitutional amendments (*Wehrverfassung*), together with the Compulsory Military Service Act (*Wehrpflichtgesetz*), paved the way for the highly controversial rearmament of the Federal Republic, and West German NATO membership in 1955/56. For observers such as Federal Minister of the Interior Gustav Heinemann, who resigned in protest, the remilitarization of West Germany also raised the specter of its renazification, and was hence a clear and present threat to the stability of West Germany's fledgling democracy. Indeed, many of the almost 200,000 *Wehrmacht* soldiers and officers who had been banned from their professional occupation by the Allied powers after 1945 now joined the ranks of the new Federal Army (*Bundeswehr*).

The security of the Federal Republic and its neighbors also played a role in Adenauer's reconciliation with France and the first steps towards European integration: the European Coal and Steel Community in 1951 and the European Economic Community in 1957. The 1958–1961 Berlin crisis and the construction of the Berlin Wall in August 1961 exacerbated the Cold War mood in Germany.

The anti-communist orientation of the Adenauer years also left its mark in the internal security realm. The "militant democracy" provisions of the Basic Law had been included as weapons against anti-democratic, totalitarian forces from the left *and* right. The Allied powers consented to the establishment of the *Bundesverfassungsschutz* (Federal Constitutional Protection Agency, BfV), the *Bundeskriminalamt* (Federal Criminal Police Agency, BKA) and the *Bundesgrenzschutz* (Federal Border Protection Agency, BGS) in 1950. However they continued to observe them closely for many years, as the danger of their infiltration by Nazis and the rise of an authoritarian police state appeared at least as threatening as the danger of communist subversion. Adenauer had opposed a rigid denazification of the public service all along, and entrusted Hans Globke, a co-author of the infamous 1935 Nuremberg Race Laws, with tasks such as the establishment of the BfV and the *Bundesnachrichtendienst* (Federal Intelligence Service, BND).

With the shift of (in)security perceptions towards the Soviet Union, the German Democratic Republic (GDR) and their sympathizers in West Germany, the rehabilitation of Nazi functional elites was increasingly viewed less as a security threat and more as a way to integrate these administrative and security "experts" into the new, democratic regime. More than 50,000 public servants and judges with a Nazi past were therefore allowed to join the public administration and justice system of the Federal Republic.[5] As a consequence, an anti-communist and state-centered, rather than an anti-totalitarian and basic rights-oriented understanding of "militant democracy" and its instruments – focused on the Communist Party of Germany (KPD), its subsidiary organizations and sympathizers – came to the fore. This was the case even though the first anti-constitutional party to be outlawed by the Federal Constitutional Court was the right-wing extremist *Sozialistische Reichspartei*; and a British commando intervened as late as 1953 on the basis of the Occupation Statute to arrest right-wing extremists who had presumably begun to infiltrate the Liberal Party (FDP).

The First Senate of the Constitutional Court resisted outlawing the KPD until 1956, and presented a more liberal, cautious and basic rights-oriented definition of "militant democracy" in its ruling. In 1953 and 1957 it confirmed the constitutionality of mass discharges in the context of the post-war denazification measures and in the context of excluding former *Gestapo* men from the police. However, the US military government had collaborated with hundreds of former members of the Nazi military and security agencies as early as 1945/46. Thousands had entered the West German police and security agencies by the time the justice system began to prosecute alleged communist organizations and individuals more systematically in 1951 on the basis of a highly illiberal *Staatsschutz* (state protection) legal doctrine. According to Rigoll, 65 percent of the management positions of the BKA were occupied by former SS men, and an ex-SS officer became the agency's president in 1965.[6] Largely unaccountable "freelancers" with an SS or Gestapo past also worked for the BfV and the Organization Gehlen (renamed and made official as the BND in 1956). The 1961 *Spiegel* Affair – in which Minister of Defense Franz Josef Strauß ordered the arrest of the news magazine's editor-in-chief based on an (unfounded) suspicion of treason – became one of the early Republic's first major political scandals.

A new phase in West German politics – characterized by the participation of the Social Democrats (SPD) in government – was ushered in with the 1966–1969 Grand Coalition of the CDU/CSU and SPD led by Chancellor Kurt Georg Kiesinger. While Kiesinger had been a member of the National Socialist German Workers' Party (NSDAP), Vice Chancellor and Foreign Minister Willy Brandt spent the Nazi regime in exile. In 1969, Brandt became the Chancellor of an SPD and FDP coalition that endured until 1982, when it was replaced by a CDU/CSU and FDP coalition led by Chancellor Helmut Kohl. In the foreign and external security policy realm, this change of government did not lead to immediate revisions of the Federal Republic's intransigent attitude vis-à-vis the Soviet bloc. Policy stances such as the non-recognition of the Oder-Neisse line as the border with Poland or the Hallstein Doctrine against the recognition of the GDR by third countries both impeded a *rapprochement* between the two German states and got in the way of the Federal Republic's NATO allies' *détente* efforts in the years after the 1962 Cuban missile crisis. Germany joined the Treaty on the Non-Proliferation of Nuclear Weapons in November 1969. Chancellor Brandt's *Ostpolitik* resulted in treaties with Moscow and Warsaw in 1970, and the *Grundlagenvertrag* with East Berlin – complemented by the Quadripartite Agreement on Berlin – in 1971/72. Both German states finally accessed the United Nations in 1973. Farther-reaching hopes of a transformation of the socialist regimes through *rapprochement* and *détente* proved unrealistic, but the objective of reunification was confirmed by the *Bundestag* (Federal Parliament) and the Federal Constitutional Court in 1972/73. Ironically, Brandt had to resign when it was revealed in 1974 that one of his closest advisers, Günter Guillaume, was an East German spy.

During the second half of the 1970s, the period of *détente* ended. It was Chancellor Helmut Schmidt (SPD) who highlighted the deterrence "gap" caused by the newly deployed SS-20 missiles of the Soviets and lobbied for the December 1979 NATO Double-Track Decision that threatened the deployment of US mid-range missiles in West Germany while, at the same time, offering the Soviets – who invaded Afghanistan in the same month – talks about nuclear disarmament in Europe.

The decision – whose implementation was initiated by Chancellor Kohl – triggered massive protests by the West German peace movement, which the Ministers of Justice Hans Engelhard (FDP) and Friedrich Zimmermann (CSU) answered with efforts to restrict the freedom of assembly. The new coalition also passed a reform of conscientious objection to military service which left the controversial investigation of conscience (*Gewissensprüfung*) in place while extending the period of alternative service to 20 months. However, the new government did not return to more confrontational policy stances vis-à-vis East Germany. Rather, Bavarian Minister-President Franz Josef Strauß organized a 1 billion DM bank loan to the crisis-ridden socialist regime, and Erich Honecker, Chairman of the State Council of the GDR, was granted an official state visit to the Federal Republic in the West. Kohl, an ardent proponent of further European integration, also established a close relationship with French President François Mitterrand and, after a rocky start, with Soviet leader Mikhail Gorbachev.

The field of legal and internal security policy across the last 20 years of the "old" Federal Republic was also characterized by more continuity than first meets the eye.[7] The Grand Coalition of 1966–1969 – which appeared quite problematic from a democratic point of view, as it reduced the parliamentary opposition to the small Liberal (FDP) caucus – was justified by the need for a large parliamentary (super-)majority to implement major, urgent reforms. Among the reform projects of the Social Democrats was an overhaul and liberalization of the Federal Republic's antiquated criminal law and of the treatment of prisoners (*Strafvollzugsreform*). Both projects were confronted with reluctance on the part of the Christian Democrats, but two reform acts (which, for instance, decriminalized homosexuality and adultery) were passed. A third reform of criminal law – with changes to § 125 on breach of the peace (punishment only for violent participants in otherwise peaceful demonstrations) – was passed by the Brandt government in 1970. Legal aid for people on low incomes was introduced by the Schmidt government in 1980.

The issue of political extremism returned to the nation's agenda with West Germany's first recession in 1966/67. The recession fostered a short-lived surge of the right-wing extremist National Democratic Party (NDP), which entered a number of *Länder* parliaments but failed to cross the 5 percent threshold in the 1969 Bundestag elections. Student protests and the rise of the so-called *Außerparlamentarische Opposition* (Extra-Parliamentary Opposition, APO) were more conspicuous domestic security threats. The APO's activities climaxed in opposition to the highly controversial *Notstandsgesetzgebung*, a constitutional amendment and legislation regulating the state of emergency and replacing Allied emergency powers. While Minister of Justice Heinemann (SPD) toned down some of his predecessors' *Staatsschutz* measures against communists and tolerated the DKP (a successor party of the outlawed KPD founded in the mid-1960s), the focus of internal security policy remained very much on the left end of the ideological spectrum. Roughly 125,000 trials against alleged KPD sympathizers were initiated until 1968, but they led to a mere 7000 condemnations. An estimated 8000 private letters sent between West and East Germany were opened per month, and 17 million "seditious" brochures sent from the GDR were destroyed annually[8] – despite a conspicuous dearth of evidence for the KPD's willingness or capacity to start a communist revolt in the Federal Republic.

The Brandt and Schmidt governments inherited the problem of extremists in public service. Brandt's reform impetus was directed at the return of Nazis to influential positions and the survival of authoritarian structures in politics and society. *Mehr Demokratie wagen!* – "Dare to be more democratic!" – was his famous slogan. Did public servants have to make their attachment to the *freiheitlich-demokratische Grundordnung* of the Basic Law explicit, or was law-abiding behavior sufficient (*Gesetzlichkeitsmodell*)?[9] Based on a restrictive line specified by the Federal Constitutional Court in 1969/70 and 1975, the Extremists Decree was passed by the *Länder* Minister Presidents' Conference in January 1972. Candidates for public service – whatever their function, including teaching staff in schools and universities – now had to show active loyalty and could not be members of parties or organizations with anti-constitutional objectives. The federal and *Länder* intelligence agencies (*Verfassungsschutzämter*) could be involved in related inquiries, although *Länder* ruled by the CDU/CSU and the SPD came to interpret these guidelines rather differently. Between 1973 and 1978 alone, 1.3 million candidates were screened by the *Verfassungsschutz*, but only about 1000 were ultimately found unacceptable for public service.[10]

While the APO fragmented into various ideological groups, left-wing political extremism and terrorism – notably the kidnappings and assassinations perpetrated by the *Rote Armee Fraktion* (Red Army Faction, RAF) – became the major testing ground for the liberalism of the SPD and FDP government in the mid-1970s, culminating in the *Deutscher Herbst* (German Fall) of 1977. The fall of 1977 saw the murder of Federal General Attorney Siegfried Buback and Dresdner Bank manager Jürgen Ponto; the kidnapping and assassination of Federal Confederation of Employers' Associations (VDA) president Hanss Martin Schleyer; the hijacking of Lufthansa airliner Landshut by a Palestinian commando allied with the RAF; and the liberation of hostages by a German special police force (GSG9) in Mogadishu, Somalia, followed a couple of days later by the suicide of RAF members Andreas Baader, Gudrun Ensslin and Jan-Carl Raspe.

Faced with an opposition majority in the Bundesrat and the judicial review of the Federal Constitutional Court, the SPD was eager to demonstrate that it was able and willing to combine a hard line against left-wing extremism in its internal security policy with its more conciliatory *Ostpolitik*. A series of restrictive anti-terror laws – such as the 1977 *Kontaktsperregesetz* (Ban on Contacts Act) and the 1978 *Gesetz zur Änderung der Strafprozessordnung* (Law on Changes in Criminal Trial Rules) – were to prove the law and order credentials of the government. The wire-tapping of nuclear physicist Klaus Traube by the BfV – with the help of the BND (which is not supposed to act on internal security matters) – led to the 1978 *Gesetz über die parlamentarische Kontrolle nachrichtendienstlicher Tätigkeit* (Parliamentary Control of the Intelligence Services Act). Paradoxically, then, a reform government that had "dared to be more democratic" and liberal came to be associated with *Berufsverbote* (job bans) and such over-reactions in internal security policy, even though the diagnosis of a growing national security state appears exaggerated in hindsight.[11] The RAF stayed active in the 1980s and 1990s, and claimed its last victim: President Detlev Karsten Rohwedder of the Federal *Treuhandanstalt* (for the Management and Privatization of Public Property in East Germany). The RAF declared its dissolution in 1998.

Democracy and security in the "new" Federal Republic of Germany

The collapse of the Socialist Unity Party (SED) regime in East Germany in late 1989 provided East and West Germany with the opportunity to reunify on 3 October 1990. The collapse of the SED may also be viewed as a critical juncture in the security policy of the Federal Republic, which shed its provisional character territorially and gained full sovereignty. Just as 40 years before, the security concerns of Germany's neighbors had to be addressed in the process of reunification. The 2 + 4 Treaty of the two German states with the four Allied powers (12 September 1990) and a Border Treaty with Poland that acknowledged the Oder-Neisse line (14 November 1990) addressed these fears. The troop size of the *Bundeswehr* was limited to 370,000 (it had fallen below 200,000 active soldiers by 2017). Moreover, Germany confirmed its renunciation of ABC weapons, and confirmed both its willingness to outlaw activities that "disturb peace and are intended to prepare a war of preparation" and to outlaw parties that threaten liberal democracy – two points already covered by the 1949 version of the Basic Law. A letter by the two Foreign Ministers confirmed that expropriations in the Soviet zone in the years 1945–1949 would not be challenged or declared invalid – an important prerequisite for internal peace in the five new *Länder.*

Although this critical juncture might have provided a window of opportunity for major constitutional reforms, no total revision of the Basic Law was undertaken in the final eight years of the CDU/CSU and FDP government led by Helmut Kohl, the architect of German reunification. Only necessary adaptations – for instance, to Germany's federalism and bicameralism, and to European integration in the wake of the 1992 Maastricht Treaty (art. 23a) – were implemented. Germany's own external and internal security context appeared to have massively changed; security threats for the country were greatly reduced. As a fully sovereign nation, Germany was free to choose its alliances, and hence to remain a member of NATO and the EU. It was now surrounded by "friends" and liberal democratic regimes, most of which also ultimately joined NATO and the European Union (EU). Germany's own commitment to disarmament had already been superseded by the multilateral Treaty on Conventional Armed Forces in Europe (1990), which established a balance between NATO and the former member states of the Warsaw Pact in Europe. Most Western Allied troops left Germany (about 54,000 US troops remain), and the Soviets (Russians) withdrew from East Germany and Europe by 1994.

On the other hand, in a multipolar world – or the unipolar world of US hyper-power – NATO lost its traditional *raison d'être* and much of its cohesion with the end of the Cold War, without an over-riding global conflict. The Clinton Administration was already less inclined to engage militarily in Europe and around the world than its predecessors. The capacity "gap" between European NATO members, especially Germany, and the US in terms of military spending and capacity soon became apparent. The gap remains a sore point in US–European relations in the Trump era. Germany, in particular, had traditionally defined itself as a *Handelsstaat*, or civil power, that promotes humanitarian objectives and democracy as well as free trade-related interests as a partner in international organizations and joint systems of security; it operates by way of (cheque book) diplomacy.

Given the increasingly tight budget situation in the wake of German reunification, the Kohl government– and the SPD–Green government led by Chancellor Gerhard Schröder (SPD) that replaced it in 1998 – were reluctant to forego the "peace dividend" of the post-Cold War era. The highly pro-American Kohl had opted against military participation in, but for generous co-funding of, George Bush Sr.'s 1991 Iraq War. Yet the fully sovereign, economically powerful and democratic post reunification Germany which appeared to have defeated the "ghosts" of its Nazi past – was increasingly confronted by calls for a more proactive, self-confident and "realist" foreign and external security policy, including peacekeeping and more "robust" peace-enforcement initiatives sanctioned by the UN. A 1994 ruling by the Federal Constitutional Court paved the way for "out of area" NATO missions, but tied them to parliamentary consent. In 1996 and 1999, respectively, the Federal Army joined missions in Bosnia and Kosovo. Ironically enough, it was Schröder (born in 1944 and hence the first Chancellor without any personal memories of the Nazi regime) and his Green Party Foreign Minister Joschka Fischer (who had cut his teeth, politically speaking, in the leftist *Sponti* milieu of 1970s' Frankfurt) who came to be associated with a more "robust" foreign and defense policy.

Although Germany has become one of the focal points of deadly Islamic terror attacks relatively late – with the attack on a Christmas market in 2016 – the devastating terror attacks on New York and Washington, DC on September 11, 2001 had already marked a turning point in German internal and external security policy.[12] The 9/11 attacks raised awareness of the growing threat represented by non-state and transnational actors such as al Qaeda and other Islamic terror groups, but also by organized crime – and by asymmetrical conflicts between them and nation states in the era of globalization: "the End of History" seemed to give way to "the Clash of Civilizations." In Germany, too, a new era began, characterized, on the one hand, by the "securitization" and even militarization of policy fields such as refugee, immigration and integration policy, energy and climate policy; and, on the other, by a broadening of the security concept – including, for instance, the notion of "human" security. With the "de-État-ization" of security challenges, or their importation from failing states, the boundary line between external and internal security threats has become fuzzy.

In the wake of 9/11, Germany quickly implemented a bundle of measures similar to those enacted by the US and other European countries, but arguably with a considerably less pronounced focus on (extra-)legal instruments (torture, so-called extraordinary renditions, secret prisons) that stretch or violate principles of the rule of law and democracy. Many of Germany's measures were subject to sunset clauses, and hence to periodical renewal given their problematic nature. Those measures included stricter anti-terror legislation that gave additional competences to the police and security agencies, enabling them to observe, prosecute and (where applicable) deport suspects and perpetrators of terror attacks more easily; to interrupt their funding streams, mobility and communication; and to facilitate data exchange between private and public as well as domestic and international actors.

The first *Antiterrorismuspaket* (Anti-Terror Package) was passed as early as 30 November 2001. Importantly, it removed the so-called *Religionsprivileg* (Religious Privilege) of the *Vereinsgesetz* (Law on Organizations). All clubs or private organizations – including religious ones and so-called *Ausländervereine* (organizations of non-citizens) – may now be screened regarding their ideological stances and compatibility with the Basic Law. They may thus be outlawed by the government. The new § 129b of the Penal Code also made membership of or sympathizing with terror organizations that have no activities or infrastructure in the country punishable under German law. This closed a legal gap that EU member states had agreed to close as early as December 1998.

Changes to the *Gesetz zur Beschränkung des Brief-, Post- und Fernmeldegeheimnisses* (Law on the Limitation of the Secrecy of Letters, Mail and Telephone Calls) facilitated data exchange between various agencies – including the *Bundesamt für Migration and Flüchtlinge* (Federal Office for Migration and Refugees) – and enabled the BND to investigate more extensively in the domestic arena. The 2002 *Terrorismusbekämpfungsgesetz* (Act on the Fight against Terrorism) changed a range of laws regulating the work of agencies such as the BKA, the BfV and the *Militärischer Abschirmdienst* (Military Intelligence Service, MAD) as well as the Foreigners Act. It also aimed at facilitating the exchange of information between agencies; established the basis for the collection of biometric data; expanded the observation mandate of the BfV; and authorized the BND and the MAD to collect more air passenger, communication, financial and postal services data.

Changes in the *Sicherheitsüberprüfungsgesetz* (Law on Security Checks) reorganized the security screening of persons working in sensitive areas. Responsibility for standard screening was transferred to Berlin. Inquiries by federal and *Länder* agencies for the protection of the constitution (*Verfassungsschutzämter*), the BKA, the BGS, the secret services and the Federal Commissioner for Stasi Documents also became possible. Implementation of this Act into the legal system was regulated in the second Security Package. Another set of criminal law instruments was added in 2009 with the *Gesetz zur Verfolgung der Vorbereitung von schweren staatsgefährdenden Gewalttaten* (Law on the Prosecution of Preparations for Serious Seditious Acts of Violence), but the 2009 legislation was criticized for vagueness.[13]

Many of the newly created legal instruments have a preventive character. Since 2002, the security agencies have begun to systematically observe so-called *Gefährder* (roughly, "potentially dangerous persons") – neither suspects nor offenders in the legal sense of the terms. About 700 of these persons – most of them in Islamist milieus and many non-citizens, but also members of the left-wing and right-wing extremist scene – are currently observed.[14] This controversial notion blurs the boundary between legal and illegal behavior. Ironically, legal behavior or minor (e.g., drug-related) offences may make a person *less* suspect as a *Gefährder*, as a surprised public learned when it came out that Anis Amri, the perpetrator of the December 2016 attack in Berlin that killed 13 persons, had long been observed by various security agencies, had taken more than a dozen identities and had been known to commit precisely such minor infractions before his attack. Checks on the mobility of *Gefährder* and their deportation were facilitated in December 2016, and such persons can now be forced to wear an electronic ankle monitor; indeed, Bavaria has introduced the possibility of their de facto unlimited preventive imprisonment. In February 2017 the BKA introduced RADAR-iTE, new software for evaluating the risk of potential offenders.

A third focus is related to organizational reforms of Germany's domestic and international security architecture. In an immediate reaction to 9/11, SPD Minister of the Interior Otto Schily called for a central coordinating agency. The *Bundesamt für Bevölkerungsschutz und Katastrophenhilfe* (Federal Office for the Protection of the Population and Disaster Management) was established in 2004, as was the *Gemeinsames Terrorabwehrzentrum* (Joint Protection against Terrorism Center) in Berlin, which brought together analytical units of the BKA and the BfV. In March 2007 an anti-terrorism data base entitled the *Gesetz zur Errichtung einer standardisierten zentralen Antiterrordatei von Polizei und Nachrichtendiensten von Bund und Ländern* was up and running, coordinating the BKA and Federal Police, the BfV, the MAD, the *Landeskriminalämter* (criminal police of the *Länder*) and various other federal and *Länder* police and security agencies. Some of these coordination and centralization efforts remain disputed because they allegedly undermine the federal architecture of German security policy. However, Interior Minister Thomas de Maizière again called for a further strengthening of the BKA, the Federal Police and the Joint Anti-Terrorism Center in the wake of the Berlin attack.

The necessity of complementing such domestic security measures with international ones and even military operations was increasingly accepted.[15] Germany sent troops to Afghanistan in the wake of the 9/11 attacks in order to support peace keeping in the troubled nation and prevent a return of the Taliban to power. The success of this mission remains disputed, but it illustrated a clear shift in German defense and external security policy. As Minister Peter Struck (SPD) famously remarked at the time, German security in the post-9/11 era "also has to be defended at the Hindukush". In contrast, Germany again did not take part in the US-led "coalition of the willing", without NATO or UN backing, that invaded Iraq and toppled Saddam Hussein in 2003. Similarly, Germany abstained, together with China, India and Russia, from the 2011 Libya resolutions. Yet Germany continues to support joint efforts in security organizations such as NATO and the UN, or organizations increasingly entering the policy field such as the G8 and the EU (with its Space of Freedom, Security and Law anchored in the 2009 Lisbon Treaty and the Schengen area), some of whose members reintroduced border controls in the wake of the 2015 refugee crisis.

In recent years, the German army or navy has participated in – or continues to support – UN or EU operations off the coasts of Lebanon and Somalia, in Mali and in the

Mediterranean Sea. German authorities have engaged in various bilateral or multilateral coordination efforts with the authorities of other nations, including the US Proliferation Security Initiative against weapons of mass destruction. Many US initiatives, however, have led to tensions between Germany, the EU and the US – including the case of the Lebanese-German Khaled el Masri, who was kidnapped in a bus in Macedonia and brought to a secret facility in Afghanistan.

Conclusions

While debates on *external* security threats such as the new assertiveness of Russia have remained comparatively subdued, there can be no doubt that the issue of *internal* security – and specifically the threat of Islamic terrorism – remained very high on the public and government agenda in the "super-election year" 2017. *Länder* elections took place in the Saarland, Schleswig-Holstein and North Rhine-Westphalia. Federal elections that took place in September 2017 humiliated the coalition partners CDU/CSU and SPD of the outgoing government, and at least in part explain the triumph of the right-wing populist *Alternative für Deutschland* (Alternative for Germany, AfD) party. The linkage of the security issue with the refugee crisis of 2015, the sexual harassment of women by – allegedly – North African young men on New Year's Eve 2015 in Cologne, a series of terror attacks culminating in the Berlin Christmas market attack by a Tunisian in 2016, and the real or perceived failure of security agencies in offering "genuine" security in media and political discourse has left its mark on public debate and policy-making.

The attention paid to Islamic terrorism may, however, distract: (a) from the threat of right-wing extremism and terrorism such as the anti-Islamic *Pegida* demonstrations and the series of murders committed by the so-called National-Socialist Underground (NSU); and (b) from the blunders – or, worse, involvement of – security agencies in these crimes. The violent protests against the July 2016 G20 Summit in Hamburg suggest that left-wing extremists – here, the so-called Autonome[16] – may represent another underestimated internal security threat. Overall, Islamic terrorism is just one of many risks. There remains a considerable gap between "objective" security threats – as measured by crime statistics, the number of victims of terror attacks and the like – on the one hand and "subjective" or "perceived" (in)security threats – in the form of highly publicized crimes such as break-ins by roaming gangs of thieves – on the other.

The robustness of liberal democracy and legal institutions has been tested; the scope of the rule of law and of what is permissible in an open society has perhaps been stretched (comparable to the stress situation of the late 1970s). But a breaking point has arguably not been reached. The arsenal of "militant democracy" has been clarified and developed, but sometimes – as with the Federal Constitutional Court's recent decision *not* to outlaw the NPD – it has been used with evident caution. The boundary line between freedom and security may have shifted towards the latter, and a consensus on the need to strengthen the key providers of security – the state and its agencies – has now arguably reached even the Greens and the Leftist Party. But there is little reason to believe that the core of the *freiheitlich-demokratische Grundordnung* is in jeopardy.

Debate on the domestic use of the Federal Army (*Bundeswehr*) may serve as a final piece of evidence for this relatively sanguine evaluation.[17] The debate gained traction with 9/11 – and the widely discussed question as to whether a hijacked passenger aircraft headed, for instance, for a nuclear power plant or crowded football stadium could be shot down. The 2005 *Luftsicherheitsgesetz* (Aviation Security Act), which aimed to regulate this situation, was immediately qualified by the Federal Constitutional Court. However, constitutional interpretations on permissible domestic use of the Federal Army have evolved. There is agreement that it may be deployed in an emergency situation against organized insurgents that threaten the *freiheitlich-demokratische Grundordnung* (art. 87 (4) GG). The deployment of the *Bundeswehr*, the Federal Police (BGS) or the police forces of several *Länder* is also permitted by art. 35 GG in catastrophic events such as natural disasters or accidents. Based on a ruling by the Federal Constitutional Court, this may be applied to major terrorist attacks as well; but the use of the *Bundeswehr* against violent demonstrators is, for instance, ruled out by the Court.

Thus, on the one hand, Germany may have come a long way from 1962 – when it was considered highly problematic that then Senator of the Interior Helmut Schmidt called in the Federal Army to provide technical aid during the devastating spring tide in Hamburg – to the 2013 Elbe river flood situation when this was considered perfectly adequate. On the other hand, unlike her colleague in France, German Defense Minister Ursula von der Leyen has not yet subjected the people of Germany to heavily armed soldiers patrolling city streets or guarding sensitive objects. In fact, the downsizing of the *Bundeswehr* and the state of its equipment make it questionable that it could be of great help: when in the summer of 2016 a young man (who turned out *not* to have an Islamist background) killed nine persons in a shopping mall in Munich, von der Leyen initially put soldiers as far away as 200 km on alert.

Arguably, Germany has come a much longer way from a time in its history when *Gegen Demokraten helfen nur Soldaten* ("Only soldiers help against democrats") became the watchword of Prussian King Friedrich Wilhelm IV as he ended the 1848/49 revolution whose protagonists had offered him the Imperial Crown of a united Germany. A long way from what was achieved about 25 years later under the auspices of a deeply authoritarian regime, or from SPD Minister Gustav Noske's *Einer muss den Bluthund machen* ("One has to be the bloodhound") in the tumultuous early days of the Weimar Republic.

Notes

1 Conze 2009.
2 See overviews in Abels 2016; Riescher 2010.
3 Landfried 1985; Schlotter 1985; Sontheimer and Bleek 1998.
4 Böckenförde and Gareis 2014; Rudzio 2015.
5 Rigoll 2017: 42.
6 Rigoll 2017: 43.
7 Landfried 1985.
8 Rigoll 2017: 44.
9 Landfried 1985: 209.
10 Landfried 1985: 45.
11 Hirsch 1980.
12 Abou-Taam 2011; Kaim 2011.
13 Abou-Taam 2011.
14 Kretschmann 2017.
15 Kahl et al. 2011.
16 Pfahl-Traughber 2017.
17 Wiegold 2017.

References

Abels, Gabriele (ed.). 2016. *Vorsicht Sicherheit! Legitimationsprobleme der Ordnung von Freiheit.* Baden-Baden: Nomos.

Abou-Taam, Marwan. 2011. Folgen des 11. September 2001 für die deutschen Sicherheitsgesetze. *Aus Politik und Zeitgeschichte* 27, 9–14.

Böckenförde, Stephan and Sven Bernhard Gareis (eds.). 2014. *Deutsche Sicherheitspolitik*. Opladen: Barbara Budrich.

Conze, Eckart. 2009. *Die Suche nach Sicherheit: Eine Geschichte der Bundesrepublik Deutschland von der Gegenwart bis zu den Anfängen*. Munich: Siedler.

Hirsch, Joachim. 1980. *Der Sicherheitsstaat: Das "Modell Deutschland", seine Krise und die neuen sozialen Bewegungen*. Frankfurt/M.: Europäische Verlagsanstalt.

Kahl, Martin, Schmid, Johann and Schneider, Patricia. 2011. Strategien zur Bekämpfung von Terrorakteuren und Aufständischen. *Aus Politik und Zeitgeschichte* 27, 14–18.

Kaim, Markus. 2011. Internationale Sicherheitspolitik nach dem 11. September. *Aus Politik und Zeitgeschichte* 27, 3–9.

Kretschmann, Andrea. 2017. Eine wissenssoziologische Perspektive auf den "Gefährder". *Aus Politik und Zeitgeschichte* 32–33, 11–16.

Landfried, Christine. 1985. Legal Policy and Internal Security. In: Klaus von Beyme and Manfred G. Schmidt (eds.), *Policy and Politics in the Federal Republic of Germany*. New York: St. Martin's Press, 198–221.

Pfahl-Traughber, Armin. 2017. Autonome und Gewalt: Das Gefahrenpotenzial im Linksextremismus. *Aus Politik und Zeitgeschichte* 32–33, 28–33.

Riescher, Gisela (ed.). 2010. *Sicherheit und Freiheit: Perspektiven einer demokratischen Sicherheit*. Baden-Baden: Nomos.

Rigoll, Dominik. 2017. Streit um die streitbare Demokratie: Ein Rückblick auf die Anfangsjahrzehnte der Bundesrepublik. *Aus Politik und Zeitgeschichte* 32–33, 40–45.

Rudzio, Wolfgang. 2015. *Das politische System der Bundesrepublik Deutschland*. Wiesbaden: Springer.

Schlotter, Peter. 1985. Military Policy and External Security. In: Klaus von Beyme and Manfred G. Schmidt (eds.), *Policy and Politics in the Federal Republic of Germany*. New York: St. Martin's Press, 222–242.

Sontheimer, Kurt and Bleek, Wilhelm. 1998. *Grundzüge des politischen Systems der Bundesrepublik Deutschland* (Völlig überarbeitete Neuausgabe). Munich: Piper.

Wiegold, Thomas. 2017. Die Debatte um einen Bundeswehreinsatz im Innern. *Aus Politik und Zeitgeschichte* 32–33, 24–27.

8

PATTERNS OF UNCERTAINTY

Security practices and quality of democracy in Italy

Antonio Zotti and Vittorio Emanuele Parsi

Introduction: a round-trip ticket to normality?

For decades, questions about whether Italy can be deemed a *paese normale* (normal country) have concerned policymakers and analysts. The issue goes beyond every nation's inherent tendency to think of – and actively (re)produce – itself as a *unicum*. The yearning for a way to finally be regarded as "normal" has been kept alive by a nagging concern about being left behind on the path towards progress that fellow European and non-European countries have seemed to walk down with comparative ease (Samuels 2003). At the same time, based on their analytical perspective and the specific aspect under scrutiny, a number of observers have come to different conclusions about whether Italy should or should not be regarded as a normal country (Andrews 2005; Newell 2010; Valbruzzi 2013). Finding traits of (ab)normality does not entail that the country has always been in every respect normal or otherwise – and neither that its status cannot more or less suddenly change, as appears to be the case with Italy over the last few years. In fact, we will identify a number of distinctive historical circumstances and structural features that have made Italy a noteworthy case as far as relationships between security and democracy are concerned.

Perhaps the subject that has been most intensively examined, at home and abroad, is the political violence Italy endured during the period of social and political turmoil from the late 1960s through the early 1980s, known as *anni di piombo* (the lead years) (Weinberg and Eubank 2019; Eubank and Weinberg 1997; Della Porta 1992; Fritszke 1989). As we will see, those events continue to affect not only the country's justice system – the famed "Special laws" are still in force – but also its democratic identity.

Another established object of analysis is the Italian *Mafias*, powerful and increasingly widespread across the national territory. The Mafia has been successful in laundering and complementing the profits generated by their traditional criminal activities through "colonization" of regular economy, infiltrating legitimate businesses, stifling competitors and steering lenders (Scaglione 2016; Paoli 2007, 2004; Behan 1996). Not even political institutions have been immune to Mafia infiltration, at least according to a number of high-profile prosecutors, political parties with strong pro-judiciary platforms (e.g. the Five Star Movement) and sections of the Italian press. All of these over the last few years have hammered away at the notion that the upper echelon of government has "come to terms" with criminal organizations, at best in order to contain the power of organizations that have literally been able to "wage war" against the established order, or, at worst, to collude with them.

A perhaps less obvious effect on the security–democracy nexus is that generated by corruption, a practice so pervasive to have become a national cultural feature (Gambetta 2018); in this respect Italy is an "abnormal country" in comparison to major Western democracies (Della Porta and Vannucci 1999). Corruption as a form criminal conduct is unusually frequent in Italy because corrupters and corruptees regard it as relatively harmless and socially acceptable, and because Italy lacks effective mechanisms to prevent and counter it. Italy's judiciary is inefficient and endemically overburdened. Remarkably though, the ultimate repercussions of high levels of corruption on the country's prosperity and growth are less severe than expected, in all likelihood because the sharing of compromising information produces cooperation and entrepreneurship as a sort of "by-product" of corruption (Gambetta 2018). Nonetheless, corruption impinges on the economic liberties of citizens, creating unfair redistributive effects. Moreover, in the long run widespread corruption has the capacity to fuel social discontent with the political establishment, with public administration and with the judicial system. The most striking outburst of resentment – if somewhat inconsequential in terms of an actual solution of the problem (Della Porta and Vannucci 2007) – was triggered by the results of *Mani pulite* ("clean hands"): the 1990s' nationwide judicial investigation into political corruption which resulted in the demise of the party system that once identified the so-called "First Republic" – a party system based on the pivotal position of the centrist catch-all Christian Democratic Party and the exclusion from government of the Italian Communist Party.

That singular political equilibrium was not just the result of statesmanship and domestic constraints. It had as one of its major foundations the country's positioning within the post-World War II international order, as evidenced by its simultaneous collapse and transformation. Indeed, the importance of the international dimension is another distinguishing aspect of the relationship between security and democracy in Italy. Democratic institutions, practices and values could take hold in the newly established Italian Republic in part on account of external anchorages (*vincoli esterni*) provided by a set of relationships, institutional arrangements and regimes with more or less direct implications for defense and security policy – e.g. the alliance with the US and NATO membership, together with participation in the Marshall Plan and the European integration process (Diodato and Niglia 2017). Moreover, the country's strategic geographical advantage permitted Italy to access the Atlantic Alliance at bargain costs (Spotts and Wieser 1986). Yet, the country's strategic and ideological alignment – underpinned by said external anchorages – made the alternation of political parties in government virtually impossible, and straitjacketed the country's foreign policy.[1] Moreover, Cold War logic spread through national politics, polarizing political and social conflicts, and acting as one trigger of domestic terrorism during the *anni di piombo* (Chiampan 2018; D'Amato 2018).

Hence, at least as far as the security–democracy nexus was concerned, the common notion that, during the Cold War/First Republic period, Italy was a "difficult" democracy seems far from groundless (Spotts and Wieser 1986). Italy appeared to be a "democratic anomaly", that is, a country failing to meet widely agreed-upon requirements to sustain a healthy participatory democracy, even as it was able to maintain the ultimate good of democratic self-governance (Newell 2010). Famously, at the beginning of the Sixties, Almond and Verba (1963) even maintained that "[t]he political culture of Italy does not support a stable and effective democratic system". Traits such as the lack of "public" or "civic spirit" (Galli 1992) and the presence of "amoral familism" (Putnam 1993; Pizzorno 2001) were all pointed out as reasons why Italy was seemingly impervious to modernity and democracy (Cavalli 2001) – not just a backward democracy in comparison to the rest of Europe (cf. Agnew 1997).

Nevertheless, by the early 1990s, many of these peculiarities and their underlying conditions had largely worn off (Leonardi 2017). Admittedly, the "transition to normalcy" was a burdensome, unaccomplished and, in many respects, disappointing process (Morlino 2013; Gilbert and Pasquino 2000; Donovan 1994; Andrews 2005). Still, despite its residual quirks and faults, the country came to be regarded as comparable with other European political systems and developed industrial democracies (Leonardi 2017; Newell 2010). In fact, Italy would even be reputed "in most respects [as] no worse than other countries in [its] category and … in some respects much better" (Newell 2010: 2).

The partial success of Italy's transition, however, has not made the country a less interesting case-study as far as the relationship between democracy and security is concerned. Recently the attention of scholars and experts has shifted towards the measures and distinctive conditions under which Italy has faced the threat of jihadist terrorism and post-9/11 global and Mediterranean security settings (Momigliano 2018; Vidino and Marone 2017). Adjustments in the country's role within the Western security community have been thoroughly analyzed, especially controversies generated by increasingly attentive public opinion paid to Italy's engagement in international missions, as well as the presence of US and NATO military facilities on Italian soil. Experts have also looked closely at the impact of immigration on the country's democratic processes: with respect to public perceptions of large and more diverse population inflows; and with respect to securitization agendas pursued by public authorities and political parties (Ceccorulli 2019).

In fact, it was with the outbreak in 2014–2015 of the so-called "migration crisis" – one that caught on in a social and political context heavily conditioned by the enduring effects of the economic crisis – that Italy was again singled out as a litmus test of the shifts in the balance between democracy and security taking place on a continental and global scale. The Italian case has been regarded as a prototype of the link between changes in security threats and the emergence of populist and/or right-wing sentiments and policies (Brubaker 2017; Gherghina et al. 2013).

The emergence of these trends in Italian national politics had in fact started to be investigated well before the topic became one of the main concerns of current scientific and public debate (Ruzza and Fella 2009; Tarchi 2008, 2003). Yet only recently has Italy effectively come to serve as a showcase for the most recent "populist moment", even gaining, as a result of the 2018 general elections, the title of country with the "first (fully) populist government of Western Europe" – the so-called "government of change", backed by a Five Star Movement–(Northern) League coalition (Garzia 2019; Chiaramonte et al. 2018; Verbeek and Zaslove 2016).

The following issues have all become objects of close analytical attention and, at least in some quarters, of political worry:

- the country's markedly securitized response to the so-called refugee crisis;
- the rise to power of right-wing and/or populist parties and the implementation of restrictive security policy agendas;
- the spread of nationalist sentiments and xenophobic attitudes in public opinion;
- deviations from Italy's traditional alliance system; and
- the emergence of revisionist views of the European integration process and the (Western) liberal international order.

Some of these issues are best taken with a pinch of salt: the chaotic developments of the League-triggered government crisis, for instance, and the formation of a new, less (or differently) populist-oriented cabinet have been regarded as evidence of a loss of momentum, if not a proper setback, of the "populist/nationalist wave" that has swept across Europe (Kupchan 2019, Bastasin 2019, Scazzieri 2019; Accetti).

Clearly, the minutiae of Italy's politics hardly square with the general purpose of this handbook. At the same time, it seems reasonable to consider whether the ongoing political instability – also due to Italy's rekindled post-bipolarism coalition politics (Bull and Pasquino 2018) – and the fluctuating political fortunes of parties overtly advocating for more severe security policies as well as stretched constitutional rules and democratic practices actually do impact the underlying balance between security and democracy.

Accordingly, this chapter will review contemporary characteristics of the relationship between democracy and security in Italy, pointing out distinctive structural aspects, but also considering whether recent developments – including major political realignments in regime, and the international context – can be identified as effects of the crisis that has blighted the country over the last decade with respect to its democratic quality. Our aim is to assess whether and under what conditions Italy – from the specific perspective of the security/democracy connection – is to be considered, alternatively, a "backward" country; a political and institutional laboratory for future trends; an anomaly compared to other European democracies; or, finally, a specific variation of common trends already characteristic of other European democracies (Sandri et al. 2013). Such changes include the transformation of the country's role within the Western collective security system, the shifting nature and modus operandi of the terrorist threat, and the emergence of regional instabilities affecting immigration flows.

Security and democratic quality in Italy

This section reviews the circumstances, institutional arrangements and policy measures that underlie coexistence between: (a) conditions enabling Italians to live their lives without worrying about dangers and risks (deemed rare or absent pre Covid-19) to their physical safety, the protection of their personal and collective property, and the environment where they live and carry out their activities; and (b) the country's adherence to democratic criteria that guarantee the universal and full enjoyment of fundamental rights. Understanding this coexistence is crucial because Italy is exposed to a dilemma affecting all regimes that qualify, to a greater or lesser extent, as "good democracies"; that is, the need to cope with the condition in which democracies' vulnerability to actions directed against individual and collective security – assumed to be higher in democracies than in other regimes – is also the result of the liberties democracies ensure.

The "quality of democracy" is a theme that has been systematically explored for quite some time, and has become a major research topic in the field of political science (Munck 2016; Pinto et al. 2012; Campbell 2008; Morlino 2010; Diamond and Morlino 2004; O'Donnell et al. 2002; Altman and Pérez-Liñán 2002). Italy has been extensively analyzed from this perspective, both in comparison with other established democracies and with respect to dramatic changes the country's politics and institutions have undergone since the early 1990s. Researchers have also tested the hypothesis that Italy is a "democracy without quality", a hypothesis emerging from of the observation of phenomena such as populism, anti-politics and lack of trust in political institutions, sometimes in connection with the study of local political culture and the country's social capital (Tebaldi 2016; Morlino et al. 2013; Almagisti 2008; Morlino 2003).

A minimal definition of democracy requires the presence of the following features: universal, adult suffrage; recurring, free, competitive and fair elections; more than one political party; and more than one source of information (Morlino 1998). A *quality democracy*, or *good democracy*, is defined as a system that "accords its citizens ample freedom, political equality, and control over public policies and policy makers through the legitimate and lawful functioning of stable institutions" (Diamond and Morlino 2004: 22). Based on three different meanings of "quality" drawn from the industrial and marketing sectors, the good democracy approach establishes that such a regime is supposed to satisfy citizens' expectations regarding governance (*quality of results*); allows citizens, associations and communities to enjoy extensive liberty and political equality (*quality of content*); and provides a context in which the whole citizenry can judge the government's performance through mechanisms such as elections, while governmental institutions and officials hold one another legally and constitutionally accountable as well (*procedural quality*) (Morlino 2004: 22).

In reality, these definitions may benefit from incorporating the evolution of new forms of political belonging, which can no longer be entirely comprised within the notion of *citizenship*, as new participatory behaviors emerge by individuals operating within certain territorial areas – especially urban ones – even though those individuals do not hold the legal status of *citizen*. The growing presence of immigrants in Italy and their relative participation in some particularly inclusive processes may therefore call for the use of concepts such as *stakeholder* – a term more apt to encompass all those who depend upon or are affected by public policies implemented within a given territory.

In accordance with a pluralistic notion of its object of analysis, this line of inquiry assesses the *quality of democracy* along the following eight dimensions which are in fact often mutually correlated and linked by trade-offs and tensions. Six dimensions are procedural; that is, albeit content-relevant, they are concerned mostly with rules and practices.

1 The *rule of law*, based on the diffusion of liberal and democratic values.
2 Strong *bureaucratic traditions* of competence and impartiality and adequate institutional and economic means.
3 *Participation*, resulting in the effective possibility to influence the decision-making process.
4 Electoral *competition* between different political parties.
5 *Vertical accountability* – i.e. the obligation of elected political leaders to answer for their political decisions when asked by voters or constitutional bodies.
6 *Horizontal accountability*, which entails the obligation by officeholders to answer to other officials and to identify institutions carrying out a monitory role.
7 Respect for *civil and political freedoms* – and the progressive implementation of greater political, *social and economic equality* – is a substantive dimension of the good democracy.
8 The last characteristic of the good democracy is *responsiveness*, which bridges procedure and substance by indicating the extent to which the public policy output (including laws, institutional performance and public expenditure) corresponds to citizens' demands and preferences (Morlino 2004: 23ff.).

Moreover, in keeping with the complex nature of democratic regimes, this approach estimates the quality of regimes and draws its logical inferences by considering three facets that, combined, make the actual functioning of a democracy possible: the *democratic politics* – i. e. the structures and processes underlying political representation and government functions, including the capacity (even via subversion) of citizens to hold powerful private interests and agents of the state to account (Luckham et al. 2003: 21); the *democratic policies* – i.e. how the government's decisions affecting the members of a political community are programmed, discussed, decided on and implemented (Howlett and Cashore 2014); and the *democratic polity*, which can be thought of as the "metaphorical space" demarcating the "political sphere" (Palonen 2003: 175) – i.e. the aggregate of all aspects concerning areas of authority, sovereignty and territorial autonomy at each level of the organized political community, which, in the case of a democratic regime, coincide with the space within which people enjoy their liberties.

Accordingly, in looking at a national case such as Italy, this multidimensional analysis investigates how the physical space in which the country's authority reifies (the polity dimension), interacts with the political processes underlying the government's activity (the policy dimension), and eventually leads to binding decisions about individual and collective security (the policy dimension).

As far as the democracy–security nexus is concerned, this democratic quality approach allows us to ask and answer a number of crucial questions. Do structures and rules that control legitimate violence (in order to enforce order and protect security in Italy) comply with the rule of law? To what extent do Italian democratic institutions provide preventive – as opposed to repressive – security policy measures? What role do security issues play within the country's party competition? How has Italy's territorial governance been reshaped to keep up with shifts in the center–periphery relations that affect virtually all Western democracies?

Criminality and democracy in Italy

Illegality and crime are prominent components of Italy's assumed "uniqueness", at least in comparison to other Western countries (Paoli 2001). As a matter of fact, the two features have long been presented as key variables in understanding the country's past and present *in spite of* official figures suggesting that, over the last twenty years, crime and illegality rates have been within the Western European average, and far below those of the United States (Lastrico 2016). Nevertheless, looking beneath the normality rendered by statistics, research has identified *contra legem* phenomena that are specifically Italian, or that manifest themselves with particular intensity and frequency in Italy (Paoli 2001). Among the most enduring are powerful Mafias (La Spina 2014), corruption (Feldman 2019; Della Porta and Vannucci 2007) and an underground economy (Taiani 2018; Nuti 2018). Legislative and policy measures have tackled such crimes, leading to varying but somewhat successful results. Yet they remain distinctive features – even more so since they have effectively combined in recent years with "newer" crimes such as migration-related smuggling and trafficking (Magri and Villa 2018; Fasani 2016; Antinori 2012).

We now assess the effectiveness and democratic adequacy of policies designed to control and prevent infractions of the law in Italy. We draw on analyses of the country's main trends in criminal behavior offered by research programs such as the "Economic crises and quality of democracies in Europe – CriEc&Demo" project, led by Leonardo Morlino, as well as by authoritative research centers such as Censis, Fondazione Unipolis, and Demos & Pi. All process official data provided by institutions such as the Italian National Institute of Statistics, the Interior Minister and Eurobarometer.[2] In addition to the actual level of criminality registered in the country, perceptions of (in)security are also extremely relevant to our analysis, as they often reflect national politics – mostly through parties pandering to people's fears. Perception may also affect the stability of the democratic polity, to the extent that the national community comes to be regarded by domestic and foreign subjects as unruly and incoherent, and the state is regarded as unable to fulfil the basic function of securing freedom from danger for its population.

Limitations typical of analyses that use yearbook statistics also must be taken into account. For example, crime rates are affected by changes in criminal law that create new types of offence, decriminalize hitherto illegal behavior or modify the penalties associated with either. This specific difficulty draws attention to the "overflowing" character of Italian criminal law, under which new norms are created with relatively little consideration of how they are going to fit into the existing penal system (Manna 2016). Relatedly, Italian criminal law has been regarded as particularly prone to oscillating between powerful "pan-penalizing" trends and attempts to decongest the penal system (Chamber of Deputies 2017; Romano 2007). Statistics are also affected by variations in the resources and effort advanced against certain crimes (which increase the number of crimes registered), possibly in connection with an upsurge in public alarm irrespective of actual criminality trends – as evidenced by the criminalization of migration-related behavior (Militello and Spena 2015; Crocitti 2014). Moreover, a relatively low number of registered offences may also indicate a general lenience towards illegality or, paradoxically, a high crime rate – as wrongdoers tend to refrain from reporting crime to avoid drawing attention to their own illegal behavior. Finally, registered crimes may also amount to just a share of crimes actually perpetrated when victims lack confidence in the institutions that are supposed to deal with them.

The contrast between Italy's relatively low crime rates (see also Spain and Poland), on the one hand, and the higher rates registered in Europe's "most mature democracy" (the United Kingdom) and the most prosperous (Germany), on the other, may be regarded as evidence of this distortion (Lastrico 2016: 72). Such distrust may be generated by the judiciary's perceived lack of independence, high costs of access to the justice system and the excessive duration of judicial proceedings, as well as the police and judiciary's ineffectiveness or undue discretion. All of these issues have been at the center of lengthy public and political debates and numerous attempts to reform the Italian justice system (Piana and Verzelloni 2016).

Common crime

After a period of increase experienced from 1992 to 2007, the number of registered crimes in Italy has flattened out, in line with the EU average trend (Ministry of the Interior 2019a; Lastrico 2016). The timing of this moderate change of direction defies the assumption that, with the outbreak of the global financial crisis, crime rates would rise. Nonetheless, the two phenomena are probably too recent for existing statistics to show a correlation. Moreover, the socioeconomic effects of the crisis, also in terms of criminality, may not have come about yet. In line with traditional security concerns, in 2018 the most common cause of crime-related insecurity in Italy was still organized crime, even though terrorism still ranked high among the people's "global" reasons for anxiety (Bordignon and Di Pierdomenico 2019). At the same time, common crime – usually referred to in Italy as *criminalità diffusa* (widespread crime) – as well as urban decay, urban security and "highly-perceivable crimes" became increasingly prominent as themes of security narratives. This is evidenced by campaigns that recently led to new norms for public security and immigration – e.g. Decreto-legge 14 June 2019, n. 53; Decreto-legge 4 October 2018, n. 113; Direttiva del ministro dell'Interno N. 11001/118/7, 17 April. Their emphasis was not only on protection and control, but also on "public decorum" (Ministry of the Interior 2019b; Algostino 2019; Corriere della Sera 2019). Concerns about common crime have also entered the debate about the right to individual and collective self-defense, including deregulation of firearm possession; reform of the proportionality requirements for legitimate defense; and neighborhood patrols – often associated with fears against certain foreign national groups (Censis 2018).

These (in)security narratives have also been fueled by intense fears about crimes against property, in particular the prospect of being the victim of home burglary – one of the few instances where risk perceptions correspond to an actual increase in the number of illegal acts, even though a remarkable turnaround has taken place over the last few years (Bordignon and Di Pierdomenico 2019; Corriere della Sera 2019). As for crimes against the person, a duality between actual figures and perceptions is confirmed. In contrast to a nuanced reality in which, since around 2000, the likelihood of being murdered has sensibly fallen, the likelihood of physical aggression has increased. The number of registered sexual assaults has also increased (possibly as a result of the victims' increasing propensity to report the crime). As a result, people living in Italy have a disproportionately strong sensation of being in danger. Remarkably, while feeling that their personal safety is increasingly under threat, people turn out to be more prepared to endure their fears – offering ground for the hypothesis of a general resignation towards security concerns (Bordignon and Di Pierdomenico 2019; Censis 2019).

Organized crime

Very few developed countries besides Italy host large-scale, enduring criminal organizations that not only engage in profit-making criminal activities but also perform quasi-political functions where they operate, heavily influencing local economy and politics. As argued by Paoli (2014: 121), the Mafia is the epitome of organized crime and a distinguishing national feature, as evidenced by numerous dramatizations of Italian Mafia (Renga 2019; Leotta 2011). In fact, there is a substantial consensus among observers, security practitioners and policymakers alike that, over the last few decades, the transnational dimension has become the increasingly favored scale of operation for organized crime. This shift dilutes the connection between organized crime and Italy – although Italian organized crime has traditionally been at the forefront of this expansion (Savona and Riccardi 2018; von Lampe 2012; Albanese 2012; Finkenauer 2005). Moreover, in recent years the press, the judiciary and public opinion have stretched the concept of "Mafia" to encompass virtually all forms of illegal behavior aimed at achieving private gains to the detriment of the public good.

Despite the presence of foreign organizations operating within and across Italy's national borders and the aforementioned transformations, organized crime in Italy is still, for the most part and distinctively embodied in, native Mafias: in particular the Sicilian *Cosa Nostra* and other local groups; the Neapolitan *Camorra*; the Calabrian *'Ndrangheta*; and the Apulian Organized Crime, frequently identified with *Sacra Corona Unita*, which is in fact only one of its manifold components. The four groups vary in origin, structure, power and focus of operations. The *Camorra* first emerged as an urban phenomenon and has generally consisted of a number of gangs that form, split and re-form. *Cosa Nostra* was born as a means of private protection for rural landlords in the context of the newly formed Italian state, and stands out today for the very high-profile and flashy lifestyle of its bosses (Allum and Allum 1996; Williams and Savona 1996). Whereas the rich and powerful *'Ndrangheta* has a dominant position in the European cocaine market given its excellent relations with drug producers, Apulian Organized Crime's traditional core business has consisted in smuggling and trafficking (Europol 2013).

These organizations share certain common traits variably linked to the cultural traditions of southern Italy, even though the organizations themselves have long taken root in the rest of the country (Allum and Sands 2004). In general, Italian Mafias have combined reverence for a few interconnected tenets – i.e. family, power, respect – with a remarkable capacity for endurance and adaptability. They can effectively instill fear and assert power across the territories they control by the use of violence, as evidenced by the systematic intimidation of private firms and ordinary citizens in order to exact money, obedience and other resources – e.g. forcing local businesses to participate in money-laundering activities. More extreme and visible examples of Mafia power were the terrorist attacks, bombings and high-profile murders carried out in the early 1990s in response to judicial investigations that had started to provide solid proof of the existence of well-structured Mafia groups. In those years, Mafias posed a credible challenge to the Italian state's legitimate control of parts of its territory. Moreover, Italian Mafias have proved quite effective in using corruption to further their interests, developing considerable links with politicians and public institutions so as to gain protection and favors – such as access to public contracts – in return for electoral support.

As for their impact on the quality of democracy, Mafias pose a real challenge to one of democracy's essential components – the *rule of law*. They exacerbate common crime and all other forms of criminal behavior normally associated with organized crime in Italy – e.g. illegal trafficking in drugs and (toxic) waste, counterfeiting, racketeering, extortion, loan-sharking and collection of protection money. These activities have impinged to a significant extent on the country's public order. Indeed, as acknowledged by the Parliamentary Anti-Mafia Commission (1993), there have been periods when organized crime was so influential, and government institutions so inadequate, that the relationships between the two came to resemble relationships between two distinct sovereignties, each careful not to upset the other for no good reason. So-called "state–Mafia negotiation" is an enduring object of public debate, the target of judicial inquiries (not all of them built on exceedingly solid ground) and indignation associated with the notion of the state coming to terms with a criminal association.

Today, however, Mafias seem to have revised their goals and the means of pursuing them. Exerting effective territorial control through a virtual monopoly of illegitimate violence – assumed as a constitutive characteristic of organized crime (Andreas and Wallman 2009; Gambetta 1996) – seems to have become a relatively less appealing goal for Mafias, one that is pursued almost exclusively in the criminal groups' respective areas of origin. In other parts of the country and across their vast transnational criminal networks, Italian Mafias now prefer to keep a low profile and pursue primarily economic goals. Those goals are not limited to "making money", but extend to all aspects of the production and consumption of goods and services. This evolution started long ago – the phrase "Mafia business" was coined more than three decades ago (Arlacchi 1986) – yet the opportunities opened up by the globalization of Italy's national economy have accelerated the process (Sergi 2019). Infiltration into the legal economy has been instrumental in reinvesting the money obtained by criminal activity. Italian Mafias regularly work at a loss in order to eliminate competition, secure public tenders and seize businesses. When Mafias work outside their traditional territory their conduct is subtler but still harmful to the security–democracy nexus, as it systematically infringes upon economic liberties – generating additional costs in terms of prosperity and squandered social capital.

The government's response to the threat posed by Mafias has also had a significant impact on Italy's quality of democracy. Over the years, Italian authorities have equipped themselves with an outstanding array of investigative, preventive and judicial instruments, including specifically designed new offences such as: criminal association of Mafia type (which makes mere membership in such as organization a crime); the power of the public prosecutor and the police chief at the district level to investigate the standard of living, income and assets of suspected Mafiosi, their families and employees; and the power to seize assets before the conclusion of inquiries – independently of the judicial process ascertaining individual criminal responsibilities – even after the death of the people under investigation or when they act through straw men. Other exceptional powers include: the police's faculty to infiltrate agents; the Bank of Italy's oversight of financial transactions; and special procedural rules for judicial proceedings against Mafia crimes (in order to ensure an effective use of evidence, its circulation among connected trials, and the protection of confidential information) (La Spina 2014). In 2002, "Art. 41 bis" was incorporated into Italy's Code of Criminal Procedure. The law conferred on the Ministry of Justice the power to enforce stricter conditions of imprisonment designed for Mafia and terrorism convicts (*carcere duro*). In the same year, the crime of "indirect collusion with Mafia criminal conspiracy" was also established – despite doubts about the legal soundness of the new crime raised by many legal practitioners and scholars.

At the time of writing, Italian public discourse was being stirred by controversies relating to the extraordinary penalties and incarceration regime destined for Mafia members and the use of information provided by Mafia defectors – *collaboratori di giustizia* (collaborators), largely referred to as *pentiti* (repentants) in public discourse since the 1980s. In October 2019, the European Court of Human Rights (ECHR) ruled that Italy's tough prison regimes (as per the 41-bis law) for Mafia bosses, and terrorists) – specifically the norm disqualifying from penalty reductions convicts who refuse to cooperate with the justice system – constituted inhumane or degrading treatment, in violation of Article 3 of the European Convention on Human Rights (ECHR 2019). The outraged reactions of a number of major figures from within ruling and opposition parties as well as the judiciary (e.g. the incumbent Minister of Justice and the former national anti-Mafia public prosecutor) revealed widespread resistance to established Western legal standards. These reactions were based on the more or less explicit assumption that penalty reduction is conditional on the convict's genuine repentance (hence the term *pentito*), to be signaled by turning state's evidence – irrespective of the potentially principled motives that might prevent him from doing so (i.e. protecting his family from the Mafia's revenge).

The debate triggered by the role of Mafia collaborators offers further insights into the assumptions underpinning Italy's justice policy. Disregard for the informants' rehabilitation in the name of judicial effectiveness is not only out of line with the notion of good democracy *per se*, but is also indicative of a tendency to regard "certainty of punishment" as an overriding principle, not to be obstructed by a "misplaced" defense of civil rights.

Traces of a bitter retributive notion of criminal justice, aimed at inflicting punishment as vengeance for a criminal act, can be found in political platforms, some police and judicial practices and public opinion orientations. In fact, since the 1988 reform of the procedure code, adversarial elements have been transplanted into the classic continental inquisitorial structural of Italy's legal system so as to put the accused and prosecutors on a more equal footing (Panzavolta 2016).[3] Yet, according to a vocal and zealous conception of criminal procedure, every component of the judiciary should first and foremost pursue the goal of finding and upholding the truth, and punishing transgressors at any cost (especially in terms of individual rights) – hence the long-standing opposition to the separation of the career paths of public prosecutors (*magistratura inquirente*) and judges (*magistratura giudicante*).

Terrorism and political violence

Political violence – i.e. "a heterogeneous repertoire of actions oriented at inflicting physical, psychological, and symbolic damage to individual and/or property with the intention of influencing various audiences for affecting or resisting political, social, and/or cultural changes" (Bosi and Malthaner 2015: 439) – can be regarded as a distinctive character of Italy's democratic development. As pointed out by Weinberg and Eubank (1987), political violence has been extraordinarily recurrent in Italian public life, manifesting either as relatively spontaneous, wide-reaching *episodes of economic and political discontent* – including bread riots, anti-tax and anti-war protests – or as *terrorism* – understood by the National Consortium for the Study of Terrorism and Responses to Terrorism as "the threatened or actual use of illegal force and violence by a non-state actor to attain a political, economic, religious, or social goal through fear, coercion, or intimidation" (START 2019).

According to Eubank and Weinberg (1997), two waves of terrorist violence beleaguered the country in the twentieth century: the first set off by Fascist *squadrismo* in the aftermath of World War I, which would then shift towards Fascist state violence; the second prompted initially by neo-Fascist groups reacting against an upsurge in leftist student and worker protests, and later by left-wing revolutionary organizations between 1969 and the end of 1982. These two waves not only made Italy an exceptional case among Western democracies, but also a worthwhile setting in which to test the hypothesis that democracy does encourage terrorism.

The Fascist squads' extra-parliamentary and paramilitary strategy of violence against the Socialist Party and the left, and general brutalization, have been regarded as pivotal in the eventual upheaval of Italy's democratic regime, as well as the singular failure of the Italian liberal governments of the time to understand the new kind of social conflict emerging in the Po Valley during the period 1900–1915 (Albanese 2014; Corner 2002; Elazar 2000). The impact of the unprecedented experience of World War I fueled an anti-democratic response to the new world order that for a brief period took hold in Europe, both informing political platforms and filling with veterans the ranks of the Fascist movement (Morgan 2002). The fascist state's police apparatus generated steadily high levels of political violence, which would come to a head in the Italian Social Republic.

As for the second wave of political violence later in the twentieth century, the so-called *lotta armata* (armed struggle) has been regarded as the most important political phenomenon of the 1970s (Della Porta 1995). According to Moss (1989), the Italian case stood out not so much for the level of violence generated (still impressive by any metrics, such as number of victims, number of incidents, damage generated) as for the singular coexistence of comparably strong, though very fragmented, left- and right-wing groups. These groups pursued primarily political agendas without significant connections to legal political organizations such as political parties or labor unions, and not in open disagreement with them. The enduring impact of past waves of political violence is evidenced by the highly ideological approaches that permeate public and political discourses about them – reinforced by the lack of a shared memory of those experiences and of a coherent historiographic reconstruction of them (Battelli and Vinci 2014; Armani 2010; Ignazi 2005). Accusations of revisionism are frequently tossed around when the question of past and present political violence is brought up in Italy, while media representations and fictionalizations of those periods reflect the continuing collective trauma experienced in those periods (Poesio 2014; Colleoni 2012).

In addition to permeating the tone of the national public debate and affecting democratic participation and political representation in general, Italy's history of political violence strongly affects the current balance between security and democracy. A major vehicle for this enduring influence is a set of statutes – known as *leggi speciali* – passed at the height of the *anni di piombo*'s terrorist threat. Designed to protect the country's democratic order and public security – at the expense of personal and collective liberties if necessary – these extraordinary norms are still law of the land, despite revisions and adjustments. Pieces of legislation such as the *Legge Reale* (Act n.152/1975) and the *Legge Cossiga* (originally the Decree Law 625/1979) created new public order and terrorism-related offences, established terrorism as a crime-aggravating factor, reduced sentences for informers and expedited judicial proceedings. The Acts also enhanced police powers – e.g. the right to use firearms, to search and arrest suspects (in given circumstances with no need for a warrant) and to compel demonstrators to make themselves recognizable.[4]

This legislation attested to a tendency to forfeit civil rights protections for the sake of public security, a move that was to turn the "emergency mode" into a constant – albeit not necessarily dominant – feature of Italy's security policy. Later legislation establishing stricter controls on foreigners and their deportation based on their "social dangerousness" – e.g. the *Legge Pisanu* (Legge n.155/2005) – adjusted this orientation to the new threats posed by radical Islamic terrorism after the early 2000s, adding to the established trends of "governing by decree", with the executive systematically bypassing Parliament (Musella 2012). Over the same period, immigration and relationships with religious, ethnic and national minorities also underwent a process of heavy securitization (Colombo and Dalla-Zuanna 2019; Cesari 2009). Ever since, arguments for urgency, exception and necessity have become common currency across the Italian party system spectrum, as evidenced by the 2007 center-right government's crackdown on foreigners, illegal immigration and crime generating social fear (Cuono and Gargiulo 2017).

As pointed out by Gambetta (2013), since the *anni di piombo*, institutions and political parties have tended to frame every (illegitimate) use of force as being contiguous and akin to terrorism and subversion. As a consequence, violent movements and manifestations that once would have been classified as "a-political" or "proto-political" were pursued as if they were terrorist in nature. Disregarding the difference between mere riots and the use of violence for political purposes has served over the years as a means of delegitimizing forms of social conflict that contest the established order. We note the latitude enjoyed today by the judiciary and the police in setting the difference between turbulent protests and instances of genuine political violence. The tendency to blur the distinction between the two circumstances is also evidenced by recent legislation such as the so-called "Security Decree" and the "Security Decree bis", of 2018 and 2019 respectively. Combining in the same bill measures designed to tackle immigration, public security issues and terrorism is a procedural expedient aimed at simplifying the approval of such legislation and conversion into law by Parliament.

Immigration

Over the last few years, immigration has significantly affected the security–democracy nexus in Italy. Not unlike other Western countries, an unsettling tension has emerged between democracy and security. On the one hand, the native population demands protection against threats posed by incoming foreigners (frequently lumped together with resident minorities) to their personal and economic safety, but also to their societal security (Uzelac 2019). On the other hand, democratic quality is also determined by the willingness to let in people who have been pushed out of their countries by need, fear of persecution, danger or just by aspiration to a different (and possibly better) life, and to prevent their unfair treatment. In this regard, Italy's status as a good democracy depends not only on its compliance with principles of openness and hospitality, but also on its adherence to the international regimes and institutional set-ups actually in force to protect immigrant rights – especially the rights of those moving for humanitarian reasons.

Italy's participation in one such arrangement – the EU migration and asylum policy – has proved crucial to the relationship between security and democracy. The so-called migration crisis of 2015 stirred old questions about the democratic deficiencies of the Union at large, and whether or not participating in the integration process was in Italy's best interests – also in security terms. So-called populist and/or Eurosceptic forces have relied heavily on a narrative that sees Italy as a "frontier province" of the Union, left alone by core Member States, and the powers lurking behind them, to bear the brunt of the alleged "invasion" (de Haas 2007). That being so, Italy's participation in EU Justice and Home Affairs policies, including the Schengen Area and the Common European Asylum System, is not only a source of security threats but also detrimental to the sovereign right of the Italian people to decide for themselves. According to this narrative, while the freedom of movement principle prevents the Italian government from controlling the borders it shares with other Schengen countries, the Dublin System – designed to harmonize the asylum policies of its Member States – serves primarily as a way to turn Italy into a cul-de-sac for undesirable asylum seekers, seekers who are systematically suspected of being "bogus refugees" only trying to live off of the country's aid and welfare systems.

Additional factors such as the country's position in the migration cycle, its economy's long-standing structural problems (e.g. North–South divide, high unemployment levels, low average productivity rates, sluggish growth), the presence of strong criminal organizations and clientelism, corrupted forms of politics – as well the remarkable number of Italians who still leave the country in search of better life and work opportunities – may appear to vindicate the idea that migration is too big a security hazard to afford Italy the luxury of abiding by the criteria of good democracy. Do the conditions of the latest migration wave really justify its framing as an emergency, with all the attendant consequences for the quality of democracy produced by measures taken to cope with that "emergency" (Ceccorulli 2019)?

In fact, the Italian democracy is far from unfamiliar with the effects of immigration. Foreign workers have regularly moved into the country since the early 1950s, in part as a consequence of Italy's rapid economic expansion. Nevertheless, it was only from the late 1980s onward that the issue became the object of a proper policy commitment designed to manage human flows. Until then, Italy's immigration regime had been primarily characterized by irregular movements and economic informality – e.g. unreported employment, especially in small-scale manufacturing companies in the north, as well as in the agricultural, care and domestic sectors. This irregular movement and economic informality was in line with traditional untaxed, unmonitored activity in the national economy, resorted to as a way to bypass labor market rigidities, high labor costs and strict working regulations (especially burdensome for typically small- to medium-sized Italian businesses). It amounted to a free ride on lax enforcement by public bodies and low levels of social control. The presence of a dual labor market – where native workers are no longer willing to engage in economic activities regarded as undesirable, or decide to move in search of work – accounts for simultaneous needs: high levels of unemployment, especially in the South, and a need for immigrated manpower.

The need for a formal and "politically driven" management of this situation became apparent when the transition from emigration to immigration was complete (except for a residual role as provider of "reserve labor" for the rest of Europe, which in its heyday resulted in creation of the Common Market). Irregular migration started to exceed the dimensions of a mere "back-door" mechanism of labor recruitment, which only required periodic regulations aimed at catching up with inflows rather than controlling them. The first piece of proper immigration legislation was the *Legge Martelli* of 1990, which tackled irregular migration through a visa system designed to limit inflows while also strengthening border controls and providing for increased deportations. The Act extended the right to asylum to include people from non-Soviet bloc countries.

The more repressive measures that would come to characterize Italy's approach to immigration emerged as a result of the mass arrivals of Albanians in the 1990s. Ever since, combating irregular migration has become the primary goal. The *Legge Turco-Napolitano* of 1998 introduced reinforced measures dealing with entry, residence and expulsion, and sought to establish a system of "managed migration" via an annual immigration quota and a sponsorship scheme. Reception centers for irregular immigrants were introduced as a compromise between the right-wing parties' request that illegal entry be classified as a crime and the leftist government's opposition to this option. The deal did not prevent the issue from becoming markedly politicized. In 1998, the newly installed center-right majority passed the *Bossi-Fini* law, which signaled a much more security-driven approach, providing stricter measures against undocumented migrants, abolition of the sponsorship scheme, and the linking of work and residence permits in the form of a *contratto di soggiorno* that would last only as long as the contract of employment.

However, the move towards a greater emphasis on security and border controls only reaffirmed the importance of back-door recruitment to dodge these controls and meet the demand for foreign workers. The result was a growth in irregular entry, which added on hundreds of thousands of migrants living in Italy. Many of them had jobs but were nevertheless irregular due to their lack of work and residence permits. Paradoxically, the result was a series of *de facto* regularizations – in the form of an extraordinary addition of entry permits for foreigners already working in Italy.

The balance between security and democracy may therefore be connected with competition between the interests of two groups: on the one hand those who call for more migrants – an expression of traditionally strong socioeconomic drivers in the country's immigration regime; and, on the other, those who demand tighter regulation out of security considerations. The latter express their sense of unsafety generated by the presence of immigrants. This view combines with and overlaps with political arguments about a people's right to decide for itself with no meddling from outsiders – whether they are immigrants or inter- or supranational entities restricting national sovereignty. In fact, until a few years ago, the emphasis on external frontier controls and relations with sending states rendered the EU an ally of the restrictive policy camp. External measures – such as EU cooperation – allowed a national authority to bypass domestic ideas, institutions and entrenched interests limiting its capacity to control human movements and making it affordable to face the political and economic costs of a more rigorous policy implementation. Things changed when, with an unprecedented surge in the number of arrivals in 2014–2015, narratives favoring securitization of the phenomenon took hold in the political and public debates. Since then migration has been increasingly politically construed with reference to the destabilizing effects of migration on domestic integration, and with reference to the dangers for public order it implies (Huysman 2000).

What is particularly remarkable is that the country's traditional ineffectiveness – covering, at least in part, its actual unwillingness to cope with large inflows – started to be increasingly reframed as a consequence of serious flaws in the EU system of migration governance. As a consequence, the *vincolo esterno* (external constraint) – one successful in empowering technocrats and giving credibility to domestic reforms (Dyson and Featherstone 1996) – started to be perceived as both a source of insecurity *and* the instrument of an unjust treatment of the Italian people and Italy as a Member State. These narratives have been actively fed by parties across the national political spectrum, though with special vehemence from right-wing parties such as the *Lega Nord* (Northern League).

With the ascent to power of the *Lega Nord–Movimento Cinque Stelle* (Five Star Movement) coalition government, the securitization process transformed from discourse alone to norms and practices. The so-called *Decreto Sicurezza* (aka *Decreto Salvini*) and the *Decreto sicurezza bis* of 2018 and 2019 respectively epitomized the pre-eminence that immigration and security issues came to occupy in the League's platform, and the extent to which Deputy Prime Minister Matteo Salvini succeeded in acquiring recognition as "owner" of the issues (Pasquino 2019). Converted into law by Parliament before the fall of Europe's "first all-populist cabinet", the measures combined two originally distinct documents (the security decree and the immigration decree). While the procedural solution was designed to expedite their approval and conversion, it also reinforced the securitization process, creating a not-so-subtle connection between the security issues the *Decretos* regulate – e.g. illegal housing, home and land invasion, new powers to fine, remove and prevent access to certain urban areas and marketplaces by those people who pose a threat to citizens and urban propriety – and migration. The measures provided, *inter alia*, for:

1 the revocation or rejection of international protection (refugee status or subsidiary protection) when certain crimes are perpetrated;
2 replacement of the humanitarian residence – a two-year permit granting a right to access work and social services and public housing – with a set of one-year special permits;
3 the undermining of the Asylum Seekers and Refugees Protection System (SPRAR) – the network of small town local authorities responsible for the implementation of integrated reception projects; and
4 the detention of asylum seekers in hotspots and first reception facilities at border crossings for up to thirty days in order to ascertain their identity and nationality.

Police forces

As already mentioned in the introductory section, trust in institutions has been traditionally low in Italy in comparison to other European countries and developed democracies (Edelman 2019; Eurofound 2018). On average, Italians have showed little confidence in governmental bodies. The legislative and executive branches have ranked lowest in the population's trust (respectively as little as 21.5 and 22.3 percent in 2018, albeit on the rise by a staggering 15.2 and 8.5 percent in 2019). Even the usually more relied-upon judiciary has not fared exceptionally well either (46.5 percent in 2019, up by 9.4 points compared to 2018, but at a lower level than in previous years). Police and armed forces, together with the intelligence agencies, are among the relatively few exceptions. The President of the Republic is the only other government entity earning the trust of more than half of the Italian population.[5] According to 2019 surveys, all law enforcement agencies and services had an approval rate above 68 percent, and have fared much more consistently across the years than other institutions in terms of reliability in the eyes of the public (Eurispes 2019). The fact that institutions defending and enforcing order are trusted more than those called on to administer justice can be regarded as evidence that Italians' approval is inversely proportional to an institution's (perceived) degree of discretion in functioning – hence the even lower level of trust put in those operating in the more fluid and less comprehensible domain of politics (Marini 2018).

As is the case with other *istituzioni di garanzia* (guarantee institutions) (e.g. the President of the Republic), which gain the highest level of trust among governmental institutions, the assumed impartiality of those who have direct control of the means of legitimate violence is regarded as more important than the citizenry's ability to control and steer this basic function of the state through democratic processes. Apart from this consistent and sizeable "nominal capital" of trust, the reputation and dependability of the police in the eyes of the population vary according to their perceived proximity to national territory and their ability to smoothly interact with and assist local actors and institutions (e.g. families, parishes, unions, civil society associations, the local public administration).

As per Act 121 of 1981, the protection of public order and safety – i.e. prevention and repression of illicit behavior and vigilance over dangerous persons and activities; protection of citizens' personal safety and property; law enforcement; provision of assistance in case of public and private accidents; and, if requested, aid in the peaceful resolution of private disagreements – is the responsibility of the Ministry of the Interior. This Ministry coordinates the tasks and activities of *forze dell'ordine* (forces of order) without prejudice to their organizational autonomy. Police forces with general authority and nationwide remit comprise: the *Polizia di Stato* (the civil national police, reporting directly to the Ministry of the Interior); the *Carabinieri* (the national gendarmerie, since 2000 the fourth branch of Italy's armed forces, also responsible for contributing to "the defense of the nation" and safeguarding state institutions); and the *Guardia di Finanza* (a militarized police force responsible for customs, tax and treasury matters, preventing and contrasting financial and economic offences). Within certain limits, police forces also include specialized civil and military forces (i.e. the Penitentiary Police Corps and the Port Captaincies – Coast Guard), while other local agencies carry out specific sets of law enforcement duties and limited maintenance of public order (e.g. municipal police). As military police corps, *Carabinieri* and *Guardia di Finanza* are part of Italy's armed forces. They depend on the Ministry of Defense and the Ministry of Economy and Finance respectively with regard to budget, recruitment, discipline, administration and equipment.

Coordination among the police forces has traditionally been less than optimal, impaired by dysfunction, mistrust, diverging historic legacies, different corporate cultures and redundancies. In particular, relations between *Carabinieri* and *Polizia di Stato* have been strained, as traditionally no general criteria have been in effect to decide which corps will obtain on a particular occasion, given the perfect coincidence of their functions concerning public order and safety and criminal investigation (Barbagli and Sartori 2004). The need for more fine-tuned instruments of coordination also arise: on the one hand, from the distinction between metropolitan and countryside areas, which has long served as the rationale for the distribution of territorial competence between Italy's civil and military police respectively (becoming less salient from the second half of the twentieth century with the boom in material and immaterial communications). On the other hand, division into "zones" with quasi-exclusive competence of either force has proved far from effective and risks reinforcing self-referential trends (Battistelli 2008). Nevertheless, to this day a disparity in numbers between larger and smaller towns remains much greater for the *Polizia* than for the *Carabinieri*.

In order to find a solution to this problem, the aforementioned Act 121 established mechanisms and certain powers meant to enhance the Minister of the Interior's ability to effectively direct and coordinate police forces. The Department of Public Safety was created, designed to provide for the technical-operative coordination of the police forces, upon which depends the Office of Police Coordination and Planning, directed by a prefect and composed of personnel drawn from *Polizia di Stato, Carabinieri* and customs services. A Data Processing Center was also created, accessible by all police forces, as well as the National Committee for Public Order and Security, a consulting body assisting the Minister of the Interior in the exercise of his functions of direction and coordination. The National Committee for Public Order and Security is composed of the top elements of the three forces – specifically the political aspects thereof, as technical aspects fall largely within the remit of the Chief of Police. Other "inter-force offices" include the Supervision of Antimafia Investigations, the Central Anti-Drug Unit and the Central Directorship of the Criminal Police Unit (Barbagli and Sartori 2004).

Research conducted among intermediate-level officers has revealed that the official policy of cooperation between police corps is actually pursued at the "basic" level and "on the street", much more so than at higher ranks of their respective organizations. Moreover, a not-always-functional competition among (and within) forces is also exacerbated by an often perfunctory application of management techniques originally designed for the private sector. It is also exacerbated by iteration of performance evaluation systems that overlook the inherent complexity of "producing security", and fail to factor in features that are not immediately quantifiable, such as the inherent "political" nature of policing (Battistelli 2008; Palidda 2017). Nevertheless, there also exists a more or less formal division of labor between the three forces, with specific areas of competence and/or specialization: *Carabinieri*, for instance, have exclusive jurisdiction over assignments such as surveillance of military bases and airports and counterespionage services. *Polizia di Stato* is solely responsible for controlling immigration and preventing illegal entry. *Guardia di Finanza* has evolved into Italy's primary agency against drug trafficking through its border patrol activities (Ministry of the Interior 2019c).

According to the classification drawn up by Calaresu and Tebaldi (2019), the Italian police's structure, functions and source of legitimacy are still largely based on a model characterized by (1) a high degree of centralization, and (2) an orientation towards governance – i.e. responsibility for aspects that go beyond law enforcement and the maintenance of public order. Those aspects include administrative duties pertaining to virtually every aspect of social life, including, among others, control of public health and commercial activities, supervision of public areas and the issuing of permits.

As for the distribution of competences among levels of government, the organization of national police forces across the country hinges primarily on provinces, Italy's second-level administrative division. A parallel territorial organization of military police corps exists, based on (inter-)regional commands. At the level of provinces responsibility for the protection of public order and security lies with the *Questore* (police commissioner), a *Polizia di Stato* superintendent who oversees and coordinates all police forces performing these duties. The *Questore* manages the technical and operational aspects of policing, in pursuit of the goals set by the *Prefetto* (the provincial representative of national government), who ensures, at least formally, that the center keeps a steady hold on public security and order issues. In order to gain a more accurate understanding of the local state of affairs, since 1981 the Prefect has availed himself of the Provincial committee for the protection of public order and security, an advisory body including: the mayor of the province's capital municipality; the president of the province; the district commanders of the *Carabinieri* and *Guardia di Finanza*; the mayors of any other municipalities involved; and, if necessary, any other public security local authority, state officials and members of the judiciary.

Yet, the Italian central government's substantial failure to run the country as a strong centralized state – together with the municipal and regional governments' successful intent to gain larger *de facto* responsibilities in urban security matters (mostly in the northern and central areas of the country) – ultimately led, in the second half of the 1990s, to the devolution of a significant share of administrative powers and local policing competences. While the national executive remained in charge of dangerous, far-reaching crimes (e.g. corruption and offences committed by criminal organizations), local governments effectively shifted the boundaries and the main focus of security policy with their newly acquired competences, concentrating their efforts on local and mundane crimes, among them routine petty theft, mugging, burglary and drug dealing – all of which ended up being classified under vague categories such as "urban disorder" that would soon feed feelings of insecurity among citizens (Selmini 2017).

When by the end of the 2000s the central government started to retrieve much of its power in the domain of urban security (now largely ruled by national law and related Minister of Interior decrees imposing strict guiding principles for local authorities at all levels), the emphasis put on urban disorder, public decorum and street violence was largely retained. The Ministry of the Interior's "tough" approach to crime hinged on more stringent control measures and criminalization of behavior, including conduct that had previously been regarded as a matter of social marginality, being handled by social policy means. The tighter grip on local government police activities was put into place, among other measures, through the so-called *patti per la sicurezza*. These are (largely one-sided) agreements between the national executive on the one hand and regional, provincial and municipal authorities on the other, stipulating the terms of local safety plans and attributing to local prefectures a leading role in defining priorities and means to be adopted.

Italy's distinctive centralization–decentralization dynamic combines with a police orientation towards governance and a shift from the traditional notion of public security to that of urban security as the pre-eminent rationale for policing. First, in addition to public security, *Polizia, Carabinieri* and *Guardia di Finanza* all perform investigative duties, acting as *polizia giudiziaria* under the authority of the judiciary. They investigate crimes, search for perpetrators and collect evidence to be used in court, in addition to other duties linked to the enforcement of criminal law (such as implementing warrants). Specifically, they support the activity of, and collaborate with, the Public Prosecution Office, which is solely responsible for initiating and directing investigations in addition to taking charge of criminal proceedings. Second, national police forces participate in the enforcement of administrative law, often by means of specialized structures, including the issuing of permits and the imposition of penalties.

As far as this facet of policing is concerned, local corps (e.g. *Polizia provinciale* and *Polizia municipale*) play a major role as they are in charge of an array of areas – including commercial transactions, construction regulation, public health and safety, the enforcement of the driving code, and urban and rural activities in general. These forces increased in number and power from the 1990s through the first half of the 2000s, the increase in numbers and power coinciding with the expansion of the role of cities in local governance of crime. The constitutional reform of 2001 further reinforced the regional level of government competences concerning the coordination, organization and professional training of municipal police, who remained, however, dependent on the municipality (Selmini 2017). As a result, while endowed with comparatively minor powers in terms of maintenance of public order, local police may have an impact on a local population's perceptions, especially in terms of "urban security" – that is, the condition in which the state guarantees not only personal safety and the protection of private property *but also* the possibility of fully enjoying the urban space and a satisfactory quality of life. Municipal police have greater flexibility, the capacity to perform both proactive and reactive roles, a deep knowledge of local contexts and close relationships with citizens.

In general, as a response to the emergence of this broader, more nuanced and comprehensive notion of security, the Italian police have been trying to meet as well as possible new security needs typical of a post-industrial society (which have to do, among others things, with environment, people's self-fulfillment, their expressiveness, the possibility of critical political participation, and private and public aesthetics). Yet, post-materialistic concerns have not replaced "rougher" aspects of (in)security such as the effects of the decay of an urban space increasingly deregulated, no longer structured by social norms and common experiences, and often exposed to various forms of exploitation. The Italian police have tried to respond to these fears by increasing their presence on the streets – or at least their visibility – and by offering an approachable point of access to the state as a security provider.

Closely related to the notion of urban security, *presidio del territorio* (which conveys the idea of "defense of *proximate space*") has significantly become a buzzword among Italian policymakers, municipal administrators and citizens' associations, indicating the authorities' commitment to a widespread activity of risk management in a range of areas: from human and natural disaster relief, in support of civil protection and the armed forces (Alexander 2010) to petty crime; indeed, to any circumstance triggering moral panic or social unease. In this context, the Italian police have been serving as a visible proxy of the state within society, enacting traditional outreach practices carried out by rule of thumb by *Polizia di Stato* area patrol units (the so-called *autoradio*) and mobile squads (*squadra volante*) as well as by the over 4500 *Carabinieri* stations located throughout the national territory. In addition, police forces have implemented fledgling community policing strategies (e.g. the *poliziotto/carabiniere di quartiere*) (Battistelli 2008).

Yet, unlike in other European countries, attempts to create a more comprehensive reform of the relationship between police forces and local levels of government, informed by notions of the "subsidiarity" (i.e. the principle that a central authority should only perform those tasks that cannot be executed at a more local level), has proved of little avail. The central government – the Ministry of the Interior in particular – has resisted these projects, while citizens' potential participation in some police tasks has been thwarted not only by lack of coordination and resources, but also by the very sense of public alarm pervading public discourse, a discourse often filled with intolerant and racist tones.

As in other parts of world, in Italy realignment of relationships between the public and the private spheres – combined with the shift from a "negative" conception of security (i.e. mere law enforcement) to a "positive" conception of security aimed at creating conditions conducive to better standards of living (Ceri 2003) – has resulted in the pluralization of policing. "Urban security services" have been complementarily provided by agencies other than traditional police forces (Salmini 2017; Battistelli 2013). On the one hand, the role of private security companies has increased as a consequence of cuts in public spending which have led central and local administrations to contract services and outsource certain functions in response to growing demands for private security by ordinary citizens and companies. According to Battistelli (2013), private security has also set a qualitative benchmark that has, at least to some extent, influenced the public security agencies' organizational culture and behavior. It is also for this reason that the police attitude towards crime has shifted from an emphasis on law enforcement and a reactive approach – primarily aimed at restoring the violated order – to an emphasis on the victim (the "client") and the proactive prevention and/or prohibition of damage.

On the other hand, as maintained by Selmini (2017), the ongoing process of centralization of local government – through Prefects' narrower control, the implementation of administrative orders and "security contracts" – has very much limited the impact of privatization of some (para)police activities. Finally, the police have also been supported by other government security agencies – specifically the armed forces – in their task to protect collectivity, maintain public order and fight crime.

The first experiences of *blurring* between the police and the armed forces date back to the 1990s, when the *Vespri Siciliani* operation was carried out against Mafia in Sicily, vastly supported by national public opinion. However, it is only since the launch of the *Strade sicure* (Safe streets) operation in 2008 that military instruments (mostly the Army) have been used to prevent crime in Italy. The operation – currently the Army's most onerous in terms of soldiers, vehicles and equipment – deploys over 7000 troops in more than 50 cities. Its main activities consist in providing stationary surveillance of sensible targets, as well as patrolling, reconnoitering and surveilling migrant reception centers (Ministry of Defense 2017).

The *Strade sicure* operation has been the object of a long debate about its effectiveness – in particular, whether its success should be measured by the number of offences actually prevented/stopped, or rather by the degree to which people feel reassured by the state's vigilant presence at the urban level through its military embodiment. Given its (necessarily) narrow legal premises, as well as the frustration that both the police corps and the Army have occasionally expressed for the distortion of their respective *raison d'être* and expertise, *Strade sicure* remains problematic. Yet the operation has also raised questions about whether a de-differentiation between the military (ideally responsible for the state's *defense* from external threats) and the police (in charge of internal *security*) is to be regarded as a safe and acceptable process. This distinction had long been regarded as a basic prerequisite of the democratic identity of a country – even more so in light of Italy's past experience of military conspiracies. The issue also has an international component, connected to Italy's engagement in global missions, which is the theme of the next section.

International operations

Both the armed services and the police forces have benefited, in terms of public opinion support, from their engagement in operations addressing issues of national security. To an increasing extent these issues straddle the internal/international divide (Friesendorf 2016). This is particularly true with regard to so-called "second-generation" international operations, operations characterized by: (1) a holistic approach to conflicts, based on comprehensive mandates with a high impact on the social, political, institutional and economic spheres of the host country; and (2) a progressive interaction of peacekeeping, peacebuilding, and capacity- and institution-building functions, with an emphasis on the nexus between peace and development (Mackinlay and Chopra 1992). Over the years, such operations have evolved from the relatively passive role of monitoring individual host state police officers to supporting the reform and reorganization of entire police agencies, and, exceptionally, standing in for ineffective or absent local police and performing law enforcement functions while establishing new capacities.

Italy has engaged in over thirty ongoing operations, deploying almost 6000 police and armed forces personnel, mostly across an area spanning the Maghreb to Afghanistan through the Balkans, the Middle East, the Horn of Africa and the Persian Gulf. Italy has thus established itself as a leading contributor to the highly complex and specialized sector of international policing (Carati and Locatelli 2017; Ruffa 2016).[6] This distinguishing role affects Italy's security–democracy nexus. For example, a critical phase of international policing – such as police training, which involves purging, recruiting, vetting, depoliticizing and training personnel, coupled with provision of infrastructure and equipment – is part of a broader peace- and institution-building process aimed at reforming, restructuring and rebuilding effective, legitimate and sustainable indigenous police and law enforcement capacities for the recipient country. This "transformational approach" to police-training activities is consistent with a democracy-assistance agenda for post-conflict societies insofar as it rests on *democratic policing* values and practices.

Democratic policing complies with the same criteria expected from police forces in established democracies, namely accountability to the people, reliance on public support, transparency and legitimacy (Wiatrowski and Goldstone 2010). According to Foradori (2018), one of the main reasons for Italy's success in this regard is the *Carabinieri*'s dual nature as a gendarmerie, together with its specific skills, training, equipment, experience, work ethos and motivations. The *Carabinieri*'s nature and skills have made the corps capable of operating in an environment still unstable and possibly in need of high-end military capacities (combat, peacekeeping or counterinsurgency), while also performing police tasks such as crowd control, criminal investigations, procuring and securing evidence or making arrests.[7] In addition to filling the "security gap" between the cessation of military hostilities and the re-establishment of civil authority, *Carabinieri* can also rely on highly specialized competences (as in the case of cultural heritage protection) and excellent skills in the training of local police personnel and international officers.

Hence, international policing can be regarded as a niche that offers a country with relatively limited foreign policy capabilities the opportunity to generate distinctive added value to itself and its allies (Tercovich 2016). Italy has not only operationalized its domestic experience of the security–democracy nexus embedded in the *Carabinieri*'s capabilities and capacities, turning the agency into one of its (few) foreign policy strong suits; it has also promoted liberal democratic principles and institutions in a crucial area such as international policing. As pointed out by Caffarena and Gabusi (2017), among the assumptions underlying foreign policymaking in Italy is the notion that democracy promotion, together with state responsibility, is a tool to foster security and development. Hence, to the extent that the democratization of transitional and post-conflict countries helps create a more stable and a safer international system, and acknowledging the fact that the latter is a precondition of (good) democracy, it is reasonable to expect positive domestic feedback with respect to Italy's quality of democracy as a result of the country's international engagement.

The reputation gained for the country by its international policing operations reinforces the position of peacekeeping as a core building block of Italy's post-1989 strategic culture. That strategic culture has enhanced and combined with two post-World War II components: multilateralism and the country's strong relationship with the United States (Marrone and di Camillo 2013). The emergence of terrorism as a major threat to national security, and terrorism's connections with the prolonged social and political upheavals that have plagued the Mediterranean and the Middle East area (an increasingly prominent focal point of Italy's foreign policy), has resulted in a reassessment of the nation's foreign policy priorities. The military instrument has been reconceived as a predominantly expeditionary, mission-oriented force. It operates within constraints imposed by Italy's traditional scarcity of resources in this policy area and resistance offered by deep-rooted strategic cultures perpetuating themselves through the socialization of political elites (Coticchia et al. 2016).

The need to move beyond a purely military intervention framework has been narratively framed – especially with reference to the International Security Assistance Force in

Afghanistan – within the more general foreign policy goal of facing new security threats through the promotion of human rights and democracy, although relatively few or mixed effects have resulted in terms of specific measures and initiatives (Caffarena and Gabusi 2017). The promotion of democratic governance, human rights protection and, more generally, the preservation of peace have constantly informed the domestic political debate, resulting in a strong normative orientation of the country's foreign policy, most conspicuously evidenced by active participation in international operations. In this context, the commitment to international military operations has always been framed in terms of peacekeeping and human rights protection. Utilitarian considerations are no stranger to the foreign and defense policymaking process – especially in light of Italy's geographical location and its scant endowment in terms of energy resources (Carati and Locatelli 2017).

However, as maintained by Ruffa (2016), even when strong economic reasons and broader national interests are taken into consideration – as was the case with the EU Naval Force (NAVFOR) Atalanta project and the NATO-led Operation Unified Protector in Libya – Italy's foreign policy obeys a logic of appropriateness. "Being there" is primarily a way to meet the perceived expectations of allies and partners about the country's commitment to multilateralism and the values underpinning the international order – as well as preferences expressed by domestic public opinion. In this sense, the idea of followership as a driver of the Italian engagement in international operations (Carati and Locatelli 2017) bridges the gap between material and ideational aspects; the pursuit of international prestige (credibility and reliability) by a middle power such as Italy is primarily undertaken through engagement in humanitarian actions and multilateral strategies.

The strong normative frame of Italy's foreign and defense policy does not imply that decisions are taken a-critically or without democratic control. Italy's participation in Operation Iraqi Freedom, for instance, was largely consistent with the pillars of Italian strategic culture, with a particular emphasis on the alliance with the US. Yet, the decision-making process that led to participation in Operation Iraqi Freedom proved exceptionally controversial. Italy's involvement was staunchly opposed by public opinion, which broadly perceived the mission as illegitimate. It was also opposed by center-left political parties. As argued by Coticchia (2015), public support for military interventions abroad has been more likely when the engagement has been framed as a strategic narrative, so as to enhance the perceived legitimacy of the military operation. Strategic narratives have proved to be "successful" when the following elements were present: bipartisan consensus over central values (peace, humanitarianism and especially multilateralism); a limited degree of violence on the ground; constant attention to non-military aspects; and the absence of effective counter-narratives.

In fact, it is only since 2016 – when the first *legge quadro* (comprehensive law) on military missions was finally adopted – that Parliament's oversight powers and the type of missions allowed were set down in a structured legal form, superseding the manifold and ambiguous procedures previously in force. As per Article 11 of the Constitution, "Italy rejects war as an instrument of offense against the freedom of other peoples and as a means of resolving international disputes." Yet, beginning with the 1990–1991 crisis in Iraq, these constitutional constraints have been regularly bypassed by denying the nature of "war" associated with military interventions abroad. Interventions were instead cast as "police operations" aimed at providing a contribution to multilateral institutions, and were therefore deemed in compliance with the second part of Article 11, providing for the exceptions to the anti-war stance of the Constitution. With the entry into force of Act 25/1997, parliamentary approval of the executive's deliberations on security and defense issues assumed by the cabinet became obligatory. Nevertheless, the types of deliberation actually required to receive legislative approval, as well as the nature thereof, remained unclear, enabling the executive to effectively circumvent parliamentary (*ex ante*) control.

Accountability has improved to some extent since 2001, when a parliamentary resolution introduced the binding practice of holding a vote on the law decrees whereby the missions were (re-)funded every twelve or six months. In practice, oversight has remained limited because the decree does not allow for proper and detailed debate, and little information has been provided to the legislature about detailed funding, rules of engagement and tasks. Moreover, the (re-)financing requests for all missions are submitted by the cabinet in one single bill. It is therefore virtually impossible for Parliament to vote against single missions. In fact, pre-2016, parliamentary approval on a new mission often occurred after its launch, by means of a vote on an executive decree. Today Parliament gets to debate and vote on each operation prior to its start (Coticchia and Vignoli 2018).

The pre-2016 procedure can be regarded as detrimental to democratic quality, as the government–opposition dynamic was in fact restrained with regard to parliamentary scrutiny. Expectedly, parliamentary support for military operations decreased on average after the new procedure was established (Coticchia and Vignoli 2018). This is consistent with the expectation that parties may have different opinions about each mission, depending on a number of factors: the aim of the operation; the types of troops and military assets deployed; the kind of activities undertaken (e.g. combat tasks, humanitarian rescue, peacekeeping, etc.); the number of casualties and "collateral damage" anticipated; and the multilateral nature of the mission. On the other hand, opposition parties may choose to offer a "strategic" dissent in order to gain visibility and media coverage for the vote and to undermine the government's public support.

However, both before and after 2016, the voting patterns concerning international military operations have been characterized by bipartisan consensus – all the more so when operations have been conducted within the UN multilateral framework and have consisted of non-combat activities. An almost permanent agreement between center-left and center-right main parties has prevailed. A decreased level of support for such missions has been evident towards the far-left end of the political spectrum (a little less so on the far right, owing to the presence of "nationalist parties" that conceive the deployment of armed forces abroad as a symbol of national pride). Nowadays far-right populist parties often take an isolationist stance on security and defense policy (Verbeek and Zaslove 2015).

Conclusions: a "normally" inadequate country

No amount of critical insight is likely to dispense any time soon with the impressive array of clichés through which Italy is still perceived and represented (Casillo 2006: 83–143). Benevolent or not, these commonplaces are usually deemed undesirable. They offer a static and oversimplified image of the country, if not just a false one, that can result in discrimination and misunderstanding. Even if this is the case, stereotyping does not represent, *per se*, an abnormality in social behaviors or a disvalue. In fact, we all seem predisposed to recognize differences and to develop ideas about others and their behavior based on our understanding and expectation of self. Hence, stereotyping may serve as a process or method of becoming more familiar with new realities.

Accepting this reality, however, does not entail attesting to clichés' conformity to "real facts". Indeed, at least in educated circles, the notion that national identities have an essential basis has been increasingly questioned. Instead they are regarded as creations, as narratives that arrange selected cultural elements in order to generate togetherness (Bhabha 1990). In fact, even essentialist conceptions of national identities themselves have been seen as rhetorics to which people and social movements resort in order to advance their agendas (Calhoun 1994). No matter how inaccurate, stereotypes are suited to the contrastive context in which national identities are built: people turn to hackneyed ideas of the other as they are forced to contend with typified images of themselves as presented by other groups (Rezende). Because national identities are generally based on the assumption of a uniform, commonly shared culture, stereotyped images help elaborate homogeneous national figures – e.g. "the Italian" – as opposed to equally homogeneous others. Stereotypes reinforce the idea that nations have a "character". Among the most recurrent commonplaces about Italy is the persuasion that the country's alleged national "character" includes the ability to scrape by in any situation, no matter how serious.

Every time an Italian oddity is reacted to with the argument that "after all, we are in Italy", the assumption is iterated that "there is an *Italian* way of doing things, which seems to consist of crafty muddling through and a healthy disrespect for the law and institutions in general" (Foot 2014: 6). The tacit assumption that many problems in Italy can be disregarded on the basis of a *eppur si muove* – "nevertheless it works" mentality (Bull and Rhodes 1997) – is even more significant when applied to an aspect so delicate as the democracy–security nexus. There is a striking tension between, on the one hand, the dilemmatic nature of the relationship between democracy and security and, on the other, the appeal to expediency which informs the idea that the country will eventually find a way to "make do".

Is this attitude to be regarded as a feature of a matchless Italian national character? Apparently, a "colorful" country like Italy lends itself to being treated as the unchanging result of unique circumstances. In fact, there are convincing arguments against the customary analytical treatment of Italy as a *sui generis* country. As argued by Anderson (2014), Italy might well be "a disaster", but "not an anomaly within Europe. It is much closer to a concentrate of it." Evangelista (2017) as well, while accepting the idea that Italy has managed, with guile and deception, to pass from one crisis to the other, disagrees with the idea that this makes the country one of a kind, not comparable to its European and world partners.

The stereotype of a country cunningly muddling through problems instead of solving them (or perishing in the attempt) in fact reveals a significant ambivalence. According to Herzfeld (1997), when we look behind the façade of unanimity that clichés seem to buttress, we see that they are not just ageless truisms, to be confirmed or refuted; instead, stereotypes are the result of a ceaseless re-elaboration of the meaning of national identity by the government *and* regular people. Although citizens often contravene official ideology in reshaping national identity, citizens and government actually share common ground that Herzfeld (1997: 3) accounts for through his notion of cultural intimacy: "those aspects of a cultural identity that are considered a source of external embarrassment but that nevertheless provide insiders with their assurance of common sociality." Self-stereotyping offers citizens a sense of "defiant pride in the face of a more formal or official morality and, sometimes, of official disapproval as well." This notion of clichés offers a rationale for the apparent inconsistency between the actual ranking of the Italians' most pressing concerns – among which, according to the 2018 Censis report, crime comes after unemployment, tax evasion and excessive fiscal burden – and the appeal that securitizing narratives and measures seem to exert on voters.

The most recent reforms of the judicial system championed by the *Movimento Cinque Stelle* resonate with a retributive conception of justice that seems to pander to the people's indignation. It is also at odds with the Constitution, and therefore the rule of law, leading to the creation of illiberal criminal law (Dolcini 2019). Migration is exemplary of this ambivalence.

On the one hand, regularization has long been resignedly seen as "the most suitable instrument to repair the dysfunctionalities of the Italian migration regime and … an important element of continuity between the policies of centre-left and centre-right governmental majorities" (Finotelli 2013: 49–50). On the other hand, the platforms of so-called populist parties such *Lega Nord* and *Movimento Cinque Stelle* have been built around the promise to break away from conventional patterns – not only in the immigration policy area, but also across a wide spectrum spanning fiscal policy to Italy's relationship with the EU. Then-Minister of the Interior Salvini's famous announcement – that "the free ride is over (*la pacchia è finita*) for clandestine immigrants" – is emblematic of this "new" forces' desire to mark a watershed in a domain where discontent among the population with the current state of affairs is deemed high. Yet, it only takes a cursory glance to notice the continuity between the current and the previous government's approach and measures – in particular, the ubiquitous framing of the immigration issue in terms of security and public order. This was indeed acknowledged to some extent by Matteo Salvini himself when he declared that, as far as immigration is concerned, "some good was done". Moreover, even the casual observer is reminded of that statement when (s)he stumbles upon the long-standing debate within the *Partito Democratico* (PD) about the effectiveness and moral adequacy of the quite restrictive immigration policy measures implemented when the PD was the leading force of the executive.

The generally less-than-impressive results achieved by populist parties in the 2019 European elections, at least compared to expectations, suggests disenchantment among a people that has "got used" to feeling vulnerable. This detachment does not lead to apathy or indifference towards politics, but rather results in a negotiating and selective approach to new political options and a readiness to backtrack in case of disappointments (Marini 2018). The populist offer confirms and defies at the same time Italy's a-normality, which is not "in the thing", but as a productive stereotype which can nevertheless have a significant political effect on so delicate an aspect as the relationship between security and democracy.

Notes

1 Del Pero (2003) argues against the notion of a "suspension of sovereignty" at least not a complete one – seeing how Christian Democratic Party-dominated governments effectively managed to "contain America's containment".

2 LUISS, "Economic crisis and quality of democracy in Europe (CriEc&Demo)", https://scienzepolitiche.luiss.it/en/ricerca/research-centers/icedd/projects/economic-crises-and-quality-democracy-europe; Censis, www.censis.it/sicurezza-e-cittadinanza; Fondazione Unipolis, www.fondazioneunipolis.org/osservatorio-europeo-sulla-sicurezza/; Demos & Pi, www.demos.it/.

3 The traditional difference between adversarial and inquisitorial legal systems has been largely put into question by experts, both conceptually and as a result of the reforms that have blurred much of the once agreed-upon correspondence with, respectively, common law and civil law countries – and Italy is a significant case of convergence (Spencer 2016; Ogg 2012). Conventionally, however, in the adversarial model representatives from each party take opposing positions to debate and argue their case, whilst the judge's role is to uphold principles of fairness and equality and to remain neutral until the very end when judgment is delivered. Conversely, in an inquisitorial legal system the judge takes a much more active role in preparing evidence, questioning witnesses in order to pursue the ultimate goal of "finding the truth" (Panzavolta 2016).

4 Significantly, on 11 June 1978 the *Legge Reale* was submitted to a repeal referendum. The Italian Communist Party, despite originally opposed to the bill, campaigned against the repeal. Eventually, only 23.5 percent of voters were in favor of repeal, and the Act remained in force.

5 In fact, if civil services are included, a number of institutions have fairly good approval rates: from the National Firefighters Corps' staggering 87.3 percent to Civil Defence's 73.6 percent, and to universities (73.5 percent), schools (67.4 percent) and the national health system (62.3 percent) (Eurispes 2019).

6 Ministry of Defense, *Operazioni Militari*, www.difesa.it/OperazioniMilitari/Pagine/OperazioniMilitari.aspx.
7 Ministry of Defense, Carabinieri, *Il contributo dell'Arma alle Operazioni militari all'estero*, www.carabinieri.it/arma/oggi/missioni-all'estero/oggi/missione_fuori_area.

Bibliography

Accetti, C.I. 2019. "Italy's new experiment in populist technocracy." *FT*, 5 September. www.ft.com/content/415474b2-cf29-11e9-b018-ca4456540ea6.

Agnew, J. 1997. "The myth of backward Italy in modern Europe." In Allen, B. and Russo, M. eds. *Revisioning Italy: National Identity and Global Culture*, Minneapolis: University of Minnesota Press: pp. 23–42.

Albanese, G. 2014. "Brutalizzazione e violenza alle origini del fascismo." *Studi Storici* 55 (1): pp. 3–14.

Albanese, J.S. 2012. "Deciphering the linkages between organized crime and transnational crime." *Journal of International Affairs* 66 (1): pp. 1–16.

Alexander, D.E. 2010. "The L'Aquila earthquake of 6 April 2009 and Italian government policy on disaster response." *Journal of Natural Resources Policy Research* 2 (4): pp. 325–342.

Algostino, A. 2019. "Sicurezza urbana, decoro della smart city e poteri del prefetto note intorno alla 'direttiva Salvini sulle zone rosse' (n. 11001/118/7 del 17 aprile 2019) e ad alcune recenti ordinanze dei prefetti di Bologna, Firenze e Siracusa." *Costituzionalismo.it* 1: pp. 104–130.

Allum, F. and Sands, J. 2004. "Explaining organized crime in Europe: are economists always right?" *Crime, Law & Social Change* 41: pp. 133–160.

Allum, P. and Allum, F. 1996 "The resistible rise of the new Neapolitan Camorra." In Gundle, S. and Parker, S. eds. *The New Italian Republic: From the Fall of the Berlin Wall to Berlusconi*, London: Routledge.

Almagisti, M. 2008. *La qualità della democrazia in Italia: capitale sociale e politica*. Rome: Carocci.

Almond, G.A. and Verba, S. 1963. *The Civic Culture: Political Attitudes and Democracy in Five Nations*, Princeton, NJ: Princeton University Press.

Altman, D. and Pérez-Liñán, A. 2002. "Assessing the quality of democracy: freedom, competitiveness and participation in eighteen Latin American countries." *Democratization* 9 (2): pp. 85–100.

Anderson, P. 2014. "The Italian disaster: 'Italy is not an anomaly within Europe. It is much closer to a concentrate of it'." *Europe Solidaire Sans Frontières*, 22 May. http://europe-solidaire.org/spip.php?article32068.

Andreas, P. and Wallman, J. 2009. "Illicit markets and violence: what is the relationship?" *Crime, Law and Social Change* 52 (3): pp. 225–229.

Andrews, G. 2005. *Not a Normal Country: Italy after Berlusconi*. London: Pluto.

Antinori, A. 2012. "The Italian Mafias and migrant smuggling." In Palmer, D., Berlin, M.M. and Das, D.K. eds. *Global Environment of Policing*, London: Routledge: pp. 221–236.

Arlacchi, P. 1986. *Mafia Business: The Mafia Ethic and the Spirit of Capitalism*, New York: Schocken Books.

Armani, B. 2010. "La violenza della politica. Letture e riletture degli anni Settanta." *Contemporanea* 13 (4): pp. 753–759.

Barbagli, M. and Sartori, L. 2004. "Law enforcement activities in Italy." *Journal of Modern Italian Studies* 9 (2): pp. 161–185.

Bastasin, C. 2019. "Italy's political turmoil shows that parliaments can confront populists." *Brookings*, 9 September 2019, www.brookings.edu/blog/order-from-chaos/2019/09/09/italys-political-turmoil-shows-that-parliaments-can-confront-populists/.

Battelli, G. and Vinci, A.M. eds. 2014. *Parole e violenza politica. Gli anni Settanta nel Novecento italiano*, Rome: Carocci.

Battistelli, F. 2008. "Produttori di sicurezza. I Corpi di polizia in Italia tra competizione e cooperazione." *Quaderni di Sociologia* 46: pp. 169–172.

Battistelli, F. 2013. "Sicurezza urbana 'partecipata'. Privatizzata, stabilizzata o pubblica?" *Quaderni di Sociologia* 63: pp. 105–126.

Behan, T. 1996. *The Camorra*, New York: Routledge.

Bhabha, H.K. ed. 1990. *Nation and Narration*. London: Routledge.

Bordignon, F. and Di Pierdomenico, M. 2019. "Sintesi dei principali risultati." *La banalità della paura. Lavoro, percezioni e insicurezze in Europa. Rapporto sulla sicurezza e l'insicurezza sociale in Italia e in Europa. XI edizione*, Fondazione Unipolis and Demos & Pi.

Bosi, L. and Malthaner, S. 2015. "Political violence." In Della Porta, D. and Diani, M. eds. *The Oxford Handbook of Social Movements*, Oxford: Oxford University Press: pp. 439–451.

Brubaker, R. 2017. "Why populism?" *Theory and Society* 46: pp. 357–385.
Bull, M.J. and Pasquino, G. 2018. "Italian politics in an era of recession: the end of bipolarism?" *South European Society and Politics*, 23 (1): pp. 1–12.
Bull, M. and Rhodes, M. 1997. *Crisis and Transition in Italian Politics*, London: Routledge.
Caffarena, A. and Gabusi, G. 2017. "Making sense of a changing world: foreign policy ideas and Italy's national role conceptions after 9/11." *Rivista Italiana di Scienza Politica/Italian Political Science Review* 47 (2): pp. 125–147.
Calaresu, M. and Tebaldi, M. 2019. "The comparative analysis of European national police systems: a theoretical and methodological proposal for a new research agenda." *Police Practice and Research*. DOI: 10.1080/15614263.2019.1677231
Calhoun, C. ed. 1994. *Social Theory and the Politics of Identity*, Oxford and Cambridge, MA: Blackwell.
Campbell, D.F.J. 2008. "The basic concept for the democracy ranking of the quality of democracy", Vienna: The Democracy Ranking of the Quality of Democracy. https://nbn-resolving.org/urn:nbn:de:0168-ssoar-290631.
Carati, A. and Locatelli, A. 2017. "Cui prodest? Italy's questionable involvement in multilateral military operations amid ethical concerns and national interest." *International Peacekeeping* 24 (1): pp. 86–107.
Casillo, R. 2006. *The Empire of Stereotypes: Germaine de Staël and the Idea of Italy*, New York: Palgrave Macmillan.
Cavalli, A. 2001. "Reflections on political culture and the 'Italian national character'." *Dedalus* 130 (3): pp. 119–137.
Ceccorulli, M. 2019. "Così è (se vi pare): talking migration to Italians." *International Spectator* 54 (3): pp. 18–36.
Censis. 2018. *Sicurezza. Il 39% degli italiani favorevoli alla pistola facile per la difesa personale.* www.censis.it/sicurezza-e-cittadinanza/sicurezza-il-39-degli-italiani-favorevoli-alla-pistola-facile-la-difesa.
Ceri, P. 2003. *La società vulnerabile. Sicurezza e libertà.* Rome: Laterza.
Cesari, J. 2009. "Securitization of Islam in Europe." In Cesari, J. ed. *Muslims in the West after 9/11: Religion, Politics and Law.* London: Routledge: pp. 9–27.
Chamber of Deputies. 2017. "Giustizia. Nuovi reati." *Temi dell'attività parlamentare XVII legislatura.* https://temi.camera.it/leg17/temi/nuovi_reati_d.html.
Chiampan, A. 2018. "Encountering violence: the movement and the legitimation of violence at the eve of Italy's anni di piombo." *Studies in Conflict & Terrorism* 43(1): pp. 24–46.
Chiaramonte, A., Emanuele, V., Maggini, N. and Paparo, A. 2018. "Populist success in a hung parliament: the 2018 general election in Italy." *South European Society and Politics* 23 (4): pp. 479–501.
Colleoni, F. 2012. "Spettri della violenza politica. Gli anni Settanta in alcuni romanzi del nuovo millennio." *Enthymia* 7: pp. 425–442.
Colombo, A.D. and Dalla-Zuanna, G. 2019. "Immigration Italian style, 1977–2018." *Population and Development Review* 45: pp. 585–615.
Committee of Enquiry on Mafia and other Criminal Associations. 2018. *Final Report.* http://documenti.camera.it/_dati/leg17/lavori/documentiparlamentari/IndiceETesti/023/038/INTERO.pdf.
Corner, P. 2002. "The road to fascism: an Italian *Sonderweg*?" *Contemporary European History* 11 (2): pp. 273–295.
Corriere della Sera. 2019. "Dimezzati i reati, ma il 78% della popolazione pensa che siano in aumento. Ecco il perché." www.corriere.it/dataroom-milena-gabanelli/sicurezza-reati-dimezzati-italiani-senso-insicurezza-armi-legittima-difesa/647419e6-89da-11e9-9b3f-2459a834d32d-va.shtml.
Coticchia, F. 2015. "Effective strategic narratives? Italian public opinion and military operations in Iraq, Libya, and Lebanon." *Rivista Italiana di Scienza Politica/Italian Political Science Review* 45 (1): pp. 53–78.
Coticchia, F. and Vignoli, V. 2018. "Italian political parties and military operations: an empirical analysis on voting patterns." *Government and Opposition* 10: pp. 1–18.
Coticchia, F., Locatelli, A. and Moro, F. 2016. "Continuity and change in Italian defence policy." EUI Working Paper RSCAS 2016/01.
Crocitti, S. 2014. "Immigration, crime and criminalization in Italy." In Bucerius, S.M. and Tonry, M.H. eds. *The Oxford Handbook of Ethnicity, Crime and Migration*, Oxford: Oxford University Press: pp. 791–833.
Cuono, M. and Gargiulo, E. 2017. "Emergenza, crisi, sicurezza. Decisioni extra-ordinarie tra governo centrale e amministrazioni locali." *Diritto e questioni pubbliche* 2: pp. 15–36.
D'Amato, S. 2018. "From BR to ISIS. 'The Italian domestic and international response to terrorism'." *European Politics and Society* 9 (4): pp. 416–434.

De Haas, H. 2007. "Turning the tide? Why development will not stop migration." *Development and Change* 38 (5): 819–841.
Del Pero, M. 2003. "Containing containment: rethinking Italy's experience during the Cold War." *Journal of Modern Italian Studies* 8 (4): pp. 532–555.
Della Porta, D. 1992 "Institutional responses to terrorism: the Italian case." *Terrorism and Political Violence* 4 (4): pp. 151–170.
Della Porta, D. 1995. *Social Movements, Political Violence, and the State: A Comparative Analysis of Italy and Germany*, Cambridge: Cambridge University Press.
Della Porta, D. and Vannucci, A. 1999. *Un paese anormale*, Rome: Laterza.
Della Porta, D. and Vannucci, A. 2007. "Corruption and anti-corruption: the political defeat of 'Clean Hands' in Italy." *West European Politics* 30 (4): pp. 830–853.
Diamond, L. and Morlino, L. 2004. "The quality of democracy: an overview." *Journal of Democracy* 15 (4): 20–31.
Diamond, L. and Morlino, L. eds. 2005. *Assessing the Quality of Democracy*, Baltimore: Johns Hopkins University Press.
Diodato, E. and Niglia, F. 2017. *Italy in International Relations: The Foreign Policy Conundrum*, London: Palgrave Macmillan.
Dolcini, E. 2019. "La pena ai tempi del diritto penale illiberale." *Diritto Penale Contemporaneo*, 22 May. www.penalecontemporaneo.it/d/6693-la-pena-ai-tempi-del-diritto-penale-illiberale.
Donovan, M. 1994. "The 1994 election in Italy: normalisation or continuing exceptionalism?" *West European Politics* 17 (4): pp. 193–201.
Dyson, K. and Featherstone, K. 1996. "Italy and EMU as a 'vincolo esterno': empowering the technocrats, transforming the state." *South European Society and Politics* 1 (2): pp. 272–299.
ECHR. 2019. "The applicant's irreducible life sentence breached the Convention." European Court of Human Rights Press Release 217. www.jurist.org/commentary/wp-content/uploads/sites/3/2019/10/Judgment-Marcello-Viola-v.-Italy-no.-2-irreducible-life-sentence-breached-the-Convention.pdf.
Edelman. 2019. *2019 Edelman Trust Barometer*. www.edelman.com/sites/g/files/aatuss191/files/2019-02/2019_Edelman_Trust_Barometer_Global_Report_2.pdf.
Elazar, D.S. 2000. "Class, state, and counter-revolution: the fascist seizure of power in Italy, 1919–1922." *European Sociological Review* 16 (3): pp. 301–321.
Eubank, W.L. and Weinberg, L.B. 1997. "Terrorism and democracy within one country: the case of Italy." *Terrorism and Political Violence* 9 (1): pp. 98–108.
Eurispes. 2019. *Sintesi rapporto Italia 2019*. https://eurispes.eu/pdf-reader/web/viewer.html?file=https://eurispes.eu/wp-content/uploads/2019/01/eurispes-sintesi-rapporto-italia-2019.pdf#page=91&zoom=auto,-113,214.
Eurofound (2018), *Societal Change and Trust in Institutions*, Luxembourg: Publications Office of the European Union.
Europol. 2013. "Threat assessment: Italian organised crime." file:///C:/Users/MM/AppData/Local/Temp/italian_organised_crime_threat_assessment_0.pdf.
Evangelista, M. *Italy from Crisis to Crisis: Political Economy, Security, and Society in the 21st Century*, London: Routledge.
Fasani, F. 2016. "The quest for la dolce vita? Undocumented migration in Italy." In Triandafyllidou, A. ed. *Irregular Migration in Europe: Myths and Reality*, London: Routledge: pp. 167–186.
Feldman, D.L. 2019. "Corruption in Italy: indigenous impediments to reform." In Jurkiewicz, C.L. ed. *Global Corruption and Ethics Management: Translating Theory into Action*, Lanham, MD: Rowman and Littlefield: pp. 53–62.
Finkenauer, J.O. 2005. "Problems of definition: what is organized crime?" *Trends in Organized Crime* 8 (3): pp. 63–83.
Finotelli, C. 2013. "Italy: regional dynamics and centralistic traditions." *Imis-Beiträge* 43: pp. 83–98.
Foot, J. 2014. *Modern Italy* (2nd edn.), New York: Palgrave Macmillan.
Foradori, P. 2018. "Cops in foreign lands: Italy's role in international policing." *International Peacekeeping* 25 (4): pp. 497–527.
Friesendorf, C. 2016. "Police assistance as foreign policy: explaining donor practices." *Review of International Studies* 42 (2): pp. 377–400.
Fritszke, P. 1989. "Terrorism in the federal republic of Germany and Italy: legacy of the '68 movement or 'burden of fascism'?" *Terrorism and Political Violence* 1 (4): pp. 466–481.
Galli, C. 1992. "La cultura politica degli italiani." *II Mulino* 41: pp. 401–411.

Gambetta, D. 1996. *The Sicilian Mafia: The Business of Private Protection*. Cambridge, MA: Harvard University Press.

Gambetta, D. 2013. "Sparano alla democrazia. La lotta armata nei manifesti dei partiti italiani." *Zapruder* 32: pp. 40–45.

Gambetta, D. 2018. "Why is Italy disproportionally corrupt? A conjecture." In Basu, K. amd Cordella, T. eds. *Institutions, Governance and the Control of Corruption*, London: Palgrave Macmillan: pp. 133–164.

Garzia, D. 2019. "The Italian election of 2018 and the first populist government of Western Europe." *West European Politics* 42 (3): pp. 670–680.

Gherghina, S., Mişcoiu, S. and Soare, S. eds. 2013. *Contemporary Populism: A Controversial Concept and Its Diverse Forms*, Newcastle upon Tyne: Cambridge Scholars.

Gilbert, M. and Pasquino, G. eds. 2000. *Italian Politics: The Faltering Transition*, New York: Berghahn Books.

Giudici, C. 2016. "Perché l'Italia è ancora immune dal terrore." *Il Foglio*, 15 July. www.ilfoglio.it/esteri/2016/07/15/news/perche-litalia-e-ancora-immune-dal-terrore-98420/.

Herzfeld, M. 1997. *Cultural Intimacy: Social Poetics in the Nation-State*, New York: Routledge.

Hibberd, M. 2004. "Italian democracy gone mad? Public service broadcasting in the Berlusconi era." *Trends in Communication* 12 (1): pp. 15–31.

Howlett, M. and Cashore, B. 2014. "Conceptualizing public policy." In Engeli, I. and Allison, C.R. eds. *Comparative Policy Studies*, London: Palgrave Macmillan.

Huysman, J. 2000. "The European Union and the securitization of migration." *Journal of Common Market Studies* 38 (59): pp. 751–777.

Ignazi, P. 2005. "Gli anni Settanta e la memoria monca." *Il Mulino* 418: pp. 385–394.

Istat. 2018. "La percezione della sicurezza." Istat report. www.istat.it/it/files/2018/06/Report-Percezione-della-sicurezza.pdf.

Kupchan, C. 2019. "In Europe, nativism and nationalism may be reaching their limits." *Foreign Policy*, 24 September. https://foreignpolicy.com/2019/09/24/in-europe-nativism-and-nationalism-may-be-reaching-their-limits/.

La Spina, A. 2014. "The fight against the Italian Mafia." In Paoli, L. ed. *The Oxford Handbook of Organized Crime*, Oxford: Oxford University Press: pp. 593–611.

Lastrico, V. 2016. "Criminalità Comune, criminalità organizzata e violenza politica. Evoluzione delle minacce della sicurezza in Europa." In Tebaldi, M. ed. *Sicurezza, libertà e democrazia. Analisi comparata di sei paesi europei*, Bologna: Il Mulino.

Leonardi, R. 2017. *Government and Politics of Italy*, London: Palgrave Macmillan.

Leotta, A. 2011. "Do not underestimate the consequences of love: the representation of the new Mafia in contemporary Italian cinema." *Italica* 88 (2): pp: 286–296.

Luckham, R., Goetz, A.M. and Kaldor, M. 2003. "Democratic institutions and democratic politics." In Bastian, S. and Luckham, R. eds. *Can Democracy Be Designed? The Politics of Institutional Choice in Conflict-Torn Societies*, London and New York: Zed Books.

Mackinlay, J. and Chopra, J. 1992. "Second generation multinational operations." *Washington Quarterly* 15 (3): pp. 113–134.

Magri, P. and Villa, M. 2018. "Gestire le migrazioni." ISPI Commentary, 26 February.www.ispionline.it/it/pubblicazione/gestire-le-migrazioni-19735

Manna, A. 2016. "Alcuni recenti esempi di legislazione penale compulsiva e di ricorrenti tentazioni circa l'utilizzazione di un diritto penale simbolico." *Proceedings of the conference promoted by the Italian Association of Criminal Law "La Società Punitiva. Populismo, Diritto Penale Simbolico e Ruolo del Penalista"*21 December. www.penalecontemporaneo.it/d/5087-la-societa-punitiva-populismo-diritto-penale-simbolico-e-ruolo-del-penalista.

Marini, D. 2018. "Gli italiani, il senso civico e la politica." *Il Mulino* 1: pp. 116–124.

Marrone, A. and di Camillo, F. 2013. "Italy." In Giegerich, B., Biehl, H. and Jonas, A. eds. *Strategic Cultures in Europe*, Vienna: Peter Lang.

Militello, V. and Spena, A. eds. 2015. *Il traffico di migranti. Diritti, tutele, criminalizzazione*, Turin: Giappichelli.

Ministry of Defense. 2017. *Relazione sullo stato della disciplina militare e sullo stato dell'organizzazione delle Forze Armate*. www.senato.it/service/PDF/PDFServer/DF/343378.pdf.

Ministry of the Interior. 2019a. "*La nuova normativa su immigrazione e sicurezza pubblica*." www.interno.gov.it/it/speciali/nuova-normativa-immigrazione-e-sicurezza-pubblica.

Ministry of the Interior. 2019b. "Direttiva del ministro dell'Interno N. 11001/118/7 del 17 aprile 2019." www.interno.gov.it/it/amministrazione-trasparente/disposizioni-generali/atti-generali/atti-amministrativi-generali/documenti/direttiva-ministro-dellinterno-n-110011187-17-aprile-2019.

Ministry of the Interior. 2019c. *Direzione centrale per i servizi antidroga. Relazione annuale 2019.* https://antidroga.interno.gov.it/wp-content/uploads/2019/07/relazione-annuale-2019.pdf.

Momigliano, A. 2018. "Italy is safe from, and for, jihadis." *Foreign Policy.* https://foreignpolicy.com/2018/05/03/italy-is-safe-from-and-for-jihadis/.

Morgan, P. 2002. "The First World War and the challenge to democracy in Europe." In Spering, M. and Wintle, M. eds. *Ideas of Europe since 1914: The Legacy of the First World War*, London: Palgrave Macmillan.

Morlino, L. 1998. *Democracy between Consolidation and Crisis: Parties, Groups and Citizens in Southern Europe*, Oxford: Oxford University Press.

Morlino, L. 2003 "What is a 'good' democracy? Theory and the case of Italy." *South European Society and Politics* 8 (3): pp. 1–32.

Morlino, L. 2004. "What is a 'good democracy'?" *Democratization* 11 (5): pp. 10–32.

Morlino, L. 2010. "Legitimacy and the quality of democracy." *International Social Science Journal* 60: pp. 211–222.

Morlino, L. 2013. "The impossible transition and the unstable new mix: Italy 1992–2012." *Comparative European Politics* 11 (3): pp. 337–359.

Morlino, L., Piana, D. and Raniolo, F. eds. 2013. *La qualità della democrazia in Italia*, Bologna: Il Mulino.

Moss, D. 1989. *The Politics of Left-Wing Violence in Italy, 1969–85*, Basingstoke: Macmillan.

Munck, G.L. 2016. "What is democracy? A reconceptualization of the quality of democracy." *Democratization* 23 (1): pp. 1–26.

Musella, F. 2012. "Governare senza il Parlamento? L'uso dei decreti legge nella lunga trasizione italiana." *Rivista italiana di scienza politica/Italian Political Science Review* 3: pp. 459–480.

Newall, J. 2000. *Parties and Democracy in Italy*, Aldershot, UK: Ashgate.

Newell, J. 2010. *The Politics of Italy: Governance in a Normal Country*, Cambridge: Cambridge University Press.

Nuti, V. 2018. "Economia sommersa vale 210 miliardi, il 12,4% del Pil." *Il Sole 24 Ore*, 12 October. www.ilsole24ore.com/art/economia-sommersa-vale-210-miliardi-124percento-pil-AE4eNwLG.

O'Donnell, G., Cullell, J.V. and Iazzetta, O.M. eds. 2002. *The Quality of Democracy: Theory and Applications*, Notre Dame, IN: University of Notre Dame Press.

Ogg, J.T. 2012. "Italian criminal trials: lost in transition? Differing degrees of criminal justice convergence in Italy and Australia." *International Journal of Comparative and Applied Criminal Justice* 36 (3): pp. 229–244.

Palidda, S. 2000. *Polizia postmoderna. Etnografia del nuovo controllo sociale.* Milan: Feltrinelli.

Palidda, S. 2008. "Appunti di ricerca sulle violenze delle polizie al G8 di Genova." *Studi sulla questione criminale* 3 (1): pp. 33–50.

Palidda, S. 2017. "Polizie, sicurezza e insicurezze ignorate, in particolare in Italia." *Revista Critica Penal y Poder* 13: pp. 233–259.

Palonen, K. 2003. "Four times of politics: policy, polity, politicking and politicization." *Alternatives: Global, Local, Political* 28 (2): pp. 171–186.

Panzavolta, M. 2016. "Of hearsay and beyond: is the Italian criminal justice system an adversarial system?" *International Journal of Human Rights* 20 (5): pp. 617–633.

Paoli, L. 2001. "Crime, Italian style." *Dedalus* 130 (3): pp. 157–185.

Paoli, L. 2004. "Italian organised crime: Mafia associations and criminal enterprises." *Global Crime* 6 (1): pp. 19–31.

Paoli, L. 2007. "Mafia and organised crime in Italy: the unacknowledged successes of law enforcement." *West European Politics* 30 (4): pp. 854–880.

Paoli, L. 2014. "The Italian Mafia." In Paoli, L. ed. *The Oxford Handbook of Organized Crime*, Oxford: Oxford University Press.

Pasquino, G. 2019. "Representing microcosms." *Political Quarterly* 90 (3): pp. 578–579.

Piana, D. and Verzelloni, L. 2016. "Dal centro disperso al centro ritrovato? Riflessioni a partire dalle riforme della giustizia in Italia." *Quaderni di Scienza Politica* 2: pp. 237–273.

Pinto, A.C., Magalhães, P.C. and de Sousa, L. 2012. "Is the good polity attainable? Measuring the quality of democracy." *European Political Science* 11 (4): 447–455.

Pizzorno, A. 2001. "Familismo amorale e marginalità storica, ovvero perché non c'è niente da fare a Montegrano (1967)." *Quaderni di Sociologia* 3: pp. 349–362.

Poesio, C. 2014. "Violenza, repressione e apparati di controllo del regime fascista." *Studi storici* 1: pp. 15–26.

Putnam, R. 1993. *Making Democracy Work: Civic Tradition in Modern Italy*, Princeton, NJ: Princeton University Press.

Ragnedda, M. 2014. "Censorship and media ownership in Italy in the era of Berlusconi." *Global Media Journal: Mediterranean Edition* 9 (1): pp. 13–26.

Renga, D. 2019. *Watching Sympathetic Perpetrators on Italian Television*. Cham: Palgrave Macmillan.

Ricotta, G. 2012. "Sicurezza urbana e tolleranza zero." *La Rivista delle Politiche Sociali* 1: pp. 117–133.

Romano, B. 2007. *Guida alla parte special del diritto penale*. Padua: Giuffré.

Ruffa, C. 2016. "Just deploy and always call it peacekeeping! Italian strategic culture and international military operations." In Britz, M. ed. *European Participation in International Operations: The Role of Strategic Culture*, London: Palgrave Macmillan: pp. 101–122.

Ruzza, C. and Fella, S. 2009. *Re-inventing the Italian Right: Territorial Politics, Populism and "Post-Fascism"*. London: Routledge.

Samuels, R.J. (2003) *Machiavelli's Children: Leaders and their Legacies in Italy and Japan*, Ithaca and London: Cornell University Press.

Sandri, G., Telò, M. and Tomini, L. 2013. "Political system, civil society and institutions in Italy: the quality of democracy." *Comparative European Politics* 11 (3): pp. 261–279.

Savona, E.U. and Riccardi, M. eds. 2018. *Mapping the Risk of Serious and Organised Crime Infiltration in European Businesses: Final Report of the MORE Project*. Milan: Transcrime and Università Cattolica del Sacro Cuore.

Scaglione, A. 2016. "Cosa Nostra and Camorra: illegal activities and organisational structures." *Global Crime* 17 (1): pp. 60–78.

Scazzieri, L. 2019, "The EU should seize the chance to stop Italy's eurosceptic drift." *Centre for European Reform*, 5 September 2019. www.cer.eu/insights/eu-should-seize-chance-stop-italys-eurosceptic-drift.

Selmini, R. 2017. "Urban policing in Italy: some reflections from a comparative perspective." In Devroe, E., Edwards, A. and Ponsaers, P. eds. *Policing European Metropolises: The Politics of Security in City-Regions*. London and New York: Routledge: pp. 167–181.

Sergi, A. 2019. Traditional organised crime on the move: exploring the globalisation of the Calabrian 'ndrangheta." In Talani, L. and Roccu, R. eds. *The Dark Side of Globalisation*. Cham: Palgrave Macmillan, pp: 123–145.

Spencer, J.R. 2016. "Adversarial vs inquisitorial systems: is there still such a difference?" *International Journal of Human Rights* 20 (5): pp. 601–616.

Spotts, F. and Wieser, T. 1986. *Italy: A Difficult Democracy. A Survey of Italian Politics*, Cambridge: Cambridge University Press.

START. 2019. *Global Terrorism Database. Codebook: Inclusion Criteria and Variables*. College Park: National Consortium for the Study of Terrorism and Responses to Terrorism, University of Maryland. www.start.umd.edu/gtd/downloads/Codebook.pdf.

Taiani, L.S. 2018. "Assessing the relation between the underground economy and irregular migration in Italy." *International Spectator* 54 (2): pp. 102–122.

Tarchi, M. 2003. *L'italia populista. Dal qualunquismo ai girotondi*, Bologna: Il Mulino.

Tarchi, M. 2008. "Italy: a country of many populisms." In Albertazzi, D. and McDonnell, D. eds. *Twenty-First Century Populism*, London: Palgrave Macmillan: pp: 84–99.

Tebaldi, M. ed. 2016. *Sicurezza, libertà e democrazia. Analisi comparata di sei paesi europei*, Bologna: Il Mulino.

Tercovich, G. 2016. "Italy and UN peacekeeping: constant transformation." *International Peacekeeping* 23 (5): pp. 681–701.

Uzelac, A. 2019. "Migration and security." *Clingendael Strategic Monitor* 2018–2019. www.clingendael.org/pub/2018/strategic-monitor-2018-2019/migration-and-security.

Valbruzzi, M. 2013. "Not a normal country: Italy and its party systems." *Studia Politica: Romanian Political Science Review*, 13 (4): pp. 617–640.

Verbeek, B. and Zaslove, A. 2015. "The impact of populist radical right parties on foreign policy: the Northern League as a junior coalition partner in the Berlusconi governments." *European Political Science Review* 7 (4): pp. 525–546.

Verbeek, B. and Zaslove, A. 2016. "Italy: a case of mutating populism?" *Democratization* 23 (2): pp. 304–323.

Vidino, L. and Marone, F. 2017. "Terrorism and Italy: roots and challenges of an 'exception'." *ISPI*, 13 November. www.ispionline.it/en/pubblicazione/terrorism-europe-foreign-fighters-and-prevention-18785.

Von Lampe, K. 2012. "Transnational organized crime challenges for future research." *Crime, Law and Social Change* 58 (2): pp. 179–184.

Weinberg, L. 1996. "The Italian revolution: the end of politics Italian style? The crisis of the Italian state: from the origins of the cold war to the fall of Berlusconi." *American Political Science Review* 90 (3): pp. 670–672.
Weinberg, L. and Eubank, W.L. 1987. *The Rise and Fall of Italian Terrorism*, Boulder, CO: Westview.
Weinberg, L.B. and Eubank W.L. 2001. "Terrorism and democracy: perpetrators and victims." *Terrorism and Political Violence* 13 (1): pp. 155–164.
Weinberg, L.B. and Eubank W.L. 2019. *The Rise and Fall of Italian Terrorism*, New York: Routledge.
Wiatrowski, M.D. and Goldstone, J.A. 2010 "The ballot and the badge: democratic policing." *Journal of Democracy* 21 (2): pp. 79–92.
Williams, P. and Savona, E.U. 1996. eds. *The United Nations and Transnational Organized Crime*, London: Frank Cass.

9

ENDING ETA'S TERRORISM IN SPAIN

Trade-offs between democracy and security?

Rogelio Alonso

Introduction

This chapter analyses an issue often underestimated when considering security threats to democracy: the effects of certain policies towards political parties associated with terrorist organizations, and the consequences of such policies for security challenges posed by democracies. When looking at the terrorist campaign waged by ETA in Spain from the late sixties onwards, scholars often focus on the terrorists' motivations for the beginning, the continuation and the end of violence, which finally occurred in Spain in 2011.[1] Various authors have already done this work. It is equally important to consider a related but key issue which has received less attention: how the Spanish State and other democratic parties in Spain that, throughout ETA's campaign condemned violence, dealt with political parties related to the terrorist organization post-2011. By attending to this issue, we broaden the framework within which a security challenge to democracy such as the one posed by ETA must be analyzed.

This approach takes into consideration the fact that one of the most controversial measures implemented by the Spanish State against ETA was the banning of its political wing, formerly known as Batasuna. In 2002 the Spanish parliament approved new legislation that allowed the executive, upon request of the legislature, to demand judicial procedures to outlaw political groups unwilling to condemn terrorism or continuing to maintain links with a terrorist organization. Based on the belief that Batasuna was part of the network of organizations ultimately led by ETA, comprising a movement that shared objectives as well as membership, the Spanish judiciary and the executive acted against it.[2] Following the suspension of Batasuna's activities through the Penal Code in September 2002, the Government also asked the Supreme Court to outlaw the party. The Supreme Court's decision took effect in March 2003. This State reaction came at a time when terrorist intimidation had reached extraordinary levels following ETA's campaign of "socialising the suffering", as termed by the organization. ETA's campaign targeted representatives and supporters of non-nationalist parties in an attempt to push them to the margins of the political system. This strategy coincided with ETA's concerns about the need to establish a "national census" as well as a "definition of who is a citizen of Euskal Herria"[3] and who was therefore entitled to vote.[4] The ideological hunt that followed the terrorist campaign resulted in the premeditated harassment and intimidation of more than 42,000 people, as estimated by the NGO *Gesto por la Paz* (Gesture for Peace).[5]

Under these circumstances the Spanish State decided to act, implementing the draconian measure of banning a political party to protect a section of society that felt vulnerable and defenceless. The banning of Batasuna was strongly criticized by all the nationalist parties in the Basque Country, which saw the proscription as a serious violation of fundamental rights and liberties. Nevertheless, the proscription was endorsed by the Spanish Supreme and Constitutional Tribunals as well as by the European Court of Human Rights. The former declared in March 2003 that the benefit derived from banning ETA's political wing was the protection of democracy and the rights of society; the latter described it as a "pressing social need".[6] In a historic ruling in June 2009 the European Court of Human Rights (ECHR) stated that:

> a political party whose representatives incite to the use of violence, or put forward a political project which does not respect one or several rules of democracy, or which pursues the destruction of democracy and the ignorance of the rights and freedoms that the latter recognises, cannot shield itself under the protection of the [European] Covenant [of Human Rights] against the sanctions envisaged for these motives.[7]

Banning Batasuna was controversial, but proved to be extremely positive in democratic terms and managed to considerably weaken the terrorist organization, as ETA itself acknowledged.[8] This is why ETA demanded the measure be reversed when it engaged in negotiations with the Spanish Government in 2006. The demand became one of the conditions put forward by ETA in return for a cessation of its campaign of terrorism, a demand that was ultimately satisfied. A thorough analysis of ETA's campaign to reinstate its political arm demonstrates that, after the end of its campaign of violence, the terrorist group was denied its main strategic aims; but at the same time terrorism was rewarded with significant political and social concessions from which political parties related to the terror group benefited.

Therefore, this chapter will analyze how the ending of ETA's terrorist campaign occurred in parallel with a significant trade-off between democracy and security, the latter understood in a restrictive way rather than in a broader sense as ontological security. This approach is particularly appropriate when referring to terrorist threats because of the psychological impact, in addition to the physical impact, that political violence in a democracy like Spain entails. The chapter will also assess the consequences such a trade-off has had for democratic procedures and values upheld during the security threat. Although some argue that concessions given to parties related to terrorism may have contributed to the ending of the terrorist campaign, the political, social and moral costs of such an approach are significant. As the analysis will show, the concessions offered to ETA and its political arm are relevant to the security of democracies that have faced protracted terrorist campaigns inspired by nationalist ideology. As this chapter demonstrates, concessions created important challenges for democracy that are often underestimated because they emerged in the context of a terrorist cessation that is given priority over other considerations. Even though ETA disbanded itself in a letter made public on 2 May 2018, having relinquished its weapons a year before, much is to be learned from its later history.

The implicit legitimization of terrorism

Perception of the terrorism perpetrated by ETA changed during the first and second decades of the twenty-first century to the point that Spanish society no longer considered this problem to be a primary concern. Years before, terrorism was regularly identified as one of the most important problems facing Spanish society; but after 2011 other issues were of greater social concern, as documented by regular sociological research.[9] This change of attitude towards terrorism was accompanied by a gradual decline in violence, ending in the "definitive cessation of armed activity" announced by ETA in October 2011. ETA had by then killed 858 people and injured thousands.[10]

While a change in social perception is logical in view of the above-mentioned reduction in the level of violence, it should be noted that consequences arising from the terrorist campaign perpetrated by ETA from the end of the 1960s onwards are still present in Spanish society. In addition to the terrible cost in human lives, terrorism damaged the political and social fabric of the country, affecting the governance of the Basque Autonomous Community and influencing the behaviors of a citizenry long cowed by the threat of terrorism. The testimony of Euskadi's Socialist Party Senator Roberto Lertxundi, offered in 2012, illustrates the point. Lertxundi recognized the "widespread fear" that still reigned in some localities in the Basque Country, localities which still could not be considered "free" of the state of intimidation consolidated following decades of terrorist threats. Thus, he warned: "Fear, if it lasts, will be ETA's victory."[11]

In the words of Francisco José Llera, the director of Euskobarómetro, a social survey produced by the University of the Basque Country, the "voluntary withdrawal strategy" pursued by the terrorist movement caused a "bleeding out of human lives, destruction and havoc, extortion and financial uncertainty, whose economic and commercial effects are yet to be assessed". It also caused:

> the loss of freedom and fundamental rights of an important and relevant part of the citizenry and, even worse, the institutional and moral corruption of a society that, even if not taking direct advantage of this situation, at least looks the other way since it doesn't feel engaged.[12]

Without a doubt, the political system and social relationships in the Basque Country were and have been affected by the violence of a terrorist organization which, although it put a brake on its campaign of systematic killings post-2011, still refused to disappear entirely. ETA's continued presence, as analysed below, including participation in democratic politics via political parties that still justified and legitimized terrorism, affected a citizenry whose attitudes and behaviors had been severely conditioned by fear for decades.

It was no exaggeration, therefore, to warn against "the fragility of democratic values in Basque society" after decades of terrorist intimidation.[13] For decades the terrorist movement – composed of ETA and a grouping of political and cultural associations that supplemented the group's activities – sought "political advantage" and sought to "weaken their rivals" through crime, threats and other forms of social intimidation.[14] In announcing the end of its "armed activity", ETA renounced exercising some of its most intimidating practices even as it retained and maintained other approaches to power, approaches it obtained through the institutional access secured by its political representatives in 2011 and 2012.

We must, therefore, bear in mind the diverse nature of the challenges to security that ETA's terrorism still posed in the period between the cessation of violence and the disbanding of ETA itself, and, consequently, the range of responses the effort to contain those challenges still required. The risks arising from ETA's existence were not limited to a hypothetical but unlikely resumption of terrorist activity, a fear that was more intense in the aftermath of the cessation of terrorism. If the potential risks arising from ETA's presence on the political scene were judged to be solely limited to active terrorism, that would be to ignore the fact that terrorism uses a medium – violence – in the pursuit of an aim: obtaining power to impose its nationalistic goals.

ETA was able to temporarily renounce certain terrorist manifestations – but not its underlying menace – when it attained its aspirations through supplementary approaches.[15] In other words, political acceptance of the so-called "abertzale left" (Basque nationalists) as a normal democratic party, without ETA's disappearance, produced an unfair situation from a democratic standpoint since it trivialized the meaning of the close relationship between differing branches of the terrorist movement. It also underestimated the extent of the intimidation suffered by citizens who had been unable for decades to enjoy basic rights and freedoms in a democracy where non-nationalist parties, threatened by ETA, suffered considerable political disadvantages. A clear trade-off emerged from the controversial legalization in 2011 and 2012 of Bildu and Sortu, political parties widely regarded as heirs of the terrorist organization ETA.

Bildu and and Sortu were accurately described as "ETA's lobbyists".[16] These political representatives returned to participation in democratic institutions in a context where political criteria were given precedence over judicial criteria. Bildu and Sortu avoided being outlawed. Legalization of parties linked to the terrorist organization took place because the relevant authorities implemented a double and contradictory message enabling their decriminalization. On the one hand, there was an insistence that they should be outlawed, as evidenced by the then Interior Minister who declared that "Bildu is part of ETA's strategy" and that "some of its members are directly linked to the illegal Batasuna".[17] But the Minister himself then engaged in a series of revealing inconsistencies. He repeatedly extolled generic pronouncements by Bildu and Sortu appearing to indicate distancing from ETA as "steps forward" in the correct direction taken by the "abertzale left".[18]

Paradoxically, the "steps" the Minister valued as positive merely constituted formal statements about the rejection of violence. They did not deserve a positive assessment, for they represented only cosmetic gestures meant to mislead the authorities, as the State Prosecution and Advocacy Services argued at the Government's behest.[19] We should recall that the Constitutional Court had already highlighted years before that a "generic" condemnation of the violation of human rights in no case could be equated with an unequivocal condemnation of terrorism, since in Basque society terrorism did not constitute a "mere abstraction", but a "concrete reality".[20]

Thus, when the Spanish Interior Minister praised certain gestures made by Batasuna while he was allegedly attempting to outlaw Bildu, the organization succeeding Batasuna, he was deliberately ignoring the fact that ETA and Batasuna had been using Bildu to gain access to democratic institutions. In other words, the Minister ignored the strong police evidence that eventually led the Supreme Court to outlaw Bildu by decree, a decision that was later reversed by the Spanish Constitutional Tribunal. As summarized by Constitutional Court Judge Manuel Aragon,

> the Supreme Court found – in terms that cannot be constitutionally censored – that the existence had been proven of a political operation by the so-called ETA/Batasuna complex, to use, for the purpose of political succession, a large number of

> electoral candidacies of the legal parties EA and Alternatiba. This operation was accomplished with the setting up of the Bildu electoral coalition [which agglutinated all those formations].[21]

This renowned expert in fundamental rights held therefore that the Constitutional Court had "clearly exceeded" its "constitutional mandate", and rejected as unfounded the criticism of the Constitutional Court of "evidentiary insufficiency" in the judgment of the Supreme Court when the latter outlawed the political representatives of ETA.[22]

Alfredo Pérez Rubalcaba, Interior Minister during this period, showed himself, in public at least, to be inflexible when dealing with Bildu. However, in fact he helped promote the victimhood and even legitimacy of the party linked to ETA. He did so through a double discourse which was complemented by that of the Basque Government when the latter delivered public outbursts against the Supreme Court, thus presenting itself as the guarantor of the legalization aspirations of ETA's political branch.[23] This double discourse, which accepted as legitimate the grievances of ETA's political wing, generated a climate of opinion favorable to legalization while strengthening the suspicion that the Spanish Government covertly encouraged the Constitutional Court judges to influence their vote in favour of legalizing Bildu. The reality of such encouragement has since been confirmed by ministerial sources who acknowledged that the Tribunal's decision was a "political" one.[24] The suspicion is also consistent with the attitude Government negotiators had shown in their dealings with ETA in 2006 when the organization demanded that the Law on Political Parties that had banned ETA's political representatives be revoked.[25]

A political communications campaign orchestrated by the Spanish Government favored the legalization of ETA's political representatives against the Constitutional Tribunal's own jurisprudence and against the criteria of the most relevant court on the subject, the Spanish Supreme Tribunal.[26] Manuel Aragón, a magistrate at the Constitutional Tribunal who voted against the decision to legalize ETA's political representatives, described the move as a "grave mistake by democracy and the State", a decision that "made him ashamed".[27] Bildu and Sortu were legalized because a political elite decided that one of the most important defense mechanisms the State has in its armory, outlawing political parties, had to be neglected in favor of the successors to Batasuna. Consequently, the Spanish Constitutional Court broke with its own jurisprudence and exceeded its powers by taking a decision that was beyond its scope, particularly after the Supreme Tribunal had already taken the decision to outlaw ETA's political wing.[28] It is worth remembering that the banning of ETA's political wing had been validated by the European Human Rights Tribunal in a historic ruling that stressed the unacceptable threat that Batasuna posed to democracy. In that historic ruling in 2009 the Tribunal stated that "the legitimisation of terrorist actions and the exculpation and minimisation of their anti-democratic meaning, as well as the violation of fundamental rights they entail can also occur in an implicit way".[29]

Another Government Interior Minister under which legalization took place later acknowledged the political, rather than judicial, rationale behind the decision. Antonio Camacho admitted months after the legalization of Bildu that it was time to "start translating into deeds the words that had enabled the courts to allow the parties its legalisation".[30] His testimony reflected the fact that the Constitutional Court interpreted favorably a discourse totally at odds with the facts that the Supreme Court, basing its decision on abundant police evidence, defined as part of ETA's strategy. The admission by the then Minister of the Interior showed that a simple discourse promising a break with ETA, unsupported by the facts, disabled one of the most effective measures that could have been taken against the terrorist group, allowing its return to Spain's set of democratic institutions.

The trade-off between democracy and security that legalization implied had obvious consequences for Spain's democratic political system that have been underestimated in the context of the cessation of ETA's terrorist campaign, and, consequently, the cessation of ETA itself.

From ETA's operational weakness to the political strengthening of its lobbyists

As some observers have pointed out,

> Batasuna and Bildu do not interpret what happened [legalization] as the outcome of their renouncing their political-military strategy, but rather as the outcome of a build-up of forces with which they have defeated the State, for whom criminalizing them was unsustainable. That's the key point which must be borne in mind.[31]

This decisive assertion requires that statements made recently celebrating ETA's defeat and attributing it to the negotiation with the terrorist group from 2006 onwards must be qualified. A wider analysis reveals that the operational weakness preceding the "definitive cessation of armed activities" in October 2011 had already existed for years.[32] Intelligence analysis described ETA's situation and that of its network as one of serious "decline",[33] characterized by "structural and functional weakness"; "economic precariousness" due to the huge financial losses derived from the banning of ETA's political wing; a loss of motivation for its militants; and a diminishing social and political influence. The situation led to "a shrinking of the political space" occupied by ETA and its network of political, social and cultural fronts in the early years of the twenty-first century. To this should be added "the loss of virtually all its power, always essential to its strategy", which placed the "abertzale left" in "a position of ineffectiveness and political irrelevance".[34]

Therefore, in the period prior to the ending of ETA's campaign, the terrorist movement did not have the political strength it subsequently gained with its return to the legal fold. Legalization in effect strengthened the terrorist movement formed by ETA and its political wing, allowing it to rebuild radical nationalism even as it upheld the political project of institutional acceptance pursued through terrorist means, and thus contaminated by it. As the Chairman of the Popular Party in the Basque Country, Alfonso Alonso, stated as late as 2016, the ETA project "is still alive: ETA has still not dissolved itself and can still be heard at the heart of institutions seeking to destroy everything that we have built from the inside out".[35]

An analysis of the evolution followed by the terrorist movement – from the middle of the first decade of the twenty-first century to the middle of the second – reveals that ETA managed to minimize the evident impact of its deep weakening at the police level between 2001 and 2003 by achieving a political victory, neutralizing the instrument that enabled the isolation of their political representatives. This conclusion requires that the positive assessments relied on during the Spanish Government's negotiations with ETA be corrected, since in some sectors they are wrongly attributed to ETA's defeat. Bearing that in mind, there has been an attempt to camouflage the counterproductive costs of the above-mentioned counter-terrorism policy by deploying discourse that describes the negotiations as "a tactical error, but a strategic success" which, according to this version, led to the evolution of the "abertzale left" and its confrontation with ETA.[36] On the other hand, rigorous analysis of the group's evolution allows another hypothesis to be put forward: that counter-terrorism policy between 2004 and 2011 served to postpone defeat by the police, which was already possible and evident prior to that period. The result was a strengthening of ETA's political arm, which then had to be confronted by the democratic state.

Serious tactical and strategic errors committed by the Spanish Government in counter-terrorism policies prior to the legalization of ETA's political representatives are now evident. By way of example we can cite the deactivation of an important potential disagreement among ETA prisoners. Doubting the effectiveness of the continuation of terrorism, six leading ETA prisoners came to recognize ETA's failure. In a letter written in 2004 they demanded that the group discontinue its campaign of violence, arguing that its "political-military strategy" had been "overwhelmed by the enemy's repression".[37] This could be regarded as highly significant since a prominent activist such as Francisco Múgica Garmendia, and another five inmates who had broader support among the prisoners' group,[38] admitted that "never, in the history of this organization, have we been in such a bad position".[39] This critical admission led them to accept that "the inability to boost the armed struggle and the impossibility of accumulating forces which will make it possible to negotiate with the central power ultimately forces us to rethink the proactive strategy we have defended up to this point".[40]

In this delicate context for ETA the Spanish Government opted for a counter-terrorism policy which, contrary to what had been raised by the above-mentioned ETA prisoners, offered negotiations. Shortly afterwards, Múgica Garmendia and his group were suspended from their militancy and kicked out of the group after ETA forced them to rectify. Thus, the Government, which later insisted on the so-called "via Nanclares" project to open fractures within the terrorist group,[41] only managed to get a minimum number of prisoners to sign up to it. By contrast, it thwarted an excellent opportunity to encourage a critique of violence from within ETA itself and by respected leaders within the terrorist movement. Consequently, it can be said that the Spanish Government managed to "defeat" those who already wanted to surrender within ETA, while strengthening those who wanted to continue supporting violence.[42]

This contradiction must be highlighted because other initiatives, developed between late 2012 and 2016 by the Government headed by Former Prime Minister Mariano Rajoy, were conditioned upon the uncritical premise that the counter-terrorism policy of the previous Government between 2004 and 2011 had brought about the end of ETA. The rhetorical insistence on considering that ETA had been defeated had two effects. On the one hand, it diverted attention away from the negative consequences legalization of ETA's political arm had on counter-terrorism policy. On the other, it produced an underestimation of the challenges a counter-terrorism policy still needed to face in terms of defeating the political project pursued by the terrorist movement composed of ETA, Batasuna and other related groupings which, as the Spanish Supreme Court flagged up, acted as the terrorist group's "frontmen".[43]

In analyzing both effects we must take into account the situation facing ETA and Batasuna following the group's boast that, once the party had been legalized again, "Euskal Herria has won the political and ideological battle against the ban".[44] Some politicians and academics tend to underestimate the setback posed for democracy by the return to legality of ETA's political arm. This is an issue that should have been stressed if we were to rigorously meet the challenges of constructing a counter-terrorism policy to confront an operationally weakened ETA, whose subculture of hatred and violence nevertheless still permeated society even as it strengthened itself politically.

To summarize: legalization of ETA's political representatives served to offset the terrorist groups' operational weakness, strengthening those parties that continued to defend ETA's project in social and political spheres. The authorities who placed so much emphasis on police successes thus failed outright, as evidenced by the electoral success of the "abertzale left" after its return to electoral politics and the democratic process. Circumstances were favorable before legalization, and authorities then had an advantage: if ETA were able to overcome its operational exhaustion and hypothetically be capable of returning to violence, the authorities could have persuaded it from doing so for fear of the price they would have to pay on the political front. But the authorities failed to understand this option. Instead, fear of a hypothetical return to violence was indeed a major consideration for politicians in choosing to accept a major concession such as legalization of ETA's political representatives, Bildu and Sortu.

In addition to the shortcomings of such an approach from a democratic point of view, if in the future ETA threatened to carry out a terrorist attack, ETA's political representatives could have demanded further concessions – relying on a discourse, fueled by some political and media representatives, that differentiated the *political* from the *militant* branches of ETA despite actual coordination between them. At such a juncture, the Government could have found itself subject to blackmail in the following terms: it is necessary to reinforce the political branch, the "abertzale left", in order to silence ETA's *militants*. Under such circumstances the democratic authorities would be faced with the challenge of demanding responsibility from the "abertzale left" when they had already exempted it from responsibility. This exemption from responsibility in fact led to the undeserved whitewashing of the "abertzale left", enabling it to conveniently dodge its close links with ETA. To ETA's coercion of the Government could be added the pressure of those who would demand that the executive take the initiative to prevent murders and not ruin a sort of peace that raised so many social expectations.

In the period prior to, and in the aftermath of the legalization of ETA's political representatives, it was common for some politicians and opinion formers to reward those responsible for the terrorist campaign – those who at some point stopped advocating full continuation of the violent campaign, albeit without delegitimizing the violence committed up until then.[45] They did it by constructing a narrative that would attribute to themselves prevention of the recurrence of violence while accepting consolidation of a discourse that legitimized and ennobled those justifying it. This was evidenced by elections held in the Basque Country after 2011, where those who had yet to condemn the systematic violation of human rights perpetrated by ETA were rewarded at their victims' expense.

Political immunity as a political price for the end of terrorism

ETA's political representatives were legitimized and legalized even though the terrorist group had not been dismantled; and nothing more than a simple formal estrangement from violence had been required of them to overcome the outlawing enforced since 2002. These circumstances limited the effectiveness of democratic speech which claimed that the Spanish State had accomplished ETA's defeat. Representatives of radical and violent nationalism acted in politics: the wrongful presence of a terrorist organization in their shadow – without delegitimization of ETA's brutal violation of basic human rights, and with the connivance of political parties which, since their return to legality, wielded significant municipal power. Those political parties acquired a strong parliamentary representation in the Basque Autonomous Parliament, where they became second in political force.

The fact that ETA's political representatives were allowed to take part in the democratic process without condemning ETA, and without producing any evidence of an unambiguous delegitimization of terrorism, constituted a significant political price for democracy. The head of the Euskobarómetro survey pointed out the following:

> What ETA now has is a guaranteed immunity and obliviousness of its past of blood and terror because it seems that no one is going to require that they account for it; it's been treated as if it has been cancelled out by the electoral and institutional success of Bildu, as if it were the "dove of peace".[46]

As an editorial in *El Correo* recognized, one key to the electoral successes of ETA's political representatives lay precisely in "the institutional return of an 'abertzale left' that had not been required to demonstrate its democratic nature, by either condemning or censoring ETA's trajectory, as a price for accessing its legal whitewashing".[47] Historian Santos Juliá corroborated this analysis, asserting that there are parties today broadcasting and socializing the discourse of the legitimization of terror until it becomes a social memory.[48] Former ETA member Eduardo Uriarte summarized well the dangers of the situation derived from legalization of political formations related to ETA when he recognized that "their very active presence in the Basque Country, where their denials of reality enjoy excessive media attention", and the wide "social acceptance of many of their proposals" by major political parties and society amount to an "euphoric conquest of the democratic space by radical nationalism", and thus made it "very difficult to politically channel" the problems of Basque society.[49] In such a context it becomes daunting to correct and counteract an already solidifying memory that denies the social and political implications of ETA's terrorism.

That significant deficit should act as a point of departure when constructing a fair memory of ETA's terrorism, which is nowadays recognized as one of the major challenges to Spanish democracy. Two writers define and question limitations on efforts to construct memory of ETA's actions. María del Mar Blanco, Chair of the Victims of Terrorism Foundation (from 2012) and sister of the Popular Party (PP) councillor murdered by ETA in 1997, writes: "It is immoral that those who have failed to condemn my brother's death are now in Government."[50] Given such clear confirmation of the failure of the democratic parties to voice objection, the next question writes itself: What was done to stop this immorality? Already in 2007, scholar Aurelio Arteta warned:

> What I most fear is that when ETA meets its end, is that a simplistic and comfortable belief that without terrorist attacks everything is now permissible will impose itself. In other words, that the only downside of all these horrors is the means used by the terrorists, but not the nationalistic ends.[51]

The radical nationalist left linked to ETA achieved important propaganda victories, spreading a specific terminology that helped interpret ETA's end of violence in terms favorable to it. As noted by academic Manuel Montero in 2012, "it controls the vocabulary", and therefore "dominates the stage" "because everybody seems to be waiting with bated breath: what will it do now, what will it say later, will it approve of what we are doing, if it will be enough or will it want more, and when".[52] Investing in the attribution of blame, supporters of terrorism managed to blame society and democratic political leaders for ETA's end. They did this by imposing a narrative demanding that active democratic institutions make "gestures" and take "steps" defined as necessary to achieve peace, while in fact concessions by those democratic institutions legitimized a terrorist group that refused to go away and worked to ensure its own continuity politically and *at the level of discourse*. Such an existence, albeit without continuation of the group's murderous campaign, remains relevant in the context of decades of psychological intimidation and coercion through terror. Misleading language reproduced by the "abertzale left" convinced a number of democratic institutions that they should "guide" ETA's end with political initiatives and concessions which, as experience shows, only served to strengthen ETA's political branch politically and socially. *This chapter, written shortly before ETA's self-declared demise, defines contradictions in the actions and intentions of the "abertzale left" with respect to discourse, memory and democratic asymmetries.*

Misleading language was often justified by referencing variation in sensitivities towards terrorism in Basque society and the rest of Spain. But to do so was also to implicitly accept the effects of terrorist intimidation which, logically, molds perceptions. It should have been unacceptable to support less democracy for the Basque Country than the rest of Spain. It should have been unacceptable that the issue of legality be subject to the opinion of cowed social majorities under conditions of coercion. Quite the opposite, so that intimidation carried out by ETA and its supporters would not pay off or become effective. This challenge remained evident as late as 2017 in a political context that constantly raised the need for Government to make "gestures" towards the radicals and to modify its counter-terrorist policy to avoid damaging the electoral expectations of Basque parties which had been the victims and targets of ETA's terrorism. A political, social and cultural hegemony is exerted by nationalism in the Basque Country, even though a terrorist organization inspired by nationalism used terrorism for decades against Basque citizens, leaving its victims in an even political competition.

Given such political and cultural hegemony, a widespread belief consolidated itself in 2007–2015 allowing the legitimization of those who simply said they wanted terrorism to disappear while preventing its clear delegitimization. When those who systematically violate human rights are relieved of the political consequences their track record should have imposed upon them in a democratic society, incentives to bring about the complete disappearance of a terrorist group are reduced since the group's existence ceases to be a price it needs to pay. ETA's perpetuation became a cost-effective weapon it used to keep generating advantages even as it continued to exploit the promise of its disappearance.

As the IRA and Sinn Féin did in Northern Ireland, ETA and Batasuna resorted to a communication strategy of whitewashing their track record and seducing the public. The words of Garret FitzGerald, Prime Minister of the Republic of Ireland in the 1980s, allow us to draw a parallel with ETA and Batasuna's propaganda efforts: "Their propaganda system is very focused. 'We are the peace party.' If you murder enough people and then stop, then you become the peace party."[53] Bildu and Sortu, the political parties that emanated from ETA, following the example of Sinn Féin, attempted to regain control of the political agenda by using language to redefine a reality marked by the continued existence of a terrorist organization that refused to go away and insisted on legitimizing its campaign of terror. For ETA's "lobbyists", as well as for the IRA and Sinn Féin, it was fundamental to use "a language of peace", making it into a "style" and using it as "a weapon for the insurgency".[54]

Some democratic players adopted that "style", as evidenced by the generous treatment representatives of the "abertzale left" received from influential politicians and the media. They justified its use by referring to the need to avoid victimizing the "abertzale left", an approach which ignored the fact that complacency towards terrorist organizations increases their respectability, credibility and prominence without requiring them to exercise the self-criticism and refusal of terror that would be logical within a democratic framework. This places unfair pressure on society, whose members are coerced into voting for radicals, radicals presented as committed pacifists who should be rewarded for championing the end of terrorism. A dangerous impunity is evident when we treat as genuine democrats those who have supported terrorism for decades, as happened when prestigious media groups offered the "abertzale left" a platform from which to expound their propaganda, uncritically and without a right to reply. This choice lent credibility to the left, implicitly placing those who did not respect the law on the same level as victims of violence and genuine supporters of democracy. A decrease in the level of demand imposed on the left contributed to strengthening parties associated with ETA while they stiffly refused to accept the illegitimacy and injustice of the violence in which they were complicit.

Finally, in Spain decreasing the level of demand imposed on the left, based on the argument that a decrease in demand prevents the left from being victimized, in reality strengthened the movement. By contrast, it would have been logical to expose the manipulative intentions of the movement by revealing the identity of those genuinely victimized by ETA's violence.

One of Batasuna's internal newsletters set the situation out clearly when it assessed the interview given by Arnaldo Otegi, an imprisoned terrorist leader, to an influential media organization in 2010:

> El País recognizes not only the abertzale left, but their imprisoned leader as valid political interlocutors. In this way, the flagrant contradiction of a State, which claims to be democratic but which imprisons political interlocutors for the fact of being so, is highlighted. The interview in El País forced the President of the Government himself to reply, and let's not forget, he sent a personal reply to a Basque political prisoner, even though it may hurt to recognize that.[55]

A journalist's concern to prevent society from being deprived of the knowledge of the full reality of events cannot ignore that, occasionally, terrorist discourse is awarded a dangerous credibility and legitimacy by a distorted presentation of its aspirations. This is what happened when Batasuna spokesmen obtained the benefit of a media presence through which they reproduced their propaganda. Using a deceptive language of peace, they confused certain audiences about the nature of their relationship with ETA, focusing on formal declarations of their estrangement from violence without delegitimizing the terrorist project.

The presumed neutrality of the media thus enabled the spread of misinformation and a distortion of reality about political parties that acted as "lobbyists" for ETA. Regular interviews with Batasuna spokesmen allow them to present a favorable portrait of themselves since the media exonerated them from the requisite questioning their track record and unreliability should have elicited. Some journalists seem fascinated by those who violate basic democratic principles, providing them with a useful opportunity to rehabilitate their image in the public eye. Association with terrorism brought them rewards rather than penalties, affording them a coercive power they could use to condition peace to the satisfaction of their demands. Sometimes the media's apparent impartiality and objectivity becomes a subjective value concealed beneath an asymmetric neutrality, which should be contrary to the role of the journalist. As Hannah Arendt wrote, "describing the concentration camps *sine ira* is not being objective, but forgiving."

Further, such political and moral impunity was evident in, and favored by, certain forms of political conduct which confused tactical compliance with standards that should have been necessary to gain access to the democratic political system. A full and true assumption of democracy requires unequivocal condemnation of terrorism and active delegitimization of it. Hence, in establishing institutional relationships with ETA's political representatives, it was critical that Government and democratic parties not ignore that fact that Bildu's and Sortu's achievement of legal status did not turn exhaustive factual police reports describing interactions between ETA and Batasuna into fiction.

When those supporting democracy agreed to normalize their relationship with ETA's representatives, justifying the same by saying that legislation demanded it, they diminished and damaged the requirements of a democratic system. As jurisprudence on the outlawing of political parties demonstrates, democracies must penalize those who lack the necessary legitimacy to partake in it with full rights unless they fully delegitimize terrorism. By opting for the strategies described above, democratic parties do not assist the democratic integration of radicals. Rather, they allow radicals to access democracy under the appropriate conditions, and with the intent to undermine it.

Conclusions

Spain's democracy applied successful coercive politics to ETA, resulting in ETA's enormous operational weakness. That success was diminished, mitigated and devalued by certain political and social gains achieved by the group's political wing, which leveraged political and social gains to counteract an unfavorable situation in the operational field. Weakness was evident in the political field as well until electoral empowerment took place in the aftermath of the terrorist cessation. One of the "abertzale left's" leaders, writing in *Gara* in 2011 under the pseudonym Mikel Etxeberria, declared:

> Over the past years they have sold us their political victory over the abertzale left and ETA's military defeat. Reality has wiped out that fallacy … . They have failed because we invested effort in the situation, and following the so-called defeat we have progressed to a show of force and taken back the political initiative. … While the Spanish–French offensive was in full swing we turned the tables on them in the operational sphere and earned ourselves a political advantage. Of course, let us not forget that the State is them, which means that the only thing that we have done so far is to position ourselves well for the next cycle.[56]

The same author argued: "The State has lost control of the political stage and also, notably, their specific standing in Basque society. They have lost the political initiative and social support."[57] He highlighted the "spiral of delegitimization [of the State] in Basque society", claiming that was precisely "what [the State had been] seeking to stir up against the abertzale left". He concluded that "the increased strengthening of the sovereignty of the left is something that may eventually overwhelm them".[58]

Aside from the obvious, intentional, propaganda value such reflections of an "abertzale left" militant may have had in 2011, Etxeberria's analysis also highlights factors exacerbating the terrorist movement's weakness. He therefore reveals what strengthens the State and, consequently, the variables that an effective counter-terrorist policy should and could have addressed. As he pointed out, "the first objective in any confrontation, whatever form it might take, is always to cause discomfort to the adversary and put them at a disadvantage".[59]

The ETA member further argued that "this is precisely what the abertzale left has achieved with their strategic shift, in such a way that it is now the State which is feeling discomfort having lost its politically advantageous position".[60] In his opinion, the recovery of radical nationalism, internationalization and the generation of a climate of opinion that accepts as necessary some of the grievances of the "abertzale left" in relation to prisoners and the implementation of policy initiatives on the side-lines of the democratic institutions had created "a sufficiently uncomfortable scenario so that they [the Government and the PP] [would have] no choice but to run with it or be left behind by history".[61]

The analysis offered in this chapter exposes the motives for this "discomfort", motives that prevented the State from transforming into a clear political victory the police defeat feared by ETA. Indeed, as stated by the above-mentioned "Etxeberria": "ETA's goal when it began its armed campaign in the 1960s was not victory over enemy forces, which was unthinkable given the absolute inequality between the parties. Its goal was always political."[62] Therefore, it was somewhat pointless to emphasize ETA's defeat at the hands of the police when defeat by the police had not been accompanied by a true political defeat – which the State must still pursue.

We must ask ourselves what the Spanish State's strategic plan against ETA's subversive terrorism was. Only when we understand that plan can we assess whether Spain's democracy achieved its policy objectives by using the legal means at its disposal. To do so we can apply the strategic thinking of authors whose theories were confined in practice to the military sphere, a limitation which also provides an interesting perspective when extended to asymmetrical conflicts such as terrorist movements with significant political dimensions. This analytic move makes sense because, according to Collins, "Strategy is no longer an exclusively military art … nor does it deal solely with armed combat."[63] For example, General Alonso Baquer defines the concept of strategy as "the art of designing operational plans, consistent with the legitimate purposes of a political community, like the art of driving armies towards decisive objectives".[64]

If we apply to asymmetric conflicts such as ETA's terrorist campaigns, the strategic thinking developed by French military strategist André Beaufre, we would interpret the strategy of the Spanish State and that of the terrorist organization as "the art of the dialectic of wills using force to resolve their conflict".[65] Beaufre distinguishes two essential elements in any strategy: the choice of turning point that it is sought to achieve (the adverse vulnerability function); and the choice of the preparatory maneuvers allowing that turning point to be reached. Both opponents try to prevent adverse maneuvers in order to make progress towards their aim in the pursuit of what is conveniently referred to as "freedom of action". Beaufre concludes: "the struggle of wills is reduced, then, to a fight for freedom of action, with each party attempting to retain it while depriving the adversary of the same". In achieving that "freedom of action", it is crucial to "make certain to secure the initiative".[66]

Certainly, ETA renounced its systematic terrorism campaign in 2011. In that sense, the State achieved one of the main goals it set itself. That goal was achieved by ensuring that the opponent, i.e. ETA, had been significantly limited in its "freedom of action" since it had to pay a large price for violence. However, in achieving this goal, the State at any given time provided the insurgents with considerable freedom of action through their political front. In other words, while intense coercion was being exercised in the operational field, pressure was being reduced in another domain, enhancing the terrorist group's freedom of action.

Therefore, it is difficult to talk about a complete strategic success since the State itself contributed to the fact that the insurgents transformed their weaknesses – political and social side-lining due to terrorism – into strengths: political and social rehabilitation and strengthening of their political standing. From this perspective – and taking into account that the conflict between terrorist organizations and democratic States is part of a confrontation not exclusively resolved through one of the main approaches of terrorist activities (i.e. systematic terrorist attack campaigns) – it seems necessary to opt for a more comprehensive analytical framework.

The measure used to assess the outcome and efficiency of democracies against terrorism is often premised on two variables: *victory* or *defeat*. Instead of using such categorical terms, it seems appropriate to adopt more proportionate parameters in order to assess an asymmetric conflict such as terrorism. In this regard, it is reasonable to measure outcomes in terms of *achievements* and *failures*, both at the strategic and tactical levels, given circumstances under which neither of the contenders has been physically eradicated or has objectively surrendered to the opponent.

Thus, while ETA did not achieve its primary objective – creating an entity whose limits would have been defined by the nationalistic organization known as Euskal Herria – it obtained some gains, thereby supplementing some of its losses. Among those gains were:

- political and social rehabilitation through tactics favored by the State itself – i.e. changing public opinion and perceptions of the terrorist movement, its nature, composition and aims;
- political reinforcement and success in accessing democratic institutions, guaranteeing to itself symbolic amounts of power;
- a subsequent trivialization of the suffering inflicted upon victims of terrorism and trivialization of the seriousness of the challenge posed to democracy, some of whose representatives were for decades at a clear disadvantage due to the terrorist threat;
- a successful resistance to any attempts to completely eradicate terrorism, preventing the State from making political concessions of any kind;
- a successful resistance of any attempts to completely eradicate terrorism; and
- resisting efforts to fully and thoroughly delegitimize the terrorist movement and its terrorist discourse.

Despite minimal explicit support it received during the last stages of its campaign of violence, ETA has managed to overcome these difficulties and enable parties that justify and legitimize terrorism (although they do not currently advocate it) to obtain a considerable political advantage.

These consequences should now be framed in the context of the expectations citizens of the Basque Country had regarding the terrorist threat which for decades threatened their safety. ETA's terrorism supplemented physical violence with tactics based on psychological violence, significantly decreasing the safety of many Basque citizens and citizens in the rest of Spain. It should be remembered that safety is one of the most urgent needs of any human being. As General Ballesteros recalls, if we look at Maslow's hierarchy of needs any human being seeks to meet we find, in the following order: physiological needs, the need for safety, belonging to a group, self-esteem and self-actualization.[67] Taking into account the fact that the term "safety" links risks, dangers and threats, we must ask ourselves wheter the citizen who is a victim of terrorism, both directly and indirectly, could feel safe in the social and political context following the announcement of the definitive cessation of armed activity by ETA. As psychologist and victim of terrorism Javier Gómez Segura observed, terrorist victimization implies a primary, secondary and tertiary level, dimensions which are directly influenced by the political and social context in which terrorism occurs and, thus, by the implicit and explicit legitimization of terrorism that some political and social conducts entail.[68]

ETA's terrorism can be distinguished from other types of social violence by its psychological impact and by the political and social consequences arising from its use. The group's violence was inspired by a nationalist ideology that sought to change the social order and the political and legal framework through fear and coercion, and its cost in human and political terms must be underlined.[69] The political nature of ETA's terrorism and its huge impact in human terms explains the effects of terrorism on a society that has suffered extreme pressure in the form of, among other expressions, the so-called strategy of "socialising suffering".[70] Given these precedents, citizens' safety should be analyzed from the perspective of ontological security. As explained by Anthony Giddens:

> ontological security is a form, but a very important form, of a sense of security in a broader sense than the one used until now. The expression refers to the confidence that most human beings have in the continuity of their self-identity and the constancy of their social and material environments. Basic to a feeling of ontological security is a sense of the reliability of persons and things; so that both are closely linked psychologically.[71]

Terrorism is characterized by the asymmetry defining the confrontation between the State and the terrorists. As explained by Ekaterina Estepanova, terrorists need "to employ a form of violence serving as a multiplier of forces in a confrontation with an enemy that is incomparably stronger whom they cannot challenge effectively by conventional means".[72] Therefore, by using non-conventional approaches, such as those used by terrorism – approaches which also limit the types of instruments to which the State can resort – the terrorist aims to become a subject of negotiation to legitimize the terrorist's position. Both terrorist and State harmonize the goals they are seeking to achieve and the means available to achieve them. In other words, tactics are selected and accommodated with the intention of contributing to strategic goals. Therefore, terrorism is used, modulated and abandoned with the aim of contributing to the achievement of a strategy that is fundamentally political. As Clausewitz asserted, "war is not an independent phenomenon, but the continuation of politics by other means".[73]

This same logic can be extended to the asymmetric conflict that terrorism implies, and which clearly constitutes a political phenomenon. The implied political nature of terrorist violence imposes a balance of the elements that terrorism's opponents use against it. That must be the case because the terrorist has a political aim. Consequently, the political dimension is also relevant when we analyze the outcomes obtained by terrorist movements. These considerations impose upon us an interpretation of the balance achieved by the Spanish State in its confrontation with ETA's terrorism, in realistic terms that scholar Aurelio Arteta summarized in an illustrative way by referring to "the victor's defeat".[74]

Notes

1 See, for example, Rafael Leonisio, Diego Muro and Fernando Molina, *ETA's terrorist campaign from violence to politics, 1968–2015*. London: Routledge, 2017; Theresa Whitfield, *Endgame for ETA: Elusive peace in the Basque Country*. Oxford: Oxford University Press, 2014; Rogelio Alonso, "Why do terrorists stop? Analyzing why ETA members abandon or continue with terrorism", *Studies in Conflict and Terrorism*, 34, no. 9 (2011), pp. 696–716.

2 A thorough analysis of the complex system of organisations linked to ETA, their actions and the nature of such relationships can be found in José Manuel Mata, *El nacionalismo vasco radical. Discurso, organizaciones y expresiones*. Bilbao: Universidad del País Vasco, 1993.

3 Euskal Herria, the ethno-linguistic unit claimed by Basque separatists as their homeland, is made up of the three Spanish provinces that conform the Basque Country (Guipúzcoa, Álava and Vizcaya), as well as another Spanish province outside the Basque Autonomous Community, Navarre; it also includes the former French departments of Labourd, Soule and the Lower Navarre portions of the Pyrenees.
4 Florencio Domínguez, *Las raíces del miedo: Euskadi, una sociedad atemorizada*. Madrid: Aguilar, 2003, pp. 260–261.
5 "Gesto por la Paz estima que 42.000 personas sufren la amenaza directa de los etarras", *El País*, 9 November 2002.
6 European Court of Human Rights, Fifth Section, *Herri Batasuna and Batasuna v. Spain*, demands n° 25803/04 and 25817/04, Sentencing, Strasbourg, 30 June 2009, articles 73, 83, 85, 91, 93, 94.
7 Ibid.
8 Rogelio Alonso, "Confronting terrorism in Northern Ireland and the Basque Country: Challenges for democracy and legitimacy", in Martha Crenshaw (ed.), *The consequences of counterterrorism*. New York: Russell Sage Foundation, 2010, pp. 213–254.
9 This evolution can be seen in the barometer carried out periodically by the Centre of Sociological Investigations (CIS) at www.cis.es.
10 For an analysis of the evolution ETA's terrorism and its victimization patterns, see Rogelio Alonso, Florencio Domínguez and Marcos García, *Vidas rotas. Historia de los hombres, mujeres y niños víctimas de ETA*. Madrid: Espasa, 2010.
11 Roberto Lertxundi, "¿Isaías Carrasco? 'No lo sé. EZ dakit'", *El Correo*, 7 March 2012.
12 Francisco Llera, "La red terrorista. subcultura de la violencia y nacionalismo en Euskadi", p. 272, in Antonio Robles (ed.), *La sangre de las naciones. Identidades nacionales y violencia política*. Granada: University of Granada, 2003, pp. 265–296.
13 Ibid.
14 Reyes Mate, "Justicia de las víctimas y reconciliación en el País Vasco", Working document, 96/2006, Fundación Alternativas, 2006, p. 52.
15 As pointed out by a military analyst, "War makes no sense as of itself; it has both a political goal and meaning, it is politics that endows war with *purpose*. And in this sense, the nature of the goals is affected by the nature of the means", p. 29, Federico Aznar, *Entender la guerra en el siglo XXI*. Madrid: Editorial Complutense, 2010.
16 Maite Pagazaurtundúa, "La espiral del silencio sobre ETA", *El Mundo*, 20 October 2016.
17 Luis Rodríguez Aizpeolea, "Rubalcaba avala impugnar Bildu porque está en la 'estrategia de ETA'", *El País*, 27 April 2011.
18 See for example, O.B. Otálora, "Los Ejecutivos central y vasco y el PNV ven 'pasos' en la buena dirección de Batasuna", *El Correo*, 13 April 2011.
19 Supreme Court, Judgment Special Chamber, Art. 61 Organic Law on the Judiciary (LOPJ), Contentious-electoral appeal 2/2011 and 4/2011, Electors Groupings, 1 May 2011.
20 See for example, Constitutional Court of Spain, Second Chamber, Supreme Court Judgment (STC) 068/2005, 31 March 2005.
21 Individual opinion formulated by Judge Manuel Aragón Reyes, in respect of the judgment, granting the requested protection, dictated by the Bench in electoral appeal no. 2561–201, 5 May 2011, p. 10.
22 Ibid., p. 4.
23 See for example, "El papelón del gobierno", Editorial, *Abc*, 28 April 2011.
24 Interviews by the author with Spanish Government and counter-terrorism officials during his time as advisor to the Minister of the Interior between January and July 2012.
25 *Crónica*, Vasco Press Agency, no. 1565, pp. 3–4; 1566, pp. 8–9; 1567, pp. 10–13.
26 Pablo Fernández de Casadevante, "La prohibición de formaciones políticas como mecanismo de defensa del Estado y el debilitamiento de dicha protección tras las polémicas decisiones sobre Bildu y Sortu", *Revista europea de derechos fundamentales*, 26 (2015), pp. 111–137.
27 Manuel Aragón, "La legalización de partidos políticos que no condenan el terrorismo", Seminar held at Universidad Rey Juan Carlos, Madrid 16 April 2015.
28 Fernández de Casadevante, 2015.
29 ECHR, *Herri Batasuna and Batasuna v. Spain*.
30 M. Balín, "Camacho recuerda a Bildu que debe justificar su legalización", *El Correo*, 27 August 2011.
31 Florencio Domínguez, "El objetivo de ETA no es la vuelta a la legalidad", p. 157, *Cuadernos de Alzate*, 44 (2011), pp. 153–162.

32 "El declive de ETA", Lieutenant Colonel Gonzalo González, Instituto Universitario de Investigación sobre Seguridad Interior, March 2004, pp. 1–7, www.uned.es/investigacion/publicaciones/Cuadernillo%20Marzo2004%202.pdf.
33 Ibid.
34 Paper produced by a representative of the Spanish National Intelligence Centre, "Perspectivas políticas de ETA y su entramado de apoyo", p. 2, Instituto Universitario de Investigación sobre Seguridad Interior, March 2004, pp. 1–3.
35 Koldo Dominguez, "Alonso: 'La paz no puede ser el tiempo de destruir el Estatuto'", *El Correo*, 26 October 2016.
36 Luis R. Aizpeolea, "Un acierto estratégico", *El País*, 30 March 2011.
37 Published in leading Basque newspaper *El Correo*, 3 November 2004.
38 "Los notables de ETA expulsan a Pakito", *La Vanguardia*, 6 December 2005.
39 *El Correo*, 3 November 2004.
40 Ibid.
41 For an analysis of the serious deficits of the so-called via Nanclares program and its failure to entice a sizeable number of ETA prisoners away from the terrorist group, see Rogelio Alonso and Javier Díaz Bada, "What role have former ETA terrorists played in counterterrorism and counterradicalization inititatives in Spain?, *Studies in Conflict & Terrorism*, 39, no. 11 (2016), pp. 982–1006.
42 Santiago González, "A qué llaman proceso de paz", Santiago González, pp. 53, *Cuadernos de Pensamiento Político*, 10 (2006), pp. 43–53.
43 Supreme Court, Ruling Special Chamber, Art. 61 LOPJ, Contentious-electoral appeal 2/2011 and 4/2011, Electors Groupings, 1 May 2011, pp. 113 and 116.
44 "ETA se muestra 'plenamente convencida' de poder alcanzar un escenario de paz y libertad", *Gara*, 13 July 2011.
45 A similar pattern was also seen in Northern Ireland in relation to Sinn Féin, as analyzed in Rogelio Alonso, "Terrorist skin, peace-party mask: the political communication strategy of Sinn Féin and the PIRA", *Terrorism and Political Violence*, 28, no. 3 (2016), pp. 520–540.
46 Francisco J. Llera, Rafael Leonisio and Jonatan García y Sergio Pérez, "Las elecciones locales y forales de 2011: Bildu mueve el tablero y provoca una debacle socialista", p. 116, *Cuadernos de Alzate*, 44 (2011), pp. 85–117.
47 "Elecciones más libres", *El Correo*, Editorial, 5 December 2012.
48 Quoted in Eduardo Uriarte, *Tiempo de canallas. La democracia ante el fin de ETA*. Vitoria: Ikusager, 2013, pp. 356–357.
49 Ibid., p. 357.
50 "Víctimas de ETA recuerdan a Miguel Ángel Blanco entre críticas a la presencia institucional de Bildu", *Deia*, 18 March 2012.
51 Interview with Aurelio Arteta, "ABCD de las Artes y las Letras", *Abc*, 3 March 2007.
52 Manuel Montero, "Las palabras y los hechos", *El Correo*, 6 March 2012.
53 Quoted in Mark Hennessy, "Republicans woo young voters with softer image", *Irish Times*, 31 July 2001.
54 Quoted in Peter Shirlow and Mark McGovern, "'Language, discourse and dialogue': Sinn Fein and the Irish peace process", *Political Geography*, 17, no. 2 (1998), pp. 171–186.
55 Batasuna internal newsletter, 18 October 2010.
56 Mikel Etxeberria, "Una reflexión", *Gara*, 29 December 2011.
57 Mikel Etxeberria, "Nutrir el proceso", *Gara*, 6 March 2012.
58 Ibid.
59 Ibid.
60 Ibid.
61 Ibid.
62 Mikel Etxeberria, "En términos", *Gara*, 9 February 2012.
63 Quoted in Miguel Ángel Ballesteros, "Las estrategias de seguridad y defensa", p. 23, in *Fundamentos de la Estrategia para el Siglo XXI*, p. 23, CESEDEN Monographs, number 67, Superior Centre for National Defense Studies, Ministry of Defence 2003, pp. 15–64.
64 Ibid.
65 André Beaufre, *Introducción a la estrategia*. Madrid: Ediciones Ejército, 1990, p. 66.
66 Ibid., pp. 66–67, 69.
67 Ballesteros, 2003, pp. 28–29.

68 Javier Gómez Segura, "La evolución en la percepción de las víctimas del terrorismo", Unpublished Master's Dissertation, Universidad Rey Juan Carlos, 2012.
69 On the different expressions and mechanisms of terror used by ETA to extend fear, see, Florencio Domínguez, *Las raíces del miedo. Euskadi, una sociedad atemorizada*. Madrid: Aguilar, 2003.
70 Javier Martín-Peña, Álvaro Rodríguez-Carballeira, Jordi Escartín Solanelles, Clara Porrúa García and Frans Willem Winkel, "Strategies of psychological terrorism perpetrated by ETA's network: Delimitation and classification", ,*Psichothema*, 22, no. 1 (2010), pp. 112–117.
71 Anthony Giddens, *Consecuencias de la modernidad*. Madrid: Alianza, 1994, pp. 80–98.
72 Ekaterina Estepanova, "El terrorismo en el conflicto asimétrico. Aspectos ideológicos y estructurales", p. 34, *Cuadernos de Actualidad en Defensa y Estrategia*, Ministerio de Defensa de Argentina, 2009.
73 Ballesteros, 2003, p. 21.
74 Aurelio Arteta, "La derrota del vencedor", *El País*, 24 February 2014.

10

FINDING THE DEMOCRATIC BALANCE

Australian and New Zealand national security coordination

Rouben Azizian and Terry Johanson

Introduction

Australia and New Zealand face a complex new security environment which challenges their security sector architecture and the democratic pillars of their societies. The two nations' relative geographic isolation no longer protects them from security challenges that transcend conventional borders. The need to focus on domestic sources of extremism and transnational crime objectively enhances the role and monitoring responsibilities of national security agencies in both countries. Australia and New Zealand's increased economic dependence on authoritarian China also potentially compromises their adherence to democratic values and human rights.

According to Australian National University's Rory Medcalf, Australia's security environment has deteriorated: "From terrorism to resource insecurity, from the assertive rise of China to the impact of disruptive technologies, especially cyber – Australia faces a crowded horizon of risk, requiring a whole-of-nation response and long-term planning."[1] New Zealand's Defense White Paper, 2016, states that New Zealand's geographic distance from other countries does not insulate it from external threats: "Physical distance bears little relevance to the threats associated with terrorism and cyberspace."[2]

The increased emphasis Canberra and Wellington now place on domestic sources of terrorism as well as cyber security has resulted in a series of legislative and organizational responses intended to meet the unique challenges these issues raise. While publics in both countries share in general their governments' security prioritization, the more intrusive role of security agencies is raising questions.

Australia and New Zealand both undertook significant reexaminations of their national security operations in the post-9/11 period. In 2008 and 2009 respectively, the Australian and New Zealand governments completed reviews of their intelligence and security sectors.[3] On the basis of these reviews, both states articulated broadened concepts of national security that sought to encapsulate events and activities outside the traditional understanding of preserving sovereignty and territorial integrity. Australia and New Zealand chose to maintain the central frameworks of their existing security machinery, but emphasized a more effective whole-of-government approach to the greater complexity of contemporary national security challenges.

Australia's national security strategy

Australia formalized its national security system in 2008 when Prime Minister Kevin Rudd delivered the country's "first national security statement".[4] In his address Rudd outlined Australia's national security environment and introduced a broader spectrum of national security operations. Rudd's statement also articulated changes within Australia's national security architecture, including the creation of the position of National Security Advisor, the need for regular national security statements and the need for national security operations to be accountable to the nation. Rudd's national security statement was followed by the release of *Strong and Secure: A Strategy for Australia's National Security* (2013) under Prime Minister Julia Gillard.[5] *Strong and Secure* formalized the inaugural national security statement into an operational architecture for security agencies within Australia's strategic environment. But, despite initial enthusiasm for promoting the importance of national security, subsequent national security statements occurred only sporadically in response to international terror events, and the National Security Advisor position was effectively disestablished in 2013 under Prime Minister Tony Abbott.[6]

Australia's national security focus reflects that country's proximity to Asia and the external threats it perceives emerging from that region. Even though it is an island, Australia has proven susceptible to border incursions by asylum seekers originating from the Middle East who transit through South-East Asia to avoid detection. Much of Australia's national security discourse is centered on human-based threats to its citizens. In particular, its discourse focuses on how radicalization by fundamentalist, ideologically based groups is realized in terrorist acts against Australian peoples within the country's national borders.

Strong and Secure, Australia's 2013 national security strategy, was its first. The strategy articulates the 'pillars of Australia's national security' and presents the government's vision for a unified security mechanism.[7] *Strong and Secure* explains Australia's transition from a traditional threat–response model to a methodology that anticipates, protects and influences the country's strategic environment in support of Australia's national interests. The basis for Australia's national security strategy was developed during the years following the 2008 National Security Statement through a substantial program of White Papers across the spectrum of relevant security areas.[8] The focus for enhancement efforts gleaned from these examinations was the strengthening of interagency coordination mechanisms through legislative change and improved strategic direction by central government. A focus on consolidating and improving the relationships between central government and states, territories and business was identified as a key element in developing a more comprehensive approach to national security operations.[9] Improved strategic direction was achieved by articulating Australia's four national security objectives: to ensure a safe and resilient population; to protect and strengthen state sovereignty; to secure national assets, infrastructure and institutions; and to promote a favorable international environment.[10] These objectives were seen not only to span the interests of traditional security agencies, but also to necessitate the participation of 'non-national security agencies' within Australia's contemporary security context.[11]

During the period 1999–2013, Australia was required to respond to several events that challenged its perception of national security operations. Military operations in East Timor, Afghanistan and Iraq, the strategic shock of the September 2001 attacks on the United States, the 2002 and 2005 Bali bombings, and the 2008 global financial crisis all demanded responses that went beyond the expertise of defense, intelligence and security agencies. The greater complexity of Australia's contemporary security environment affirmed the country's need for a whole-of-government approach to national security. To achieve its national security objectives, the Australian government posited eight pillars or principles to ground national security operations.[12]

The first pillar – countering terrorism, espionage and foreign interference – dominates the Australian discussion of national security, particularly with respect to the challenges modern terror groups pose within the country's current security context. In fact terrorism, and Australia's response to it, has been the dominant theme in that country's national security discourse since the 1970s.[13] Following the Hilton Hotel bombing in Sydney in 1978, then Prime Minister Malcolm Fraser announced the establishment of a committee which included Australian government, state and territory agencies. The committee's principal aim was to establish a set of national arrangements and agreements to respond to threats or acts of politically motivated violence. The Standing Advisory Committee on Commonwealth and State Cooperation for Protection Against Violence (SAC-PAV) held its first meeting in February 1979.[14]

Prior to 2001, terrorist events occurring within Australian borders were in support of international issues and targeted symbols of external protagonists. But, in the aftermath of the 9/11 attacks which precipitated the 'Global War on Terror', Australia itself became the specific target of domestic and external terrorist action.[15] In the decade preceding 2001, over 100 Australian citizens had been killed in terrorist attacks across the globe.[16] More recently, threats have emerged within the country's national borders, albeit from lone actors inspired by fanatical ideologies imported from abroad. The stabbing of two police officers and the Martin Place siege in in Sydney in 2014 illustrate the insecurity that can be generated by unhinged individuals incited to violence by digital and social media.

Australia's Counter-Terrorism White Paper, released in 2010, states that the main source of international terrorism and the primary terrorist threat to Australia and Australian interests is from a global violent jihadist movement – extremists who follow a distorted and militant interpretation of Islam that espouses violence as the answer to perceived grievances. This extremist movement comprises al-Qa'ida, groups allied or associated with it, and other groups and individuals inspired by a similar worldview. While the threat is persistent, the challenge has evolved since the last counter-terrorism White Paper in 2004 in two respects.[17]

First, while there have been counter-terrorism successes – most notably pressure on al-Qa'ida's core leadership in Afghanistan and Pakistan, and action against terrorists in South-East Asia – these successes have been offset by the rise of groups affiliated with, or inspired by, al-Qa'ida's message and methods. New areas such as Somalia and Yemen have joined existing areas of concern in South Asia, South-East Asia, the Middle East and the Gulf.

A second shift apparent since 2004 has been an increase in the terrorist threat from people born or raised in Australia, people who have become influenced by the violent jihadist message. The bombings in London on July 7, 2005, which were carried out by British nationals, brought into stark relief the real threat of globally inspired but locally generated attacks in Western democracies, including Australia. A number of Australians are known to subscribe to this message, some of whom might be prepared to engage in violence. Many of these individuals were born in Australia and come from a wide range of ethnic backgrounds. The pool of those committed to violent extremism in Australia is not static – over time some move away from extremism, while others become more extreme.

Indeed, the violent ideology of Sunni Islamist terrorist groups – such as the Islamic State of Iraq and the Levant (ISIL) and al-Qa'ida – continues to appeal to a small number of people in Australia. These groups use the power of the internet to provide propaganda to an existing audience, and also aim it at those susceptible to radicalization. The broad body of propaganda continues to grow. Some releases specifically celebrate terrorist attacks overseas, including the methods and tactics used in attacks, while others feature tailored messaging referencing specific countries or individuals. Australia has been specifically mentioned in ISIL's online magazines, most recently in February 2017. Such propaganda releases add to a large body of material that encourages terrorism.[18]

Today the primary terrorist threat in Australia is from a small number of Islamist extremists, principally lone actors or small groups who use simple attack methodologies enabling them to act independently and with a high degree of agility. The simple nature of such attacks means preparation may not involve activity overt enough or concerning enough to pique the attention of authorities – meaning there is no guarantee of early detection or disruption. Islamist terrorist attacks and plots aim to inflict maximum casualties, and perpetrators often aim to be killed during the attacks. Previous overseas incidents have been perpetrated by small groups and have featured multiple attackers and targets; even more complex plots have featured the use of relatively simple weapons and tactics.

Despite recent ISIL setbacks in the Middle East, the Australian government remains vigilant. The 2015 *Review of Australia's Counter-Terrorism Machinery* document asserts that global terrorism is growing and diversifying.[19] Ideologically based terror groups have become more able to exploit digital technology to promulgate their narrative to a global audience. In Australia's case this has not only encouraged domestic terror events, but has also drawn an estimated 120–250 of the country's citizens into the conflict zones of Syria and Iraq.[20] This cadre of foreign fighters creates security challenges for the Australian government in deciding how to prevent more of its citizens from joining fundamentalist groups, how to prevent radicalized individuals from acting domestically and how to reintegrate returning foreign fighters into Australian society. To meet these challenges, the Australian government has significantly enhanced its counter-terrorism arrangements, raised its national security expenditure and enacted new legislation to enhance security agencies' powers to act against suspected individuals and groups.

Before 2001, Australia's response to terrorism was one dimensional. It focused primarily on its national intelligence agencies collecting information in order to undermine terrorist activities.[21] In the face of increased terror threats and greater scrutiny of government responses to such threats, Australia raised its national security expenditure and developed specific counter-terrorism machinery to enhance its approach to these challenges. Over the period 2001–2014, Australia significantly increased the budgets of its major security agencies. The Australian Security Intelligence Organisation (ASIO)'s overall budget grew by 500 percent; the Office of National Assessments funding increased fourfold; the Australian Secret Intelligence Service (ASIS) budget tripled; and the Australian Federal Police (AFP) received double its former amount of funding.[22] The National Counter-Terrorism Committee (NCTC) was established in 2002, along with Joint Australian Federal Police – local police counter-terrorism teams in each of the six states and three internal federal territories. To support the NCTC, the National Threat Assessment Centre (NTAC) was created within ASIO, and a Counter-Terrorism Ambassador appointed within the Department of Foreign Affairs and Trade.[23] These new institutions assisted the NCTC through regular threat assessments and enhanced collaboration between Australia and its international partners.[24]

This counter-terror framework was further strengthened in 2008–2009 by the establishment of the Crisis Coordination Centre within the Attorney General's Department and the National Security College at Australian National University, which aimed to improve the situational awareness and operational functionality of the national security community through education.[25] In concert with such new structures, the Australian Parliament approved 12 new pieces of legislation to broaden the powers of its security agencies in response to contemporary terror threats and issues.[26] Specifically, these bills define a range of terrorism-related offences; permit the detention and/or questioning of individuals in relation to terrorism offences; and allow the arrest, monitoring and/or prosecution of returning foreign fighters.[27]

The combination of focused counter-terrorism agencies and empowering legislation described above has allowed Australia to deepen its approach to combating contemporary terror issues. The spectrum of Australian counter-terrorism operations now not only has the capacity to undermine terrorist activities; it also has the capability to disrupt detected attacks and strengthen community resilience through greater cohesion and awareness. Changes in Australia's national security architecture have allowed the country to evolve its counter-terrorism machinery from a reactionary response to an emergent threat mechanism, to a proactive 'systems' approach. Australian counter-terror efforts involve government agencies, but also seek to encourage community engagement – engagement able to identify low-level precursors to terrorist activity, thereby providing early detection and response. This new approach has successfully prevented five terror attacks within Australia since 2001.

Nevertheless, the new measures have not escaped criticism. Primary concerns revolve around the impact the new legislation has on the civil liberties of Australian citizens given increased powers of surveillance and enhanced government authority to question or detain terror suspects without normal liberal democratic checks and balances.[28] Australia's Human Rights Commission president, Gillian Triggs, has openly stated that democratic rights and freedoms have been infringed upon by the new laws which expand executive powers. Triggs claims that the laws passed by Australia's Parliament over the last decade have undermined a healthy, robust democracy: "What are the options for democracy when both major parties, in government and opposition, agree upon laws that violate fundamental freedoms?" According to Triggs, the overreach of the executive is clear in the proposal to strip citizenship from people accused of being jihadists fighting against Australian interests if they are dual nationals. "This proposal strikes at the heart of Australia as a largely migrant nation," she said.[29]

Criticism of Australia's new legislative powers highlights the tension between the government's need to protect its citizens and the right of those citizens to exercise their liberty. Terrence McCoy, writing in the *Washington Post*, labelled Australia a "national security state". He asserts that Australia has "mortgage[d] civil liberties for a broader sense of security", and has criticized the National Security Legislation Amendment Bill (No 1) 2014 for legalizing "surveillance of the entire Australian Internet" and endangering freedom of speech by potentially sentencing "whistleblowers and journalists" to prison for publishing classified information. McCoy also challenges the new laws regarding the detention and 'coercive questioning' of Australian citizens without charge.[30]

McCoy has not been alone in expressing concern over the potential impingement upon Australian liberal democratic values. The *Sydney Morning Herald* and other Australian press agencies, as well as academics, have questioned the lack of definition within the new legislation, and have suggested that the vagueness of the bill allows ample room for the Australian government to extend its powers and control the security agenda.[31] In response to this criticism, Attorney-General George Brandis did not attempt to ease concerns, but stated that such measures were 'vital' in equipping Australia's security agencies with the power and capability needed in a "newly dangerous age".[32]

New Zealand's national security coordination

New Zealand's geographic isolation and volatile natural environment shape the country's national security lens. Geographic isolation is a boon in that it removes the likelihood of an existential military threat to New Zealand's sovereignty. But isolation is a double-edged sword since New Zealand relies on expansive physical and electromagnetic lines of communication that enable the state to interact both politically and economically within the global community. New Zealand's national security discourse is centered on preservation of these lines of communication and maintenance of a rules-based international order based on democratic institutions. These foci are not surprising given New Zealand's position as a small, liberal democratic state reliant on soft power to influence other actors in pursuit of its national interests. Accordingly, New Zealand's national security machinery is geared towards protecting its physical and cyber lines of communication and the natural resources that are the foundation of its economy.

The themes presented in Australia's 2008 national security statement are echoed in *New Zealand's National Security System* (NSS) document, produced in 2011 by the New Zealand Department of the Prime Minister and Cabinet (DPMC). The 2011 document identifies itself as the first comprehensive presentation of New Zealand's national security interests. It emphasizes a whole-of-government approach to national security operations, and establishes the position of National Security Advisor. The National Security System identifies the broadening of New Zealand's concept of national security from an essentially defensive, police and intelligence agency orientation to an approach that encompasses all hazards to New Zealand's people, resources and sovereignty.[33] The definition of national security currently presented in the New Zealand's national security system is expansive. It demonstrates intent by the New Zealand government to respond to the evolving nature and greater complexity of the global security environment. This definition requires New Zealand's national security system to encompass all significant risks and hazards, both natural and man-made, to the nation's population and environment.[34] Yet the *New Zealand's National Security System* document is not a national security strategy; and, although it identifies desired ends by stating its national security objectives, it fails to articulate the ways and means necessary to achieve them.

In August 2016, the DPMC released the *National Security System Handbook* (NSS Handbook), which describes "New Zealand's arrangements with respect to both … the governance of national security and in response to a potential, emerging or actual national security crisis."[35] The NSS Handbook provided an update of New Zealand's national security architecture and formalized changes to operational structures made in response to the NSS of 2011. The Handbook's intended audience is public service members, ranging from chief executives to officials, public service members likely to be involved in national security system operations. But it also offers critical insight into security discourse and governance. The NSS Handbook provides detailed descriptions of the governance structures that oversee the operation of the NSS, including the composition and roles of key advisory boards and (as mentioned above) the expectations of contributing agencies in response to potential, emerging or actual events. Despite several operational changes, the foundational tenets and highest levels of authority articulated in the NSS of 2011 remain unchanged. The system's core principles, the definition of national security, and key security objectives remain firmly embedded in the national security system through their reiteration in the NSS Handbook.[36]

The 2011 NSS and 2016 NSS Handbook, taken together, attempt to facilitate a whole-of-government approach to security issues by describing the New Zealand government's aspirations for individuals and agencies involved in the national security system. These documents establish levels of authority within the system, and provide a basis for interagency cooperation. The information and direction provided by the NSS and the NSS Handbook are focused very much on clarifying the process the system will follow in response to a security event. What is lacking is a critical analysis of New Zealand's security context, and an articulation of the unique problem space within which New Zealand's security agencies are expected to operate. The 2016 *Report of the First Independent Review of Intelligence and Security in New Zealand* identifies the challenges the current definition presents to government departments that are seeking to understand where security responsibilities begin and end.[37]

The absence of a comprehensive national security strategy leaves New Zealand's security agencies reactionary in nature, inhibited in their ability to reduce risks and achieve readiness within the security field. Furthermore, the breadth of issues encompassed by New Zealand's definition of national security leaves significant room for misinterpretation and misunderstanding by agencies as to what the government's expectations of them are. The 2014 New Zealand Intelligence Community (NZIC) Performance Improvement Framework report stated that New Zealand's national security and intelligence priorities were inadequately defined, and that the NZIC did not understand the needs and priorities of the key decision-makers.[38] Lacking appropriate definition and direction from central government, agencies will continue to function under their institutionalized perceptions of the security environment. Without the development of a complete New Zealand national security strategy, agencies involved in national security activities will struggle to operate in a coherent, whole-of-government fashion. At the same time, in the absence of an existential military threat, the term 'security', and the emotive value attached to it, remain important political tools. Therefore, the omission of a national security strategy may be a deliberate mechanism for increasing the New Zealand government's control over its national security discourse.

New Zealand's DPMC represents the office of the Prime Minister, who assumes his or her role by virtue of leading the political party that received the majority of votes from the New Zealand electorate. The Prime Minister's leadership is enhanced by the charisma of office that his or her political appointment holds with the New Zealand public. The strength of the Prime Minister's charisma of office in the security sector allows the PM's office to determine the major threats to New Zealand's national security. The DPMC constructs national security threats for the New Zealand government agencies and the nation's citizens by shaping the national security discourse. As the chair of the Cabinet National Security Committee (NSC), and by positioning the Chief Executive of their own office as chair of the Officials Committee for Domestic and External Security Coordination (ODESC), New Zealand's Prime Minister has the power not only to set the national security agenda, but also to control its execution through the ODESC system. By leading the major components of the national security system, New Zealand's Prime Minister and Chief Executive DPMC have created a national security context in which they are the dominant securitizing agents within the nation's national security discourse.

Tensions arise between New Zealand's liberal democratic institutions and the reality of a single agency dominating the national security discourse. The legitimacy of the NSS comes from its origins in New Zealand's democratic system of government. Democratic legitimation asserts that a state's citizens are the highest authority within their territory, and views the institutions of state as necessary mechanisms for coordinating the actions of society. State office holders, as elected representatives of the people, enact policy on behalf of the electorate in pursuit of agreed national interests. Liberal theorist John Locke asserted that the direct influence of the state should be minimized to allow constituents the liberty to realize their individually determined interests. Locke contends that the institutions of a state exist to facilitate the rights and liberties of its citizens. He presents the people as the best judge of their own interests. Therefore the state must be restricted in its scope and practice to provide the greatest possible freedom for its citizens.[39] Locke proposes that freedom and equality are possible given an individual's capacity for rational thought that follows the laws of nature. He states that the right to govern one's affairs and uphold 'natural laws' is as inherent as respect for the rights of others.

Locke's 'state of nature' is undermined by 'inconveniences' that exist within a societal group. Not all individuals respect the rights of others. When individuals are left to enforce the laws of nature, different interpretations cause disagreement over the meaning of law, and loosely organized individuals are vulnerable to external aggression.[40] Locke's proposed solution for these 'inconveniences' is the creation of both an independent society and a political society or government. These bodies accept the concept that authority is bestowed upon government to pursue the interests of the governed. Its authority is contingent upon its maintenance of the people's approval. This contract does not transfer all rights of the citizens to the state. It permits the state to undertake law making and enforcement on behalf of its constituents, as long as the state's actions preserve natural rights.

The dominant roles of the Prime Minister and Chief Executive DPMC within New Zealand's security mechanisms, amplified by their charisma of office, make any articulation of a security threat immediately accepted by government departments and the nation's public audiences. The 2014 national security speech by then Prime Minister John Key is an example of such construction of a national security threat used to achieve policy aims. The Prime Minister's speech presented the Islamic State organization (ISIL) as an existential threat to New Zealand's national security in order to rapidly introduce new counter-terrorism laws. By using the strength of the Prime Minister's charisma of office, combined with the power inherent in linking an issue to the security discourse, the New Zealand government could potentially circumvent or minimize the scrutiny of any legislation related to a securitized issue. The Power to Act allows the NSC to act without further reference to the full cabinet should urgency or operational reasons necessitate an immediate response.[41] This authorization is understandable given the dynamic and unpredictable nature of security, yet it carries greater risk when one agency exercises significant control within this field. By declaring a national security threat 'extreme' or' imminent' New Zealand's government can shorten the time during which any legislation with respect to security is debated in Parliament or open to public consultation.

During 2013 the New Zealand Parliament debated the Government Communications Security Bureau and Related Legislation Amendment Bill. The legislation clarified the GCSB's three functions:

- information assurance and cyber security;
- foreign intelligence; and
- assisting other agencies.

The New Zealand Green Party protested against the new legislation, suggesting that a fundamental constraint on freedom had become law.[42] It called it a fundamental attack on the right to privacy and the right to be free of mass state surveillance. According to the Green Party statement, the GCSB bill gives the GCSB the power to:

- spy directly on New Zealanders to assist the Police, the Defence Force and the Security Intelligence Service (SIS);
- get warrants, not just for a specified individual, but also for a "class of people" – without saying which individuals might be included; and
- share what they find out about ordinary Kiwis with other spy agencies around the world.[43]

In response to criticism, a revised version of the bill, entitled the Security and Intelligence Act (ISA), was approved by Parliament in 2017. The new bill states that the purpose of the Act is to protect New Zealand as a free, open and democratic society by establishing intelligence and security agencies that will effectively contribute to the protection of New Zealand's national security. It emphasizes the need: to give the intelligence and security agencies adequate and appropriate functions, powers and duties; to ensure that the functions of the intelligence and security agencies are performed in accordance with New Zealand law and all human rights obligations recognized by New Zealand law, with integrity and professionalism and in a manner that facilitates effective democratic oversight; and to ensure that the powers of the intelligence and security agencies are subject to institutional oversight and appropriate safeguards.[44]

Key features of the legislative changes contained in the Intelligence and Security Act of 2017 are as follows:

- A single law to cover the agencies, replacing the existing four laws;
- A new warrant system, including a "triple lock" protection for any New Zealander placed under surveillance;
- More effective cooperation between the Government Communications Security Bureau (GCSB) and the Security Intelligence Service (SIS).

Commenting on the new security legislation of 2017, then Prime Minister John Key admitted that "some will always feel a bit nervous about privacy and their own rights", but gave his assurance that the government would be very careful and cautious about what it does as a state.[45] The New Zealand Green Party has described the proposals for the expansion of spy agency powers as "one of the most significant erosions in New Zealanders' privacy in recent times".[46] The New Zealand Labour Party supported the new legislation but has problems with some elements of it, including the definition of national security and the level of privacy protections.[47]

New Zealand's Intelligence and Security Bill primarily increases the powers of surveillance government agencies exercise over persons they identify as risks to national security. The National Assessments Bureau, a unit of the DPMC, determines potential threats and monitors any further action that is coordinated through the ODESC system.[48] As a result, all the agencies involved in counter-terror operations are subordinate organizations of the Prime Minister's office. Ironically, while the DPMC maintains that the NSS and other security-oriented policies are designed to protect the institutions, principles and values that underpin New Zealand society,[49] the structure of these new measures blurs some of the checks and balances inherent within the UK's Westminster system – checks and balances intended to prevent such a concentration of power in any single individual or agency.

It is important to remember in this context the content of the Prime Minister's 2014 speech which identified ISIL as a threat of sufficient magnitude to warrant special legislation to counter its potential threat, and claims that the magnitude of the threat required the Head of State to inform the citizens personally. A degree of security theatre surrounded the delivery of the Prime Minister's speech. The fact that the Prime Minister himself introduced the proposed new measures is significant since it indicated to the audience the PM's direct support for the policy and the prominence of the threat in New Zealand's national security spectrum. Media coverage of the speech was extensive. All New Zealand's broadcast media were represented at what was officially a New Zealand Institute of International Affairs event. The Prime Minister announced that the government's response to counter ISIL outside New Zealand focused only in Iraq, and would not extend into Syria. This suggested that the defeat of ISIL may not have been the actual objective of the introduction of increased powers of surveillance within New Zealand. Yet, as the Prime Minister and his officials are the initiators and controllers of New Zealand's national security discourse, which other actors are able to challenge the validity of the threats they portray?

The dominance of New Zealand's national security discourse by the Prime Minister and their department prevents an effective sub-discourse from occurring among government agencies involved in New Zealand's security field. This lack of a sub-discourse prevents necessary translation of strategic or political concepts into effective cross-agency initiatives, initiatives through which successful national security operations could be implemented. Senior officials in government agencies possess the expertise and experience to provide effective advice, both upwards and down, to create realistic expectations of what particular support and capabilities their agency offers to a security response. Such bureaucrats play an important role in the Westminster system, ensuring that key decision makers within central government fully comprehend the implications of their decisions, and that frontline agencies have a clear appreciation of political expectations attendant to their contribution to national security activities.

The New Zealand government's response to the Christchurch mosque shootings on March 15, 2019 provides a more recent example of the Prime Minister's ability to dominate both discourse and actions in New Zealand's national security field. Despite New Zealand's counter-terrorism precautions, its security was shattered when an Australian citizen, Brenton Tarrant, who had been living in New Zealand for two years, entered the Masjid Al Noor and Linwood mosques in Christchurch during Friday prayers and proceeded to kill 51 worshippers, leaving another 40 people wounded. These murders shocked most New Zealanders and much of the world beyond the country's borders. The day after the shootings Prime Minister Jacinda Ardern announced that New Zealand's firearms laws would change, and that the legal status of semi-automatic weapons would be reconsidered. The New Zealand government quickly enacted legislation that severely restricted access to handguns and other weapons. On March 21, 2019, less than a week after the mosque attacks, New Zealand's Governor General signed an order banning military-style semi-automatic and assault rifles, as well as large-capacity magazines. The rapid enactment of these law changes was viewed by opponents as an emotive overreaction that lacked appropriate consultation in a democratic society. Gun owners, however, have supported the government's actions and participated in the buyback events that have occurred. New Zealand's firearms law changes remain a contentious issue, and the prospect of further amendments is likely to ensure that the debate continues.

Conclusion

The nexus between security and democracy in Australia and New Zealand is overall balanced, and has not disrupted the traditional adherence of the two nations to democratic governance and human security. The majority of the public in both countries is becoming more aware of increased transnational security risks, and expects their governments to effectively protect each country and its population from violence and crime. Recent terrorist attacks all over Europe are perceived by the Australian and New Zealand public as dangerous international trends which could potentially reach their countries. The alleged Russian hacking interference in the US and European elections has raised concerns both in Australia and New Zealand about their vulnerability to such attacks.

Australian society, for obvious reasons, seems to be particularly concerned about transnational security threats. New Zealanders have not been affected by extremism in the same way yet. Australia's close security involvement with the United States and NATO is broadly accepted by its public. That leads to general acceptance of Canberra's alignment with the security policies and legislation of its Western allies. New Zealand's relatively autonomous foreign policy, cherished by its public, regularly clashes with the country's security cooperation with Western allies, especially through the Five Eyes arrangement. Internal security legislation and policy decisions are often viewed by New Zealand's public as being imposed by Western nations, and not necessarily driven by the country's national interests.

This dilemma is exacerbated by the absence of a comprehensive national security strategy in New Zealand. Australia's national security strategy of 2013 emphasizes the importance of a whole-of-society approach to national security, even if that system remains inadequate. The absence of a national security strategy, which in a democratic society also implies broad public consultation, hampers the mitigation of tension between security and democracy in New Zealand more than it does in Australia.

Notes

1 Simon Benson, "'Crowded horizon of risk' requires strategy and long-term planning, says key government adviser," *Daily Telegraph*, May 24, 2016, www.dailytelegraph.com.au/news/crowded-horizon-of-risk-requires-strategy-and-longterm planning-says-key-government-adviser/news-story/fa4a2565f19afaa2622f8551f5f286b2.

2 New Zealand Defence White Paper, 2016, p. 29, www.nzdf.mil.nz/downloads/pdf/public-docs/2016/defence-white-paper-2016.pdf.

3 Ric Smith, "Summary and Conclusions Report of the Review of Border and Homeland Security", December 4, 2008. http://ict-industry-reports.com.au/wp-content/uploads/sites/4/2013/10/2008-Review-Homeland-and-Border-Security-Ric-Smith-June-2008.pdf; Department of the Prime Minister and Cabinet, *New Zealand's National Security System*, 2011 [hereafter DPMC, *NSS*].

4 Kevin Rudd (Hon.) The Prime Minister. "The First National Security Statement to the Australian Parliament", Australian Government, Canberra, December 4, 2008.

5 Australian Government Department of the Prime Minister and Cabinet, *Strong and Secure: A Strategy for Australia's National Security*. January 2013. http://apo.org.au/system/files/33996/apo-nid33996-44191.pdf.

6 Ben Grubb, "Terror laws clear Senate, enabling entire Australian web to be monitored and whistleblowers to be jailed." *Sydney Morning Herald*, September 25, 2014. www.smh.com.au/digital-life/consumer-security/terror-laws-clear-senate-enabling-entire-australian-web-to-be-monitored-and-whistleblowers-to-be-jailed-20140925-10m8ih.html.

7 Australian Government, *Strong and Secure*, p. vi.
8 Ibid p. 10.
9 Ibid p. vi.
10 Ibid p. 4.
11 Ibid.
12 Ibid p. 15.
13 Australian Government Department of the Prime Minister and Cabinet, *Counter-Terrorism White Paper: Securing Australia Protecting our Community*, 2010. www.dst.defence.gov.au/sites/default/files/basic_pages/documents/counter-terrorism-white-paper.pdf, p. 7.
14 Australian Government, "What Australia is Doing: Australian National Security", www.nationalsecurity.gov.au/WhatAustraliaisdoing/Pages/Australia-New-Zealand-Counter-Terrorism-Committee.aspx.
15 Australian Government, *Counter-Terrorism White Paper*, p. 7.
16 Australian Government, *Strong and Secure*. p. 9.
17 Australian Government. *Counter-Terrorism White Paper*.
18 Australian Government, "Australian National Security: National Terrorism Threat Advisory System", www.nationalsecurity.gov.au/Securityandyourcommunity/Pages/National-Terrorism-Threat-Advisory-System.aspx.
19 Australian Government Department of the Prime Minister and Cabinet, *Review of Australia's Counter-Terrorism Machinery*, January 2015. www.dpmc.gov.au/sites/default/files/publications/190215_CT_Review_1.pdf, p. 10.
20 The Soufan Group, "Foreign Fighters: An Updated Assessment of the Flow of Foreign Fighters into Syria and Iraq", 2015. http://soufangroup.com/wp-content/uploads/2015/12/TSG_ForeignFightersUpdate_FINAL3.pdf.
21 Australian Government, *Australia's Counter-Terrorism Machinery*, p. 13.
22 Ibid p. 3.
23 Ibid pp. 5–6.
24 Ibid p. 6.
25 Ibid p. 8.
26 Ibid pp. 5–9.
27 Ibid p. 9.
28 Terrence McCoy, "How Australia just became a 'national security state'." *Washington Post*, October 7, 2014. www.washingtonpost.com/news/morning-mix/wp/2014/10/07/how-australia-just-became-a-national-security-state/?utm_term=.64807ac1ec28; Grubb, "Terror laws clear Senate".
29 Stefanie Balogh and Tessa Akerman, "Democracy undermined by new laws says Gillian Triggs", *Weekend Australian*, June 6, 2015, www.theaustralian.com.au/news/democracy-undermined-by-new-laws-says-gillian-triggs/news-story/04a8d873b8c04b96a7bae954c44adbb0.
30 McCoy, "How Australia just became a 'national security state'."
31 Ibid.
32 Grubb, "Terror laws clear Senate".
33 DPMC *NSS*, pp. 3–4.
34 Ibid.
35 Department of the Prime Minister and Cabinet, *National Security System Handbook* (2016), p. 5, https://dpmc.govt.nz/sites/default/files/2017-03/dpmc-nss-handbook-aug-2016.pdf [hereafter DPMC, *NSS Handbook*].
36 Ibid pp. 6–8.
37 Hon Sir Michael Cullen, KNZM and Dame Patsy Reddy, DNZM, *Intelligence and Security in a Free Society: Report of the First Independent Review of Intelligence and Security in New Zealand* (2016), pp. 92–93.
38 Peter Bushnell and Garry Wilson, *Performance Improvement Framework: Review of the Agencies in the Core New Zealand Intelligence Community (NZIC)* (State Services Commission, July 2014), p. 6.
39 Gregor McLennan, David Held and Stuart Hall, *The Idea of the Modern State* (Milton Keynes: Open University Press, 1984), p. 41.
40 Ibid p. 38.
41 DPMC, *NSS Handbook*, p. 14.
42 Audrey Young, "GCSB bill passes after final reading", *New Zealand Herald*, August 21, 2013.
43 "Stop the GCSB Bill", Green Party Statement, https://home.greens.org.nz/stop-the-gcsb-bill.
44 Intelligence and Security Bill, New Zealand Legislation, www.legislation.govt.nz/bill/government/2016/0158/latest/DLM6920829.html.

45 "New GCSB bill allows spying on Kiwis", stuff.co.nz, August 15, 2016, www.stuff.co.nz/national/politics/83160725/New-GCSB-bill-allows-spying-on-Kiwis.
46 Ibid.
47 Vernon Small, "Proposed new spooks law hands GCSB power to spy on New Zealanders", stuff.co.nz, August 15, 2016, www.stuff.co.nz/national/politics/83166880/proposed-new-spooks-law-hands-gcsb-power-to-spy-on-new-zealanders.
48 DPMC, *NSS Handbook*, p. 34.
49 DPMC, *NSS*, p. 3.

11

ISRAEL'S DEMOCRACY AND SECURITY

Raphael Cohen-Almagor and Amos N. Guiora[1]

Introduction

Israel is a small country. Comprised roughly of 21,200 square kilometers, Israel is more or less the size of Massachusetts (21,456 sq km), ranked 45th of the 50 US states in land mass.[2] This size does not include the West Bank (5,607 sq km),[3] which is not officially part of Israel. Israeli law does not apply in the West Bank, where the majority of the population consists of about 2.5 million Palestinians and 360,000 Jewish settlers.[4] On the eve of Rosh Hashana (Jewish New Year) 2014, Israel's population was 8,904,373; of that number about 75 percent were Jews.[5]

Israel's national security environment is volatile, extreme in the breadth and frequency of change in its level of uncertainty.[6] Israel has four Arab neighbor states: Egypt, Syria, Lebanon and Jordan. Israel has signed peace treaties with two of its neighbors, Egypt and Jordan. But permanent hostility defines Israel's relationships with Syria, Lebanon, Hamas in Gaza and the Palestinian Authority in the West Bank. In recent years, Israel has witnessed new non-state actors in Syria with the potential to interfere with the integrity of the State of Israel and pose threats. Israel differs from its neighbors in many crucial respects: religion, culture, language and regime. Over time its neighbors have refused to accept it, perceiving Israel as a bone in their throats. Many Palestinians and Arabs in the neighboring states still consider Israel a foreign element that needs to be removed. As the Arab states are collectively many times stronger and larger than Israel in means, size and population, Israel takes every threat most seriously. Israel's history is thus the history of survival.

Since its establishment, Israel has had to fight. Between 1948 and 2010, some 23,000 Israelis were killed in wars and terror attacks.[7] This loss is felt in every home in Israel. Israel's objectives have been to continue its existence, to provide a home for the Jewish people and to uphold the political prerogatives of nationality. Facing an unequal balance of power, unfavorable geo-strategic conditions and the constant threat of physical annihilation, Israel has been compelled to develop a strong army capable of withstanding the siege. Since the 1970s, few of its neighbors have been willing to recognize Israel's existence, or achieve some form of reconciliation with Israel. Violence was to be expected. During the early period Israeli security policy was dictated by an Arab strategy that aimed to undermine the country's very existence.[8] Thus, until the 1970s wars were perceived as an inevitable eruption and expansion of the constant violence. Periods between wars were perceived in Israel as latent wars. Given its lack of economic resources, its limited geo-strategic depth and the psychological effects of a nation recovering from the trauma of the Holocaust, Israel developed a defensive strategy that relied first and foremost on its strong army. Its reasoning was: the world did not rush to save European Jewry. There is no reason to think that anything significant has changed. The outside world still will not feel compelled to come to Israel's rescue in case of need. Thus, the development of a strong military power has been, and remains, the nation's most important priority.

Today all Zionist political parties, from the far left to the far right, recognize security needs and acknowledge the necessity to maintain a strong army in order to sustain Israel's sovereignty. Security is a basic necessity, *sine qua non* to the promotion of other ends, including peace. The country unites in the face of security challenges.

Israel's security policy

Israel began to formulate its security policy in the early 1950s under its first leader, David Ben-Gurion. The three pillars of its defense doctrine were deterrence of possible threats; detection of impending attacks; and decisive military defeat of the enemy when deterrence failed.[9] Until the 1990s, the major perceived threat was an Arab military invasion of Israel and a war between states. But in the early 1990s, Israel started to formulate a new security concept according to which the main threat might not emanate from states but from sub-state organizations such as Hamas and Hezbollah.[10] Israel is surrounded by non-state actors: Hamas, Hezbollah, rebel organizations in Syria, jihadist elements in the Golan Heights, Sinai and in Gaza, and the Palestinian Authority. Since the mid-2000s, much attention has been given to the Iranian nuclear threat and to rocket and missile attacks from Gaza, Lebanon and potentially other hostile areas, perpetrated by non-state actors and proxies of other nations. Israel's security policy therefore has the following characteristics:

- It is aimed at securing the country's ability to overcome single-handedly challenges posed by neighboring states.
- There is an inherent asymmetry between Israel and the Muslim and Arab countries around it. Thus a significant part of Israel's annual budget is dedicated to security issues.
- At the same time, Israel has always sought the support of influential international players and aspired to develop security relationships with many countries across the globe.[11] Since the 1973 Yom Kippur War, Israel has developed special relationships with the United States.
- There is no clear borderline between times of war and times of relative peace.[12]
- Peace is a desired end, a value in itself. But, important as peace undoubtedly is, security is the prime consideration; nothing should undermine Israel's security.
- A zero sum game exists between Israel and its enemies. Gains for the one necessarily mean loss for the other.
- Thus, violations of the status quo by Israel's enemies are unacceptable. Such violations are met by active steps to restore the status quo ante.
- Nearly 80 percent of Israel's population resides along the Mediterranean Sea, and much of its essential infrastructure facilities are built along the coastline. Thus, protecting the shores from attack is crucial. Furthermore, the discovery of large offshore gas resources remains a huge potential for the economy, and 97 percent of Israel's exports and imports are conducted via the sea. Freedom of navigation is crucial. For many years, the sea was

the only gateway that did not pass through hostile territory. The sea must remain open in accordance with international laws.[13]

- Threats and intimidation are necessary tactics to achieve and ensure deterrence. Threats, of course, need to correspond to the stakes at any given point. They need to be credible and sufficient to overcome the challenge posed by the aggressor.[14]
- Deterrence is primarily an act of hostility rather than an act motivated by fear. Such a behavioral model is based on the stick rather than the carrot. In 1963 Schelling explained: "Deterrence is concerned with the exploitation of potential force. It is concerned with persuading a potential enemy that he should in his own interest avoid certain courses of activity."[15]
- Thus, Israel wishes to be perceived as a resolute and determined actor willing to protect its interests, building an image of insistence and will to apply sanctions, including force when it deems necessary.[16] As Claude explained: "Deterrence is a psychological phenomenon, deriving from the belief that the power situation does not favor aggressive action."[17]
- When measures of deterrence have failed, military force on varying scales has been used to secure the integrity of the state and its sovereignty.
- Israeli leaders are well aware of the country's geo-strategic vulnerability and its inferiority compared to the Arab world, parts of which wish to destroy it. Israeli leaders know that Israel cannot match Arab quantitative abilities. There is no comparison between Israel's size and population and the size and population of the Arab countries that surround it. Israel lacks strategic depth, and it lacks natural resources which are in abundance in Arab lands.[18]
- Israel has thus developed and produced both defensive and offensive capabilities (as well as sophisticated weaponry) in order to maintain "a permanent qualitative advantage over Arab confrontation states".[19] Israel aspires to have clear qualitative and technological superiority.[20] In recent years, it has developed enhanced cyber capabilities to protect its infrastructure: water, energy, communication, transportation, economy, technology and security. Israel's cyber defense includes attacks on its opponents' cyber systems in order to undermine their offensive capabilities.[21]
- Israel would try to disrupt potential war coalitions by damaging the core of their offensive capability.[22] Israel would launch military attacks against targets that might seek to undermine its security.
- Israel's existential imperative leads to ruthless conduct if it is attacked or threatened.[23]
- Israel wishes to have a regional monopoly on the possession of nuclear capabilities. It attacked Iraq under Saddam Hussein in 1981, and Syria under Bashar Assad in 2007 and in 2013 to maintain this monopoly. It threatens to attack Iran if the Ayatollah's regime continues to develop its nuclear program or acts on its threat to annihilate Haifa.
- The "worst case scenario" is always in the minds of Israeli decision-makers since they always believe that the state is under siege. Consequently, their aim is to secure the widest possible security margins.
- Israeli leaders maintain a "power politics" orientation, rejecting juridical and moral codes of behavior that seem contradictory to the above characteristics.[24]

The radical Arab stand against Israel of neither peace nor reconciliation, or even mere recognition of its right to exist, has brought about a high level of sensitivity to each declaration and action against Israel. Understanding the "crazy" and irrational characteristics of the Arab nations has been crucial for Israeli strategy,[25] leading its leaders to think that the only language its Arab neighbors understand is force. Virulent, unabashed hostility towards Israel has undermined common features of deterrence policies that customarily assume that rivals act rationally, calculate risks and benefits, avoid taking high risks and are repelled by strong sanctions. Israeli leaders have thought in the past, and still think today, that Arab and Muslim leaders are willing to take very high risks to destroy Israel. They assume that Muslim extremists have norms of rationality different from norms that guide western leaders. This combination of insecurity and lack of trust in the other's ability to act rationally leads to the frequent collapse of deterrence in the Middle East, and brings about sporadic eruptions of violence.

While Israeli leaders believe that Israel should remain capable of withstanding any challenge against its sovereignty and basic rights, they have always sought powerful allies who might come to its aid. During the 1950s, France was the sought-after major power. Indeed, the close relationship between Israel and France during this period led to the 1956 Sinai War. Until the June 1967 Six Day War, France was the main supplier of Israel's weapons; but on 3 June, two days before the beginning of the war, President Charles de Gaulle decreed an arms embargo on Israel, and the supportive relationship came to an end. From then on Israel allied itself first and foremost with the United States. This bond and strategic alliance between the two countries deepened thereafter, and, although the relationship has had its ups and downs, the bond is still said to be unshakeable. On 22 May 2011, President Obama remarked that "the bonds between the United States and Israel are unbreakable, and the commitment of the United States to the security of Israel is ironclad".[26] The bond has been reaffirmed under President Trump, who has moved the US Embassy to Jerusalem and recognized the Golan Heights as part of Israel.

In times of crisis Israel had usually taken three steps that constitute the basis of its deterrence policy: verbal threats by its leaders; mobilization of reserve soldiers; and negotiations with allies in order to receive their support and approval (public or discreet) to use force against the enemy.[27] As mentioned above, Israeli leaders understand that they are not able to compete equally with the Arabs with respect to resources since the Arab nations enjoy capabilities Israel simply does not have, primarily land, population and oil. Thus Israel relies on developed military skills, enhanced technology and superior weapons, supplied by the United States, to withstand aggression.

The centrality of Israel's attitude toward defense leads to the formation of many ties and links between the military and the civilian sectors.[28] The tendency of the military elite to gather and keep power makes the army an important player in the economy and politics of Israel.[29] Retired generals enjoy high esteem and are well positioned to start a second successful career in business or politics. Indeed, some generals try both.[30] At the same time, up until now the army has always supported Israel's democratic institutions and has always subordinated itself to the elected governments. As Horowitz explained, although Israel is a "Fortress Nation", it is much closer to the Athenian model of governance than to the Spartan model as the prominence of security issues does not lead to limitations on society's openness, and does not threaten to resolve civil conflicts via military force.[31]

Occupation

The occupation is a black mark in Israeli and Jewish history.[32] The occupation undermines Israeli democracy and its security. It puts soldiers in a tenuous position vis-à-vis the Palestinians and the Jewish settlers, and it is an obstacle to building trust between Israel and the Palestinians. Trust is essential for reaching peace, and peace should be seen as a significant factor in bolstering Israel's security. Indeed, one may argue that peace is the key to Israel's present and future security.

The occupation is immoral and increasingly leads to Israel's isolation among the community of nations. In 2012, Human Rights Watch (HRW) released a report which exposed the ways in which Israel controls immigration and nationality in the occupied Palestinian territory (OPT) – especially through the population registry, which Israel established in September 1967. The first census conducted after establishment resulted in the exclusion of at least 270,000 people. Israel excluded a further 130,000 West Bank Palestinians who stayed abroad for long periods of time, between 1967 and 1994. In 2000, Israel effectively "froze" the registry's functions altogether, preventing the Palestinian authorities from issuing identity and travel documents or updating information for residents of the OPT.[33]

The Human Rights Watch report details Israel's policies and practices since the beginning of its occupation of Palestinian territory with respect to control of population and movement in and outside of the occupied territory – including removal of individuals from the population registry, denial of child registration and denial of residency in the West Bank for Palestinians from the Gaza Strip. Implementation of these policies has resulted in the depopulation of large groups of Palestinians.

The report holds that Israel's policies violate human rights to freedom of movement, including the right to choose one's place of residence and the right to family life (or family unity, as stated in the report). The report further states that these policies violate a person's rights to a nationality and to prohibition of collective punishment, given the sweeping character and indiscriminate effects of Israel's policies.

In its final section, the report briefly discusses Israel's authority under the law of occupation, recalling the limits placed by the international law of belligerent occupation on an occupying power's ability to administer and implement changes in the daily life of an occupied territory. The international law of belligerent occupation strictly prohibits an occupier from undertaking adjustments in the life of the occupied territory that would outlive the occupation. Premised on a conservational purpose, the law of belligerent occupation exists to ensure that an occupier does not transcend its administrator-type mandate and does not use the slogan of "the benefit of the local population" as a pretext for a hidden agenda. Controlling the population in the occupied territory by regulating immigration and nationality, and by granting or revoking citizenship and permanent residency, not only resembles the powers of sovereign governments but, most pressingly, also has the effect of changing the demographic composition of the territory. Dilution of the Palestinian population is also perpetuated through the continual expansion of Jewish settlements in the Palestinian territory.

On 6 February 2012 Sarah Leah Whitson, Middle East director at Human Rights Watch, stated that "Israel [had not] put forth any concrete security rationale for blanket policies".[34] It can be added that, however serious the security rationale may be, there is no rationale that would allow Israel to legally implement blanket policies of the kind it does, particularly by controlling the registry and effectively rendering it defunct. In all cases, such measures cannot include expulsions from the occupied territory, which are absolutely prohibited. At most, Israel could use security measures when a real necessity for them can be shown on the basis of the specific merits of the case, particularly in order to prevent measures taken under the guise of security, which actually result in the suppression and punishment of the local population.[35]

It is impossible to maintain the occupation without adversely impacting democracy. The occupation dehumanizes the Palestinians and desensitizes Israelis to the harms they inflict on the occupied. The occupiers are mostly young Israeli soldiers who implement the policies of the occupation. It is impossible to maintain a Dr Jekyll and Mr Hyde duality: on the one hand, an occupier who denies basic human rights to others; and, on the other, a democratic citizen who understands and promotes human rights. There is a zero sum game between the occupation and democracy. One comes at the expense of the other. Because the occupation has continued to be part of Israeli life for almost 50 years, Israelis have grown used to it. They accept it, legitimize it, and at the same time deny it. Many Israelis do not speak about the occupation, do not acknowledge it, and rebuff its existence. The Supreme Court considers petitions protesting against the harms of the occupation, and sometimes decides that security considerations do not trump basic human rights; but the occupation should not exist in the first place. The Supreme Court cannot fix something that is inherently wrong.

The Israeli Democracy Index 2013 shows that the greatest share of respondents identified the tension between Jews and Arabs as the most serious area of friction in Israeli society.[36] The tensions relate to the Palestinians in the West Bank and Gaza as well as to the Palestinians inside the Green (1967) Line. The Jewish public is divided as to whether Jewish citizens should be given more rights than non-Jewish citizens. The fact that roughly half of the respondents consider the latter to be an acceptable policy is extremely problematic since the essence of democracy is the principle of equal rights for all citizens.[37] A large proportion of the Jewish sample believes that Arabs should not take part in a referendum to approve a peace treaty with the Palestinians, if and when such a referendum is held:[38] 27.5 percent of the Jews in the sample "Agree totally" and a further 16.3 percent "Agree somewhat" with the statement "The government should encourage Arabs to emigrate from Israel."[39] The survey also reveals that a majority of the Jewish public considers the Jews to be the "chosen people" (50.1 percent believe this "Very strongly" and a further 14.2 percent believe this "Quite strongly"), and that there is a direct correlation between this view and support for excluding Arabs from a possible peace referendum.[40] This sense of "chosenness" entails the exclusion of others. Unsurprisingly, only a minority of the Israeli-Arabs, less than one-third of the sample, feel part of Israel.[41]

Human rights organizations that stand to protect the rights of Palestinians are under increased pressure and are often portrayed as enemies of Israel.[42] Their activities are closely monitored. After the last round of violence during the summer of 2014, Israeli parliamentarians warned civil rights groups that they could be branded as delegitimizers if they insist on promoting rights for Israel's Arab minority and oppose the definition of Israel as the nation state of the Jews.[43]

The fence

On 27 March 2002, on the eve of Pesach, when Jews all around the world celebrate the Seder, a Palestinian Hamas suicide bomber murdered 30 people and injured 140 others, 20 of them seriously, in a brutal attack at Hotel Park in Netanya. This attack shook the nation. The Israeli leadership decided to stop working with the Palestinians on security matters. Israel began construction of a barrier that would separate most of the West Bank from areas inside Israel. The fence (as Israel terms it; others call it the wall) was deemed necessary to block terrorists from entering Israel. At an emergency special session of the UN Security Council on 20 October 2003, Israel argued that the fence was consistent with the right of the State to self-defense, as enshrined in Article 51 of the UN Charter.[44] Indeed, the fence/wall has proved a security success story. The facts are conclusive: before the fence/wall was erected, the average number of terrorist attacks was 26 per year. After its partial construction, this number dropped to between three and zero per year as Israel was able to foil every suicide bombing originating from the northern West Bank, specifically from the cities of Nablus and Jenin, areas that had previously been infamous for exporting suicide bombers. However, according to the UN Office for the Coordination of Humanitarian Affairs Occupied Palestinian Territory (OCHA), 85 percent of the entire fence/wall passes inside Palestinian territory. Were the fence to be completed as planned, some 25,000 Palestinians were expected to live between the barrier and the Green Line.[45]

Because of the barrier's route, which passes through Palestinian living space, 47 gates have been established that are supposed to enable daily movement of farmers to their lands, students and teachers to their schools, businessmen and merchants to their places of work, and more. As a practical matter, freedom of movement for Palestinians has been drastically restricted, and their lives are now run against their will on both sides of the barrier.

On 9 July 2004, the International Court of Justice (ICJ) dismissed the applicability of the law of self-defense which Israel claimed in constructing the fence. In its Advisory Opinion, the Court ruled that the destruction of enemy property is permitted only if it is absolutely necessary for military operations, which was not the case here. The Court argued that the West Bank separation barrier contravenes international law, that it must be dismantled, and that compensation must be paid to the Palestinian owners of property confiscated for its construction. An almost unanimous 14 justices supported the decision. The sole opponent was the American judge, Thomas Buergenthal. In building the barrier, the ICJ opined, Israel violated international humanitarian law by infringing Palestinians' freedom of movement, freedom to seek employment, education and health. It also found Israel in violation of international treaties it had signed, noting: "The construction of such a wall accordingly constitutes breaches by Israel of its various obligations under the applicable international humanitarian law and human rights instruments."[46]

The judges rightly questioned the route of the wall as determined by Israel, saying they were "not convinced that the specific course Israel has chosen for the wall was necessary to attain its security objectives".[47] The ruling further says:

> The wall, along the route chosen, and its associated regime, gravely infringe a number of rights of Palestinians residing in the territory occupied by Israel, and the infringements resulting from that route cannot be justified by military exigencies or by the requirements of national security or public order.[48]

On the issue of compensating Palestinians harmed by construction of the wall, the ICJ ruled that "Israel is under an obligation to make reparation for all damage caused by the construction of the wall in the Occupied Palestinian Territory, including in and around East Jerusalem."[49] The Hague decision was not binding. As expected, Israel immediately reacted by saying that it would not honor the ICJ advisory opinion.

The separation barrier should have been built along the 1967 Green Line, with some accommodation necessary to include a large settlement in the Jerusalem area and Ariel inside the fence/wall, as well as compensation of the Palestinians in other areas. The idea of using the barrier to create geographic facts that in effect make Israel greater and Palestine smaller was unfair, discriminatory, unwise and unjust. The fence/wall should be moved, and continued international pressure is expected to be exerted to ensure that it will actually be moved.

Israeli security: through the lens of the Supreme Court

Israeli security concerns significantly changed in the aftermath of the 1967 Six Day War. In addition to threats from neighboring countries, decision-makers increasingly had to develop counterterrorism measures relevant to Palestinian terrorism in the West Bank and also in the Gaza Strip up until Israel evacuated the settlers and withdrew its army in 2005 (Sharon's Disengagement Plan, known also as Gaza First). This section of the chapter focuses on Palestinian terrorism, Israeli counterterrorism and the balancing of national security and individual rights.

The Israel Supreme Court, sitting as the High Court of Justice (HCJ), is the primary Israeli institution that balances national security and individual rights. The HCJ hears cases initiated by petitions claiming that government action injures individuals and their interests. The Court may issue temporary restraining orders, thereby halting, at least temporarily, planned government actions. In addition, given the acuity of some measures, the Court may convene a hearing immediately upon submission of a petition. With respect to Palestinians living in the West Bank, the HJC hears petitions filed by Palestinians or by human rights organizations on behalf of aggrieved Palestinians.

To date, Israel has not annexed the West Bank (conquered in the 1967 Six Day War). The areas under Israeli control are subject to military rule. Legislation regarding the occupied territories is drafted by officers of the Judge Advocate General Corps and signed into being by the Commander of the Central Command or by the Commander of the Southern Command. Both Commanders are Major Generals. Their decisions may be scrutinized by the Supreme Court, which applies Israeli and international law in its decisions. The Court seeks to ensure that decision-making by these actors reflects respect for international law and is conducted and enforced in accordance with international treaties to which Israel is signatory. Israel's decades-long controversial "State of Emergency" – subject to extension by vote of the Knesset (Parliament) – reflects the primacy of security concerns for decision-makers.

Under President (akin to Chief Justice) Aharon Barak, the Supreme Court significantly minimized the standing requirement and greatly expanded justiciability. In April 2002, during Operation "Ebb and Flow" – when the Israel Defense Forces (IDF) were involved in intensive fighting in the West Bank – over 40 petitions were filed against the IDF in the HCJ regarding military action in the West Bank city of Jenin.

Issues raised in petitions include: potential demolition of a suspected terrorist's home; alleged firing by IDF soldiers on ambulances transporting wounded and sick Palestinians; the need to enable the local population to have a normal water supply; and burial of terrorists. The Court's decisions are rooted in both Israeli law and international humanitarian law. Generally, the Court notes that military matters are not within its area of expertise, whereas issues of humanitarian law are; and the Court will intervene if it determines the IDF has violated domestic or international law.

The principle of judicial activism in Israel can be defined by analyzing five petitions that highlight judicial balancing of national security and individual rights.

I Detainees: Marab v. IDF Commander in the West Bank

According to Military Order 378, as amended in 1997, a Palestinian may be held for eight days before seeing a judge.[50] Upon initiation of Operation Ebb and Flow (April 2002) by the IDF, the detention period before the initial judicial review was extended to 18 days. Iad Ashak Mahmud Marab, a Palestinian detainee, filed a petition before the HCJ against this

Order in *Marab v. IDF Commander in the West Bank* (2002). Marab's counsel argued that the Order results in collective detention without judicial review, and prolonged mass detention rather than individual review. Counsel argued that the Order was neither preventive nor administrative, and violated the principles of proportionality and due process.[51]

The State argued that standard detention law was unsuitable for combat situations: screening of detainees is a time-consuming process; keeping detainees from meeting with counsel prevents passing of messages that endanger soldiers; detentions were individualized rather than collective; unique circumstances of armed conflict dictated unusual measures; and detention standards were proportional and reasonable.[52]

The HCJ held the Order illegal, arguing that detaining individuals for 12 or 18 days without bringing them before a judge conflicted with "fundamentals of both international and Israeli law". The Court also held that judicial review is not separate from detention, but rather is "an integral part of the detention process" and as such cannot legally be separated.[53]

II *Timeliness of the Court's action with respect to humanitarian obligations*

Physicians for Human Rights et al. v. Commander of the IDF Forces in the Gaza Strip

In response to the widespread smuggling of arms and ammunition through an intricate series of tunnels dug between Egypt and the city of Rafah (located in the southern part of the Gaza Strip), the Israel Defense Forces conducted a military operation intended to locate and destroy the tunnels and weaken the terrorist infrastructure in Rafah. During the course of the fighting, civilians were injured and the water supply was affected. Complaints were lodged that the IDF was not allowing basic supplies, such as medication, to enter the city.

A petition was filed by Physicians for Human Rights, the Association for Civil Rights in Israel, the Center for the Defense of the Individual and human rights NGO B'Tselem asking the Court to order the IDF to enable critical humanitarian supplies to be received by the local population and to ensure that the water supply was adequate.[54] As in *Marab*, the Court heard the case during the course of the armed conflict. A senior IDF commander was present in the courtroom to respond directly to the HCJ's questions. The petition was filed on a Thursday and the hearing was held the following day. The State argued that the Court should exercise judicial restraint given the operation's twin goals: preventing additional arms smuggling and destroying terrorist infrastructure.[55] The State also argued that humanitarian measures were occurring within the confines of a military operation, and efforts were being made to minimize danger to innocent civilians while Palestinian terrorists were using civilians as "human shields".[56]

The Court wrote that it would not rule on the manner in which combat is conducted, as that is the responsibility of military commanders when "soldiers' lives are in danger".[57] The decision whether or not to take military action was not a judicial question. Rather, the question before the Court was whether the operation met international humanitarian legal obligations. The Court assumed the operation was a military necessity.[58]

In granting a majority of the petitioners' requests, the Court held that rules of conduct must be taught to, and internalized by, all combat soldiers, regardless of rank.[59] The Court also required "procedures be drawn up that allow implementation of these rules, and which allow them to be put into practice during combat".[60] It ruled that the military commander had an obligation to prevent his troops from "harming lives and dignity of the local residents".[61]

III House demolition

In an effort to quell the Palestinian Intifada (1987–1993), the Israeli government instituted a number of counterterrorism measures, including a policy of demolishing houses in which suspected terrorists resided – predicated on deterring other Palestinians from committing similar acts of terrorism. Israel viewed the policy as an administrative sanction distinct from criminal law process, whereby suspected terrorists are tried either in a civilian or military court. In response to a terrorist attack, the Israel Security Agency (ISA) recommends to the commanding general of the West Bank that the suspected terrorists' homes be demolished.

Section 119 of the Emergency Defense Regulations 1945 authorizes house demolitions under the following circumstances:

> 1 A Military Commander may by order direct the forfeiture to the Government of Palestine of any house, structure, or land from which he has reason to suspect that any firearm has been illegally discharged, or any bomb, grenade or explosive or incendiary article illegally thrown, or of any house, structure or land situated in any area, town, village, quarter or street the inhabitants or some of the inhabitants of which he is satisfied have committed, or attempted to commit, or abetted the commission of, or been accessories after the fact to the commission of, any offence against these Regulations involving violence or intimidation or any Military Court offence; and when any house, structure or land is forfeited as aforesaid, the Military Commander may destroy the house or the structure or anything growing on the land.
>
> 2 Members of His Majesty's forces or of the Police Force, acting under the authority of the Military Commander may seize and occupy, without compensation, any property in any such area, town, village, quarter or street as is referred to in subregulation (1), after eviction without compensation, of the previous occupiers, if any.[62]

When the IDF conquered the West Bank and the Gaza Strip in June 1967, the British Mandatory 1945 Defense Emergency Regulations were in effect. Accordingly, commanders were authorized, according to section 119, to order the forfeiture, sealing and demolition of houses. From 1967 to 1989, IDF commanders ordered the demolition of homes without granting prior notice to the homeowners or tenants.

In *Association for Civil Rights in Israel and Others v. Central District Commander* (1989), the HCJ ordered the Israel Defense Forces to establish a mechanism whereby written notice shall be given to the family regarding the intent to demolish the home. The family was granted the right to appeal to the commanding officer prior to the actual demolition. In those cases where the appeal was denied, the family could petition the HCJ.[63]

A number of criteria were established to determine application of the measure in response to a specific act of terrorism. If the suspected terrorist committed an act resulting in the death of innocent civilians, the home would be immediately sealed and the family would be simultaneously notified of the commanding officer's intent to demolish the house. The purpose of immediately sealing the house was to deter others in the terrorist's community from committing a similar act of terrorism. Simultaneous to the sealing, the relevant authorities gathered information – classified and unclassified – regarding the following issues: (1) whether the terrorist actually lived in the house; (2) how many family members resided in the dwelling; (3) who owned the house; (4) whether the terrorist received assistance (active or passive) from family members; (5) whether demolition of the house would cause structural damage to neighboring homes; and (6) the severity of the terrorist acts committed. After the decision was made to seal or demolish the house, the authorities would determine the extent of the sanction to be imposed. An Arabic-speaking officer serving in Civil Administration would give the family written notice of the commander's decision.

The 1989 High Court's ruling ordering prior due notice fundamentally changed the process, substantively and procedurally. The Court's decision ensured both a process and a more balanced approach to implementation of the sanction. Decision-makers were forced to articulate a house demolition policy. Once the policy was in place, the HCJ largely gave the IDF a free hand in implementing the house demolition sanction. Therefore, the issue was not the legality of the policy; the HCJ had decided that. Rather, the relevant concern was the policy's effectiveness.

A high-level IDF Commission recommended to the Minister of Defense that the policy be frozen. The Commission concluded that house demolitions had not acted as a deterrent and did not meet the policy's stated purpose. Prime Minister Sharon accepted the recommendation, though he indicated the policy could be reactivated if an extreme change in circumstances warranted such a decision.[64]

IV The security fence

According to the Israeli government, the security fence was constructed for strategic and topographical reasons rather than as a border demarcating boundaries between Israel and a future Palestinian state.[65]

In a petition filed to the HCJ, petitioners from the West Bank village of Beit Sourik argued that the fence prevents access to their land; impacts their ability to move freely without excessive bureaucracy; makes use of local wells almost impossible; greatly hinders access to water for crops; uproots olive trees; harms the livelihood of farmers; and does not benefit the local population. The real purpose of the fence is annexation of land exclusively benefiting the IDF and the Jewish population living in the West Bank. Furthermore, the petitioners argued that due process had been violated since military orders regarding the construction of the fence had not been published, denying those injured the right to appeal the decision.[66]

In its response to the petition, the state argued that affected landowners were both offered compensation and entitled to appeal to the West Bank military commander against an order to use their land for the fence. Additionally, the state argued that the primary purpose of the fence was self-defense, intended to protect Israeli citizens against Palestinian terrorists who could easily infiltrate Israel proper. Israel proper refers to lands not captured in the 1967 Six Day War – the West Bank, Gaza Strip, Golan Heights, Sinai Peninsula and East Jerusalem, including the Old City of Jerusalem. The state argued that commanders balanced national security and individual rights, concluding that Palestinian terrorism justified the measure in the context of self-defense.[67] The state did not deny that injury had been incurred by Palestinians, but argued that efforts had been made to minimize damage and rejected claims the decision was intended to annex Palestinian lands for political purposes.

The HCJ developed a three-pronged proportionality test for determining the legality of state action. According to the Court: the objective must be related to the means (a rational means test); the means used must injure the individual to the least extent possible (least injurious test); and the means used must be of proper proportion to the benefit gained (proportionality test). According to the Court, the state failed to meet this test. Therefore, while upholding the legality of the fence's construction, the Court ordered the government to re-contour the fence's route in order to minimize its impact on Palestinians.

A second petition was filed to the HCJ regarding the fence's effect on the residents of the town of Bil'in, *Yassin v. Israel and Military Commander in the West Bank* (2005).[68] The petitioners argued that the fence directly impacted construction of housing projects and access to agricultural lands, and therefore villagers' livelihoods. In addition, the petitioners argued that construction of the security fence on Palestinian lands violated public international law. The military commander (respondent) argued that the fence, as contoured, was necessary from a security perspective for the purpose of protecting Israeli citizens. The Court held that security considerations were within the purview of the military commander. However, in applying a proportionality test, the Court concluded that the military commander did not sufficiently examine alternatives that would have enabled meeting legitimate security requirements while minimizing harm to village residents.

V Targeted killing

In the original petition filed against the policy of targeted killings, the HCJ determined that the issue was not justiciable, thereby dismissing the case. Upon filing a second petition – *Public Committee Against Torture v. Government* – the Court decided to hear the parties' arguments.[69] Here the State argued that, first, the conflict between the State of Israel and Palestinian terror organizations is defined as "armed conflict" (this definition had been previously accepted and adopted by the Israel Supreme Court in a number of decisions). Second, according to the law of armed conflict, terrorists taking part in attacks against civilian or public targets are illegal combatants, not civilians, and are therefore legitimate targets. Third, the principle of proportionality must be respected when implementing targeted killing. Fourth, targeted killing is used only when the targeted terrorist cannot be arrested using reasonable means, in accordance with international principles requiring exhaustion of all reasonable alternatives. The HCJ held that:

> The approach of customary international law applying to armed conflicts of an international nature is that civilians are protected from attacks by the army. However, that protection does not exist regarding those civilians "for such time as they take a direct part in hostilities" (§ 51(3) of The First Protocol). Harming such civilians, even if the result is death, is permitted, on the condition that there is no other less harmful means, and on the condition that innocent civilians nearby are not harmed. Harm to the latter must be proportionate. That proportionality is determined according to a values based test, intended to balance between the military advantage and the civilian damage. As we have seen, we cannot determine that a preventative strike is always legal, just as we cannot determine that it is always illegal. All depends upon the question whether the standards of customary international law regarding international armed conflict allow that preventative strike or not (¶40).

The opinion, written by Court President Aharon Barak, articulates the limits of operational counterterrorism by holding that the targeted killing of known terrorists is legal if done in accordance with international law. This means that the decision and order for a terrorist's targeted killing must be rooted in the principles of proportionality, collateral damage and alternatives. The decision, the last in Barak's corpus of rulings on fighting terrorism, is the final piece in a puzzle of judicially mandated rules in Israel for how an army should conduct operational counterterrorism. Rather than engaging in broad, academic discourse, the ruling establishes clear criteria: a checklist of how the state is to make operational considerations. Harming civilians who "take direct part in hostilities", as defined in the decision, "is permitted":

> even if the result is death … on the condition that there is no other means which harms them less, and on the condition that innocent civilians nearby are not harmed. Harm to the latter must be proportional. That proportionality is determined according to a values-based test, intended to balance between the military advantage and the civilian damage (¶60).

Iran

In recent years, Israeli leaders have portrayed Iran as the greatest threat to Israel; a threat not only to its security but to its very existence. This is because, from time to time, Iranian leaders have uttered their commitment to destroy Israel and, at the same time, their commitment to develop nuclear capabilities. Iranian leaders had also voiced their desire for hegemony in the Middle East and the Muslim world at large. To achieve this hegemony, Iran has been developing a nuclear policy that poses an existential threat to Israel. Iran's leaders have a long history of uttering explicit threats against "the Zionist entity", a history which makes Iranian nuclear aspirations extremely dangerous for Israel, and for the Middle East at large.

The threat is threefold. First, terrorist organizations supported by Iran may enjoy a larger scope for violent activity against Israel and against Jewish targets in the world as they feel more secure given Iran's capabilities. Second, via its proxies in Lebanon, Syria, Gaza and other places, Iran might challenge the Israeli Defense Forces. Third, and most significantly, Iran has a large stock of nuclear reactor fuel that is enriched to 3.5 percent fissionable uranium as a fraction of total uranium content. "Fissionable" means the individual atomic nuclei can be split, yielding usable energy. Iran also has a smaller stock of 20 percent enriched uranium, which it claims to need for medicine and research. Iran has installed 12,000 centrifuges in its large Natanz enrichment plant and its smaller underground and heavily fortified Fordow plant.[70] Iran also has a uranium conversion facility in Esfahan, a uranium mine in Gachin, a uranium enrichment plant in Qom, a heavy water production plant in Arak and nuclear power plants in Bushehr, Darkhovin and Parchin.

Iran's enrichment capability is much greater than required for its announced peaceful purposes. Its leaders wish to exert pressure on Israel, whose nuclear capacity is known, although Israeli leaders have never admitted this capability in explicit terms. Israel's leaders maintain opaque policy on this matter. Reports have claimed that Israel developed its 100–200 nuclear weapons during the 1960s, and today has a secure "triad" of delivery systems (land missiles, bombers, submarines). Israel's plutonium-producing reactor at Dimona is similar to Iran's Arak reactor, except that Israel also has a reprocessing facility to convert plutonium to bomb-usable form. Like Iran, Israel also has a uranium-enrichment facility.[71]

On 13 July 2015, an historic agreement was signed between Iran and a group of six nations: Britain, China, France, Germany, Russia and the United States. The agreement limited Tehran's nuclear ability for more than a decade in return for lifting international oil and financial sanctions against Iran. The agreement outlined: how much nuclear fuel Iran could keep in the country for the next 15 years (until 2030); what kind of research and development it could perform on centrifuges and other nuclear equipment; and the redesign of both a nuclear reactor and a deep-underground enrichment site. Most of Iran's nuclear infrastructure remained intact under the agreement, although much of it was to be disassembled and put in storage. Some restrictions limiting Iran's program would begin to be phased out after ten years. Then, after 15 years, Iran would be free to produce as much enriched uranium as it wants.[72]

A nuclear Iran poses a problem first and foremost for Israel, but it is not a concern for Israel alone. A nuclear Iran might lead to nuclear proliferation as additional countries (among them Saudi Arabia, Turkey and Egypt) might opt to develop their own nuclear programs to offset Iranian capabilities. Iran should continue to be encouraged to adhere to the Convention on Nuclear Safety, adopted on 17 June 1994 by a Diplomatic Conference convened by the International Atomic Energy Agency (IAEA), and to engage with its Gulf neighbors over nuclear safety concerns about reactors in seismic zones.[73] Iran should also be invited to Nuclear Security Summits, encouraged to ratify the Comprehensive Nuclear-Test-Ban Treaty, and play a part in pursuing a weapon of mass destruction (WMD)-free zone in the Middle East.[74]

These "shoulds" were reasonable, but the situation has changed dramatically. In 2018 the Trump administration unilaterally withdrew from the multilateral agreement with Iran and re-imposed economic sanctions, thereby placing continued adherence by Iran in jeopardy. By the middle of 2019 the entire relationship between Iran and the other signatories was unraveling, and by the beginning of 2020 open hostilities between the United States and Iran had taken place. How much longer Iran will limit its uranium enrichment to safe levels remains unclear.

Conclusion

Zionism aims to secure a Jewish home for all Jews in Israel. The Zionist idea has remained contested. Hamas does not recognize the Zionist venture. It wishes to eradicate Israel from the map and establish Palestine at Israel's expense. Leaders of a major Islamic nation, Iran, voice the same desires. Two of Israel's neighbors, Syria and Lebanon, remain in a state of war with the Jewish state and contest its borders. For more than 60 years since its establishment, Israel has withstood many challenges and overcome sturdy opposition. To be successful, Zionism must find a way to integrate into the Middle East and to garner acceptance, especially among the nations surrounding Israel.

At present, many Israelis are still quite content with satisfying security needs, and see no urgency or need to establish peace with Israel's neighbors. They believe that the status quo is good for Israel. In reality there is no status quo, as Israel continues to build settlements, hampering the possibility of striking a deal with the Palestinians in the future. The situation on the ground keeps changing, supposedly in favor of Israel. The Palestinians remain observers as their future state shrinks in front of their eyes and there is very little they can do about it. Furthermore, the occupation remains a reality and is undermining the vital ingredients needed for peace talks: good faith and trust. Under occupation, Palestinians lack freedom and control over their lives. Their economic activities, the allocation and management of their natural resources, their health and well-being, their ability to move are all in the hands of Israel.[75]

The situation is becoming more and more complicated as nearby countries develop long-range ballistic missiles and nuclear capabilities. The potential for attack might come not only from Israel's neighbors but also from remote countries like Iran. Israel has dominated the balance of power with its neighbors in terms of modern conventional systems, recapitalization and foreign military support.[76] But dramatic regional geo-political changes, the post-Arab Spring turmoil and techno-military-cyber advances introduce further weighty challenges to Israel's deterrence and defensive capabilities. Israel's ability to overcome such fateful tests and challenges alone is questionable. Powerful allies do not rush to involve themselves in conflicts with significant regional powers such as Iran. The worst case scenario includes total nuclear annihilation, against which wide security margins are difficult to ascertain. Other scenarios involve conventional threats emanating from Israel's neighbors and/or terror organizations wishing to plant chaos, undermine Israel's security and/or escalate the situation into a regional war.

Achieving a democratic and secure Israel requires bold steps. Israeli leaders need to define its borders. They should abolish the ever-present "State of Emergency" that has been in place since the establishment of the State.[77] The continued renewal of the Emergency Laws enables the government and its security forces to put security considerations above human rights and the democratic principle of upholding civil liberties. Israel should end the occupation and make a sincere and audacious effort to sign a peace treaty with the Palestinians, attempting to address their rights and needs, making the necessary compromises in order to achieve just and lasting peace.[78] Peace should be Israel's security strategy. Finding ways to integrate into the Middle East and to bring to a halt the continued cycle of violence and war are essential. Without resolving the Palestinian problem, Israel's existence will continue to be threatened.

Notes

1 We thank Chuck Freilich, former Israeli deputy national security adviser, for his constructive comments.
2 www.city-data.com/states/Massachusetts-Location-size-and-extent.html.
3 Including East Jerusalem the size is 5,900 sq km. See *American Heritage Dictionary*, "West Bank", www.answers.com/topic/west-bank.
4 Dror 2011, p. 102; BBC 2012. There are roughly 150,000 Jews in East Jerusalem.
5 Gravé-Lazi 2014.
6 Freilich 2012, p. 13.
7 Dror 2011, p. 16.
8 Gissin 1982.
9 Freilich 2015.
10 Ben-Israel 2013.
11 Dror 2011; Kalb 2013.
12 Horowitz 1984, p. 107.
13 Alon 1959, p. 347; Minz and Shai 2014.
14 Craig and George 1983; Shalev 2006.
15 Schelling 1963, p. 9.
16 Yaniv 1985.
17 Claude 1967 p. 57. See also Maniv 1987, p. 185.
18 See Alon 1959, pp. 55–60; Sharon 1981.Freilich commented that this is a false comparison. Israeli military capabilities should not be compared to the combined power of the entire Arab world. We need to compare the Israeli might to specific Arab countries. Vis-à-vis each and every such country, Israel has qualitative and quantitative superiority.
19 Alon 1959, p. 342.
20 Sharon 1981; Cordesman 2010.
21 Minz and Shai 2014.
22 Sharon 1981.

23 Dror 2011, p. 25.
24 Horowitz 1984, p. 107.
25 Dror 1973.
26 Obama 2011.
27 Bar-Joseph 2001; Yaniv 1985, p. 43.
28 Lasswell 1941.
29 Levy 2012.
30 Peri 1985.
31 Horowitz 1977, p. 75.
32 Bregman 2014.
33 Human Rights Watch 2012a.
34 Human Rights Watch 2012b.
35 In his comments, Chuck Freilich wrote on 10 October 2014 that there are "real security concerns – 'eastern threat', terrorism", an irredentist Palestinian state, threat to Jordan, the fact that the Palestinians "have rejected every offer – and Israel made dramatic ones" in 2000 (Camp David and the Clinton Parameters), former Israeli Prime Minister Ehud Olmert in 2008 and Netanyahu in 2014. We have offered almost 100 percent of territory, division of Jerusalem, Palestinian state, "and they have refused repeatedly. Only area where we didn't make dramatic proposals was on refugees and that won't happen. So not all Israel's fault, occupation, actually most of the fault is the pal's, as much as I wish to see the 'occupation' end."
36 Hermann et al. 2013, pp. 13, 150.
37 Ibid, p. 14.
38 Ibid: 47 percent "Agree totally" that "Decisions crucial to the state on issues of peace and security should be made by a Jewish majority." Further, 19.7 percent "Agree somewhat". Ibid, p. 148.
39 Ibid, p. 148.
40 Ibid, p. 152.
41 Ibid, p. 78.
42 Ibid, p. 105: 31.8 percent of the sample "Agree totally" that "Human rights and civil rights organizations, such as the Association for Civil Rights in Israel and B'Tselem, cause damage to the state"; 18.4 percent "Agree somewhat"; 37.1 percent of the sample "Agree totally" that "Speakers should be prohibited from harshly criticizing the State of Israel in public"; 15.3 percent "Agree somewhat". Hermann 2013, p. 142.
43 Economist 2014.
44 UN Doc A/ES-10/PV.21, 6, https://unispal.un.org/DPA/DPR/unispal.nsf/0/534E668989 EA4AE685256E1500708DAF. Article 51 of the Charter holds that: "Nothing in the present Charter shall impair the inherent right of individual or collective self-defense if an armed attack occurs against a Member of the United Nations, until the Security Council has taken measures necessary to maintain international peace and security. Measures taken by Members in the exercise of this right of self-defense shall be immediately reported to the Security Council and shall not in any way affect the authority and responsibility of the Security Council under the present Charter to take at any time such action as it deems necessary in order to maintain or restore international peace and security." See www.un.org/en/documents/charter/chapter7.shtml.
45 UN OCHA 2011.
46 International Court of Justice 2004.
47 Ibid.
48 Ibid.
49 Ibid; see also Okimoto 2011.
50 In Israel, according to section 9.3.3 of the Penal Code, a detainee must be brought before a judge within 24 hours. See Sebba et al. 2003.
51 Marab v. IDF Commander in the West Bank, HCJ 3239/02, 2002, ¶¶8–10.
52 Ibid, ¶¶11–14.
53 Ibid, ¶32.
54 Physicians for Human Rights v. Commander of the IDF Forces in the Gaza Strip, HCJ 4764/04, 2004, ¶7.
55 Ibid, ¶9.
56 Ibid., ¶22.
57 Ibid, ¶16.

58 Ibid, ¶17.
59 Ibid, ¶66.
60 Ibid.
61 Ibid.
62 Emergency Defense Regulations 1945, www.hamoked.org/Document.aspx?dID=2204; Dinstein 1996.
63 Association for Civil Rights in Israel and Others v. the Central District Commander and Another, HCJ 358/88, 1989.
64 Guiora 2013.
65 Association for Civil Rights in Israel and Others, ¶¶12–15.
66 Beit Sourik Village Council v. the Government of Israel, HCJ 2056/04, 2004, ¶13.
67 Ibid.
68 Yassin v. Israel and Military Commander in the West Bank, HCJ, 8414/05, 2005.
69 Public Committee Against Torture in Israel, Palestinian Society for the Protection of Human Rights and the Environment v. the Government of Israel, and Others, HCJ 769/02, 2006.
70 Hobson 2013a. See also Norman and Mitnick 2014; Haaretz 2014; Ploughshares Fund 2014.
71 Hobson 2013b; Cohen 2010.
72 Friedman 2015; Sanger and Gordon 2015; Sanger 2015.
73 Convention on Nuclear Safety, www.iaea.org/publications/documents/infcircs/convention-nuclear-safety.
74 Comprehensive Nuclear-Test-Ban Treaty, www.state.gov/t/avc/c42328.htm; Jenkins and Dalton 2014.
75 Cohen-Almagor 1991 and 2012.
76 Cordesman 2010, p. 44.
77 Sucharov 2013.
78 Cohen-Almagor 2014.

References

English

Bar-Joseph, Uri (ed.), *Israel's National Security Towards the 21st Century* (New York: Routledge, 2001).

BBC, "West Bank Jewish Settlers Agree to Relocate from Migron" (12 March2012), www.bbc.co.uk/news/world-middle-east-17335633.

Bregman, Ahron, *Cursed Victory* (London: Penguin, 2014).

Claude, L. Inis, *Power and International Relations* (New York: Random House, 1967).

Cohen, Avener, *The Worst-Kept Secret: Israel's Bargain with the Bomb* (New York: Columbia University Press, 2010).

Cohen-Almagor, R., "The Intifada: Causes, Consequences, and Future Trends", *Small Wars & Insurgencies*, Vol. 2, No. 1 (1991): 12–40.

Cohen-Almagor, R., "The Failed Peace Process in the Middle East 1993–2011", *Israel Affairs*, Vol. 18, No. 4 (2012): 563–576.

Cordesman, Anthony H., *The Arab-Israeli Military Balance* (Washington DC: Center for Strategic and International Studies, 2010).

Craig, A. Gordon and Alexander L. George, *Force and Statecraft* (New York and Oxford: Oxford University Press, 1983).

Dinstein, Yoram, *Israel Yearbook of Human Rights* (Leiden: Martinus Nijhoff, 1996).

Dror, Yehezkel, *Israeli Statecraft: National Security Challenges and Responses* (Abingdon and New York: Routledge, 2011).

Economist, "Us and Them" (2 August2014), www.economist.com/news/briefing/21610312-pummelling-gaza-has-cost-israel-sympathy-not-just-europe-also-among-americans.

Freilich, Charles D., *Zion's Dilemmas* (Ithaca: Cornell University Press, 2012).

Freilich, Charles D., "Why Can't Israel Win Wars Any More?" *Survival*, Vol. 57, No. 2 (2015): 79–92.

Friedman, Thomas L., "Obama Makes His Case on Iran Nuclear Deal", *New York Times* (14 July2015), www.nytimes.com/2015/07/15/opinion/thomas-friedman-obama-makes-his-case-on-iran-nuclear-deal.html.

Gravé-Lazi, Lidar, "Israeli Population Climbs to 8,904,373 Ahead of Jewish New Year", *Jerusalem Post* (21 September2014), www.jpost.com/Israel-News/Politics-And-Diplomacy/Israeli-population-climbs-to-8904373-ahead-of-Jewish-New-Year-375927.

Guiora, Amos, *Legitimate Target: A Criteria-Based Approach to Targeted Killing* (New York: Oxford University Press, 2013).

Haaretz, "Kissinger: Iran Is a Bigger Threat than Islamic State" (7 September2014), www.haaretz.com/news/middle-east/1.614569.

Hermann, Tamar*et al.*, *Israeli Democracy Index 2013* (Jerusalem: Israel Democracy Institute, 2013).

Hobson, Art [2013a], "The Iranian Nuclear Weapons Deal", *Northwest Arkansas Times* (1 December 2013).

Hobson, Art [2013b], "Iran and a Mideast Nuclear-Free Zone", *Northwest Arkansas Times* (22 December 2013).

Horowitz, Dan, "Is Israel a Garrison State?", *Jerusalem Quarterly*, Vol. 4 (Summer 1977): 58–75.

Human Rights Watch [2012a], *"Forget About Him, He's Not Here": Israel's Control of Palestinian Residency in the West Bank and Gaza* (New York: Human Rights Watch, 2012), www.hrw.org/sites/default/files/reports/iopt0212webwcover.pdf.

Human Rights Watch [2012b], "Israel: End Restrictions on Palestinian Residency", *World Post* (6 February 2012), www.huffingtonpost.com/human-rights-watch/israel-end-restrictions-o_b_1257576.html.

International Court of Justice, *Legal Consequences of the Construction of a Wall in the Occupied Palestinian Territory* (2004), www.icj-cij.org/docket/index.php?p1=3&p2=4&k=5a&case=131&code=mwp&p3=6.

Jenkins, Peter and Richard Dalton, *Iran's Nuclear Future* (London: Chatham House, 2014).

Kalb, Marvin, *The Road to War* (Washington DC: Brookings Institution, 2013).

Lasswell, Harold D., "The Garrison State", *American Journal of Sociology*, Vol. 46, No. 4 (1941): 455–468.

Norman, Laurence and Joshua Mitnick, "Israeli Leader Says Iran Nuclear Program, Islamic State Twin Threat", *Wall Street Journal* (29 September2014), http://online.wsj.com/articles/netanyahu-says-iran-nukes-islamic-state-twin-militant-threat-1412019938.

Obama, Barack, "Remarks at the AIPAC Policy Conference 2011" (22 May2011), www.whitehouse.gov/the-press-office/2011/05/22/remarks-president-aipac-policy-conference-2011.

Okimoto, Keiichiro, *The Distinction and Relationship between Jus ad Bellum and Jus in Bello* (Oxford and Portland, OR: Hart, 2011).

Peri, Yoram, *Between Battles and Ballots* (Cambridge: Cambridge University Press, 1985).

Ploughshares Fund, *World Nuclear Stockpile Report* (28 August2014), www.ploughshares.org/world-nuclear-stockpile-report?gclid=CjwKEAjw5ZKiBRDhqa-YjcmI9kYSJABia-Rn4FworwPigPa-YLQWf dOFHCbsjsM2IMHS1II6IUqTLRoC8jDw_wcB.

Sanger, David E., "Ex-Advisers Warn Obama That Iran Nuclear Deal 'May Fall Short' of Standards", *New York Times*(24 June2015), www.nytimes.com/2015/06/25/world/middleeast/former-advisers-caution-obama-on-iran-nuclear-talks.html?_r=1.

Sanger, David E. and Michael R. Gordon, "Iran Nuclear Deal Is Reached after Long Negotiations", *New York Times* (14 July2015), www.nytimes.com/2015/07/15/world/middleeast/iran-nuclear-deal-is-reached-after-long-negotiations.html?emc=edit_na_20150714&nlid=33802468&ref=cta&_r=0.

Schelling, C. Thomas, *The Strategy of Conflict* (New York: Oxford University Press, 1963).

Sebba, Leslie, Menachem Horovitz and Ruth Geva, *Criminal Justice Systems in Europe and North America: Israel* (Helsinki: European Institute for Crime Prevention and Control, Affiliated with the United Nations, 2003).

Sharon, Ariel, "Address by Defense Minister at the National Defense College" (15 December1981), www.mfa.gov.il/MFA/Foreign%20Relations/Israels%20Foreign%20Relations%20since%201947/1981-1982/84%20Address%20by%20Defense%20Minister%20Sharon%20at%20the%20Natio.

Sucharov, Mira, "Israel's Perpetual State of Emergency", *Daily Beast* (4 December2013), www.thedailybeast.com/articles/2013/04/12/israel-s-perpetual-state-of-emergency.html.

UN OCHA, *Barrier Update* (East Jerusalem: Office for the Coordination of Humanitarian Affairs Occupied Palestinian Territory, 2011), https://reliefweb.int/sites/reliefweb.int/files/resources/Full%20Report_44.pdf.

Hebrew

Alon, Yigal, *A Curtain of Sand* (Tel Aviv: Hakibbutz Hameuchad, 1959).

Ben-Israel, Itzhak, The Security Concept of Israel (Tel Aviv: Modan, 2013).

Cohen-Almagor, Raphael, "*Suggestions for Israeli-Palestinian Agreement*", Kivunim Hadashim (New Directions), No. 30 (June 2014): 144–159.

Dror, Yehezekel, *Crazy States* (Tel-Aviv: Maarachot, 1973).
Gissin, Raanan, "Israel's Defensive Strategy: Continuity or Change", *Maarachot* (February 1982): 2–8.
Horowitz, Dan, "Israeli Perception of National Security (1972–1948)", in Benjamin Neuberger (ed.), *Diplomacy in a Shade of a Conflict* (Tel-Aviv: Open University, 1984): 105–148.
Levy, Yagil, "Public Responsibility of the IDF Senior Command", in Raphael Cohen-Almagor, Ori Arbel-Ganz and Asa Kasher (eds.), *Public Responsibility in Israel* (Tel Aviv and Jerusalem: Hakibbutz Hameuchad and Mishkanot Shaananim, 2012).
Maniv, Asher, *The Weakness of Force* (Yad Tabenkin: Hakibbutz Hameuchad, 1987).
Minz, Alex and Shaul Shai, "The Need for Reconsolidating Israel's Defence Concept", Policy Paper No. 1, Herzliya Forum for Consolidating Israel's Defence Concept (March 2014).
Shalev, Aryeh, *Failure and Success in Deterrence* (Tel Aviv: Maarachot, 2006).
Yaniv, Avner, "Intimidation and Defence in Israeli Strategy", *State, Government, and International Relations*, No. 24 (Summer 1985): 27–62.

PART II

Challenged democracies: India, South Africa, Brazil, Argentina, Romania

12

PUBLIC SECURITY CHALLENGES IN INDIA

Ajay K. Mehra

Public security and strategies to ensure it, in all their dimensions, are extensions of a society, its polity, its domestic politics, its neighborhood and global geopolitics. Since the beginning of the millennium the United Nations (UN) has redefined security as an empowering, grassroots-based process, and as an inter-disciplinary, people-centered, multi-sectoral, comprehensive, context-specific, prevention-oriented concept. The term 'security' encompasses economic security (persistent poverty and unemployment); food security (hunger and famine); health security (deadly infectious diseases, unsafe food, malnutrition and lack of access to basic health care); environmental security (environmental degradation, resource depletion, natural disasters and pollution); personal security (physical violence, crime, terrorism, domestic violence and child labor); community security (inter-ethnic, religious and other identity-based tensions); and political security (political repression and human rights abuses).[1] Given the wide range of the UN definition, this chapter will primarily focus on the last two categories, though reference to the first two will also appear indirectly. Given contemporary complexities in conceptualizing security, the intricacies of India's public security challenges can best be comprehended from the perspectives of geography, demography, diversity and democracy, the latter including India's Constitution and institutions established to ensure public security.

Geography

Ranked seventh in the world in terms of landmass, India comprises 3,287,263 square kilometers of territory and 15,106.7 km of land border. Measuring 3,214 km from north to south and 2,933 km from east to west, India shares its border with Bangladesh (4,096.70 km), China (3,488 km), Pakistan (2,910 km), Nepal (1,751 km), Myanmar (1,643 km) and Bhutan (699 km). India also has a 7,516.6 km coastline washed by the Bay of Bengal, the Indian Ocean and the Arabian Sea. India's borders with Pakistan and Bangladesh are the result of a retreating British colonialism. Other borders drawn by the British – such as the McMahon Line (Sino-Indian border, 1914) and the Durand Line (drawn by British and Afghani rulers in 1893, now the border between Pakistan and Afghanistan) – have implications for security challenges across the entire subcontinent.

Geography impinges on a nation's security and on global security, generally and in specific ways. Pre- and post-Columbian human history offers a panoptic view of how geography invited explorers, conquerors, crusaders and sailors to shape and reshape boundaries across the globe, over centuries. Discovery of the Cape Route to the Indies connected western and coastal navigation, and laid the foundation for the advent of colonialism in its various manifestations in the Americas, Asia and Africa. In 1904 geographer and politician Halford John Mackinder considered the actual balance of political power the product of geographical conditions, both economic and strategic, and of the relative number, vitality, equipment and organization of competing peoples.[2] Naval historian Alfred Mahan viewed the sea as the great 'commons' of civilization, and saw the Indian and Pacific oceans as the hinges of geopolitical destiny, allowing a maritime nation to project power around the Eurasian rim, affecting political developments in Central Asia as well.[3] Kaplan argues that geography in the era of globalization:

> serves to qualify human freedom and choice with a modest acceptance of fate. Rather than eliminating the relevance of geography, globalization reinforces it. Mass communications and economic integration currently are weakening many states, exposing a Hobbesian world of small, fractious regions.[4]

The Indian subcontinent, according to Kaplan – "defined on its landward sides by the hard geographic borders of the Himalayas to the north, the Burmese jungle to the east, and the somewhat softer border of the Indus River to the west" – puts India at the center of a crucial geopolitical surround that heightens its public security concerns. Here Kaplan factors in India's border, demography and geography to explain subcontinental geopolitics: "Because these geographic impediments are not contiguous with legal borders, and because barely any of India's neighbors are functional states, the current political organization of the subcontinent should not be taken for granted."[5] Kaplan echoes earlier opinions. For example, Lord Curzon, Viceroy of India in 1899–1905, observed that "frontiers were the razor's edge on which suspended the modern issues of war or peace, life or death for nations". Curzon said in his 1909 essay 'The Place of India in the Empire':

> The central position of India, its magnificent resources, its teeming multitude of men, its great trading harbors, its reserve of military strength, supplying an army always in a high state of efficiency and capable of being hurled at a moment's notice upon any point either of Asia or Africa – all these are assets of precious value.[6]

Artificially created borders in South Asia during and after British rule "across the nations, across the communities and at times even across the families … [have] played a substantial role in the subsequent problems".[7] Thus, within the subcontinent the borders between India and Pakistan (in Kashmir and in Sir Creek in Gujarat), between India and Bangladesh (largely solved now), between India and Nepal (over Kalapani), and between India and Sri Lanka (over maritime boundaries and fishing rights in the Palk Straits) continually cause tensions which sometimes become serious.[8]

A regional concept, 'northern South Asia', is based on the understanding that the region from Gujarat and Rajasthan in western India to Bengal and Orissa in the east, as well as many parts of Nepal, displays "interesting cultural commonalities across the region so named, despite its division into different nation-states".[9] Recent tension between India and Nepal following adoption of a new constitution in the Himalayan nation that has left some communities dissatisfied is an example of overlapping ethno-cultural borders becoming an issue of public security.[10]

Oscar Martinez's four models for understanding borders – *alienated borderlands* (routine cross-border infiltrations do not take place because of enmity between the bordering states), *coexistent borderlands* (some cross-border interactions exist in spite of enmity between the bordering states), *interdependent borderlands* (economic and social interactions are common across the border) and *integrated borderlands* (cross-border movements are legally recognized) – underline the significance of geography even in the Indian context.[11] The India–Pakistan borders in Jammu and Kashmir (J&K) and Punjab reflect the first model; the India–Pakistan borders in Rajasthan and Sind and the Indo-Myanmar borders, when relations between these two countries were not good, represent the second model; the borders between India and Bangladesh, India and Sri Lanka, and India and Bhutan where cross-border movements of people take place (likewise social and economic interactions, though they are not officially sanctioned) would come under the third category; and the India–Nepal border, which is legally and effectively open, falls under the fourth category.

In short, India's geography imposes enormous public security responsibilities on the Indian state and agencies tasked with keeping the country and its people safe. Since India's border dispute with China is not resolved, there is a perpetual eyeball-to-eyeball contact between the armies, hence their preparedness, and diplomatic brouhaha. Despite friendly relations, Nepal and India also engage in rough diplomatic tussles, as the land-locked Himalayan kingdom resents 'big brother' and India is cautious, if not suspicious, of Nepal's Chinese tilt. The porous border between the two countries invites vigilance. Pakistan has been a rough west for India since partition. The Kashmir imbroglio has only added to it. Three and a half wars since 1947 have been followed by a terror proxy war in Punjab and Jammu and Kashmir. Use of non-state actors exposed a crevasse in India's coastal security when Ajmal Kasab and nine others sneaked unnoticed into Mumbai and wreaked havoc on the city on 26 November 2008; and coastal boundaries continue to be vulnerable.[12]

Even though India and Bangladesh recently resolved their border issues relating to enclaves on both sides of the fence (on 6 June 2015), illegal migration across the long border contiguous with five states (including West Bengal, Assam and Meghalaya) has created public security challenges for India. The Indo-Myanmarese border is porous; its most contentious aspect is the free movement of Naga rebels who have been leading a secessionist insurgency since 1949.[13] All these issues have implications, as stated, for internal and national security. The maritime boundary with Sri Lanka has been quiet since the annihilation of the Liberation Tigers of Tamil Eelam (LTTE, or Tamil Tigers) by Sri Lankan forces.

Demography

Demography by itself appears unlikely to become a public security challenge. Nevertheless, population size, density, composition in terms of age and quality of life (i.e. human development, economic status, education, employment) and dynamics (i.e. natural increase, sex ratio, child and infant mortality, and migration) all have the potential to raise public security challenges for India.[14] Kaplan reinforces this thesis: "The other force driving the revenge of geography is population growth."

India's population (1,210,193,422 according to the 2011 census) – territorially divided into 29 states and 7 Union Territories (UTs) – exemplifies diversity on a continental scale, a fact that creates complex public security issues.[15] While the overall population density of the country had risen from 324 to 382 per square kilometer according to the 2011 census, density in fact varied dramatically, from 17 per square kilometer in Arunachal Pradesh to 11,320 in the Union Territory of Delhi. Bihar, with 1,106 persons per square kilometer, is the most densely populated state. Mumbai (population 18,394,912), Delhi (16,349,831) and Kolkata (14,035,959) are the three 10 million-plus cities. There are 50 more million-plus cities in India, and urban India consists of 31 percent of the Indian population.[16] A large section of the urban population lives in slums, places where urban poverty is concentrated[17] and where tremendous economic inequity persists.[18] Urbanization is perceived as a sign of economic development. Increase in the 'urban' occurs at the cost of the 'rural' in a variety of ways, the most significant of which is the political economy of land. Industrial development and economic activity-led urbanization take place at the cost of natural resources that are often claimed by the rural. The process of urbanization produces conflict; police and security structures are drawn willy-nilly into conflicts and must be prepared to meet emerging challenges.[19]

The 69 percent of Indian citizens living in villages are highly diverse socially and economically. Poverty in India is predominantly rural; rural areas are populated by disadvantaged and dispossessed landless and casual laborers. The rural poor have limited ownership of land and assets. Scheduled Castes and Scheduled Tribes (SCs and STs), matriarchal families, the old and female children face relatively greater deprivation than others. Many villages across the country witness seasonal migration of young males to cities for employment. Nearly 42 percent of the rural poor are among the most economically disadvantaged. And more than half of this group comprises Scheduled Castes and Scheduled Tribes, who constitute 25 percent of the rural population and who live at the margins of social and economic power structures.[20] Pranab Bardhan says that among the three negative impacts caused by the emerging global economy is

> the damage caused to jobs, wages and incomes of poor people by the dislocations and competition of international trade and foreign investment and the weakening of the ability of the state to compensate for this damage and in general to alleviate poverty and inequality.[21]

The nature of India's rural demography, the geography of poverty and the processes unleashed by globalization make the task of public order complex, putting great social and constitutional responsibility on the police.

The demography of age, of youth and the old, creates public security challenges of differing kinds. Without gainful employment, the young may devote themselves to protest politics or illegal activities, while the elderly need care and protection from criminal attacks. Nearly one-third of India's population is in the 15–34 age group; increased life expectancy means that nearly 15 percent of the population are senior citizens.[22] Challenges to public security emanating from both groups cannot be understated.

The diversity of India's religious demography also poses security challenges given socio-political and economic controversies. Memories of partition (15 August 1947) based on a two-nation theory (Hindus and Muslims), and the violence that preceded and followed partition, have allowed tensions to erupt from time to time. Three characteristics of this demographic are worth noting. First, Muslims are a large, visible and vocal minority who constitute a larger percentage of the population than the national average in some states. In Jammu and Kashmir Muslims constitute the majority; India has the second largest Muslim population in the world after Indonesia. Second, the rate of growth of Muslims has been faster than that of Hindus and the national average. Third, India's division based on religion created Muslim majority states on its western and eastern borders. Pakistan impacts religious sentiments to the west, while Bangladesh is a source of illegal migration to neighboring Indian states, particularly West Bengal, Assam Meghalaya and Tripura. In the 1951 census, the first after partition, Muslims accounted for 9.8 percent of the country's population. The 2011 census numbered Muslims as 14.2 percent of the population, 4.4 points higher than six decades earlier. A growth rate among Muslims higher than the national average, and higher than that of Hindus, has stirred controversies. That the growth of the Muslim population dipped in 2011 as compared to 2001, and that the recent decline in growth has been sharper than that of the Hindus, has been missed in the din of controversies.

Migration is linked to urbanization as well as to the process of globalization. In the context of public security, the following three issues enhance challenges to the country. First, in 2007 the United Nations Population Fund (UNFPA) regarded the concentration of poverty, slum growth and social deprivation in cities as the major challenges to development in less developed countries.[23] Amitabh Kundu has pointed out serious stress involved in the 'withdrawal or displacement' of labor from rural to urban economies.[24] Urban centers have limited capacity to assimilate rural transplants in employment, access to land or basic amenities. Second, agitation in certain parts of the country – particularly in the financial capital Mumbai and Maharashtra State (including the campaign for 'sons of the soil' that has targeted non-Marathi migrants since the 1960s) – poses a serious challenge to public order. Though lately dormant, such campaigns erupted in 2008, 2012 and 2014.[25] Third, globalization processes have been positive in creating employment opportunities but negative in creating economic inequality. India faces both consequences.[26]

Demography is a public security issue in absolute terms as well. An adequate number of security personnel must be provided to protect diverse populations, and public security agencies need to be created to meet multifarious needs. International standards on the ratio of police personnel to population cannot be met. In India, the latest data indicates a shortage of police officers even with respect to the sanctioned strength determined by the government.[27]

Diversity

India is a diverse, modernizing society. Intersecting on several axes, socio-cultural diversity in the country offers inherent and innumerable possibilities for friction and conflict as well as for reconciliation and conflict resolution within India's constitutional framework. The most ominous impact of diversity could be, and at times has been, when the police and other security agencies entrusted to intervene in conflicts carry deeply entrenched social biases.[28]

India's billion-plus population comprises all racial types, and practices all major religions of the world, as it has done for centuries.[29] Indians practice Islam, Christianity, Judaism and Zoroastrianism as well as religions of Indian origin such as Hinduism, Jainism, Sikhism and Buddhism. Animism of various kinds and sects and sub-sects of religious beliefs also abound.

George Grierson's multi-volume survey of languages spoken in India in the early 20th century (1903–28) listed 179 languages and 544 dialects. The Constitution of India recognized 11 major languages initially, then added 11 more to the list in the form of 4 Amendments (the 21st in 1967, the 71st in 1992, the 92nd in 2003 and the 96th in 2011), bringing the total number of languages recognized by the Constitution to 22. Nearly half a dozen additional linguistic groups are currently striving for constitutional status.

The People of India project of the Anthropological Survey of India generated comprehensive data about the socio-cultural diversity of the country during 1985–2000, identifying 4,694 communities in its 43-volume work. It prepared a database of 17,129 entries, of which

8,530 refer to castes/communities. The remaining 8,566 relate to sub-groups (3,123), surnames (2,729) and the names of deities, places and titles. The project identified 2,619 as the actual number of castes, nearly 4,599 languages and dialects in 12 language families, and some 24 scripts.[30] Diversity of kinship, marriage rites and customs, inheritance and general modes of living – as well as patterns of rural and urban settlements, community life, forms of land tenure, agricultural operations and so on – abound in India.[31]

As ethnicities strive to assert their identities – seeking either territorial demarcation or caste, language and religion-based recognition in one form or another – frictions arise that result either in confrontation with the state or inter-community collective violence. Two forms of violence differ in scale but are equally troubling for India's security: *collective violence* and *communal violence*. Collective violence is rooted mostly in social stratification. Communal violence denotes violence between two religious communities, mostly between majority Hindus and the largest religious minority, Muslims. Communal violence has confounded the public security establishment due to it socio-political dimensions, and an institutionalized system.[32] Though in most cases communal riots have been rooted in specific local problems, episodically and over minor issues, they have had political ramifications, dragging the police into indiscretion and revealing the proclivity and vulnerability of police to be used by the powers that be.[33] Economic interests and rivalries, however small, on many occasions have been at the root of communal violence. Since the late 1980s and during the 1990s rioting has also been a result of a majoritarian mobilization in India's electoral politics, mainly driven by electoral politics.[34]

Asghar Ali Engineer has listed the following problems associated with the police role in communal violence:[35]

- Police do not come to the rescue of the minority community despite complaints.
- The police have been instrumental in killing members of the minority community, not only rioters amongst them, but also innocents, often in blatant fashion. In many cases they dragged people from homes, took them to a desolate spot and killed them.
- The police led the mob in looting and killing members of the minority community. Curfew orders were discriminately applied.
- The police also misused powers and, displaying partisanship, arrested innocent persons from the minority community and tortured them in custody.
- The police not only turned a blind eye and deaf ear to requests and pleas for protection, they in fact encouraged perpetrators to act against the minority community.[36]

Collective violence against the poor of the lower castes in the Hindu hierarchy (known as Dalits or Scheduled Castes) and against indigenous people (referred to as Adivasi or Scheduled Tribes) also has not received adequate attention from the police.[37] Complaints against the police for siding with the higher castes are very common.[38] Even though atrocities and violence against these groups are cognizable as well as non-bailable under The Scheduled Castes and Scheduled Tribes (Prevention of Atrocities) Act, 1986,[39] police performance in protecting lower-caste rights in state after state has been far from exemplary. Despite their legal and statutory protections, Dalits have witnessed a 15–20 percent annual increase in crimes against them, and police discriminate against them as well.[40]

From the perspective of micro-managing a major governmental organization, namely police forces that interface with the public on a quotidian basis, the lack of minority officers in security organizations has raised concerns for experts. Absence of minority officers creates an avoidable trust deficit.[41] In fact, a committee of three Directors General of Police (DGP) has said that people in general, and minorities in particular, find the police to be 'communal, biased and insensitive … ill-informed, corrupt and lacking professionalism'. The 2015 report prepared by the DGPs of Maharashtra, Uttar Pradesh and Tamil Nadu, titled 'Strategy for Making Police Forces More Sensitive Towards Minority Sections', argues that:

> Poor representation of the minorities in the police forces has contributed to this distrust and suspicion. It has to be admitted that the conduct of some members of the police forces in various states during communal riots had only served to strengthen and heighten these suspicions and distrust in the minority communities.[42]

Despite the mandatory 15 percent reservation for the Scheduled Castes and 7.5 percent reservation for the Scheduled Tribes in public employment, these communities have not received fair treatment from the police during caste violence that is a regular feature of Indian society. By contrast the reservation for Other Backward Castes (OBC)[43] since 1990 has created a 27 percent job quota for them, changing the profile of many public services including the police. The 'backward' and 'lower' castes have also used the electoral process to wrest power in several states.[44] Their success has caused a rise in social and caste conflict, complicated by the partisan and unprofessional behavior of the police.

Democracy

The structure and processes of Indian democracy revolve around the Constitution of India that came into operation on 26 January 1950, and a politics that shaped itself during the struggle for independence against British colonialism. In the interim period after independence – between the framing of the constitution and since 1951–52, when the first general election took place – an electoral party politics and a politics of governance emerged.

Article 1 of India's 'federal' Constitution states: "India, that is Bharat, shall be a Union of States." In emphasizing the 'indestructibility' of the territorial entity of the country inherited following decolonization and partition of the subcontinent, the provision sought to discourage centrifugal forces, even as India's state structure was rigidly cast. In a Constituent Assembly debate, B.R. Ambedkar, Chairman of the Drafting Committee, defined the basis for the division of power between the Union and its States thus:

> Though India was to be a federation, the federation was not the result of an agreement by the States to join in a federation, and that the federation not being the result of an agreement, no State has the right to secede from it. The Federation is a Union because it is indestructible. Though the country and the people may be divided into different States for convenience of administration, the country is one integral whole, its people a single people living under a single *imperium* derived from a single source.

By contrast, public security in India's constitutional framework was arranged in the context of 'life and personal liberty'. This led to an elaborate debate to determine whether it would be best to place public security under a 'due process of law' framework (as in the USA) or under a 'procedure established by law' (as in the UK). Since the latter framework was adopted (Article 21), with some discomfort, Dr. Ambedkar introduced Article 22, which detailed protection due to individuals against detention by the state.[45] The framework of personal liberty as propounded in these two articles is key to the operationalization and functioning of police powers in India.

The division of power mentioned in the three lists in the Seventh Schedule in the Indian Constitution is also key to understanding the police powers of the Indian state.[46] That division was quite neat until 1976. Entry 1 in List II (State List) in the Seventh Schedule makes 'public order' the responsibility of states. List I (Union List) and List III (Concurrent List) incorporate public security as a larger concept denoting the Union's responsibility for national security and attendant legal support in the task of overall public security. Three controversies that arose during 1967–72 raised issues: this was when the coalition experience in the states following the first electoral setback to the Indian National Congress in seven states (governments of Kerala and West Bengal) objected to the Union Government's deployment of central paramilitary forces even to protect its own properties from rioting trade unions.[47]

Changes to entry 2A of List I and corresponding changes to entries 1 and 2 of List II in the Seventh Schedule were brought about by the controversial 42nd Amendment of the Constitution. The 42nd Amendment was enacted in 1976 during the state of emergency declared by then Prime Minister Indira Gandhi. Retention of these changes by the Janata Party Government that succeeded Ghandi in the post-emergency 1977 general election redefined state police powers in India with a greater tilt towards to the Union Government. Entry 2A inserted in List I reads:

> Deployment of any armed forces of the Union or any other force subject to the control of the Union or any contingent or unit thereof in any State in aid of the civil power; powers jurisdiction, privileges and liabilities of the members of such forces while on such deployment.

To make the Union's central role even more unambiguous, List II was also altered in the same Amendment by making additions to 'Public order' in entry I and 'Police' in entry 2:

1 Public order (but not including [the use of any naval, military or Air Force or any other armed force of the Union or of any other force subject to the control of the Union or of any contingent or unit thereof] in aid of the civil power).
2 [Police (including railway and village police) subject to the provisions of entry 2A of List I.][48]

These three provisions in Lists I and II made the role of the Union Government in the exercise of police powers unambiguous. The fact that further revisions made by the 43rd and 44th Amendments to the Constitution did not alter the changes brought in by the 42nd Amendment reflected a political consensus that the police powers of the Union Government could override those of the states if circumstances so demanded.[49] Nevertheless, the deployment of central Union forces has been discrete in states affected by insurgency and/or terrorism or Maoist revolutionary movement.

Public security structure in India: internal security

Public security agencies in India, leaving aside the defense forces (Army, Navy and Air Force), have a dual structure that has evolved historically as well as by constitutional design. Even before the 42nd Amendment tweaked the federal tilt towards the Union Government, Article 355 of the Constitution of India ordained that "It shall be the duty of the Union to protect every State against external aggression and internal disturbance and to ensure that the government of every State is carried on in accordance with the provisions of this Constitution." In both respects the Union needed to create agencies to fulfill its constitutional duty of protecting the states. Hence, while each of India's 29 states and 7 Union Territories has its own police force,[50] the Union Government has its own police structure as well: 7 security forces and 6 specialized agencies.[51] State police organizations are under the direct organizational and operational authority of their respective state governments. The Indian Police Service (IPS) is a unique federal cadre serving both the Union and state governments.[52]

Let us now briefly survey the evolution of India's security systems and structures. Like other administrative systems, police administration evolves in relation to political systems and societal needs – societal needs as perceived by a political system at a particular historical juncture.[53] Police forces represent a widely accepted need for public security and social consensus about that need – despite perceptions of the police and policing as state mechanisms for the use of legitimized violence.

The police in post-independence India trace their legacy to their colonial origins. Following the granting of *diwani* (revenue rights) in Bengal to the East India Company in 1765 (after the Battle of Buxar, 1764), colonial police forces developed as an amalgam of existing structures and requirement-based innovations in different parts of the country.[54] The Indian Police Act of 1861 (enacted in the wake of the revolt of 1857 that ended the century-old rule by the East India Company and transferred power to the Queen in Parliament) laid the foundation of present-day police organization in India. Supported by the Indian Penal Code (IPC), the Criminal Procedure Code (CrPC) and the Indian Evidence Act that came soon after, the modern Indian police came into existence as part of the colonial criminal justice system.[55]

The intent and purpose of the new police force in India was clear: it was created in response to political exigencies consequent to revolt, but also in response to a new requirement of the colonial government that was to be controlled directly by the British Parliament and government. The Indian government emphasized cost control, keeping the police poorly paid and turning a blind eye to corruption and brutality enacted on the front lines and intermediary levels of police work – despite reports made by various commissions the government appointed to evaluate police performance. Those commissions pointed out the dangers of police policies as described above; but still those policies shaped police organization.[56] Foundations were thus laid for a police culture not desirable for a democracy. Further, since the government of British India ran on a model of decentralized centralization, the provinces of British India and the princely states had their own police organizations as well.

The founding of the modern Indian police followed, *inter alia*, the founding of the Indian National Congress in December 1885. Though promoted by the British – Allan Octavian Hume, a retired British civil servant worked tirelessly to create a platform for the Indian urban intelligentsia to vent their feelings so that events of 1857 were not repeated – police forces became the cornerstone of the Indian national movement, and later the party system. From a democratic perspective this was the beginning of political challenges to civil and police administrations in India because police administrations were initially led entirely by British officers drawn from the army, but staffed almost entirely by Indians. The police had a mixed record during the national movement as well as during partition. Riots preceding and following partition created tough times for the police, who emerged from them with a mixed record.[57]

The post-independence shaping of India's public security architecture according to the Westminster model – adapted on the lines of Canadian parliamentary federalism but constructing India as an indestructible 'Union of States' (Article 1) fixed in the framework of 'strong-center' federalism – impacted the way police administration has been situated.[58] When the government turned to reforming police administration following the reorganization of states in 1956, the spotlight was on the states to take initiatives in this direction. There is no evidence to suggest that the Union Government pushed in this direction; but, given the Congress system that existed until the fourth general election of 1967 (whereby both at the national and state levels the Congress party led governments), a consensus on leaving the initiative of police reforms to the states appears to have existed.

During the1960s and 1970s most states appointed police commissions to suggest reforms. As a result, the critical question of whether to break from provisions of the colonial Indian Police Act of 1861 and remodel police forces with a new organizational structure based on democratic culture was not even considered.[59] State police commissions did consider critical issues of police reforms, but without questioning the colonial foundation of police forces itself. Each state commission suggested a wide range of measures to enhance efficiency through better training, rationalization of existing organizational structure and improvement of service conditions for police at various ranks.[60] Little improvement resulted, given two factors: (1) most commissions consisted of police officers and administrators recruited, trained and organizationally acculturated by the colonial government; (2) hence, though commissions were all for improvement in police administration in the respective states, they did not think out of the box, and therefore did not break free from the colonial mold.

The Union Government first turned its attention towards the police in the country in 1971 when it appointed a committee chaired by noted sociologist Madhav Sadashiv Gore to review police training. The committee found several professional constraints in the existing methodology of police training and suggested several ways to ameliorate them.[61] However, the government of India was limited in its power to effect change. The central government could only recommend reforms to state governments, taking measures to develop consensus and using it for the training of state police leadership as well as of personnel in its own Union police organizations (none of which participated in day-to-day grassroots policing).

Obviously, though alert to the challenges state police faced in independent India and the critical role that training played in their work, the committee led by M.S. Gore produced only another government report post-independence that was put on ice. No wonder then that, in less than a decade, the experience of the police during the internal emergency imposed by Indira Gandhi in 1975 and during post-emergency dilemmas arising from accountability of the police and administrative systems during that period a new government – led by a new coalition of old political parties named the Janata (People's) Party – appointed a National Police Commission (NPC) chaired by a widely respected civil servant, Dharma Vira, in 1977. But the NPC report was only issued after Indira Gandhi returned to power in 1980 after a disastrous faction-ridden performance by the Janata Party government.[62] Obviously, indictment of the Gandhi administration during the emergency was unlikely, and the NPC report also met a predictable fate.

Still it would be fair to say that the Commission comprehensively underlined the challenges faced by India's police: politically, organizationally, but also in terms of issues such as communal and collective violence, widely prevailing custodial crimes and new facets of crime that had begun to emerge by then. Though only a few recommendations made by the NPC (mostly of a routine organizational or procedural nature) were implemented by some states, the NPC report has continued to be the rallying point for comprehensive reform. A Public Interest Litigation (PIL) filed by a retired civil servant and two retired police chiefs – H.D. Shourie, Prakash Singh and N.K. Singh – in 1996 with the Supreme Court of India emphasized implementation of the NPC recommendations. Ultimately the Government of India appointed two committees to suggest concrete steps for police reforms. In 2006 the Supreme Court directed the central and state governments to comply with its order to enact police reforms, and appointed a Monitoring Committee to look into the matter. Later, a blueprint for an Indian Police Act as suggested by the NPC was also drafted by a committee led by jurist Soli Sorabjee.[63] Despite some small changes and expansion through the years, organization of the Indian police forces continues to evidence its colonial design. Resistance to change is equally visible in political and police leadership. Security forces' capacity to meet contemporary challenges remains dependent on police reform.

Incongruities within: internal issues

Corruption and brutality have marked police behavior since colonial rule. Corruption has generally been described as extortion of bribes (petty and large), occurring both where police interact with citizens on the front lines of police work and at intermediate levels. Citizens may offer bribes either to distort a process of the law in their favor or to gain favor during the process of enforcement. Filing a Registration of First Information Report (FIR) is required in registering a case, and comes at a cost. Reports of investigations can be distorted in favor of a bribe payer. Traffic violators can be let off for a consideration.

These are relatively small examples of corruption. David Bayley, in his classic study *The Police and Political Development in India* (1969), referred to involvement and intervention by the police in politics, in the form of active persuasion and passive behavior. In a later work Bayley asserted that the police in India play a much larger role than enforcement of law and order. He pointed out cases of non-enforcement when criminal sanctions were involved or when police responded to calls for general assistance.[64] Larger dimensions of these aberrations have emerged over the decades, including police collusion with local politicians on the one hand and commercial and business interests on the other. Real estate in big cities and metropolises is a multi-million rupee sector. Almost yearly events indicate a nexus between builders, city corporations and the police.[65] Such nexuses between the police and district administration on the one hand and local contractors on the other have also been reported in labor cases.[66] These emerging nexuses have been rooted in the politicization of the police; the ugliest among them occurred during the emergency years June 1975–April 1977. The 'use' of the police to serve political purposes, and evidence of police officers currying favor at multiple levels, has become more acute given increasingly competitive politics.

Police brutality has been a byword in India since colonial rule. Under colonial rule, the police were perceived, and also acted, as agents of an alien power. The agency's fierceness was symbolic of an alien force. Following independence, recognition of police brutality became a tool to embarrass the ruling party rather than a reason to explore correctives for an Indian public institution. Obviously, initiatives for reform have not been forthcoming from within the police. Consequently, police brutality has continued to be a complaint, reflected in a wide range of organizational behaviors as police deal with people and their issues. The underprivileged have suffered especially: police officers have been rude to people in the course of day-to-day policing; have functioned at the behest of the rich and powerful against the dispossessed; have enacted custodial crimes and partisan behavior; and have used excessive force during collective and communal violence, an issue discussed earlier in this chapter.

Rude behavior by police forces has been discussed since independence. Research during the 1970s by the Indian Institute of Public Opinion (IIPO) pointed out that those who have interacted with the police have held a better opinion of them.[67] But a more recent report published by the Centre for the Study of Developing Societies (CSDS) on Indian democracy finds that the police are still not trusted and that people who need to go to the police depend on community elders instead.[68] The impression that the Indian police are not people-centric prevails despite seven decades of democracy. That impression exists and is widespread. Efforts to ameliorate police–public relationships have been made at the level of training; the report of the Committee on Police Training referred to above has been very useful in this project.

Custodial crimes such as torture, murder and rape have been reported in India regularly since independence,[69] but government reports show gross underreporting of these malpractices.[70] It has been pointed out that, in most cases, either victims do not report such crimes for fear of reprisal or the police avoid registering such cases to avoid damaging their professional record. This behavior mixes a low level of professionalization (despite being upgraded and revised, police training is identified as a major lacuna in this context) with a lack of scientific investigative techniques and the pressure and stress of police work in a situation of constant understaffing. Instead of employing scientific investigative techniques, the police too often are alleged to resort to 'third degree methods' to extract confessions. Such methods lead to custodial crimes, and also impact the processes of the criminal justice system when cases fail in courts of law. Civil society interventionists and active human rights groups have uncovered several cases of police misconduct, and courts of law have also pointed out investigative deficiencies with grim regularity, pressing for change from without. These deficiencies invite self-correction from within rather than outside intervention. Accountability structures, lately discussed by the District Police Complaints Authority, would be useful in solving the problem of custodial crimes as well.

The prevalence of custodial rape is indeed a continuation of the trend discussed above, reflecting both the organizational incongruities already addressed and the larger question of gender in Indian society. Finally, a large number of personnel at the front lines of police work – i.e. the constabulary – receive postings in non-family stations and situations. Police on the front lines thus do not experience the sustenance of family after a socio-politically hostile working day, a fact but not an excuse. Social and organizational anomalies contribute to the unpardonable problem of custodial rape and need to be ameliorated.

Terrorism and the police

India experiences terrorism from within and without. A complex psycho-sociological phenomenon, terrorism finds political expression in extreme violence, violence which creates multilayered and multifaceted insecurity in a society.[71] Terrorism's larger political sociology is not normally the concern of security establishments in any part of the world; but the threats political sociology causes to public security – with respect to immediate consequences, and intermediate and long-term reactions – compels the police to counter suicidal actors.[72]

During the second decade of the 21st century, the onset of a new phase of global terror – the Islamic State of Iraq and al-Sham (ISIS) waging a war for an Islamic Caliphate, situated as much in West Asia as in the Middle East – found expression in conflicts between western and non-Islamic civilizations and certain forms of Islamism. Terrorist attacks to express solidarity with ISIS took place twice in Paris – *Charlie Hebdo* (7 January 2015) and public places (13 November 2015) – and in California on 2 December 2015. Comparable attacks have occurred in Libya, twice in Tunisia, Yemen, Egypt (including the blowing up of a Russian passenger plane) and Turkey.[73] The demolition of the World Trade Center's twin towers in New York, with 3,000 dead and 6,000 injured, and partial damage to the Pentagon on 11 September 2001 (9/11) first compelled world powers to address terrorism's new ferocity:

> This new war was chaotic ... It was a conflict where gain and loss had been determined as much by the relative venality or brutality of participants as by courage or resourcefulness ... marked by violence to civilians, to prisoners and by an appalling ignorance among many decision-makers of the local conditions.[74]

As mentioned earlier, terrorism has defied a preventive strategy, making it difficult for the world to balance safety and human rights concerns. It has exposed hypocrisies of the world community, and not allowed the UN to be defined precisely since 1945.[75]

The ISIS phenomenon has affected India's public security scenario, and the globalization of terrorism has produced glocal consequences. As stated above, India includes the second largest Muslim population in the world. Its demography and diversity are highly significant in relation to the charged atmosphere of international religious extremism. Since the beginning of the millennium, India has faced not only home-grown terrorism but also cross-border attacks, most notably the terrorist attack on Mumbai on 26 November 2008 (26/11). Ten members of Pakistan-based Lashkar-e-Taiba 'attacked' Mumbai via the sea route, undetected. For four days the terrorists coordinated attacks with impunity, killing 164 people at multiple locations. The Coast Guard and the Mumbai police were stunned. India's federal security structure took an inordinately long time to reach Mumbai and counter the attackers. State/federal police coordination was for a time inefficient and ineffective. In the aftermath, when India identified 42 alleged terrorist camps and some talked about an Indian counterstrike, a video warned that "were Delhi to carry out its threat, it would hit targets in India – an under-policed country where security is lax and soft targets abound".[76] Studies on the Indian Mujahedeen refer to a bleak security scenario in India.[77] Indian security forces could not mobilize quickly enough during the Mumbai attack, a problem still to be fully addressed. Indian security agencies are currently working to devise measures to prevent the radicalization of youth, a preventive measure.[78]

Regional issues are also worth mentioning. When terrorism surfaced in India during the 1980s the police were the first line of defense.[79] In the seven northeastern states, insurgency has raged almost since independence; there insurgents have used terror techniques since the 1970s. Despite large-scale army deployment in those states on India's borders with China and Myanmar, the police remain the first line of defense and have to be prepared. Unfortunately, their training and weapons do not equip them to deal with the situations they face. The diverse demography of the region requires separate planning and execution for each state, given the complex nature of political interests and insurgent/terrorist groups that often indulge in fratricide. Ved Marwah's detailed account of local politics, national politics, corruption and regional security issues shows how the enmeshing of interests and people in the northeastern states endangers public security.[80]

Marwah's analyses from 1995 and 2009 of the politics of terror in Punjab during the 1980s reveal that rising unemployment drew a sub-group of youths to separatist politics in search of an independent nation of Khalistan for the Sikh community. Pakistan exploited this movement, highlighting the complexity of South Asian geopolitics. During the 1980s the discourse on the role of the police in countering terrorism had not even begun, and the Indian establishment was confused.[81] The Punjab police eventually developed a strategy that obliterated terrorism, despite human rights concerns.[82]

Jammu and Kashmir, central to Indo-Pakistan wars and skirmishes since 1948, have faced terrorism since December 1989.[83] It has been a complex situation and operation for the government to keep the police focused, given infiltration of terrorists across the porous border. Despite the presence of the army and India's Central Reserve Police Force (CRPF) in Jammu and Kashmir, the J&K police have been the principal security actors there. It is difficult to keep a police organization focused when a significant section of a population is either hostile or skeptical; rebellion in the ranks has not been unexpected.[84] In such a persistently violent situation the police and security forces have both faced charges of human rights abuses, mass killings and mass rape.[85]

The Maoist movement

The Maoist revolutionary movement has been a major challenge to India's public security since 1946. In May 2010 then Prime Minister Manmohan Singh described it as "the biggest internal security challenge", and in May 2015 the Indian Minister of Home Affairs promised a strong strategy against it. Between those dates, in November 2009, the Government of India launched an offensive, codenamed Operation Green Hunt, along the Maoist 'red corridor'.[86] The history of the Maoist movement in India is worth detailing.

The Indian 'revolution' began when the Communist Party of India (CPI) started an armed struggle against local landlords in the Telangana region of the Princely state of Hyderabad in 1946, a revolution 'withdrawn' on the advice of Stalin in 1951. The movement resurfaced in 1966–67 in West Bengal, erupting in a village called Naxalbari (hence Naxalism); this revised revolution was crushed by 1972. A concurrent revolution, simmering in the Srikakulam district of Andhra Pradesh after 1969, developed from the late 1970s onward. It became a serious public security challenge when the People's War Group emerged as a well-trained guerrilla revolutionary organization, ferociously attacking the police, local landlords and anyone opposing them. They were also divided into several groups (*dalam*), some indulging in fratricide. The Andhra Pradesh government organized 'Greyhound' commandos from within the state police to combat them, with some notable success. Still the revolutionary groups were able to extend their tentacles to other states, at one time operating across one-third of the 600-plus districts if India.

Three major groups merged to create the Communist Party of India (Maoist), which in 2004 emerged as a lethal force, attacking security forces and civilians – even the poor, whom they suspected to be agents of the police – thus expanding and consolidating the red corridor. Some major features of the Maoist movement post-1946, from the perspective of public security, are as follows:

- The first three major strands – Telangana, Naxalbari and Srikakulam – were focused on land relations and the iniquitous intersections between, and relations and economic and human exploitation by, brutal landlords. The focus on human security was relatively successful.
- From the 1980s onward, the 'revolutionaries' consolidated, attacking the police, the security establishment, and public institutions and properties. The Maoists mustered greater popular support. The government attempted a variety of security counter-strategies, with mixed results.
- The Maoist expansion affected mainstream Indian politics, muddling the country's security scenario.
- Becoming a multi-state phenomenon along a north–south corridor stretching from the Nepalese border in the north to Andhra Pradesh in south, the Maoist movement made the tasks of the public security establishment especially difficult. Interstate cooperation was necessary, even cooperation with Nepal.

- Consolidation in 2004 produced both expansion and fierceness for the Maoist movement. Expansion of private enterprise and big business as a means of exploiting rich tribal areas, post-liberalization, meant that the Indian economy intensified the conflict between the Indian government and Maoist challengers. Expansion of private enterprise swelled the ranks and intensified the activities of the Maoists. Public security forces were on the receiving end of aggression, and suffered several losses.
- The government of Chhattisgarh State organized a tribal voluntary force called Salwa Judum, which turned into a vigilante group. The force had to be disbanded on the orders of the Supreme Court of India on a Public Interest Litigation.
- Concerted action by security forces in 2010 and thereafter led to leadership losses amongst the Maoists, sending the movement into disarray.[87]

Conclusion

India inherited its public security structure and its criminal justice system from the British colonial administration. Following independence, the republican Constitution, enacted in 1950, designed India's public security architecture as part of a strong-center federalism. While the organizational basics of India's police force, at federal and state levels, has not changed substantially since independence (the Indian Police Act 1861 as well as the Criminal Procedure Code, the Indian Penal Code and the Indian Evidence Code continue to guide functioning of the criminal justice system), challenges thrown up by democratic processes have continually mounted and become increasingly complex. The best efforts of the country's policing system – which is still concurrently administered by the respective 29 state governments and by the Union Government in the 7 Union Territories – to reduce this complexity to order have not fully succeeded. Strains in the system show both in daily policing and under circumstances arising out of democratic protests, which require sensitive handling. India's geography, demography and diversity continue to produce demands for police reform. Security challenges from within and without remain troubling for a democracy that has prevailed for more than 70 years.

Notes

1 United Nations, 2009.
2 This brilliant old article offers a good analysis of the opening of the sea route to Africa and India. See Mackinder 1904: 437.
3 As discussed by Robert Kaplan 2009. Mahan extended his argument that British control of the seas, combined with a corresponding decline in the naval strength of its major European rivals, paved the way for Great Britain's emergence as the world's dominant military, political, and economic power to suggest that these lessons could be applied to U.S. foreign policy, particularly in the quest to expand U.S. markets overseas. See US Department of State, n.d.
4 Kaplan 2009.
5 Ibid.
6 Quoted in Raja Mohan 2006: 204–205.
7 Suba Chandran 2013.
8 Ghosh 2016: 130–137.
9 Gellner 2013: 7.
10 Gellner 2007 and Singh 2015.
11 Martinez 1994: 5–10.
12 Singh 2012: 223–225. See also Rao and Prabhu 2015.
13 Hazarika 2011.

14 Fair et al. (2005: 54) rightly point out that, seen from this perspective, population pressure, environmental degradation, resource depletion, urbanization and nationalism (or sub nationalism) could cause armed conflict, territorial disputes, ethnic rivalries and ideological divides, and exacerbate tensions and violence and create security risks.
15 www.censusindia.gov.in/2011-prov-results/data_files/india/paper_contentsetc.pdf (accessed on 26 April 2011). Latest figures put India's population at almost 1.353 billion (https://en.wikipedia.org/wiki/Demographics_of_India).
16 www.census2011.co.in/density.php (accessed on 9 December 2015).
17 *The Report of the Working Group on Urban Poverty, Slums, and Service Delivery System* by the erstwhile Steering Committee on Urbanization Planning Commission (2011) pointed out that, in 2004–05, 80.8 million people out of an estimated urban population of 309.5 million were below the poverty line in that their monthly consumption was less than 538.6 rupees. Further, the numbers of urban poor rose by 34.4 percent and the share of total urban poor from 18.7 percent in 1973 to 26.8 percent in 2004–05. This had implications both for conflict and crime. See also http://planningcommission.nic.in/aboutus/committee/wrkgrp12/hud/wg_Final_Urb_Pvt.pdf (accessed on 9 December 2015).
18 The 2011 census of India enumerated 13 million urban slum households; if a household is estimated at five members, the urban slum population would be around 65 million. This was estimated to surge to 104 million by 2017 (Dash 2013).
19 See Misra 2009 and Todhunter 2012.
20 "Rural Poverty in India", http://shodhganga.inflibnet.ac.in/bitstream/10603/9697/7/07_chapter%202.pdf (accessed on 9 December 2015). For a discussion and analysis of left-wing 'revolutionary politics' caused by agrarian poverty see Mehra (2008); more about this aspect later.
21 Bardhan n.d.: 2.
22 http://censusindia.gov.in/Census_And_You/age_structure_and_marital_status.aspx (accessed on 11 December 2015).
23 UNFPA 2007.
24 Kundu 2007.
25 See Mehra 2008a.
26 Bardhan n.d.
27 The sanctioned and actual strength of police personnel at the all-India level per 100,000 population was given as 181.47 and 136.42 to Lok Sabha (House of the People in Indian Parliament) on 22 July 2014 (http://zeenews.india.com/news/nation/police-public-ratio-in-india-is-13642-per-one-lakh-population_949338.html; accessed on 17 December 2015). Data from *Crime in India* – published annually by the Indian Government's National Crime Records Bureau (NCRB) – for 2013 (the latest available at the time of writing) gives the "actual strength of civil police (including district armed police) in 28 states (after the creation of Telangana by bifurcating Andhra Pradesh on 2 June 2014 the number of states in India increased to 29) and seven UTs in India 1.73 million against the sanctioned strength of 2.24 million of total police force (civil and armed combined), rendering 22.8 percent posts vacant. The Armed Police at 382,563 constitutes over one-fourth of the total strength." See http://ncrb.gov.in/ (accessed on 17 December 2015).
28 The second Administrative Reforms Commission appointed by the Government of India said in its second report: "In a pluralistic democracy like ours, political polarization sometimes throws up issues leading to conflicts which escalate into public disorder. Even demonstrations held on legitimate grounds can sometimes degenerate into public disorder. Given our historical inequities on the basis of caste and other social factors, these can easily lead to conflicts that may degenerate into public disorder. Similarly, divisive impulses based on ethnicity, religion, region, language and the sharing of natural resources can exacerbate tensions." http://arc.gov.in/5th%20REPORT.pdf (p. 2; accessed on 8 December 2015).
29 Srinivas 1965.
30 Singh 1996. See also Singh 2000.
31 Srinivas 1965: 501.
32 Brass 2006.
33 Bryjak 1986: 46.
34 Guha 2007: 633–659.
35 Engineer 1994.
36 Khalidi (2010) has candidly captured the failure of the police to display professional neutrality during post-partition riots in 1947–48. Rajeshwari (2004) offers a chronology of communal riots since

independence, and lists a number incidents in which most major political parties emerge as guilty of fanning violence and the police failed to measure up to the challenge. Jabalpur (1961), Varanasi (1977), Jamshedpur (1979), Moradabad (1980), Bihar Sharif (1981), Hazaribagh (1983), Delhi (1984), Meerut (1987) and Gujarat (2002) are some of the major riots in which the police did not emerge with spotless khaki. An analysis of communal violence in India during 1947–86 by Graff and Gallonier (2013) also brings out police inaction, complicity and hostility against Muslims during communal riots. Banerjee (1990) succinctly revealed police double standards in Kanpur (a city in Uttar Pradesh, a north Indian state). It has also been argued by Khalidi (2010), among others, that low representation of minority and other vulnerable communities in the police and security forces has led to communalization of these institutions.

37 Some major violence, physical or otherwise, against Dalits emanates from the practice of 'untouchability', which was abolished by Article 17 of the Constitution of India (part of the Fundamental Rights chapter). This provision also makes the practice punishable by law.

38 See for example, Economic and Political Weekly 1974.

39 See http://tribal.nic.in/WriteReadData/CMS/Documents/201303131039493105468poaact989E4227472861.pdf (accessed on 8 December 2015).

40 See the NCRB's *Crime in India*. The latest issue at the time of writing was 2014, with earlier issues also available on the web. Chapter 7 of the report is devoted to atrocities against SCs and STs. See http://ncrb.gov.in/ (accessed on 8 December 2015).

41 Das 2014.

42 See Nair 2014.

43 The Constitution of India mentions 'backward classes' in Articles 15(4), 16(4) and 340(1). Articles 15 (4) and 16(4) empower the State to make special provisions for any socially and educationally backward class of citizens, while Article 340(1) provides for the appointment of a Commission to investigate the conditions of backward classes. Article 46 casts upon the State an obligation to promote with special care the educational and economic interests of the weaker sections of the people. Even though the framers of the constitution and the post-independence political leadership looked at backwardness as an economic category, the political sociology of India's electoral and party politics has made backwardness synonymous with caste.

44 Jaffrelot and Kumar 2009.

45 He reopened the issue nine months later. For a comprehensive discussion see Mehra (2006).

46 Article 245(1) empowering Parliament 'to make laws for the whole or any part of the territory of India' and the Legislature of a State to 'make laws for the whole or any part of the State' is the source of the Seventh Schedule that organizes subjects elaborately and neatly in three lists – Union List;, State List and Concurrent List. Article 248 assigns residuary powers of legislation exclusively to Parliament.

47 The Union Government deployed the Central Reserve Police Force (CRPF) *suo motu* on three occasions during this period: in Kerala in September 1968 to protect government offices in Trivandrum during the strike of Union Government employees; and twice in West Bengal in 1969 to protect the Farakka Barrage and the Durgapur Steel Plant. http://interstatecouncil.nic.in/Sarkaria/CHAPTERVII.pdf (accessed on 14 December 2015).

48 The text in square brackets in both entries was inserted by the 42nd Amendment. For details see http://indiacode.nic.in/coiweb/amend/amend42.htm (accessed on 14 December 2015).

49 For details of the 43rd and 44th Constitutional Amendments see http://indiacode.nic.in/coiweb/amend/amend43.htm and http://indiacode.nic.in/coiweb/amend/amend44.htm (accessed on 14 December 2015). For a commentary on the Amendments that are crucial to understanding the discourse on police powers of the Indian state see Mehra (2015a).

50 The Union Territories in India emerged when the States Reorganisation Commission (SRC) was redrawing the internal map in 1955. Aside from 'States' that the Constitution recommended, it suggested "'Territories' which, for vital strategic or other considerations, cannot be joined to any of the States and are, therefore, centrally-administered.' The SRC recommended their representation in the 'Union legislature', but '(D)emocracy in these areas should take the form of the people being associated with the administration in an advisory rather than a directive capacity.' The SRC based its recommendation of 'federally administered' areas on international experience, particularly of security considerations in other federations and of national capitals such as Washington DC, Ottawa, Canberra, and so on" (Mehra 2015: 81–82, internal citation omitted).

51 The seven central forces are: Assam Rifles, Border Security Force, Central Industrial Security Force, Central Reserve Police Force (including the Rapid Action Force and Commando Battalion for

Resolute Action/CoBRA), Indo-Tibetan Border Police, National Security Guard and Sashastra Seema Bal. These agencies have around 600,000 personnel. The specialized security and support agencies of the Union Government are the Intelligence Bureau, the Central Bureau of Investigation, the Research and Analysis Wing, the National Crime Record Bureau, the National Institute of Criminology and Forensic Science, and the Bureau of Police Research and Development. In 1978, the Government of India constituted the Indian Coast Guard to police its coastline under the Ministry of Defense. It has close to 11,000 active personnel.

52 Independent India inherited two all-India cadres from the colonial administration – the Indian Civil Service and the Imperial Police. After independence these were renamed and retained as the Indian Administrative Service (IAS) and the IPS as the steel frame of Indian bureaucracy. They were given statutory support in Articles 310–312 of the Constitution. Entry to the IPS is through a national competitive examination conducted by the Union Public Service Commission, recruited and trained by the Union Government and allocated to state cadres; thence they are under administrative and operative control of the respective state government, unless on deputation to the Union Government. Deputation to the Union Government is under a formula and rule meant to ensure rotation between the Union and the states.

53 This argument emerges clearly from studies in Mehra and Lévy (2011).

54 Mehra 2011.

55 The IPC, the CrPC and the Indian Evidence Act now figure in the Concurrent List (III) in the Seventh Schedule of the Constitution referred to earlier.

56 The second police commission set up under the chairmanship of Sir A.H.L. Fraser in 1902 concluded that: 'The police force is far from efficient, it is defective in training and organization, it is inadequately supervised, it is generally regarded as corrupt and oppressive, and it has utterly failed to secure the confidence and cordial cooperation of the people' (Government of India 1903: 15). The legacy continues to this day.

57 Khalidi 2010.

58 For the most current discussion on this issue see the Centre-State Commission's *Internal Security, Criminal Justice and Centre-State Cooperation* report and Task Force reports (Government of India 2010a and 2010b).

59 Mehra 1985.

60 Mehra 2011.

61 Government of India 1971.

62 For a discussion on features of the NPC report, which is still considered a good report, see Mehra (2007 and 2011). The full, multi-volume report is available on the web. Since each volume has a separate web address, they can be checked selectively, or entirely, by discerning researchers.

63 The full text of the report submitted to the government in 2006 is available at www.prsindia.org/uploads/media/vikas_doc/docs/1241499712~~mpolice_act.pdf (accessed on 20 December 2015).

64 Bayley 1971.

65 See for example a discussion on house collapses and the police–builder nexus in Mumbai in the 1990s (Roy 1991).

66 For a discussion on the gangster–police nexus in India's largest state, Uttar Pradesh, see Economic and Political Weekly 1981. Also see Singh and D'Mello (1989).

67 I have pointed this out in a study of the Indian police quoting the IIPO study (Mehra 1985).

68 Lokniti 2015: 64–66.

69 Dasgupta (1990) gives a typical example from Calcutta (now Kolkata).

70 *Crime in India*, an annual government publication by the National Crimes Records Bureau (NCRB), devotes a chapter to custodial crime, divided into: (i) deaths in police custody/lock up of persons remanded in police custody by a court; (ii) deaths in police custody of those not remanded in custody; (iii) reasons for custodial deaths; and (iv) escapes from police custody. Archive copies from 1953 onwards are available at http://ncrb.gov.in and are rich sources of data for researchers.

71 Ved Marwah (1995: 1–30) describes the psychological make-up of a few involved in terrorist activities who had neither fear nor remorse for the killings.

72 Gupta (2008: 182) describes a terrorist's mental make-up and strategy thus: "Facing a huge asymmetry of power a dissident group adopts shock tactics to achieve certain short- and long-term goals. In the short run, through these atrocities a terrorist group announces its existence and signals its commitment to its political goal to its adversaries, support base, and to the world, which it sees largely as ignorant or apathetic to its cause." However, the globalized terror of today goes beyond this limited definition.

73 According to the *New York Times*, "ISIS demonstrated a significant leap in its ability to coordinate operations against the West when it directed two major attacks that killed hundreds: an assault across Paris and the downing of a Russian passenger jet in Egypt." See Yourish et al. 2015.
74 Burke 2011: 495.
75 Alex P. Schmid's detailed research guide to terrorism listed 109 definitions of terrorism provided between 1936 and 1981 (see Schmid and Jongman 1984). See also Mehra and Sharma 2006: 7–14.
76 Hiro 2011: xix.
77 Gupta 2011.
78 See the *Times of India* of 28 December 2015 on the busting of an Indian Mujahedeen (IM) module and on the National Investigation Agency's admission that youth were being lured (pp. 2, 9).
79 Mehra and Sharma 2006.
80 Marwah 2009: 162–249. See also Marwah 1995.
81 In the wake of terrorism in Punjab, I was among the first to stress that the police is the agency that should be trained as the first and effective line of defence against terrorism (Mehra 1982).
82 Laws and Lacopino 2002; Singh 2002.
83 Bose et al. 1990; Guha 2007: 242–262.
84 Marwah 1995: 80–85.
85 Ongoing complex situations of public security involving contentious claims, baffled responses and mortifying protests leading to daily misery for the people would need volumes to record and analyze. It is only possible here to provide links to some of references for the discerning to follow (all were accessed on 18 December 2015): www.bgverghese.com/KunanPoshpora.htm;www.warscapes.com/reportage/kunan-poshpora-mass-rape-case-notes-hearing;http://kafila.org/2014/01/20/kunan-poshpora-the-other-story-shrimoyee-nandini-ghosh/;www.hrw.org/sites/default/files/reports/INDIA935.PDF;https://kashmirsolidaritymumbai.wordpress.com/tag/press-council-of-india/.
86 The red corridor as drawn up tentatively for 2015 appeared short compared to how it had been shown in much of the early years of the millennium. The government offensive has borne results. For a map see www.satp.org/satporgtp/countries/india/database/conflictmap.htm (accessed on 20 December 2015).
87 The literature on the Maoist movement spanning seven decades is comprehensive on each of its aspects. I am not referring to any in this text, but the references at the end of the chapter contain many, and my works listed there have comprehensive bibliographies. My arguments from them are condensed here. See Gupta 2011; Mehra 2009, 2011.

References

Banerjee, Ashis. 1990. '"Comparative Curfew": Changing Dimensions of Communal Politics in India', in Veena Das (ed.). *Mirrors of Violence: Communities, Riots and Survivors in South Asia*. New York: Oxford University Press, pp. 37–68.

Bardhan, Pranab. n.d. 'Globalization, Inequality, and Poverty: An Overview'. http://eml.berkeley.edu/~webfac/bardhan/papers/BardhanGlobalOverview.pdf (accessed on 17 December 2015).

Bayley, David H. 1969. *The Police and Political Development in India*. Princeton: Princeton University Press.

Bayley, David H. 1971. 'The Police in India', *Economic and Political Weekly*, 6 (45), 6 November, pp. 2287–2291.

Bose, Tapan, Dinesh Mohan, Gautam Navlakha and Sumanta Banerjee. 1990. 'India's "Kashmir War"', *Economic and Political Weekly*, 25 (13), pp. 650–662.

Brass, Paul. 2006. 'Collective Violence, Human Rights, and the Police of Curfew', *Journal of Human Rights*, 5, pp. 323–340.

Bryjak, George J. 1986. 'Collective Violence in India', *Asian Affairs*, 13 (2), p. 44.

Burke, Jason 2011. *The 9/11 Wars*. London: Allen Lane.

Chandran, D. Suba. 2013. 'Border Management in South Asia: Volatile, Violent and Porous'. Institute of Peace and Conflict Studies, South Asia, Articles # 4096, 22 August.www.ipcs.org/article/south-asia/border-management-in-south-asia-volatile-violent-and-porous-4096.html (accessed on 23 November 2015).

Das, Madhuparna. 2014. 'Skewed Representation of Muslims in Police behind Trust Deficit: Islam', *Indian Express*, 22 July. http://indianexpress.com/article/cities/kolkata/skewed-representation-of-muslims-in-police-behind-trust-deficit-islam/ (accessed on 8 December 2015).

Dasgupta, Rajshri. 1990. 'Death under Police Protection', *Economic and Political Weekly*, 25 (5), 3 February, pp. 245–246.

Dash, D.K. 2013. 'By 2017, India's Slum Population Will Rise to 104 Million', *Times of India*, 20 August. http://timesofindia.indiatimes.com/india/By-2017-Indias-slum-population-will-rise-to 104-million/articleshow/21927474.cms (accessed on 10 December 2015).

Economic and Political Weekly. 1974. 'Police in Action', 9 (5), 2 February, pp. 113–114.

Economic and Political Weekly. 1981. 'Politics, Police and Crime', 16 (34), 22 August. www.epw.in/journal/1981/34.

Engineer, Asghar Ali. 1994. 'Communal Violence and Role of Police', *Economic and Political Weekly*, 29 (15), 9 August, pp. 835–840.

Fair, C. Christine, Clifford Grammich, JulieDaVanzo and Brian Nichiporuk. 2005. 'Demographics and Security: The Contrasting Cases of Pakistan and Bangladesh', *Journal of South Asian and Middle Eastern Studies*, 28 (4), pp. 53–76.

Gellner, David N. 2007. 'Caste and Ethnicity in Nepal', *Economic and Political Weekly*, 19 May, pp. 1823–1828.

Gellner, David N. (ed.). 2013. *Borderland Lives in Northern South Asia: Non-State Perspectives*. Durham, NC: Duke University Press.

Ghosh, Partha S. 2016. *Migrants, Refugees and the Stateless in South Asia*. New Delhi: Sage.

Government of India. 1903. *Fraser Report of the Indian Police Commission, 1902–03*. Simla: Government Printing Office.

Government of India. 1971. *The Gore Committee Report on Police Training*. New Delhi: Ministry of Home Affairs, Government of India. http://police.pondicherry.gov.in/Police%20Commission%20reports/THE%20GORE%20COMMITTEE%20REPORT%20ON.pdf.

Government of India. 2010a. *Commission on Centre-State Relations Report: Internal Security, Criminal Justice and Centre-State Cooperation*. http://interstatecouncil.nic.in/wp-content/uploads/2015/06/volume5.pdf.

Government of India. 2010b. *Commission on Centre-State Relations Supplementary Volume-I: Task Force Reports*. http://interstatecouncil.nic.in/wp-content/uploads/2015/06/Suppl_VolI_Task_Forces.pdf.

Graff, Violette and Juliette Gallonier. 2013. 'Hindu Muslim Communal Riots in India I', *Online Encyclopaedia of Mass Violence*. Paris: Sciences Po. www.massviolence.org/IMG/article_PDF/Hindu-Muslim-Communal-Riots-in,736.pdf. (accessed on 9 December 2015).

Guha, Ramachandra. 2007. *India After Gandhi: The History of the World's Largest Democracy*. London: Macmillan.

Gupta, Dipak K. 2008. *Understanding Terrorism and Political Violence: The Life Cycle of Birth, Growth, Transformation and Demise*. Oxford and New York: Routledge.

Gupta, Shishir. 2011. *Indian Mujahedeen: The Enemy Within*. Gurgaon: Hachette India.

Hazarika, Sanjoy. 2011. *Strangers of the Mist: Tales of War and Peace from India's Northeast (1994)*. New Delhi: Viking.

Hiro, Dilip. 2011. *Jihad on Two Fronts: South Asia's Unfolding Drama*. New Delhi: HarperCollins India.

Jaffrelot, Christophe and Sanjay Kumar (eds). 2009. *Rise of the Plebeians? The Changing Face of Indian Legislative Assemblies*. New Delhi: Routledge.

Kaplan, Robert D. 2009. 'The Revenge of Geography', *Foreign Policy*, 172, pp. 96–105. www.foreignpolicy.com (accessed on 20 November 2015).

Khalidi, Omar. 2010. *Khaki and Ethnic Violence in India: Armed Forces, Police and Paramilitary during Communal Riots* (2nd edn). New Delhi: Three Essays Collective.

Kundu, Amitabh. 2007. 'Migration and Urbanisation in India in the Context of Poverty Alleviation'. www.networkideas.org/ideasact/jun07/Beijing_Conference_07/Amitabh_Kundu.pdf (accessed on 12 December 2015).

Laws, Ami and Vincent Lacopino. 2002. 'Police Torture in Punjab, India: An Extended Survey', *Health and Human Rights*, 6 (1), pp. 195–250.

Lokniti. 2015. *Democracy in India: A Citizens' Perspective*. New Delhi: Centre for the Study of Developing Societies.

Mackinder, H.J. 1904. 'The Geographical Pivot of History', *Geographical Journal*, 4 (23), pp. 421–437; reproduced in *Geographical Journal*, 170 (4), 2004, pp. 298–321.

Martínez, Oscar J. 1994. *Border People: Life and Society in the U.S.-Mexico Borderlands*. Tucson: University of Arizona Press.

Marwah, Ved. 1995. *Uncivil Wars: Pathology of Terrorism in India*. New Delhi: Indus.

Marwah, Ved. 2009. *India in Turmoil: Jammu and Kashmir, the Northeast and Left Extremism*. New Delhi: Rupa & Co.

Mehra, Ajay K. 1982. 'Dealing with Police Unrest', *Mainstream*, 20 November.
Mehra, Ajay K. 1985. *Police in Changing India*. New Delhi: Usha.
Mehra, Ajay K. 2006. '"Due Process" or "Procedure Established by Law"', in Pran Chopra (ed.), *The Supreme Court versus the Constitution: A Challenge to Federalism*. New Delhi: Sage.
Mehra, Ajay K. 2007. 'Police Reforms at Sixty', *Mainstream*, 55 (35), 18 August. www.mainstreamweekly.net/article286.html.
Mehra, Ajay K. 2008. 'India's Experiment with Revolution'. Working Paper No. 40. Heidelberg Papers in South Asian and Comparative Politics. South Asia Institute. Department of Political Science. University of Heidelberg. http://archiv.ub.uni-heidelberg.de/volltextserver/8710/1/Heidelberg_Paper_Mehra.pdf. (accessed on 15 December 2015).
Mehra, Ajay K. 2008a. 'Mumbai's Cloistered Hearth: A Mockery of the Very Idea of India', *The Statesman*, 10 November.
Mehra, Ajay K. 2009. 'Left-of-Left: The Link between Revolutionary and Mainstream Politics', *The Statesman*, 29 May.
Mehra, Ajay K. 2011. 'Police Reforms in India: Imperatives, Discourse and Reality', in Ajay K. Mehra and René Lévy (eds.), *The Police, State and Society: Perspectives from India and France*. New Delhi: Pearson India, pp. 263–286.
Mehra, Ajay K. 2015. 'Comment: Sharing Sovereignty', *Seminar*, 671, July, pp. 80–82.
Mehra, Ajay K. 2015a. 'The Emergency Deserves Larger Reflections', *Mainstream*, 53 (34) 15 August.
Mehra, Ajay K. and René Lévy (eds.). 2011. *The Police, State and Society: Perspectives from India and France*. New Delhi: Pearson India.
Mehra, Ajay K. and O.P. Sharma. 2006. *Terrorism and the Rule of Law: An Indian Perspective*. New Delhi: KAS-CPA.
Mishra, Subhash. 2015. 'IS Influencing Youth in South India: NIA', *Times of India*, 28 December. http://timesofindia.indiatimes.com/articleshow/50347550.cms?utm_source=contentofinterest&utm_medium=text&utm_campaign=cppst.
Misra, Neelesh. 2009.'Biggest Land Grab after Columbus', *Hindustan Times*, 14 November. www.hindustantimes.com/india/biggest-land-grab-after-columbus/story-YpgiVcJlO5BW86Kdk496II.html (accessed on 11 December 2015).
Nair, Smita. 2014. 'Muslims Think We Are Communal, Corrupt: Police', *Indian Express*, 17 July. http://indianexpress.com/article/india/maharashtra/muslims-think-we-are-communal-corrupt-police/ (accessed on 8 December 2015).
Raja Mohan, C. 2006. *Impossible Allies: Nuclear India, United States and the Global Order*. New Delhi: India Research Press.
Rajeshwari, B. 2004. 'Communal Riots in India A Chronology (1947–2003)'. *ICPS Research Papers* 3. New Delhi: Institute of Peace and Conflict Studies. www.nagarikmancha.org/images/1242-Documents-Communal_Riots_in_India.pdf (accessed on 4 December 2015).
Rao, Srinath R. and Vasant Prabhu. 2015. '7 Years after 26/11, Face of Coastal Security: 8 Bamboo Poles, 2 Cops, 1 Aluminium Roof', *Indian Express*, 26 November.
Roy, Krishna. 1991. 'House Collapses and Police-Builders Nexus'. *Economic and Political Weekly*, 26 (27–28), pp. 1655 1656.
Schmid, Alex P. and Albert J. Jongman. 1984. *Political Terrorism: A New Guide to Actors, Authors, Concepts, Data Bases, Theories and Literature*. Amsterdam: North-Holland.
Singh, Gayatri and Bernard D'Mello 1989. 'Policing Firing at Chandrapur Thermal Power Station', *Economic and Political Weekly*, 24 (41), 14 October, pp. 2293–2295.
Singh, K. Suresh. 2000. 'A Perspective on the ASI', *Seminar*, 495, November. www.india-seminar.com/2000/495/495%20k.%20suresh%20singh.htm (accessed on 3 November 2015).
Singh, K.R. 2012. *Coastal Security: Maritime Dimensions of India's Homeland Security*. New Delhi: United Services Institute of India and Vij Books.
Singh, K.S. 1996. *Communities, Segments, Synonyms, Surnames and Titles*. People of India, National Series, 8, Anthropological Survey of India. New Delhi: Oxford University Press.
Singh, Pritam. 2015. 'Nepal's Time for Plural Democratic Socialism', *Tribune* (India), 2 November.
Singh, Ujjwal Kumar. 2002. 'Amnesty for Police Officers: Politics of Truth and Reconciliation', *Economic and Political Weekly*, 37 (32), pp. 3326–3328.
Srinivas, M.N. 1965. 'Social Structure'. in *The Gazetteer of India, Volume 1: Country and People*. New Delhi: Publications Division, Government of India Ministry of Information and Broadcasting, pp. 501–577.

Steering Committee on Urbanization Planning Commission. 2011. 'Report of the Working Group on Urban Poverty, Slums, and Service Delivery System'. New Delhi, 19 September.

Todhunter, Colin. 2012. 'Modernisation, Injustice and Social Resistance in India', *Global Research*, 31 August. www.globalresearch.ca/modernisation-in-india/5302731?print=1 (accessed on 11 December 2015).

UNFPA. 2007. *State of World Population 2007: Unleashing the Potential of Urban Growth*. New York: United Nations Population Fund.

United Nations. 2009. *Human Security in Theory and Practice*. New York: Human Security Unit, UN Office for the Coordination of Humanitarian Affairs (OCHA). www.undp.org/content/dam/turkey/docs/news-from-new-horizons/issue-41/UNDP-TR-HSHandbook_2009.pdf (accessed on 15 December 2015).

US Department of State. n.d. 'Mahan's The Influence of Sea Power upon History: Securing International Markets in the 1890s'. https://history.state.gov/milestones/1866-1898/mahan (accessed 23 November 2015).

Yourish, Karen, Derek Watkins and Tom Giratikanon. 2015. 'Where ISIS Has Directed and Inspired Attacks Round the World', *New York Times*, 17 June. www.nytimes.com/interactive/2015/06/17/world/middleeast/map-isis-attacks-around-the-world.html?_r=0 (accessed on 16 December 2015).

13

DEMOCRACY AND SECURITY IN SOUTH AFRICA

Jeffrey A. Griffin and Robert L. Ostergard Jr.

Introduction

In 1994, the Nationalist Party voluntarily relinquished control of the racist apartheid government it had firmly controlled since 1948. After 27 years of imprisonment, African National Congress (ANC) leader Nelson Mandela was released from prison by the apartheid government, and soon thereafter became the first black president of South Africa. When the opposition party, the ANC, ascended to power, the South African government fundamentally transformed from a white-minority controlled government to a majority government based on free and open elections. While the change initiated a new era in South Africa's history, shifting political control from a minority-led to a majority-led government, problems have lingered in the country that continue to pose potential security and stability issues for its democratic regime. These problems include economic inequality, land distribution issues, endemic poverty, unemployment, issues of political party governance and representation, issues associated with protest rioting, and issues associated with South Africa's large-scale private security industry. Such problems have become interconnected, challenging South Africa's human security as well as its democratic order.

Although historical remnants of colonization and British rule still affect the governance capacity of the state, the legacy of colonization cannot be pinpointed as the only source of South Africa's contemporary security concerns. In fact, South Africa's security issues have reversed a typical pattern of post-colonial African state rule. Sub-Saharan African states typically have not faced external threats that could lead to interstate war. Their greatest security threats have been *internal*, emanating not only from weak institutional constructs but also from their own militaries via military coups d'état. In South Africa, the apartheid government held firm control over its military and enjoyed relatively stable governing institutions. But, in the wake of its democratic transition, South Africa's regime has faced internal institutional weakness (due to high levels of inefficiency and corruption) and economic problems that still linger from the apartheid regime. In the period after South Africa's democratic transition, institutional weakness, corruption, income inequality, poverty, and ethnic conflict, alongside social welfare and race issues, have threatened the stability and sustainability of South Africa's democracy by fostering antidemocratic attitudes and movements.[1] While South Africa is a long-standing state and a major power on the African continent, it is still in its democratic infancy. It is still trying to find its balance and achieve sufficient stability to ensure that democracy and security thrive.

South Africa and the triumph of the African National Congress

South Africa's relatively modern history began roughly in the mid-1600s, at a time when expansionism vis-à-vis colonization and the subsequent monopolization of political, economic, and social power were all controlled by Dutch traders (beginning in 1652). Dutch traders utilized the country as a mid-point in their trade routes to Asia and beyond. Two centuries later South Africa experienced British involvement, beginning in 1860 after British seizure of the Cape of Good Hope.[2] Two colonial powers were then in play: Dutch settlers, known as Afrikaners or Boers, and British subjects. The colonizing powers began to confiscate land previously ruled by the indigenous peoples of the country, and white South Africans from both national groups were able to develop "the richest and most industrialized society in Africa".[3] Settlers discovered natural resources, specifically gold and diamonds, which led to greater immigration, wealth, and further suppression of South Africa's indigenous populations.[4]

In recent times, from 1948 until 1994, the National Party ruled South Africa, employing a governance structure of legal and systemic racial segregation known as "apartheid" that corresponded with principles of white supremacy. The Afrikaner-dominated National Party ruled until the dismantling of apartheid in 1994, when the first multiracial elections were held and a new South African constitution was adopted. The African National Congress took the reins of power through those elections. The issue of how the ANC would rule came to the fore as South African society transitioned from decades of racist oppression to a new period of democratic reform.

Since the transition, the ANC has dominated the country's political environment, with little substantial political opposition. How South Africa became a one-party state has as much to do with the ANC's active role against apartheid as it does with how the new post-apartheid South Africa evolved. During the latter years of apartheid, the majority of the black populace viewed the ANC as a group of legitimate freedom fighters led by dominant figures who deserved support. Nelson Mandela was arguably the most well-known of the major figures of the movement. Released after 27 years of imprisonment, Mandela ran under the political party platform of the ANC and easily won election to become South Africa's first post-apartheid president. Since the 1994 election, South Africa's black majority has viewed the ANC as "victors" who fought for the black majority, a primary reason why the ANC has dominated South Africa's national elections for more than two decades.

In the aftermath of apartheid, the Republic of South Africa became a constitutional multiparty democracy. However, based on the final constitution of 1996, a weak form of federalism emerged which helped the ANC consolidate power and the national decision-making process. While change of government went smoothly, change in society lagged, partly because of the strength of the ANC itself and the resulting over-centralization of the national government. The ANC not only garnered significant national electoral strength, but also captured control of the nine provincial governments. The ANC became the dominant national party, similar in circumstances to parties in other one-party dominant states such as the Kuomintang in Taiwan, the Institutional Revolutionary Party in Mexico, and the United Malays National Organization in Malaysia.[5]

The strength of its national appeal allowed the ANC to centralize much of the decision-making process without significant input from provincial leadership. While this may have been a strong political move for the ANC in the short term, it became a political liability during the ANC's long-term control of South Africa. After the ANC took control of the national government, local and provincial governments barely stayed afloat as their ability to deliver services declined and their authority within their territories eroded. According to Giliomee, "of the approximately seven hundred local governments, about a third [could] manage, another third [were] salvageable, and the remaining third [were] collapsing to one degree or another".[6]

Decay in provincial and local institutions, and decline of public confidence in them, has had significant political and economic effects. The inability of provincial and local institutions to provide services to people strained national services' capacity as the national government attempted to fill the services gap at those levels. A suggestive measure of public confidence in the national government has been how well, and the degree to which, the government has been able to provide needed services to its people. The ANC has not met the challenge effectively, and the strain of such failure has been evident upon national and provincial ANC leaders. Symptoms of the state's ineffectual governance emerged quickly and have lingered, creating significant problems for South Africa's democratic consolidation and stability. Regrettably, the innate structural inequality that dominated the apartheid era remained intact.

The electoral process has also been at issue. Since the first post-apartheid elections in 1994, the ANC has been able to render competitive elections in the country effectively non-existent. Large portions of the electorate have remained loyal to the ANC. Even in the face of allegations of corruption and ineffective governance during South Africa's 2014 national election cycle, the ANC still managed to capture 62.1 percent of the seats in the National Assembly (though its majority declined slightly from the 2009 election results when it captured 65.9 percent of the parliamentary seats). The winner of the 2009 and 2014 elections, Jacob Zuma, became the focus of over two decades of discontent with ANC rule, causing people to question the ANC's dominance and the very nature of the ANC as a democratic party.

While there has been no sense of widespread authoritarianism in South Africa, the ANC has shown corrupt and anti-democratic tendencies.[7] These tendencies are no longer latent. They came to the fore under Jacob Zuma's presidency and persist now that he is no longer president. Zuma resigned his office on February 15, 2018 under charges of corruption and wrongdoing. The National Assembly appointed Cyril Ramaphosa president that same day. National elections took place during May of 2019. Though Zuma is no longer president, the security challenges developed over two decades of ANC rule, and specifically under Zuma's tenure, remain in place and are worth examining in detail.

President Zuma

As head of the executive branch and the face of the ANC, President Zuma governed South Africa after 2009. Voters re-elected him in 2014. The national elections of 2014 began to expose the president's vulnerabilities; the ANC vote dropped to just 49 percent in Pretoria and Port Elizabeth and 51 percent in Johannesburg. Opposition leaders claimed that in these elections the ANC actually lost, but was declared the winner due to fraud. The Independent Electoral Commission confirmed the ANC victory, but its decision was tainted since Zuma had appointed his former advisor to head the Commission.[8] Subsequent events showing signs of internal dissent and strife, coupled with allegations of corruption and ineffective governance, indicated that Zuma's position may have been more tenuous than under any previous

ANC president. Dissent within the party over policy and leadership may have been signs that Zuma was losing the allegiance of some followers and losing the firm grip over the party that had helped propel him to the presidency. Zuma's own popularity with rank-and-file members of the ANC decreased.[9] His ability to govern South Africa was repeatedly called into question by a more vocal opposition which sensed the ANC president's vulnerability. A corresponding drop in the president's popularity lent further credence to the idea that Zuma's grip on power was more fragile than that of his predecessors.

In December of 2015, President Zuma blazed through three finance ministers in one week, leaving commentators to speculate that "the President is losing control".[10] Ahead of local elections in 2016, opposition parties were expected to give the ANC its first significant challenge at the polls. The impending challenge from opposition groups led some to anticipate a major electoral realignment that would change South Africa's political landscape, which was becoming unstable under Zuma's control. Potential ANC losses in 2016 included major cities such as the financial capital of Johannesburg, the administrative capital Pretoria, and Port Elizabeth, whence many top ANC leaders emerged.[11]

One of the dominant opposition parties in the country, the Democratic Alliance (DA), appeared as a challenger with the greatest chance to capitalize on the ANC's political misfortunes. Within the context of the ANC's loosening grip on power, in May 2015 the DA elected the first black leader in the party's history, Mmusi Maimane. Maimane's election brought about a significant shift in South African party politics. The Democratic Alliance traced its roots to the origins of the anti-apartheid Progressive Party. The Progressive Party emerged in 1959 as a federalist and free market party that sought to end the practice of apartheid and guarantee the powers and rights of the provinces. Before Maimane's election, whites had dominated the DA's leadership. Maimane quickly struck out at Zuma, referring to the president as a "broken man presiding over a broken country".[12]

Unfortunately for Zuma, one of the hallmarks of his tenure was the prevalence of corruption within his administration. While accusations of corruption have become standard in South African politics, under Zuma the issue of corruption came to the fore in a much more pronounced way than in previous ANC administrations. Polling conducted by Afrobarometer in 2015 demonstrated that more than two-thirds of the population expressed distrust of the president, with an almost equal number disapproving of his overall performance.[13]

On the face of it the Zuma administration cracked down on corruption at the public-official and governmental level. But evidence suggests that such investigations and claims were speculative and superficial at best. Zuma himself came under investigation for allegations dating to 2009 that "millions of rand [South African currency] of taxpayers' money were spent on a swimming pool and other facilities at his private home".[14] Mismanagement of public funds became the latest in a string of corruption problems for Zuma. In fact, before Zuma's election in 2009, more than 700 corruption, fraud, money-laundering, and racketeering charges against him were dropped.[15] The following year he fathered a child out of wedlock in another scandal.

While Zuma was able to hold onto power until 2018, public perceptions of corruption, mismanagement, and ineffective governance developed during his tenure with respect to a long legacy of perceived ineffective ANC rule after the end of apartheid. South Africa's population stood in awe of Nelson Mandela's victory over apartheid; they waited for his successors to show that they had earned the right to stay in power. The ANC's legacy of poor governance has fostered much of the frustration and insecurity South Africans feel today.

Democracy and (in)security in South Africa: the legacy of the African National Congress

In a traditional sense, South Africa does not have foreign enemies. Geographically situated on the southern tip of the African continent, South Africa has had long-standing contact, positive and negative, with states around the world. In the post-colonial period, South Africa's military was a dominant force that had no serious challengers regionally or continentally. Likewise, South Africa had little expansionistic ambition, with the exception of its 75-year occupation and control of Namibia. Thus, while its democratic transition was underway, the South African government had little to fear from external threats. In the post-transition period, internal problems of state capacity have been the primary challenges to South Africa's democratic rule and stability. To be more specific, internal issues that have manifested as potential security issues over time have emerged from institutional arrangements put in place under the former apartheid regime. Many originate in the economic disenfranchisement of the majority black population under apartheid rule.

Black economic disenfranchisement is closely linked to land distribution problems that remain from the apartheid era, when whites controlled South Africa's business and investment capital. The Natives' Land Act of 1913, exacerbated by the 1936 Native Trust and Land Act, enabled the apartheid government to block the majority black population from access to land and capital, thus creating a fundamental disjuncture in economic and political power between the white ruling class and black labor. According to Lahiff,

> The 1913 Act represented … not the final act of dispossession, but rather the formalization of a dual system of property rights whereby the majority black population would be granted limited and conditional access to land, greatly inferior to those of their white counterparts, in urban areas, on white-owned farms and, above all, in the ethnically-based "Native Areas".[16]

In this context, the Acts of 1913 and 1936 deprived the majority black population of both economic and political power.

Land distribution issues plagued the ANC-controlled government after the transition. These issues have remained politically sensitive, if not explosive, for the ANC government and potentially its successors. According to Hall, "land reform is one way in which the 'new' South Africa set out to redress the injustices of apartheid and, by redistributing land to black South Africans, to transform the structural basis of racial inequality".[17] But, given the politically sensitive nature of the problem, economic rationales for land reform, and associated problems of justice and equity, have made limited progress.[18] As O'Laughlin et al. show, progress in the redistribution of land has been staggeringly slow. Initially the ANC government planned to redistribute 24.6 million hectares, roughly equivalent to 30 percent of white-owned agricultural land, through a combination of grants and rights-based distribution schemes. But by 2000 only 1.2 percent of white-owned land had been redistributed, and target dates had been pushed back to 2014. By 2011, 7.2 percent of white-owned land had been reassigned, and the date for achieving full distribution of the 30 percent had been moved to 2025, more than 30 years after the transition from apartheid.[19] While the transfer process has been slow, research shows that land that has been transferred tends to be underutilized, given high initial startup costs, lack of access to capital, and poor planning by officials and hired consultants.[20]

These problems demonstrate clearly that land redistribution and issuance policies are not as simple as taking away land and giving it to others, a lesson Zimbabwe's late Robert Mugabe learned when he stripped white landowners of their land and redistributed it to his country's black population without establishing institutional and policy mechanisms to support or properly maintain the new arrangements. Zimbabwe, once known as the breadbasket of Africa, became dependent upon foreign food imports as agricultural output plummeted.

President Jacob Zuma recognized these interrelated issues, making land reform, agrarian change, and rural development issues priorities of the ANC government in 2009.[21] Seven years later, at the Annual Opening of the National House of Traditional Leaders in Cape Town in March of 2016, Zuma addressed the myriad problems the ANC had experienced related to land distribution, focusing on the creation of multi stakeholder Agri-Parks that promised to bring underutilized land into full production within three years and proposing to expand agricultural irrigation at the same time.[22] This proposal highlighted the lack of progress made since 2009 and additional related problems that mounted for the ANC government over time. The land problem remained a vital issue throughout the Zuma presidency, an issue that exacerbated poor economic performance, poverty, discrimination, and social and racial tension.[23] According to a South African news report, a three-year drought threatened the country's long-term food security and had the potential to precipitate food crises.[24]

In the face of a growing population, economic growth has not kept up with current and future population needs. Slow economic growth has resulted in high levels of unemployment (about 25 percent officially) and has condemned most black South Africans to an impoverished existence. South Africa's dire economic conditions have further hastened a growing interest in land distribution, land seizures, and the nationalization of the country's mineral wealth.[25] A substantial part of the country's economic structure—businesses, corporations, and the mining industry—remains in the hands of the white minority. Witness the comments of Dr. Ali A. Mazrui in 2008: "You take the crown, and we'll keep the jewels … Black people should assume the crown of political power, and white people should retain the jewels of economic prosperity."[26]

Poverty is a dire and endemic issue that plagues a majority of South Africa. According to the World Bank, the poverty headcount ratio at the national poverty line was 53.8 percent in 2010, down from 66.6 percent in 2000. But this progress in reducing the poverty rate may have come at a substantial cost; social welfare rolls have grown since 1994, when 4 million people received some form of social welfare support, to 16.9 million people in 2015. Seeing the trend, President Zuma declared that the government "[could] not sustain a situation where social grants are growing all the time and think it can be a permanent feature".[27] Even though the situation was unsustainable, the government continued to see social welfare expenditures increase.

Unemployment has been closely related to poverty. South Africa's most recent unemployment rate was at about 24.5 percent of the work force, with expanded unemployment and real unemployment estimates placing that number above 35 percent.[28] Over 50 percent of African and colored youth remained unemployed, constituting the hardest-hit demographic in the country.[29] These unemployment rates are not new to South Africa; in fact, they have been a chronic condition for much of the post-apartheid period and a significant feature that has exacerbated the country's poverty rates. Similarly, wage and income inequality is among the highest in the world, driven predominantly by wage inequality between those in the 90th percentile and those in the 50th percentile,[30] and falling along racial lines, with black South Africans being worse off than other racial groups. In other words, the gap widened between those at the top, where a premium is paid for high-skilled labor, and those in the middle, dominated by low-skill employment. This gap contributes to overall wealth inequality, which has wage and income components but which has institutional and structural roots as well.

Food security issues parallel endemic poverty in South Africa. While food security is guaranteed by South Africa's Constitution (Articles 27 and 28(1) (c)), as a practical matter the country has had a difficult time guaranteeing food security to large segments of the population. Although research on the issue is somewhat limited, hunger and food security problems have existed in a country that should be food secure.[31] Data are notoriously inconsistent and fluctuate with research methodologies and definitions. Some estimates place the food insecure population at 14 percent of the total population;[32] other estimates show that 26 percent of the population possibly suffers hunger on a regular basis, while another 28 percent are at risk of hunger.[33] The sources of food insecurity and hunger vary, but research has focused on factors such as poverty, unemployment, development, health, education, agricultural sustainability, fuel prices, food prices, tariffs, and interest rates all playing roles.[34] The ability of the population to have access to adequate food is based on economic assumptions and structures that, for large segments of the population, may still be unattainable in South Africa's current economic climate.

While issues related to land distribution, economic growth, unemployment, poverty, inequality, and food security contribute to a growing sense of uneasiness and instability among the population, they are, by themselves, problems that all governments face. Collectively, however, they represent a vast array of policy areas that the ANC government mismanaged, reflecting deep-seeded problems of state capacity, inefficiency, and corruption that promoted resentment and backlash over time. That resentment was ultimately directed at the government of Jacob Zuma. What was at the root of the resentment, surprisingly, were not absolute conditions and problems such as poverty and inequality, but the Zuma government's handling of day-to-day operations within South Africa.

After the democratic transition, rioting and protests were resurgent, though certainly not at the levels found under the apartheid regime. Pinpointing definitive causes for the riots and protests has been difficult.[35] In South Africa, protests seemed to be rooted in a series of social and economic maladies such as xenophobia and education issues, but, most importantly, widespread poverty and inequality.

While conditions in South Africa may lie at the roots of social unrest, one study appears to confirm that government inaction may be definitive for people as well. Research documenting civic protests in South Africa found that protests hit a high point in 2009, the year of President Zuma's accession to power, and then declined until 2014 when they spiked back to 2009 levels. During that same period, the number and percentage of violent protests increased. In 2009 violent protests occurred at slightly more than 40 percent of the total 204 protests. In 2014 the total number of protests increased to 218; 83 percent (181) of them were classified by researchers as violent.[36] Of all the protests, approximately 56 percent focused on the lack of municipal government services, or problems with municipal government services. While this may seem like a "local" problem, it is most likely that the protests reflected resentment toward the federal government, given the tight reign that the ANC imposed on provincial and local governance. As Powell, O'Donovan and De Visser state, "protesters often treat municipalities as a proxy responsible for the failures of higher tiers of the state [... which] includes grievances relating to services at schools and the quality of policing." The outcome of these findings is that the ANC government may have been its own worst enemy in trying to stabilize its governing problems.

The ANC's perceived ineffectual governance has given rise to social and political problems that hinder democratic and security stability. For instance, racism and anti-foreign sentiments have been present in South Africa for decades. The end of the apartheid era did not erase those sentiments. After apartheid, South Africa attracted immigrants from other parts of the world who sought to improve their own economic and political status. However, the stagnation of South Africa's economy under ANC governance helped create backlash conditions against such immigrants. South African nationalists expressed more severe anti-immigrant tendencies than they had previously, helping to spawn riots and attacks on foreign nationals, attacks which resulted in the displacement of immigrants and even their deaths.

Multiple incidents of xenophobic violence have occurred in South Africa. In 2008, anti-immigrant violence killed 62 people in Johannesburg. In April 2015 in the port city of Durban, as many as 5000 people participated in xenophobic riots that engulfed the city, with attacks perpetrated on immigrants from Malawi and Mozambique. The rioting subsequently spread to Johannesburg, targeting small business owners and shopkeepers. Immigrants who were victims contended that the police were powerless to stop the violence. But, more importantly, the riots broke out after South Africa's Zulu King Goodwill Zwelithini demanded that immigrants get out of the country, lending a powerful voice to anti-immigrant nationalist rhetoric,[37] and further fostering public perceptions of the authorities as ineffectual. Such perceptions have contributed to an overwhelming sense of personal and communal insecurity rooted in individual understanding of personal risk.

Xenophobic tendencies that have emerged in South Africa may appear simply to target ethnic or cultural groups; but individual economic security issues may in fact play a substantial role in constructing attitudes because poverty and income inequality undermine individual security. During the April 2015 riots, people did not protest because of an instinctive sense of threat from a particular ethnic group or community. As Wilkinson pointed out, "With every outbreak of xenophobic violence … the refrain is the same: the *kwerekwere* [foreign visitors] are stealing our jobs".[38] Thus, the rising tide of South African xenophobia is not linked to cultural insecurity; rather, it is intricately tied to the feeling of personal economic insecurity manifested in the social and economic problems the ANC government was not able to overcome.

Protests are not only attributable to xenophobia. In 2015 some of South Africa's universities were rocked by violent protests and clashes that eventually spread to universities throughout the country. In October 2015, violent protests over a proposed hike in tuition fees corresponded with a week of demonstrations at South African universities.[39] In the economic climate then present in the country, the decision to increase tuition fees proved to be a breaking point for South Africa's frustrated youth. As in the xenophobic riots in Durban and Johannesburg, the inability of the police and security forces to control the protests became problematic.[40]

The inability of security forces to control protests and riots further plays into the narrative of ineffective government control and services. Beyond the more recent protests, crime generally has been at epidemic proportions in South Africa. Intertwined with the problems of poverty, development, and inequality, crime rose under ANC rule. In fact, crime has been a chronic problem for more than two decades. Even as economic crimes such as robbery and theft intensified, violent crimes became so prevalent that South Africa had some of the highest murder and rape rates in the world.

In 1996, the South African government launched a National Crime Prevention Strategy (NCPS) in an attempt to curtail violent crime.[41] Analysts deemed the program a failure because the strategy suffered from "a lack of understanding and insight of the intricate relationship between crime and its underlying causes (socio-economic and other risk factors) by political leaders and other principals" and, "as a result, a lack of conviction, commitment and support to implement the NCPS".[42] The failure of the NCPS starkly represented the government's inability to put forward a comprehensive plan for local safety and security.

In that context, the demand for domestic security forces and policing patrol forces rose substantially, further demonstrating a lack of confidence in South Africa's government to provide security to its population. South Africa has become home to one of the world's largest private security industries. Although not the world's largest, statistics from the Private Security Industry Regulatory Authority (PSIRA) in 2013 indicate that the South African private security industry had become (and remains) one of the largest in existence. Persistent high rates of violent and aggressive crime in the country fueled this phenomenon, alongside what has been documented as corrupt policing or weak or ineffective policing.

In 2013, estimates showed that nearly 9000 private security companies were active in the country. Over 400,000 active private security guards were registered; many of the active guards who worked for and alongside the private security agencies also had a background with the military or police, or had extensive military training.[43] For example, one of the leading private security companies in South Africa has been TSU Protection Services. The organization's stated purpose is "to address a gap in the private security market in South Africa for highly trained professionals".[44] Its founder and chief executive officer is Chris Beukes, a former member of the South African Police Services. Several of TSU's directors or individuals in managerial positions have backgrounds in the South African security services or related fields. The emergence of a significant presence for private security in South Africa is a further indictment of the ANC's ineffective governance, calling into question the ANC's ability to govern South Africa.

Democracy and security in South Africa: an assessment

While the transition to democracy in 1994 marked a turning point for South Africa, the ANC faced significant challenges initially in trying to hold together a country fractured on racial lines. Hence the party faced problems and issues that tested its strength and abilities to govern. While these problems have been and remain enormous obstacles to South Africa's democratic development, it is worth noting that the country is still in its democratic infancy. The road to transition from an opposition revolutionary party to a governing party has proven difficult to navigate by its nature, but the ANC's governance style exacerbated problems needlessly in some cases.

Almost a decade after the transition from apartheid, Mattes suggested that South Africa would endure significant problems on its democratic journey. He observed that "Cross-national analysis has highlighted three broad sets of factors crucial to democratic consolidation: a growing economy that steadily reduces inequality; stable and predictable political institutions; and a supportive political culture."[45] The issues Mattes raised still linger. Just a decade into the transition, South Africa showed signs of trouble in achieving the conditions for democratic consolidation Mattes articulates. Economic stagnation that has deepened unemployment, poverty and inequality has become the norm in South Africa. Wage and income inequality remain serious issues and contribute to the larger problem of wealth inequality that is endemic throughout the South African economic landscape.

The consolidation of political power at all levels of government under ANC rule has led to an entrenched, inflexible governing structure that is still unresponsive to the South African people. If people are supposed to look to political institutions for stability and predictability, the performance of South Africa's government under Jacob Zuma elicited dynamic shifts in public opinion that ultimately questioned Zuma's governing ability and the logic of allowing the ANC to remain in power. The ANC's absolute grip on power in South Africa helped promote corruption as an overarching characteristic of the political leadership and the institutions it controls. The result is a political culture that has become divisive, hostile, and intolerant of opposition voices.

Lastly, the ANC's two decades in power led to an opposition that sees political culture as having rotted under ANC rule. Given an underperforming economy and an intolerant political climate that punishes dissent, South Africa's opposition parties and certain large portions of the country's population see drastic change from ANC rule as the only way for South Africa to extricate itself from its political and economic problems. They have not yet succeeded at the ballot box.

Still, given these conditions, South Africa has reached a point of instability unmatched since the period of transition away from apartheid. While the state remains nominally democratic, conditions are present that could undercut South Africa's progress toward greater democratic gains. Those conditions include: endemic corruption; an unchallenged and unresponsive one-party state; stagnant long-term economic performance; high levels of chronic unemployment; and significant levels of wage and income inequality. After more than two decades with the same results, South Africans were ready to acknowledge the removal of President Zuma from power, and seemed potentially to be ready for substantial change in who governs their country. While the ANC has been able to count on loyalty to the party because of its significant role in ending apartheid, it has squandered some of that loyalty, attenuating its continued dominance over South African politics.

The important question for South Africa remains whether the ANC is willing to share power with others seeking a better future, or whether the party will need to be dragged from power altogether. The conditions that have brought about this question remain dire concerns for maintaining security and sustaining democracy for South Africa's future. As of this writing, the ANC remains in power, but with a reduced majority (58 percent) post the elections of May 2019, elections in which the Democratic Alliance received 21 percent of the vote. President Cyril Ramaphosa called on the people of South Africa to build a united country.

Notes

1 Cilliers 1995.
2 Davenport and Saunders 2000.
3 Furlong 1996.
4 Davenport and Saunders 2000.
5 Giliomee 1998.
6 Gilomee 1998: 139–140.
7 Butler 2005.
8 African Research Bulletin February 2016.
9 African Research Bulletin January 2016.
10 African Research Bulletin February 2016.
11 African Research Bulletin February 2016.
12 African Research Bulletin June 2015.
13 AllAfrica 2015; Africa Research Bulletin January 2016.
14 Smith 2013; Rossouw 2009.
15 Smith 2013.
16 Lahiff 2014: 587.
17 Hall 2004: 213.
18 O'Laughlin et al. 2013: 8.

19 O'Laughlin et al. 2013: 8.
20 Hall 2009 in O'Laughlin et al. 2013: 8.
21 O'Laughlin 2013: 8.
22 Zuma 2016.
23 Hall 2004; Hendriks 2005.
24 eNCA 2016; Zuma 2016.
25 Campbell 2012.
26 Turkington 2008.
27 Ferreira 2017.
28 BusinessTech 2015.
29 African Development Bank 2013.
30 Bhorat et al. 2009: 57.
31 Rose and Charlton 2002; Hendriks 2005).
32 Koch 2011.
33 Oxfam 2014.
34 Labadarios et al. 2011: 891; Altman et al. 2009.
35 Claassen 2014: 1.
36 Powell et al. 2015: 11.
37 Ruble 2015.
38 Wilkinson 2015.
39 Cohen and Vollgraaff 2015.
40 Allison 2015.
41 Burger and Boshoff 2008.
42 Burger and Boshoff 2008, citing Burger 2007: 79.
43 Eastwood 2013.
44 TSU Protection Services 2016.
45 Mattes 2002: 22.

Bibliography

Ferreira, Louise. 2017. "Factsheet: Social Grants in South Africa—Separating Myth from Reality." Africa Check, February 28. Accessed March 5, 2016. <https://africacheck.org/factsheets/separating-myth-from-reality-a-guide-to-social-grants-in-south-africa/>.

eNCA. 2016. "Parliament Warned: Food Riots Possible." February 20. Accessed March 5, 2016. <www.enca.com/south-africa/parliament-warned-food-riots-possibility>.

Africa Research Bulletin: Political, Social and Cultural Series. February 2016. "South Africa: Prospects for 2016." 53 (1): 20855–20857.

Africa Research Bulletin: Political, Social and Cultural Series. June 2015. "South Africa: New DA Leader." 52 (5): 20568–20569.

Africa Research Bulletin: Political, Social and Cultural Series. January 2016. "South Africa: Stunning Flip-Flop." 52 (12): 20811–220812.

African Development Bank. 2013. "Republic of South Africa Country Strategy Paper, 2013–2017." Southern Africa Resource Center (SARC). Accessed February 25, 2016. <www.afdb.org/fileadmin/uploads/afdb/Documents/Project-and-Operations/2013-2017_-_South_Africa_-_Country_Strategy_Paper_01.pdf>.

AllAfrica. 2015 "South Africa: Most South Africans Distrust Zuma—Survey." Accessed March 5, 2016. <http://allafrica.com/stories/201511240629.html>.

Allison, Simon. 2015. "South African Police Fire Teargas at Students in University Fees Protest." *Guardian*, October 21. Accessed March 1, 2016. <www.theguardian.com/world/2015/oct/21/riot-police-tear-gas-student-protest-south-africa-university-fees-cape-town>.

Altman, Miriam, Tim Hart and Peter Jacobs. 2009. "Food Security in South Africa." Human Sciences Research Council. Accessed February 10, 2016. <www.hsrc.ac.za/en/research-outputs/ktree-doc/2643>.

Bhorat, H., Carlene Van der Westhuizen, and Toughedah Jacobs. 2009. "Income and Non-Income Inequality in Post-Apartheid South Africa: What are the Drivers and Possible Policy Interventions?" Accessed March 5, 2016. <http://ssrn.com/abstract=1474271>.

Burger, Johan. 2007. *Strategic Perspectives on Crime and Policing in South Africa*. Pretoria: Van Schaik.

Burger, Johan and Henri Boshoff. 2008. "The State's Response to Crime and Public Security in South Africa." Institute for Security Studies. Accessed February 15, 2016. <www.isn.ethz.ch/Digital-Library/Publications/Detail/?lang=en&id=128739>.

BusinessTech. 2015. "The Real Employment Rate in SA." February 10. Accessed March 5, 2016. <http://businesstech.co.za/news/general/79373/the-real-employment-rate-in-sa/>.

Butler, Anthony. 2005. "How Democratic is the African National Congress?" *Journal of Southern African Studies* 31 (4): 719–736.

Campbell, John. 2012. "Africa in Transition: South Africa's Land Issue Not So Simple." Accessed March 4, 2016. <http://blogs.cfr.org/campbell/2012/07/02/south-africas-land-issue-not-so-simple/>.

Cilliers, Jakkie. 1995. "Security and Transition in South Africa." *Journal of Democracy*, 6 (4): 35–49.

Claassen, Christopher. 2014. "Who Participates in Communal Violence? Survey Evidence from South Africa." *Research & Politics* 1 (1): 1–8.

Cohen, Michael and Rene Vollgraaff. 2015. "Post-Apartheid Disenchantment Fuels S. African Student Riots." *Bloomberg Business*, October 22. Accessed March 4, 2016. <www.bloomberg.com/news/articles/2015-10-22/post-apartheid-disenchantment-fuels-south-african-student-riots>.

Davenport, Rodney and Christopher Saunders. 2000. *South Africa: A Modern History*, 5th ed. New York: St. Martin's Press.

Eastwood, Victoria. 2013. "Bigger than the Army: South Africa's Private Security Forces." CNN, February 8. Accessed March 4, 2016. <www.cnn.com/2013/02/08/business/south-africa-private-security/>.

Furlong, Patrick J. 1996. "South Africa," in April A. Gordon and Donald L. Gordon (eds), *Understanding Contemporary Africa*, 2nd ed. Boulder: Lynne Rienner.

Giliomee, Hermann. 1998. "South Africa's Emerging Dominant-Party Regime." *Journal of Democracy* 9 (4): 128–142.

Hall, Ruth. 2004. "A Political Economy of Land Reform in South Africa." *Review of African Political Economy* 31 (100): 213–227.

Hall, Ruth. 2009. "Land Reform for What? Land Use, Production and Livelihoods," in Ruth Hall (ed.), *Another Countryside: Policy Options for Land and Agrarian Reform in South Africa*. Belville: Institute for Poverty, Land and Agrarian Studies, School of Government, University of the Western Cape, pp. 23–61.

Hendriks, Sheryl L. 2005. "The Challenges Facing Empirical Estimation of Household Food (In)security in South Africa." *Development Southern Africa* 22 (1): 103–123.

Koch, Josee. 2011. "The Food Security Policy Context in South Africa." International Policy Centre for Inclusive Growth Country Report, United Nations Development Program. Accessed February 26, 2016. <www.ipc-undp.org/pub/IPCCountryStudy21.pdf>.

Labadarios, Demetre, Zandile June-Rose Mchiza, Patricia Steyn*et al.*2011. "Food Security in South Africa: A Review of National Surveys." *Bulletin of the World Health Organization* 89: 891–899.

Lahiff, Edward. 2014. "Review Essay: Land Reform in South Africa 100 Years after the Natives' Lands Act." *Journal of Agrarian Change* 14 (4): 586–592.

Mattes, Robert B. 2002. "South Africa: Democracy without the People?" *Journal of Democracy* 13 (1): 22–36.

Turkington, Tara. 2008. "In Conversation with Ali Mazrui." Nelson Mandela Foundation, March 28. Accessed March 4, 2016. <www.nelsonmandela.org/news/entry/in-conversation-with-ali-mazrui>.

O'Laughlin, Bridget, Henry Bernstein, Ben Cousins, and Pauline E. Peters. 2013. "Introduction: Agrarian Change, Rural Poverty and Land Reform in South Africa since 1994." *Journal of Agrarian Change* 13 (1): 1–15.

Oxfam. 2014. *Hidden Hunger in South Africa*. Oxford: Oxfam. Accessed March 5, 2016. <www.oxfam.org/sites/www.oxfam.org/files/file_attachments/hidden_hunger_in_south_africa_0.pdf>.

Powell, D.M., M. O'Donovan and J. De Visser. 2015. "Civic Protests Barometer, 2007–2014." Accessed March 2, 2016. <http://mlgi.org.za/talking-good-governance/20150219%20Civic%20Protest%20Barometer%20Published%20%20DP.pdf>.

Rose, Donald, and Karen E.Charlton. 2002. "Prevalence of Household Food Poverty in South Africa: Results from a Large, Nationally Representative Survey." *Public Health Nutrition* 5 (3): 383–389.

Rossouw, Mandy. 2009. "Zuma's R65M Nkandla Splurge." *Mail & Guardian*. Accessed February 27, 2016. <http://mg.co.za/article/2009-12-04-zumas-r65m-nkandla-splurge>.

Ruble, Kayla. 2015. "Deadly Xenophobic Durban Riots Spread to Other South African Cities." *Vice News*. Accessed March 4, 2016. <https://news.vice.com/article/deadly-xenophobic-durban-riots-spread-to-other-south-african-citie>.

Smith, David. 2013. "Jacob Zuma Accused of Corruption 'on a Grand Scale' in South Africa." *Guardian*, November 29. Accessed February 27, 2016. <www.theguardian.com/world/2013/nov/29/jacob-zuma-accused-corruption-south-africa>.

TSU Protection Services. 2016. "Private Security Companies in South Africa." TSU Private Security Company. Accessed March 4, 2016. <www.tsuafrica.com/AboutUs/tabid/74/Default.aspx>.

Van Onselen, Gareth. 2015. "Jacob Zuma's Top Ten Quotes on Corruption." *BDlive*. Accessed February 25, 2016. <www.bdlive.co.za/opinion/columnists/2015/03/09/jacob-zumas-top-ten-quotes-on-corruption>.

Wilkinson, Kate. 2015. "South Africa's Xenophobic Attacks: Are Migrants Really Stealing Jobs?" *Guardian*, April 20. Accessed March 4, 2016. <www.theguardian.com/world/2015/apr/20/south-africa-xenophobic-violence-migrants-workforce>.

World Health Organization. 2016. "Food Security." Accessed February 25, 2016. <www.who.int/trade/glossary/story028/en/>.

Zuma, Jacob. 2016. "Land Dispossession Source of Poverty and Inequality Today." *Politicsweb*. Accessed March 4, 2016. <www.politicsweb.co.za/news-and-analysis/land-dispossession-source-of-poverty-and-inequalit>.

14

DEMOCRATIC POLITICS IN BRAZIL

Advances in accountability mechanisms and regression in civil–military relations

Thomas C. Bruneau[1]

Introduction

The doyen of democratization studies and American policies in support of democratization globally, Professor Larry Diamond, recently published an article in *The American Interest* entitled "The Liberal Democratic Order in Crisis". The header correctly states the main message of the article: "We are at a tipping point. Around the world, many democracies are hanging by a thread and autocrats are preparing more savage assaults on what remains of freedom."[2] This chapter focuses on Brazil, primarily on how democratic politics ironically have led to vast improvements in accountability mechanisms while also leading to regression in civil–military relations. It is important to emphasize from the outset that the regression in civil–military relations, with implications for democracy, is due mainly to the dynamics of democratic politics and not to the supposed nefarious plans and plots of the Brazilian Armed Forces.[3]

The Constitution of 1988

To understand the current political situation in Brazil, including accountability mechanisms and civil–military relations, one must begin with the Constitution of 1988 which marked the formal consolidation of democracy following 21 years (1964–85) under a military regime. Scholars who study the process whereby the Constitution of 1988 was formulated, and the resulting document, are extremely critical. In my writing I argue that the Constitution did not represent an "elite settlement" ensuring democratic consolidation, as was the case in Spain, for example.[4] Law professor Keith S. Rosenn states the following: "The process by which Brazil's 1988 Constitution was adopted practically assured that the end product would be a hodgepodge of inconsistent and convoluted provisions."[5] Despite 3 years of work, resulting in a document of 245 articles and 70 transitional provisions, the 559 framers were unable to resolve whether Brazil would be a monarchy or a republic, and, if the latter, a presidential or parliamentary regime. These fundamental decisions were left to a referendum in 1993 that favored a presidential republic. The framers of the Constitution, who were the 559 members of the Brazilian Congress, maintained intact both the institutional defects of the political system and the extensive prerogatives of the armed forces that governed Brazil between 1964 and 1985. Whereas the institutional defects of the political system continue to the present, accountability institutions have become robust and active. The prerogatives of the armed forces were diminished, but recently have increased depending on a political situation dominated by civilians.

Although the Constitution of 1988 included a great many items that could lead to an improved socio-economic situation for Brazilians, it changed nothing regarding the political institutions that put those 559 politicians in the position of writing the constitution, and have made only minimal changes in the intervening 28 years. As Rosenn states, "The constituent assembly also did nothing to reform the malfunctioning of the political party system, which is one of the world's worst."[6] They did not establish a minimum number of votes for a party to be recognized, resulting in the current situation: 35 political parties at the national level, with 19 having deputies in the lower house, the Câmara. They did not change the open-list system of proportional representation in which each state is a single, and at-large, multi-member district. They did not change the gross misrepresentation whereby all states, and the federal district, have three senators, or the provision stipulating that all states, regardless of population, would have a minimum of 8 and a maximum of 70 deputies in the Câmara.

There was supposed to be a wholesale revision of the Constitution in 1993 that would require only an absolute majority of the deputies. That revision never happened. Instead, there have been piecemeal revisions. In reviewing the various initiatives to revise the Constitution between 1988 and today, we find that they amount to very little. This is the consensus of recognized experts on the issue, including David Fleischer, Alfredo Montero, Timothy Power, and Keith Rosenn. The Constitution of 1988 was full of contradictions. The issue of parliamentary vs. presidential form of government was never fully resolved, neither in the constituent assembly nor after. On the one hand, the Constitution gave the Congress a role in approving annual budgets and allowed them to overrule presidential vetoes with absolute majorities rather than a two-thirds vote. On the other hand, it gave the presidency the exclusive right to initiate and execute annual budgets and to force 45-day limits on the Congress to review bills defined as "urgent" by the president; the power to appoint a cabinet, subject to Senate approval; and the power to issue executive decrees (*medidas provisórias*) which had the force of law while Congress had 30 days to review the measure.[7] Post-1990 presidents utilized these measures, and others, to govern.

Politics as usual

Even with these gimmicks, the need to assemble a coalition remained: no president since the first directly elected, Fernando Collor de Mello in 1989, has belonged to a party with a majority in either house of Congress, all presidents would have to obtain the support of other parties. Brazil has one of, if not the most fractured, party systems of any democracy. This form of government – commonly called coalitional presidentialism (*presidencialismo de coalizão*) – could, and did, easily evolve into corruption. The most famous, but not the only, corruption scandal of President Luis Inácio Lula da Silva's administration (2003–2010) was the "big monthly" (*mensalão*) scandal – as in big monthly payments to members of Congress to support his government's policies. Alfred Montero has this to say on the topic. "The need to engage in vote-buying emerged from the limited options the Lula administration had for composing the same kind of legislative coalition that Cardoso [president, 1995–2003] enjoyed."[8] Several top Workers' Party (PT) officials were implicated in this vote-buying scheme. The scandal ultimately led to the convictions of 25 people, including Lula's former chief of staff, José Dirceu de Oliveira e Silva, who has more recently been sentenced to 23 years in jail in the *Lava Jato* (car wash) corruption scheme.

There are so many corruption scandals currently in play in the investigation and sentencing phases that only experts can keep straight the modalities of *Mensalão, Lava Jato, Petrolão, Zelotes*, and *Operation Aequalis*, to mention only the biggest and most recent. So far the wave of illegal, extralegal, and simply corrupt practices has resulted in the impeachment of President Dilma Vana Rousseff, the conviction of ex-President Lula, the conviction of 84 persons for crimes associated with *Lava Jato*, and dozens more in other corruption scandals. While not all of the crimes involve politicians, most of them do; and virtually all of them involve sources of funds, as in Petrobras, under the control of the Brazilian State, and thus of necessity involve politicians.[9]

It must be acknowledged that corruption is nothing new in Brazil. In fact, according to the late Samuel Huntington in his influential *Political Order in Changing Societies*, corruption was seen in positive terms in the process of modernization, and Huntington called specific, and positive, attention to Brazil.[10] Further, there is a highly influential article by Anna Maria Campos, published in 1990 in the important *Revista de Administração Pública* of the Fundação Getúlio Vargas, which argues in great detail why there is no concept or meaning for the term "accountability" in Portuguese.[11] Most Brazilian and foreign authors refer to the Brazilian propensity to use "angles" or "gimmicks" (*jeitinhos*) to get around laws. Or, as was said in positive terms of a mayor of São Paulo, "he robs but he accomplishes things" – *Rouba mas faz*.

Accountability mechanisms to the fore

While politics has not changed, including the use of corruption to govern, what is now permissible in politics and business in general in Brazil is changing. There is no single cause for the change, and I have identified at least five.

First, the 1988 Constitution created, or recreated, a large spectrum of oversight and investigation mechanisms, and these have been expanded in number during the intervening 29 years. Today they include the Comptroller General, the Accounting Tribunal, the Federal Police, the Public Ministry, and the courts. There is a huge literature on these institutions in both Portuguese and English, and the approach that I find most convincing to explain their increasing influence, culminating in the current wave of imprisonments, is that of Sérgio Praça and Matthew Taylor, who demonstrate that the capacity of these institutions increases not by a single event or factor, but through bureaucratic interaction.[12] The increase in capacity is thus contingent and interactive. In short, these oversight, investigatory, and punishment institutions can only be understood in a specific national and international context, which is why I include the following four factors.

Second, whereas in the past the main weakness of the accountability mechanisms was the inability or unwillingness of the courts, especially the Supreme Court, to process and convict individuals, today this is changing given personalities and the gradual modification of processes similar to those noted in the preceding paragraph. This change is best highlighted by the actions of Judge Sérgio Moro of Curitiba, who has taken the lead in the *Lava Jato* scandal. He is extremely active not only in pursuing corruption, but also in writing on the importance of plea-bargaining (*delação premiada*) and the Italian experience in countering the Mafia. He is also something of a hero in Brazil today, as described in Watts' article. In addition to the changes in this point, the use of plea-bargaining is also a key mechanism for enhancing accountability.

Third, much of the momentum to impeach President Rousseff is related to allegations of corruption involving the Workers' Party, established by the information provided by Senator Delcídio do Amaral, who was the leader of the party in the Senate. He was arrested, and in plea-bargaining he provided information on the spread of corruption throughout the Brazilian government. Those familiar with criminal law in the United States emphasize that plea-bargaining is the single most important mechanism for gathering evidence on white-collar crime. Plea-bargaining was established in Brazil only in 2013 with law 12,850/2013. I have been informed by Brazilian lawyers involved in the introduction of plea-bargaining that it was one of several laws that were required for Brazil to reach Organisation for Economic Co-operation and Development (OECD) standards. Since June 2015 there has been a Co-Operation Agreement in place between Brazil and the OECD, which has been followed by an OECD–Brazil Programme of Work. Ironically enough it was implemented by President Rousseff, who was later impeached.[13]

Fourth, Brazil's population of over 200 million is increasingly invested in the system. An important indicator of this is their paying taxes. According to one source, in 2013 over 50 percent of those who declared income paid income tax, whereas a decade earlier only 36 percent paid income tax.[14] Just as important, according to data analyzed by the Instituto Brasileiro de Planejamento e Tributação, of the 30 countries where taxes are the highest, Brazil is the worst in terms of return to the population of investments in the quality of life.

Fifth, Brazilians today are keenly aware of the low return on investment for their high taxes. Indeed, the huge anti-government demonstrations in June 2013 were mainly caused by public awareness of high taxes and mediocre public services in health, education, and transportation, failures of allocation which took place while the government invested massively in stadiums and other infrastructure for global prestige sporting events – the soccer World Cup in 2014 and the Olympics in 2016. In addition to all-pervasive radio and television stations there is today extremely high penetration by social media. According to Comscore, which claims to be the global leader in digital analysis, Brazil led the world with a 99.9 percent reach of social media. And, with 8.8 hours of use in the month of June 2015, Brazil was the world leader in that similar data for Europe, for example, was 6.1 hours and the U.S. 5.2 hours.[15]

In sum, traditional politics, in which the lubricant is public funds, has now encountered a wide spectrum of accountability mechanisms, supported by processes and attitudes that no longer tolerate the traditional lackadaisical approach to ethics in politics. While the incentives to reform politics are not as obvious, they are nevertheless present in the expectations of the Brazilian population and international organizations.

Prerogatives of the Brazilian armed forces

Both Rosenn and I detail the extensive prerogatives of the armed forces that resulted from the very long and negotiated transition from military to civilian rule and the reliance of President José Sarney on the armed forces during his five-year tenure (1985–90). The most extensive work on this topic, however, is found in Alfred Stepan's *Rethinking Military Politics: Brazil and the Southern Cone*, where he demonstrates, by describing 11 prerogatives, that Brazil had progressed little between military and civilian rule.[16] More recently, 26 years after Stepan published his book, my colleague Scott D. Tollefson and I demonstrated that the prerogatives that were mainly high when Stepan wrote became either low or moderate.[17] Some of the main developments of the process whereby the prerogatives were diminished or eliminated include the creation of a civilian-led ministry of defense in June 1999, which resulted in the decrease of military-led ministries from six to zero; and a large package of laws in 2011 which further delimited and restricted the autonomy of the armed forces.

Illustrative of the change from the military regime was President Collor's abolition in 1990 of the National Information Service (*Serviço Nacional de Informações*, SNI), which was the intelligence arm of the military regime, and the creation, only after nine years, of the Brazilian Intelligence Agency (*Agência Brasileira de Inteligência*, ABIN). ABIN is prohibited from conducting intercepts, has a minimal budget, and lacks a direct link to decision-makers. In short, the politicians had incentives to diminish the influence and roles of the armed forces, thereby increasing their own. Table 14.1 describes the progress of these prerogatives.

Table 14.1 Selected prerogatives of the military as institution in a democratic regime, Brazil 1946–2014

Prerogative	*Stepan 1946–64 (Civilian Rule)*	*Stepan 1969–72 (Intense Repression)*	*Stepan 1974–79 (Controlled Opening)*	*Stepan 1985–87 (Democratic Transition)*	*Authors 2014 (Democratic Consolidation)*
1. Constitutionally sanctioned independent role of military in political system	High	High	High	High	Low
2. Military relationship to chief executive	Moderate	High	Moderate	Moderate	Low
3. Coordination of defense sector	High	High	High	High	Moderate
4. Active-duty military participation in cabinet	High	High	High	High	Low
5. Role of military vis-à-vis legislature	Moderate	High	High	High	Low
6. Role of senior career civil servants or civilian political appointees	High	High	High	High	Moderate
7. Role in intelligence	Moderate	High	High	High	Moderate
8. Role in police	Moderate	High	High	Moderate	Moderate
9. Role in military promotions	Moderate	High	Moderate	High	Moderate
10. Role in state enterprises	Moderate	High	High	Moderate	Low
11. Role in legal system	Moderate	High	High	High	Low

Source: Adapted from Alfred Stepan, *Rethinking Military Politics: Brazil and the Southern Cone* (Princeton: Princeton University Press, 1988), pp. 93–114, especially Table 7.1 and p. 103. Authors' update based on documents and interviews in Brazil with civilians and military officers in 2012 and 2013, and by e-mail in 2014.

Note: "Close to high" for 1969–72 is interpreted as "high". For 1985–87, variables 8 and 10 "were reduced", according to Stepan (p. 103), and are placed here in the "moderate" category.

Utilizing a conceptual framework that includes not only democratic civilian control, as exemplified by the prerogatives listed in Table 14.1, but also military effectiveness, Scott D. Tollefson and I documented how control had been asserted by diminishing the prerogatives. Military effectiveness, however, had not been achieved.[18] We demonstrate that Brazil lacks a national security strategy; does not have a functioning joint staff that could interface with the civilian-led ministry of defense; and invests only 1.29 percent of gross domestic product (GDP) in defense, 73 percent of which goes to salaries and pensions. This minimal military effectiveness is not a popular or political issue, however, since Brazil is situated in a "zone of peace" with no obvious enemies. For example, the Introduction to the National Defense Strategy of 2008 states: "Brazil is a peaceful country, by tradition and conviction. It lives in peace with its neighbors"; and its guidelines section notes that "Presently, Brazil does not have any enemies."[19]

The lack of effectiveness would not matter if Brazil did not harbor aspirations to be recognized as a global power. It is commonplace to state, as President Lula did in 2003, that Brazil is ready to "assume its greatness". There is a huge outpouring of reports and documents giving evidence of Brazil as a regional, if not global, actor, a BRIC (Brazil, Russia, India, and China), an important interlocutor with the United States, and more. For example, then U.S. Secretary of Defense, Robert Gates, and Brazilian Minister of Defense, Nelson Jobin, signed a Security of Military Information Agreement on November 21, 2010. Significant and recent U.S. government documents highlight Brazil's importance. As President Barack Obama's *National Security Strategy* stated, "We welcome Brazil's leadership and seek to move beyond dated North–South divisions to pursue progress on bilateral, hemispheric, and global issues."[20] In its most recent 20-year prospective, the U.S. National Intelligence Council (NIC) states, "Brazil will play an outsized role on the region's future. Its resources and scale could offer benefits and insulation others lack."[21] In addition to the Congressional Research Service, which issues periodic reports on Brazil, many important U.S. and European think tanks and non-governmental organizations (NGOs) publish reports heralding Brazil's emergence into greatness. The issue whether any country – even Brazil, with the 5th largest population and 5th largest area – can realistically aspire to global status without credible "hard power" is responded to in the negative by many observers.[22]

Regression in military prerogatives

Currently, nothing has changed regarding military effectiveness. If anything, with the economic crisis the armed forces have fewer resources, which results in fewer ships, airplanes, and tanks available for deployment.[23] What has changed, however, is regression concerning the prerogatives, or democratic civilian control. Today, for the first time since its founding in June 1999, the Ministry of Defense (MOD) is headed by an army general. The Secretariat for Institutional Security (Gabinete de Segurança Institucional, GSI) has been recreated, and is also headed by an army general; and the Brazilian Intelligence Agency (Agência Brasileira de Inteligência, ABIN) is under the GSI. Another army general heads the Civilian Household (Casa Civil) of the President of Brazil; and another army general is the president of the Indian Foundation (FUNAI). In addition to these important changes in leadership of key security and domestic policy institutions are changes in the legislation whereby military personnel accused of crimes that occur in pacification programs will be judged by military justice rather than normal, civilian, justice.

These are all major changes, for the worse, in terms of military prerogatives, and thus civilian control of the armed forces. These could have been short-term changes in that, with another president after the elections in October 2018, these important security positions could again be filled by civilians. However, the MOD was never really staffed by civilians, and the GSI, until it was disbanded between 2014 and 2016, was always under the leadership of a general. The precedent of staffing of what were civilian positions by senior military officers is very serious.

What is very unlikely to change, and can have an ongoing impact, is both the creation of the Ministry of Security (Ministério Extraordinário da Segurança Pública) – now headed by Raul Jungmann, who was previously Minister of Defense – and the federal intervention in Rio de Janeiro. The *interventor* (one who intervenes) designated by former President Michel Temer, is an army general; essentially the Brazilian army is now in charge of security, including control over the Polícia Militar (state police) and the prisons in Rio de Janeiro. The media reports that this military intervention may be extended to other cities and states.[24]

Utilizing the same table of prerogatives, and updating those changed by recent decisions by President Temer regarding the Brazilian military, will better document the regression in democratic civil–military relations. The most relevant ones, while all to a greater or lesser degree regress, are 2, 4, 6, 7, 8 and 11 (see Table 14.1).

Prerogative #2: Military relationship to the chief executive. Stepan writes that this prerogative is low when "The Chief executive (president, prime minister, or constitutional monarch) is de jure and de facto commander-in-chief" (p. 94).[25] This was low in Brazil in 2014. Since 1985 all presidents of Brazil have been civilians. Since 1989 the presidents have been elected by the population in national elections every four years. However, President Rousseff was impeached in August 2016, and Vice-President Michel Temer, also accused of corruption, assumed the presidency. The MOD was headed by a civilian between its creation in 1999 and February 2018, when General Silva e Luna was appointed Minister of Defense by President Temer. Today this prerogative would be high.

Prerogative #4: Active duty military participation in the Cabinet. This prerogative is low, in Stepan's analysis, when there is normally no active duty military participation in the Cabinet. This rating was low in Brazil in 2014. None of the 27 members of the cabinet were military. Today the Minister of Defense is a general. Of the 14 officials in the expanded cabinet, the head of the Secretariat for Institutional Security, GSI, is a member of the military, as is the National Secretary of Public Security and the Chief Secretary of the Civil Cabinet (Casa Civil). Today this prerogative is high.

Prerogative #6: Role of senior career civil servants or civilian political appointees. To Stepan, this prerogative is low when a "Professional cadre of highly informed civil servants or policy-making civilian political appointees play a major role in assisting [the] executive branch in designing and implementing defense and national security policy" (p. 95). In 2014 this prerogative was moderate. The civilian bureaucracy in Brazil is unequivocally strong. However, as there is neither a civilian career nor the required *concurso* (public academic competition) in the MOD – and with the paucity of civilians with expertise – the military fills the vacuum, and thereby assumes larger roles in the MOD itself. The Planning Ministry is the entity that could create civilian career positions, but it has not done so to date, alleging the lack of funds. From what we have been able to determine, the issue is mostly financial, and not political. Today, with the Minister himself a general, and with other generals in key positions – GSI, FUNAI, Casa Civil, and Public Security – this prerogative is high.

Prerogative #7: Role in intelligence. For Stepan, this prerogative is low when "Peak intelligence agencies [are] de jure and de facto controlled by civilian chains of command." In addition, there are "Strong civilian review boards" (p. 96). This prerogative was moderate in 2014. The National Information Service (SNI), which was the military regime's intelligence service, was abolished by President Collor in 1990. The Brazilian Intelligence Agency (ABIN), which is led by a civilian who is nominated by the president and confirmed by the Senate, replaced it in 1999. In 2015 and 2016 ABIN reported directly to the president. Today, the GSI has been recreated, and ABIN reports to the Chief Minister of the GSI, who is a general officer in the Brazilian Army. Then too, the Brazilian military intelligence system is generally intact. Today this prerogative is high.

Prerogative #8: Role in police. This prerogative is low when, according to Stepan, "Police [are] under control of nonmilitary ministry or local officials" and there are "No active-duty military allowed to command a police unit." In 2014 this prerogative was moderate. The control of the *Polícia Militar* (Military Police, PM) is a state responsibility, under the democratically elected civilian governors of the states. The *Polícia Federal* (Federal Police, PF) is under the Ministry of Justice. The domestic roles of the armed forces in Brazil are defined in Article 142 of the Constitution of 1988 and in subsequent laws. The conditions are very precisely defined in Complementary Law 97 of June 9, 1999. Specifically, a state governor, who is responsible for security in the state, can request of the president of the Republic that the armed forces be used to support the police. In February of 2018 President Temer named General Braga Netto as *interventor* for security in the state of Rio de Janeiro. This is the first intervention under the 1988 Constitution, and Temer could have named a civilian. The intervention is distinct from, and far more serious than, the frequent deployment of the Brazilian armed forces under Article 142 of the Constitution, which provides for the military to guarantee law and order (GLO).

In addition, the Brazilian armed forces have police powers along the border, to a distance of 150 kilometers from it. This police power is exercised especially in the Amazon, where the Brazilian Army is often the sole representative of the state along the porous borders. The total amount of land that corresponds to the 150-kilometer corridor is actually larger than any other single country in South America, with the exception of Argentina. This prerogative is high today.

Prerogative #11: Role in legal system. According to Stepan, this prerogative is low when the "Military have almost no legal jurisdiction outside of narrowly defined internal offenses against military discipline." In all areas outside this domain, civilians and military are subject to civil laws and civil courts. In 2014 this rating was low as the military's legal system was changing. Today, however, the military still have their own legal system, and in October of 2017 President Temer decreed the law that transferred from civil law to military law crimes committed by military personnel during public security operations. Consequently, this prerogative is moderate today.

Whereas in 2014 the ratings on the 11 prerogatives were 6 low and 5 moderate (with no highs), in early 2018 they were 3 low, 3 moderate, and 5 high.

These presidential decisions, illustrated by the 11 prerogatives, can have very serious and long-lasting negative consequences. They must be seen in terms of political dynamics. As stated by ex-president and famous political sociologist, Fernando Henrique Cardoso, "it is mainly weak governments that end up appealing for military [support]".[26] President Michel Temer apparently wanted to run for election for the presidency in October 2018 on a public security platform. Temer suffered a major political setback in his inability to reform the pension system, and one of the leading candidates for the presidency was Jair Bolsonaro, a very conservative retired military officer. Furthermore, when asked in surveys to evaluate Temer's administration, whereas 14 percent of respondents said good or excellent in July 2016, in January 2018 this figure was 6 percent; on the other hand, whereas 31 percent said bad or terrible in July 2016, in January 2018 this was 70 percent.[27] In opinion polls for the

October 2018 presidential elections (including simulations), of 11 potential candidates, Temer had the third lowest amount of support (0.9 percent) and by far the highest rejection rate, at 88 percent (Table 14.2).[28]

Michel Temer was, in short, a *very* unpopular president who also carried a huge amount of baggage for graft and corruption. In the end he declined to stand in the 2018 election and was succeeded by Bolsonaro. Temer, like all politicians in Brazil, was aware that public security is by far the most important issue concerning the population. In addition, according to all public opinion polls, the military, in stark contrast to politicians, is highly regarded. Even before the most recent scandals, in 2014, 44 percent of the population trusted the president and 43 percent the federal government, whereas 62 percent trusted the military. And, in a World Values Survey (WVS), 58.6 percent stated they had confidence in the armed forces, while only 41 percent had confidence in the government.[29] Further, according to a very credible poll by the Brazilian Instituto de Pesquisa Econômica Aplicada (Institute of Applied Economic Research, IPEA), when asked about using the military for public security, whereas 92 percent of respondents said always or in some situations (47 and 45 percent), only 8 percent said never.[30]

Conclusions: the Bolsonaro presidency

The 1988 Constitution in Brazil was formulated by politicians who sought to guarantee their own welfare. In the intervening decades the prerogatives of the Brazilian military were gradually reduced, thereby increasing the control of civilians over the military. Brazil's strategic landscape and domestic politics never required military effectiveness, and the civilian politicians – while utilizing rhetoric to the contrary – never provided strategy, institutions, or

Table 14.2 First-round election opinion polls, October 2018

Candidate (Party)	*A*	*B*	*Rejection Rate*
Lula (PT)	33.40%	–	46.70%
Haddad (PT)	–	2.30%	–
Bolsonaro (PSC)	16.80%	20.00%	50.40%
Marina (Rede)	7.80%	12.80%	53.90%
Alckmin (PSDB)	6.40%	8.60%	50.70%
C. Gomes (PDT)	4.30%	8.10%	47.80%
A. Dias (Podemos)	3.30%	4.00%	–
Collor (PTC)	1.20%	2.10%	–
Temer (MDB)	0.90%	1.30%	88.00%
M. D'Ávila (PCdoB)	0.70%	1.30%	–
R. Maia (DEM)	0.60%	0.80%	55.80%
Blank/Null	18.20%	28.20%	–
DK/NR	6.40%	10.50%	–

Source: Information provided by David Fleischer, March 7, 2018, drawn from poll results released by the Brazilian National Transportation Confederation (CNT), March 6, 2018.

Note: The CNT-commissioned poll was carried out by the MDA polling organization between February 28 and March 3 among 2,002 voters in 137 *municípios* in 25 states with a 2.2 point margin of error. A and B are different scenarios, different simulations.

resources that could result in military effectiveness. The nature of Brazil's political institutions, in combination with a culture of impunity, resulted in mass graft and corruption. Due to a series of domestic and international factors, however, a robust set of accountability mechanisms emerged, which resulted in massive penalties for corrupt politicians, bureaucrats, and prominent businessmen. In this context, when even a president who took office on the impeachment of his elected predecessor in August 2016 defined public security as the main issue of concern to the Brazilian population, he turned to the only security institution with its reputation intact – the Brazilian military – to take on important roles at all levels of government in an attempt to achieve public security. The challenge – in view of a lack of demand for an external role and the weakness of the institutions of civilian control of the military – would become whether civilian control could be reasserted in a future political context.

In the wake of a succession of scandals involving his predecessors, Brazilian voters elected Jair Bolsonaro to the country's presidency in 2018. Bolsonaro, an ex-army officer, ran as a self-described outsider, although he had spent years as a member of the country's parliament. Some have described Brazil's president as the "Trump of the tropics" because of his contempt for the rules of liberal democracy and his right-wing nationalism. Illustratively, at one point Bolsonaro expressed nostalgia for Brazil's military dictatorship (1964–1985), as well as contempt for women's rights and the concerns of the country's indigenous Amazonian population. An advocate of "law and order", with a strong emphasis on the latter, Bolsonaro at one point endorsed the extra-judicial killing of suspected drug dealers in Rio de Janeiro and elsewhere.

In office, despite world-wide condemnation, President Bolsonaro supported the decision of large-scale landowners to burn down significant parts of the Amazon rain forest to make way for more farming. After the COVID-19 pandemic struck Brazil, Bolsonaro expressed contempt for those, including a succession of health ministers, who warned the public about the threat of the disease. As a consequence, Brazil, like the United States and India, has developed one of the world's worst rates of infection. Despite what appear to be calamitous decisions, Bolsonaro continues to enjoy high approval ratings (2020) in public opinion polls.

Notes

1 The views expressed here are the author's alone and do not necessarily represent those of the U.S. Navy or Department of Defense.
2 February 16, 2018. Available at www.the-american-interest.com/2018/02/16/liberaldemocratic-order-crisis/. Accessed March 6, 2018.
3 The dynamics, and resistance, of senior Brazilian Army officers to some of the political decisions described in this chapter are vividly captured in Fabio Victor, "Mal-estar na Caserna," *Piauí*, 138, March 2018. Available at http://piaui.folha.uol.com.br/materia/mal-estar-na-caserna/. Accessed March 12, 2018.
4 Thomas Bruneau, "Brazil's Political Transition," in John Higley and Richard Gunther, eds. *Elites and Democratic Consolidation in Latin America and Southern Europe* (Cambridge: Cambridge University Press, 1992), pp. 257–281.
5 Keith S. Rosenn, "Conflict Resolution and Constitutionalism: The Making of the Brazilian Constitution of 1988," in Laurel E. Miller, ed. *Framing the State in Times of Transition: Case Studies in Constitution Making* (Washington, D.C: United States Institute of Peace, 2010), p. 458.
6 Ibid.
7 In 2001 this was changed to 60 days.
8 Alfred P. Montero, *Brazil: Reversal of Fortune* (Cambridge, MA: Polity Press, 2014), p. 43.
9 For a very thorough, if somewhat sensational, review of this issue see Jonathan Watts, "Operation Car Wash: Is This the Biggest Corruption Scandal in History?" *Guardian*, June 1, 2017. Available at www.

theguardian.com/world/2017/jun/01/brazil-operation-car-wash-is-this-the-biggest-corruption-scandal-in-history. Accessed March 9, 2018.

10 Samuel P. Huntington, *Political Order in Changing Societies* (New Haven, CT: Yale University Press, 1968).

11 Anna Maria Campos, "Accountability: quando poderemos traduzi-la para o português?" *Revista de Administração Pública* 34, 2 (1990), pp. 30–50.

12 Sérgio Praça and Matthew M. Taylor, "Inching toward Accountability: The Evolution of Brazil's Anticorruption Institutions, 1985–2010," *Latin American Politics and Society* 56, 2 (2014) pp. 27–48.

13 According to Jonathan Watts, 2017, President Rousseff implemented it in an attempt to placate an angry public in the wake of nationwide anti-corruption demonstrations in June 2013.

14 *Pulsamérica*, available at www.pulsamerica.co.uk/2013/02/25/brazil-over12-million-currently=pay-income-tax/. Accessed June 2, 2016.

15 Comscore & Shareablee (2015) "The State of Social Media in Brazil," available at www.comscore.com. Accessed June 2, 2016.

16 Alfred Stepan, *Rethinking Military Politics: Brazil and the Southern Cone* (Princeton: Princeton University Press, 1988).

17 Thomas Charles Bruneau and Scott D. Tollefson, "Civil–Military Relations in Brazil: A Reassessment," *Journal of Politics in Latin America* 2 (2014), pp. 107–138.

18 For the conceptual framework see Florina Cristiana Matei, "A New Conceptualization of Civil–Military Relations," in Thomas C. Bruneau and Florina Cristiana Matei, eds. *The Routledge Handbook of Civil–Military Relations* (New York: Routledge, 2013), pp. 28–38.

19 Brazil Government, *National Strategy of Defense: Peace and Security for Brazil* (Brasilia: Ministry of Defense, 2008), pp. 8, 16. Available at www.files.ethz.ch/isn/154868/Brazil_English2008.pdf. For the argument on control and effectiveness, see Bruneau and Tollefson, "Civil–Military Relations in Brazil." See also our conceptual framework.

20 Barack Obama, *National Security Strategy* (Washington, DC: White House, 2010), p. 44.

21 National Intelligence Council, *Global Trends 2030: Alternative Worlds* (Washington, D.C.: NIC, 2012), p. 82.

22 For the most balanced and credible negative assessment see David R. Mares and Harold A. Trinkunas, *Aspirational Power: Brazil on the Long Road to Global Influence* (Washington, D.C.: Brookings Institution, 2016).

23 For concrete data on this see Juliano da Silva Cortinhas, "Brazil and the Construction of Its Power to Defend the South Atlantic," in Érico Duarte and Manuel Correia de Barros, eds, *Navies and Maritime Policies in the South Atlantic* (Cham: Palgrave Macmillan, 2019), pp. 151–185. According to a media report on information provided by Professor Octavio Amorim Neto, in 2011 only 48 percent of Brazilian Navy ships were operational, as were 55 percent of Brazilian Army tanks and 41 percent of Brazilian Air Force planes. See *Valor Econômico* June 9, 2015.

24 As David Pion-Berlin and Rafael Martínez state in their recent book: "A military (Brazil) that exploits its constitutional right to enforce internal law and order and can, under certain conditions, exert command authority over the police is not one consistent with a mature polyarchy." *Soldiers, Politicians, and Civilians: Reforming Civil-Military Relations in Democratic Latin America* (Cambridge: Cambridge University Press, 2017), p. 381.

25 This and other quotations from Stepan in the following paragraphs on prerogatives draw on *Rethinking Military Politics*, Table 7.1.

26 Rubens Valente and Gustavo Uribe, "Temer dá a militares controle sobre áreas sensíveis do governo," *Folha de São Paulo* March 5, 2018.

27 *Brazil Report* of David Fleischer Jan 27–Feb 2, 2018.

28 Information provided March 6, 2018 in e-mail from David Fleischer.

29 IBOPE Inteligência, "Após queda acentuada em 2013: Índice de Confiança Social se estabiliza," September 1, 2014; World Values Survey, *WVS Database*, 2014.

30 Instituto de Pesquisa Econômica Aplicada, *Sistema de Indicadores de Percepção Social: Defesa Nacional 29 January 2012* (Brasília: Secretaria de Assuntos Estratégicos da Presidência da República, 2012), p. 6.

15

ARGENTINA

Old and new military missions, security and democracy

David Pion-Berlin

Introduction

Argentina has faced a number of security challenges during its modern history. The threats that these challenges posed—both real and perceived—invited different kinds of responses. During the 1970s, the emergence of left-wing guerrilla insurgents prompted the military to overthrow a democratically elected government and impose an authoritarian regime. Driven by geopolitical, national security and counter-insurgency doctrines, the military leaders launched a reign of state terror on society that was disproportionate to the threat, and which did grave harm to the nation and the military institution itself. A return to democratic rule prompted diplomatic solutions to geopolitical problems, resulting in an easing of inter-state tensions and the elimination of the risk of external war, which in turn removed at least one excuse for military re-intervention. During democratic rule, historic legislation on defense and security prohibited the armed forces from engaging in internal security operations of any kind. Argentina became a regional leader in this regard, but that may have changed with the new administration, which has sought to insert the armed forces into the fight against drug trafficking and terrorism. While these new ventures are ill-conceived, it is doubtful they will erode civilian control or jeopardize the democracy.

Threats, threat perceptions and state responses under military rule in Argentina

When Argentina was under military rule from 1976 to 1983, national security thinking and planning dominated the policy-making agenda. Dubbed *El Proceso*, for the Process of National Reorganization, the military regime dealt harshly with its enemies, both real and imagined.[1] The generals of the *Proceso* were wed to the idea that security should be the yardstick by which all policies are measured, the beginning and end of politics. Anyone thought to be interfering with the state's security objectives was "fair game." This drove the junta to attack guerrilla forces, Marxists, other left-wing elements and fellow travellers—be they armed or unarmed, unionists, students, professionals or just those who turned up in an address book of a detained individual. The *Proceso* went to coercive extremes hitherto unwitnessed in that nation to "cleanse" Argentina of its problems. Unprecedented levels of state terror directed at a cross-section of the population resulted in some 20,000 deaths and disappearances, making this the worst example of mass human rights abuses in South America at the time.

Through the early 1980s, the perception that Argentina faced security threats was driven by two modes of thought. The first was geopolitics, which often dominated military thinking at the time and accentuated national competitiveness. Geopolitics is generally thought of as the "science that studies the influence of geographical and historical factors on the life and evolution of the states."[2] Situated in a competitive and sometimes hostile environment, states, according to this view, had to prevail over rival states to survive, and did so by acquiring territory or fiercely defending land already acquired. Naturally, this placed nations in competition with others over disputed boundaries, and helps explain a country's preoccupation with threats originating from across the border. This marriage of geographical and political factors would become central to military thinking during the Cold War era. It was geopolitical thinking that helped motivate the fierce territorial rivalries between Argentina and Chile that brought those two countries to the brink of war in 1978. That same mode of thought was at the cognitive center of Argentina and Brazil's competition for regional domination.

The second kind of thought was ideological: a blend of national security and counter-insurgency doctrine that grew out of French experiences in Algeria and U.S. Cold War thinking, with a strong anti-communist thrust and a focus on internal threats aided and abetted by the Soviet Union and Cuba. While militaries distrusted their geopolitical neighbors, they hated the radical left. Thus, enemies of enemies became friends; and, prodded on by Washington, they joined forces against the internal left-wing "menace" in a hemispheric-wide effort, termed "Operation Condor," to hunt down, torture and execute "enemies of the state."[3] They were rewarded handsomely by the U.S. for their cooperation, with generous military aid, financial assistance and foreign investments.

The Argentine military regime was unsparing in its public rhetoric against alleged domestic enemies of state. It frequently said it was at war, referred to its policies of extermination. Its continued public expression of extremist language gave force to the idea that its perception of threat was quite high.[4] Was that perception justified? What was the level of security threats at the time?

Beginning just prior to the military's assumption of power, insurgent groups did operate in Argentina. Principal among them were the People's Revolutionary Army (Ejército Revolucionario del Pueblo or ERP) and the Montoneros. The ERP operated in the rugged mountainous region of Tucumán. The Montoneros were self-styled urban revolutionaries, occasionally staging poorly planned raids on military installations. Neither organization ever posed a serious military threat. Both groups (especially the Montoneros) were poorly trained, badly equipped and greatly outnumbered. Most accurate estimates placed the armed combatants at no more than 5000 men and women, compared to the 200,000-strong Argentine armed forces, a proportion that far exceeded the 10:1 parity thought necessary to win a guerrilla war.[5] The Argentine revolutionaries exhausted their forces quickly. Unlike their Vietnamese counterparts, these insurgents were like "fish out of water," never having built a secure base of mass support from which to recruit new personnel. They crumbled easily under the weight of the army's offensive, never putting the military to a full test.

"Operation Independence," fought in 1975 in Tucumán province against the ERP guerrillas, was an unmitigated success. In what appeared to have been a textbook display of counter-guerrilla strategy, the armed forces destroyed the ERP's rural *foco* while absorbing few casualties of its own—all in the space of just 11 months.[6] The Tucumán operation was of course followed by the infamous 'Dirty War' which dealt the final blow to the Peronist-affiliated

Montonero guerrillas. For all intents and purposes, the Montoneros were finished by the end of 1976, having abandoned organized combat. Any rational assessment of the security threat at that time would have concluded that the worst was over for the Argentine military regime.

One would not have known that, viewing the carnage that was to take place over the next several years.[7] The Argentine junta ratcheted up its campaign against enemy forces that had no military capacity. The number of victims of state violence rose in 1977 and, while leveling off in 1978, remained extremely high. In April 1977, President Jorge R. Videla drew up a secret order to pursue "bands of delinquents." In that same order, he admitted that 90 percent of the so-called subversive organizations had already been destroyed.[8] At a time when it would have been logical to de-escalate, the military expanded its coercive operations, intervening in industrial, educational, cultural, professional and religious organizations with a full show of force. Militaries are, after all, trained to carefully assess the strength of their adversaries. What reason would they have for attacking largely unarmed, defenseless groups?

The Argentine leaders were guided by threat perceptions that were less a careful calculation of the balance of forces and more a prior image of reality driven by beliefs about the nature of subversive revolutionaries.[9] They believed themselves to be in an unconventional war where the enemy operated in disguised form. Once driven from the battlefield, the enemy would reorganize, penetrate and assimilate into Argentina's social and political fabric to prepare for the next phase of the struggle. The struggle was multi-dimensional, reaching into schools, factories, government offices and homes. Convinced that the enemy's chameleon-like transformations would help widen their attack and prolong their life span indefinitely, the Argentine military thrust themselves into a "war" they perceived to be total and permanent. The actual threat was an illusion. There was no war, just a witch hunt against perceived enemies of state; there was no organized resistance to the regime, and no counter-state violence. Insurgents had been vanquished, and the internal security threat had vanished. To this day, the nation faces no concerted security threat from inside its borders.

The military dictators might have well perpetuated the illusion and the repressive response to it for many more years had it not been for their ill-conceived attempt to reclaim the Malvinas Islands on the 150th anniversary of the British seizure. The war they sparked in April of 1982 ended in disaster for them, as they went down to a crushing defeat after two months of combat. The war exposed a plethora of deficiencies in Argentina's ability to fight: there was no unified planning or any operable, unified command. There was no logistical coordination or any sharing of intelligence between the three branches. Army, navy and air force operated on their own, as though each were fighting a separate war. That defeat spelled the beginning of the end for the Argentine military regime. By the following year, the transition to democracy was in full force. The Malvinas war also marked the last time that Argentina would face a serious threat from a foreign state power.

The return to democracy and the end of inter-state security threats

During the Cold War (and prior to the 1982 Malvinas conflict), the closest Argentina came to trading blows with a foreign adversary was in 1978, when tensions between it and Chile over disputed claims to the Beagle Channels reached boiling point. Only last-minute arbitration by the Vatican forestalled what looked like a probable war. For decades, Argentina and its other nemesis, Brazil, had competed for regional domination and often clashed over boundaries, water rights and nuclear power. Rivalry had been particularly pronounced in the nuclear area, since these were the only two Latin American nations with nuclear capabilities.

A move by one from the production of energy to the production of nuclear arms would deal the other a decisive military disadvantage.

With the return to democratic rule, the Argentine government showed a willingness to use diplomacy as a first resort in the making of foreign policy. Beginning in 1985, vigorous diplomatic efforts were launched by Argentina and Brazil to improve relations, most notably in the realm of nuclear power. The Foz de Iguazú Joint Declaration on Regional Nuclear Policy of 1985 committed both nations to develop nuclear power for peaceful uses only. The significance of these accords reached well beyond the nuclear issue. Through the process of diplomatic recognition, Argentina and Brazil broke down the political and psychological barriers which had separated them, paving the way for other kinds of bilateral talks and mutual understandings.

Argentina and Chile went through a similar thawing of once-frozen relations. Argentine President Raúl Alfonsín (1983–1989) signed the 1984 Treaty of Peace and Friendship with Chile, which put an end to the Beagle Channel feud. The two nations went on to sign accords that resolved all standing border disputes. Rather than threaten each other, Argentina and Chile now collaborate in joint military exercises. Argentina has been in the lead in fostering confidence-building measures (CBMs) between erstwhile foes that include military visitations, greater budgetary transparency, joint exercises and student exchange programs. CBMs reduce the risk of armed confrontation between states by making available information regarding each other's military capabilities and intentions.

Argentina's original motivation for vigorously pursuing tension-reducing measures lay in its comparative military disadvantage vis-à-vis Chile and Brazil. It had spent far less and had failed to modernize its forces, and its combined forces were unprepared to defend the country. Argentina, along with the other Southern Cone states, has settled for modes of security cooperation. As practiced in South America, security cooperation is predicated on making military intentions and processes transparent. Unlike strategic balancing, the nations do not depend on the build-up of dissuasive forces to deter aggression from others. That does not mean that countries forego the opportunity to update and enlarge their defense systems. It means that they are not principally motivated to do so out of fear they would be vulnerable to the offensive designs of nearby states should they opt not to. And, unlike a security alliance, there is no joining of resources, intelligence and command systems to confront an external aggressor. In the cooperative arrangement the objective is to reduce or eliminate the sources of security anxiety by increasing military-to-military contacts, exchanging information and making defense intentions and processes transparent.

Today, hypotheses of conflict have been discarded. None of the Southern Cone countries visualize their neighbors as potential foes. For example, Argentina's last national defense strategy rejected hypotheses of conflict, and instead opted for readiness (capacity) in the face of a spectrum of generic threats.[10] Likewise, Brazil no longer considers its southern neighbor a military threat. Once the region's primary competitors for geopolitical domination, Brazil and Argentina now share a common strategic vision.[11] Inter-state security threats of any magnitude have virtually vanished from the Southern Cone, certainly in comparison to other subregions of Latin America.

These diplomatic moves helped strengthen democracy in Argentina by removing a military excuse to re-intervene. Political leaders quickly realized that the survival of democratic rule hinged on keeping the military out of politics and subordinate to civilian control. Removing the threat of external war was one means of doing so. The military could no longer claim there were geopolitical reasons for them to assume power, on the premise that civilian governments were not up to the task of defense planning against potentially dangerous foes.

With tensions having dissipated between the three countries, the military did not have to be called upon to advise on strategy; nor could it justify placing as many men under arms or commanding the same share of the government budget as it had done earlier.

At the time of transition to democracy (1983) the number of men under arms was sizeable in proportion to the nation's territory. When compared to several other very large states in and outside of Latin America, only Mexico had deployed more troops per square kilometer. Argentina's ratio of soldiers to land was twice that of Brazil's, and seven times greater than those of Australia and Canada, two nations it is often compared with in terms of size, natural endowments and economic structure. That same year, the Argentine armed forces still retained a 21.4 percent share of public sector outlays, compared to 17.9 and 19.1 percent for Chile and Peru respectively.[12] The contrast is even greater when examining Brazil. Argentina's military share of Central Government Expenditures averaged 5–6 times that of its northern neighbor during the early 1980s.[13]

But with the election of Raúl Alfonsín, the first post-authoritarian president, priorities would change. Alfonsín used his newfound strength to weaken the armed forces politically by paring down their size, power and prerogatives. His goal was to create an appropriate defense for a democratic nation at peace. The government could justify a peace dividend, shifting resources away from defense toward other priorities. His argument was practically unassailable: since defensive needs are assessed in proportion to risk, and since the risks of regional conflict had greatly subsided, then spending reductions were warranted. Cuts to military spending would continue unabated during the two terms of Alfonsín's successor, Carlos Menem (1989–1999). Reducing the military's economic and thus its political power at home, while forging peace with neighbors, were two sides of the same coin—a joint strategy designed to eliminate nearly all excuses for military coups against democratic governments.

Democratic rule, the military and internal security threats

Even though the external threat posed by neighboring states had disappeared, as had the geopolitical rationales for military rule, Argentine democratic leaders still worried about the military's propensity to intervene internally to suppress alleged threats to security at home. Here, Congress stepped up to the plate, enacting historic legislation that has limited the military's role. Thanks in large part to the work of staff members on the defense commissions in Congress, Argentina passed landmark legislation in 1988—*Ley de Defensa Nacional* (the Law of National Defense)—which stipulated that military force be used to confront aggressions by other states only.[14] Previous laws had reserved for the military a significant and ongoing role in facing down domestic threats under the rubric of national security. This law represented a huge loss for the armed services, one they had lobbied vigorously to forestall. Never had the legislative branch taken so active a role in defense matters with such an unexpected emphasis on long-term national interests rather than the sectarian politics of defense patronage.

This legislation was followed up in 1992 with another landmark piece of legislation: the *Ley de Seguridad Interior* (Law of Internal Security).[15] For the first time, the system of internal security was defined in a way that omits mention of the armed forces: it is comprised of the president, governors, Congress, ministers of interior, defense and justice, the federal and provincial police, and the two special security services—the *Gendarmería* and the *Prefectura Naval.* The military plays no official role in internal security. According to the law, the military cannot intervene domestically unless and until the president orders them to do so, and only then under exceptional circumstances. Those circumstances arise when other security forces are completely overwhelmed by a formidable force or insurrection that endangers the security of the nation—something that has not occurred in decades. However, the armed forces are permitted to lend logistical support to (not take control of) internal security operations, but only when requested by the appropriate authorities.[16]

The governments of Néstor Kirchner (2003–2007) and Cristina Fernández de Kirchner (2007–2015) stood fast in refusing to allow the armed forces to deploy internally. They had the law on their side, sufficient civilian control to make that a reality, and were backed by civilian security specialists who published a manifesto in 2014 warning of the tremendous risks associated with a return to military internal operations, and of the failures that have occurred where other militaries have been employed to fight the "war against drugs."[17] The armed forces have fully complied with government orders, not to mention the spirit and letter of the two laws. The country has made great progress in reducing military autonomy in the realm of internal security. For all intents and purposes, internal security has been demilitarized. Soldiers have not been seen on the streets of Argentina's cities, pursuing criminals or cracking down on citizen protests.

For several decades, these legislative initiatives set Argentina apart from all other states in the region for their rigorous demarcation of two spheres: defense and internal security. That was unusual, considering regional trends beginning in the mid-1990s that began to question whether the separation was still valid, and whether the armed forces should be tightly walled off from venturing into internal security operations. New threats were emerging which were transnational in scope, criminal in intent, oftentimes highly lethal, and which operated across borders and inside states. If criminal organizations regularly cross over territorial limits, then a security challenge may be neither purely domestic nor purely external; it could be both, thus blurring the line between defense and public security spheres. Harold Trinkunas and I have defined these as mid-level or intermediate challengers who pose threats that do not rise to the level of an invading army or insurgent force, but which are formidable nonetheless.[18] These challengers are found in the middle, lodged between common crime at the low end and insurgencies (guerrilla or otherwise) at the high end. They include high-powered criminal gangs, drug syndicates, arms and human smugglers, and the like. Criminal elements can be extremely violent, large, well-armed and well-funded. Police forces can be quickly overwhelmed by mid-level challengers, and sometimes captured by the very elements they are supposed to suppress. Intermediate challengers elevate the stakes because they compel deadlier or numerically massive responses than police are normally capable of mustering. When the threat looms that large, politicians are tempted to define it as a national security issue, and that *may* justify a military-like response.

If in fact the line between the domestic and the external has blurred, it could also mean that police work and military tasks have meshed. Some scholars believe this is so, with police becoming more militarized and soldiers becoming more police-like.[19] But others maintain that a blurring of domestic and international security spheres does not automatically conflate police and military roles.[20] And then there are numerous scholars who have urged that the roles *should not* be conflated.[21]

The matter is not clear-cut, not black and white. There are numerous, well-documented instances where military immersion in internal security operations has resulted in human rights violations. But, as I have argued elsewhere, this is not always the case, and very much depends on the precise nature of the operation, where and how soldiers are deployed, and whether they can respect international principles designed to mitigate harm to civilians.[22] There are occasions, albeit not many, where the level of threat is so great that it leaves governments with few options, and so governments may call upon soldiers to intervene as a last resort. In these instances, it is possible for soldiers to pursue criminal elements without threatening the surrounding population.[23] To do so, there must be compatibility between the demands of the operation, the military's skill set, its professional inclinations and its ability to conform to international principles of engagement in urban-styled operations. If, on the other hand, soldiers are forced to do policing, they have a more difficult time coping, and may break with standards of conduct designed to protect civilians.

While these debates continue, one matter has been settled: in Latin America the use of armed forces personnel in internal security operations has, over the last decade or more, become widespread. Guaranteeing internal order is now a constitutional provision in ten Latin American nations.[24] By 2014, 94 percent of Latin American armed forces were regularly performing operations related to public security, 65 percent had a program related to citizen security and 76 percent possessed regular programs for combatting drugs and crime:[25] 13 countries have military, counter-crime, counter-narcotic operations; 14 have frontier operations against trans-border criminal activity; and 10 conduct military citizen security operations, including foot patrols, riot control and response to demonstrations.[26]

Yet, amidst all this change, there seemed to be one hold-out: Argentina. With its laws of defense and internal security, it has established a starker delineation between defense and internal security, and between military and police operations, than any other Latin American country. And, with its alternative security forces like the *Gendarmería*, it can respond to most border incidents and public security crises without having to call upon the military.[27] But, with the coming to power of President Mauricio Macri in 2015, all of that seems to have changed.

The new Argentine military role: a solution in search of a problem

It appears as if President Macri (2015–19) has embraced the concept of "new threats," drug trafficking and terrorism included among them. He insists that the Argentine armed forces can no longer operate based on worn-out 20th-century concepts; that in this century, as the nature of security threats have changed, so too must the policies governing military conduct, not to mention the mindset that has prevailed since the late 1980s.[28]

Within weeks of assuming office, President Macri, through Decree 228/16, declared a public security emergency, calling narcotrafficking a threat to national sovereignty since it is a crime that is transnational in origin and scope.[29] He has even invoked the dubious terminology of referring to the battle against drug traffickers as a "war."[30] Once these terms are used, they "up the ante," legitimizing the potential use of military force to counter a threat of such magnitude that it could endanger the very sovereignty of a nation.

Macri has denied that utilizing the military to confront drug trafficking and terrorism would cross any legal line, insisting that the defense and security laws would be respected.[31] But the president has made a subtle change, widening the scope of "external threat" to include non-state actors. Article 1 of Decree 727/2006 issued under the Kirchner administration that regulated the law of defense, thus permitting its implementation, said that the armed forces would be deployed to "counter foreign originated aggressions perpetrated by the armed forces of other states."[32] The latest decree, 683/2018, issued on 23 July 2018, modifies that article, saying that the military will be deployed in a dissuasive manner against aggressions of external origin. By dropping the language about *state* foes, the new decree permits military responses to non-state actors such as transnational criminal organizations—organizations which include drug, human and arms traffickers, along with terrorists who cross territorial borders.[33]

With new decrees in hand, the government aimed to send some 4000 military personnel to the country's northern border by the end of 2018. The first phase has already been completed with the dispatch of 450 army soldiers and 40 air force pilots.[34] The same decree also allows for adjustments to be made in doctrine, planning and training that the government says would be consistent with operations framed in the law of internal security and other operations in support of the national and international community. So, whereas the law regulating defense aimed to limit the military's preparation to classic defense in all its aspects, this new decree would permit retraining to allow the military to assume other unconventional roles.[35]

Is any of this justified? Does the scope and severity of the threat warrant such a response? In any realistic comparison with other states from Latin America or elsewhere, neither narcotrafficking nor terrorism—the two principal rationales for a change in military mission—are of sufficient gravity in Argentina to cause alarm, let alone a dramatic change in military posture. Argentina is not a drug-producing country like Colombia, Bolivia, Peru or Mexico; nor is it afflicted with drug-related violence on a scale seen in Brazil, Mexico or Central America. It is principally a transhipment point for drugs, especially cocaine, that originate in Bolivia and Peru and are destined for European and Asian markets.[36] Argentina is neither an exit port nor an internal market for heroin, morphine and other opiates, or meth.

Criminal organizations in Argentina are relatively small, having local but not national or international reach. They do not rise to the level of intermediate challengers I defined earlier.

Though drug consumption has risen in Argentina in recent years, Argentina could not be described as a large consuming nation. In 2016, among the top 20 countries in the world, Argentina ranked 17th in cocaine seizures, accounting for 1 percent of the total. Though 60 percent of cocaine seizures worldwide do occur in South America, and although Argentina is the 3rd most populous country in that region, Colombia, Brazil, Chile, Ecuador and Peru all ranked higher in terms of cocaine apprehensions. In fact, Argentina placed 15th within the Americas as a whole.[37]

There are no accurate statistics on the number of drug-related homicides for Argentina, or any nation for that matter. The United Nations (UN) does not break down deaths attributable to drug-related crimes. But the overall homicide rate serves as a proxy, since deaths attributable to drug violence track with the overall homicide rate. On that score, Argentina's homicide rate is one of the lowest in South America, at 6.53 per 100,000 in 2015. Of 13 nations, only Chile had lower murder rates (3.59).[38]

This is not to say that Argentina does not have a problem. Its borders are porous, allowing not only drugs but also arms to flow across from other states. That is compounded by widespread corruption as traffickers have been able to bribe truck drivers and customs agents to allow drugs to be snuck into container shipments.[39] Criminal groups have infiltrated some security and political institutions, and have successfully bribed political officials and judges in certain locales.[40]

Terrorism does not pose a problem for Argentina—at least not any longer. The last major terrorist attack occurred on 18 July 1994 against the Jewish Welfare and Community Center, known as AMIA. The culprits have never been punished, but it is suspected that Iran was behind the bombing that left 85 dead and hundreds wounded, and that Hezbollah operators carried out the attack, aided and abetted by Argentine provincial police. That attack followed a 1992 bombing of the Israeli embassy in Buenos Aires, and seemed to be tied to a string of worldwide attacks on Israeli and Jewish targets.

Argentina may have been chosen in part because it was a soft target, easily penetrable by agents who probably crossed over from the tri-border area that connects Paraguay, Brazil and

Argentina. That region has long been suspected of being a haven for Islamic-sponsored terrorist activities because of a hospitable Arab and Muslim population mostly centered on Ciudad del Este, Paraguay. With government controls being as lax as they are, it has been alleged that Hezbollah has used the city as an operational, logistical and financial center, raising and laundering millions to finance terrorist activities worldwide. The city is certainly awash with criminal activity, mostly related to the smuggling of contraband, arms and drugs across the borders. It is reasonable to suspect that Hezbollah has engaged in these activities to raise funds for terrorism.[41]

Nevertheless, since 1994, there have been no actual terrorist attacks launched against Argentina originating from the triple frontier, or from anywhere else.[42] Many suspect that the "threat" from this region has been exaggerated, prompted by Washington's obsession with fighting terrorism and its insistence that the triple frontier does pose a serious risk. The latest State Department Report on Terrorism describes the tri-border area as "an important regional nexus of arms, narcotics, pirated goods, human smuggling, counterfeiting, and money-laundering—all potential funding sources for terrorist organizations."[43] And yet, neither the State Department, Homeland Security or the United States Southern Command (Southcom) have been able to find any convincing evidence that such illicit funding has been used to support terrorist plotting directed at Argentina or the other Southern Cone nations.

The complete absence of terrorist actions may also be the result of enhanced security and surveillance operations at the border area. All three nations have stepped up their initiatives, Argentina having gone the furthest in the realm of intelligence gathering and surveillance. It has improved its abilities to detect suspicious aircraft with the installation of new aerospace radar systems in the north.[44] None of these combined efforts, however, depend on direct military intervention; rather, they depend on improved technology and its installation, information sharing, enhanced law enforcement, anti-corruption measures, improved salaries for police, border, immigration and customs officials, as well as increased armed border patrols.[45] Securing the border area does not depend on any sizeable military presence, at least not for Argentina. Unlike many countries, the nation has not one but two non-military organizations that effectively patrol land and water routes at the frontier. These are, respectively, the *Gendarmería* and the *Prefectura Naval*.

Clearly then, neither drug trafficking nor terrorism constitute sufficient threats to Argentina to warrant a military response. Why then did President Macri choose this path? There are several explanations. The first is that the government was searching for a rationale to build up the defense budget in order to modernize the armed forces.[46] By imposing new, expansive responsibilities on soldiers, budget enlargement becomes easier to justify. The need to invest in military readiness, equipment and training was long overdue, and moves in that direction are commendable. The executive has repeatedly noted the need to upgrade the military in order to fulfill its primary mission. But thrusting the military head first into internal security operations does nothing but *divert* it from its primary mission—defense.[47] Such a diversion is costly, measured in combat training time foregone and in tanks, ships, submarines and heavy artillery gone idle, or never purchased. Such ventures do nothing to fortify the defensive capabilities of the nation.

The second rationale for Macri's path is that the government wanted to soften the boundary between defense and security to justify an eventual repressive role for the armed forces. Considering his administration's turn towards austere economic adjustments, as mandated by a standby agreement with the International Monetary Fund (IMF), it is not surprising that social protests have erupted. These are bound to continue; and if they cannot be contained, and in fact grow more disruptive, then Macri may have wanted the option of sending troops to urban areas to reestablish public order. This seems a less likely scenario, since the scheduled deployment of troops to the northern frontier would logically free up men from the *Gendarmería*'s border patrol units, who are also especially well-trained in handling public demonstrations, to be redeployed to the cities. The Gendarmes have been used effectively on many occasions in the past in precisely these situations, and would be joined by police.

A third possibility, one with greater plausibility, was that the president had another agenda entirely, one tied to the country's improved relations with the United States. As Ernesto López has convincingly argued, the shift in missions could be a quid pro quo: Argentina furthers Washington's counter-narcotic, counter-terrorist agenda in exchange for economic benefits.[48] The Macri government forged closer ties with the U.S. after relations had chilled under the previous Kirchner administrations. Presidents Macri and Trump knew each other well, having had business dealings that went back decades. Argentina made the first moves, signing agreements to construct U.S. military bases at its southernmost point, in Neuquén province to the west, as well as up north near the tri-border region.[49] The northern base was to be set up on the pretext of helping Argentina combat drug trafficking and terrorism. The government claimed that the U.S. presence would be limited to providing technical assistance and intelligence on criminal activity. In addition, Argentina would allow U.S. Drug Enforcement Administration (DEA) and Federal Bureau of Investigation (FBI) agents to operate on Argentine soil to help in these endeavors.[50] President Macri hoped the U.S. would return these favors by opening its markets to Argentine goods and encouraging more direct investment and financing in Argentina. Whether Washington holds up its end of the bargain remains to be seen.

Do these new military roles necessarily threaten civilian control and democracy? Based on extensive research I have conducted in the past on numerous countries, the answer is no. There is no sound evidence that a reorientation of the military to assume internal security roles results in a loss of civilian control.[51] Whether civilian leaders can exert authority over their armed forces or not depends less on the location of the mission or its content, and much more on the capacity to build stronger institutions, accumulate greater expertise and exert more oversight. When those goals are accomplished, they can be applied to any military mission or operation anywhere.

Democracy is not imperilled either, simply because governments have their militaries operate inside their borders. There is a logical fallacy to the assumption that inward-oriented missions cause militaries to become politicized, throwing their weight around in ways that could infringe on democratic processes and institutions. Governments may certainly gain politically from operations that eliminate threats, reduce crime and enhance public well-being. But it does not follow that armies are therefore politicized solely by their participation in such operations. Militaries are obligated to execute the policies handed to them by the legitimate political authorities, however those policies are conceived. But doing so does not naturally or inevitably lead militaries to politically exploit their mission for their own gain.[52] In sum, while these latest military deployments are ill-conceived, they do not pose any inherent risks to the Argentine democracy.

Notes

1 On the military regime and its motivations for using repression, see David Pion-Berlin and George Lopez, "Of Victims and Executioners: Argentine State Terror, 1975–1979," *International Studies Quarterly* 35, 1 (1991): 63–86; David Pion-Berlin, "The National Security Doctrine, Military Threat Perception and the 'Dirty War' in Argentina," *Comparative Political Studies* 21, 3 (1988): 382–407.

2 Joseph Comblin, "La Doctrina de la Seguridad Nacional," *Mensaje*, 25 (1976): 96–104; Golbery Do Cuoto e Silva, *Geopolítica de Brasil*. Mexico: El Cid, 1978.
3 J. Patrice McSherry, *Predatory States: Operation Condor and Covert War in Latin America*. Lanham, MD: Rowman & Littlefield, 2005.
4 Pion-Berlin, "National Security Doctrine."
5 Richard Gillespie, *Soldiers of Perón: Argentina's Montoneros*. Oxford: Clarendon, 1982, p. 178.
6 Familiares y Amigos de los Muertos por la Subversión (FAMUS), *Operación Independencia*. Buenos Aires: FAMUS, 1988, pp. 217–220.
7 Ernesto López, *Seguridad Nacional y Sedición Militar*. Buenos Aires: Legasa, 1987, pp. 137–144. Also see Pion-Berlin and Lopez, "Of Victims and Executioners."
8 David Pion-Berlin, *The Ideology of State Terror: Economic Doctrines and Political Repression in Argentina and Peru*. Boulder, CO: Lynne Rienner Publishers, 1989, p. 5.
9 David Pion-Berlin, "The Ideological Governance of Perception in the Use of State Terror in Latin America: The Case of Argentina," in Vladimir Shlapentokh and Christopher Vanderpool, eds. *State Organized Terror: The Case of Violent Internal Repression*. Boulder, CO: Westview Press, 1991, pp. 135–152.
10 República Argentina, Decreto 1714/2009, 10 November 2009.
11 Agencia Estado, "Brazil-Argentine Military Accord Said to Show 'Common Strategic Vision'", 27 April 1997, *Global Newsbank*, http://infoweb.newsbank.com, accessed 25 March 2015.
12 David Pion-Berlin. *Through Corridors of Power: Institutions and Civil-Military Relations in Argentina*. University Park: Pennsylvania State University Press, 1997, p. 115.
13 David Pion-Berlin, "Between Confrontation and Accommodation: Military and Government Policy in Democratic Argentina," *Journal of Latin American Studies* 23, 3 (1991): 543–571.
14 República Argentina, Ley de Defensa Nacional 23.554, *Boletín Oficial*, 5 May 1988.
15 República Argentina, Ley de Seguridad Interior 24.059, *Boletín Oficial*, 6 January 1992.
16 Ibid., article 27.
17 Consejo Argentino para las Relaciones Internacionales, *La Opinión Pública Argentina Sobre Política Exterior y Defensa 2010*. Buenos Aires: CARI 2011, pp. 37–39; A. Colombo Sierra, N. Comini, E. del Percio, R. Diamint, A. Fohrig, E. López, J. López Chorne, P. Martínez, P. Paradiso, R. Sánchez Antelo, L. Tibiletti, M.P. Tibiletti, J.G. Tokatlian, J.M. Ugarte and J.M. Vázquez Ocampo, *La Argentina y la cuestión de las drogas: una propuesta para repensar el debate político*. Buenos Aires, 6 May 2014.
18 The following section borrows from David Pion-Berlin and Harold Trinkunas, "Latin America's Growing Security Gap," *Journal of Democracy* 22, 1 (2011): 41–42; and David Pion-Berlin, "Neither Military nor Police: Facing Heterodox Security Challengers and Filling the Security Gap in Democratic Latin America," *Democracy and Security* 6, 2 (2010): 109–127.
19 Peter Andreas and Richard Price, "From War Fighting to Crime Fighting: Transforming the American National Security State," *International Studies Review* 3, 3 (2015): 31–52.
20 B.K. Greener-Barcham, "Crossing the Green or Blue Line? Exploring the Military Police Divide," *Small Wars and Insurgencies* 18, 1 (2007): 90–112.
21 Rut Diamint, "A New Militarism in Latin America," *Journal of Democracy*, 26, 4 (2015): 155–168; D. Zimmerman, "Between Minimum Force and Maximum Violence," *Connections: The Quarterly Journal* 4 (2005): 43–60.
22 David Pion-Berlin, "A Tale of Two Missions: Military Police Patrols vs. High Value Targeted Operations," *Armed Forces & Society* 43, 1 (2017): 53–71.
23 Ibid.
24 Red de Seguridad y Defensa de America Latina (Latin American Security and Defence Network, RESDAL), *A Comparative Atlas of Defence in Latin America and Caribbean: 2014 Edition*. Buenos Aires: RESDAL, 2014, p. 41. www.resdal.org/.
25 Ibid., pp. 70, 80.
26 RESDAL, *A Comparative Atlas of Defence in Latin America and Caribbean: 2016 Edition*. Buenos Aires: RESDAL, 2016, p. 74. www.resdal.org/.
27 Argentina's *Gendarmería* can also be redeployed to maintain public order. It is relatively well-trained in that regard, has a good (though not perfect) record of treating public protesters humanely and with minimal force, and is not at all beholden to the armed forces. Thus, when the regular police forces fail to perform, the political authorities can call on the *Gendarmería* rather than hitting the military trip wire, as is often the case in other countries.
28 "Mauricio Macri, en el Día del Ejército," *Todo Noticias*, 29 May 2018.

29 República Argentina, Decreto 228/2016, *Boletín Oficial*, 1 January 2016.
30 Anna-Catherine Brigida, "To Battle Drug-Traffickers, Argentina Takes a Risk and Uses Military," *Christian Science Monitor*, 17 November 2016.
31 "Macri: These Are the Armed Forces of All Argentines," *Notas: Periodismo Popular*, 1 August 2018.
32 República Argentina, Decreto 727/2006, *Boletín Oficial*, 13 June 2006.
33 República Argentina, Article 1, Decreto 683/2018, *Boletín Oficial*, 23 July 2018.
34 "Macri" *Notas: Periodismo Popular*.
35 Article 2, Decreto 683/2018.
36 According to the UN, it is the 5th largest trafficking point for cocaine en route to Europe and Asia.
37 UN Office on Drugs and Crime (UNODC), "Global Seizures of Drugs 2016," https://dataunodc.un.org/drugs/global_seizures.
38 UNODC, "Intentional Homicide Counts and Rates per 100,000 Population," https://data.unodc.org/#state:0.
39 Caroline Stauffer, "Argentina Shifts Drug Trafficking Offensive to Private Ports," *Reuters*, 15 November 2016.
40 InSight Crime, "Argentina Profile," 21 May 2018. www.insightcrime.org/argentina-organized-crime-news/argentina-profile/.
41 Felipe Umaña, "Threat Convergence: Revisiting the Crime-Terrorism Nexus in the Tri-Border Area," *Fund for Peace*, 11 April 2012. http://library.fundforpeace.org/ttcvr1208.
42 Arie M. Kacowicz, "Regional Peace and Unintended Consequences: The Peculiar Case of the Tri-Border Area of Argentina, Brazil, and Paraguay," in Maiah Jaskoski, Arturo C. Sotomayor, and Harold A. Trinkunas, eds. *American Crossings: Border Politics in the Western Hemisphere*. Baltimore: Johns Hopkins University Press, 2015.
43 United States Department of State, *Country Reports: Western Hemisphere, Chapter Two*, 2016. www.state.gov/j/ct/rls/crt/2016/272234.htm.
44 "Argentina: Tightening Air Surveillance in the North," *Security & Strategic Review*, February 2017. www.latinnews.com/component/k2/item/71298.html?period=2017&archive=26&Itemid=6&cat_id=806168:argentina-tightening-air-surveillance-in-the-north.
45 Umaña, "Threat Convergence," p. 18, says: "the triple frontier, thusly, would benefit from the implementation of high-intensity crime policies, anti-corruption measures, and stronger financial regulations, along with greater attention to border control and immigration between the three border cities."
46 "El presidente Macri habló en la cena de camaradería anual de las fuerzas armadas," 31 July 2018. www.argentina.gob.ar/noticias/el-presidente-macri-hablo-en-la-cena-anual-de-camaraderia-de-las-fuerzas-armadas.
47 Ernesto López, "Una operación de gato por liebre," *Pagina 12*, 3 August 2018.
48 Ibid.
49 "The Expansion of U.S. Military Installations in Argentina and their Implications for Argentine Sovereignty," *Impact News Service*, 26 July 2018; Global Security, "Argentina–U.S. Relations," www.globalsecurity.org/military/world/argentina/forrel-us.htm.
50 Ibid.
51 David Pion-Berlin and Craig Arceneaux, "Decision-Makers or Decision-Takers? Military Missions and Civilian Control in Democratic South America," *Armed Forces & Society*, 26, 3 (2000): 413–436.
52 David Pion-Berlin, *Military Missions in Democratic Latin America*. New York: Palgrave Macmillan, 2016, pp. 146–147.

16

THE QUEST FOR A TRADEOFF BETWEEN DEMOCRACY AND SECURITY

The case of post-Communist Romania[1]

Florina Cristiana Matei

Romania, a fairly new democracy,[2] underwent a bloody transition in 1989 from one of the most oppressive non-democratic regimes in Central and Eastern Europe.[3] Romania's rating from non-governmental organization (NGO) Freedom House for 2017 was 3.46 for democratization on a 1–7 scale, with 1 being the highest and 7 the lowest.[4] Its endeavors and developments have disproved the skepticism of some experts on democratization (e.g. Samuel Huntington and Mary Ellen Fischer), who claimed Romania had infinitesimal chances for achieving democracy.[5]

In its path to democratic consolidation, Romania has also striven to find an appropriate balance between democracy and security. In fact, Romania's democratic institution building has effected a comprehensive reform of its security organizations, strengthening their capabilities to face current security threats more effectively.[6] In addition, Romania is currently a member of various multinational, regional and sub-regional security organizations, including the United Nations (UN) and Organization for Security and Cooperation in Europe (OSCE), the North Atlantic Treaty Organization (NATO), and the European Union (EU). It has contributed to the allied forces' operations in the first Gulf War, and to peace operations in Afghanistan, Bosnia, Kosovo, Albania, Iraq and Mali. Since the end of hostilities, Romania has been involved in security and reconstruction activities.[7]

This chapter assesses Romania's legislative and institutional quest to find a tradeoff between democracy and security since the transition to democracy in 1989. It finds that Romania's journey to a free, yet secure, society has been long drawn out and challenging. But, notwithstanding a series of glitches, Romania has achieved progress in building basic democratic institutions. The chapter also finds that, despite these efforts, maintaining a reasonable democracy–security balance in Romania remains a work in progress.

Romania's transition from a non-democratic regime to democracy

Between 1947 and 1989 Romania was a Communist regime—totalitarian under Gheorghe Ghiorghiu Dej (1947–1965) and totalitarian-cum-sultanistic under Nicolae Ceausescu (1965–1989)[8]—characterized by one-party rule (Romanian Communist Party, PCR, extreme centralization, a cult of personality (worsened during the Ceausescu regime) and egregious human rights violations. Those violations of human rights included harsh social and economic conditions,[9] as well as prohibition of any contraceptive measures.[10] All policies were advanced under the pervasive watch of the Securitate, Ceausescu's political police.

The Ceausescu regime ended in December 1989 when a political coup attempt turned into a mass revolt against Ceausescu's dictatorship and abolished the non-democratic regime. Ceausescu and his wife were executed after a brief ad hoc trial. The Securitate was dismantled and placed under command of the military. Since then, Romania has embarked upon democratic consolidation.[11] New institutions and practices have emerged and developed: free and fair elections, the peaceful transfer of power from one political party to another; the establishment of a legal framework for democracy and security; security strategies and policies; democratic reform of the security sector; free and active civil society and press; and a free market economy.

Security and democracy developments since 1989

Romania's quest for security and democracy has been a long process, characterized by ups and downs. Nevertheless, unlike other new democracies from other regions (most notably Latin America) whose civilian elites have more or less discounted national security threats and the role of the security sector, Romania's elected and appointed officials have "invested" in security. Policymakers have been well aware of Romania's geostrategic position (the country's turbulent neighborhood includes the Former Yugoslavia and Former USSR) and the impact of globalization on national security and defense. In addition, Romania—which unanimously articulated its wish, will, and pledge to join the European and Euro-Atlantic collective security organizations as soon as these institutions announced their willingness to accept new members—worked hard to comply with these organizations' membership demand that new members find a balance between security and democracy. Romania joined these organizations respectively in 2004 and 2007.

In line with the "European environment of freedom, prosperity, security and justice,"[12] Romania has channeled its efforts to achieve

> [Full] acceptance of political pluralism, political, ideological and cultural differences, ethnic diversity, respect for human rights, which shape the activity of the 'rule of law' state institutions in eliminating any forms of marginalization on ethnic, religious, social, sexual or political orientation criteria, the uncontestable political stability and the example-setting experience of the peaceful, democratic alternatives to power.[13]

Romania has also attempted to complement these democracy building related endeavors by undertaking legal and institutional developments aimed to avert national security threats—of both domestic and international nature—that can jeopardize democracy if not contained.

Romania's security threats since the transition to democracy

Romania's security environment includes overlapping domestic and transnational threats, mostly of a non-military nature. Domestically, threats to Romania's national security stem from economic, financial, social, and environmental challenges.[14] These include: demographic decline; population migration; deteriorating living standards; precarious health, education, and environment protections; unnecessarily bureaucratic public services; poor territorial infrastructure and public transportation; and precarious and corruption-prone political, economic, and business environments.[15] In addition, the lackadaisical response, adaptation, and amendment of the public law and order and national security system to current types of criminality—coupled with serious flaws in the management of the justice system—have increasingly endangered the safety of Romanian citizens.[16]

Corruption, endemic in Romania, is another challenge to national security. As Romania's National Defense Strategy stipulates, "[c]orruption makes the state vulnerable, generates prejudices to economy and alters the country's development potential … governance … [and] decision-making processes … as well as … confidence in justice and state institutions."[17]

Transnational threats are an outcome of Romania's geographical and strategical position. Romania lies in a region plagued by both active and frozen conflicts, a situation which affects its citizens' security. Transnational threats "have led to a loss of traditional economic relations, [and] caused important financial losses to Romania."[18] Moreover, Romania is at the crossroads of many routes favored by transnational organized crime. Illegal trafficking in people, drugs, arms and ammunition, and strategic and radioactive materials occurs across its territory.[19] In this regard, the CIA *World Factbook* notes that Romania lies at a

> major transshipment point for Southwest Asian heroin transiting the Balkan route and small amounts of Latin American cocaine bound for Western Europe; although not a significant financial center, [its] role as a narcotics conduit leaves it vulnerable to laundering, which occurs via the banking system, currency exchange houses, and casinos.[20]

Terrorism is not a major threat to Romania's security. Nonetheless, Romania could become a terrorist target for multiple reasons. Among them are its Eastern border of almost 1,600 km and its current membership in NATO and the EU, whose countries have often become terrorist targets, Romania's unstable geographical surroundings have harbored terrorist groups. A relatively high Middle Eastern representation in Romania may have the capacity to transform the country into a hub for terrorist traffic targeting both Romania and other nations. Romania's friendly relationship and close security cooperation with the United States may also potentially make it a target for terrorist attack.[21]

One of the most significant foreign threats to Romania's national security has come from the Russian Federation. Security experts highlight Russia's protean, multilayered, and multifarious actions aimed at undermining both Romania's security and its democracy, ranging from daily (military) aggressions in the Black Sea to more subtle covert operations (in the form of disinformation and propaganda as well as political and economic actions, often supported by cyberattacks), resulting in political meddling, instigation of minorities, and the like.[22]

Legal and institutional arrangements intended to balance democracy with security

All of these issues call for concerted action on the part of elites, security sectors, and citizens in order to maintain an appropriate security and democracy tradeoff. Post-communist governments have brought about changes in Romania's legal framework and in policies related to security, as well as institutional redesign.

Laws, strategies and policies

Romania's Constitution, adopted in 1991 and amended in 2003 (by Law No. 429 on the revision of the Constitution of Romania), is the law of the land. It establishes the structure and roles of the country's government, its citizens' rights and responsibilities, and the country's method of enacting laws.[23] The Constitution provides for a system of national defense and security; interagency coordination and cooperation of the security institutions; and democratic control and oversight of security agencies.[24] In addition, it stipulates the conditions under which the Romanian president can declare a "state of exception"—which involves the declaration of a state of siege and/or a state of emergency. The president of Romania may declare a state of siege or state of emergency across Romania's entire territory or over specific regions or zones, but needs Parliament's approval of his or her action within five days of the declaration. An executive order declaring a state of siege or state of emergency must be countersigned by the Prime Minister and published in the Romanian Official Gazette.[25]

The Romanian Constitution prohibits the creation of special courts.[26] In addition, the state of siege and emergency is regulated by Law No. 453 of 2004, which provides mechanisms to approve the Government Emergency Ordinance on the state of Siege and Emergency No. 1 of 21 January 1999.[27] In line with the law, a state of siege involves "all the exceptional measures of a political, military, economic, social, and other nature applicable throughout the country or in some administrative-territorial units, established for the adaption of the defense capability of the country to serious, current or imminent threats." A state of emergency is similar to a state of siege, but imposes non-military measures to address threats to national security and function of government, and crises due to natural disasters.[28] The law allows the armed forces to take over responsibilities of public administration throughout the crisis.[29] Between 21 and 22 January 1999, Romania actually declared a state of emergency during strikes initiated by miners protesting against harsh political and work conditions.[30] Romania also declared a state of emergency on 6 August 2018 in the aftermath of the outbreak of African swine fever.[31]

Law No. 39/1990 established the National Defense Supreme Council (CSAT) as the body that coordinates all national defense- and security-related activities. It also regulates Romanian participation in international security efforts, collective defense within military alliances, and peace and reconstruction operations.[32] CSAT is composed of ten members: the non-partisan president as chair (who is also the Supreme Commander of the Armed Forces); the prime minister as deputy chair; the minister of industry and trade; the minister of defense; the minister of foreign affairs; the minister of the interior; the head of the Political Analysis Department of the Presidency; the director of the Romanian Intelligence Service; the director of the Foreign Intelligence Service; and the chief of general staff.[33] The CSAT's responsibilities include:

- informing and advising the president on issues pertaining to national security and defense;
- coordinating the activities of all security institutions;
- producing security-related documents (for example, national security strategy and military strategy);
- integrating all information provided by the intelligence agencies and other national security institutions; and
- initiating measures vis-à-vis declaring a state of siege and/or emergency, declaring and canceling a state of war, and/or initiating, suspending or terminating specific military actions.
- The National Defense Supreme Council also:
- coordinates policies developed by the executive branch together with the legislative branch (for example, in the event of war the CSAT will submit a plan to mobilize the national economy and a budget for the first year of war for parliamentary approval);
- endorses various draft policies initiated by the government on national security topics;
- organizes all security institutions;
- manages the organization and functions of the CSAT itself;
- prepares the populace, economy, and territory for defense;
- drafts budget proposals and allocations for the security institutions;
- handles foreign relations—for example, CSAT approves the circumstances under which foreign troops are allowed to enter, pass through or deploy on Romanian territory; and
- endorses draft international treaties and agreements relevant to Romania's national security.

Finally, CSAT monitors the implementation of CSAT decisions and fulfills other functions with regard to national security and defense.[34]

National Security Law, or Law No. 51 of 1991, enumerates national security threats and challenges (which, unfortunately, have remained unmodified since 1991). Law 51 defines the institutions in charge of achieving national security; stipulates the need, and conditions, for interagency cooperation; and creates the framework for democratic civilian control of the security institutions.[35] In addition, the Romanian government has enacted laws on the organization and functioning of each ministry and institution involved in national security and defense.

Additional rules and regulations pertaining to national security and defense include: Law 182 of April 2002 on the Protection of Classified Information, which provides for the right of access to public information, but continues to restrict access to classified information; Romania's National Doctrine of Security Intelligence, adopted by the CSAT in July 2004; specific doctrines established by each national security-tasked agency (for example, the Doctrine of Combating Terrorism, Military Strategy and Doctrine); and other laws and policies enacted and used to combat terrorism and organized crime.[36] In 2004, the government issued Executive Order No. 21/200 on the National System of Management of Emergency Situations, which established a system of coordination during emergency situations, including consequence management and resource allocation.[37] Romania's policymakers also enacted laws and established rules and regulations on transparency and freedom of information, including: Law No. 544 of 2001 on Free Access to Public Information; Law No. 16 of April 1996 (updated in July 2002) on the National Archive; Law No. 677 of 2001 for the Protection of Persons concerning the Processing of Personal Data and Free Circulation of Such Data; the 2003 Law on Certain Steps for Assuring Transparency in Performing High Official

Positions, Public and Business Positions, and for Prevention and Sanctioning the Corruption; and Law No. 187 of 1999 on Access to the Personal File and the Disclosure of the Securitate as a Political Police.[38]

Additional norms and regulations include the latest National Security Strategy (NSS) of Romania, adopted by the CSAT. Those norms and regulations address post-Cold War security risks and threats, including global security trends that emerged with and after the terrorist attacks of 9/11. In addition, the Defense Strategy, adopted in 2015, highlights the military and non-military threats to Romania security, and sets the objectives and courses of action for defense, public order, intelligence, counterintelligence and security activity, education, healthcare, economy, finances, tourism, environment, and critical infrastructure.[39]

Security institutions

Romania's security sector includes several organizations covering military, law enforcement, and intelligence roles. The Romanian Armed Forces—comprised of the Army, Air Force and Navy—ensure Romania's national defense, and operate under the Ministry of Defense (MOD).[40] The Romanian Police (which is a national police force) and the Gendarmerie (which is a military police agency akin to the Chilean Carabineros or French Gendarmerie) ensure Romania's law enforcement, and operate under the Ministry of Administration and Interior (MAI). The intelligence community in Romania includes four independent agencies—the Romanian Intelligence Service (SRI), the Foreign Intelligence Service (SIE); the Guard and Protection Service (SPP), and the Special Telecommunications Service STS)—and two ministerial agencies (the MOD's General Intelligence Directorate of the Armed Forces/DGIA and the MAI's Directorate for Intelligence and Internal Protection/DIPI). Since 1989, Romania has devoted considerable resources to strengthening the professional norms of its security forces. Such endeavors have involved new standards for recruitment, education, training, and promotion—all aimed at increasing the expertise, corporateness, and responsibility of each institution, in line with the standards and practices of their western counterparts.[41]

The security institutions, in compliance with the legal framework and security and defense strategies and policies outlined above, can fulfill the following roles and missions: fighting external wars; fighting internal wars (if any); fighting terrorism; fighting crime; participating in peace operations; participating in humanitarian assistance/disaster relief/civil affairs operations; safeguarding and preserving national identity and culture; defense diplomacy; and research and development.[42] Under the strategic coordination of the National Defense Supreme Council these institutions cooperate in support of national security. These institutions have also established avenues of communication, information, and collaboration with representatives of civil society.[43]

Romania has also established democratic control and oversight mechanisms for the security sector. Executive control involves direction and guidance by the National Defense Supreme Council, as well as management, direction, and control by the civilian-led ministries or agencies. Legislative control and oversight encompasses enacting legislation, investigations, interpellations, hearings, supervisions, motions, etc., all of which are exercised by Romania's bicameral Parliament through permanent and ad hoc committees.[44] Judicial control and oversight of the security sector consists of verification by the Constitutional Court of the constitutionality of the normative documents related to defense and security.[45] The Romanian civil society and media, the ombudsman (advocate of the people), as well as the European Court of Human Rights, have exercised informal control over the armed forces, police, and intelligence agencies. In this context, although often sensationalist and profit-oriented, the Romanian media has revealed actions and inaction related to reforms of the security institutions to both domestic and international audiences, including NATO and the EU—institutions which could block or postpone Romania's accession—and has hence forced the hand of the executive and legislative bodies to deal with reported problems in order to join the two organizations. Intervention by the media has proved to be a more effective oversight mechanism as compared to initiatives by the formal bodies.[46]

Is there a balance between democracy and security in Romania?

Security can exist without democracy, but no democracy can survive without security. In this context, since the transition to democracy in 1989, Romania has striven to find a balance between democratic requirements and security roles in preserving these demands—legally and institutionally. With regard to security, Romania has developed new legal bases, and has created and transformed its armed forces, police, and intelligence agencies to avert and counter the national security threats and challenges as well as possible. These institutions have often received accolades from the international community, including their counterparts in other countries. For instance, in the fall of 2017, US Secretary of Defense Jim Mattis "praised fellow NATO member nation Romania as a valued ally in alliance efforts to deter Russian aggressive actions in Eastern Europe and in the campaign to defeat terrorist groups, including the Islamic State of Iraq and Syria."[47] On the same note, *GardaWorld* highlights the progress and role of intelligence and police forces in the fight against crime, noting that Romania's "[i]mproved law enforcement funding, additional legal powers combined with greater collaboration with European counterparts has led to a gradual decline in criminal activity in Romania."[48]

Nevertheless, despite progress, keeping democracy and security in balance remains a work in progress, particularly with regard to staying on the democratic consolidation path. While, unlike other countries from the former Soviet bloc—most notably Hungary and Poland—Romania has not undergone democratic erosion, its democracy has most recently been in jeopardy for several reasons. Lack of trust in democratic institutions and democracy itself, according to a study by Visan, is the number one danger to Romania's democracy. The author notes that "Romanians do not feel that their elected representatives are interested in promoting the public's agenda and concerns."[49] This challenge derives directly from a troubled cohabitation within the coalition government since 2014 and difficult interagency cooperation, also reflected by the fight between the prime minister and the president.[50] In Romania the president is from one political party, the prime minister from another. Hence a challenging "cohabitation" prevails, not only from a partisanship perspective but also because, in a semi-presidential system, infighting between the prime minister and the president with respect to security can occur. In this context, Freedom House reports that:

> A general mistrust in the ruling coalition lingered throughout 2017 as events from the beginning of the year remained fresh in the memory of both magistrates and the public. Several scandals erupted around the National Anticorruption Directorate (DNA), and several prosecutors left the unit or were laid off.[51]

Corruption is another obstacle to democratic—as much as security—progress. Visan argues that corruption "undermines the rule of law and denies citizens the full exercise of their right as well as access to public services."[52] Despite accolades by the EU and other watchdogs for its anti-corruption measures, Romania's policymakers—particularly in Parliament—do not concur. Rather, political elites embrace and attempt to perpetuate corruption.[53] As such, legislative control and oversight were more rigorous and effective before 2004, the date of Romania's accession to NATO and the EU, when these institutions' accession requirements became the "only game in town" for Romanians, and political divergences were put aside for the sake of NATO/EU integration.[54]

Admittedly, during that time legislators attached greater importance to both democracy and security. On the downside, in 2017, the legislative branch postponed draft laws on the transformation of the judicial framework.[55] On the upside, on 18 April 2018, the Romanian Parliament established an ad hoc committee to review the national security laws package that has been maintained and followed by the legislature since the mid-2000s.[56]

On the same note, while the EU Commission's most recent Cooperation and Verification Mechanism report praised the National Anticorruption Directorate (DNA) and other Romanian institutions for "improving the fight against corruption, which has recently brought a number of high-profile convictions ranging from a former prime minister and parliamentarians to mayors and businessmen,"[57] the firing of Laura Codruța Kövesi, Prosecutor General of the DNA, in the summer of 2018 and the government's responses to the ensuing riots have cast doubt on the future of anti-corruption efforts in the country. On 10 August 2018, anti-government protests occurred in Bucharest and other major cities in Romania. Termed "Diaspora at Home," the protests were organized by the Romanian diaspora, who went to Romania specifically for the riots.[58]

The protesters demanded the resignation of the prime minister on grounds of corruption (in particular related to the government's attempt to modify the penal code to allow for corruption). Also at issue was the firing of Kövesi; the political blunders of the prime minister; and allowing Liviu Dragnea, convicted on grounds of incitement to abuse of office during his time as chair of a county council, to remain head of the Chamber of Deputies.[59] Peaceful riots in Bucharest were met with violence by the Gendarmerie as soon as the protesters tried to enter a government building by force, while other protesters were reportedly violent themselves.[60] The Romanian president, Klaus Iohannis, along with human rights groups, condemned the way the gendarmerie handled the protests, which angered Dragnea.

Another danger to democracy in Romania is the rise of populism and populist politics, coupled with political polarization. Both respond to corruption and variation in the way people from various societal strata view the issue.[61] George Visan warns that, domestically, "Romania faces the threat of political instability in the short and medium term" as a domino effect of the regress to illiberal democracy status in Romania's neighborhood. He further notes that:

> Political polarization over combatting corruption endangers the entire effort [against corruption] and there is a serious risk of rolling back reforms undertaken until now. Weak [*sic*] institutions, nationalism and corruption increase the risks of illiberal outcomes … of the democratic system" [and enhance] the "vulnerability to hybrid warfare—for example, Russian propaganda.[62]

Freedom House also stresses Romania's "poor governance demonstrated by sustained attempts to decriminalize corruption and infighting within the ruling coalition, as well as … the promotion of populist policies and an escalation of illiberal discourse."[63]

All in all, the case of Romania demonstrates that while the country has found a convenient tradeoff between democracy and security, its effort is a work in progress. The fact that

Romania's Democracy Score according to Freedom House's assessment declined from 3.39 in 2016 to 3.46 in 2017 is a case in point. Freedom House's forecast for 2018 was similar:

> Attempts to weaken judicial independence and the anticorruption framework are expected to continue in 2018, accompanied by an increasing illiberal discourse against groups that oppose those changes. In preparation for the presidential elections scheduled for 2019, the government's populist and clientelistic behavior will also continue, including attempts at buying influence at the local level with public funds. A referendum to change the constitution to redefine "family" could be instrumental in energizing socially conservative groups. The year 2018 also marks 100 years of Romania's existence as a unified state. Major celebrations are planned inside and outside the country. This will increase the nationalist sentiment building upon the existent political narrative.[64]

Indeed, finding the balance between democracy and security is not a linear process, and past accomplishments do not guarantee enduring success.

Notes

1 The views expressed in this chapter do not reflect the policy or view of the United States Government, Department of Defense or Department of Navy. The author would like to credit Mr. Christopher Ketponglard for the research on the State of Exception in Romania.

2 I used the conceptual framework of five arenas which Linz and Stepan introduced as *sine qua non* for achieving democracy and democratic consolidation: free civil society, political society, rule of law, state bureaucracy, and economic society. See Juan J. Linz and Alfred Stepan, *Problems of Democratic Transition and Consolidation: Southern Europe, South America, and Post-Communist Europe* (Baltimore: Johns Hopkins University Press, 1996).

3 For thorough discussions on the various types of non-democratic regimes, see the following scholarly literature: Barbara Geddes, *Paradigms and Sand Castles: Theory Building and Research Design in Comparative Politics* (Ann Arbor: University of Michigan Press, 2003); Linz and Stepan, *Democratic Transition and Consolidation*.

4 See https://freedomhouse.org/report/nations-transit/2018/romania.

5 See Samuel Huntington and Mary Ellen Fischer, as cited by Melanie Ram, "Romania's Reform through European Integration: The Domestic Effects of European Union Law," www.ksg.harvard.edu/kokkalis/GSW1/GSW1/20%20Ram.pdf.

6 Romania's security forces include the armed forces (Army, Navy, Air Force) under the Ministry of Defense (MOD), the police force and Gendarmerie, under the Ministry of Internal Affairs (MIA) and six intelligence agencies. Of the latter, the Romanian Intelligence Service (SRI), Foreign Intelligence Service (SIE), Guard and Protection Service (SPP) and Special Telecommunication Service (STS) are independent; and the MAI General Directorate for Intelligence and Internal Protection (DGIPI) and MOD General Directorate of the Armed Forces (DGIA) are ministerial.

7 Thomas C. Bruneau and Florina Cristiana Matei (eds.) *The Routledge Handbook of Civil Military Relations* (London: Routledge 2012); Cristiana Matei, "Romania's Transition to Democracy and the Role of the Press in Intelligence Reform," in Thomas C. Bruneau and Steven C. Boraz (eds.) *Reforming Intelligence* (Austin: University of Texas Press, 2007), pp. 219–240; Florina Cristiana (Cris) Matei, "Romania's Intelligence Community: From an Instrument of Dictatorship to Serving Democracy," *International Journal of Intelligence and Counterintelligence* 20/4 (2007), pp. 629–660; Larry Watts, "Control and Oversight of Security Intelligence in Romania," Geneva Centre for Democratic Control of Armed Forces (DCAF) Working Papers, 111, February 2003; Florina Cristiana (Cris) Matei, "Balancing Democratic Civilian Control with Effectiveness of Intelligence in Romania: Lessons Learned and Best/Worst Practices before and after NATO and EU Integration," *Intelligence and National Security*, 29/4 (2014), pp. 619–637.

8 Linz and Stepan, *Democratic Transition and Consolidation*.

9 As a way to pay off Romania's national debt, which Ceausescu actually succeeded in doing by 1989, but at the expense of the population and without trying to improve living conditions after the full pay.

10 This is one of the most tragic consequences of Ceausescu's dictatorship. Far from actually increasing the number of Romanians, Ceausescu's idea for increasing the population led to numerous sad consequences. For example, an increase in illegal abortions (performed in non-hygienic conditions, sometimes by amateurs rather than medical professionals) correlated with the death of women, as well as the birth of lots of unwanted children. Many of them ended up in orphanages because their mothers had died during illegal abortions or their parents were incapable of raising them.

11 Juan Linz and Alfred Stepan, *Problems of Democratic Transition and Consolidation: Southern Europe, South America, and Post-Communist Europe* (Baltimore: Johns Hopkins University Press, 1996).

12 www.presidency.ro/files/userfiles/National_Defense_Strategy_2015_-_2019.pdf.

13 Ministry of National Defence, "Romania's National Security Strategy," www.files.ethz.ch/isn/15286/ROMANIA.pdf.

14 www.files.ethz.ch/isn/15286/ROMANIA.pdf.

15 Ibid.

16 Ibid.

17 www.presidency.ro/files/userfiles/National_Defense_Strategy_2015_-_2019.pdf.

18 www.files.ethz.ch/isn/15286/ROMANIA.pdf.

19 Ibid.

20 www.cia.gov/library/publications/the-world-factbook/geos/ro.html.

21 There is a US military base in Romania, and Romania is also more pro-US than its neighboring countries.

22 Alison Mutler, "Romania Minister Says Country Facing Cyber-Attacks," *Fifth Domain*, 25 June 2018, www.fifthdomain.com/international/2018/06/25/romania-minister-says-country-facing-cyber-atta cks/; author's discussion with Romanian intelligence community professionals during a Center for Civil-Military Relations (CCMR) residential course, Monterey, Naval Postgraduate School, 5–7 September 2018.

23 Florina Cristiana (Cris) Matei, "The Legal Framework for Intelligence in Post-Communist Romania," *International Journal of Intelligence and CounterIntelligence*, 22/4 (2009), pp. 667–698.

24 Ibid.

25 In line with the Constitution, Parliament must function—and cannot be dissolved—during the entire state of siege or state of emergency. For more information, see Alexandru Stoian, "Considerations Regarding the Legal Regime of the State of Siege in Romania," *Revista Academiei Forţelor Terestre/Land Forces Academy Review*, 22/4(88) (2017), pp. 239–243, www.armyacademy.ro/reviste/rev4_2017/STOIAN.pdf.

26 European Commission for Democracy Through Law (Venice Commission), "Emergency Powers," 1995, www.venice.coe.int/webforms/documents/default.aspx?pdffile=CDL-STD(1995)012-e.

27 "Ordonanţa de urgenţă a Guvernului nr. 1/1999 privind regimul stării de asediu şi regimul stării de urgenţă," *Monitorul Oficial*, Part I, No. 22, 21 January 1999.

28 Marian Zulean, "The Normative Aspects of Building Democratic CMR in Post-Communist Romania: Romanian Case," Peace Research Institute Frankfurt (PRIF) Research Paper No. I/13-2007, 2007, p. 7, www.hsfk.de/fileadmin/HSFK/hsfk_downloads/Romania_13.pdf.

29 Ibid.

30 Larry L. Watts, "Stressed and Strained Civil–Military Relations in Romania, but Successfully Reforming," https://outlook.office.com/owa/?realm=nps.edu&exsvurl=1&ll-cc=1033&modurl=0&path=/attachmentlightbox.

31 https://phys.org/news/2018-08-romania-outbreaks-african-swine-fever.html.

32 Thomas C. Bruneau, Florina Cristiana (Cris) Matei and Sak Sakoda, "National Security Councils: Their Potential Functions in Democratic Civil-Military Relations," *Defense & Security Analysis*, 25/3 (2009), pp. 255–269.

33 Ibid.

34 Ibid.

35 Matei, "Legal Framework for Intelligence in Post-Communist Romania."

36 Ibid.

37 D. Paicu and I. Petroman, "'Alert State' in a State of Emergency," www.usab-tm.ro/pdf/2010/xii3/fin_tur_47.pdf.

38 Matei, "Legal Framework for Intelligence in Post-Communist Romania."

39 www.presidency.ro/files/userfiles/National_Defense_Strategy_2015_-_2019.pdf; Anna Khakee, "Securing Democracy? A Comparative Analysis of Emergency Powers in Europe," Geneva Centre for the Democratic Control of Armed Forces (DCAF), Policy Paper No. 30, 2009, www.um.edu.mt/library/oar/handle/123456789/16054.
40 The Army hosts the Military Police, which performs law enforcement functions for the Army. It cooperates with the other law enforcement agencies and the intelligence community, and participates in international missions.
41 Bruneau and Matei, *Handbook of Civil–Military Relations.*
42 Ibid. Of these roles, three were included based on the input provided to the author by her US and international military and civilian students in NPS NS4225 (Civil-Military Relations and Transitions to Democracy) class (2015–2018); Matei, "Romania's Transition to Democracy"; Matei, "Romania's Intelligence Community"; Watts, "Control and Oversight"; Matei, "Balancing Democratic Civilian Control."
43 Author's discussions with intelligence, military and police personnel.
44 See Matei, "Romania's Transition to Democracy"; Matei, "Romania's Intelligence Community"; Watts, "Control and Oversight"; Matei, "Balancing Democratic Civilian Control"; Bruneau and Matei, *Handbook of Civil–Military Relations*; Liviu Muresan and Marian Zulean, "From National, through Regional …': Security and Defense Reforms in Romania," in Thomas Bruneau and Harold Trinkunas (eds.) *Global Politics of Defense Reform* (New York: Palgrave Macmillan, 2008), pp. 155–176; Simon Johnson, John McMillan and Christopher Woodruff, "Entrepreneurs and the Ordering of Institutional Reform: Poland, Slovakia, Romania, Russia and Ukraine Compared," *Economics of Transition and Transitional Change*, 10 January 2003, https://doi.org/10.1111/1468-0351.00034; Thanos P. Dokos, *Security Sector Transformation in Southeastern Europe and the Middle East* (Amsterdam: IOS Press, 2006).
45 Muresan and Zulean, "From National, through Regional."
46 Florina Cristiana Matei, "The Media's Role in Intelligence Democratization," *International Journal of Intelligence and CounterIntelligence*, 27/1 (2014), pp. 73–108.
47 "Mattis Praises Romania for Defense Partnership," 20 September 2017, https://dod.defense.gov/News/Article/Article/1317769/mattis-praises-romania-for-defense-partnership/. Romania pledged to reach 2 percent of GDP in 2018 for NATO. In addition, Romania would add more soldiers to the 700 troops on the NATO-led Resolute Support mission in Afghanistan that provides training, advice and assistance to local security forces. Mutler, "Minister Says Country Facing Cyber-Attacks."
48 GardaWorld, "Romania Country Report: Executive Summary," www.garda.com/crisis24/country-reports/Romania.
49 George Visan, "Romanian Defense and Security in an In-Depth Perspective," Romania Energy Center Research Paper, June 2016, p. 3, www.roec.biz/wp-content/uploads/output/2016/06/ROEC_George_Visan-Romanian_Defense_and_Security_EN-__output.pdf.
50 Ibid.
51 Freedom House, *Nations in Transit 2018: Romania*, 11 April 2018, www.refworld.org/docid/5b3cc273a.html.
52 Visan, "Romanian Defense and Security," p. 3.
53 Visan, "Romanian Defense and Security."
54 Bruneau and Matei, *Handbook of Civil–Military Relations*; Matei, "Romania's Transition to Democracy"; Matei, "Romania's Intelligence Community"; Watts, "Control and Oversight"; Matei, "Balancing Democratic Civilian Control."
55 Freedom House, *Nations in Transit.*
56 Romania Insider, "Romania Creates Parliament Commission to Change National Security Laws," 19 April 2018, www.romania-insider.com/parliament-commission-national-security-laws/.
57 European Commission, "Assistance to Bulgaria and Romania under the CVM," https://ec.europa.eu/info/policies/justice-and-fundamental-rights/effective-justice/rule-law/assistance-bulgaria-and-romania-under-cvm_en.
58 Jennifer Hauser and Laura Smith-Spark, "Anti-Government Protesters and Police Clash in Romania," CNN, 11 August 2018, https://edition.cnn.com/2018/08/11/europe/romania-protest-intl/index.html; AGERPRES, "Romanians from Abroad to Gather in Bucharest: Rally in Piata Victoriei Announced on Social Media," 10 August 2018, www.agerpres.ro/english/2018/08/10/romanians-from-abroad-to-gather-in-bucharest-rally-in-piata-victoriei-announced-on-social-media–158677; *Deutsche Welle*, "Romanian Expats Return Home for Major Anti-Government Protest, Clash with Police," 10 August

2018, www.dw.com/en/romanian-expats-return-home-for-major-anti-government-protest-clash-with-police/a-45034900; Kit Gillet, "Violence Erupts as Tens of Thousands Protest Corruption in Romania," *New York Times*, 10 August 2018, www.nytimes.com/2018/08/10/world/europe/romania-protests.htm l; *Deutsche Welle*, "Mitingul Diasporei: 100.000 de protestatari şi incidente violente serioase," 11 August 2018, www.dw.com/ro/mitingul-diasporei-100000-de-protestatari-%C8%99i-incidente-violente-serioase/a-45041717.

59 Radu-Sorin Marinas, "Romania's President Removes Chief Anti-Corruption Prosecutor," Reuters, 9 July 2018, https://uk.reuters.com/article/uk-romania-corruption/romanias-president-removes-chief-anti-corruption-prosecutor-idUKKBN1JZ0MK; www.hotnews.ro/stiri-esential-22307168-proteste-pentru-sustinerea-dna-laurei-codruta-kovesi-anuntate-bucuresti-mai-multe-orase-sub-sloganul-tudorele-pleaca-hotii-tai.htm; www.hotnews.ro/stiri-esential-22479469-protest-anun-azi-bucure-dup-decizia-ccr-privind-revocarea-efei-dna.htm; https://stirileprotv.ro/stiri/actualitate/protest-anuntat-miercuri-seara-in-piata-victorie-dupa-decizia-ccr.html.

60 AP News, "Israel Protests to Romania after Tourists Beaten by Police," 13 August 2018, https://apnews.com/5a3c051f83444b638dea8ef7319b28dc; Digi24, "Explicaţiile Jandarmeriei după violenţele de la miting: Am acţionat defensiv," 11 August 2018, www.digi24.ro/stiri/actualitate/evenimente/jandarmeria-da-explicatii-dupa-violentele-de-la-mitingul-diasporei-978800; Ziare, "Jandarmii raniti la protestele din Piata Victoriei se recupereaza: Doi din trei vor fi externati astazi"; *Deutsche Welle*, "Romania: Tens of Thousands Protest for Second Night Running," 12 August 2018, www.dw.com/en/romania-tens-of-thousands-protest-for-second-night-running/a-45049450; SBS News, "Hundreds Injured in Romania Protests," 11 August 2018, www.sbs.com.au/news/hundreds-injured-in-romania-protests; www.digi24.ro/stiri/actualitate/evenimente/usr-cere-demisia-ministrului-de-interne-si-a-sefului-jandarmeriei-romane-978536; Cristina Scutaru, "Protest 10 august: manipulare cu diaspora şi Vama Nădlac, DCNews, 6 August 2018, https://m.dcnews.ro/protest-10-august-manipulare-cu-diaspora-i-vama-nadlac_606394.html; Bogdan Bolojan, "Protest 10 august. Ovidiu grosu: revoluţia a fost deja declarată: dacă făceam ceva ilegal, mă arestau deja. Exclusiv," Stiri Diaspora, 7 August 2018, www.stiridiaspora.ro/protest-10-august-ovidiu-grosu-revolu-ia-a-fost-deja-declarata-daca-faceam-ceva-ilegal-ma-arestau-deja-exclusiv_3473.html; Iulia Moise, "Dezvăluiri de ultim moment despre mitingul din 10 august. terorism urban la Bucureşti?", EVZ, 13 August 2018, https://evz.ro/miting-10-august-chris-terhes-terorism-urban-antifa.html. Some 452 people were injured, of whom 70 were hospitalized, including 3 gendarmes.

61 Visan, "Romanian Defense and Security."

62 Ibid., p. 12.

63 Freedom House, *Nations in Transit.*

64 Ibid.

PART III

Fragile democracies: the Philippines and Nigeria

17

THE PHILIPPINES FACE THE NEW PEOPLE'S ARMY

Fifty years in the field

Christopher C. Harmon

The ongoing story of the Filipino Republic's struggle with violent communist extremism has had two interwoven themes: the insurgents' challenge, and the state's effort to survive and thrive as a liberal democracy. The challengers, at times divided and always short of good weapons, have proven incapable of victory, yet after a half-century are still fighting. The republican government, for its part, has shown grit, persistence, and ability to learn, but also occasional incompetence; in this the Philippines may be typical of how free states usually respond to armed internal ideological challengers.

The threat to security: national more than international

As a militant challenger to the status quo, communism had a stutter-start in the Philippines.[1] Its roots in labor movements were fertilized by ideological activists, including communists from China and the United States. Filipino communists always had *some* guidance from Moscow; indeed, the official date of founding for the party in 1930 is 7 November—an intended echo of the month and day in 1917 so important to Russians. The Communist Party of the Philippines (CPP) proved slow to garner popularity, and at times had as few as mere hundreds on its formal rolls. It merged with the Socialist Party by 1946. This was also insufficient; a counterinsurgency campaign by the estimable Defense Secretary-turned-President, Ramon Magsaysay, defeated the party's Hukbalahap or "Huk" army by 1955. By then, Maoist communism, sited so geographically close to the Philippines, had completed its long drive to power on the Chinese mainland, attracting Filipino militants increasingly towards Maoist thinking and Maoist methods.[2] Under the influence of university professor Jose Maria Sison (a.k.a. "Joma"), they set aside all ideological ambiguities, published a constitution, and marked it all with a particular date of late 1968: 26 December—Mao's birthday.

Early cadres faced the predictable problems of domestic law and law enforcement. The party was outlawed in 1932 and again in 1957. There were many natural noncommunist political rivals. More troubling for communist leaders was the reluctance, and even antipathy, in a population that was moderate, Catholic, and pro-democratic. Finally, there were the nasty divisions between communist activists, often on display, and enlivened by fierce rhetorical sallies. The ideological discipline of Vladimir Lenin's Bolsheviks was rarely characteristic of communist movements in these islands. One can see, in the public stridency of the Maoist Sison against the pro-Soviet insurgent military leader Luis Taruc and CPP General Secretary Jose Lava,[3] the natural fear of division that all clandestine drivers towards power have (we recall Chinese obsessions with "splitism").

On the other hand, severe economic inequalities, and corruption and inefficiency in government, were perpetually encouraging radical movements in the Philippines. Land reform efforts were minimal, or token; and labor agitators naturally found common cause in some areas with communist revolutionaries. It was not surprising that party cadres would see close parallels between the revolutionary potential of Filipino peasants and that encouraged and empowered by Mao Tse-tung on the Chinese mainland. Sison's seminal book of 1970, *Philippine Society and Revolution*, may have hidden its author under a pseudonym ("Amado Guerrero") but it repeatedly announced itself as Maoist work, as in the inside cover script about its initial appearance "in mimeograph by the Revolutionary School of Mao Tse tung Thought."[4] From that moment, through today, Maoism has been an ideological weapon that the renewed party steadily uses against leftists favoring other ideological lines, not just rightists and noncommunist rivals in Filipino politics.

Sison's re-founding of the Communist Party came at a low point for revolutionary prospects in his native country. Dissolution of the Huks and the passage of time had left no more than 170 armed guerrillas. Their field commander, Luis Taruc, had quit, and written without embarrassment *about* quitting. To lead a "protracted people's war," Sison found Bernardo Biscayno, an able, dynamic man. The "New People's Army" (NPA) took shape around him. NPA bylaws of 29 March 1969 dictate that "the road of armed revolution is the only road" and, "as Comrade Mao Tse-tung has said, 'political power grows out of the barrel of a gun.'" That gun is to be gripped and aimed by the political party; there would be no "militarists" or "roving rebel bands" or others wandering down "incorrect" paths. Almost incredibly, given Sison's displacement to Holland in 1987 (where he still lives), and the lengthy and unsatisfying run of party fortunes in the Philippines, rank indiscipline or corruption or political deviations are not endemic to the New People's Army. It has varied in strength: from several hundred, to 22,000 or more, to today's 3,000-plus; but it has not collapsed or surrendered. American observers have a propensity to claim that the NPA is merely criminal and has lost its ideological direction, but such claims are rarely supplemented by evidence. Nor is the author persuaded.

While its Maoist ideological compass needle has not varied since 1968 and 1969, the severity of the threat the movement presents to the democratic nation has varied much. The strategic threat to the republic was profound in the 1980s. Much of the country had in-place NPA combatants; forces at platoon or even company strength were often challengers to police and armed services; hundreds of communities were effectively ruled by shadow governments of the CPP/NPA; and larger rural areas showed strong traces of the party's ideological virus. Anti-U.S. feelings, a general popular spirit for change, and contempt for domestic governance by the Ferdinand Marcos regime all gave the communist movement strength. Recruiting was relatively easy, and staffing of guerrilla and terrorist operations was not difficult. "Sparrow" killing teams seemed to enjoy impunity as they slipped about in big cities such as Davao. The Armed Forces of the state and nation were hard-pressed, and most veterans of Army duty agreed that the NPA was the country's major internal threat.[5]

Almost universally, in 1980 or 1985, outside observers of the Filipino low-intensity conflict could not see how the government would prevail against the enlarged "liberated zones" and no-go areas.[6] Then mass graves of purged communist militants came to light.[7] Dread of communist fanatics crystallized in Ross H. Munro's powerful *Commentary* article of December 1985, "The New Khmer Rouge." An educator from party schools who defected advised in a Manila interview that one may trust another account of the brutality and purges—the essay by insider Patricio N. Abinales, "When the Revolution Devours Its Children before Victory" in that author's volume provocatively titled *Fellow Traveler*.

What most checked the communist drive for power was the dramatic rise to the presidency of Corazon ("Cory") Aquino, spouse of a beloved politician who was murdered—probably at Marcos' direction. Her "Yellow Revolution" was among the finest and healthiest moments of late 20th-century politics in Asia. The present author was in the visitor's gallery during a 1986 joint session of the U.S. Congress in which politicians long troubled by Marcos' politics welcomed in the first female president of the Philippines. Their ovation was sustained, and thunderous, and tears ran freely for some. U.S. aid flowed more freely thereafter, but that was less important than the geyser of optimism and idealism among proud Filipinos who came together to make their new political life. Nor did it help the NPA that Muslim leaders in Mindanao were able to strike a 1996 accord with Manila, tendering limited self-governance to certain central and western provinces of that island expanse. This success in pacific politics underscored the New People's Army's status as the main enemy of the state. It meant that state resources could be redirected against that main enemy, further darkening the future of the NPA and diminishing the internal threats to democratic governance in the country.

The real but lesser threat, from the party and its New People's Army, is of the international sort. The ideology of a fighting organization matters deeply since it usually defines means as well as ends. As democratic leaders well know, communists traditionally call for, and often promise, international support to fighting comrades—even if the only deliveries are in rhetorical stores. Luis Taruc and his Hukbalahap fighters dreamed of Soviet-bloc material support in the early 1950s; but if they ever got it, it was insubstantial. The guerrillas were poorly armed and equipped in most areas and in most periods of fighting. U.S. assessment, during this part of the deep cold war, recognized a limited but significant menace to Manila: first because Washington is a treaty ally, and second because of the dangers posed by regional and global communist enterprises inimical to American and democratic causes. None the less the international threat was always seen as one of secondary status and one with a "low-intensity" character. The United States had far more concern—just as it does today—about prospects of North Korean invasion of the south; for decades after 1945 that threat always came teamed with fears of support—for such an action by Pyongyang—from Moscow, Beijing, or both.

In the 1970s, 1980s, and 1990s, security analysts watched for foreign arms deliveries to Filipino guerrillas of the NPA. Twice came attempts to land major shipments from China by boat on Philippine shores; only one delivery succeeded, and only 1000 weapons were salvaged from the lot.[8] Maoist guerrillas and terrorists used mainly what they could steal or buy on the black market. Corrupt units or soldiers did indeed sell arms to their "red" enemies. The general shortage of good arms hobbled operations by the NPA, who were dutifully following the Maoist protracted war in its textbook three phases. Of those, the first begins with propaganda, organization, and small attacks—making logistics requirements minimal. But Mao's phases two and three demand immense amounts of armaments, as well as safe zones to store and refurbish them, and secure space to train soldiers to use them. Phase two is semi-conventional; phase three is a fully conventional war (and an accurate description of how Chinese Maoists won in 1949).

Sison, resourceful in so many ways, must have called out to China, and even Albania—then communist and an ally of Beijing. But if money moved, or words were plentiful, supplies and arms were not incoming. War "stuck" in a gully between phases one and two, and the communists knew it. Any dream of Soviet support had of course passed by the end of the 1980s. And earlier, about 1975, Chinese diplomacy embraced Manila in formal bilateral country relations—placing "revolution" beyond the pale of policy options, at least officially. Thereafter, Chinese support to comradely strugglers for Filipino communism has been limited, rhetorical, and channeled through party-to-party lines.

Today's People's Republic gravely disappoints most foreign revolutionaries, including Filipino Maoists. For all its power, China today only rarely acts abroad to help revolutionaries—e.g. indulging several of Myanmar's current insurgent groups of separatist character. The New People's Army is in a perilously weakened state, and China is not stepping in to bridge the capabilities gap. Outside powers do not and should not perceive an existential threat to national sovereignty from Sison's party or army. And certainly outside analysts, as in South East Asia, see little to no region-wide threat from the attenuated Communist Party or NPA in the Philippines.

Meeting the security challenge with law and policy

The communist Hukbalahap insurgency of the post-World War II years (1946–1955) was defeated by original and good grand strategy, including adjustments of governmental practice and law.[9] It was not only skillful repression of the guerrillas and terrorists but also affirmation of the institutions of the free republic that made the victory. In the eyes of many citizens, the disappointment and discredit of past elections, especially of 1946, was remedied in part by former president Ramon Magsaysay in having his Secretariat of National Defense help supervise balloting. Thousands of Reserve Officer Training Corps cadets were mobilized. As important were the thousands of volunteers who formed units of NAMFREL, the new national movement for free elections. Nuns gained notice, and many others volunteered as generously. These legions of fellow citizens were a most reassuring presence for voters—whether angry at past vote fraud or fearful of imminent militant attacks on voting places. NAMFREL and the government-controlled COMELEC, the Commission on Elections, continue on today in the Philippines. To be sure, electoral fraud may still occur, but no more than in other democracies. The communists' dogmatic and predictable derision of "bourgeois elections" sounds hollow under such conditions. Filipino elections work.

Political leadership was vital to the saving of the post-war republic. Magsaysay himself, the man and the personality, evoked the fresh spirit of affirmative counter-revolution. He had evolved from working-class mechanic to anti-Japanese guerrilla in World War II to anti-communist counter-guerrilla, and then politician of national standing and international repute. His personality won over some prickly political rivals as surely as it did one or two communist assassins sent to stalk and kill him. He was lauded in the world press, pictured in *Life Magazine*, and increasingly famous among Filipinos, whether they were pro-American or not. Charismatic leadership works as well in democratic institutions—not just revolutionary undergrounds. Great leaders bring legitimacy—and insurgency is usually a battle for legitimacy. Charisma and legitimacy are not measured readily; they cannot be put into one side of a balance and weighed against other factors such as campaign money or numbers of voters, yet both have distinctive political and psychological power.

This republic, born in 1946 in an era of global interest in the self-determination of peoples, did defeat its first communist challenger handily in the 1950s, but then went through years of inattention, decline, and drift. Democracy's slide came to parallel the self-assertion of Ferdinand Marcos. The martial law imposed in 1972 came with a new constitution that conveniently collapsed the bicameral legislature into a "national assembly" dominated by Marcos' "New Society Movement." In a classic lesson on the interrelationship between state power and insurgency, the concentration of the former *did not* quell the latter. In fact, the New People's Army grew, and fast, emboldened by the losses of the democratic ethos and democratic institutions. For the republic this political erosion was psychological and functional. Despots often distract their subjects with news of great new achievements, as in material infrastructure; although the Marcos regime drove some such advances, it became better known at home and abroad for damaging democracy, for corruption, for excess.

In the long history of truly democratic polities, emergency powers are sometimes necessary. The U.S. in the early 1860s, the U.K. in the early 1940s, and Canada in 1970 are examples in which moderate statesmen backed by working congresses remained accountable and in good charge during national emergencies, lived under strict temporary measures, and then restored peacetime norms and liberties after the emergency had been dealt with. In Ferdinand Marcos' Philippines this was not the case: a limited NPA challenge elicited martial law, which only added to the new challenges. In the Philippines the Marcos experiment became the Marcos method. Clarion calls about "emergency" were cover for dictatorship: civilians in police forces were suborned to martial direction; the Armed Forces of the Philippines were all but conscripted into the defense of one man's rule.

But while the powers of both Marcos and his communist enemies gathered in the late 1970s and early 1980s, citizens of the Philippines were not quelled. Many flatly refused to accept political dictatorship of the right or the left as a necessary answer to anything. Citizen opposition was a tangible display of what security practitioners always talk of and often hope for: "a whole-of-nation response." In 1984, the rising indignation of citizens was very evident, pressing against Marcos' authority. Elections that year demonstrated general disquiet—even if the regime appropriated to itself most of the offices offered in balloting. For two more years dissent proliferated via healthy civic organizations, and the influence of the Roman Catholic Church with its stolid Radio Veritas. In old Spanish colonial days, had authorities of the church too often aided foreign state power? Not so in the mid-1980s, when the Roman Catholic Church was a very different sort of political actor: a liberal force.[10]

Free-thinkers in the Armed Forces constituted another critical link in the road towards anti-Marcos revolt. Martial law had warped civil–military relations, one of the central piers of sound democratic polities: cronyism and promotion by age and by loyalty to named leaders rather than energy or martial skill were among the regime's sins. Emerging in 1982 as "Reform the Armed Forces of the Philippines Movement," RAM represented military men who were healthy citizens. They captured something optimistic in the officer corps—which was increasingly well-educated, professional, and exposed to wider democratic practices. RAM officers and thousands of others in national uniform declined to be tin soldiers lined up smartly by Ferdinand Marcos. Open mutiny showed itself in several places; and, strangely, masses of citizens then hurried to the aid of the soldiers, physically buffering the uniformed rebels from forcible government reaction. This combined civil–military opposition to Marcos crested in famous moments surrounding the 1986 elections. Popular rebelliousness had the eventual support of Washington as well; the second Ronald Reagan administration shared the citizens' aspiration for lifting the Marcos stain from Filipino democracy.

As all these forces combined, it became possible for Filipinos to close out the unnecessary and destructive martial law period, 1972 to 1986. From then on, however, the dangers of self-assertion by parts of the Armed Forces would dog the polity; rebellion of some kind, large or small, visited the military in July 1986, January 1987, April 1987, August 1987, and December 1989. Such a record becomes a specter: elected officials fear to see it; it may produce confusion and unhealthy deliberations within military ranks; it hands revolutionary propagandists of the left a plum—they can argue that democracy is feeble and ever-ready to fall to a "Bonapartist coup." The right balance in civil–military relations in democracies is never easy, or even permanent perhaps; but to be healthy it must be just, and it must not be transient.

The ethics and vigor of police are vital parts of the response to major security challenges as well. It is a most important moment whenever countering violent political activity is taken out of police hands and given over to martial authorities. The truth of this is demonstrated by the earnestness of Filipino officials and military officers associated with "Bayanihan," the country's penultimate strategic plan for internal peace and security. The strategy was introduced for the years 2012–2016 by General Emmanuel Bautista, Chief of Staff of the Armed Forces when Benigno Aquino III was president. Its commitments were to: "*human* security" and not mere killing of guerrillas; local governments in the "lead" in counterinsurgency as against the armed forces leading; a domestic military posture as protector of the *people*, not only protector of the state; a whole-of-nation approach, including rural economic development as surely as martial operations; and the gradual return of most counterinsurgency duties to the police from the military. In such ways may political and military policy contribute directly to a nation's physical security. *Bayanihan* means "a coming together" and it was liberal, thoughtful, sophisticated.[11]

Recent years have seen fulfillment of only some of these aspirations. Armed forces are still in action against the NPA—and absolutely had the lead in the hard counterinsurgency against Islamists (a) in western and central Mindanao in 2013–2017, and (b) in the important islands just to the west: Sulu and Basilan, especially. Foreign fighters and others clustered around the brothers Maute, the Bangsamoro Islamic Liberation Fighters, the Moro National Liberation Front, the Islamic State in Iraq and Syria, and Abu Sayyaf have all contributed to the deferral of any police lead against insurgency. The Philippine National Police, even with their highly trained Special Action Force (SAF),[12] are neither ready for nor strong enough to handle such well-armed and motivated internal challengers.[13]

Benigno Aquino's years in the presidency ended in mid-2016 with progress but not a conclusion, in this respect; his successor, Rodrigo Duterte, has swung civil–military relations violently to the right since his term opened in June 2016. The bare-knuckle war on drug dealers and drug users, in particular, with its overt invitations to vigilantism, is more brazen and unsettling than anything in Filipino politics since Marcos turned his elected post into a gilded throne. The Duterte "war on drugs" may be popular with some, but discredits Duterte's own police forces and is a virtual repudiation of the rule-of-law principles natural to Filipinos. By October 2017 the president was facing such harsh criticism, at home and abroad, that he announced he was giving the war on drugs over to his Drug Enforcement Agency and keeping the police out of it for the future.

President Duterte carries on now under an announced new internal security plan, "Kapayapaan." In it the Armed Forces of the Philippines clearly have the lead in countering armed political militancy, and under executive authority the Marines and Army have been waging war against Islamists in Mindanao. Defense Secretary Delfin Lorenzana had pledged to "finish this problem (of terrorism) once and for all" by mid-2017;[14] but, like so many earnest counterinsurgency commanders of recent decades in other countries, he was flagrantly optimistic. Yet Duterte's drive, and the unpopularity of insurgents among most Filipinos, suggests little domestic opposition to the concept of military primacy in the kind of national emergency created when Islamists seized and held swaths of the city of Marawi in Lanao del Sur province in May 2017. The national codes themselves permit the military to take the lead when the chief executive hands it to them.

When the comprehensive law for National Police was finalized in 1998 it carried a short but important clause in Title Two permitting martial authority over policing when national emergency seemed to dictate. Then, as he famously does on occasions, Duterte went further than expected, placing the whole land mass of Mindanao under martial law in the summer of 2017, with no indication of when it might be lifted. At this writing in October 2017, martial law thus extends over even the lands and affairs of the existing Autonomous Region in Muslim Mindanao, as well as the mature political forces of the rival Moro Islamic Liberation Front, with whom Aquino III signed the Bangsamoro Accord for a new form of semi-autonomy. Viewed critically, and expressed in language of political psychology or public diplomacy, the new president *might have divided* the fighting terrorists from the mainstream Muslim political leaders who were still committed to negotiated settlement with the central government; but instead *Duterte cast them all together* as inveterate opponents of Manila—which they are not.

Security forces evolve in the contest with the NPA

The growth of Filipino abilities at counterinsurgency has been evolutionary, rarely revolutionary. Periodically, new forces have been invented, and incorporated; but the larger pattern is in long-term learning and gradual enhancement of capabilities, both in low-intensity combat and in the equally important political and psychological sides of such conflict. Yet clearly there is a paradox. Are presidents of the Philippines cursed with long-running guerrilla wars in which military victories are many but so small that political victory eludes the government? Or is each new Filipino president fortunate to inherit security forces with years of experience countering terrorists and guerrillas? The latter is the fairer expression of the situation facing incoming presidents of the late 20th and early 21st centuries. The armed forces' officer corps are highly professional, well-educated, acquainted with the outer world, schooled to protect human rights, and (for the most part) politically balanced. They always need reinforcement on aspects of civil–military relations. They may have too few Muslims in uniform, given the endless "low-intensity" conflicts in the deep south; but, as armed forces go, those of the Philippines are modern, smart, and serious. And they have not shirked the political and military difficulties of fighting unconventional or low-intensity wars within their own country.

Philippines military commanders today enjoy the benefit of multiple forms of light infantry skilled in reconnaissance, intelligence, and pursuit of small enemy units. Usually such forces are central to low-intensity conflict. But another of the reasons for them dates back a century to the U.S. colonial period. United States officers—perhaps reflecting practice in their previous Indian wars at home—saw wisdom in drawing in volunteers from Filipino tribes who had immense skill in local affairs and geography, and who may have harbored distaste for the proximate enemy of Manila at that time. "Scouts" quickly became a bright point for American officers smart enough to know their own ignorance of local terrain—both physical and human. From hundreds of these Filipinos who served well in American-led forces in 1899 and 1900, Scouts became an official subsection of U.S. Army units—50 companies of them fought alongside all-American units against Filipino nationalist countrymen, greatly improving counterinsurgency performance.[15] Scouts were later amalgamated in ever-larger units of their own countrymen, somewhat obviating their original purpose.

But the sense of specialization and virtue-in-smallness returned with Scout units, and specifically Scout Rangers, serving in the Army in the late 1980s and early 1990s. Today there is a "First Scout Ranger Regiment," which trains at San Miguel, Bulacan, and carries on the century-long legend and cultivates the skills known to other special operating forces around the globe, especially U.S. Army Rangers. Drawn from the Army alone, these Filipinos are a treasured national asset and, with Philippines Marines, led the anti-insurgent ground battles of Marawi City in 2017.

Other infantry with specialized training and unique roles have included the Army's "Special Operations Teams (SOTs)." In this conception, introduced in the early 1980s and perfected in that decade, regulars from Army battalions had the opportunity to take special courses befitting them for counterinsurgency—which usually meant combating the NPA or, less frequently, Islamist opponents in the south—and then serve in the field in small teams. SOT personnel had political training that ranged from understanding democracy to understanding Mao's answer to it. They were neither a "strike force" nor a transient patrolling-and-presence force; SOTs were intended as ambassadors to the civilian population, and they embedded themselves within villages—living beside the civilians. They saw themselves as "community organizers" or "community workers," and pictured their efforts as including "development" rather than just military dominance and destruction of NPA forces. A doctrinal handbook stated their concept as "a combination of the triad action of Intelligence, Civil-Military (Psychological) and Combat Operations to undertake the primary objectives of isolating the enemy from the populace. This effort aims to reverse the Maoist practice."[16]

SOT forces thus mimic the techniques of their NPA enemies. Such uniformed grouplets were at the center of the regular Army's efforts in NPA-strong areas of the Philippines from the late 1980s through the 1990s. Until 2016 or 2017—when auditors heard ministers and senior generals of the Philippine Armed Forces speaking proudly of sophisticated counterinsurgency "involving all stakeholders" and as "a whole-of-society effort" to "win the peace"—the speakers were often referring to the mindset and practice of SOT teams working among the people.[17] Today such Army teams often go by a newer moniker: "Peace and Development Teams," but the concept is little changed.

Citizen militias engaged in countering insurgency receive very little attention from foreign analysts but are a key force in counterinsurgency in the Philippines, as in many other countries. Militias—Winston Churchill called his the "Home Guard"—know well and want to protect their home turf against intruding forces. The concept is thus most natural. Over time, citizen militias also make a "renewable" security force, for governments prepared to build and deploy them, as they may feed good men and women into the uniformed permanent security forces. The National Defense Act of 1935 of the Philippines foresaw a professional army of limited size but supported by the spirit and physical mass of the citizenry through varied reserve forces: a formal "Reserve Officer Training Corps" is one variant; another is the less formal yet semi-professional citizen militia. At their best, such civilian forces can be among the most effective of counterinsurgency tools, if judged over time and in many countries. If Mao found strength and revolutionary spirit in "Red Guards," citizen militias may prove as strong against Maoists. Hmong tribesmen in Laos during the U.S./South Vietnamese war against the Viet Cong in Indochina are one early example of success.

The militias of course require professional training and equipment. And their potential for sinning is well known and begins with uncontrollability and abuse of some unarmed civilian opponents. In Colombia, some of the "United Self-Defense Militias" organized to fight communism went off the rails into abuse of the citizenry, malpractice, or the cocaine business. Happier stories include the use of civilian militias called "rondas" against Shining Path

Maoists in Peru. Under President Fujimori, Peruvian authorities were wary of arming villagers; but when the hard-driving executive saw citizens stepping forward, ready to serve *whether or not* the state armed them, the government determined to arm them. Results were excellent—in part because the Shining Path guerrillas were usually minimally armed.

Communist theorists such as Jose Maria Sison wax indignant when describing such "counter-revolutionary" militias; ideologues such as Prof. Sison can only conceive of "people power" working for revolution. They have reason to fear the success of anti-revolutionary militias and the ways village self-defense can aid larger plans for rural reform and development in terrain under insurgent threat. In 1950, American intelligence expert Edward Lansdale and Philippine Defense Secretary Ramon Magsaysay cooperated to create a sort of "land for the landless guerrilla" program. It included not just farming and electrification but self-defense for the villages (barrios or, later, barangays).

This Economic Development Corps is well-known to have undermined communist messaging about oligarchy, democratic paralysis, and oppressive landlords. Accordingly, each generation of communist thinkers led by Jose Maria Sison has been primed to react rhetorically against any creation or use of local pro-government militias; the professor's books and interviews occasionally explode with denigrations of "fascists" and "anti-riot squads" and "rondas" and "provisional strike forces." Nor is the charge of indigenous fascism enough; "Joma" Sison once added (correctly) that some money for the citizen militias was coming from the United States Agency for International Development (U.S.A.I.D.). America's development agency was attacked for such practice in Latin America: the 1972 Costa-Gavras film *State of Siege* depicts development assistance as a mere guise for getting policing experts into the country (Uruguay) to help the indigenous government repress leftists. That is the film's story, inspired by the director's view of the profession and purpose of American Daniel Mitrione, a man who in fact was taken hostage and killed by Uruguayan Tupamaros guerrillas.

Emphasis on citizen militias in the Philippines appears to come and go. One round of systematic work on them in the republic began in 1969. In that year of the New People's Army's creation, the national government introduced the "Home Defense Program." Professional military units helped local citizen volunteers build roads and schools, protected utilities, and did other deeds keeping them in concord with local people. This genre of national service has the moniker "civic action"—a term invented by Edward Lansdale during the Magsaysay administration, and it has ever since been a part of life for the Armed Forces of the Philippines. Home defense meant militias, lightly armed and lightly trained locals ready to be combatants if necessary. The Marcos administration said it hoped to have one for each of the country's 40,000 barrios—a guard of earnest citizens under direction of a noncommissioned officer. These "Civilian Home Defense Forces" were actually created only in especially troubled areas of Luzon and Mindanao, and some of those, ill-supervised, engaged in theft or violence against villagers. A government more interested in effect and less in despotic powers would have extended the system swiftly, for after only three years NPA guerrilla war, terrorism, and hostility were a presence in an as many as 63 of 73 provinces.[18]

The Cory Aquino government, which began with an outstretched hand and wide amnesty for communists, felt circumstances turning sour, and Aquino's government resumed the national war against New People's Army. Revamped, the local village militias reemerged in 1988 as "Citizens Armed Forces Geographical Units (CAFGUs)." Locals were given training by the Army's Special Operations Teams. In the largest sense, these militias are an important addition of manpower to security forces. In 1990, when the CAFGU program was growing, the professional armed forces numbered just 153,000, to which formal reserves added another several hundred thousand, in a nation of over 9 million militarily eligible males. Counter-insurgency is manpower-intensive, and driven by intelligence collection; militias were a help in both ways. In a republican form of government, nothing is so logical as an understanding that citizens must aid in security. Local militias remain a continuity of this Filipino understanding.

The foregoing has illuminated a few special dimensions of the many security forces in the Philippines. These instruments of national power all exist and find use today, in some form or another, in the effort against Maoist insurgency. The specialized forces and instruments help set in place the psychological and political conditions for success. Paralleling such efforts are the more traditional martial units. Said differently: while today the NPA has skilled snipers, saboteurs, and guerrilla fighters who move easily and quietly among the rural people, so does Manila.

The New People's Army Maoist infantry are decreasingly important today. They are never seen in company-size, except perhaps when local civilians are dragooned into temporary and tactical service for a given operation. The Armed Forces of the Philippines units are usually as well-trained, faster-moving due to technical advantages, and better-fed and provisioned. The NPA would be a frightening force if it could conduct naval attacks or shift a force of multiple platoons by sea among islands; they cannot, because the Philippine Navy, Coast Guard, and Marines have craft and riverine commandos that have no sizeable counterpart in the NPA. Manila's Air Force possesses abilities in reconnaissance and signals interception that make ground movement in large NPA formations too dangerous, and where the Maoist forces do hold ground, they may be struck by aerial attack. In Maoist "phase two" warfare, the NPA would be acting like Islamists have in Zamboanga City in 2013 and Marawi city in 2017—infiltrating, preparing, and then seizing and holding territory, if only for weeks or months.

But the NPA threat is not semi-conventional; it is merely lower "presence" and "influence" in innumerable areas throughout the archipelago. The New People's Army cannot mass large forces for decisive attacks without risk of pulverization. Its officers surely long to use geography and guerrilla skills to stage great battles and shift forces within theater, but this cannot be done without logistical and naval assets. Nor can the New People's Army turn to foreign military help; there is none on offer, beyond the financial and political, often from weak or disparate partners abroad. The stamina of the guerrilla organization approaching its fiftieth year in the field is remarkable, given such a balance of forces against it.

National legal evolution

Whether to proscribe a political party or entity for its anti-democratic policy ends is one of the difficult open questions for democratic polities. Nearly every country bans a party or two—but only after deliberations, and rarely permanently. The Communist Party of the Philippines is legal today. And, despite its flagrant practices, the New People's Army is no longer on official "terrorist" lists of the government in Manila (since 2011).

Although Filipino communists and international allies founded their new party openly in 1930, authorities could—and sometimes did—arrest leaders on charges of "sedition" or "illegal association."[19] Modern law in the Philippines allows prosecutions for crimes of violence committed for political ends in at least three realms. There are laws against rebellion. Criminal codes bar such (typical terrorist) acts as extortion, murder, and theft. And most recently, in accord with the expanded practices of many countries, "terrorism" has been banned by name in certain newer laws of the Philippines, including those aimed at criminal money laundering: 2012 saw passage of Republic Act 10168, "Terrorism Financing Prevention and Suppression Act."

Several limits impede state power against its domestic opponents. For one, there is no equivalent of British "Diplock Courts" staffed solely by military judges and conducted with strictly controlled information flows in closed chambers. When the armed services capture an insurgent today, they turn him over to the Philippine National Police, who jail and try him (or her) in civil courts. Second, an older legal tool against insurgency is no longer available: useful, and rightly controversial, it was the "Anti-Subversion Law," Act No. 1700, passed in 1957. This permitted the arrest and prosecution of armed militants and the civilian networks supporting them, the latter being essential engines for full-blooded insurgency.[20] But some charged that the law was too often used against mere dissenters—whose rights must always be guaranteed under "rule of law" principles governing the Philippines. After the rise of Cory Aquino in the Yellow Revolution, Act 1700 was retracted; so from 1992 onward the Communist Party of the Philippines was effectively legal—a dream for party members since the 1930s.

This law ending proscription of the party did something further: it removed shadows over the legitimacy of the National Democratic Front, created in 1973 and now called NDF-Philippines (NDFP). This is the party's above-ground vehicle for running communists for election to public office. The Front has hundreds of thousands of members, and distinguishable sub-organizations such as "Gabriella," an all-women political organization successful in domestic politics. The NDFP's other services include providing capable lawyers who contest the prosecution of insurgents and terrorists of the party and the NPA. Behind the national Communist Party and NDFP are "Barrio Revolutionary Committees," shadow governments that seek to run the villages, sometimes doing so invisibly, sometimes nearly openly, depending on circumstances. This formidable combination of political layers secured many areas of the Philippines to the communist cause in past decades. In certain areas, counter-insurgency strategists sought to break apart this political structure. But the revocation of Law 1700 in 1992 made that too difficult. The Army's handbook, called *Army Concern on Community Organizing for Development*, or ACCORD, clarified the situation for service members: not only is the CPP now legal, but "it follows that the Barrio Revolutionary Committee, the basic political party of the CPP at the barangay [village] level is also legal."[21]

The Filipino nation is thus in the same living dilemma as other democratic peoples—that between freedom and security. The Communist Party by its doctrine and charter is committed to the violent overthrow of the government, as the reasonable citizen knows. But their balancing concern is that no Filipino be arrested and tried solely for his opinions of politics. This legal dilemma manifested itself in political terms in the presidency of Gloria Macapagal-Arroyo. In 2002 she declared all-out war against the New People's Army. Not long thereafter she theorized publicly about prospects for eventually welcoming Jose Maria Sison into some new sort of "national unity" government—an idea he later ridiculed as desperate, a grasp at political support as her own base declined when the 2004 elections were impending.[22]

Of equal significance to the law and security of the Republic of the Philippines are ongoing considerations of granting semi-autonomy to certain of the Moro peoples in central and western parts of Mindanao—traditional Muslim areas. There has been and remains an "Autonomous Area of Muslim Mindanao," achieved by years of elaborate negotiations and continuously dominated by the Moro National Liberation Front. More recent plans—in most respects formalized in 2014—have been to replace that structure with a newer model under different leaders from the rival Moro Islamic Liberation Front. Culture, and especially religion, seems to speak for this reasonable bargain, the Bangsamoro Accord. But any yielding in matters of sovereignty can be dangerous, and contagious. Spain appears frightened by Catalonian moves towards independence. The option of semi-independence was tried for communist insurgents in Colombia by President Andrés Pastrana and ended in his fulsome discredit. It is not being tried by the national governments of Nepal or India as a means of dealing with ongoing Maoist extremism. And it is not seriously suggested as a way of dealing with the New People's Army—nor could it be, as government policy ends are national, not provincial or separatist. Yielding national authority over some NPA-strong region is not ever on the bargaining table in Malacañang Palace in Manila.

A new and significant aspect of national law in the Philippines is the "Human Security Act" of 2007. In contemporary parlance and practice, that phrase suggests that it is not only the government that must be secure but all the citizenry as well—secure in their homes, their rights, their economic futures, etc. "Human security" underscores how rule of law and other civilian expectations are to be maintained even during harsh counterinsurgency campaigning—in which the Army and Marine Corps are continuously engaged in the Philippines. United States Department of State commentaries indicate this 2007 law is the main tool affecting prosecutions for terrorism. As President, Benigno Aquino III was a strong supporter but wanted several amendments, including alterations of the definition of "terrorism" to be more in line with international norms. At least one current government minister suggests that the Human Security Act is too liberal towards revolutionaries, as when it prescribes high financial penalties against anyone making what proves to be a "false arrest" of a suspected revolutionary.

The country wrestles with real problems of proper employment of the legal structure. The U.S. reported in 2013 that the law enforcement system working against terrorism is "under resourced and understaffed," while the justice system is "coupled with widespread official corruption," leading to few investigations and few prosecutions. Four years later, in 2017, the department's *Country Reports on Terrorism* noted that there were no convictions during all of 2016 under the Human Security Act. Massive counterinsurgency efforts in Mindanao have contributed to sidetracking the transfer of martial authorities to national police, the change anticipated in the "Philippine National Police Reform Reorganization Act" of 1998. Legislators aspired to completing the full transition in two years; in 2017 it was nowhere near accomplished. Finally, there is the troubling character of the Rodrigo Duterte presidency: wildly unconventional, unpredictable, and at times contrary to Filipino law and wider democratic practice around the globe. No observers today would argue that civilian police, rather than the military, are leading counterinsurgency, if not also counterterrorism. Ideally, they would be—but, in the face of Marawi City battles and martial law throughout Mindanao, analysts have shelved expectations for any such transition to police primacy.

These legal matters are no mere administrivia. A Marxist/Leninist/Maoist cause enunciated by a founding leader who is still stoking the flames has generated over 40,000 deaths in the Philippines since 1969. The national legal structure for fighting back—with force when necessary and with restraint and transparency whenever possible—is important, and it is malleable. The Marcos interval showed how dramatically a democracy may change in its character. The Duterte presidency is showing, if less dramatically, how the challenges of meeting insurgent force with civilized and superior means is a perpetual trial for democracies. One might have hoped that the NPA would now be defeated—as thoroughly as the Hukbalahap were defeated by Ramon Magsaysay. Instead, a half-century on, the national "trial" in the matter of NPA and CPP power grinds on. At least 3,000 armed guerrillas remain in the field, supported by hundreds of thousands of friendly civilian allies and sophisticated political structures. A negotiated solution, rumored in the first year or more of the Duterte presidency, seems unlikely.

Democracy versus military rule

A five-decade long drama was initiated in 1968 and 1969 by the creation of the Communist Party of the Philippines and its New People's Army. Liberal democracy, secured in the 1950s, overpowered by Marcos and authoritarianism, reemerged and has had great success—but not perfect triumph. There has been a dramatic decline in NPA numbers from a 1980s' apex of over 22,000 to today's scrappy force of 3,000–4,000. Symbolic of the passing of the existential threat to the republic would be continued work towards the enunciated end of national police as leading, countrywide, in counterinsurgency against NPA.

Yet certain causes of communist insurgency remain—especially the concentration of lands and wealth in too few hands. So the party and its guerrilla army endure, generation after generation. The CPP (Maoist) survived the isolation of its founder, Jose Maria Sison, in exile in Holland, as well as the resignation or capture of apparent successor Rodolfo Salas in 1986. A man named Adelberto Silva had a primary role in the party in 2014 and 2015, but no more. Sison remains energetic but distant; Holland may be friendly, but it is a difficult spot from which to rule. As for martial operations, New People's Army leaders have suffered capture. In 1976 the government nabbed the founder, "Kumander Dante" or Bernabe Buscayno. He later abandoned the cause for pacific work in labor and land reform—a principled and widely admired decision.[23] Romulo Kintanar served well in his stead as operational chief of the NPA but was captured in 1992; released, he was killed in an ambush in January 2003. The year 2014 brought yet further disappointments with loss of successor operational leaders Benito and Wilma Tiamzon, a formidable couple caught in Cebu and jailed.[24] Ironically, all these martial and policing successes seem to show what Filipino governors already know: "decapitation" only rarely ends deep-seated insurgency, and the principle applies to the NPA. Operational-level decentralization, archipelagic geography, long fighting traditions, and ideological patience all buffer the New People's Army from the impact of arrests of national communist leaders. "Decapitation" is an alluring option for strategists thinking about "How Terrorist Groups End," but in decades of counterinsurgency it has always been an uncommon result.[25]

Counterinsurgency and political reform must reach more widely, and new ways must be found to discredit the party's overt political front (the NDFP). As the map of violent incidents from 2009 through 2012 demonstrates (Figure 17.1), even under the successful Benigno Aquino presidency, NPA activities declined yet continued. Regularly there were violent instances, and larger armed contacts, in areas from eastern and southern Luzon down through Bicol and the Visayas and elsewhere. Few outsiders realize it, but NPA activism, extortion, and other violence remained fixed in the far south as well: western Mindanao may be known for Abu Sayyaf presence and splinters of Moro groups, but eastern Mindanao, including the environs outside Davos City, show muscular NPA presence. Maoists there draw upon natural resources such as mines and related businesses.

Extortion remains a way of life. Many of the cases of guerrilla violence arise when some courageous citizen, property owner, or businessman refuses to submit to direct warnings. Intriguingly, the country's famous breadbasket and seat of the Hukbalahap insurgency of the early 1950s, south-central Luzon, is among the least "red" Filipino areas. The NPA has kept a central objective at the operational level of war: they resolved to not be confined to Luzon, as the Huks largely were. In the end they are spread about, but with fewer than 4,000 under arms this translates to lack of power in almost all areas of the country. NPA has devolved; it was the primary threat to the nation and is now only one of the primary pests.

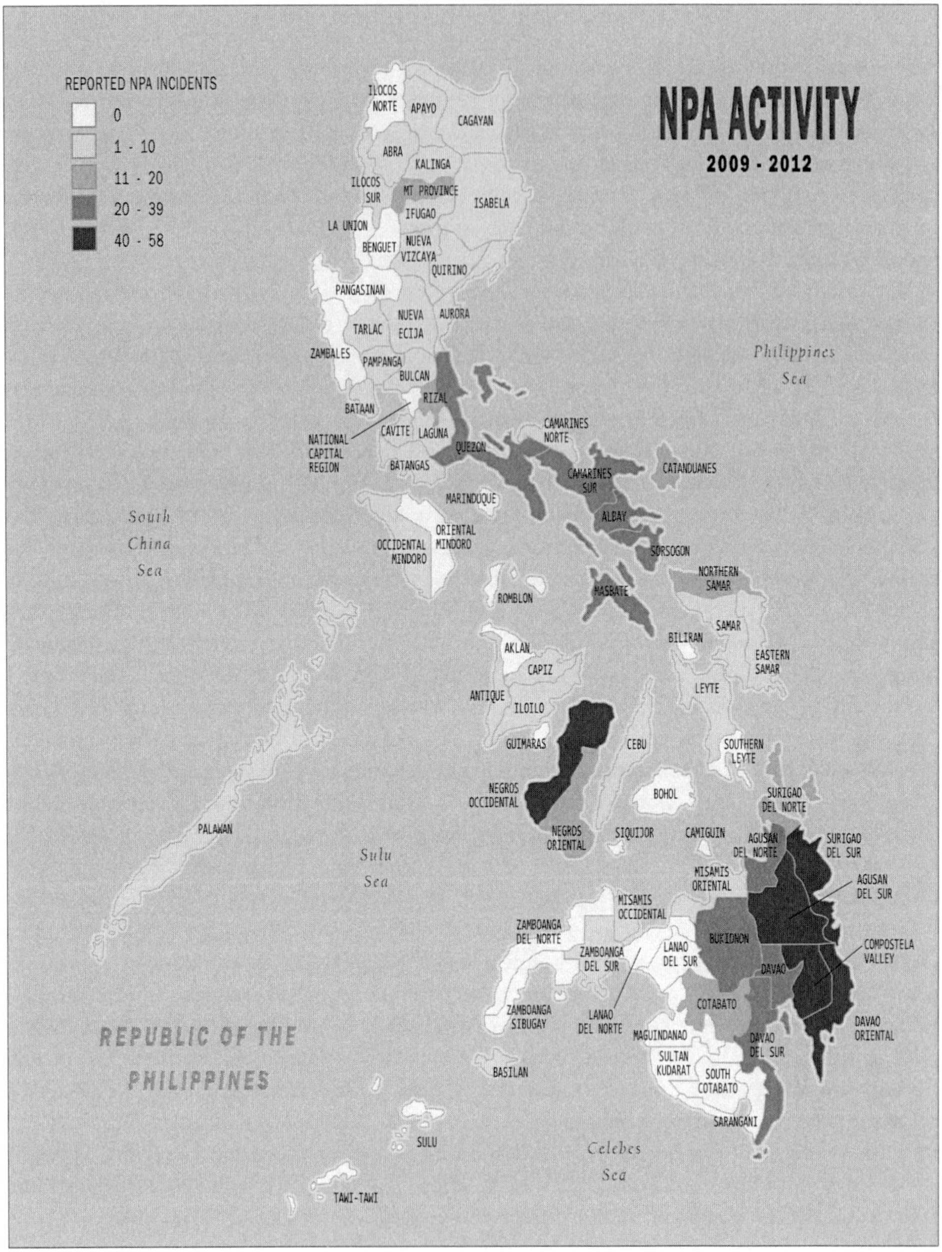

Figure 17.1 New People's Army (NPA) activity, 2009–2012
Source: I created the map in 2013 with Justin Klein and a graphics specialist. Its database came from Richard Ward of the Institute for the Study of Violent Groups, at the University of New Haven, Connecticut.

The years 2016 and 2017 were ambiguous for the NPA and its democratic enemies. The Duterte administration assuming power on 30 June 2016 initially was non-confrontational. Philippine press stories indicated that Sison, from exile, had made friendly contact. There was speculation he might wish to return home. Then Professor Sison began putting it about that he had taught the younger Duterte at university decades earlier. The president thus merited watching as he attempted to free a handful of important NPA and party people from prison but was blocked by the Supreme Court, which determined he had no powers to make the release. It also seemed revealing that when the military's new "Development Support and Security Plan Kapayapaan" was rolled out in January 2017, its designated targets did not include the New People's Army. Abu Sayyaf, Bangsamoro Islamic Freedom Fighters, and other Islamists were marked for defeat under the plan. It could be that the plan was ill-considered; it could be that the new administration wished to concentrate on the deadliest enemies and hoped to reel the NPA in on a peace deal.

No matter: the cease fire between the government and the NPA announced in 2016 did not survive two months of 2017. Incidents, and presidential rhetoric, spiked. As with several past presidents of his country, Duterte apparently learned that peace with the NPA is unlikely, and perhaps even illusory. Indeed, communist forces might take advantage of the new president's full military engagement with the ruins of Marawi City, and the ineradicable Abu Sayyaf Islamists associated with Al Qaeda in the extreme southwest of Mindanao and adjacent islands. Duterte continues to have war on both hands, all complicated by questions of peace-making in the middle.

Notes

1 While this is my description, an interested reader may consult the document collection by Alfredo B. Saulo, *Communism in the Philippines: An Introduction* (Quezon City, PI: Ateneo de Manila University Press, 1990). Also valuable are the writings of Patricio N. Abinales, such as "Filipino Communism and the Specter of *The Communist Manifesto*," in his *Fellow Traveler: Essays on Filipino Communism* (Quezon City: University of the Philippines Press, 2001).

2 An indicator of early warmth between Chinese and Filipino communists is in the memoires of a General Secretary of the party in the Philippines, Dr. Jesus B. Lava. He relates that the Chinese had advisors strategically placed in every party department, and that "The Filipino communists were friendly and comradely toward the Chinese. This was true internationalism in practice. We viewed the anti-fascists struggle in global terms. To us, the Soviets and the Chinese party people were one of us." Jesus B. Lava, *Memoirs of a Communist* (Pasic City, PI: Anvil, 2002), 20.

3 A typical subheading (within a volume by Sison) is "Lavaites are Not Only Careerists But Super-careerists, Conspirators and Double-dealers;" reprinted in Jose Maria Sison, *Defeating Revisionism, Reformism and Opportunism: Selected Writings, 1969 to 1974* (Netherlands: International Network for Philippines Studies, 2013), 168–179.

4 Amado Guerrero (Jose Maria Sison), *Philippine Society and Revolution* (Hong Kong: Ta Kung Pao, 1971). There are many editions of this book by the chairman of the central committee of the CPP.

5 Throughout the 1990s I had the honor of teaching at U.S. military colleges where Filipino officers attended. Nearly all I met made this point, or would do so if asked an open-ended question.

6 Analytical literature was deeply pessimistic, and some experts could not imagine how the republic would prevail. Typically sobering was a research paper covering the growth of NPA numbers, the weaknesses of government forces opposing them, and the sense that "the political war in the countryside is going the NPA's way in many areas." Robert B. Stephan, "Counterinsurgency in the Philippines: Problems and Prospects," CLIC Papers (Langley Air Force Base, VA: Army-Air Force Center for Low Intensity Conflict, October, 1989), 2.

The republic has prevailed, in part due to good clear thinking. In the same year that saw printing of the above research paper, Victor N. Corpus published his monograph on appropriate counter-insurgency operations for beating the NPA, *Silent War* (Quezon City, PI: VNC Enterprises, 1989). The new theory was put into practice by some commanders, such as Emmanuel Bautista (author's interview, Manila, 28 Sept. 2017).

7 An insider's account of the mid-1980s' purges by the CP and NPA is Robert F.B. Garcia, *To Suffer Thy Comrades: How the Revolution Decimated its Own* (Manila: Anvil, 2001). A ranking civil servant in

the Philippines and former CPP member who knew Garcia in the underground, while wishing to remain anonymous, confirms for me the veracity of Garcia's account (interview, Fall 2017).

8 There are many partial or cloudy accounts of attempts by China to aid this revolution. Some clarity was attained in 2012 by a news service collaboration with the ultimate insider, Victor Corpus, who had been an NPA intelligence officer present at the first landing of arms, in northern Luzon, in 1972. When a plane spotted the arms-bearing ship, the Philippine Navy brought in men to interrupt off-loading. A second shipment two years later sank in the South China Sea. Chinese officials at high levels approved the arms aid, but assistance efforts halted in June 1975 when formal diplomatic ties were created between the two capitals; *Gulf News Philippines*, 15 March 2012.

9 The strongest short account of the defeat of the Huks is the monograph by Maj. Lawrence M. Greenberg, *The Hukbalahap Insurrection: A Case Study of a Successful Anti-Insurgency Operation in the Philippines, 1946–1955* (Washington, D.C.: U.S. Army Center of Military History, 1987). And one always does well to study memoirs of principals of the campaign, such as Luis Taruc and Edward Lansdale (advisor to the Filipino government and an intelligence officer of the U.S.). Despite its celebrity, the later book, *In Our Image* by Stanley Karnow, is in my view too polemical to be valuable history.

10 William Chapman, *Inside the Philippine Revolution* (New York: Norton, 1987), ch. 11.

11 "Internal Peace and Security Plan 'Bayanihan'," a lecture by Emmanuel Bautista at the Asia-Pacific Center for Security Studies, Honolulu, HI, 10 Dec. 2014. The general retired in 2014 and graciously permitted me to refer to his work.

12 The SAF (within the Philippine National Police) is built around eight-man teams who undergo tough physical conditioning and much specialized training. Highly selective, they wear Army-style fatigues and black berets with red flashing and a jungle knife insignia. Their base is Camp Bagong Diwa Bicutan in Taguig City, south-east Manila.

13 Of course, insurgency has bubbled in the "Moro" south for centuries, but in the last few decades it had been well managed by the state and some Moro leaders. Several years ago I heard a very senior Army officer declare generally that "there is no way the insurgent groups can threaten the security of our state." But we have seen the temporary occupation of Zamboanga City in 2013, followed by the larger and more persistent Islamist takeover of Marawi in 2017. Even with a hard, focused man in the presidency, suppression of this ISIS-assisted uprising in Marawi has been laborious and destructive. For a short military appraisal see Jasminder Singh and Muhammad Haziq Jani, "The Siege of Marawi City: Some Lessons," RSIS Commentary no. 153/2017 (22 Aug. 2017); accessed 22 August 2017 on the web site of the S. Rajaratnam School of International Studies, Singapore.

The Islamist challenge is a recurring one for the Philippines. There are local drivers of insurgency, especially religion and culture, which have no comparison to the NPA/CPP challenge. There are important intrusions of foreign fighters, allying with local belligerents. Maoist "phase two" warfare (semi-conventional) and the occupation of towns indicate real martial power in the contest—not just terrorism and "bite and flee" attacks.

For the 2017 offensive by Islamists, President Duterte's response was more martial than "whole of society, whole of government." It was hard power, not a mix of soft and hard; and its use of security forces—while necessary and fully justified—will be resented and disturbing for the region for years to come. For the Filipino nation it will be tragic if the cauterizing spirit of the present contest discredits the long-running Bangsamoro peace process. It had all but successfully concluded as Duterte stepped onto the national stage, but during 2017 one hardly heard of it, and few to none were pretending the peace process, aimed at semi-autonomy for some of the Muslim-dominated provinces—was soon to conclude successfully.

14 Frances Mangosing, "AFP's 'Innovative' Plan Aims to Crush Terror Groups in 6 Months," *The Inquirer* (Manila), 9 Jan. 2017. See also Amita Legaspi, "Bayanihan to Kapayapaan: AFP Adopts New Security Plan under Duterte," GMA News Online (Manila), 6 Jan. 2017.

15 John M. Gates, *Schoolbooks and Krags: The United States Army in the Philippines, 1898–1902* (Westview, CT: Greenwood Press, 1973), 212–213.

16 Army of the Philippines, *ACCORD Handbook* (*Army Concern on Community Organizing for Development*) (Makati City, PI: Office of the Assistant Chief of Staff for CMO, n.d. [circa 1995]), 2.

17 Another source on SOT troops is Adolpho B. Espuelas Jr., "Examining the Capacity of the Philippine Army's Enlisted Corps" (Ft. Leavenworth, KS: Command and General Staff College, 2008).

18 In the mid-1970s there were 35,000 army regulars serving in Mindanao and another 15,000 in the government's village defense forces, says the *Area Handbook for the Philippines*, 2nd ed. (Washington, D.

C.: Foreign Area Studies, American University, 1976), 379. Moro rebellion, especially by the Moro National Liberation Front (MNLF), was their main concern, and one of the most troublesome places of the early 1970s was Marawi City.

19 Jose Maria Sison, "Impact of the Communist International on the Founding and Development of the Communist Party of the Philippines," an address in Brussels in May 2006, with the text reprinted in *Crisis of Imperialism and People's Resistance*, ed. Sison (Philippines: Aklat ng Bayan, 2009), 245.

20 The law was used in arrests of the NPA military chief, "Dante," and the political party chief, Sison, in 1976 and 1977 respectively.

21 *ACCORD Handbook*, 4.

22 Jose Maria Sison with Ninotchka Rosca, *Jose Maria Sison: At Home in the World: Portrait of a Revolutionary* (Manila: IBON Books, 2004), 231. Looking back, Sison mocked the president for her seeming reversal. But he understands the maneuver; communists are often themselves experts at working war and peace tracks in parallel and simultaneously.

23 "Bernabe 'Kumander Dante' Buscayno," I Report EDSA 20/20, Philippine Centre for Investigative Journalism, 2 Feb. 2006.

24 One principal in the duo's capture was Gen. Emmanuel Bautista, then Armed Forces Chief of Staff; another was his subordinate in charge of intelligence, Gen. Ano, the 2017 Chief of Staff. As for the Tiamzons, both were released as gestures during ongoing discussion of peace prospects with the NPA.

25 The whole politburo in Manila was arrested in 1950 but the Huks carried on; they had another politburo in their rural fastness! I always discussed decapitation options in my rubric of a half-dozen ways that terrorist groups end in a lecture series of 2003–2006: Sandhurst; hearing rooms of the U.S. Congress; the Pentagon's Office of Net Assessment; the Woodrow Wilson International Center for Scholars. This author's first publication using the rubric was an analysis of "How Al Qaeda May End," *Backgrounder # 1760*, Heritage Foundation, printed on 19 May, 2004 and remaining on the think tank's website; another print form was "What History Suggests about Terrorism and Its Future," my chapter for a volume edited by historians Williamson Murray and Richard Hart Sinnreich, *The Past as Prologue: The Importance of History to the Military Profession* (Cambridge University Press, 2006), 217–246.

18

DEMOCRACY AND SECURITY IN NIGERIA

A history

Robert L. Ostergard, Jr. and Jeffrey A. Griffin

Introduction

For more than 50 years, Nigeria has sought peace and stability in one of the most complex regions of the world. Nigeria faces historical, cultural and demographic issues that few other states face. Nigerians' search for peace and stability has been a fight against themselves, and rarely, if ever, a battle against an external enemy. Like so many other African states, Nigeria's history of colonial occupation and British rule has left the country weak and vulnerable to internal strife. The British system of governance bequeathed by the crown to Nigeria was insufficient to deal not just with the usual complexities of Nigerian ethnic and religious divisions, but also with the system of privilege and favoritism that has promoted further divisions within the state.

While Nigeria has been dealt a bad hand historically, its leaders have also given the country a legacy of brutal repression, underdevelopment, and inequality which has left the country in shambles. After emerging from its colonial period, its military quickly became a political player in the absence of having any true purpose for existence. The military's inability to leave politics to civilian leaders led to the collapse of three Nigerian republics after military coups, and to successive coups that have brought military rule to Nigeria for more years than the country has had civilian rule. While the military has pointed to ineffective and corrupt civilian leaders as the rationale for ongoing military rule, the military has shown itself to be equally corrupt and ineffective at governance. In short, Nigeria has never had effective leadership free of repressive measures and corruption. Consequently, Nigeria's democracy and security position have the country teetering on the brink of being a failed state.

Background

In order to understand Nigeria's security condition one has to appreciate its geographic, demographic and historical background. Located on the Gulf of Guinea in West Arica, Nigeria borders Benin, Cameroon, Chad and Niger. While it is not Africa's largest country geographically, it is the largest by population (181,562,000); and in 2014, it surpassed South

Africa as the continent's largest economy, with an estimated 2015 gross domestic product (GDP) of $1.1 trillion. As Africa's most populous country, it is also one of the most demographically complex. Nigeria is a young country; the median age of both its men and women is 18. Nigerians belong to more than 250 ethnic groups that speak over 500 indigenous languages. The Hausa and Fulani (29 percent of the population), the Yoruba (21 percent) and the Igbo (18 percent) groups have been the most notable and influential in Nigeria's post-colonial history. Nigeria is also a religiously complex country; 50 percent of the population is Muslim, 40 percent Christian and another 10 percent comprises indigenous belief systems. Geographically, Northern Nigeria is predominantly Muslim, while the southern parts of the country are mostly Christian. In the middle region, substantial Christian minorities in Muslim majority states have led to some of Nigeria's most violent social clashes across its post-colonial history.

Despite the country's substantial economic wealth and oil reserves (8th largest in the world), Nigeria's people suffer from some of the most crippling poverty on the African continent. While Nigeria has earned billions of dollars from decades of oil production, little of that money has been invested to diversify the country's economy or develop its population. Its GDP per capita in 2015 was $6400, ranking it 157th in the world, while nearly 61 percent of the population live in poverty (earning less than $1 per day).[1] Nigeria also suffers from an unequal level of development that has provided substantially more resources for the south than for the north. Nigeria's poverty and development challenges are also indicative of governance and corruption problems that have been endemic in its history.

The richness and diversity of Nigeria's history and people have been at the center of its troubled post-colonial governance issues. Indeed, the country's rulers have encountered significant difficulty in accommodating Nigeria as a highly divided society. Some of Nigeria's issues date to the colonial period, but certainly the post-colonial period has exacerbated them and even introduced new ones to the country. In the post-colonial period, Nigerian society has been divided on economics (haves vs have-nots; oil producers vs the revenue dependent), class (traditional rulers and elites vs colonial meritocratic principles), geography (north vs south), and ethnicity (Hausa-Fulani in the north, Yoruba in the west, and Igbo in the east). Along with these established chasms within Nigerian society, the most dominant division in the country is on religious identification (Muslim vs Christian). In fact, by 2006 a majority of Nigerians identified not as a nation of Nigerian people, but by their religious group.[2]

If there has been one constant in Nigeria's history over the past 150 years, it is foreign influence that has had a definitive impact on the country's political, economic, and social structure. During the mid-19th century, Christian missionaries, European traders and imperialists exerted pressure to abolish the use of slaves in the production of palm oil and kernel in the region.[3] The British decision to abolish slavery in 1807 led to a new era of gunboat diplomacy characterized by the use of naval power to negotiate favorable treaties and benefits for British traders, missionaries, and explorers. The treaties stipulated the end of the slave trade by local rulers; the adoption of normalized trade practices that did not trade in slaves; customs duties; and subsidies the British paid to local rulers for giving up the slave trade.[4] The new relationships fundamentally restructured the Niger delta region by weakening control of local rulers.

The introduction of Christian missionaries also had a lasting impact on the region. The local rulers had mixed reactions to the missionaries. Some welcomed the missionaries as a way their children could be educated and learn English, which would facilitate commercial interests. Some also hoped that allowing the missionaries would improve overall relations with the British crown, which would have helped with ongoing internal local struggles. For these exact same reasons, other local rulers shunned the introduction of missionaries to the region.[5] Despite British influence, local customs did not disappear as the British preferred a system of indirect rule that left in place local customs and local leaders who had positions of influence inside British-controlled areas. However, as British influence and imperial control gained in strength, the expansion of Christianity also grew.

Up until governor Lord Frederick Lugard's consolidation of Nigeria as a colony in 1903, private companies exercised the greatest influence as the British expanded inward from the coastal regions of West Africa, from the Niger delta in particular. Some 100 years prior to Lugard's conquest, the area that would become the protectorate had been consolidated through war launched by the Fulani sheikh Uthman dan Fodio, a Sufi Qadiriyya Muslim. While the war had imperialist overtones, it was also both theologically a classic jihad to purify Islam and an attempt to impose the administration of law and justice in the areas under Uthman's control.[6] Most of the Hausa leaders that the jihad targeted in the area had already been believers and practitioners of Islam. The resulting Uthmani dynasty took Sokoto as its capital, and the Sokoto caliphate stood as the primary resistance to Lugard's conquest.[7]

In 1902, Lugard made overtures to incorporate the caliphate into British rule without resorting to bloody, protracted war.[8] Caliph Attahiru rejected Lugard's overture, saying:

> From us to you. I do not consent that any one from you should ever dwell with us. I will never agree with you. I will have nothing ever to do with you. Between us and you there are no dealings except between Muslims and the unbelievers, war, as God Almighty has enjoined on us. There is no power or strength save in God on high.[9]

The rejection represented, in words, a strong renunciation of British control in the protectorate. Despite Attahiru's rhetoric, Lugard quickly took control of Sokoto, and Attahiru fled. British forces caught up with him and killed him.[10]

For a long time, under British rule, the official British policy regarding the Muslim north was to remain neutral amongst the different Muslim brotherhoods present there. But the very nature of British indirect rule meant that the British had to favor a group that tended to support its governance arrangement. In Northern Nigeria, the dominant form of Islam is Sunni, but the two most important brotherhoods are Sufi – the Qadiriyya and the Tijaniyya. The Qadiriyya, of which Uthman dan Fodio was a member, had created the existing political and legal system after his jihad. Thus, the Muslim ruling class, the *Masu Sarauta* (possessors of governance), had also descended from the Sokoto caliphate and was Sufi Muslim.[11] As such, the principles of British indirect rule allotted a certain acceptance and defense to the Qadiriyya, which helped entrench the Qadiriyya firmly in power.[12]

During the 1930s, a reformist Tijaniyya movement spread from the Nigerian city of Kano to other areas of the north.[13] However, the British perceived the Tijaniyya as dedicated to the resistance to the state. Other non-Sufi Muslims, Sunnis and millennial Mahdiyya, joined with the Tijaniyya in their resentment of the Qadiriyya, who they increasingly perceived as elitists. By the late 1930s and 1940s, violent clashes erupted as the Qadiriyya tried to consolidate Northern Nigeria while the Tijaniyya spread further spread in the region.[14]

The British colonial administration helped solidify ethnic and religious identity in Northern Nigeria through indirect rule. At the same time, the restructuring of the Nigerian economy and the introduction of a governing bureaucracy put average northern Muslims at a disadvantage. Muslim Quranic education dominated schools located in the north by the 1920s.[15] But fear that Muslims would not have a role in Nigeria's economy prompted

Muslim leaders to encourage people to attend Western-oriented schools by the 1930s and into the 1940s.[16] Nigeria's economy underwent changes; Europeans and other foreign interests promoted investment, while indigenous Nigerians established interests in manufacturing and trading.[17]

The 1950s also brought additional external influence. Not only did Nigeria become an investment target, but external forces also came to Nigeria to strengthen aspects of its cultural identity. That external influence strengthened in the post-independence period. The Islamic world sought to strengthen Islamic identity: Iran, Iraq, Saudi Arabia, and Libya provided teachers and materials, missionaries, and money to support Nigerian Islam.[18] More controversially was Saudi Arabia and Egypt's influence in Nigeria. The Saudis provided substantial numbers of scholarships for students to attend Arab and Muslim schools in Egypt and Saudi Arabia, students who brought back with them Wahhabi influences. A significant Wahhabi presence in Northern Nigeria resulted. There is disagreement about the nature of the influence, which was in fact mixed. For instance, Winters implies that the Wahhabi influences were more Saudi (and thus a more radicalized form of Islam), while Lapidus directly contradicts this proposition, arguing that the Wahhabi influence resembled other Wahhabi influences in West Africa, which tended to be reformist instead of radical.[19] Nonetheless, into the 1970s, greater contact from the Arab Middle East further spread Islam and Arabic instruction while opening greater ties between Nigeria and the Islamic world overall. Greater contact also helped solidify the gulf between Westernized Muslims and tradition-oriented Muslims.

Politically, Nigerian independence was on the horizon, and an ethnically dominated tripartite federal system emerged: the north (Hausa-Fulani dominated), the west (Yoruba dominated), and the east (Igbo dominated). While traditional leadership and belief systems helped stymie the creation of an independent state, the emerging federalist system promoted ethnic identities.[20] The 1954 constitution gave considerable governance power to the regions, leaving foreign policy and large-scale economic issues, such as transportation, to the federal government. Political parties that formed promoted themselves as representations of the major ethnic groups.[21] In Northern Nigeria, the political parties that emerged reflected the dangerous conditions that prevailed between the Qadiriyya and Tijaniyya. The Northern Peoples' Congress, under the Sardauna (Crown Prince) of Sokoto, Alhaji (Sir) Ahmadu Bello, attempted to consolidate the legitimacy of the Masu Sarauta, constructed around the dominance of the Qadiriyya and the legacy of the Sokoto caliphate.[22] Later, after independence, the most serious challenge to this hegemony came from formation of the pro-Tijaniyya Kano People's Party in 1963. While Northern Nigerian identity split in the face of competing Islamic identities, when Britain granted Nigeria its independence the conflict in Nigeria elevated to reflect the tripartite federal division under the constitution.

Post-independence Nigeria

Britain granted Nigeria its independence in 1960, and attention immediately went from the range of cleavages across the north and south to the tripartite division implemented under the constitution. A new economic factor – oil – also played a role in consolidating the emerging differences between the regions. The north held political dominance, while the south held economic power based on oil as the new domestic economic engine.

As Diamond notes, antagonisms amongst the tripartite groups made Nigeria's government dysfunctional.[23] The British Westminster system of governance entrenched ethnic divisions. Southern Yoruba and Igbo had gained privilege and status under British rule, giving them great advantages in education, trade and the economy. The Hausa-Fulani elite dominated the north and the formal political aspects of governance. Like many post-independent African states, Nigeria's politicians were their own worst enemies. Corruption, intolerance, distrust, brutality and incompetence turned the first elections and the subsequent governing of Nigeria into a fraud-ridden struggle for power.[24] As a result, Nigeria's first republic succumbed to the greatest threat that most sub-Saharan African states faced after independence – its own military.

The political strength of the north and resistance to federal rule in the West led to a bloody and violent military coup d'état in 1966 that left Nigeria with a much more contentious political scene.[25] In the coup, military officers assassinated most of the post-independence northern leadership, including the Prime Minister, Abubakar Tafawa Balewa, and the Sardauna of Sokoto, Alhaji Amadu Bello. Coup leaders also killed four of the highest military officials in the north. Targeting of the northern leaders led to the widespread popular conception that the coup was an Igbo conspiracy.[26] The blowback against the Igbos and Christians living in the north led to a mass exodus from that region. Subsequently, Igbos seceded from the Nigerian state and established the state of Biafra, dominated by Christians. General Yokubu Gowon, who came to power after a second military coup in 1966, was able to defeat the attempted Biafran secession despite external support for Biafra from France, South Africa and Portugal.

The cost of retaining the Nigerian state was high. On a human scale, the war killed up to 1 million people and showed the world the horrors of poverty and war in West Africa. Additionally, during the civil war period, the military also grew significantly in numbers. Prior to the war Nigeria had an army of about 10,000 soldiers; after the war 250,000 soldiers made up Nigeria's army.[27] Without much of a purpose in the post-war period, the Nigerian military became the dominant and most corrupt political player in the country, while also becoming the supreme veto player in Nigerian politics. Gowon himself succumbed to the military in a coup it carried out against him in 1975. Another military coup in 1976 ousted the government, and Olusegun Obasanjo became the new military dictator. To his credit, Obasanjo established the framework that transitioned Nigeria to a democracy once again.

In 1979 Shehu Shagari, a northern Muslim, was elected president of Nigeria's Second Republic. His time in office was short, but displayed the immaturity of Nigeria's political environment. For Nigeria, Shagari's National Party of Nigeria had little concern for building the country's democracy, but instead saw Shagari's election as an opportunity to build its own wealth and to launch a power grab against its opponents.[28] Even frustrated northern politicians, who were not party elites, advocated for change. The military stepped in and overthrew Shagari in 1983, ushering in a 15-year period of military rule (1983–1998) and a period of religious tension that continues to this day.

A transformation of religious tensions during both Shagari's presidency and during military rule occurred in Nigeria as a result of the government's perceived favoritism toward the Muslim north and southern Christian reaction to it. The general fear was that the government was moving toward turning Nigeria into an Islamic state.[29] Many government appointments were given to Muslims, money went to support the annual hajj to Mecca, and support was given to anti-Christian literature and sermons by Islamic writers.[30] Islamic youths and youth movements became more radicalized and drew support from Libya, Saudi Arabia and Iran.

In 1988, a reissued pamphlet originating in a 1935 Cairo publication provided guidelines for punishing and humiliating Jews and Christians, referring to them as third-class citizens.[31] A book entitled *Black Gold and Holy War* proclaimed that there were only three ways to deal with non-Muslims: "(1) they must be converted, (2) they must be subjugated, (3) they must be eliminated."[32] The decision to ban Salman Rushdie's novel *Satanic Verses* (1988) gave further credence to Christian fears that the Nigerian government was favoring Islamic causes, and even kowtowing to Iran's Islamic agenda.

Another central issue at the heart of the Christian–Muslim divide concerned education across Nigeria. Universal Primary Education (UPE) had been implemented in the 1970s, and provided support to Christian mission schools. With the influx of oil money, northerners argued that there was no need for the mission schools, and that oil could finance schools that taught national values.[33] In response, northern politicians saw the education system as promoting the influence of Western Christian values while diminishing Islamic values.[34] Muslims firmly opposed variants of Western education that did not teach Arabic and Islamic religious information. In doing so, they insisted that teaching be done in Hausa, that the influence of Christianity be reduced in northern schools, and that indigenous religions be banned.[35] As the Muslim north became more integrated into a national Nigeria, it promoted Islam as a path for social order and organization; such arguments also received a sympathetic hearing in the Yoruba west.[36]

After a number of missteps in the transition to democracy, the military finally turned control of Nigeria over to a democratically elected government led by the former military dictator Olosegun Obasanjo. By the end of military rule in 1998, Nigeria had become an international pariah for its rampant human rights abuses and for its level of corruption, often deemed some of the worst in the world. The military rigged the 1999 elections in favor of Obasanjo, and did so in such a blatant way that international observers, including former US President Jimmy Carter, left the country so as not to be identified in any way with support for the electoral process.[37]

Despite its rocky start, the Fourth Republic has been a strong turn in favor of democratic processes that have now seen the succession of Obasanjo by peaceful means three times since the transition. In 2007, Umaru Musa Yar'Adua succeeded Obasanjo as president. When Yar'Adua died in office in 2010, Vice President Goodluck Jonathan ascended to the presidency without incident; but his reelection in 2011 was again marred by vote rigging.[38] In 2015 the incumbent, Jonathan, for the first time in Nigeria's history, lost the election to an opposition party candidate – former military dictator Muhammadu Buhari. Obasanjo, Yar'-Adua and Jonathan had been members of the People's Democratic Party; Buhari was a member of the All Progressives Congress, a merger of Nigeria's three largest opposition parties – the Action Congress of Nigeria, the Congress for Progressive Change and the All Nigeria People's Party.

While the People's Democratic Party controlled Nigerian politics for 15 years, its governing was not without problems and challenges. Chief amongst them were poverty, resource management, corruption and an increasingly violent Islamist agenda that emerged in the 2000s. Those challenges continue to affect the nation.

Security in Nigeria's Fourth Republic

Poverty

Nigeria's Fourth Republic began with the political, economic and social baggage acquired over the prior 150 years. At the top of the government's list should have been the political and economic problems faced by all Nigerians, and particularly Northern Nigerians. By most indicators, Nigerians, though living in the most populous and one of the wealthiest (in natural resources) countries on the African continent, have not enjoyed the benefits of their wealth. Nigeria's impoverishment at the hands of its own government has not been a general impoverishment across the country. Northern Nigeria has borne the cost of the developmental retardation brought about by the nation's politicians. Testifying before the US House of Representatives Subcommittee on Africa, Global Health, Human Rights, and International Organizations and Subcommittee on Terrorism, Nonproliferation, and Trade, US Assistant Secretary of State for African Affairs Linda Thomas-Greenfield explained that:

> Northern Nigeria has long lagged behind the south in education and economic development. In 2011, Nigeria's national unemployment rate was 24 percent, but the unemployment rate in six of the twelve far northern states exceeded 30 percent. In 2010, Nigeria's rate of absolute poverty was 62 percent, but in eight of the twelve far northern states the figure exceeded 70 percent. Of Nigeria's estimated 10.5 million children who do not attend school, 92 percent are estimated to be in the north.[39]

Resource management

At the heart of Nigeria's poverty crisis has been the country's inability to manage its own resources for the benefit of the Nigerian people. As a large oil producer, Nigeria has reaped billions of dollars in revenue from the global oil markets. While historically Nigeria had an agriculturally based economy, after the discovery of oil in the 1950s oil production became the dominant force behind Nigeria's economy. In fact, oil has been generally become the only force in Nigeria's economy, as other sectors faded in comparison to the oil sector. Oil comprises 70 percent of the Nigerian government's revenues, 80 percent of its total exports, and 90 percent of foreign exchange earnings.[40] While recent downturns in the oil markets have hurt Nigeria's economy, the country's long-term dependence on the oil sector and its failure to develop other economic sectors have damaged the country's economic stability by making it subject to fluctuations in a single economic market.

Corruption

At the intersection of Nigeria's oil industry and its political oversight has been the problem of corruption and theft. In a modern context, analysts and business people perceive Nigeria as one of the most corrupt political systems in the world. Transparency International, an independent corruption-monitoring organization, ranked Nigeria 136th out of 168 countries, with a score of 26 out of 100 on its Corruption Perceptions Index (with 0 being highly corrupt and 100 being clean of corruption).[41] The country's reputation for corruption has had an impact on its general political and economic climate. The World Bank's Ease of Doing Business measure ranked Nigeria 170th out of 189 countries, indicating that corruption, bureaucracy and other obstacles to the private sector exist at a high level in the country.[42]

While President Muhammadu Buhari promised during his 2015 campaign and during his administration to crackdown on corruption, doing so has been a difficult task. Nigeria's political system has been the perfect storm for the breeding and festering of a corrupt environment. In part, elites in Nigeria have for decades encouraged and participated in the system of corruption that emanates from the construction of the Nigerian state itself. Highly concentrated political, economic and bureaucratic power, combined with an opportunity for large-scale economic growth, provides the basis for corrupt systems.[43] In Africa and other regions of the world, corruption has manifested in four ways: cost-reducing corruption (civil servants reducing regulation costs); cost-enhancing corruption (civil servants increasing costs for businesses); benefit-enhancing corruption (civil servants permitting more public benefits to be given to people than permitted, and then taking a cut of the excess benefits); and benefit-reducing corruption (civil servants illegally appropriating benefits due to citizens for themselves).[44]

The issue of corruption has multiple roots that make Nigeria's problems of poverty, resources and corruption a vicious circle. A number of structural problems promote Nigerian corruption. Low wages across all sectors of Nigeria's economy make taking payments and bribes attractive, particularly to low-paid civil servants. The lack of economic development in Nigeria across its modern history also makes alternative means to earn a living difficult to find and cultivate. Lack of investment opportunities may also promote a climate where corruption is used to amass investment capital in order to start businesses. Lack of social safety nets also provides motives and incentives. While many of these problems are linked to formal governing issues, Nigerian corruption also has cultural roots.[45]

As discussed previously, loyalty to one's ethnic group or religion in Nigeria is a strong incentive that opens political cleavages in the country. It also opens up problems of economic dysfunction linked to corruption. Identification with one's ethnic group may override any sense of national obligation or identity. Moreover, loyalty to one's family is paramount. The better one does financially, the more one is expected to do for one's family.[46] While the Nigerian people voice displeasure at corruption, they are also less likely to fault public officials, thinking of them as successful when they steal from public coffers.[47] Thus, a culture of corruption exists that is entrenched, not just in Nigeria's political and economic institutions but also in social and cultural structures that strongly emphasize sub-national identities.

The impact of corruption is more than just a perceptual problem. In March of 2016, the Nigerian National Petroleum Corporation (NNPC) failed to pay the government over $16 billion in revenues in a suspected fraud case.[48] While this is the most recent problem with the NNPC, the corporation has been involved in large-scale problems of corruption and fraud that go back years. Under President Goodluck Jonathan, an audit of the NNPC's books found $1.48 billion that the corporation did not pay to the government.[49] Such problems with the NNPC predate the 1999 transition. Likewise, the theft of oil by the Movement for the Emancipation of the Niger Delta (MEND) has cost the government millions of dollars since the transition.

At the intersection of Nigeria's political and economic issues of poverty, resource management and corruption has been a violent backlash in Nigerian society that the government has often dismissed, in both the north and south, as the work of criminals and gangs. That backlash has flared up during Nigeria's more than 50 years of post-independence history. During its post-independence period, the military has led the state and cared little about issues of poverty and human rights. In fact, the Nigerian military has too often been the greatest security threat facing the people and the state as its role expanded from being the country's premier security institution to being the country's premier political force. In the Fourth Republic, Nigeria's corrupt military has taken on a more traditional role as protector of the state and constitution, though it is important neither to overstate that role nor to dismiss the military's current political role.

Violence and security in Southern Nigeria

While the 1980s saw an upswing in religious conflict in the north, the Niger Delta became the first global focal point for conflict in the post-independence period. Most conflicts in the

Niger Delta pitted rival ethnic communities against each other. By 2003, the delta had become a conflict zone over the sharing of resources, the haves vs the have-nots.[50] After the 1999 transition, the number of insurgent groups and criminal gangs burgeoned to at least 40, while the Nigerian government appeared increasingly weak in being able to protect its oil infrastructure and resources in the delta region.[51] By 2006, the activity in the delta region became more violent and radicalized when the Movement for the Emancipation of the Niger Delta claimed responsibility for the kidnapping of four foreign oil workers.[52] Subsequent attacks on oil pipelines and additional kidnappings reduced Nigeria's oil output by as much as a third.[53]

Global attention further turned to the delta region when piracy became a more prominent method of attacking the government's oil interests. In 2009, President Yar'Adua proposed amnesty for MEND members; following Yar'Adua's death, President Jonathan, who was from the Niger Delta's Bayelsa state, formalized the amnesty program. He infused billions of dollars into development projects in the delta region and gave patronage to local insurgent leaders.[54] With the election of President Buhari in 2015, insurgent leaders feared that his anti-corruption campaign would end the amnesty program, as Buhari wanted to move the government away from such deals. Attacks in the delta region resumed in January 2016 in what appears to be an apparent response to an arrest warrant issued against a former MEND commander on corruption charges. Though attacks resumed, it is unlikely that MEND would be able to reprise its attacks to levels prior to the 2010 amnesty, given that the organization was essentially dismantled as part of the amnesty agreement.

Violence and security in Northern Nigeria

The outbreak of violence in Northern Nigeria during the post-transition period has direct links to the intra-religious, inter-religious and developmental problems that have plagued Nigeria's history for over a century. The most prominent manifestation of these problems has come with the emergence of Boko Haram (BH). The violence between BH and Nigerian police and military forces has taken its toll on the people in the north: over 17,000 dead, 1000 schools destroyed and 1.5 million people displaced.[55]

Followers of Mohammed Yusuf started BH in the Railroad Quarter of a Maiduguri neighborhood. Yusuf was a political and religious entrepreneur who built a large following and attracted their donations. The BH movement was not a single movement; the Nigerian government gave the groups their moniker of Boko Haram, providing a collective identity to an initially localized bunch of revolts.[56]

Yusuf's ideology reflects the newest manifestation of an intra-Muslim war in Northern Nigeria. That conflict dates back to the 1940s (see above) when opposition to the emerging Muslim ruling structure erupted. But its ideology and objectives remain a bit murky. By mobilizing people against the secular government, Yusuf contended that an Islamic state could be achieved without violence.[57] His deputy, Abubakar Shekau, rejected this interpretation of strategy and strongly advocated violence against the state. While the movement started as a non-violent struggle for an Islamic state, it slowly gravitated toward violence, particularly after the 2009 insurrection. The army hastened BH's movement toward violence with repeated violent and bloody attacks against the group.[58]

What ideology BH holds appears to be a hybrid that is opportunistic in many ways. The group has espoused anti-Western views and has contested the secular post-colonial state.[59] While some have claimed that BH is a Saudi Wahhabist sect and a theofascist organization,[60] the group's ideology and actions place it in contradiction to Saudi Wahhabism, and its ties to

Saudi Arabia are almost non-existent. Nonetheless, its ideology is radicalized against the Nigerian secular state.

Within Nigeria, BH has decried Muslim clerics and leaders as "infidels," often putting them in conflict with Wahhabi (Salafist) fundamentalists and more tolerant Sufis that dominate Northern Nigeria.[61] As such, BH poses a direct threat to the Muslim political order and Islamic establishment, even going so far as attempting to assassinate the Sultan of Sokoto and the Shehu of Borno.[62] Moreover, ties to Saudi Arabia remain unproven, particularly given that Yusuf broke off from the main Salafi group in Northern Nigeria. The operational elements of BH have reflected this ideology. The initial targets of the attacks were government forces and "bad" Muslims, and not Christians. Boko Haram targeted both Tijaniyya and Qadiriyya Muslims (the former the most popular form of Islam in Northern Nigeria, the latter the embodiment of elitist Islam in the region). As Sufi brotherhoods, both groups were "infidels" in the eyes of Boko Haram.

In 2009, the BH uprisings in northeast Nigeria marked a turning point for the group and its campaign. When security forces and BH clashed in Maiduguri, security forces arrested Yusuf and carried out his murder and the extrajudicial killing of several hundred of his followers.[63] The movement disappeared until it reemerged, expanding its base of operation and adding to its tactical toolbox. In 2010, BH attacked churches in the ethnic and religious tinderbox city of Jos in the middle belt region. In 2011, the group attacked the United Nations offices in the Nigerian capital of Abuja. In that attack, Nigeria experienced its first suicide terrorism attack, with more that followed.[64]

By 2012, BH's tactics led to a doctrinal split in the organization, specifically over the killing of fellow Muslims: Abubakar Adam Kambar split from the group and formed Ansaru.[65] Initially, Ansaru's signature tactic was the kidnapping, ransoming and killing of Western nationals. Ansaru also expanded its geographic influence into Algeria and Mali, and its tactical fighting into Chad and Niger.[66] Despite the split, more recent events indicate that Ansaru may have merged back into BH.[67]

Internationally, BH has extended its operational influence into the neighboring countries of Chad, Niger and Cameroon. Between 2010 and 2012, BH members are reported to have received training by the al-Shabaab group in Somalia.[68] Leaders of BH also sought to open relations with al-Qaeda,[69] but formal connections between the two groups never fully materialized – though Ansaru holds an ideology and connections that are close to al-Qaeda in the Islamic Maghreb (AQIM). In 2015, BH leader Abubakar Shekau pledged his allegiance to the Islamic State of Iraq and al-Sham (ISIS), and to its leader Abubakar al-Baghdadi. Leaders of BH even started to refer to BH as the West African Province of ISIS. At the time, the fear was that ISIS and BH would be able to collaborate to further destabilize Nigeria and other regional states. This fear has not materialized. President Muhammadu Buhari, who was inaugurated in May of 2015, launched an anti-Boko Haram campaign that he believes has been successful in reducing BH to a regional group similar to the Lord's Resistance Army in Uganda. Critics, however, claim that Buhari's victory claim was premature and that BH has consistently returned to fight another day.[70]

For the government's part, the response to BH has been less than ideal. In fact, human rights organizations contend that the government security forces have committed serious human rights violations. The government has used heavy-handed responses to BH and to security in Northern Nigeria in general, including arbitrary and unlawful killings, forced disappearances, torture, beatings, abuse, arbitrary arrests and excessive use of force in dealing with BH. For instance, in March of 2014, the Nigerian military carried out the extrajudicial execution of 622 people following BH attacks on Nigerian military barracks.[71] The government's response to BH has fallen into the long pattern of human rights abuses the military has enacted over time in Nigeria. By adopting these tactics, the government is itself making BH's case against the secular government as abusive and indifferent to Muslim populations in the north. While in the short-term the government may have made progress against BH, the long-term damage to the government's credibility and reputation is making it certain that if the government does vanquish BH, another group will be right behind it to take up the cause against the Nigerian government.

Notes

1 BBC 2012.
2 Hanson 2007b.
3 Alagoa et al. 1989: 741.
4 Ibid: 730.
5 Ibid: 730–734.
6 Miles 2000: 210.
7 Ibid.
8 Ibid.
9 Ibid.
10 Ibid: 211.
11 Reynolds 2001: 601.
12 Miles 2000; Reynolds 2001.
13 Lapidus 2002: 747.
14 Lapidus 2002: 748; Miles 2000: 213–214.
15 Winters 1987: 175.
16 Ibid; Falola 1998: 38.
17 Falola 1998: 52.
18 Ibid: 30.
19 Winters 1987; Lapidus 2002: 755.
20 Falola 1998: 52–53.
21 Ibid.
22 Reynolds 2001: 618.
23 Diamond 1991.
24 Ibid: 55.
25 Lapidus 2002: 750.
26 Campbell 2013: 6.
27 Ibid: 8.
28 Falola 1998: 60.
29 Ibid: 163.
30 Ibid: 164
31 Ibid: 165.
32 Ibrahim 1983, cited ibid.
33 Falola 1998: 172.
34 Lapidus 2002: 752.
35 Falola 1998: 172.
36 Lapidus 2002: 753.
37 Campbell 2013: 9.
38 Ibid: 123.
39 Thomas-Greenfield 2013: 4.
40 National Bureau of Statistics 2016.
41 Transparency International 2016.
42 US Department of State 2015: 9.
43 Eker 1981: 174.
44 Agiboa 2012: 328–329.
45 Ibid: 334–335.

46 Ibid; see also Eker 1981, who noted this problem in earlier research.
47 Agbiboa 2012: 334–335.
48 BBC 2016.
49 Ibid.
50 Akpan and Umoh 2016: 99.
51 Ibid: 99–100.
52 Hanson 2007a: 1.
53 Ibid: 2.
54 Stratfor 2016.
55 BBC 2015.
56 Campbell 2013: 131.
57 Ibid: 133.
58 Ibid: 131–133.
59 de Montclos 2014.
60 Bederka 2014.
61 Campbell 2014.
62 Ibid.
63 Ibid: 2.
64 Murray and Nossiter 2011.
65 Campbell 2014: 2; de Montclos 2014: 139–140.
66 Campbell 2014: 2.
67 Ibid.
68 Busari 2016.
69 Office of the Director of National Intelligence 2016.
70 BBC 2015.
71 US Department of State 2014.

Bibliography

Agbiboa, Daniel Egiegba. 2012. "Between Corruption and Development: The Political Economy of State Robbery in Nigeria." *Journal of Business Ethics* 108 (3): 325–345

Akpan, Otoabasi, and Ubong Essien Umoh. 2016. "Nigeria: State Capacity and Insurgency in the Niger Delta since the 1990s." *Conflict Studies Quarterly 14*: 92–110.

Alagoa, E.J., L.Z. Elango, and M. Metegue N'Nah. 1989. "The Niger Delta and the Cameroon Region." In *General History of Africa*, Vol. 6: *Africa in the 19th Century until the 1880s*, edited by J.F. Ade Ajayi. Paris: UNESCO, 724–748.

BBC. 2012. "Nigerians Living in Poverty Rise to Nearly 61%." February 13. www.bbc.com/news/world-africa-17015873.

BBC. 2015. "Nigeria Boko Haram: Militants 'Technically Defeated'." December 24. www.bbc.com/news/world-africa-35173618.

Bederka, Alan. 2014. "Wahhabism and Boko Haram." June 2. www.scarrdc.org/projects/.

Busari, Stephanie. 2016. "Boko Haram Training in Somalia: Security Chief." *CNN*, February 26. www.cnn.com/2016/02/25/africa/boko-haram-al-shabaab-somalia/.

Campbell, John. 2013. *Nigeria: Dancing on the Brink*. New York: Rowman & Littlefield.

Campbell, John. 2014. "Boko Haram: Origins, Challenges and Responses." Oslo: Norwegian Peacebuilding Resource Centre Policy Brief. http://mercury.ethz.ch/serviceengine/Files/ISN/184795/ipublicationdocument_singledocument/8b7fa46e-ce9b-47a5-ae4f-6ab13bdd01a4/en/5cf0ebc94fb36d66309681cda24664f9.pdf.

Central Intelligence Agency. 2016. *The World Factbook*. www.cia.gov/library/publications/the-world-factbook/geos/ni.html.

Hanson, Stephanie. 2007a. "MEND: The Niger Delta's Umbrella Militant Group." Council on Foreign Relations, March 21. www.cfr.org/nigeria/mend-niger-deltas-umbrella-militant-group/p12920.

Hanson, Stephanie. 2007b. "Nigeria's Creaky Political System." Council on Foreign Relations, April 12. www.cfr.org/nigeria/nigerias-creaky-political-system/p13079.

de Montclos, Marc-Antoine Pérouse. 2014. "Boko Haram and Politics: From Insurgency to Terrorism." In *Islamism, Politics, Security and the State in Nigeria*, edited by M.-A.P. de Montclos. Leiden: African

Studies Centre, 135–157. http://horizon.documentation.ird.fr/exl-doc/pleins_textes/divers15-04/010064363.pdf.
Diamond, Larry. 1991. "Nigeria's Search for a New Political Order." *Peace Review* 3 (4): 32–37.
Eker, Varda. 1981. "On the Origins of Corruption: Irregular Incentives in Nigeria." *Journal of Modern African Studies* 19 (1): 173–182.
Falola, Toyin. 1998. *Violence in Nigeria: The Crisis of Religious Politics and Secular Ideologies*. New York: University of Rochester Press.
Lapidus, Ira M. 2002. *A History of Islamic Societies*. Cambridge: Cambridge University Press.
Miles, William F.S. 2000. "Religious Pluralisms in Northern Nigeria." In *The History of Islam in Africa*, edited by Randall Pouwels and Nehemia Levtzion. Columbus: Ohio University Press, 210–224. www.africabib.org/rec.php?RID=I00001252.
Murray, Senan, and Adam Nossiter. 2011. "Suicide Bomber Attacks U.N. Building in Nigeria." *New York Times*, August 26. www.nytimes.com/2011/08/27/world/africa/27nigeria.html.
National Bureau of Statistics. 2016. "Nigeria Data Portal." http://nigeria.opendataforafrica.org/.
Office of the Director of National Intelligence. 2016. "Bin Laden's Bookshelf: 'Praise Be to God the Lord of All Worlds'." www.dni.gov/files/documents/ubl2016/english/Praise%20be%20to%20God%20the%20Lord%20of%20all%20worlds.pdf.
Rahman, Fazlur. 2002. *Islam*. 2nd ed. Chicago: University of Chicago Press.
Reynolds, Jonathan. 2001. "Good and Bad Muslims: Islam and Indirect Rule in Northern Nigeria." *International Journal of African Historical Studies* 34 (3): 601–618.
Stratfor. 2016. "In Nigeria, Militant Attacks Made in Vain." www.stratfor.com/analysis/nigeria-militant-attacks-made-vain.
Thomas-Greenfield, Linda. 2013. "Countering the Threat Posed by Boko Haram." US Department of State, November 13. www.state.gov/p/af/rls/rm/2013/217653.htm.
Transparency International. 2016. *Corruption Perceptions Index*. www.transparency.org/cpi2015.
US Department of State. 2014. *Investment Climate Statements 2015: Nigeria*. www.state.gov/e/eb/rls/othr/ics/2015/index.htm.
US Department of State. 2015. *Country Reports on Human Rights Practices for 2014: Nigeria*. www.state.gov/j/drl/rls/hrrpt/humanrightsreport/#wrapper.
Winters, Clyde Ahmad. 1987. "Koranic Education and Militant Islam in Nigeria." *International Review of Education* 33 (2): 171–185.

19

SECURITY AND THE RULE OF LAW IN NIGERIA

The role of the Nigerian judiciary

Honorable Ari Tobi-Aiyemo

The last two decades have witnessed the emergence of enormous security threats in Nigeria, threats that have introduced primary challenges to a democracy which is still struggling for recognition. Rule of law, the main indicator of democracy, is yet to adequately grasp its balance and fit into the socio-political puzzle of Nigeria. The unique and complex nature of Nigeria, with its diverse population and historical impact of military rule, has amplified security threats and made embracing the rule of law difficult. Since the resumption of democracy in Nigeria, the government has faced unwavering difficulty in upholding the rule of law as the return to democracy was not matched with a concomitant democratic culture.[1] Between 1979 and 1983 Nigeria's first democratic government prevailed but was overturned by a military junta. Nigeria returned to democratic rule in 1999 after 33 years of predominantly military rule.[2]

Over the past two decades of 'uninterrupted' democratic governance, Nigeria's security challenges have questioned the impact of rule of law on the country's unstable democracy; indeed, rule of law as a central tenet and indicator of democratic rule. Threats range from the destructive and piercing practices of corruption to the Boko Haram insurgency; Niger Delta militancy and piracy; upheavals caused by ethno-religious conflicts, tribal tussles; secession demands from the Indigenous People of Biafra Movement; random abductions and demands for ransom; and numerous criminal activities.[3] The government itself has faced internal conflicts in understanding, accepting and applying the rule of law.

In 2018 the president of Nigeria, Muhammadu Buhari, was accused of "assaulting" the rule of law at a Nigerian Bar Association annual conference when he said, "The Rule of law must be subject to the supremacy of the nation's security and national interests."[4] In fact the burden of eradicating security threats has too often caused the government to use unconstitutional means to eliminate social opposition rather than depend on the courts and due process to resolve conflict. Courts themselves have made false starts and faced legal distractions in the effort to articulate and enforce the rule of law.

Part I of this chapter assesses security threats to Nigeria's democracy. Part II offers an overview of the rule of law in Nigeria. Part III explains how security threats impact the rule of law in relation to dilemmas Nigeria's government faces in adhering to the rule of law. Part IV addresses the role of the Nigerian judiciary in resolving this quagmire.

I Major security threats in Nigeria

Corruption

Corruption is the mother of all threats to democracy in Nigeria, the source from which most security threats emanate, thrive and persist. Corruption has eaten so deeply into Nigerian society that it has become 'real' culture, central to the psyche and polity of the country. Corruption operates through two basic types of actor: active and passive. The former are directly involved in corrupt acts; the latter either benefit from corrupt acts or aid and abet those who commit them. This is why eradicating corruption is the most difficult venture the Nigerian government currently faces. According to Justice of the Supreme Court (JSC) Niki Tobi,

> In sum one innate and cancerous problem in Nigeria is corruption. It is one problem, which virtually the whole country seems to disclaim and detest, but which unfortunately is the bane of the country. It is the issue most talked about in the country, particularly in contemporary times, and yet no solution has been found and none is proximate or in sight. Corruption is a social malady that is fastly eating up the fabrics and the dynamics of the Nigerian economy. It blinds the eyes of the corrupt persons to do the wrong thing most of the time if not all the time. It is an evil, a complete evil. It must be destroyed from the society for the good of the society and mankind. When that happens society will be happy. Man in society will be happy too. Sociology and economics will triumph to egalitarian advantages of the entire nation.[5]

Corruption spreads across the executive, the judicial and the legislative arms of government, and even into the private and public sectors. In the past, corruption was allegedly common amongst governing parties and lawmakers who sought to advance their own political interests and desires. Corruption within the courts was less well recognized, since it was taboo to think that a judge would dare to be corrupt, but a reality nevertheless. Former JSC Chukwudifu Oputa said that a corrupt judge is thus the greatest vermin, the greatest curse ever to afflict any nation.[6] Unfortunately, that taboo has been enacted. Currently a number of judges are now under investigation for corrupt practices.[7] Some judicial cases have been prosecuted, while some have been dismissed.[8] It is especially unfortunate that certain judges entrusted with tackling corruption and upholding the rule of law are allegedly corrupt as well.

Corrupt judges in the public legal system strangle the efforts of un-corrupt people, who may not be able to sustain their idealism in the face of rottenness.[9] Ironically, society may falsely assume that the entire judiciary is corrupt, based on the actions of a few corrupt judges, and come to distrust the rule of law and political idealism associated with it. In *Re Olafisioye*, the court held,

> A corrupt society definitely will trouble the peace, stability, order and good government of the country. In a country where public officers freely dip their hands in the treasury and steal government money at will, the masses will complain and such complains could threaten the stability and social equilibrium of the nation.[10]

The Supreme Court also stated in *Attorney General of Ondo State v Attorney General of the Federation* that corruption is not a disease that afflicts public officers alone, but society as a whole; so, if it is to be eradicated effectively, the solution must be pervasive enough to cover every segment of society.[11]

Boko Haram insurgency

It is no longer news that Boko Haram, which originated from the northeastern states of Borno, Yobe and Adamawa in Nigeria, has become one of the most powerful terrorist movements in the world.[12] Since 2009, this group has grown to torment the Nigerian government and populace. So far Boko Haram (which translates as 'western education is forbidden') has executed dozens of attacks in various regions of northern Nigeria, raiding villages and towns, killing and abducting people (including foreigners), and bombing and burning public places. Boko Haram has killed tens of thousands, injured many and displaced over 2.3 million from their homes. The surge of attacks in these regions has also claimed the liberty of several women and children; indoctrinated children into becoming suicide bombers; stalled the right to education as many have stopped attending school for fear of public bombings; and led to the abduction of women and children.[13]

By the beginning of 2019 the Nigerian government had made little progress in its fight against this resilient insurgent group. About 20 percent of Nigeria's territory was under the insurgents' control.[14] Since investigations commenced, more than 20,000 people had been arbitrarily arrested in connection to terrorism in Nigeria.[15] The first prominent arrest was of four suspects after the bombing of a UN building in Abuja. These suspects were arraigned before a court in Abuja. The first mass trial of suspected terrorist began on October 10, 2017 when the court remanded 1,669 suspected terrorists for 90 days. About 575 of the suspects were arraigned in a Federal High Court in Kainji, Niger State. The court discharged 468 suspects who had no case to answer: 34 cases were struck out and 28 of the suspects were remanded for trial in Abuja and Minna; 45 were convicted and sentenced to between 3 and 31 years in jail. The court ordered that the 468 discharged should be de-radicalized and rehabilitated.[16]

The arrests of suspected Boko Haram members attracted international criticism – criticism which asserted that, in a bid to curb the insurgency, the Nigerian Army itself committed human rights abuses, arresting some innocent people without due process and killing many others.[17] In short, government responses to this threat, including use of the courts, raise legal and ethical questions.

Niger Delta militancy

The Niger Delta conflict formally began in the early 1990s and has since escalated to a nightmare between militants, government, multinational corporations and communities.[18] Conflicts and attacks are unique to specific states in the South-South geopolitical zone (Bayelsa, Delta and Rivers) mainly comprising the Ogoni and Ijaw tribes.[19] The militants adopt all sorts of vices to express their grievances against the abuse, exploitation and 'illegal' exploration of oil in their region. The tactics of the Niger Delta militants include destruction of oil platforms using improvised explosive devices (IEDs); kidnapping of foreign oil workers; sabotage of oil facilities; and vandalizing of oil pipelines – with the serious consequence of environmental pollution.[20]

As early as 1966 such grievances led to the creation of armed groups when a former police officer from the region, Isaac Adaka Boro, recruited, trained and armed men, founding an organization known as the Niger Delta Volunteer Force. Then came the Niger Delta People's Volunteer Force (headed by Alhaji Mujahid Asari Dokubo), the Movement for the Emancipation of the Niger Delta (headed by Henry Okah) and the Niger Delta Vigilantes (led by Ateke Tom), which brought together a plethora of smaller militants. Eventually they were cumulatively allied as Niger Delta militants, comprising young and energetic men from tribes within the region.[21]

Suppressed grief at the failure of historic attempts by men like Isaac Boro to save the region from oil exploitation (in 1966) lies at the heart of the conflict. In particular, the 1990 Saro-Wiwa saga represents historical proof of Nigeria's outright disregard for the rule of law.[22] Ken Saro-Wiwa was a foremost human rights activist from Ogoni who led others in the Movement for the Survival of the Ogoni People (MASOP) to protest the 'illegal' oil exploration in Ogoni land. A Special Military Tribunal tried Saro-Wiwa and his Ogoni associates upon allegations by the government. They were found guilty of masterminding the gruesome murder of certain Ogoni chiefs during a political rally. Saro-Wiwa's 1995 execution by hanging provoked international outrage and led to the suspension of Nigeria from the Commonwealth of Nations for over three years.[23]

When military rule ceased and democratic rule resumed the government granted the militants amnesty.[24] Most were granted monthly stipends from the government. Cash incentives and training were also given to them. Such gifts reduced the level of violence and attacks for a time – until the administration decided to revoke the amnesty. Threats of violence have taken on different dimensions and now extend to piracy, kidnapping and human rights abuses by soldiers who are supposed to curb the violence.[25]

Increasing violence has led to the creation of additional militant groups with various motives and interests, all under the guise of a campaign against oil exploration. Those groups include the Niger Delta Liberation Force (NDLF), the Niger Delta People's Volunteer Force (NDPVF), the Joint Niger Delta Liberation Force (JNDLF) and the Niger Delta Republic Vigilante (NDV).[26] In 2018 a new militant group, the Niger Delta Avengers (NDA), took militancy to a more destructive level. Its goal was "to cripple Nigeria's economy".[27] Unlike their predecessors, the NDA is more vicious. They caused a shutdown of oil terminals and a fall in Nigeria's oil production to its lowest level in 20 years. Although militant groups suspended attacks in early 2017, a coalition now known as Reformed Niger Delta Avengers (RNDA) resumed an 'operation no mercy' attack, claiming the Nigerian government is apathetic towards the interests and welfare of the Niger Delta region.[28] They also threatened secession so that the Niger Delta region could manage its own resources.[29]

Despite violent protests and the amnesty granted militants in the past, the oil-rich region is still impoverished. Alleged abuse of the rights of the Niger Delta community persists. The Nigerian government is still unable to secure the rights of the region's inhabitants. Nor can it justify unjust exploitation of an oil-rich region which contributes about 90 percent of the Nigerian economy.[30] In addition, security forces seeking to arrest members of militant groups in the region have engaged in human rights abuses such as arbitrary arrests and detention, forced disappearances and extra-judicial killings.[31] As a result, rule of law and democratic practices remain under threat, and the central government is caught in a cycle of ambiguity as it responds to challenges in the nation and the region. The level of insecurity caused by the activities of these militant groups has reached a point where the whole world has become apprehensive of the nature of the calamity.[32]

Ethno-religious conflicts

These are a combination of conflicts between different ethnic groups – especially in the north, where, fault-line conflicts persist in the contexts of faith, ethno-linguistic identities and inter-communal tensions over resources and power on the one hand, and between Christians and Muslims on the other.[33] These conflicts are intertwined because somehow one introduces or heightens the other. More often than not, religious conflicts arise from tribal tussles between northerners and southerners; when there is conflict between Muslims and Christians, tribal conflicts occur as well. A series of religious riots, massacres and conflicts have ensued in many states in the northern region of Nigeria, especially Plateau, Kaduna and Borno.[34] These religious conflicts have transformed into tribal tussles that have since extended to other states, threatening the security of Nigeria as a whole.

In 2017 conflicts ensued between the Hausas and Igbos who lived in some northern states. The Hausas insisted that the Igbos leave the north and return to their place of origin in the east.[35] Earlier, in 2016, some Fulani herdsmen from the north reportedly killed about 40 Igbos in Enugu state.[36] The killings, which have increased in number since then, have generated spates of violence, retaliation and strife between both tribes.

A farmers-herders' conflict within the North-Central zone, the most ethno-nationally and religiously diverse geopolitical zone in the country, has also produced violence. The North-Central states mostly affected by such conflicts are Benue, the Federal Capital Territory, Kogi, Nasarawa, Niger, Kwara and Plateau. Political tensions have arisen between some ethnic and religious communities, resulting in uncontrolled mob violence.[37] Environmental resource scarcity-induced movement of herders from the northern part of the country southward has also produced conflict. Ethnic or religious differences, sociopolitical differences and communal 'insecurities' which have led some regions to believe the government does not treat all regions equally are some of the reasons for such conflicts (see Ostergard and Griffin, Chapter 18 this volume).[38]

Infringements of freedom of expression and freedom of movement by one ethnic group over another stifle the rule of law and contravene Section 38 of the Constitution of the Federal Republic of Nigeria 1999, as amended, which provides for freedom of religion.

The court in *Medical and Dental Practitioners Disciplinary Tribunal v Okonkwo* stated that:

> The right to freedom of thought, conscience or religion implies a right not to be prevented without lawful justification from choosing the course of one's life, fashioned on what one believes … The limits of these freedoms as in all cases are where they impinge on the rights of others or where they put the welfare of society or public health in jeopardy.[39]

Secession movements

Nigeria comprises over 300 ethnic groups, the most prominent of which are the Yoruba, Hausa and Igbo. Within these groups several tribes and multi-tribal differences have, over time, generated skirmishes. Given the liberties offered by democracy, some tribal groups have taken advantage of freedom of speech and expression rights to demand separation from the rest of Nigeria. During their early agitation against oil exploration, the Niger Delta militants threatened to separate from Nigeria so they could have full and independent control of the oil from their region.[40] The Yoruba Liberation Command (YOLICOM) from the Yoruba ethnic groups have demanded an Odudwa Republic, advocating for secession as the best solution to the tribal clashes in Nigeria.[41]

The most prominent secessionist agitation that has threatened Nigeria's security and challenged the existence of the rule of law was the Independent People of Biafra (IPOB), led by Nnamdi Kanu. Continuing to the present day, this Igbo ethnic group of South-East Nigeria is vying for an independent republic comprised of various states within their region.[42] Igbo agitation for a referendum has been incessant; as have spates of violence and human rights abuses evolving from it. Such complex demands for secession have threatened Nigerian democracy. Yet the government continues to abide by Section 2 of the Constitution, which states that Nigeria is one indivisible and indissoluble sovereign state.

In the bid to curb the violence, the government arrested Nnamdi Kanu, the leader of the IPOB, and charged him with treasonable felony. He was detained for over 18 months while awaiting trial, despite court orders that he be released. This unlawful detention exemplified the government's disregard for the rule of law. The government's reactions in the matter have attracted global criticism for violations of international standards of human rights. In fact the Nigerian army extra-judicially executed some members of the IPOB.[43]

In short, complex demands for secession have challenged and threatened Nigerian democracy. Threats to the nation's unity have ironically exposed an endemic disregard for the rule of law on the part of the government and citizens on both sides of the conflict. The IPOB leader, who was expected in court to commence his treason trial, failed to show up and reportedly jumped bail, supporting by his actions the government's initial refusal to release him from custody.

Abduction for ransom and other criminal activities

Initially an insurgent tactic initiated by Niger Delta militants in the South-South region of Nigeria, kidnapping today serves the economic advancement of its practitioners. From protesting militants and insurgent terrorists to opportunistic youths seeking economic advantage, kidnappers invoke survival strategies.[44] Kidnapping has now taken on multiple motivations and produced varying outcomes in wider regions. The militant kidnap is a socio-political act motivated by political objectives, including the objective of enforcing the government's obligation to address pervasive poverty in the oil-rich yet poorly funded oil region.[45] The reference here is to socio-economic kidnapping for ransom. This is most prominent in South-Eastern region states like Imo, Abia, Anambra, Enugu, Ebonyi and Rivers, but has now extended to other parts of the country, even in the north.[46]

Kidnapping threatens the peace, security and welfare of the citizenry. It also threatens the socio-economic development of Nigeria as a whole. In their quest to alleviate poverty, young, idle and mostly unemployed graduates take to the streets and highways to abduct rich and prominent personalities or their family members, demanding ransoms before the victims are released. The ransom demanded for a victim's release is subject to negotiation between the kidnappers and the victim's relatives.[47]

No longer is kidnapping used to advance communal interests, contest human rights violations, claim constitutional rights or address issues inherent to the national economy. Instead kidnapping has become a business that recruits employees, hoodlums who share ransom money amongst themselves and spend it as they please.[48] Ongoing is the trial of notorious alleged kidnapping kingpin Chukwudumeme Onwuamadike, also known as Evans, on charges of armed robbery and kidnapping. Evans allegedly confessed to the crime of kidnapping, and stated that proceedings from his kidnappings were his livelihood.[49]

Socio-economic kidnapping has physical and mental impacts on its victims, causes fear amongst citizens and interferes with the economic development of the country.[50] It is a fast-growing threat, driving local and foreign investors away from doing business in the regions/states where this social vice predominates.

II The rule of law in relation to security challenges in Nigerian democracy

Overview of rule of law in Nigeria

Rule of law is a most enigmatic concept in Nigeria's democracy. Like a silhouette, it is indeterminate in practice yet expressly stated in principles of law as a basic yardstick and watchword of democratic governance. No matter how democratic Nigeria becomes, the absence or failure of the rule of law negates its democracy. Presently the Nigerian government is in a dilemma: efforts to eradicate or fight threats to the country's security and democracy constrain strict application of the rule of law; and the need to fight security threats tempts authorities to violate the very principle they are supposed to value. The government denies certain rights in order to uphold certain rights, robbing Peter to pay Paul – e.g. denying the right to bail in order to uphold the right to national security.

In an ideal democratic setting rule of law should define the actions of both the government and the governed; but in Nigeria the actions of the government and the governed too often define rule of law. Rule of law in Nigeria is complicated: a form of governance which has accomplished positive change for Nigerian society but which has been marred by discrepancies in implementation and adoption. Rule of law speaks with one voice in a given case, in a different voice in another. In one act it is revered, and in another act it is disregarded. After decades of military rule and familiarity with practices developed under military rule, the government supposes that simple due process mechanics cannot deal sufficiently with threats to the country's security.[51] So, quasi-military tactics considered effective in the past are still often applied to fight corruption, the Boko Haram insurgency, the IPOB movement, the Niger Delta militants and other threats to security. Hence the ardent use of security forces that resort to human rights abuses, clearly breaching the constitution.

What rule of law means in principle differs from what it means in practice. As British jurist A.V. Dicey explained in his 1885 *Introduction to the Study of the Law of the Constitution*, in principle, rule of law is supremacy of the law, equality before the law and inherent and inalienable rights.[52] In Nigerian practice and in reality it is doubtful whether the principle prevails since the government incessantly disregards court orders, as in the military era. To Nigeria's citizenry rule of law means independence, human rights, freedom of speech, freedom of the press, freedom of expression, freedom of association, accountability – and an 'it's all about me and not my neighbor' mentality. Further, the average Nigerian believes rule of law guarantees, or should guarantee, social, political and economic rights – rights which include food, water, energy and shelter. The citizenry also believes that individual rights should be upheld even if upholding them means trampling on the rights of others. This 'illusion' constitutes a major problem for the government and the courts.

The concept of the rule of law in Nigeria has changed over the years and in modern times; it is now identified with the rights of man in society. It is argued that this modern concept is entrenched in Chapter IV of the 1999 Constitution, as amended; in its generally accepted sense Section 17 of the Constitution also enunciates the concept of rule of law.[53] Since Chapters II and IV of the Constitution stipulate, respectively, the government's obligation to ensure society/socio-economic rights and socio-political rights accruable to citizens, it will be safe to conclude that the definition of rule of law in Nigeria is encapsulated in both chapters.

Ongoing arguments about which of these rights supersedes the other arise from the above provisions. According to Falana, there is continuing tension between national security and respect for human rights. While human rights and the rule of law are concerned with limitations on state power, national security is intertwined with the assertion of state power. The result has often been the marginalization of human rights in the name of national security by successive governments. The subordination of human rights to national security has been a permanent feature of Nigeria's political history.[54]

A reasonable expectation would have been that, with a deliberate return to democracy, rule of law would thrive in Nigeria. In fact, abuse of the principle and disregard for its use persist at all levels of society. The government and certain citizens deploy the principle according to their own interests, with little or no regard for the rights of others. Hence, adherence to the rule of law is too often based on the convenience of the actor involved – government or governed. Still, the rule of law is better professed in Nigeria today than it was during the military era, which was characterized by gruesome human rights abuses, suspension of certain constitutional provisions by decree, manipulation of court powers and jurisdiction, and outright disregard for court orders.[55]

Rule of law has navigated numerous twists and turns to find a place in Nigeria's nascent democracy. Ambiguities and contradictions remain. Responses have varied from acceptance and recognition to partial acceptance and disregard or abuse. Although the government recognizes this concept as imperative to its democratic success, it sometimes applies the principle as a manipulative tool when the principle favors government rights and interests. We can distinguish between reliance and compliance. The government relies on the rule of law as a benefit for personal or political interests, but fails to comply with the rule of law as a constitutional requirement and obligation. A vivid example occurred in Oyo state, where the former governor, Rashidi Ladoja, violated a court order asking his administration to recognize and swear in a local government chairman who had won the election but was denied office due to pending political conflicts. A few years later, the same governor ran to the courts invoking rule of law against his unconstitutional and illegal impeachment.[56]

Rule of law is also used as a tool for vendetta. Some government officials have resorted to it as a mechanism to avenge political opponents or antagonists. Under the guise of anti-corruption campaigns or human rights abuse enforcement, such opponents have been impeached, arrested or prosecuted.[57] Under these circumstances the principle of equality is abused and misused.

Rule of law has also been invoked as a tool for vindication, or at other times ignored or jettisoned altogether. Examples arise when government officials allegedly siphon money from the government's treasury or coffers into foreign accounts without adhering to established bureaucratic practice, or when a governor misappropriates government funds in plain violation of established standards. Such acts breach the rule of law. But when perpetrators are caught or fall under investigation by security forces, the Economic and Financial Crime Commission or any other anti-graft agency – when their bank accounts or properties are seized – they invoke the rule of law to intervene, a process they failed to respect or acknowledge previously. For example, IPOB leader Nnamdi Kanu invoked the rule of law to plead that his human rights had been breached, and to vindicate himself from government allegations; but just when the government complied with the rule of law, he violated the rule by jumping bail and absconding from court proceedings.[58]

Nevertheless, despite these setbacks, respect for the rule of law has improved over the history of Nigeria's democracy, although with wavering and inconsistent strides. Corruption has been exposed at all levels. Highly placed government officials, judges and the rich have been investigated, prosecuted or convicted. A vivid example is the unprecedented arrest of certain judges on charges of corruption. Charges of corruption for judges entrusted with enforcing the rule of law have been deeply troubling. But so also was the spate of arrests that followed raids upon the homes of judges to obtain incriminating evidence, an historic affront to the rule of law. The action of the Department of State Security (DSS) was an abdication of due process, and clearly negated the concept of rule of law.[59]

These and other cases have introduced an interesting dimension to rule of law in Nigeria. They have generated arguments for and against strict adherence to rule of law with respect to socio-political and socio-economic crimes. Some have argued that rule of law should only apply to those who 'deserve it'. Culprits who embezzle public funds and deny citizens basic human rights, or terrorists who outright violate human rights, should equally be denied the protection of rule of law.[60] According to Adejumo, Nigeria is not uniformly ripe for strict adherence to the stipulations and requirements of the rule of law, and rule of law should therefore not apply to all Nigerians equally.

In short, despite progress under democracy, Nigeria's commitment to the rule of law is caught in contradictions. General commitment to the principle is still a work in progress. Strict application of the principle for all citizens is a necessary element of democratic process, but Nigeria is yet to settle into pure democracy and be fully alienated from an indelible military past. This endemic part of the country's history adds complexity to Nigerian democracy and makes embracing rule of law equally complex. Those who flout the principle claim to be victims, and seek the rule of law when indicted. Conversely, beneficiaries of rule of law flout the principle to avoid prosecution. Thus, the rule of law has itself become a political football in Nigeria's democracy. Even when government attempts to sustain the rule of law, it violates due process to attain adequate process. Rule of law is infringed in order to attain rule of law. The ironies are obvious.

The impact of security on rule of law in Nigeria

Rule of law is a valuable requirement and leveling factor in the preservation of security and democratic development. When the security of a country is threatened, rule of law is also threatened. Social vices that constitute security threats challenge maintenance of rule of law, which becomes susceptible to governmental and societal manipulation. Too often, the freedoms and rights guaranteed by the rule of law, as enshrined under Chapter IV of the 1999 Constitution, have undermined the concept they represent. Liberties long denied under military rule, released under Nigeria's Constitution, have been used to justify secession, which breaches Section 2 of that same Constitution, which clearly states that Nigeria is one indivisible nation. Yet citizens feel free to advocate for secession under the guise of exercising their fundamental rights.

In another instance, even though the Niger Delta militants have justified to a large extent their reasons for demanding enforcement of the rights of the region, their violent approach questions the justifiability of such rights (rule of law). The militants were granted amnesty in 2009.[61] More recently the amnesty was revoked on the grounds that paying or negotiating with violent actors violates the rule of law. So, even as on one side of the scene groups advocate for and demand constitutionally guaranteed rights to life, safe environment, freedom of expression, etc., on the other government simultaneously decries protestors' unjust violence, and itself applies unjust means to combat militants to defend national security and safeguard the Constitution. Instead of waiting for due process from the courts, the government responds to internal threats by implementing arbitrary arrests as well as unlawful detention and prosecution. It allows its soldiers to ambush and kill civilians without court orders, to rape and to enact inhumane treatment of citizens.

Furthermore, due process as a fundamental mechanism of fair hearing appears not to be trusted or fully understood in Nigeria. In May 2014 a bombing in Abuja killed 75 people and wounded 100 others. The alleged mastermind of the attack, who denied links to Boko Haram, was arrested but then released by the court. Terrorism charges against the suspect were struck for lack of diligent prosecution. Nevertheless the government continued to detain the suspect. Citizens at times distrust what is perceived to be a 'gentlemanly' attitude of the courts towards litigants who appear to threaten public safety yet are deemed not guilty after trial. In other words, citizens who have become more assertive in demanding for themselves full benefits of the rule of law nevertheless distrust due process, its delays and outcomes, as a mechanism for ensuring the rights they seek.

The Nigerian judiciary has been fairly consistent in its role as a reservoir of rule of law; but the government, responsible for ensuring enforcement of judicial pronouncements, often flouts court orders. Too often court orders have been unenforceable, or only enforced at executive convenience. Four recent deviations from the rule of law have attracted international audiences and intervention. The first involved the aforementioned arrest and unlawful detention of IPOB leader Nnamdi Kanu sometime in 2015 and his continued detention for more than 18 months.[62] In a bid to prevent an upsurge of violence resulting from the group's demand for secession, the government disregarded court orders and hoped to detain Kanu until his trial commenced or finished. He was detained in custody for over a year before he was released on bail.[63]

The second case was the random arrest of a suspected terrorist after the 2016 raid on the Sambisa Forest (Boko Haram's former base), when some of the suspects were killed without trial, and those arrested were detained without bail pending trial.[64] The third was the arrest and unlawful detention of a former national security adviser (NSA), Sambo Dasuki, who was charged with fraud from 2015 onward in spite of court orders to allow his bail. The Economic Community of West African States (ECOWAS) court ordered his immediate release and fined the Nigerian government N15m but the government did not obey.[65] In fact the Abuja Federal High Court declared the continued detention illegal, and the court dismissed the claim of the federal government that the ex-NSA was being detained for the sake of national security.

A fourth case of shameful disregard for the rule of law was the detention for over two years of Ibrahim El-Zakzaky, leader of the Shiite Islamic Movement of Nigeria, despite court orders to free him.[66] The danger with such executive lawlessness is that, as political analyst Justice Malala rightly put it when South Africa flouted the rule of law in its refusal to arrest Sudanese President Omar Al-Bashir, "where government disobeys a court order, then South Africa has begun its descent".[67]

Security agents lack respect for the rule of law in their dealings with culprits or suspects when they detain without due process and do not observe constitutionally guaranteed procedures. An example is the aforementioned illegal search and arrest of judges by the DSS in 2016. The excuse for such illegality is that waiting for due process will alert the suspects and create an opening for evidence to be confiscated. The likelihood that suspects will abscond and stall trials makes it difficult for the government to abide by due process. A recent example occurred when IPOB leader Nnamdi Kanu was released on bail in 2017, pending his trial for treason, after local and international intervention. He was absent from court on the date set for his trial and has not been located.

In such instances the safety and security of the nation is at stake, whilst the rights of citizens and integrity of rule of law are also at sake. All signs indicate that government actors believe using democratic measures in the strict sense would not be effective in fighting security threats. The government's rationale is that although the continuous detention of an accused pending trial contravenes the accused's constitutional right to liberty as stipulated in Section 38 of the Constitution, continuous detention is in compliance with Section 2, the requirement to safeguard national unity and security.

Breaches of national security militate against the rule of law, while disregard for rule of law enhances attacks on the security of a nation and inevitably threatens democracy. The Nigerian government has ridden the crest of a campaign for rule of law by making strides in various socio-political pursuits. But the question remains as to whether this observable progress justifies contravening the Constitution by repeatedly breaching due process under the pretext of ensuring security, and whether extra-judicial efforts by the Nigerian government are not detrimental to democracy. In assessing attempts to curb security threats, some believe that due process is as damaging as extra-judicial process. Due process may delay a trial. It may lead to a suspect's escape or evasion of justice. In some cases it may lead to enhanced violence in society. Should Nigeria adhere strictly to the requirements of rule of law? The answer for some is problematic.

The role of the Nigerian judiciary in sustaining the rule of law

That the judiciary is a key player in upholding the rule of law in the pursuit of national security is unequivocal. Section 14(4) (b) of the Nigerian Constitution stipulates that "the security and welfare of the people shall be the primary purpose of the government." Thus, national security and public interest are correlated agendas in the preservation of democracy in Nigeria. The judiciary is vested with the function of interpreting this and any other provision of the Constitution justly, according the due process rights to those who come before the courts. It is the role of the judge to interpret laws and constitutional provisions with adequacy and consistency, taking into account social developments as well as the shifting interests of the nation, and recognizing that rule of law is not the exclusive preserve of a particular government or historical moment. Another primary task of the judiciary is to exercise judicial functions and responsibilities to protect human rights.

Rule of law, like democracy, is a universal concept; it is not the exclusive preserve of a particular government. At every level, with respect to diverse cases, the rule of law abides or should abide by the same consistent process. It is a concept measured by reliable forms and standards so judges are not at liberty to give it personal or varied interpretations. But laws, which are dynamic, are in fact subject to interpretation, even though judges are not at liberty to bring personal perspectives to bear. At times, unique or diverse interpretations of the law can produce conclusions that align with basic social views. It is the role of the judge to interpret the rule of law with adequacy and consistency. When government contravenes rule of law it is entirely up to the judiciary to ensure that rule of law prevails.

Nigerian judges face the reality that public understanding of court proceedings and public perception of outcomes do not always acknowledge the reasoning of the court against the backdrop of relevant legal principles. Nigerian citizens often possess misleading information about why a judge reached a particular decision, and how courts interpreted or upheld the rule of law. Furthermore, there is widespread social misconception of legal principles and procedures that enable courts to adopt unique approaches to different cases under similar circumstances. In this regard, media reports of court proceedings and public perception of the outcomes too often do not include the reasoning of the court against the backdrop of relevant legal principles. Thus, society possesses wrong and misleading information on why a judge took a particular decision and how courts interpret or uphold rule of law. Hence the unique approaches courts adopt under particular circumstances create the illusion that even the judiciary lacks genuine understand of the concept 'rule of law'.

Social perception of the rule of law has not improved in recent times, especially as the judiciary is now in the spotlight regarding allegations of corruption against some judges. Corruption within the judiciary makes judges pay lip service to fairness, neutrality and unbiased decision-making even as judicial officers enact corruption themselves. Judges who have been accused of and prosecuted for corruption in multiple parts of the country have brought ridicule and distrust to the judiciary. In 2016 armed officers of the Department of State Security (DSS) arrested judges suspected of corrupt practices, leading to about 18 coming under investigation.[68] Between 2016 and 2017 at least ten judges were sacked for professional misconduct relating to corruption. This gives the impression that judges pay lip service to their appointed role but cannot be entrusted to uphold the rule of law themselves. This situation threatens democracy and puts Nigeria "on the threshold of anarchy".[69]

To safeguard the integrity of the judiciary, the Chief Justice of Nigeria established the National Judicial Policy to check corrupt practices amongst judges. Fear of indictment has revamped the rule of law. A shift from a relatively conservative judicial philosophy has given way to an agenda which includes radical ethical measures. At the same time we should note that the 2016 raid on the houses of some judges by the DSS created insecurity within the judiciary. In addition to disregarding court orders, the DSS bypassed the courts in order to execute searches and arrests. This outright disregard for due process undermined judicial authority and the independence of the judiciary. Where due process appears slow and sometimes ineffective, government actors remain tempted to resort to extra-legal means and extra-judicial outcomes, threatening democracy and risking anarchism. A DSS siege at the national assembly where senators were assaulted also affronted the rule of law.[70]

On the other hand, despite charges of corruption, and political upheaval, Nigerian courts have striven to sustain and uphold the rule of law in the face of human rights abuses in recent years. The Nigerian judiciary overall has remained consistent and assertive on this issue.

The struggle to maintain the judiciary's independence was visible even under military rule. In *Lakanmi & Ors v A.G. West & 2 Ors* (1971), the Supreme Court nullified a military decree that sought to forcibly acquire a property without compensation based on the fact that a person had committed acts of impropriety. Pats Acholonu, JCA, in the Court of Appeal stated in *Nwosu v Imo State Environmental Sanitation Authority and Ors*, that:

> Courts are not frightened of an ouster clause. They respect it but when an ouster clause seeks to make it impossible for the court to protect the common man and make laws which cannot stand the test of reason or that is an affront to decency and intelligence then a court should be careful not to lend its weight to a law that would make it an enemy of the common man and not the last hope of the common man.

Many years later, in the case of *Miscellaneous Offences Tribunal v Okaroafor* (2001), the Supreme Court stated that: the rule of law demanded that government should be conducted within the framework of recognized rules and principles which restrict discretionary power; and that disputes as to the legality of the acts of government are to be decided by judges who are wholly independent of the executive.[71] Still there is little the judiciary can do to ensure the government's compliance with court orders. Many examples come to mind, such as the aforementioned cases of former NSA Dasuki and Shiite Islamic Movement of Nigeria leader Ibrahim El-Zakzaky.

Rule of law empowers the judiciary to uphold democratic values, and today the record shows a proactive judiciary taken as a whole. Part of the role of the judiciary in maintaining the rule of law can be determined by understanding judicial perceptions of national security, and the extent to which judicial involvement can avert challenges to democracy, national security and the rule of law. So far the Nigerian judiciary perceives national security as fundamental, prevailing over other rights. On balance the judiciary has given more weight to safeguarding national security than to upholding human rights. In *Alhaji Mujahid Dokubo-Asari v. Federal Republic of Nigeria* (2007), the appellant, charged with treasonable felony, appealed against a ruling of the trial court denying him bail. In that case the Supreme Court held that:

> I therefore agree with the Court of Appeal that there is a threat to national security. There is instability in the Niger Delta area and I do not think the appellant will assist in reducing the instability and turbulence there. On the contrary, it is clear from his statement that there is every likelihood for him to foment or instigate more trouble. This is certainly not in the interest of the region and Nigeria as a whole. The appellant should therefore be where he is to take his trial.

The implication of this decision is that the fundamental rights of citizens enshrined in Chapter IV of the Constitution can be justifiably infringed to sustain or uphold Section 45 of the Constitution – the interest of defense, public safety and public order.[72]

Still the judiciary protects the rights of citizens in appropriate circumstances. According to Falana, "In Babankura Fugu v. President, Federal Republic of Nigeria (2009–2010) … the Borno State High Court awarded N100 million [in] damages to the applicant to atone for the extra-judicial murder of his father, an alleged terrorist suspect."[73] Therefore, even while the judiciary defends citizens' fundamental rights to associate, move, assemble, express themselves or join any religion, it also considers, determines, establishes and reiterates the boundaries where an individual's rights end and national interests begin. Nigerian courts are in the process of defining such boundaries.

Although rule of law has evolved to become a more acceptable/reliable concept Nigeria identifies with, there is still need for improvement. The extent to which judicial involvement can avert challenges to democracy, national security and the rule of law will in part determine the future role of the judiciary in sustaining rule of law in Nigeria. Only when the nation is secured is it likely that individual rights will be fully realized. For example, the people who died in explosions or from violence in the Niger Delta communities cannot exercise their rights from the grave. Although the family of Ken Saro-Wiwa received an out-of-court settlement in the case of *Wiwa v Royal Dutch Petroleum Co.*, 15 years after his execution, the environmental and human rights abuses over which he fought persist.

Frustration remains. Sustainable democratic development can only be achieved when the executive branch of government is fully committed to honoring all branches of government. With respect to separation of powers, the judiciary cannot do much more than it is already doing. Under present circumstances the judiciary is in a dilemma with respect to executive interference. The executive's disobedience of court orders and disregard for judicial powers undermine judicial independence.

Therefore, a revamp of the system is paramount, beginning with a review of the penal code. The security challenges facing the country are more advanced than existing laws anticipate; antiquated laws do not address the present state of affairs. A revamp would enable Nigeria to deal with advanced socio-economic crimes, such as cyber crimes, and thus assist the courts, limiting unfettered discretion. This would limit use of discretion as much as possible, especially as debate on judicial discretion is a controversial issue.

Furthermore, Nigerian judges need advanced training in criminal justice as a matter of exigency. The level of insecurity threatening Nigeria requires judges to have more than elementary knowledge of criminal law. The Latin maxim *nemo dat quod non habet* best expresses the point here: the judiciary *cannot give what it does not have.* We need knowledge, and we also need new laws to guide us and abide by. That knowledge needs to be relevant to the times. The judiciary cannot give justice in criminal matters (or threats to insecurity) without advanced, relevant knowledge of such crimes; and there is no way the judiciary can adequately uphold the rule of law with antiquated and irrelevant laws. As crimes advance, the law should equally develop. Additionally, most perpetrators of enhanced 'threats' to Nigerian society rely on the rule of law to protest and demand restoration of their allegedly abused human rights. And this may well be justified by constitutional provisions. There is need for a unified and more activist judiciary that would err on the side of substantial justice based on 'realism' rather than technical justice based on 'legalism'. Judges need laws to guide their discretion so the judiciary can speak with one voice. This would ensure that judicial pronouncements acknowledge prevailing social norms and standards.

Conclusion

Although rule of law is a plausible concept in Nigeria, the concept is currently not fully functional. Its implementation is at times more cosmetic than surgical. The concept that security threats can only be countered by autocratic means must be jettisoned for good. The functioning of the country's system of government needs to be reimagined, based on a strong understanding of principled relationships among democracy, security, constitutionality and the rule of law. Despite recent ethical and legal lapses within the executive and the judiciary, progress has been made. Citizens who at one time were ruled by dictatorship, their freedom of speech stifled within the walls of incarceration, now freely express their views and opinions. The current government defers to the Constitution in most matters, and the judiciary is now actively involved in governance as an arm of government, no longer merely a tool used to forcefully execute the desires of military dictatorship.

Notes

1 Lawal-Rabana (n.d.).
2 Nwekeaku (2014), p. 27.
3 Arewa (2011), p. 137.
4 Sote (2018).
5 Tobi (2008), pp. 57–58.
6 See Jegede and Olawale (1993), p. 231.
7 Adesomoju (2018).
8 Nigerian Observer (2016); Soniyi (2016).
9 See Tobi (1996), p. 50.
10 (2004) 1 SC (pt I) 27 at 54, per Niki Tobi, JSC.
11 (2002) 9 NWLR (pt 772) 222.
12 Dambazau (2014).
13 CNN (2020).
14 Amnesty International (2018).
15 Amnesty International (2017).
16 Vanguard (2017a).

17 Amnesty International (2017).
18 Tobi (2004).
19 Ibid.
20 Dambazau (2014).
21 Oyewo (2016). pp. 63–64.
22 Ibid, p. 63.
23 Ogundamisi (2015).
24 Oyewo (2016), p. 63.
25 Dambazau (2014).
26 Nwakalor (2016).
27 Amaize and Brisibe (2016).
28 Ibid.
29 Nwachukwu (2017).
30 Tobi (2004), pp. 2–3.
31 Human Rights Watch (2017).
32 Ibid, p. 64.
33 Institute for Peace and Conflict Resolution (IPCR) (2017), p. 16.
34 Ibid, p. 38.
35 Punch (Nigeria) (2017).
36 Mamah et al. (2016).
37 IPCR (2017), p. 30.
38 Ibid.
39 (2001) FWLR (pt 44) 542.
40 Tobi-Aiyemo (2019), p. 15.
41 Vanguard (2017b).
42 BBC (2017).
43 Amnesty International (2018).
44 Ibrahim and Mukhtar (2017), p. 143.
45 Arewa (2011), pp. 142–143.
46 Ibid, p. 143.
47 Ibid, pp. 187–188.
48 Ibid.
49 Hanafi (2017).
50 Ibrahim and Mukhtar (2017), p. 140.
51 Adejumo (n.d.).
52 See Tobi (2008), pp. 3–4.
53 Ibid, pp. 10–11.
54 Falana (2014).
55 Akanbi and Shehu (2012), p. 3.
56 Yusuf (2010).
57 Akinola (2006).
58 Adesomoju (2020).
59 Akanbi and Shehu (2012).
60 Adejumo (n.d.).
61 VOA News (2018).
62 Vanguard (2017a).
63 Ibid.
64 Amnesty International (2017).
65 Akinloye (2017).
66 Human Rights Watch (2017).
67 Malala (2015).
68 Nwakanma (2016).
69 Guardian (Nigeria) (2018).
70 Ibid.
71 18 NWLR (pt 745), 295.
72 Falana (2014).
73 Ibid.

References

Adejumo, A. (n.d.). Democracy, Corruption and the Rule of Law in Nigeria. www.gamji.com/article6000/NEWS7022.htm. Retrieved November 2017.

Adesomoju, A. (2018). Alleged Corruption: NJC Raises Panels to Probe 25 Judges. *Punch* (Nigeria), May 11. https://punchng.com/alleged-corruption-njc-raises-panels-to-probe-25-judges.

Adesomoju, A. (2020). Don't Restore Nnamdi Kanu's Bail, FG Tells Court. *Punch* (Nigeria), January 26. https://punchng.com/dont-restore-nnamdi-kanus-bail-fg-tells-court.

Akanbi, M.M. and Shehu, A.T. (2012). Rule of law in Nigeria. *Journal of Law, Policy and Globalization*, 3, pp. 1–8.

Akinloye, B. (2017). ECOWAS Threatens to Sanction Nigeria over Dasuki. *Punch* (Nigeria), March 19. https://punchng.com/ecowas-threatens-to-sanction-nigeria-over-dasuki. Retrieved December 27, 2017.

Akinola, A.A. (2006). The Conflict of Creed and Vendetta. www.gamji.com/article6000/NEWS6360.htm. Retrieved December 20, 2017.

Amaize, E. and Brisibe, P. (2016). Who are the Niger Delta Avengers? *Vanguard*, May 15. www.vanguardngr.com/2016/05/niger-delta-avengers. Retrieved September 19, 2018.

Amnesty International (2017). *Amnesty International Report 2016/17: The State of the World's Human Rights*. London: Amnesty International. www.amnesty.org/download/Documents/POL1048002017ENGLISH.PDF.

Amnesty International (2018). *Amnesty International Report 2017/18: The State of the World's Human Rights*. London: Amnesty International. www.amnesty.org/download/Documents/POL1067002018ENGLISH.PDF.

Arewa, J.A. (2011). Core National Values as Determinant of National Security Panacea for the Crime of Kidnapping and Abduction in Nigeria, in Azinge, E. and Bello, F. (eds), *Law and Security in Nigeria*. Lagos: Nigerian Institute of Advanced Legal Studies, pp. 127–196.

BBC (2000), General Attacks Obansanjo 'Vendetta'. news.bbc.co.uk/2/hi/africa/1070382.stm. Retrieved December 20, 2017.

BBC (2017). 'Nigeria Treats Us Like Slaves' – But is Biafra the Answer?July 6. www.bbc.com/news/world-africa-40506251.

CNN (2020). Boko Haram Fast Facts. September 7. https://edition.cnn.com/2014/06/09/world/boko-haram-fast-facts/index.html.

Constitution of the Federal Republic of Nigeria 1999, as amended.

Dambazau, A. (2014). Nigeria and Her Security Challenges. *Harvard International Review*, 35 (4), pp. 63–70. http://hir.harvard.edu/nigeria-and-her-security-challenges/. Retrieved November 24, 2017.

el-Kurebe, A. (2017). Rule of Law: Why ECOWAS Must Apply the Gambia Experience on Nigeria. *PRNigeria*, October 5. https://prnigeria.com. Retrieved December 20, 2017.

Falana, F. (2014). Insecurity in Nigeria: The Legal Challenge. *Vanguard*, November 18. www.vanguardngr.com/2014/11/insecurity-nigeria-legal-challenge-femi-falana. Retrieved December 25, 2017.

Guardian (Nigeria) (2018). DSS, Democracy and the Rule of Law. August 14. https://guardian.ng/opinion/dss-democracy-and-the-rule-of-law.

Hanafi, A. (2017). I Collect Ransom in Dollars, Says Evans, Notorious Kidnapper. *Punch* (Nigeria), June 12. https://punchng.com/i-collect-ransom-in-dollars-says-evans-notorious-kidnapper. Retrieved September 24, 2018.

Human Rights Watch (2017). World Report 2017: Nigeria: Events of 2016. www.hrw.org/world-report/2017/country-chapters/nigeria. Retrieved December 31, 2017.

Ibrahim, B. and Mukhtar, J.I. (2017). An Analysis of the Causes and Consequences of Kidnapping in Nigeria. *African Research Review*, 11 (4), pp. 134–143. www.ajol.info/index.php/afrrev/article/download/163979/153468. Retrieved September 26, 2018.

Institute for Peace and Conflict Resolution (IPCR) (2017). *2016 Strategic Conflict Assessment of Nigeria: Consolidated and Zonal Reports*. Abuja: IPCR. www.ng.undp.org/.../nigeria/.../Strategic%20Conflict%20Assessment%20of%20Nigeria. Retrieved September 19, 2018.

Jegede, M.I. and Elias, T.O. (eds) (1993). *Nigerian Essays in Jurisprudence*. Lagos: MIJ Professional Publishers.

Lawal-Rabana, R.A. (n.d.). The Nigerian Bar Association and Protection of Rule of Law in Nigeria. www.ibanet.org/Document/Default.aspx?DocumentUid=36600E1C-9C7B. Retrieved August 6, 2018.

Malala, J. (2015). *We Have Now Begun Our Descent: How to Stop South Africa Losing Its Way*. Johannesburg and Cape Town: Jonathan Ball. www.energiaci.com/we-have-now-begun-our-descent-english.pdf. Retrieved December 31, 2017.

Mamah, E., Ndujihe, C., Nkwopara, C. and Ozor, C. (2016). Bloodbath in Enugu as Fulani Herdsmen Kill 40. *Vanguard*, April 26. www.vanguardngr.com/2016/04/bloodbath-enugu-fulani-herdsmen-kill-40.

Manok, J. (n.d.). Vendetta as State Policy. www.gamji.com/article5000/NEWS5141.htm. Retrieved December 20, 2017.

Nigerian Observer (2016). Alleged Corruption: Court Varies Bail Conditions of Judge, San. December 9. http://nigerianobservernews.com/2016/12/alleged-corruption-court-varies-bail-conditions-of-judge-san/#.WE7ZbaIrKAw.

Nwachukwu, J.O. (2017). Why We're Resuming 'Operation No Mercy' on Oil Facilities: Niger Delta Militants. *Daily Post* (Nigeria), November 5. https://dailypost.ng/2017/11/05/resuming-operation-no-mercy-oil-facilities-niger-delta-militants. Retrieved November 26, 2017.

Nwakalor, M. (2016). The Major Players in the Niger Delta Dispute Identified. *Ventures Africa*, August 11. http://venturesafrica.com/we-identify-the-major-players-in-the-niger-delta-dispute. Retrieved September 19, 2018.

Nwakanma, O. (2016). The DSS Arrest of Judges. *Vanguard*, October 16. www.vanguardngr.com/2016/10/dss-arrest-judges.

Nwekeaku, C. (2014). The Rule of Law, Democracy and Good Governance in Nigeria. *Global Journal of Political Science and Administration*, 2 (1), pp. 26–35. www.eajournals.org/…/The-Rule-of-Law-Democracy-and-Good-Governance-in-Nigeria. Retrieved August 6, 2018.

Ogundamisi, K. (2015). The Legacy of a Nigerian Human Rights Hero. *Al Jazeera*, November 10. www.aljazeera.com/indepth/opinion/2015/11/legacy-nigerian-human-rights-hero-151109083731968.html. Retrieved September 17, 2018.

Oviasuyi, P.A. and Uwadiae, J. (2010). The Dilemma of Niger-Delta Region as Oil Producing States of Nigeria. *Journal of Peace, Conflict and Development*, 16 (November), pp. 110–126. www.peacestudiesjournal.org.uk.

Oyewo, H.T. (2016). Nigeria: The Challenges of Reintegrating Niger Delta Militants. *Conflicts Studies Quarterly*, 17 (October), pp. 57–72. www.csq.ro/wp-content/uploads/Hussain-Taofik-OYEWO.pdf. Retrieved September 18, 2018.

Punch (Nigeria) (2017). Igbo Dare Arewa: We Won't Leave North … Demand Ango Abdullahi's Arrest. June 11. https://punchng.com/igbo-dare-arewa-we-wont-leave-north.

Soniyi, T. (2016). NJC Sacks Appellate Court Judge, Two Others for Corruption. *This Day*, October 1. www.thisdaylive.com/index.php/2016/10/01/njc-sacks-appellate-court-judge-two-others-for-corruption. Retrieved August 8, 2018.

Sote, L. (2018). Buhari Assaults Rule of Law. *Punch* (Nigeria), September 5. https://punchng.com/buhari-assaults-rule-of-law. Retrieved September 15, 2018.

Tobi, A. (2004). Exploring a Rights-Based Approach to Development and Poverty Alleviation in Delta State. Report on the Social and Economic Rights Action Centre (SERAC) Legislating for the Poor Summit.

Tobi-Aiyemo, A. (2019). The Wealth and Pain of Nigeria's Niger Delta Region: Moving from Exploitation to Accountability. *ESR Review*, 20 (2), pp. 14–18.

Tobi, N. (1996). *The Judiciary in a Democracy*. Enugu: Enugu State University of Science and Technology.

Tobi, N. (2008). The Rule of Law and Anti-Corruption Crusade in Nigeria. Lecture delivered at the 9th Justice Idigbe Memorial Lecture, Benin City, Nigeria.

Vanguard (2017a). 45 Boko Haram Members Convicted, Jailed for 31 Years. October 14. www.vanguardngr.com/2017/10/45-boko-haram-members-convicted-jailed-31-years. Retrieved November 25, 2017.

Vanguard (2017b). Give Us, Kanu Oduduwa, Biafra Republics: Too Late for Restructuring. July 31. www.vanguardngr.com/2017/07/breaking-yoruba-group-demand-oduduwa-republic-says-late-restructuring. Retrieved December 26, 2017.

VOA News (2018). Nigeria's Buhari Fires Head of Niger Delta Amnesty Program. March 13. www.voanews.com/africa/nigerias-buhari-fires-head-niger-delta-amnesty-program.

Yusuf, H.O. (2010). *Transitional Justice, Judicial Accountability and the Rule of Law*. New York: Routledge.

INDEX

Page numbers in italics refer to figures. Page numbers in bold refer to tables. Page numbers followed by 'n' refer to notes.

Printed in Canada
PGCA2024